Conflict in the Classroom

Conflict in the Classroom

The Education of At-Risk and Troubled Students

FIFTH EDITION

Nicholas J. Long,
William C. Morse,
and
Ruth G. Newman

pro·ed   8700 Shoal Creek Boulevard • Austin, Texas 78757-6897

pro·ed

© 1996 by PRO-ED, Inc.
8700 Shoal Creek Boulevard
Austin, Texas 78757-6897

Library of Congress Cataloging-in-Publication Data

Conflict in the classroom : the education of at risk and troubled
    students / [edited by] Nicholas J. Long, William C. Morse, Ruth G.
    Newman. — 5th ed.
        p.   cm.
    Includes bibliographical references and index.
    ISBN 0-89079-682-3 (pbk. : alk. paper)
    1. Emotional problems of children.   2. Mentally ill children-
    -Education—United States.   I. Long, Nicholas James, 1929–
II. Morse, William Charles.   III. Newman, Ruth G.
LC4181.C65   1996
371.9′4—dc20   95-48366
                                                                        CIP

Production Manager: Alan Grimes
Production Coordinator: Karen Swain
Managing Editor: Tracy Sergo
Art Director: Thomas Barkley
Reprints Buyer: Alicia Woods
Editorial Assistant: Claudette Landry
Editorial Assistant: Martin Wilson
Copyeditor: Maryan Malone, Publications Development Company

Printed in the United States of America

1   2   3   4   5   6   7   8   9   10   99   98   97   96

We dedicate *Conflict in the Classroom* to our wives, Sunny and Jody, and children, who provided continual support; to our professional colleagues, especially teachers, who shared their efforts and insights; and most of all, to the troubled youngsters who told their stories of growing up in an abusive and fragmented society and expressed their need to be understood, respected, and helped.

This book also is dedicated to the memories of Ruth G. Newman, Ph.D. Ruth was our lifelong friend, writer, and creative therapist who brought personal comfort to her many clients in conflict.

N.J.L.
W.C.M.

Contents

3   The Challenge of Reeducating Troubled Students:
Understanding the Interaction Between a Student and
His Community, Family, and Staff • 149

4   The Power of Group Forces in the Classroom:
Strategies and Skills of Promoting Positive Group Behavior • 185

9   Beyond the School: Enhancing Family Support   •   539

Preface

This fifth edition of *Conflict in the Classroom* continues the psychoeducational fusion of relevant educational and mental health practices used by teachers to help troubled students. When our earlier editions were published, this area of special education was preoccupied with such issues as identification criteria, emotional vs. social maladjustment, proper settings and services, appropriate curricula, the nature of school therapy, and preparation of special teachers. There was much explication of contrasting theories. None of these matters has been resolved; they are all still with us. But, as we approach the year 2000, the focus of the field is undergoing drastic revision in response to changes in American society. These changes have put us at or near the top of the list of western countries that have multiple indicators of family instability and disintegration. Schools are being expected to take the lead in helping to resolve a national crisis in child upbringing. There is a virtual revolution in educational practice as the schools adjust to this new reality. This edition of our book reflects the impending changes.

What factors are altering the face of education for troubled children even as the schools struggle to restructure themselves to better meet the needs of all children? There are two primary conditions. Of first concern is the *significant increase in the number* of already troubled and seriously at-risk students in our schools. No letup is in sight, and there are now too many to accommodate in traditional special education. The presence of these special-needs students is ubiquitous, as every regular and special teacher and administrator knows. Second, along with increased numbers has come the *deeper and more profound nature* of the personal and ecological difficulties of these students. More students are deeply depressed, despairing, and suicidal; others turn defiant, angry, violent, and homicidal. Many will travel well-marked trails to gang membership, delinquency, drugs, or the occult. When we hear their stories, we wonder how they survived at all, and they make us aware of those who did not. Larger numbers of students are trying to cope with fearsome family and community conditions and are failing in life as well as in school. The schools reap the harvests of poverty, neglect, and abuse. Inappropriate schooling adds to the students' struggle when proper schooling could contribute to a solution.

Even in the best of times, special education never included all of the disturbed and disturbing students and never was designed to include those at risk. Today, these students can be half the members of a given class. Special education services once awaited certification rituals for proper "fit" and were not geared to prevention or early intervention. But, along with the current national thrust for school reorganization has come a profound change in special education philosophy regarding traditional exclusionary services: as a basic civil right, to the maximum extent possible, all special children are to be taught in the mainstream at their local school and with their age peers. This change makes *all* teachers responsible for educating *all* students, including the seriously troubled. The philosophy of full- and part-time inclusion presents special problems both for troubled students, who act out their struggles, and for their already overburdened teachers. Coping with individual differences and diversity takes on a new aspect, and the accommodation that is implied requires new skills. As the wall between regular and special education is breached, all teachers become special teachers. The previously designated special teachers become team teachers in regular classrooms, collaborators, and consultants. When needed, they continue their "hands on" service as well. Particularly for troubled students, this philosophical turnabout requires expanded teacher education and system reorganization to provide back-up crisis support.

Another change that affects all teachers is the increased power parents and community representatives have in the educative process. As school reorganization brings local school autonomy, teachers find new faces at the decision-making table. Parents of special pupils continue to exercise their right to decide the content of their children's educational program as well as where it should be taught. A few parents inevitably will resort to the courts for a redress. Fear of litigation has become a strong political force in some school systems. Concurrently, there is a new focus in working with families: *family preservation* has become the central goal in providing support for distraught families and their children. Teachers are expected to reach out to families as intensively as possible, to accomplish conjoint efforts in helping all students to find school success.

Another far-reaching change involves accountability. As though there were no multiple causes for children's troubles, evaluation of the schools' programs is changing from "Are we doing the right things?" to "Are we getting the desired results?" This change presents a particular problem for those working with our clientele. In addition, stringent budgets for school and community agencies are resulting in fewer support services for teachers to call on for their troubled students.

Schools can do much to meet the new expectations, but it is axiomatic that, alone, they cannot meet the child-raising crisis that has invaded the classroom. Even the available community resources are most often fragmented. One encouraging change that deserves our support is the movement to bring agencies together in what are called Full Service Schools, one-stop neighborhood centers for children and families. The hope for meeting the crisis requires this type of collaboration. As Full Service Schools evolve, all parties will have to learn skills for a new collegiality.

The forces outlined above, along with others in contemporary society, are modifying education—particularly special education. Some observers think we will not recognize special education by 2000, but we can count on still recognizing troubled children in our classrooms. The pace and nature of change are not uniform in our variegated schools. Indeed, there are competing and antagonistic directives in the proposals for change. For teachers, one of the most contentious conflicts in proposed educational goals is academic excellence vs. equity-based meeting of needs. Response in one school may differ drastically from what is going on in another nearby.

One text cannot cover *all* aspects of teaching troubled and at-risk students. This fifth edition of *Conflict in the Classroom* has benefited from advice offered by teachers and from the authors' own experiences. Teachers have shared with us their trials in helping troubled students in their classrooms. They have suggested less theory and more practical strategies, especially strategies from other colleagues, to keep the book reality-based. They didn't want just a series of articles. Teachers proposed putting the individual pieces of each chapter into a meaningful context. This would account for the introductory essays and the interfacing paragraphs. While keeping certain selections from the last edition, we have added much new material that is tuned to the current nature of the field.

In each chapter, the articles are bound together by the humanistic ties of psychoeducation, a concern for both the inner life and the external behavior. All students deserve our caring, our respect, and the most astute individualized interventions we can generate. Follow-up studies tell us we have a long way to go. Although we do not command the resources to save all of the troubled children, we can get much better results than present practice is delivering. A recent film (L. G. Fitzgerald et al., *Perspectives on Emotional and Behavior Disorders: A Problem Solving Program for Teachers*, Jonesboro, AK: Arkansas State University) follows the same student mainstreamed in four classes. In two, he shows the expected behavior and really messes things up. In the other two, he is a top student. What are we to make of the transformations? Redl (*When We Deal with Children*, New York: The Free Press, 1966) demonstrated the power of the ecology and emphasized the potency of helping troubled children through interacting with them in their daily activities. Compared to teachers, what trained professionals spend more time with children in their living space, with a wide variety of possible activities? This book is about how to make school time effective enough to empower troubled and high-risk students to manage their lives more successfully.

The first chapter contains selections that describe how it feels to be upset: These stories have been a hallmark of *Conflict* since its first edition. When we read a case record—or better still, hear a student's story from his or her own lips—the youngster becomes transformed in our understanding. We become symbiotic in common cause to reduce the troubles and the risks. This empathy may not make our task easier but it makes our work more meaningful. Great literature penetrates the life of an "other" and generates empathy for his or her plight, often with deeper effect than a case study. For that reason, the text opens with stories from literature to sensitize readers to the significance of the turmoil in troubled lives.

Chapter 2 examines the nature of the helping process. In Chapter 3, we consider strategies for understanding our students and their families, and we reflect on what we, as professionals, bring to the interaction. Many of the experiences of troubled students are foreign to our own lives, and it takes effort to incorporate their impact without becoming merely sentimental.

A school is a matrix of groups, both formal and informal. Most youngsters are addicted to being in groups, and they play a variety of roles in group life. Groups exert strong forces and can be a teacher's enemy or aid. Although teachers are by definition group leaders, many have not been trained in positive strategies for utilizing group life (the topic of Chapter 4). Knowledge of a student is not an end: it is only the starting point. Chapter 5 moves to generic strategies for providing student support based around Long's conflict cycle. Chapter 6 presents intervention strategies for dealing with common behavior patterns ranging from aggression to suicide. These days, no matter how carefully one plans, there will be crises in any setting with troubled students. Hygienic management of crises offers a most promising avenue to help many troubled youngsters, as indicated in Chapter 7. A crisis can be converted to a high-voltage learning situation.

The therapeutic potentials of curriculum have been largely ignored in favor of concentrating on workbooks, dull drills, and catch-up academics, because troubled students are so often below grade level. Yet, many examples of enriched curricula are more motivating and useful to our students. These curricula are the focus of Chapter 8. Finally, because we work ever more diligently with parents, the book ends with strategies for supporting families (Chapter 9). Included are specifics to use with aggressive parents who often make interaction more difficult than do their offspring.

It was painful to have to leave out many challenging articles because of space limitations. In spite of the difficulties facing schools in meeting the needs of troubled and high-risk students, our many years in the field leave us upbeat about the possibilities. We see so many teachers exploiting the potential of education by doing exceptional things to help these students by redirecting their lives. Think of what even one life change means to one youngster, one family, one community at large. It is our hope that readers will enjoy using this different kind of text, and will find ideas that can be transformed to become part of the educational practices of "tomorrow." High hopes and intense anxiety form the background of the schools' extended role. There can be no promise of quick or easy solutions, only the knowledge that there is much teachers can do. The intent of this book is to inform newcomers to the profession, revitalize the battle-weary, and broaden the vision of teachers already coping successfully.

We thank the PRO-ED staff for their encouragement and substantive help, which made this new edition possible. It is a distinct pleasure to be part of PRO-ED's expanding leadership in the field of special education publication.

NICHOLAS LONG
WILLIAM MORSE

1

Walking in the Footsteps of Troubled Students: How Classical Literature Portrays the Struggle

Students' emotional problems are not a new phenomenon. Although scientists argue about the causes of emotional problems and the relative importance of genetic, constitutional, and environmental factors, all agree that their occurrence is in some degree dependent on the cultural and social values of the times.

Each of us contains the whole range of emotional health and disease within ourselves. Our nightmares, if they serve no other purpose, enable us to share the ways in which many psychotics experience life. If our legs "go to sleep" and refuse to behave as they should, we can briefly experience the helpless and often outraged feelings of the organic spastic. The sudden loss of temper nearly all of us have experienced gives a momentary empathy with the feelings of uncontrollable rage, helplessness, confusion, and self-hate of a student who has no impulse control. Most of us have shared a variety of symptoms: the terrifying fear of something that we know rationally should not in itself cause fear, the magical, protective cloak of knocking on wood, crossing fingers, counting to ten, holding our breath; the compulsive need to get one thing done, no matter how inane or how inconvenient, before we can do something else; the piece of work that can never be finished because it is never good enough; the headaches, stomach pains, or unexplained shortness of breath that often occurs at a family reunion, at exam time, or at the appearance of a certain person; the need to eat greedily though we are not hungry, or the reverse, the inability to swallow a mouthful; the uncontrollable blush or stutter; the immobilizing lapse of memory; or the urge to take something, to break something, to say the very thing that will get us into trouble, or to be silent when speaking up might simplify our lives and reduce the hostility of others.

Such illogical behavior does not mean that we are disturbed—only that some emotional problems are as much a part of everyone's life as the common cold. It is not surprising, therefore, that emotional problems play so great a role in childhood periods of dependence and change, in which the world and its demands are new and often confusing, conflicting, and frustrating.

Many literary artists have chronicled the actions of troubled children and adults whose disturbances were rooted in their childhood. Writers were describing these people long before Freud; and because good writers are skilled in conveying pictures and feelings, their descriptions often have greater impact than the clinical descriptions in textbooks. This chapter includes excerpts from a variety of fictional and autobiographical works to illustrate the kinds of emotional problems that beset children. Mostly, the stories are about children of various ages, but some descriptions of adult behavior have been included to show clearly the final development of a childhood disturbance.

The chapter is divided into three parts. The first part pictures basic internal difficulties that can be found anywhere, anytime. The second part presents certain aspects of society—its deprivations, restrictions, and human devaluations—that breed disturbed behavior or, when in conflict with inner needs, cause destructive reactions. Some people react by withdrawing into themselves; some separate feeling from thought; some resort to body language, get headaches or ulcers, or become psychologically deaf or paralyzed; some eat compulsively to build a wall of fat between themselves and others; some drink to numb their pain. The third part discusses drug use. Many young people take drugs, some to such excess that they delude themselves into a state of "nonfeeling" or believe they have grasped the import of their lives or expanded their awareness of the world.

The fundamental purpose of this chapter is to offer the reader an intense and accurate experience of *how it feels* to walk in the shoes of troubled students.

ARTICLE 1.1

The Use of Force

William Carlos Williams

They were new patients to me, all I had was the name, Olson. Please come down as soon as you can, my daughter's very sick. When I arrived I was met by the mother, a big startled looking woman, very clean and apologetic who merely said, Is this the doctor? and let me in. In the back, she added, You must excuse us, doctor, we have her in the kitchen where it is warm. It is very damp here sometimes.

The child was fully dressed and sitting on her father's lap near the kitchen table. He tried to get up, but I motioned for him not to bother, took off my overcoat and started to look things over. I could see that they were all very nervous, eyeing me up and down distrustfully. As often, in such cases, they weren't telling me more than they had to, it was up to me to tell them; that's why they were spending three dollars on me.

The child was fairly eating me up with her cold, steady eyes, and no expression to her face whatever. She did not move and seemed, inwardly, quiet; an unusually attractive little thing, and as strong as a heifer in appearance. But her face was flushed, she was breathing rapidly, and I realized that she had a high fever. She had magnificent blonde hair, in profusion. One of those picture children often reproduced in advertising leaflets and the photogravure sections of the Sunday papers.

She's had a fever for three days, began the father, and we don't know what it comes from. My wife has given her things, you know, like people do, but it don't do no good. And there's been a lot of sickness around. So we tho't you'd better look her over and tell us what is the matter.

As doctors often do I took a trial shot at it as a point of departure. Has she had a sore throat? Both parents answered me together, No . . . No, she says her throat don't hurt her. Does your throat hurt you? added the mother to the child. But the little girl's expression didn't change nor did she move her eyes from my face. Have you looked?

I tried to, said the mother, but I couldn't see. As it happens we had been having a number of cases of diphtheria in the school to which this child went during that month and we were all, quite apparently, thinking of that, though no one had as yet spoken of the thing.

Well, I said, suppose we take a look at the throat first. I smiled in my best professional manner and asking for the child's first name I said, come on, Mathilda, open your mouth and let's take a look at your throat. Nothing doing.

Aw, come on, I coaxed, just open your mouth wide and let me take a look. Look, I said opening both hands wide, I haven't anything in my hands. Just open up and let me see.

Such a nice man, put in the mother. Look how kind he is to you. Come on, do what he tells you to. He won't hurt you.

At that I ground my teeth in disgust. If only they wouldn't use the word *"hurt"* I might be able to get somewhere. But I did not allow myself to be hurried or disturbed but speaking quietly and slowly I approached the child again. As I moved my chair a little nearer suddenly with one cat-like movement both her hands clawed instinctively for my eyes and she almost reached them too. In fact she knocked my glasses flying and they fell, though unbroken, several feet away from me on the kitchen floor.

Both the mother and father almost turned themselves inside out in embarrassment and apology. You bad girl, said the mother, taking her and shaking her by one arm. Look what you've done. The nice man . . .

For heaven's sake, I broke in. Don't call me a nice man to her. I'm here to look at her throat on the chance that she might have diphtheria and possibly die of it. But that's nothing to her. Look here, I said to the child, we're going to look at your throat. You're old enough to understand what I'm saying. Will you open it now by yourself or shall we have to open it for you?

Not a move. Even her expression hadn't changed. Her breaths however were coming faster and faster. Then the battle began. I had to do it. I had to have a throat culture for her own protection. But first I told the parents that it was entirely up to them. I explained the danger but said that I would not insist on a throat examination so long as they would take the responsibility.

If you don't do what the doctor says you'll have to go to the hospital, the mother admonished her severely.

Oh yeah? I had to smile to myself. After all, I had already fallen in love with the savage brat, the parents were contemptible to me. In the ensuing struggle they grew more and more abject, crushed, exhausted while she surely rose to magnificent heights of insane fury of effort bred of her terror of me.

The father tried his best, and he was a big man but the fact that she was his daughter, his shame at her behavior and his dread of hurting her made him release her just at the critical moment several times when I had almost achieved success, till I wanted to kill him. But his dread also that she might have diphtheria made him tell me to go on, go on though he himself was almost fainting, while the mother moved back and forth behind us raising and lowering her hands in an agony of apprehension.

Put her in front of you on your lap, I ordered, and hold both her wrists.

But as soon as he did the child let out a scream. Don't you're hurting me. Let go of my hands. Let them go I tell you. She shrieked terrifyingly, hysterically. Stop it! Stop it! You're killing me!

Do you think she can stand it, doctor? said the mother.

You get out, said the husband to his wife. Do you want her to die of diphtheria?

Come on now, hold her, I said.

Then I grasped the child's head with my left hand and tried to get the wooden tongue depressor between her teeth. She fought, with clenched teeth, desperately! But now I also had grown furious—at a child. I tried to hold myself down but I couldn't. I know how to expose a throat for inspection. And I did my best. When finally I got the wooden spatula behind the last teeth and just the point of it into the mouth cavity, she opened up for an instant but before I could see anything she came down again and gripping the wooden blade between her molars she reduced it to splinters before I could get it out again.

Aren't you ashamed, the mother yelled at her. Aren't you ashamed to act like that in front of the doctor? Get me a smooth-handled spoon of some sort, I told the mother. We're going through with this. The child's mouth was already bleeding. Her tongue was cut and she was screaming in wild hysterical shrieks. Perhaps I should have desisted and come back in an hour or more. No doubt it would have been better. But I have seen at least two children lying dead in bed of neglect in such cases, and feeling that I must get a diagnosis now or never I went at it again. But the worst of it was that I too had got beyond reason. I could have torn the child apart in my own fury and enjoyed it. It was a pleasure to attack her. My face was burning with it.

The damned little brat must be protected against her own idiocy, one says to one's self at such times. Others must be protected against her. It is social necessity. And all these things are true. But a blind fury, a feeling of adult shame, bred of a longing for muscular release are the operatives. One goes on to the end.

In a final unreasoning assault I overpowered the child's neck and jaws. I forced the heavy silver spoon back of her teeth and down her throat till she gagged. And there it was, both tonsils covered with membrane. She had fought valiantly to keep me from knowing her secret. She had been hiding that sore throat for three days at least and lying to her parents in order to escape just such an outcome as this.

Now truly she *was* furious. She had been on the defensive before but now she attacked. Tried to get off her father's lap and fly at me while tears of defeat blinded her eyes.

· ·

Editors' Commentary ·

> DIAGNOSIS: Behavior problem—resistance to adult authority, hostility, aggressiveness—leading to character problems.

This child has had many struggles with her parents. She has immobilized and terrorized them. She has been the unhappy victor with her parents—unhappy because she would be greatly relieved to know she was not all-powerful, and to know that the adults on whom she *must* depend *can* be depended on to make and carry out decisions that she cannot make. A child feels helpless at best in the adult world, and when parents—and teachers and doctors—are rendered helpless, the result is increased anxiety, panic, and rage. This rage often comes out in a defiant, aggressive onslaught. It makes adults more fearful or angry, and it further isolates the child and makes her feel more unloved. Thus, she develops a circular pattern of helplessness, panic, and anger, which also includes the adults in her life. For this child, the circle spirals into misery, isolation, and trouble with the world.

The parents, as Williams says, are incompetent. Their words are ill-chosen, frightening, threatening, and shaming—effective only in arousing fear, not compliance. Even in a matter of life and death such as this, they are so defeated by the child that they are unable to facilitate the throat examination.

Williams' reaction to the child illustrates the feelings that such parental behavior arouses in other adults. He secretly admires the courage and determination of the little girl. At the same time, her defiance evokes rage in him, a need to counterattack, and a need simply for "muscular release." He is ashamed that such a little child can make him lose control and poise. His ambivalence in being both on the side of the willful and unhappy child and on the side of necessary adult behavior has increased his own violence and therefore his consequent guilt and self-disgust. He has to complete the throat examination for the sake of the child's very life, and he is aware that his excuses to himself for the way he accomplishes this task are rationalizations to cover up his own primitive rage.

This couple clearly needs family counseling for resolving the child's and the family's interlocking dilemmas. One or both of the parents may have a need, because of problems rooted in their own background, to keep the child all-powerful; or, some unsatisfactory aspect of their marriage may encourage them to make the child act out their own unverbalized conflict. If the family is seen as a unit, then proper decisions on treatment can be made.

ARTICLE 1.2

The Day of the Last Rock Fight

Joseph Whitehill

Fallbrook Academy May 16, 195-

Dear Dad,

I expect this will be a very long letter, so I am sending it to your office marked Personal. I know you don't like to do family business at the office, but I wanted you to have a chance to read this all by yourself and I didn't want Mother or Sue reading it before you did.

Thank you for sending my allowance, and also for the subscription to the home paper. Thank you also for the nice new wallet for my birthday. I really needed it, as my old one was afflicted with rot and falling apart.

I apologize for not having written sooner. As you said in your last letter, "Something must have happened in the last two months worth writing down." I have been very busy with things here at school, but mainly I haven't written because I didn't know how to say what I wanted to say. I hope this letter will make up for the long delay.

You keep asking me what I think of Fallbrook Academy and if I'm happy here, and so on. Well, I don't like it here, and I want to come home. That's what this letter is for—to tell you that now it's all right for me to come back home. I guess I know why you sent me here, and I admit that I wanted very much to come when I did. It's not that the people here aren't nice or anything. They are. They're so nice it's phony. In all the catalogues of the school they call it a Special School, but the boys here call it Goodbar. (Mr. Goodbar is a chocolate bar full of nuts.) They all kid about it, and pretend they don't care about being put in a school for misfits and boys with emotional problems. I guess most of them like it here. Most of them say they hate their parents, one or both, and are really glad to get away from them. All the faculty are so sweet and kind and sympathetic that a lot of the boys get away with murder. (That last word was sort of a poor choice, I suppose, but I'll leave it there anyway.) But I don't feel like I belong here any more.

It is going to be very complicated to explain everything in just one letter, because there are lots of different ways of looking at that mess that happened there at home, and I suppose I am the only one who knows the whole story. I guess you sent me here because you thought I was terribly upset by Gene Hanlon getting killed out there at Manning Day School at home, and seeing his body lying in the creek, and so on. Well, that was part of it, but only a little part. The rest of it I couldn't tell anybody until Detective Sergeant Gorman put the story in the paper last week. I got that paper in the mail yesterday and I have been reading the story over and over, and feeling relieved and awful at the same time.

I'm sure you read the same story, so you already know that Gene Hanlon was murdered, instead of getting killed accidentally as they said at first. But neither you nor anybody else knows that I saw the murder done, and knew all the time who did it. I guess if I acted upset afterwards it was from knowing all this and not being able to tell anyone about it. I'm going to work on this letter all night, if it takes that long, because I have to get all this out of my system. (When you stay up after curfew around here they don't actually make you go to bed, but the doctor who is on duty looks in on you every half hour or so to see what you're doing, and to try to make you want to go to bed.)

I suppose the beginning is the best place to start, so I will tell you first about Gene Hanlon, the boy who got killed. He came to Manning Day School last fall as a senior. They said he was fired from his last school, but I don't know about that. I didn't like him just from looking at him. I know you hate judgments that way on first impressions, but I couldn't help it. I wouldn't ever bring him over to our house, but if I had, you might have seen what I was talking about. He was big and beefy, and he played on the first string last fall. He was also blond, and the girls thought he was cute and from what I heard they fought over him for dates. But he was a bully, and he cheated in the classroom and he borrowed your stuff without asking you and then left it some place where you had to go hunt it up for yourself.

In a school like Manning Day there are always a number of tight little groups—cliques, I guess you call them—that move around independently and generally stay out of the way of the others. I mean there is a football group, and a group of boys who drink beer, and a group who studies hard, and a group who loafs and tries to avoid everything that looks like work, and a group that meets in the locker room to talk about sex and tell dirty jokes. It was probably the same way when you yourself went to school, but you may have forgotten. When you go to a school like that, you pretty soon find the group that suits you best, and you stay there and don't try to mix with any of the others, because if you do you won't be let in.

What I am getting at in this long explanation is that Gene Hanlon was the Big Man in all the groups I wouldn't be seen dead in. He was tops among the football players and their fans. He could tell filthier stories and, he said, hold more liquor than anybody else. And he told stories about the things he had done to girls that you wouldn't believe if anybody else had told them, but with him telling them, you knew they were all possible. I guess he was feared more than he was liked, but one thing sure, he never went anywhere alone. There was always a loud bunch along with him horse-laughing and beating him on the shoulders.

I stayed out of his way. There is something about me that brings out the worst in bullies. That's what Peter Irish used to say. I guess it's because I'm slightly built, and because of those glasses I have to wear. Once, I was going upstairs to lab, and Gene Hanlon was coming down and we met halfway, and for no reason I could see, he belted me as hard as he could on my shoulder. My glasses flew off and bounced halfway down the stairs along with a whole armload of books and papers. I had to grab the banister to keep from following them down myself. Two other guys with him saw him do it and didn't say anything at first, but then they looked at Gene and knew they'd better laugh, so they did. So I sat there on the stairs all confused inside, holding my shoulder to make it stop hurting. Gene Hanlon and the others went on down the stairs laughing to beat all at how I looked there with everything scattered around me. On the way down, Gene kicked my physics book ahead of him, bouncing it all the way to the bottom. When I could stand up all right I went down and got it. When I picked it up it fell apart in my hands with its binding broken and I guess I started to cry. I hate to see books treated that way.

When I had about got everything picked up, Peter Irish came up to where I was and wanted to know what had happened. Peter being my best friend, I told him all about it. Probably there were still tears in my eyes about the physics book because Peter said, "Do you want me to get him for you?"

I thought for a minute how swell that would be, but then I said no. It was almost yes because Peter was the only one in school who could have whipped Gene under any rules, and it was a very satisfying thing to think about. But then I thought about afterwards, when Gene would have gotten over his beating and would begin to wonder why Peter had done it, and he would remember that Peter was my best friend. Then he would put one and one together and start out after me seriously. So I said no.

Peter Irish was a good friend to have. I suppose he was the strongest kid in school, but he didn't ever use his strength to bully people, but just for things that were fun, like squashing a beer can in one hand. You knew him pretty well because of all the times he came over to the house to study with me. I remember the time he beat you at Indian hand wrestling on the dining-room table, and you were a real good sport about it because Mother was watching and laughing at your expression. But anyway, you know how strong Peter was, and you can feature what he would have done to Gene if I'd told him to. Peter always stayed out of fights unless they were for fun, and if they ever got serious he'd quit because he didn't want to hurt anybody. But he would have torn Gene Hanlon apart if I had asked him to.

That was something I don't think you understood Peter and me, I mean, and why we hung around together. The simplest way to say it is that we swapped talents. I used to write a lot of his themes for him, and help him in labs so he'd finish when the rest of us did, and he'd show me judo holds and how to skin a squirrel, and such things. You would call it a good working agreement.

Now, there are just two more things you have to know about to see the whole picture. The first one is Peter Irish and Angela Pine. Peter and Angela went together all last year and the year before, and neither of them wanted anybody else. Both their folks made them date other kids because they didn't like to see them going steady, but everybody knew that Angela belonged to Peter, and Peter belonged to Angela, and that's all there was to it. He used to talk to me a lot about her, and how they were going to get married and run a tiding stable together. And he told me that he would never touch her that way until they were married. They used to kiss good night and that was all, because Peter said that when the great thing happened, he wanted it to happen just right, and it could never be really right while they were both kids in high school. A lot of the fellows thought that more went on between them than I know did, but that's because they didn't understand Peter really. He had a simple set of rules he operated under, and they suited him very well. He was good to Angela and good to animals, and all he asked was to be let alone to do things his own way.

The other thing you have to know about is the noontime rock fights. From the papers and the inquest and all, you know something about them, but not everything. I guess most of the parents were pretty shocked to learn that their little Johnny was in a mob rock fight every day at school, but that's the way it was. The fights started over a year ago, as near as I can recollect, and went on all that time without the faculty ever finding out. The papers made a big scandal out of them and conducted what they called an "expose of vicious practices at select Manning Day School." It was comical, actually, the way everybody got all steamed up over the things we knew went on all the time, not only at Manning but in all the other schools in town. Of course, we all knew the rock fights were wrong, but they were more fun than they seemed wrong, so we kept them up. (That time I came home with the mouse under my eye, I didn't get it by falling in the locker room. I just forgot to duck.)

We had a strict set of rules in the fights so that nobody would really get hurt or anything, and so the little guys could get into them too without fear of being killed. All sixty of us, the whole school, were divided into two teams, the Union Army and the Confederates, and after lunch in the cafeteria we'd all get our blue or gray caps and head out into the woods behind the school. The faculty thought we played Kick the Can and never followed us out to check up on us.

Each team had a fort we'd built out of sapling logs—really just pens about waist high. The forts were about two hundred yards apart, invisible to each other through the trees and scrub. You weren't allowed to use rocks any bigger than a hazelnut, and before you pegged one at a guy in the opposite army, you had to go chk, chk with your mouth so the guy would have a chance to find where it was coming from and duck in time. We had scouting parties and assault teams and patrols, and all the rest of the military things we could think up. The object was to storm the enemy's fort and take it before recess was up and we had to quit.

These rock fights weren't like the papers said at all. I remember the Morning Star called them "pitched battles of unrelenting fury, where injuries were frequent." That was silly. If the injuries had been frequent, it wouldn't have been fun any more, and nobody would have wanted to keep doing it. You could get hurt, of course, but you could get hurt a lot worse in a football game with the grandstand full of newspaper reporters and faculty and parents all cheering you on.

Now I guess you know everything that was important before the day Gene Hanlon got killed, and I can tell you how it happened so that you'll know why.

After our last morning class, Peter Irish and I went down to the washroom in the basement to clean up for lunch. All morning Peter had acted funny—silent and sort of tied up inside—and it was worrying me some. At first I thought I had done something he didn't like, but if I had, he'd have told me. He'd hardly said two words all morning, and he had missed two recitations in English that I had coached him on myself. But you couldn't pry trouble out of Peter, so I just kept quiet and waited for him to let me in on it.

While he was washing his hands I had to go into one of the stalls. I went in and shut the door and was hanging up my jacket when I heard somebody else come into the washroom. I don't know why, but I sat down—being real careful not to make any noise.

Somebody said, "Hi, Pete, boy." It was Gene Hanlon, and he was alone for once.

"Hi, Gene." That was Peter. (I am trying to put this down as near as I can just the way they said it.)

"Oh, man!" Gene said. "Today I am exhaust pipe!"

"Tired?"

"You said the word, man. Real beat under." "Why so?"

"Big date last night. Friend of yours, Angela Pine." Just as if that stall door hadn't been there, I could see Gene grinning at Peter and waiting for a rise out of him. Peter didn't say anything, so Gene tried again. "You're pretty sly, Pete." "What do you mean?"

"I mean about Angela. You've done a real fine job of keeping her in drydock all this time."

"She dates other guys," Peter said, sounding like he ought to clear his throat.

"Aaaah. She goes out with those meatballs and then comes home and shakes hands at the door. What kind of a date is that?"

"Well, that's her business."

Gene said, giggling, "I don't know what her business is, but I got a few suggestions for her if she ever asks me."

"What are you getting at?"

"Real coy, boy. She's crazy for it. Just crazy. Real crazy hungry chick, yeah." "Are you through?"

"What? . . . Oh, sure. Hey! You sore or something?"

Peter said, "It's time for you to go eat lunch." "All right already. Jesus! You don't have to get that way about it. A guy gives you a compliment and you go and get sore. You are an odd ball. You and your screwy horses too. See you around." And Gene went out scuffing his feet along the floor.

When I came out of the stall Peter was hunched stiff-armed over the wash-basin. He didn't even know I was around. I wished right then that I could have gone back and unlived the last five minutes. I wished they had never happened, and that everything was back just the way it was before. I was hurt and mad, and my mind was whirling around full of all the stuff Gene Hanlon had said. Just to be doing something, I got busy combing my hair, wetting and shaking the comb and all, trying to find a way to say what I was feeling. Peter was very busy turning both faucets on and off again in a kind of splashy rhythm.

Finally, I said, "If you believe all that crap, you're pretty silly. That guy's a bragging liar and you know it." Peter looked up at me as though he had just noticed I was there. "I've got to believe it," he said. I jumped on him for that. "Oh, come on," I said. "Give Angela a little credit. She wouldn't give that pile of you-know-what the right time."

Peter was looking down the basin drain. "I called her this morning to say hello. She wouldn't talk to me, Ronnie. She wouldn't even come to the phone."

Now I knew what had been eating him all morning. There wasn't any more a friend could say to Peter, so I made him let go of the faucets and come with me to eat lunch in the cafeteria. All through lunch he just pushed dishes around on his tray and didn't say anything. As we scraped our plates I asked him if he was going out to the fight in the woods, and he surprised me by saying yes, so we got our caps and hiked out to the Confederate fort.

Almost everybody, Gene Hanlon too, was there before us, and they'd already chosen today's generals. Smitty Rice was General of the Armies of the Confederacy, and Gene Hanlon was the Union Commander. Gene took all his boys off to the Union fort to wait for the starting whistle, and Smitty outlined his strategy to us.

There was to be a feint at the south side of the Union fort, and then a noisy second feint from the north to pull the defenders out of position. Then Smitty and Peter Irish were to lead the real massed assault from the south, under the lip of the hill where the first feint had come from. When five minutes had gone by on my watch, we all got up and Smitty blew the starting whistle and we piled out of the fort, leaving only five inside as a garrison, and a couple of alarm guards a little way out on each side of the fort.

I got the job I usually got—advance observation post. I was to note enemy movements and remember concentrations and directions and elapsed times between sightings. Even though you couldn't see more than a hundred feet through the woods, you could always get a fair idea of the enemy strategy by the way they moved their troops around. So all I had to do was stay in one place and watch and listen and remember, and every so often Smitty would send a runner over from field headquarters to check up on what had happened lately. I had three or four good posts picked out where I could hide and not be seen, and I never used the same one twice running.

Today's was my favorite—Baker Post, we called it. It was a dense thicket of young blackjack oak on a low hill on the inside of a bend in the creek, and because nothing grew on the gravel bars of the creek, you could see a long way to each side. The creek ran generally south, cutting the fighting area between the forts right in two, and it made a good defense line because there were only a few places you could cross it in one jump and not get your shoes wet. The east bank of the creek, directly across from Baker Post, is a vertical bluff about ten feet high so that the ground up there is right on eye level with Baker, and the creek and the gravel bars are spread out between you and the bluff bank. I always knew that Baker Post was good, because every time I took it up I had to flush out a covey of quail or a cottontail.

It was always quiet in the woods during the first few minutes of those fights. Even the birds shut up, it seemed like, waiting for the first troop contacts. Out of the corner of my eye I saw somebody jump the creek at the North Ford, and I rolled over to watch. Because of the brush up there I couldn't see who it was, but I knew he was there because once in a while a bush would stir, or his foot would slide a little on the gravel. Pretty soon he came out to the edge of the underbrush and crouched there looking around and listening. It was Gene Hanlon. His eyes crossed right over me, without finding me, and after a minute he came out and ran low along the creek. When he got even with Baker Post, he went down to his knees and began filling his cap with rocks. I had to laugh to myself at how stupid that was. He should have collected his ammunition earlier, when he and his army were on their way over to their fort. He was wasting maneuvering time and exposing himself for no good reason. It makes you feel good when a guy you hate does something dumb like that.

I got ready to go chk, chk with my mouth just to scare him and see him run. But then I looked up at the bluff above him and my heart flopped over inside me. Peter Irish was there, down on one knee, looking over at Gene Hanlon. Gene never looked up. Peter moves like that—floating in and out of the brush as quietly as if he didn't weigh anything. Peter was a good woods fighter.

So instead of going chk, chk I hunkered down lower in my thicket and thought to myself that now it wasn't a game any more. Peter looked a long time over at where I was hiding, then he looked up and down the creek bed, and then he moved back a little from the edge of the bluff. He put all his weight pulling on a half-buried boulder beside him until it turned over in its socket and he could get a good grip on it. Even from where I was I could see the cords come out in his neck when he raised it up in his arms and stood up. I hadn't heard a sound except the creek gurgling a little, and Gene Hanlon scratching around in the gravel. And also the blood roaring in my own ears. Watching this was like being in a movie and seeing the story happen on the screen. Nothing you can do or say will change what is going to happen because it's all there in the unwinding reel.

Peter held the heavy stone like a medicine ball and walked to the edge of the bluff and looked down at Gene Hanlon. Gene had moved a few feet south along the creek, so Peter above him moved south too, until he was even with Gene. Peter made a little grunt when he pushed the rock out and away and it fell. Gene heard the grunt and lifted his head to look up, and the rock hit him full in the face and bent his head away back and made his arms fly out. He sat right down in the water with his red and dirty face turned up to the sky and his hands holding him up behind. Then he got himself up with his head still twisted back like that, so he was looking straight up, and he wandered a little way downstream with the water up to his knees, and then he fell out on a gravel bar on his stomach.

His legs and arms spread out like he was asleep, but his head was up rigid and his mouth was open. I couldn't look any more.

Peter hadn't made a sound leaving, but when I looked up, the bluff above was empty. As soon as I could move without getting sick I faded out of there and went up north a ways to Able Post and lay down in the foxhole there and held myself around the knees and just shook. I couldn't have felt more upset if I had dropped that rock myself. Just like a movie reel had the ends tied together, the whole scene kept rolling over and over in front of my eyes, and I couldn't stop the film or even turn off the light in the projector.

I lay there with my head down waiting for someone to find the body and start hollering. It was little Marvin Herold, Smitty's courier, who started screaming in his high voice, "Safety! . . . Oh, God! . . . Safety safety safety!

. . . Help! . . . Help!" "Safety" was the call we used to stop the fights if anyone saw a master coming or somebody got hurt. I lay there for several minutes listening to guys running past me through the brush heading for Baker Post, then I got up and followed them. I couldn't move very fast because my knees kept trying to bend the wrong way.

When I came out of the brush onto the gravel bank, I was surprised that everything looked so different. When I had left just five minutes before, the whole clearing and the creek were empty and lying bright in the sun, and Gene Hanlon was there all alone on the gravel bar. Now, with all the guys standing around and talking at once with their backs to the body, the whole place was different, and it wasn't so bad being there. I saw little Marvin Herold go over and try to take the pulse of Gene Hanlon's body. Marvin is a Boy Scout with lots of merit badges, and I expected him to try artificial respiration or a tourniquet, but he didn't find any pulse so he stood up and shook his head and wobbled over to where we were. He looked terribly blank, as though the Scout Manual had let him down.

The assumption going around was that Gene had run off the bluff and landed on his head and broken his neck. I couldn't see Peter anywhere, so I finally had to ask Smitty where he was. Smitty said he had sent Peter in to the school to tell somebody what had happened, and to get the ambulance. Smitty was still being the General, I guess, because there was nothing less for him to do. I tried to think to myself what Peter must be feeling like now, sent off to do an errand like that, but I couldn't get anywhere. My head was too full of what I was feeling like, standing with the fellows on the gravel bar looking at Gene Hanlon spread out half in the water like a dropped doll, knowing just how he had gotten there, and not being able to say anything.

Then Smitty got an idea, and he said, "Ronnie, weren't you here at Baker Post all the time?"

I made myself look at him, and then I said, "No, damn it, I got to thinking their army might try a crossing up by Able Post, so I went up there instead."

He said, "Oh," and forgot it.

Not long after, we heard a siren. We all knew what it was, and everybody stopped talking to listen to it as it got nearer. It was the first time I ever heard a siren and knew while hearing it why it had been called, and where it was going. It was kind of creepy, like it was saying to us over the trees, "Wait right there, boys. Don't anybody leave. I'll be there in a minute, and then we'll see just what's going on." I wanted to run and keep on running, until I got away from all the things swarming around inside me. You always wish afterward you had never joggled the wasp ball.

Pretty soon we heard somebody moving in the woods on the bluff and then two big men in white pants, carrying a folded-up stretcher, and another man in a suit, carrying a black bag, came out to the lip of the bluff. They stood there looking at us a minute without saying anything until one of the stretcher-bearers saw Gene Hanlon lying there all alone on the gravel bar. The man said something to the other two, and they all three looked where he pointed. Then the doctor looked at us all bunched up where we were and said, "Well, how do we get down?" He sounded sore. None of us moved or said anything, and in a minute the doctor got tired of waiting and blasted us. "Wake up over there! How do we go to get down?" Smitty came unstuck and gave them directions, and they went back into the bush heading north.

From then on things got pretty crowded in the woods. Two uniformed policemen and a photographer and a plain-clothes man showed up, and then Peter Irish came back leading almost the whole school faculty, and later a reporter and another photographer arrived. Nobody paid any attention to us for a while, so we just sat there in a clump, not moving or saying much. I managed to get right in the middle, and I kept down, hiding behind the guys around me and looking between them to see what was going on. After the police photographer was through taking pictures of Gene Hanlon from all sides, the two ambulance men raised him onto the stretcher and covered him with a piece of canvas or something and carried him away. The photographer took pictures all around by the creek and then went up onto the bluff and took pictures of the ground up there too. The plain-clothes man poking around on the gravel bar found Gene Hanlon's blue cap half full of rocks and gave it, with the rocks still in it, to one of the policemen to save.

I finally got up nerve enough to look for Peter Irish. He was standing with Smitty and Mr. Kelly, the math teacher, and they were talking. Peter didn't look any different. I didn't see how he could do it. I mean, stand right out there in plain sight of everyone, looking natural, with all that in his head. He looked around slowly as though he felt me watching him, and he found me there in the middle of the bunch. I couldn't have looked away if I had tried. He gave me a little smile, and I nodded my head to show him I'd seen it, then he went back to his talking with the other two.

Then the plain-clothes man went over to the three of them, and I got all wild inside and wanted to jump up and say that Peter couldn't possibly have done it, so please go away and let him alone. I could see the plain-clothes man doing most of the talking, and Peter and Smitty saying something once in a while, as though they were answering questions. After a little the plain-clothes man stopped talking and nodded, and the other three nodded back, and then he led them over to where the rest of us were. Smitty and Peter sat down with us and Mr. Kelly collected all the other faculty men and brought them over.

The plain-clothes man tipped his hat back and put his hands in his pockets and said, "My name is Gorman. Sergeant Gorman. We know all about the rock fight now, so don't get nervous that you'll let on something that'll get you into trouble. You're already in trouble, but that's not my business. You can settle that with your instructors and your parents. Uh . . .

you might think some about this, though. It's my feeling that every one of you here has a share in the responsibility for this boy's death. You all know rock fighting is dangerous, but you went ahead and did it anyway. But that's not what I'm after right now. I want to know if any of you boys actually saw this (what's his name?), this Hanlon boy run over the bluff." I was looking straight at Sergeant Gorman, but in the side of my eye I saw Peter Irish turn his head around and look at me. I didn't peep.

Then Sergeant Gorman said, "Which one of you is Ronnie Quiller?" I almost fainted.

Somebody poked me and I said, "Me." It didn't sound like my voice at all.

Sergeant Gorman said, "Which?" I said, "Me," again.

This time he found me and said, "Weren't you supposed to be lying there in this thicket all the time?"

"Yes," I said. All the kids were looking at me. "But there wasn't anything doing here so I moved up there a ways."

"I see," he said. "Do you always disobey orders?"

"No," I said, "but after all, it was only a game."

"Some game," said Sergeant Gorman. "Good clean fun."

Then he let me alone. There was only one person there who knew I would never have deserted the post assigned to me. That was Peter Irish. I guess, Dad, that's when I began to get really scared. The worst of it was not knowing how much Peter knew, and not daring to ask. He might have been waiting out of sight in the brush after he dropped that rock, and seen me take out for Able Post. I had always been his friend, but what was I now to him? I wanted to tell him everything was okay and I wouldn't for the world squeal on him, but that would have told him I knew he did it. Maybe he knew without my telling him. I didn't know what to do.

Sergeant Gorman finished up, "Let's all go back to the school now. I want to talk to each of you alone." We all got up and started back through the woods in a bunch. I figured Peter would think it was funny if I avoided him, so I walked with him.

I said, "Lousy damn day." He said, "Real lousy."

I said, "It seems like a hundred years since lunch."

We didn't say any more all the way back. It took all afternoon to get the individual interviews over. They took us from Assembly Hall in alphabetical order, and we had to go in and sit across from Sergeant Gorman while he asked the questions. He must have asked us all the same questions because by the time he got to me he was saying the words like they were tired. A girl stenographer sat by him and took down the answers. "Name?" "Ronnie Quiller." I had to spell it.

"Were you at the rock fight this afternoon?" "Yes, I was."

"What side were you on?" "The Confederates."

"What were you supposed to do?" "Watch the guys on the other side." "After this whistle, did you see anyone?" "No."

"You sure?"

"No, I didn't. That's why I moved from Baker Post up to Able Post. There wasn't anything doing where I was hiding."

"In rock fights before, have you ever changed position without telling somebody?"

"Sure, I guess. You can't run clear back to the field headquarters to tell anyone anything. It's up to them to find you."

Sergeant Gorman squinted at me with his eyebrows pulled down. "You know that if you had stayed where you were supposed to be you would have seen him fall over that bluff there?" "Yes," I said.

"I wish you had."

Afterwards I ran into Smitty out in the hall and I asked him why all this fuss with the police and all. I asked him who called them.

"It was Peter, I think. He told Mr. Kelly to, and Mr. Kelly did."

"What do you suppose they're after?" I asked Smitty.

"Oh, I guess they're trying to get a straight story to tell Gene's parents and the newspapers. From what I get from Mr. Kelly, the school is all for it. They want everybody to know they weren't responsible."

"Do you think Gene fell over that bluff?" I couldn't help asking that one.

"I don't know. I suppose so." He cocked his head to one side and grinned a little at me. "Like they say in the papers, 'fell or was pushed,' huh?"

I said, "I guess nobody'd have nerve enough to do that to Gene—push him, I mean." All of a sudden I was thinking about something I had seen. Going back in my mind I remembered seeing Sergeant Gorman pick up Gene's cap half full of rocks. Gravel rocks taken from the low bank of the creek. Now, I figured that Sergeant Gorman wouldn't have been a sergeant if he was stupid, and unless he was stupid he wouldn't go on for long thinking that Gene had fallen from above—when the cap half full of rocks said he'd been down below all the time!

I got my bike and rode home the long way to give me time to think about Peter and what he had done, and what I should do. You were real swell that night, and I guess I should have told you the whole story right then, but I just couldn't. I put myself in Peter's place, and I knew he would never have told on me. That's the way he was. He hated squealers. I couldn't think about his ever learning I had squealed on him. That would put me right alongside Angela Pine in his book. To him, I would have been the second person he trusted who let him down.

I felt like a rat in a cage with no place to go and no way out. When you kept me home nights after that, I didn't mind, because I wouldn't have gone out after dark if I'd been paid to. I don't blame you and Mother for thinking I had gone loony over the whole thing. Every noon recess for two whole weeks they pulled us into Assembly Hall and one of the masters would give a speech about group responsibility or public conscience or something awful like that, and then, worst of all, they made us bow our heads for five minutes in memory of Gene Hanlon. And there I'd be, sitting next to Peter Irish on the Assembly Hall bench, thinking back to the day of the last rock fight, and how Peter had looked up there on the bluff with the cords of his neck pulled tight, holding that big rock like it was a medicine ball. I had the crawliest feeling that if anybody in the hall had raised up his head and looked over at us together there on the bench, he would have seen two great fiery arrows pointing down at us. I was always afraid even to look up myself for fear I would have seen my own arrow and passed out on the spot.

It was my nightmares that got you worried, I guess. They always started out with Peter and me on a hike on a dusty country road. It was so hot you could hardly breathe. We would walk along without saying anything, with me lagging a little behind Peter so I could always keep an eye on him. And then the road would come out on the football field there at school, and he would go over to the woodpile and pick up a thin log and hold it in one hand, beckoning to me with the other and smiling. "Let's go over to the drugstore," he'd say, and then I'd start running.

I would follow the quarter-mile track around the football field and I'd know that everything would be all right if I could only get around it four times for a full mile. Every time I turned around to look, there he'd be right behind me, carrying that log and running easily, just like he used to pace me when I was out for the 880. I would make the first quarter mile all right, but then my wind would give out and my throat would dry up and my legs would get heavy, and I'd know that Peter was about to catch me, and I'd never make that full mile.

Then I would jar awake and be sweating and hanging on tight to the mattress, and in a minute you'd come in to see why I'd screamed. Your face was always kind of sad over me, and there in my bed in the dark, with you standing beside, I would almost let go and tell you why things were so bad with me. But then as I'd come awake, and the hammering in my heart would slow up, and the sweat would begin to dry, all the things I owed Peter Irish would stand out again and look at me, and I would know that I could never tell you about it until my telling could no longer get Peter Irish into trouble.

I'm tired now, Dad—tired in so many ways and in so many places that I don't know where to begin resting. This letter took all night, as I thought it would. It's beginning to get light outside and the birds are starting up. I just reread the story in the paper where it says that Sergeant Gorman knew all along that Gene Hanlon had been murdered. I told you he wasn't stupid. He knew what that cap half full of rocks meant, and he knew what it meant to find a big damp socket in the earth on top of the bluff, and the rock which had been *in* the socket down below in the creek. And after he had talked to each of us alphabetically there in the school office, he knew the name of the only boy in school strong enough to lift up a seventy-pound rock and throw it like a medicine ball. He knew all of these things before the sun went down on the day of the last rock fight, but he was two months putting the rest of the story together so he could use it in his business.

As I read it in the paper, Sergeant Gorman went over to Peter's house last Monday and talked to him about the things he had learned, and Peter listened respectfully, and then, when Sergeant Gorman was through and was ready to take Peter along with him, Peter excused himself to go upstairs and get his toilet articles. He got his four-ten shotgun instead and shot himself. I suppose it was the same four-ten he and I hunted squirrels with.

There's only one good thing about this whole stinking lousy mess, Dad. Because Sergeant Gorman talked to Peter and Peter listened, there in the living room; when Peter Irish climbed up those stairs he did it knowing that I, Ronnie Quiller, had not squealed on him. That may have made it easier. I don't know.

Now please, Dad—please may I come home again?

RONNIE

. . . .

Editors' Commentary . . . .

DIAGNOSIS: Post stress syndrome—severe anxiety reaction.

This story deals with the severe problems brought about by clashing feelings of guilt and loyalty. Ronnie was fully aware of the guilt of concealment he shared with Peter. His conscience immobilized him. He was torn between society's demand to report a homicide to the authorities and his loyalty to his friend. Peter had many times protected Ronnie from the cruelty or bullying of other boys, particularly the star bully, Gene Hanlon. Ronnie's guilt was of shared hostility as well as concealment. Like Peter, he hated Gene Hanlon and at times may have fantasized the aggression that Peter acted out.

In the adolescent struggle for identity, Peter and Ronnie made up one whole person: each compensated for the other's weaknesses and for using the other's strength. "We swapped talents," Ronnie said—Ronnie being the intellectual performer. He considered himself a natural scapegoat and thus regarded Peter, the physical performer, with gratitude and respect. Ronnie sensed that he must not, under any circumstance, betray his friend. His emotions were complicated by partial hostility and jealousy toward Angela.

As a sensitive student, Ronnie was aware that Peter must be protected not only from the police or another betrayer, but even from knowing that he, Ronnie, knew of the crime. Thus, Ronnie felt trapped—"like a rat in a cage"—by the necessity for silence and the projection of guilt. His overt symptoms were deep depression, nightmares, sweating, and inability to be with his friends.

His letter, written to a trusted person as soon as the crime was exposed (without his having participated in its exposure), released him from his anxiety reaction. He was able to see his own part in the drama and to evaluate realistically, and without blame, the part of the adults. His trust in his father's ability to listen to him sympathetically indicates that he had a basically sound relationship and therefore the capacity to grow out of this incident.

If the father listens, good! Ronnie should come home, resume normal life, and receive professional help. Ronnie has great capacity for awareness, introspection, and meaningful relationships.

ARTICLE 1.3

Silent Snow, Secret Snow

Conrad Aiken

Just why it should have happened, or why it should have happened just when it did, he could not, of course, possibly have said; nor perhaps could it even have occurred to him to ask. The thing was above all a secret, something to be preciously concealed from Mother and Father; and to that very fact it owed an enormous part of its deliciousness. It was like a peculiarly beautiful trinket to be carried unmentioned in one's trouser-pocket—a rare stamp, an old coin, a few tiny gold links found trodden out of shape on the path in the park, a pebble of carnelian, a sea shell distinguishable from all others by an unusual spot or stripe—and, as if it were any one of these, he carried around with him everywhere a warm and persistent and increasingly beautiful sense of possession. Nor was it only a sense of possession—it was also a sense of protection. It was as if, in some delightful way, his secret gave him a fortress, a wall behind which he could retreat into heavenly seclusion. This was almost the first thing he had noticed about it—apart from the oddness of the thing itself—and it was this that now again, for the fiftieth time, occurred to him, as he sat in the little schoolroom. It was the half hour for geography. Miss Buell was revolving with one finger, slowly, a huge terrestrial globe which had been placed on her desk. The green and yellow continents passed and repassed, questions were asked and answered, and now the little girl in front of him, Deirdre, who had a funny little constellation of freckles on the back of her neck, exactly like the Big Dipper, was standing up and telling Miss Buell that the equator was the line that ran around the middle. Miss Buell's face, which was old and grayish and kindly, with gray stiff curls beside the cheeks, and eyes that swam very brightly, like little minnows, behind thick glasses, wrinkled itself into a complication of amusements.

Reprinted by permission of The World Publishing Company from *The Collected Short Stories of Conrad Aiken* by Conrad Aiken. Copyright 1922, 1923, 1924, 1925, 1927, 1928, 1929, 1930, 1931, 1932, 1933, 1934, 1935, 1941, 1950, 1952, 1953, 1955, 1956, 1957, 1958, 1959, 1960 by Conrad Aiken.

"Ah! I see. The earth is wearing a belt, or a sash. Or someone drew a line round it!" "Oh, no—not that—I mean—" In the general laughter, he did not share, or only a very little. He was thinking about the Arctic and Antarctic regions, which of course, on the globe, were white. Miss Buell was now telling them about the tropics, the jungles, the steamy heat of equatorial swamps, where the birds and butterflies, and even the snakes, were like living jewels. As he listened to these things, he was already, with a pleasant sense of half-effort, putting his secret between himself and the words. Was it really an effort at all? For effort implies something voluntary, and perhaps even something one did not especially want; whereas this was distinctly pleasant, and came almost of its own accord. All he needed to do was to think of that morning, the first one, and then of all the others—but it was all so absurdly simple! It had amounted to so little. It was nothing, just an idea—and just why it should have become so wonderful, so permanent, was a mystery—a very pleasant one, to be sure, but also, in an amusing way, foolish. However, without ceasing to listen to Miss Buell, who had now moved up to the north temperate zones, he deliberately invited his memory of the first morning. It was only a moment or two after he had waked up—or perhaps the moment itself. But was there, to be exact, an exact moment? Was one awake all at once? or was it gradual? Anyway, it was after he had stretched a lazy hand up towards the headrail, and yawned, and then relaxed again among his warm covers, all the more grateful on a December morning, that the thing had happened. Suddenly, for no reason, he had thought of the postman, he remembered the postman. Perhaps there was nothing so odd in that. After all, he heard the postman almost every morning in his life—his heavy boots could be heard clumping round the corner at the top of the little cobbled hill-street, and then, progressively nearer, progressively louder, the double knock at each door, the crossings and recrossings of the street, till finally the clumsy steps came stumbling across to the very door, and the tremendous knock came which shook the house itself. (Miss Buell was saying "Vast wheat-growing areas in North America and Siberia." Deirdre had for the moment placed her left hand across the back of her neck.)

But on this particular morning, the first morning, as he lay there with his eyes closed, he had for some reason *waited* for the postman. He wanted to hear him come round the corner. And that was precisely the joke—he never did. He never came. He never had *come—round the corner—again.* For when at last the steps *were* heard, they had already, he was quite sure, come a little down the hill, to the first house; and even so, the steps were curiously different—they were softer, they had a new secrecy about them, they were muffled and indistinct; and while the rhythm of them was the same, it now said a new thing—it said peace, it said remoteness, it said cold, it said sleep. And he had understood the situation at once—nothing could have seemed simpler—there had been snow in the night, such as all winter he had been longing for; and it was this which had rendered the postman's first footsteps inaudible, and the later ones faint. Of course! How lovely! And even now it must be snowing—it was going to be a snowy day—the long white ragged lines were drifting and sifting across the street, across the faces of the old houses, whispering and hushing, making little triangles of white in the corners between cobblestones, seething a little when the wind blew them over the ground to a drifted corner; and so it would be all day, getting deeper and deeper and silenter and silenter. (Miss Buell was saying "Land of perpetual snow.") All this time, of course (while he lay in bed), he had kept his eyes closed, listening to the nearer progress of the postman, the muffled footsteps thumping and slipping on the snow-sheathed cobbles; and all the other sounds—the double knocks, a frosty far-off voice or two, a bell ringing thinly and softly as if under a sheet of ice—had the same slightly abstracted quality, as if removed by one degree from actuality—as if everything in the world had been insulated by snow. But when at last, pleased, he opened his eyes, and turned them towards the window, to see for himself this long-desired and now so clearly imagined miracle—what he saw instead was brilliant sunlight on a roof; and when, astonished, he jumped out of bed and stared down into the street, expecting to see the cobbles obliterated by the snow, he saw nothing but the bare bright cobbles themselves.

Queer, the effect this extraordinary surprise had had upon him—all the following morning he had kept with him a sense as of snow falling about him, a secret screen of new snow between himself and the world. If he had not dreamed such a thing—and how could he have dreamed it while awake?—how else could one explain it? In any case, the delusion had been so vivid as to affect his entire behavior. He could not now remember whether it was on the first or the second morning—or was it even the third?—that his mother had drawn attention to some oddness in his manner.

"*But* my darling—" she had said at the breakfast table—"what has come over you? You don't seem to be listening. . . ."

And how often that very thing had happened since! (Miss Buell was now asking if anyone knew the difference between the North Pole and the Magnetic Pole. Deirdre was holding up her flickering brown hand, and he could see the four white dimples that marked the knuckles.) . . .

"Now Paul—I would like very much to ask you a question or two. You will answer them, won't you—you know I'm an old, old friend of yours, eh? That's right! . . ."

His back was thumped twice by the doctor's fat fist—then the doctor was grinning at him with false amiability, while with one fingernail he was scratching the top button of his waistcoat. Beyond the doctors shoulder was the fire, the fingers of flame making light prestidigitation against the sooty fireback, the soft sound of their random flutter the only sound.

"I would like to know—is there anything that worries you?" The doctor was again smiling, his eyelids low against the little black pupils, in each of which was a tiny white bead of light. Why answer him? why answer him at all? "At whatever pain to others"—but it was all a nuisance, this necessity for resistance, this necessity for attention: it was as if one had been stood up on a brilliantly lighted stage, under a great round blaze of spotlight; as if one were merely a trained seal, or a performing dog, or a fish, dipped out of an aquarium and held up by the tail. It would serve them right if he were merely to bark or growl. And meanwhile, to miss these last few precious hours, these hours of which every minute was more beautiful than the last, more menacing—? He still looked, as if from a great distance, at the beads of light in the doctor's eyes, at the fixed false smile, and then, beyond, once more at his mother's slippers, his father's slippers, the soft flutter of the fire. Even here, even amongst these hostile presences, and in this arranged light, he could see the snow, he could hear it—it was in the corners of the room, where the shadow was deepest, under the sofa, behind the half-opened door which led to the dining room. It was gentler here, softer, its seethe the quietest of whispers, as if, in deference to a drawing room, it had quite deliberately put on its "manners"; it kept itself out of sight, obliterated itself, but distinctly with an air of saying, "Ah, but just wait! Wait till we are alone together! Then I will begin to tell you something new! Something white! something cold! something sleepy! something of cease, and peace, and the long bright curve of space! Tell them to go away. Banish them. Refuse to speak. Leave them, go upstairs to your room, turn out the light and get into bed—I will go with you, I will be waiting for you, I will tell you a better story than Little Kay of the Skates, or The Snow Ghost—I will surround your bed, I will close the windows, pile a deep drift against the door, so that none will ever again be able to enter. Speak to them! . . ." It seemed as if the little hissing voice came from a slow white spiral of falling flakes in the corner by the front window—but he could not be sure. He felt himself smiling, then, and said to the doctor, but without looking at him, looking beyond him still "Oh, no, I think not—" "But are you sure, my boy?" His father's voice came softly and coldly then—the familiar voice of silken warning. "You needn't answer at once, Paul—remember we're trying to help you—think it over and be quite sure, won't you?"

He felt himself smiling again, at the notion of being quite sure. What a joke! As if he weren't so sure that reassurance was no longer necessary, and all this cross-examination a ridiculous farce, a grotesque parody! What could they know about it? These gross intelligences, these humdrum minds so bound to the usual, the ordinary? Impossible to tell them about it! Why, even now, even now, with the proof so abundant, so formidable, so imminent, so appallingly present here in this very room, could they believe it?— could even his mother believe it? No—it was only too plain that if anything were said about it, the merest hint given, they would be incredulous—they would laugh—they would say "Absurd!"—think things about him which weren't true . . . .

"Why no, I'm not worried—why should I be?" He looked then straight at the doctor's low-lidded eyes, looked from one of them to the other, from one bead of light to the other, and gave a little laugh.

The doctor seemed to be disconcerted by this. He drew back in his chair, resting a fat white hand on either knee. The smile faded slowly from his face.

"Well, Paul!" he said, and paused gravely, "I'm afraid you don't take this quite seriously enough. I think you perhaps don't quite realize—don't quite realize—" He took a deep quick breath, and turned, as if helplessly, at a loss for words, to the others. But Mother and Father were both silent—no help was forthcoming.

"You must surely know, be aware, that you have not been quite yourself of late? don't you known that? . . ." It was amusing to watch the doctor's renewed attempt at a smile, a queer disorganized look, as of confidential embarrassment.

"I feel all right, sir," he said, and again gave the little laugh.

"And we're trying to help you." The doctor's tone sharpened.

"Yes, sir, I know. But why? I'm all right. I'm just *thinking,* that's all."

His mother made a quick movement forward, resting a hand on the back of the doctor's chair. "Thinking?" she said. "But my dear, about what?"

This was a direct challenge—and would have to be directly met. But before he met it, he looked again into the corner by the door, as if for reassurance. He smiled again at what he saw, at what he heard. The little spiral was still there, still softly whirling, like the ghost of a white kitten chasing the ghost of a white tail, and making as it did so the faintest of whispers. It was all right! If only he could remain firm, everything was going to be all right.

"Oh, about anything, about *nothing*—*you* know the way you do!"

"You mean—day-dreaming?" "Oh, no—thinking!"

"But thinking about *what?*" "Anything."

He laughed a third time—but this time, happening to glance upward towards his mother's face, he was appalled at the effect his laughter seemed to have upon her. Her mouth had opened in an expression of horror. . . . This was too bad! Unfortunate! He had known it would cause pain, of course, but he hadn't expected it to be quite so bad as this. Perhaps—perhaps if he just gave them a tiny gleaming hint—?

"About the snow," he said.

"What on earth!" This was his father's voice. The brown slippers came a step nearer on the hearth-rug. "But my dear, what do you mean?" This was his mother's voice.

The doctor merely stared.

"Just *snow,* that's all. I like to think about it." "Tell us about it, my boy."

"But that's all it is. There's nothing to tell. *You* know what snow is?"

This he said almost angrily, for he felt that they were trying to corner him. He turned sideways so as no longer to face the doctor, and the better to see the inch of blackness between the window-sill and the lowered curtain—the cold inch of beckoning and delicious night. At once he felt better, more assured.

"Mother can I go to bed, now, please? I've got a headache."

"But I thought you said—"

"It's just come. It's all these questions—! Can I, mother?"

"You can go as soon as the doctor has finished."

"Don't you think this thing ought to be gone into thoroughly, and *now?*" This was Father's voice. The brown slippers again came a step nearer, the voice was the well-known "punishment" voice, resonant and cruel.

"Oh, what's the use, Norman—"

Quite suddenly, everyone was silent. And without precisely facing them, nevertheless he was aware that all three of them were watching him with an extraordinary intensity staring hard at him—as if he had done something monstrous, or was himself some kind of monster. He could hear the soft irregular flutter of the flames; the cluck-click-cluck-click of the clock; far and faint, two sudden spurts of laughter from the kitchen, as quickly cut off as begun; a murmur of water in the pipes; and then, the silence seemed to deepen, to spread out, to become world-long and world-wide, to become timeless and shapeless, and to center inevitably and tightly, with a slow and sleepy but enormous concentration of all power, on the beginning of a new sound. What this new sound was going to be, he knew perfectly well. It might begin with a hiss, but it would end with a roar—there was no time to lose—he must escape. It mustn't happen here—Without another word, he turned and ran up the stairs.

Not a moment too soon. The darkness was coming in long white waves. A prolonged sibilance filled the night—a great seamless seethe of wild influence went abruptly across it—a cold low humming shook the windows. He shut the door and flung off his clothes in the dark. The bare black floor was like a little raft tossed in waves of snow, almost overwhelmed, washed under whitely, up again, smothered in curled billows of feather. The snow was laughing: it spoke from all sides at once: it pressed closer to him as he ran and jumped exulting into his bed.

"Listen to us!" it said. "Listen! We have come to tell you the story we told you about. You remember? Lie down. Shut your eyes, now—you will no longer see much—in this white darkness who could see, or want to see? We will take the place of everything . . . . Listen—"

A beautiful varying dance of snow began at the front of the room, came forward and then retreated, flattened out toward the floor, then rose fountainlike to the ceiling, swayed, recruited itself from a new stream of flakes which poured laughing in through the humming window, advanced again, lifted long white arms. It said peace, it said remoteness, it said cold—it said—

But then a gash of horrible light fell brutally across the room from the opening door—the snow drew back hissing—something alien had come into the room—something hostile. This thing rushed at him, clutched at him, shook him—and he was not merely horrified, he was filled with such a loathing as he had never known. What was this? this cruel disturbance? this act of anger and hate? It was as if he had to reach up a hand toward another world for any understanding of it—an effort of which he was only barely capable. But of that other world he still remembered just enough to know the exorcising words. They tore themselves from his other life suddenly—"Mother! Mother! Go away! I hate you!"

And with that effort, everything was solved, everything became all right: the seamless hiss advanced once more, the long white wavering lines rose and fell like enormous whispering sea-waves, the whisper becoming louder, the laughter more numerous.

"Listen!" it said. "We'll tell you the last, the most beautiful and secret story—shut your eyes—it is a very small story—a story that gets smaller and smaller—it comes inward instead of opening like a flower—it is a flower becoming a seed—a little cold seed—do you hear? we are leaning closer to you—"

The hiss was now becoming a roar—the whole world was a vast moving screen of snow—but even now it said peace, it said remoteness, it said cold, it said sleep.

. . . .

Editors' Commentary . . . .

DIAGNOSIS: Schizophrenic breakdown—delusions and hallucinations, both visual and auditory; gradual withdrawal from world of reality into autistic or fantasy world.

Like the Sirens to Ulysses, this secret world of snow is unbearably tempting or beckoning to Paul, until this twelve-year-old boy is magnetized away from the world of home and school. Exactly what, in his middle-class home and daily life, was so painful for him that he needed to retreat? The clinging to mother or the overidentification and unconscious hostility of one of the parents, so frequently found in schizophrenic breakdowns? We are told only how his delusionary cocoon has spread from home to school. Mother, father, and teacher become aware of the increasing withdrawal of this boy, of his "not-thereness." The ways the doctor mishandles the child and the father's understandable irritation under the strain of anxiety are typical reactions to the frightening phenomenon of watching the child disappear into another world before their eyes.

The story clearly indicates the character of this type of student. In a classroom, he or she is shy, quiet, and withdrawn—not a behavior problem. Yet, more and more often, the youngster is miles away when a question is asked. Sometimes, his or her answers are puzzlingly inappropriate, rooted in the question but winding off into outer space. This is the kind of student Miss Buell would describe in a conference as being very well prepared sometimes, but just not there most of the time. The seemingly sudden onset of the illness is misleading. A keen and sensitive teacher who is prepared to see them can recognize signs of increasing withdrawal. An adequately prepared teacher would have consulted the counseling department of the school before the breakdown occurred.

THE ABUSED CHILD . . . .

The following is the true story of a boy who was born into a protected home but had experienced, by the time he was ten, all the horrors, cruelties, and bestialities humans are capable of inflicting. He was a Polish-Jewish child whose parents gave him to a peasant in order to spare him the horrors and probable death of a Nazi prison camp. His peasant helper died several months after he arrived, however, and he was left at age seven to roam for three years, homeless, helpless, ill-fed, and ill-treated. Because of his dark skin, he was thought to be either Gypsy or Jewish and therefore subjected to a variety of cruelties by the ignorant, highly superstitious peasants of the villages he wandered through. His journey from farm to village to town to city, through the Nazi and then the Russian occupations of Poland, was a living nightmare. He was exploited, beaten, mauled, sexually abused, and treated like an animal. In one episode, when he was beaten, whipped, tied, and buried deep in a human manure heap, he lost his speech. Each time he reached out for minimal sustenance and care, he met with physical violence.

Although his story reflects the intense ugliness, horror, and cruelty that people may inflict on a child, it lacks one aspect of hideousness that happens daily to children throughout our nation, it was not this boy's own parents who perpetrated the horrors on him. He thought his parents were dead, but they had survived, and after the war they fought through years of red tape to find him again. He was then living in a Russian-run orphanage, the most secure home he had found since his wanderings began. Even after his return to his parents, he did not regain his speech until caught one time in a blizzard, when his survival was once more at stake.

This author knows firsthand the abuse of children: their suffering, fantasies, susceptibility to superstition, defenses against utter invasion, vulnerability to cruelty, hope for nurturance, and immobilizing despair under the yoke of mistreatment.

Child abuse is as old as history itself. It occurs when adults who are wrapped in feelings of helplessness about their own lives take our their rage and distress, their twisted and thwarted sexual and affectional desires, on helpless children. It occurs most often in the family setting. Often, it goes too long without comment by neighbors and community, because people believe that no one should interfere in the parents' handling of their own child, that the child is the "property" of the parents. It is time we discarded the notion that others have no right to save a child from mistreatment even when death or crippling can result.

The Painted Bird

Jerzy Kosinski

Garbos was waiting for me at home. As soon as I entered he dragged me to an empty room in the corner of the house. There at the highest point of the ceiling two large hooks had been driven into the beams, less than two feet apart. Leather straps were attached to each as handles.

Garbos climbed on a stool, lifted me high, and told me to grab a handle with each hand. Then he left me suspended and brought Judas into the room. On his way out he locked the door.

Judas saw me hanging from the ceiling and immediately jumped up in an effort to reach my feet. I brought my legs up and he missed them by a few inches. He started another run and tried again, still missing. After a few more tries he lay down and waited.

I had to watch him. When freely hanging, my feet were no more than six feet above the ground and Judas could easily reach them. I did not know how long I would have to hang like this. I guessed that Garbos expected me to fall down and be attacked by Judas. This would frustrate the efforts I had been making all these months, counting Garbos's teeth, including the yellow, ingrown ones at the back of his mouth. Innumerable times when Garbos was drunk with vodka and snored open-mouthed I had counted his loathsome teeth painstakingly. This was my weapon against him. Whenever he beat me too long I reminded him of the number of his teeth; if he did not believe me he could check the count himself. I knew every one of them, no matter how wobbly, how putrefied, or how nearly hidden under the gums. If he killed me he would have very few years left to live. However, if I fell down into the waiting fangs of Judas, Garbos would have a clear conscious. He would have nothing to fear, and his patron, St. Anthony, might even give him absolution from my accidental death.

My shoulders were becoming numb. I shifted my weight, opened and closed my hands, and slowly relaxed my legs, lowering them dangerously near to the floor. Judas was in the corner pretending to be asleep. But I knew his tricks as well as he knew mine. He knew that I still had some strength left and that I could lift my legs faster than he could leap after them. So he waited for fatigue to overcome me.

The pain in my body raced in two directions. One went from the hands to the shoulders and neck, the other from the legs to the waist. They were two different kinds of pain, boring toward my middle like two moles tunneling toward each other underground. The pain from my hands was easier to endure. I could cope with it by switching my weight from one hand to the other, relaxing the muscles and then taking the load up again, hanging on one hand while blood returned to the other. The pain from between my legs and abdomen was more persistent, and once it settled in my belly it refused to leave. It was like a woodworm that finds a cozy spot behind a knot in the timber and stays there forever.

It was a strange, dull, penetrating pain. It must have been like the pain felt by a man Garbos mentioned in warning. Apparently this man had treacherously killed the son of an influential farmer and the father had decided to punish the murder in the old-fashioned manner. Together with his two cousins the man brought the culprit to the forest. There they prepared a twelve-foot stake, sharpened at one end to a fine point like a gigantic pencil. They laid it on the ground, wedging the blunt end against a tree trunk. Then a strong horse was hitched to each of the victim's feet, while his crotch was leveled with the waiting point. The horses, gently nudged, pulled the man against the spiked beam, which gradually sank into the tensed flesh. When the point was deep into the entrails of the victim, the men lifted the stake, together with the impaled man upon it and planted it in a previously dug hole. They left him there to die slowly.

Now hanging under the ceiling I could almost see the man and hear him howling into the night, trying to lift to the indifferent sky his arms which hung by the bloated trunk of his body. He must have looked like a bird knocked out of a tree by a slingshot and fallen flabbily onto a dried-out, pointed stalk.

Still feigning indifference, Judas woke up below. He yawned, scratched behind his ears, and hunted the fleas in his tail. Sometimes he glanced slyly at me, but turned away in disgust when he saw my hunched legs.

He only fooled me once. I thought he had really gone to sleep and straightened out my legs. Judas instantly bounced off the floor, leaping like a grasshopper. One of my feet did not jerk up fast enough and he tore off some skin at the heel. The fear and pain almost caused me to fall. Judas licked his chops triumphantly and reclined by the wall. He watched me through the slits of his eyes and waited.

I thought I could not hold on any longer. I decided to jump down and planned my defense against Judas, though I knew that I wouldn't even have time to lift a hand before he would be at my throat. There was no time to lose. Then suddenly I remembered the prayers.

I started shifting weight from one hand to the other, moving my head, jerking my legs up and down. Judas looked at me, discouraged by this display of strength. Finally he turned toward the wall and remained motionless. Time went by and my prayers multiplied. Thousands of days of indulgence streaked through the thatched roof toward heaven.

Late in the afternoon Garbos came into the room. He looked at my wet body and the pool of sweat on the floor. He took me off the hooks roughly and kicked the dog out. All that evening I could neither walk nor move my arms. I lay down on the mattress and prayed. Days of indulgence came in hundreds, in thousands. Surely by now there were more of them in heaven for me than grains of wheat in the field. Any day, any minute, notice of this would have to be taken in heaven. Perhaps even now the saints were considering some radical improvement of my life.

Garbos hung me up every day. Sometimes he did it in the morning and sometimes in the evening. And had he not been afraid of foxes and thieves and needed Judas in the yard, he would have done it at night too.

It was always the same. While I still had some strength the dog stretched out on the floor calmly, pretending to sleep or casually catching fleas. When the pain in my arms and legs became more intense, he grew alert as though sensing what was going on inside my body. Sweat poured from me, running in rivulets over my straining muscles, hitting the floor with regular plip-plops. As soon as I straightened my legs Judas invariably leapt at them.

Months went by. Garbos needed me more around the farm because he was often drunk and didn't want to work. He hung me up only when he felt he had no particular use for me. When he sobered up and heard the hungry pigs and the lowing cow he took me off the hooks and put me to work. The muscles of my arms became conditioned by the hanging and I could endure it for hours without much effort. Although the pain that came to my belly began later now, I got cramps which frightened me. And Judas never missed a chance to leap at me, though by now he must have doubted he would ever catch me off guard.

While I hung on the straps I concentrated on my prayers to the exclusion of all else. When my strength ebbed I told myself that I should be able to last another ten or twenty prayers before I dropped down. After these were recited I made another promise to myself of ten or fifteen prayers. I believed that something could happen at any moment, that every extra thousand days of indulgence could save my life, perhaps at this very instant.

Sometimes, to divert my attention from the pain and from my numb arm muscles, I teased Judas. First I swung on my arms as though I were about to fall down. The dog barked, jumped, and raged. When he went to sleep again I would wake him with cries and the smacking of lips and grinding of teeth. He could not understand what was happening. Thinking that this was the end of my endurance, he leapt about madly, knocking into the walls in the darkness, overturning the stool standing by the door. He grunted with pain, heaved heavily, and finally rested. I took the opportunity to straighten my legs. When the room resounded to the snoring of the fatigued beast, I saved strength by setting prizes for myself for endurance: straightening one leg for every thousand days of indulgence, resting one arm for every ten prayers, and one major shift of position for every fifteen prayers.

At some unexpected moment I would hear the clatter of the latch and Garbos would enter. When he saw me alive he would curse Judas, kick and beat him until the dog cried and whimpered like a puppy.

His fury was so tremendous that I wondered if God Himself had not sent him at this moment. But when I looked at his face, I could find no trace of the divine presence . . . .

Rough hands tore me up from the floor and pulled me toward the doorway. The crowd parted in stupefaction. From the balcony a male voice shouted "Gypsy vampire!" and several voices took up the chant. Hands clamped my body with excruciating hardness, tearing at my flesh. Outside I wanted to cry and beg for mercy, but no sound came from my throat. I tried once more. There was no voice in me.

The fresh air hit my heated body. The peasants dragged me straight toward a large manure pit. It had been dug two or three years ago, and the small outhouse standing next to it with small windows cut in the shape of the cross was the subject of special pride to the priest. It was the only one in the area. The peasants were accustomed to attending to the wants of nature directly in the field and only used it when coming to church. A new pit was being dug on the other side of the presbytery, however, because the old pit was completely full and the wind often carried foul odors to the church.

When I realized what was going to happen to me, I again tried to shout. But no voice came from me. Every time I struggled a heavy peasant hand would drop on me, gagging my mouth and nose. The stench from the pit increased. We were very close to it now. Once more I tried to struggle free, but the men held me fast, never ceasing their talk about the event in the church. They had no doubt that I was a vampire and that the interruption of the High Mass could only bode evil for the village.

We halted at the edge of the pit. Its brown, wrinkled surface steamed with fetor like horrible skin on the surface of a cup of hot buckwheat soup. Over this surface swarmed a myriad of small white caterpillars, about as long as a fingernail. Above the surface circled clouds of flies, buzzing monotonously, with beautiful blue and violet bodies glittering in the sun, colliding, falling toward the pit for a moment, and soaring into the air again.

I retched. The peasants swung me by the hands and feet. The pale clouds in the blue sky swam before my eyes. I was hurled into the very center of the brown filth, which parted under my body to engulf me.

Daylight disappeared above me and I began to suffocate. I tossed instinctively in the dense element, lashing out with my arms and legs. I touched the bottom and rebounded from it as fast as I could. A spongy upswell raised me toward the surface. I opened my mouth and caught a dash of air. I was sucked back below the surface and again pushed myself up from the bottom. The pit was only twelve feet square. Once more I sprang up from the bottom, this time toward the edge. At the last moment, when the downswell was about to pull me under, I caught hold of a creeper of the long thick weeds growing over the edge of the pit. I fought against the suction of the reluctant maw and pulled myself to the edge of the pit, barely able to see through my slime-obscured eyes.

I crawled out of the mire and was immediately gripped with cramps of vomiting. They shook me so long that my strength vanished and I slid down completely exhausted into the stinging, burning bushes of thistle, fern, and ivy.

I heard the distant sound of the organ and human singing and I reasoned that after the Mass the people might come out of the church and drown me again in the pit if they saw me alive in the bushes. I had to escape and so I darted into the forest. The sun baked the brown crust on me and clouds of large flies and insects besieged me. As soon as I found myself in the shade of the trees I started rolling over in the cool, moist moss, rubbing myself with cold leaves, and vomiting. With pieces of bark I scraped off the remaining muck. I rubbed sand in my hair and then rolled in the grass and vomited again.

Suddenly I realized that something had happened to my voice. I tried to cry out, but my tongue flapped helplessly in my open mouth. I had no voice. I was terrified and, covered with cold sweat, I refused to believe that this was possible and tried to convince myself that my voice would come back. I waited a few moments and tried again. Nothing happened. The silence of the forest was broken only by the buzzing of the flies around me.

I sat down. The last cry that I had uttered under the falling missal still echoed in my ears. Was it the last cry I would ever utter? Was my voice escaping with it like a solitary duck call straying over a huge pond? Where was it now? I could envision my voice flying alone under the high-arched, vaulting ribs of the church roof.

. . . .

Editors' Commentary . . . .

DIAGNOSIS: Massive child abuse frequently leading to paralyzing depression and little sense of self-worth.

The Dynamics of Child Abuse   Adults perpetrating child abuse often were abused themselves as children or grew up with violence as the major means of expression. These parents are reluctant to bring their children to medical facilities for treatment and loath to confess. Although the emergency room of every children's hospital or clinic sees cases of deaths caused by beatings, burnings, and maulings, only recently have medical personnel attempted to get proper records, make inquiries, and follow up on incidents. Even now, adequate protection of abused children, particularly infants, is tragically lacking. Sometimes, child abuse is an outlet for rage or a means of punishing another person in the family. The results are scarred and bruised bodies. In some cases, hair can no longer grow, because hot grease has burned the source of growth. Whip scars and bruises to face and body are everyday occurrences. Damaged penises and ripped vaginas and anuses are common in every hospital. Blindness and deafness are frequent results, as are crippling and maiming.

The psychological results, if the child survives, are every bit as scarring. The most familiar effects are lack of trust, stultification of mind and speech, inability to relate, and, most common of all, total self-hate. An abused child who survives always feels intrinsically worthless, as if he or she interprets the abusing parents' acts as a value judgment on his or her worth. A child reasons that some past action must explain the violent acts done; the ill treatment must be deserved.

One of the most paradoxical elements found in child abuse is the frequent loyalty of children to the abusing parents. Children will sometimes even defend parents within minutes after a beating. They will deny their very obvious wounds. Children can thus see the parents as good and loving despite all evidence and pain.

The best treatment, where treatment is possible, is family counseling, with much support given to the offending adult(s). Despite the repulsiveness of the acts, the parents' behavior must be looked at as an uncontrollable illness that must be stopped. Usually, one child in a family is selected as victim. However, if the selected child is placed elsewhere, it is likely that another child will be substituted. Often, the chosen child is the most vulnerable of the children: the quiet, very sensitive, or handicapped child. The offending parent perhaps sees his or her own vulnerability in the selected child.

Although only one of two parents may be engaged in actual physical abuse, the other participates or acquiesces in the act—even when he or she does not overtly know what is going on. The nonabusing parent tries to remain unaware of the facts or belittles the seriousness of them. Part of the treatment involves confronting the inactive partner with his or her own role in the family situation.

The number of child abuse cases that are reported is staggering, running into the thousands annually. The number of unreported cases is even more staggering. Conditions of poverty breed despair, and lack of education limits means of expressing frustrations—for example, the choice of verbal substitutes for physical impulses. Hence, poverty is the most fertile ground for acting out and for child abuse. Among ethnic minorities who themselves have been ill-treated, often with external violence, and where hatred cannot be turned outward for lack of power and means, it is turned inward toward self or family.

Child abuse by no means belongs exclusively to the economically deprived or to racial minorities. The middle and upper classes are better able to keep the physical scars and signs of child abuse concealed from others. Severe beatings and sadistic acts go unreported, and private doctors try to believe the lies they are told to explain peculiar and unlikely injuries; often, they have no proof to bring the cases out in the open, so they pretend to believe and go along with the families. In the more privileged groups, where violence is not the normal mode of expression and verbal skills are the major currency of communication, it is hard to tell what goes on. As long as the lie is maintained, it is next to impossible to work with the family.

The teacher, however, has a professional and legal obligation to report to the principal any unusual injuries, burns, or marks on any student. Society has a responsibility to step in and protect abused students, and the classroom teachers' observations are the first line of defense and protection.

SOME REASONS WHY IT FEELS THE WAY IT DOES
(Poverty/Slums/Racial and Ethnic Class Distinctions, and
Economic Differences) . . . .

E. R. Braithwaite, author of the first excerpt in this section, is an Oxford-trained Black engineer. Unable to find a job that made use of his professional training and experience, he took a teaching job at an experimental day school in the poorest White slums of London. The school, run by an inspired educator, admits students rejected by other schools. Braithwaite's understanding of the group dynamics of teaching is impressive.

ARTICLE 1.5

To Sir, with Love
E. R. Braithwaite

Just about this time a new supply teacher, Mr. Bell, was sent to our school as supernumerary to the Staff for a few weeks. He was about forty years old, a tall, wiry man, who had some previous experience with the Army Education Service. It was arranged that he should act as relief teacher for some lessons, including two periods of P.T. with the senior boys. One of Mr. Bell's hobbies was fencing: he was something of a perfectionist and impatient of anyone whose co-ordination was not as smooth and controlled as his own. He would repeat a P.T. movement or exercise over and over again until it was executed with clockwork precision, and though the boys grumbled against his discipline they seemed eager to prove to him that they were quite capable of doing any exercise he could devise, and with a skill that very nearly matched his own.

This was especially true in the cases of Ingham, Fernman and Seales, who would always place themselves at the head of the line as an example and encouragement to the others. The least athletic of these was Richard Buckley, a short, fat boy, amiable and rather dim, who could read and write after a fashion, and could never be provoked to any semblance of anger or heat. He was pleasant and jolly and a favorite with the others, who, though they themselves chivvied him unmercifully, were ever ready in his defense against outsiders. Buckley was no good at P.T. or games; he just was not built for such pursuits. Yet, such is the perversity of human nature, he strenuously resisted any efforts to leave him out or overlook him when games were being arranged. His attempts at accomplishing such simple gymnastic performances as the "forward roll" and "star jump" reduced the rest of the P.T. class to helpless hilarity, but he persisted with a singleness of purpose which, though unproductive, was nothing short of heroic.

Buckley was Bell's special whipping boy. Fully aware of the lad's physical limitations, he would encourage him to try other and more difficult exercises, with apparently the sole purpose of obtaining some amusement from the pitiably ridiculous results. Sometimes the rest of the class would protest; and then Bell would turn on them the full flood of his invective. The boys mentioned this in their "Weekly Review," and Mr. Florian decided to discuss it at a Staff Meeting.

"The boys seem to be a bit bothered by remarks you make to them during P.T., Mr. Bell."

"To which remarks do you refer, Mr. Florian?" Bell never used the term "Sir," seeming to think it "infra dig." Even when he granted him the "Mr. Florian," he gave to this form of address the suggestion of a sneer.

"From their review it would seem that you are unnecessarily critical of their persons."

"Do you mean their smell?"

"Well, yes, that and the state of their clothing."

"I've advised them to wash."

"These are the words which appear in one review." The Headmaster produced a notebook, Fernman's, and read:

"Some of you stink like old garbage." His tone was cool, detached, judicial.

"I was referring to their feet. Many of them never seem to wash their feet, and when they take their shoes off the stink is dreadful."

"Many of them live in homes where there are very few facilities for washing, Mr. Bell."

"Surely enough water is available for washing their feet if they really wanted to."

"Then they'd put on the same smelly socks and shoes to which you also object."

"I've got to be in contact with them and it isn't very pleasant."

"Have you ever lived in this area, Mr. Bell?" "No fear."

"Then you know nothing about the conditions prevailing. The water you so casually speak of is more often to be found in the walls and on the floors than in the convenient wash basin or bath to which you are accustomed. I've visited homes of some of these children where water for a family in an upstairs flat had to be fetched by bucket or pail from the single back-yard tap which served five or six families. You may see, therefore, that so elementary a function as washing the feet might present many difficulties." Bell was silent at this.

"I've no wish to interfere, or tell you how to do your work; you're an experienced teacher and know more about P.T. than I ever will,"—the Old Man was again patient, encouraging—"but try to be a little more understanding about their difficulties." He then turned to other matters, but it was clear that Bell was considerably put out by the rebuke.

Matters came to a head that Monday afternoon. I was not present in the gym, but was able to reconstruct the sequence of events with reasonable accuracy from the boys' reports and Bell's subsequent admissions.

During the P.T. session he had been putting them through their paces in the "astride vault" over the buck, all except Buckley, who was somewhat under the weather and wisely stood down from attempting the rather difficult jump, but without reference to or permission from Bell, who was not long in discovering the absence of his favorite diversion.

"Buckley," he roared. "Yes, Sir."

"Come on, boy, I'm waiting." He was standing in his usual position beside the buck in readiness to arrest the fall of any lad who might be thrown off balance by an awkward approach or incorrect execution of the movement. But the boy did not move, and the master stared at him amazed and angry at this unexpected show of defiance by the one generally considered to be the most timid and tractable in the whole class.

"Fatty can't do it, Sir, it's too high for him," Denham interposed.

"Shut up, Denham," Bell roared. "If I want your opinion I will ask for it." He left his station by the buck and walked to where Buckley was standing. The boy watched his threatening approach, fear apparent in his eyes.

"Well, Buckley," Bell towered over the unhappy youth, "are you going to do as you're told?"

"Yes, Sir," Buckley's capitulation was as sudden as his refusal.

The others stopped to watch as he stood looking at the buck, licking his lips nervously while waiting for the instructor to resume his position. It may have been fear or determination or a combination of both, but Buckley launched himself at the buck in furious assault, and in spite of Bell's restraining arms, boy and buck crashed on the floor with a sickening sound as one leg of the buck snapped off with the sound of a pistol shot. The class stood in shocked silence watching Buckley, who remained as he fell, inert and pale; then they rushed to his assistance. All except Potter; big, good-natured Potter seemed to have lost his reason. He snatched up the broken metal-bound leg and advanced on Bell, screaming:

"You bloody bastard, you fucking bloody bastard."

"Put that thing down, Potter, don't be a fool," Bell spluttered, backing away from the hysterical boy.

"You made him do it; he didn't want to and you made him," Potter yelled.

"Don't be a fool, Potter, put it down," Bell appealed.

"I'll do you in, you bloody murderer." Bell was big, but in his anger Potter seemed bigger, his improvised club a fearsome extension of his thick forearm.

That was where I rushed in. Tich Jackson, frightened by the sight of Buckley, limp and white on the floor, and the enraged Potter, slobbering at the instructor in murderous fury, had dashed upstairs to my classroom shouting: "Sir, quick, they're fighting in the gym." I followed his disappearing figure in time to see Bell backed against a wall, with Potter advancing on him.

"Hold it, Potter," I called. He turned at the sound of my voice and I quickly placed myself between them.

"Let's have that, Potter." I held out my hand towards the boy, but he stared past me at Bell, whimpering in his emotion. Anger had completely taken hold of him, and he looked very dangerous.

"Come on, Potter," I repeated, "hand it over and go lend a hand with Buckley."

He turned to look towards his prostrate friend and I quickly moved up to him and seized the improvised club; he released it to me without any resistance and went back to join the group around Buckley. Bell then walked away and out of the room, and I went up to the boys. Denham rose and faced me, his face white with rage.

"Potts should have done the bastard like he did Fatty, just 'cos he wouldn't do the bloody jump."

I let that pass; they were angry and at such times quickly reverted to the old things, the words, the discourtesies. I stooped down beside Buckley, who was now sitting weakly on the floor, supported by Sapiano and Seales, and smiling up at them as if ashamed of himself for having been the cause of so much fuss.

"How do you feel, old man?" I inquired.

"Cor, Sir," he cried, smiling, "me tum does hurt."

"He fell on the buck. You should have seem 'im, Sir."

"Gosh, you should've heard the noise when the leg smashed."

"Mr. Bell couldn't catch Fatty, Sir, you should've seen him."

Most of them were trying to talk all at once, eager to give me all the details.

"Bleeding bully, always picking on Fats." This from Sapiano, whose volatile Maltese temperament was inclined to flare up very easily.

"If I'd had the wood I'd have done the fucker in and no bleeding body would have stopped me." Denham was aching for trouble and didn't care who knew it. Bell had slipped away unharmed after hurting his friend, and Denham wanted a substitute. But I would not look at him, or even hear the things he said. Besides, I liked Denham; in spite of his rough manner and speech he was an honest, dependable person with a strong sense of independence.

"Can you stand up, Buckley?"

With some assistance from Seales and Sapiano the boy got to his feet; he looked very pale and unsteady. I turned to Denham: "Will you help the others take Buckley up to Mrs. Dale-Evans and ask her to give him some sweet tea; leave him there and I'll meet you all in the classroom in a few minutes."

Without waiting for his reply I hurried off to the staffroom in search of Bell.

I was in something of a quandary. I knew that it was quite possible Buckley was all right, but there was no knowing whether he had sustained any internal injury not yet apparent. The Council's rules required that all accidents be reported and logged; the Headmaster should be informed forthwith, and in the light of what he had said to Bell so very recently, there would most certainly be a row.

I went up to the staffroom and found Bell washing his face at the sink.

"I've sent Buckley upstairs for a cup of tea," I said. "I suppose he'll be all right, anyway he was walking under his own steam."

"What happens now?" His voice was querulous.

"You should know as well as I do," I replied. "Shouldn't you see the Old Man and make some kind of report?"

"Yes, I suppose I'd better get over to his office right away. I should have attended to the Buckley boy, but the other one rushed me. Thanks for helping out."

"Oh, that's all right," I replied. "But why did you insist on the boy doing the vault?"

"I had to, don't you see; he just stood there refusing to obey and the others were watching me; I just had to do something." His whole attitude now was defensive.

"I'm not criticizing you, Mr. Bell, just asking. Buckley's a bit of a mascot with the others, you know, and I suppose that is why Potter got out of hand."

"I guess it was the way he jumped or something, but I couldn't grab him. He hit the buck too low and sent it flying."

"He's a bit awkward, isn't he; anyway I'm sure the Old Man will understand how it happened."

"He might be a bit difficult, especially after what he said the other day."

"Not necessarily. After all, it was an accident and thank Heaven it's not very serious."

He dried his hands and moved towards the door. "I suppose they'll really go to town on this in their weekly reviews," he remarked.

"I'll ask the boys to say nothing about it. I don't suppose Potter is now feeling any too pleased with himself at his conduct."

As he left Clinty came into the staffroom. "What's happening, Rick?" she asked. "I just saw some of your boys taking Fatty Buckley upstairs. What's happened to him?"

I told her about the incident and added: "Bell has just gone to the Old Man's office to report the matter."

"Well, what do you know?" she chuckled.

"Fancy Potter going for Bell like that. I always thought that boy a bit of a softie, but you never know with those quiet ones, do you?"

"He was not the only one. Sapiano and Denham were just as wild, I think, but they were too busy fussing over Buckley to bother with Bell."

"He is a bit of a tyro, isn't he. This might make him take it a bit easier."

"I don't think the boys mind his being strict during P.T. It's just that Buckley's a bit of a fool and they resented his being hurt. If it had been Denham or someone like that, I'm sure they would have done nothing."

"Yes, I guess you're right. Bell is a good teacher. I wonder how long the Divisional Office will let him stay here. I hope he hasn't had too much of a fright."

"Oh, he'll get over that. Now I must go and have a word with my boys."

I left her. For some inexplicable reason I felt nervous about being alone with Clinty; I felt that there was something she wanted to say to me, and for my part I did not want to hear it.

In the classroom the boys were sitting closely grouped together, looking rather sheepish. I knew they were feeling aggrieved and, according to their lights, justifiably so; but nevertheless the matter of Potters' behavior had to be dealt with. "How's Buckley?" I asked.

"We left him upstairs with Mrs. Dale-Evans, Sir. He didn't want to stay, he kept saying he was all right. But she told him if he wasn't quiet she'd give him some castor oil, Sir. Ugh!" They all managed a smile at Seales' remark.

"Good," I replied. "I expect he'll be quite all right. But there is something I want to say to you about this unfortunate incident." I sat down on the edge of Fernman's desk.

"Potter, there is nothing I can think of which can excuse your shocking conduct in the gym."

Potters mouth fell open; he looked at me in surprise, gulped a few times and stammered:

"But it was him, Sir, Mr. Bell, making Fatty fall and that." His voice was shrill with outrage at my remark.

"Mr. Bell was the master there, Potter, and anything that happened in the gym was his responsibility. Buckley's mishap was no excuse for you to make such an attack on your teacher."

"But Fatty told him he couldn't do it, Sir, and he made him, he made him, Sir."

Potter was very near tears. His distress was greater because of what he believed was the further injustice of my censure. The others, too, were looking at me with the same expression.

"That may be, Potter. I am not now concerned with Mr. Bell's conduct, but with yours. You came very near to getting yourself into very serious trouble because you were unable to control your temper. Not only was your language foul and disgusting, but you armed yourself with a weapon big enough and heavy enough to cause very serious harm. What do you think would have happened if everyone had behaved like you and had all turned on Mr. Bell like a pack of mad wolves?" I waited for this to sink in a bit, but Potter interjected:

"I thought he had done Fatty in, Sir, he looked all huddled up like, Sir."

"I see. So you didn't wait to find out but rushed in with your club like a hoodlum to smash and kill, is that it? Your friend was hurt and you wanted to hurt back; suppose instead of a piece of wood it had been a knife, or a gun, what then?" Potter was pale, and he was not the only one.

"Potts didn't think. He was naked, we was all naked, seeing Fatty on the deck. I wasn't half bleeding wild myself."

"You're missing the point, Denham. I think you're all missing the point. We sit in this classroom day after day and talk of things, and you all know what's expected of you; but at the first sign of bother you forget it all. In two weeks you'll all be at work and lots of things will happen which will annoy you, make you wild. Are you going to resort to clubs and knives every time you're upset or angered?" I stood up. "You'll meet foremen or supervisors or workmates who'll do things to upset you, sometimes deliberately. What then, Denham? What about that, Potter? Your Headmaster is under fire from many quarters because he believes in you—because he really believes that by the time you leave here you will have learned to exercise a little self-control at the times when it is most needed. His success or failure will be reflected in the way you conduct yourselves after you leave him. If today's effort is an example of your future behavior I hold out very little hope for you."

At this moment Buckley walked in, smiling broadly and seemingly none the worse for wear. I waited until he was seated then went on:

"I've no wish to belabor this matter, but it cannot be left like this. Potter, you were very discourteous to your P.T. instructor, and it is my opinion that you owe him an apology." Potter stared at me, his mouth open in amazement at my remark; but before he could speak Denham leapt to his feet.

"Apologize?" His voice was loud in anger. "Why should Potts apologize? He didn't do him any harm. Why should he apologize to him just because he's a bleeding teacher?" He stood there, legs slightly apart, heavy-shouldered and truculent, glaring at me. The others were watching us, but agreeing with him; I could feel their resentment hardening.

"Please sit down Denham, and remember that in this class we are always able to discuss things, no matter how difficult or unpleasant, without shouting at each other."

I waited, fearful of this unexpected threat to our pleasant relationship; he looked around at his colleagues indecisively, then abruptly sat down. I continued, in a very friendly tone:

"That was a fair question, Denham, although you will agree it was put a little, shall we say, indelicately?"

I smiled as I said this, and, in spite of his anger, Denham smiled briefly too. I went on:

"Potter, are you quite pleased and satisfied with the way you behaved to your P.T. teacher?"

Potter looked at me for a moment, then murmured, "No, Sir."

"But he couldn't help it," Denham interjected.

"That may be so, Denham, but Potter agrees that his own actions were unsatisfactory; upon reflection he himself is not pleased with what he did."

"How's about Mr. Bell then: How's about him apologizing to Buckley?" Denham was not to be dissuaded from his attitude.

"Yes, how about him?" echoed Sapiano.

"My business is with you, not with Mr. Bell," I replied.

This was not going to be easy, I thought. Denham was getting a bit nasty; the usual "Sir" had disappeared from his remarks, and Sapiano was following suit.

"It's easy for you to talk, Sir, nobody tries to push you around." Seales' voice was clear and calm, and the others turned to look at him, to support him. His question touched something deep inside of me, something which had been dormant for months, but now awoke to quick, painful remembering. Without realizing what I was doing I got up and walked to where he sat and stood beside his desk.

"I've been pushed around, Seales," I said quietly, "in a way I cannot explain to you. I've been pushed around until I began to hate people so much that I wanted to hurt them, really hurt them. I know how it feels, believe me, and one thing I learned, Seales, is to try always to be a bit bigger than the people who hurt me. It is easy to reach for a knife or a gun; but then you become merely a tool and the knife or gun takes over, thereby creating new and bigger problems without solving a thing. So what happens when there is no weapon handy?"

I felt suddenly annoyed with myself for giving way to my emotion, and abruptly walked back to my desk. The class seemed to feel that something had touched me deeply and were immediately sympathetic in their manner.

"The point I want to make, Potter," I continued, "is whether you are really growing up and learning to stand squarely on your own feet. When you begin work at Covent Garden you might someday have cause to be very angry; what will you do then? The whole idea of this school is to teach you to discipline yourself. In this instance you lost your temper and behaved badly to your teacher. Do you think you are big enough to make an apology to him?"

Potter fidgeted in his seat and looked uncertainly at me, then replied: "Yes, Sir."

"It's always difficult to apologize, Potter, especially to someone you feel justified in disliking. But remember that you are not doing it for Mr. Bell's sake, but your own."

I sat down. They were silent, but I realized that they understood what I meant. Potter stood up:

"Is he in the staffroom, Sir?"

"I think he should be there now, Potter."

Denham and Seales stood and joined Potter and together they went to find Bell. I called Buckley.

"How are you feeling, Buckley?"

"Okay, Sir," he replied, as jovial as ever.

"What will your parents say about all this Buckley?" I was being devious but, I thought, necessarily so.

"I shan't tell 'em, Sir. Must I, Sir."

"It's up to you, Buckley. If you feel fine there's no need to bother; but if in the next few days or weeks you feel any pain, it would be best to mention it so that they'd know what to do."

In a few minutes the boys were back, Potter looking red and embarrassed; behind them came Mr. Bell.

"May I speak to your boys for a moment, Mr. Braithwaite?" He came in and stood beside my desk and I nodded to him.

"I want to say to all of you," he began, "that I'm sorry about what happened in the gym a little while ago. I think that one way or another we were all a bit silly, but the sooner we forget the whole thing, the better.

"How're you feeling now, boy?" He addressed himself to Buckley.

"Okay, Sir," the boy replied.

"Fine. Well, I suppose we'll see each other as usual next week." And with that he was gone, having made as friendly a gesture as his evident nervousness would allow.

The boys seemed not unwilling to let the matter drop, so we turned our attention to the discussion of other things.

· ·

Editors' Commentary ·

> DIAGNOSIS: Impulse breakthrough—group acting-out a socially and economically deprived student.

In this case, the behavior of Potter was clearly provoked. Potter's anger was aroused by injustice; and students, even troubled ones, are happily committed to justice—even though their definitions may not coincide with society's. The crucial factor in Potter's case was not his anger but the way he handled it. Rage is an overwhelming experience. Inability to handle it in an acceptable fashion leads to tragedy.

Braithwaite is careful to make this point to the students as he details the precarious life ahead for one who is at the mercy of rage instead of being its master. His handling of the problem in this group of children, where all could hear and express themselves, displays the kind of skill that comes from human understanding.

This selection highlights the contagion of rage among students. It indicates, too, that the teacher's revelation of his own deep personal feeling communicated real emotional understanding far more powerfully than intellectual reasoning. This feeling, more than the proper words, got across to the students. Students, even troubled ones, respond to genuineness. In many cases, the more troubled the student, the more therapeutic can a teacher's genuine feelings be, provided they are not overexploited or used to gain sympathy for the teacher.

ARTICLE 1.6

Doctor Jack-o'-Lantern

Richard Yates

All Miss Price had been told about the new boy was that he'd spent most of his life in some kind of orphanage, and that the gray-haired "aunt and uncle" with whom he now lived were really foster parents, paid by the Welfare Department of the City of New York. A less dedicated or less imaginative teacher might have pressed for more details, but Miss Price was content with the rough outline. It was enough, in fact, to fill her with a sense of mission that shone from her eyes, as plan as love, from the first morning he joined the fourth grade.

He arrived early and sat in the back row—his spine very straight, his ankles crossed precisely under the desk and his hands folded on the very center of its top, as if symmetry might make him less conspicuous—and while the other children were filing in and settling down, he received a long, expressionless stare from each of them.

"We have a new classmate this morning," Miss Price said, laboring the obvious in a way that made everybody want to giggle. "His name is Vincent Sabella and he comes from New York City. I know we'll all do our best to make him feel at home."

This time they all swung around to stare at once, which caused him to duck his head slightly and shift his weight from one buttock to the other.

Ordinarily, the fact of someone's coming from New York might have held a certain prestige, for to most of the children the city was an awesome, adult place that swallowed up their fathers every day, and which they themselves were permitted to visit only rarely, in their best clothes, as a treat. But anyone could see at a glance that Vincent Sabella had nothing whatever to do with skyscrapers. Even if you could ignore his tangled black hair and gray skin, his clothes would have given him away: absurdly new corduroys, absurdly old sneakers and a yellow sweatshirt, much too small, with the shredded remains of a Mickey Mouse design stamped on its chest. Clearly, he was from the part of New York that you had to pass through on the train to Grand Central—the part where people hung bedding over their windowsill and leaned out on it all day in a trance of boredom, and where you got vistas of straight, deep streets, one after another, all alike in the clutter of their sidewalks and all swarming with gray boys at play in some desperate kind of ball game.

The girls decided that he wasn't very nice and turned away, but the boys lingered in their scrutiny, looking him up and down with faint smiles. This was the kind of kid they were accustomed to thinking of as "tough," the kind whose stares had made all of them uncomfortable at one time or another in unfamiliar neighborhoods; here was a unique chance for retaliation.

"What would you like us to call you, Vincent?" Miss Price inquired. "I mean, do you prefer Vincent, or Vince, or—or what?" (It was purely an academic question; even Miss Price knew that the boys would call him "Sabella" and that the girls wouldn't call him anything at all.)

"Vinny's okay," he said in a strange, croaking voice that had evidently yelled itself hoarse down the ugly streets of his home.

"I'm afraid I didn't hear you," she said, craning her pretty head forward and to one side so that a heavy lock of hair swung free of one shoulder. "Did you say 'Vince'?"

"Vinny, I said," he said again, squirming. "Vincent, is it? All right then, Vincent." A few of the class giggled, but nobody bothered to correct her; it would be more fun to let the mistake continue.

"I won't take time to introduce you to everyone by name, Vincent," Miss Price went on, "because I think it would be simpler just to let you learn the names as we go along, don't you? Now, we won't expect you to take any real part in the work for the first day or so; just take your time, and if there's anything you don't understand, why, don't be afraid to ask."

He made an unintelligible croak and smiled fleetingly, just enough to show that the roots of his teeth were green.

"Now then," Miss Price said, getting down to business. "This is Monday morning, and so the first thing on the program is reports. Who'd like to start off?"

Vincent Sabella was momentarily forgotten as six or seven hands went up, and Miss Price drew back in mock confusion. "Goodness, we do have a lot of reports this morning," she said. The idea of the reports—a fifteen-minute period every Monday in which the children were encouraged to relate their experiences over the weekend—was Miss Price's own, and she took a pardonable pride in it. The principal had commended her on it at a recent staff meeting, pointing out that it made a splendid bridge between the worlds of school and home, and that it was a fine way for children to learn poise and assurance. It called for intelligent supervision—the shy children had to be drawn out and the show-offs curbed—but in general, as Miss Price had assured the principal, it was fun for everyone. She particularly hoped it would be fun today, to help put Vincent Sabella at ease, and that was why she chose Nancy Parker to start off; there was nobody like Nancy for holding an audience.

The others fell silent as Nancy moved gracefully to the head of the room; even the two or three girls who secretly despised her had to feign enthrallment when she spoke (she was that popular), and every boy in the class, who at recess liked nothing better than to push her shrieking into the mud, was unable to watch her without an idiotically tremulous smile.

"Well—" she began, and then she clapped a hand over her mouth while everyone laughed. "Oh, *Nancy,*" Miss Price said. "You *know* the rule about starting a report with 'well.'"

Nancy knew the rule; she had only broken it to get the laugh. Now she let her fit of giggles subside, ran her fragile forefingers down the side seams of her skirt, and began again in the proper way. "On Friday my whole family went for a ride in my brother's new car. My brother bought this new Pontiac last week, and he wanted to take us all for a ride—you know, to try it out and everything? So we went into White Plains and had dinner in a restaurant there, and then we all wanted to go see this movie, 'Doctor Jekyll and Mr. Hyde,' but my brother said it was too horrible and everything, and I wasn't old enough to enjoy it—oh, he made me so-mad! And then, let's see. On Saturday I stayed home all day and helped my mother make my sister's wedding dress. My sister's engaged to be married you see, and my mother's making this wedding dress for her? So we did that, and then on Sunday this friend of my brother's came over for dinner, and then they both had to get back to college that night, and I was allowed to stay up late and say goodbye to them and everything, and I guess that's all." She always had a sure instinct for keeping her performance brief—or rather, for making it seem briefer than it really was.

"Very good, Nancy," Miss Price said. "Now, who's next?"

Warren Berg was next, elaborately hitching up his pants as he made his way down the aisle. "On Saturday I went over to Bill Stringer's house for lunch," he began in his direct, man-to-man style, and Bill Stringer wriggled bashfully in the front row. Warren Berg and Bill Stringer were great friends, and their reports often overlapped. "And then after lunch we went into White Plains, on our bikes. Only we *saw* 'Doctor Jeckyll and Mr. Hyde.'" Here he nodded his head in Nancy's direction, and Nancy got another laugh by making a little whimper of envy. "It was real good, too," he went on, with mounting excitement. "It's all about this guy who—"

"About *a man who*," Miss Price corrected. "About a man who mixes up this chemical, like, that he drinks? And whenever he drinks this chemical, he changes into this real monster, like? You see him drink this chemical, and then you see his hands start to get all scales all over them, like a reptile and everything, and then you see his face start to change into this real horrible-looking face—with fangs and all? Sticking out of his mouth?"

All the girls shuddered in pleasure. "Well," Miss Price said, "I think Nancy's brother was probably wise in not wanting her to see it. What did you do *after* the movie, Warren?"

There was a general *"Aw-w-w!"* of disappointment, everyone wanted to hear more about the scales and fangs—but Miss Price never liked to let the reports degenerate into accounts of movies. Warren continued without much enthusiasm: all they had done after the movie was fool around Bill Stringer's yard until supertime. "And then on Sunday," he said, brightening again, "Bill Stringer came over to *my* house, and my dad helped us rig up this old tire on this long rope? From a tree? There's this steep hill down behind my house, you see—this ravine, like?—and we hung this tire so that what you do is, you take the tire and run a little ways and then lift your feet, and you go swinging way, way out over the ravine and back again."

"That sounds like fun," Miss Price said, glancing at her watch.

"Oh, it's fun all right," Warren conceded. But then he hitched up his pants again and added, with a puckering of his forehead, "Course, it's pretty dangerous. You let go of that tire or anything, you'd get a bad fall. Hit a rock or anything, you'd probably break your leg, or your spine. But my dad said he trusted us both to look out for our own safety."

"Well, I'm afraid that's all we'll have time for, Warren," Miss Price said. "Now, there's just time for one more report. Who's ready? Arthur Cross?"

There was a soft groan, because Arthur Cross was the biggest dope in class and his reports were always a bore. This time it turned out to be something tedious about going to visit his uncle on Long Island. At one point he made a slip—he said "botormoat" instead of "motorboat"—and everyone laughed with the particular edge of scorn they reserved for Arthur Cross. But the laughter died abruptly when it was joined by a harsh, dry croaking from the back of the room. Vincent Sabella was laughing too, green teeth and all, and they all had to glare at him until he stopped.

When the reports were over, everyone settled down for school. It was recess time before any of the children thought much about Vincent Sabella again, and then they thought of him only to make sure he was left out of everything. He wasn't in the group of boys that clustered around the horizontal bar to take turns at skinning-the-cat, or the group that whispered in a far corner of the playground, hatching a plot to push Nancy Parker in the mud. Nor was he in the larger group, of which even Arthur Cross was a member, that chased itself in circles in a frantic variation of the game of tag. He couldn't join the girls, of course, or the boys from other classes, and so he joined nobody. He stayed on the apron of the playground, close to school, and for the first part of the recess he pretended to be very busy with the laces of his sneakers. He would squat to undo and retie them, straighten up and take a few experimental steps in a springy, athletic way, and then get down and go to work on them again. After five minutes of this he gave it up, picked up a handful of pebbles and began shying them at an invisible target several yards away. That was good for another five minutes, but then there was still five minutes left, and he could think of nothing to do but stand there, first with his hands in his pockets, then with his hands on his hips, and then with his arms folded in a manly way across his chest.

Miss Price stood watching all this from the doorway, and she spent the full recess wondering if she ought to go out and do something about it. She guessed it would be better not to.

She managed to control the same impulse at recess the next day, and every other day that week, though every day it grew more difficult. But one thing she could not control was a tendency to let her anxiety show in class. All Vincent Sabella's error in schoolwork were publicly excused, even those having nothing to do with his newness, and all his accomplishments were singled out for special mention. Her campaign to build him up was painfully obvious, and never more so than when she tried to make it subtle; once, for instance, in explaining an arithmetic problem, she said, "Now, suppose Warren Berg and Vincent Sabella went to the store with fifteen cents each, and candy bars cost ten cents. How many candy bars would each boy have?" By the end of the week he was well on the way to becoming the worst possible kind of teachers pet, a victim of the teacher's pity.

On Friday she decided the best thing to do would be to speak to him privately, and try to draw him out. She could say something about the pictures he had painted in art class—that would do for an opening—and she decided to do it at lunchtime.

The only trouble was that lunchtime, next to recess, was the most trying part of Vincent Sabella's day. Instead of going home for an hour as the other children did, he brought his lunch to school in a wrinkled paper bag and ate it in the classroom, which always made for a certain amount of awkwardness. The last children to leave would see him still seated apologetically at his desk, holding his paper bag, and anyone who happened to straggle back later for a forgotten hat or sweater would surprise him in the middle, of his meal—perhaps shielding a hard-boiled egg from view or wiping mayonnaise from his mouth with a furtive hand. It was a situation that Miss Price did not improve by walking up to him while the room was still half full of children and sitting prettily on the edge of the desk beside his, making it clear that she was cutting her own lunch hour short in order to be with him.

"Vincent," she began, "I've been meaning to tell you how much I enjoyed those pictures of yours. They're really very good."

He mumbled something and shifted his eyes to the cluster of departing children at the door. She went right on talking and smiling, elaborating on her praise of the pictures; and finally, after the door had closed behind the last child, he was able to give her his attention. He did so tentatively at first; but the more she talked, the more he seemed to relax, until she realized she was putting him at ease. It was as simple and as gratifying as stroking a cat. She had finished with the pictures now and moved on, triumphantly, to broader fields of praise. "It's never easy," she was saying, "to come to a new school and adjust yourself to the level, the new work, and new working methods, and I think you've done a splendid job so far. I really do. But tell me, do you think you're going to like it here?"

He looked at the floor just long enough to make his reply—"It's alright"—and then his eyes stared into hers again.

"I'm so glad. Please don't let me interfere with your lunch, Vincent. Do go ahead and eat, that is, if you don't mind my sitting here with you." But it was now abundantly clear that he didn't mind at all, and he began to unwrap a bologna sandwich with what she felt sure was the best appetite he'd had all week. It wouldn't even have mattered very much now if someone from the class had come in and watched, though it was probably just as well that no one did. Miss Price sat back more comfortably on the desk top, crossed her legs and allowed on slim stockinged foot to slip part of the way out of its moccasin. "Of course," she went on, "it always does take a little time to sort of get your bearings in a new school. For one thing, well, it's never too easy for the new member of the class to make friends with the other members. What I mean is, you mustn't mind if the others seem a little rude to you at first. Actually, they're just as anxious to make friends as you are, but they're shy. All it takes is a little time, and a little effort on your part as well as theirs. Not too much, of course, but a little. Now for instance, these reports we have Monday mornings—they're a fine way for people to get to know one another. A person never feels he has to make a report; it's just a thing he can do if he wants to. And that's only one way of helping others to know the kind of person you are; there are lots and lots of ways. The main thing to remember is that making friends is the most natural thing in the world, and it's only a question of time until you have all the friends you want. And in the meantime, Vincent, I hope you'll consider *me* your friend, and feel free to call on me for whatever advice or anything you might need. Will you do that?"

He nodded, swallowing.

"Good." She stood up and smoothed her skirt over her long thighs. "Now I must go or I'll be late for my lunch. But I'm glad we had this little talk, Vincent, and I hope we'll have others."

It was probably a lucky thing that she stood up when she did, for if she'd stayed on that desk a minute longer Vincent Sabella would have thrown his arms around her and buried his face in the warm gray flannel of her lap, and that might have been enough to confuse the most dedicated and imaginative of teachers.

At report time on Monday morning, nobody was more surprised than Miss Price when Vincent Sabella's smudged hand was among the first and most eager to rise. Apprehensively she considered letting someone else start off, but then, for fear of hurting his feelings, she said, "All right, Vincent," in as matter-of-fact a way as she could manage.

There was a suggestion of muffled titters from the class as he walked confidently to the head of the room and turned to face his audience. He looked, if anything, too confident: there were signs, in the way he held his shoulders and the way his eyes shone, of the terrible poise of panic. "Saturday I seen that pitch" he announced. "Saw, Vincent," Miss Price corrected gently.

"That's what I mean," he said; "I sore that pitch. 'Doctor Jack-o'-Lantern and Mr. Hide.'"

There was a burst of wild, delighted laugher and a chorus of correction: "Doctor *Jekyll!*"

He was unable to speak over the noise. Miss Price was on her feet, furious. "It's a *perfectly natural mistake.*" she was saying. "There's no reason for any of you to be so rude. Go on, Vincent, and please excuse this very silly interruption." The laughter subsided, but the class continued to shake their heads derisively from side to side. It hadn't, of course, been a perfectly natural mistake at all; for one thing it proved that he was a hopeless dope, and for another it proved that he was lying.

"That's what I mean," he continued. "'Doctor Jackal and Mr. Hide.' I got it a little mixed up. Any-ways, I seen all about where his teet' start comin' outa his mout' and all like that, and I thought it was very good. And then on Sunday my mudda and fodda come out to see me in this car they got. This Buick. My fodda siz, 'Vinny, wanna go for a little ride?' I siz, 'Sure, where yiz goin'?' He siz, 'Anyplace ya like.' So I siz, 'Let's go out in the country a ways, get on one of them big roads and make some time.' So we go out—oh, I guess fifty, sixty miles—and we're cruisin' along this highway, when this cop starts tailin' us? My fodda siz, 'Don't worry, we'll shake him,' and he steps on it, see? My mudda's gettin' pretty scared, but my fodda siz, 'Don't worry, dear.' He's tryin' to make this turn, see, so he can get off the highway and shake the cop? But just when he's makin' the turn, the cop opens up and starts shootin', see?"

By this time the few members of the class who could bear to look at him at all were doing so with heads on one side and mouths partly open, the way you look at a broken arm or a circus freak.

"We just barely made it," Vincent went on, his eyes gleaming, "and this one bullet got my fodda in the shoulder. Didn't hurt him bad—just grazed him, like—so my mudda bandaged it up for him and all, but he couldn't do no more drivin' after that, and we had to get him to a doctor, see? So my fodda siz, 'Vinny, think you can drive a ways?' I siz, 'Sure, if you show me how.' So he showed me how to work the gas and the brake, and all like that, and I drove to the doctor. My mudda siz, 'I'm prouda you, Vinny, drivin' all by yourself.' So any-ways, we got the doctor, got my fodda fixed up and all, and then he drove us back home." He was breathless. After an uncertain pause he said, "And that's all." Then he walked quickly back to his desk, his stiff new corduroy pants whistling faintly with each step.

"Well, that was very—entertaining, Vincent," Miss Price said, trying to act as if nothing had happened. "Now, who's next?" But nobody raised a hand.

Recess was worse than usual for him that day; at least it was until he found a place to hide—a narrow concrete alley, blind except for several closed fire-exit doors, that cut between two sections of the school building. It was reassuringly dismal and cool in there—he could stand with his back to the wall and his eyes guarding the entrance, and the noises of recess were as remote as the sunshine. But when the bell rang he had to go back to class, and in another hour it was lunchtime.

Miss Price left him alone until her own meal was finished. Then, after standing with one hand on the doorknob for a full minute to gather courage, she went in and sat beside him for another little talk, just as he was trying to swallow the last of a pimento-cheese sandwich.

"Vincent," she began, "we all enjoyed your report this morning, but I think we would have enjoyed it more—a great deal more—if you'd told us something about your real life instead. I mean," she hurried on, "For instance, I noticed you were wearing a nice new windbreaker this morning. It *is* new, isn't it? And did your aunt buy it for you over the weekend?"

He did not deny it.

"Well then, why couldn't you have told us about going to the store with your aunt, and buying the windbreaker, and whatever you did afterwards. That would have made a perfectly good report." She paused, and for the first time looked steadily into his eyes. "You do understand what I'm trying to say, don't you, Vincent?"

He wiped crumbs of bread from his lips, looked at the floor, and nodded.

"And you'll remember next time, won't you?"

He nodded again. "Please may I be excused, Miss Price?"

"Of course you may."

He went to the boys' lavatory and vomited. Afterwards he washed his face and drank a little water, and then he returned to the classroom. Miss Price was busy at her desk now, and didn't look up. To avoid getting involved with her again, he wandered out to the cloakroom and sat on one of the long benches, where he picked up someone's discarded overshoe and turned it over and over in his hands. In a little while he heard the clatter of returning children, and to avoid being discovered there, he got up and went to the fire-exit door. Pushing it open, he found that it gave onto the alley he had hidden in that morning, and he slipped outside. For a minute or two he just stood there, looking at the blankness of the concrete wall: then he found a piece of chalk in his pocket and wrote out all the dirty words he could think of, in block letters a foot high. He had put down four words and was trying to remember a fifth when he heard a shuffling at the door behind him. Arthur Cross was there, holding the door open and reading the words with wide eyes. "Boy," he said in an awed half-whisper. "Boy, you're gonna get it. You're really gonna *get* it."

Startled, and then suddenly calm, Vincent Sabella palmed his chalk, hooked his thumbs in his belt and turned on Arthur Cross with a menacing look. "Yeah?" he inquired. "Who's gonna squeal on me?"

"Well, nobody's gonna *squeal* on you," Arthur Cross said uneasily, "but you shouldn't go around writing—" "Arright," Vincent said, advancing a step. His shoulders were slumped, his head thrust forward and his eyes narrowed, like Edward G. Robinson. "Arright. That's all I wanna know. I don't like squealers, unnastand?"

While he was saying this, Warren Berg and Bill Stringer appeared in the doorway—just in time to hear it and to see the words on the wall before Vincent turned on them. "And that goes fa you too, unnastand?" he said. "Both a yiz."

And the remarkable thing was that both their faces fell into the same foolish, defensive smile that Arthur Cross was wearing. It wasn't until they had glanced at each other that they were able to meet his eyes with the proper degree of contempt, and by then it was too late. "Think you're pretty smart, don'tcha, Sabella?" Bill Stringer said.

"Never mind what I think," Vincent told him. "You heard what I said. Now let's get back inside."

And they could do nothing but move aside to make way for him, and follow him dumbfounded into the cloakroom.

It was Nancy Parker who squealed—although, of course, with someone like Nancy Parker you didn't think of it as squealing. She had heard everything from the cloakroom; as soon as the boys came in she peeked into the alley, saw the words and, setting her face in a prim frown, went straight to Miss Price. Miss Price was just about to call the class to order for the afternoon when Nancy came up and whispered in her ear. They both disappeared into the cloakroom—from which, after a moment, came the sound of the fire-exit door being abruptly slammed—and when they returned to class Nancy was flushed with righteousness, Miss Price very pale. No announcement was made. Classes proceeded in the ordinary way all afternoon, though it was clear that Miss Price was upset, and it wasn't until she was dismissing the children at three o'clock that she brought the thing into the open. "Will Vincent Sabella please remain seated?" She nodded at the rest of the class. "That's all."

While the room was clearing out she sat at her desk, closed her eyes and massaged the frail bridge of her nose with thumb and forefinger, sorting our half-remembered fragments of a book she had once read on the subject of seriously disturbed children. Perhaps, after all, she should never have undertaken the responsibility of Vincent Sabella's loneliness. Perhaps the whole thing called for the attention of a specialist. She took a deep breath.

"Come over here and sit beside me, Vincent," she said, and when he had settled himself, she looked at him. "I want you to tell me the truth. Did you write those words on the wall outside?" He stared at the floor. "Look at me," she said, and he looked at her. She had never looked prettier: her cheeks slightly flushed, her eyes shining and her sweet mouth pressed into a self-conscious frown. "First of all," she said, handing him a small enameled basin streaked with poster paint, "I want you to take this to the boys' room and fill it with hot water and soap."

He did as he was told, and when he came back, carrying the basin carefully to keep the suds from spilling, she was sorting out some old rags in the bottom drawer of her desk. "Here," she said, selecting one and shutting the drawer in a businesslike way. "This will do. Soak this *up*." She led him back to the fire exit and stood in the alley watching him, silently, while he washed off all the words.

When the job had been done, and the rag and basin put away, they sat down at Miss Price's desk again. "I suppose you think I'm angry with you, Vincent," she said. "Well, I'm not. I almost wish I could be angry—that would make it much easier—but instead I'm hurt. I've tried to be a good friend to you, and I thought you wanted to be my friend too. But this kind of thing—well, it's very hard to be friendly with a person who'd do a thing like that." She saw, gratefully, that there were tears in his eyes. "Vincent, perhaps I understand some things better than you think.

Perhaps I understand that sometimes, when a person does a thing like that, it isn't really because he wants to hurt anyone, but only because he's unhappy. He knows it isn't a good thing to do, and he even knows it isn't going to make him any happier afterwards, but he goes ahead and does it anyway. Then when he finds he's lost a friend, he's terribly sorry, but it's too late. The thing is done."

She allowed this somber note to reverberate in the silence of the room for a little while before she spoke again. "I won't be able to forget this, Vincent. But perhaps, just this once, we can still be friends as long as I understand that you didn't mean to hurt me. But you must promise me that you won't forget it either. Never forget that when you do a thing like that, you're going to hurt people who want very much to like you, and in that way you're going to hurt yourself. Will you promise me to remember that, dear?"

The "dear" was as involuntary as the slender hand that reached out and held the shoulder of his sweatshirt; both made his head hang lower than before.

"All right," she said. "You may go now."

He got his windbreaker out of the cloakroom and left, avoiding the tired uncertainty of her eyes. The corridors were deserted, and dead silent except for the hollow, rhythmic knocking of a janitor's push-broom against some distant wall. His own rubber-soled tread only added to the silence; so did the lonely little noise made by the zipping-up of his windbreaker, and so did the faint mechanical sigh of the heavy front door. The silence made it all the more startling when he found, several yards down the concrete walk outside, that two boys were walking beside him: Warren Berg and Bill Stringer. They were both smiling at him in an eager, almost friendly way.

"What'd she do to ya, anyway?" Bill Stringer asked.

Caught off guard, Vincent barely managed to put on his Edward G. Robinson face in time. "Nunnya business," he said, and walked faster.

"No, listen—wait up, hey," Warren Berg said, as they trotted to keep up with him. "What'd she do, anyway? She bawl ya out, or what? Wait up, hey, Vinny."

The name made him tremble all over. He had to jam his hands in his windbreaker pockets to force himself to keep on walking; he had to force his voice to be steady when he said "Nunnya *business,* I told ya. Lea' me alone." But they were right in step with him now. "Boy, she must of given you the works," Warren Berg persisted. "What'd she say, anyway? C'mon, tell us, Vinny."

This time the name was too much for him. It overwhelmed his resistance and made his softening knees slow down to a slack, conversational stroll. "She din say nothin'" he said at last; and then after a dramatic pause he added, "She let the ruler do her talkin' for her."

"The *ruler?* Ya mean she used a *ruler* on ya?" Their faces were stunned, either with disbelief or admiration, and it began to look more and more like admiration as they listened.

"On the knuckles," Vincent said through tightening lips. "Five times on each hand. She siz, 'Make a fist. Lay it out here on the desk.' Then she takes the ruler and *Whop! Whop! Whop!* Five times. Ya think that don't hurt, you're crazy."

Miss Price, buttoning her polo coat as the front door whispered shut behind her, could scarcely believe her eyes. This couldn't be Vincent Sabella this perfectly normal, perfectly happy boy on the sidewalk ahead of her, flanked by attentive friends. But it was, and the scene made her want to laugh aloud with pleasure and relief. He was going to be all right, after all. For all her well-intentioned groping in the shadows she could never have predicted a scene like this, and certainly could never have caused it to happen. But it was happening, and it just proved, once again, that she would never understand the ways of children.

She quickened her graceful stride and overtook them, turning to smile down at them as she passed. "Goodnight, boys," she called, intending it as a kind of cheerful benediction; and then, embarrassed by their three startled faces, she smiled even wider and said, "Goodness, it *is* getting colder, isn't it? That windbreaker of yours looks nice and warm, Vincent. I envy you." Finally they nodded bashfully at her; she called goodnight again, turned, and continued on her way to the bus stop.

She left a profound silence in her wake. Staring after her, Warren Berg and Bill Stringer waited until she had disappeared around the corner before they turned on Vincent Sabella.

"Ruler, my eye!" Bill Stringer said. "Ruler, my eye!" He gave Vincent a disgusted shove that sent him stumbling against Warren Berg, who shoved him back.

"Jeez, you lie about *everything,* don'tcha, Sabella? You lie about *everything?*"

Jostled off balance, keeping his hands tight in the windbreaker pockets, Vincent tried in vain to retain his dignity. "Think I care if yiz believe me?" he said, and then because he couldn't think of anything else to say, he said it again. "Think I care if yiz believe me?"

But he was walking alone. Warren Berg and Bill Stringer were drifting away across the street, walking backwards in order to look back at him with furious contempt. "Just like the lies you told about the policeman shooting your father," Bill Stringer called.

"Even *movies* he lies about," Warren Berg put in; and suddenly doubling up with artificial laughter he cupped both hands to his mouth and yelled, "Hey, Doctor Jack-o'-lantern!"

It wasn't a very good nickname, but it had an authentic ring to it—the kind of a name that might spread around, catch on quickly, and stick. Nudging each other, they both took up the cry:

"What's the matter, Doctor Jack-o'-Lantern?"

"Why don'tcha run on home with Miss Price, Doctor Jack-o'-Lantern?"

"So long, Doctor Jack-o'-Lantern!"

Vincent Sabella went on walking, ignoring them, waiting until they were out of sight. Then he turned and retraced his steps all the way back to school, around through the playground and back to the alley, where the wall was still dark in spots from the circular scrubbing of his wet rag.

Choosing a dry place, he got out his chalk and began to draw a head with great care, in profile, making the hair long and rich and taking his time over the face, erasing it with moist fingers and re-working it until it was the most beautiful face he had ever drawn: a delicate nose, slightly parted lips, an eye with lashes that curved as gracefully as a bird's wing. He paused to admire it with a lover's solemnity; then from the lips he drew a line that connected with a big speech balloon, and in the balloon he wrote, so angrily that the chalk kept breaking in his fingers, every one of the words he had written that noon. Returning to the head, he gave it a slender neck and gently sloping shoulders, and then, with bold strokes, he gave it the body of a naked woman: great breasts with hard little nipples, a trim waist, a dot for a naval, wide hips and thighs that flared around a triangle of fiercely scribbled pubic hair. Beneath the picture he printed its title: "Miss Price."

He stood there looking at it for a little while, breathing hard, and then he went home.

. . . .

Editors' Commentary . . . .

DIAGNOSIS: Culturally and affectionally deprived student in a middle-class environment.

The story is a realistic description of how a new student in a strange environment tries to find his way. His clothes, manner, and speech make him a stranger. His difference is felt keenly by classmates, the teacher, and himself. His attempt to be like the others by lying or make-believe is understandable. Equally understandable is his well-intentioned teacher's over-involvement with him. Her seductive and sympathetic behavior, although well-meaning, singles him out and further alienates him from the class. Teacher's pet is at best a hard role, particularly when a student is starving for attention and expression.

Vincent's reaction to the teacher's moralistic, middle-class approach to him is confused. In despair, anger, loneliness, and a sense of isolation, he uses the very tools that shock middle-class society most—street language and lewd pictures.

Overinvolvement often results in a teacher's withdrawal and disappointment. The danger of the teacher's pet role is clear. A gradual welcome that would give the boy a chance to be different, and an understanding that a weekend report from him is bound to be a fiasco, one way or another, are what were needed. Even teachers who come from the same ethnic groups as their students are not always trained in an awareness of their middle-class myopia. This condition of cross-culture training is improving, but it is still much too familiar.

DRUGS: WHAT SOME PEOPLE DO ABOUT THEIR FEELINGS AND WHAT THAT DOES TO THEM . . . .

Anxiety is hard to bear but none of us can live without learning to tolerate a certain amount of it. Anxiety arises from the self-preserving instinct of fear, in which we all react with mechanisms of either fleeing or fighting. Anxiety's basic purpose is to send us unmistakable alarms and warnings, alerting us to whatever threatens, so that we can do something about it. There is a body of evidence to support the theory that, without some degree of anxiety, we would not learn to learn, and our very survival would be endangered.

As society grows increasingly complex, human-generated anxieties haunt us. Competition, anger, feelings of inadequacy and unworthiness, guilt, loneliness, confusion, problems of sexual identity, and dependence are just some of the anxieties that plague us, yet we live together and are by nature dependent on each other. When anxiety rises too high, it is sometimes more than we can handle. Immobilized, we may revert to the crudest, most primitive forms of combating danger and acute discomfort. In the moment of anxiety, everything we know can be forgotten and everything we have repressed may come pouring in. We may then give way to overwhelming bursts of anger and violence, or we may take flight. Anxiety is often the reason teenagers run away or students who have ability show apathetic lack of effort. Over the years, we all learn certain defenses, and sometimes they serve us worse than the anxiety they are combating. The particular defense we choose is determined by our temperament and our environment, past and present. Some of us develop combativeness and irritability. For others, psychosomatic illnesses such as headaches, stomach aches, and hives are outward signs of the terror inside. Many of us choose escape, perhaps in books, films, or TV. (Many people, especially preadolescents, use TV as a kind of drug.) Some escape in alcohol, which can be as effective as any drug at damaging human relationships, job effectiveness, and physical or mental health.

To escape anxiety and society's deficiencies and onslaughts many young people today have turned to drugs, just as those in earlier generations turned to alcohol. The overuse of some drugs, such as amphetamines (stimulants), barbiturates (downers), or glue-sniffing can cause long-term physical damage. Conclusive evidence suggests that the hallucinogen LSD causes permanent physical harm. Other drugs are so addictive that they become the controlling force in a person's life. For the addictive drugs, the craving is both physical and psychological. Those addicted to alcohol, barbiturates, or opiates (such as heroin, opium, and morphine) suffer not only an overwhelming desire for the drug but also extreme physical discomfort upon withdrawal—shaking, stomach cramps, and wracking pain. They also incur a great risk of death from taking unknown mixtures or an overdose. Addiction brings helplessness, abject dependence, misery to oneself and others, and self-loathing.

More and more young people are using addictive drugs, and increasing numbers of them are very young. Some children get on drugs because resisting the peer pressure is too much for their essentially conforming, infantile, and dependent social natures. Some young people take a hard drug once or twice and then leave it alone. But others become addicted with only a few exposures. Some young people may turn to drugs out of frustration at their inability to tell their parents about their unhappiness. It may be the normal unhappiness of any adolescent growing up, but it can seem especially acute in a world where so much is demanded, values often appear phony and hypocritical, and problems seem nearly insoluble. Given a sufficient sense of powerlessness, a young person in today's culture is often tempted to give up. Sometimes the adolescent then chooses an alternative life without knowing much about its terrors and consequences.

Some of the drug users have been disturbed for a long time, but, because their parents were insensitive, unprepared, or simply didn't want to see; or because their teachers were afraid of alarming someone or "overstepping boundaries," drug use was left to go on until it was too late. These youngsters found no way to tell someone they were in trouble inside, except through actions that seriously limit, if they do not end, their futures. The disturbances were always there; drugs made them manifest. Of course, drugs always make matters worse—at times irremediably worse. A familiar type of drug abuser is the gifted adolescent with middle- and upper-middle-class parents. Sensitive to the ills of the environment, unable to communicate with his or her family, the gifted adolescent sometimes shares a family tendency to avoid looking facts in the face. The drug abuser of the poor ghetto, like his wealthier counterpart, is dependent, frightened, and unwilling to grow up. Both may be disturbed in a psychiatric sense as well as for social causes. Both have little sense of self and both share an inability to be direct or to communicate feelings; they have little ability to tolerate anxiety or to foresee that the future will largely derive from their present choices—for good or bad. The younger the child (and some are only 9 to 12 years old), the more the will is affected and training for coping with life is sacrificed.

Many adults are not nearly as learned as their children are about the varieties of pills, serums, powders, and plants that will take a person up, out, or down. But there is a terrifying ignorance about the actual effects of drugs among many young users themselves as well as among adults who ought to know better, including supposed experts. So little is known that there is still a great deal of work to be done. The realistic handling of young drug abusers requires the active engagement of physicians, psychologists, researchers, lawyers, educators, and law enforcement officers in evaluating, preventing, and treating drug abuse—not simply in punishing it. Whatever other needs drug use may fill, its illegality has given it the added attraction among young people of being another channel for the common adolescent rebellion against authority. It is a very complicated issue and we cannot begin to understand it without making a differentiation among the drugs, their effects, and the individuals and groups who use them.

Teachers and school officials seeking a sensible approach to student drug use will probably adopt at least one principle: Certain things are appropriate to do in school or during work hours, and others are not; some things are appropriate to bring to school, and others are not. A person does not drink in school or at work or come drunk to school or work without consequences. Likewise, a person does not get high on drugs in school. When a student fails to abide by this principle, as many do, it should be a major concern of the school to assist the drug abuser in coping with the sources of the problem.

Though heavy drug users often fantasize great creations, they seldom act on them; the act of creation itself seems to require too much effort, to make too great a demand on the infantile orientation of the drug user. The addictive drugs reduce the appetite, so that undernourishment and consequent lack of energy make productivity the exception rather than the rule among addicted users. Article 1.7 below describes this seductive and enervating state where, if the drugs take hold, particularly in children and youth, they can burn out a zest for learning and living. Although the literature on drug use among the young is increasing, remarkably little has been written that accurately conveys the experience and helps adults to recognize and deal with the problem. However, teachers are now aware of certain signals of student drug use: large pupils and heavy eyelids, leaden or slack bodies, atypical or inappropriate speech, excessive giggling or tears, or reports of fantasies.

ARTICLE 1.7

Down These Mean Streets

Piri Thomas

I sat down on the edge of the roof ledge. My mind refused to get off its kick of reminiscing. Man, like how many times some cat's come up to me with his old man's watch or sisters coat and swap for a three-cent bag. Heh, a

---

three-cent bag—like a grain of rice crushed to powder, that's how much it is for a cost of three dollars, and you couldn't beat down that hell-like look as the begging took place in exchange for that super-tranquilizing ca-ca powder. I sniffed back a tear that came out of my nose. And how about the time I plowed through that falling snow with no pride at all in my Buster Brown shoes—like brown on top and bustered on the bottoms—knowing without a doubt in the world that the only thing that would get me warm again so I could care about being cold was the connecting—the blending of my vein's blood and dogie drug.

Shit, man, how far can pride go down? I knew that all the help in the world could get that stuff out of my system, but only some kind of god would be able to get it out of my swinging soul and mind. What a sick murder scene! If you didn't get gypped outta your stuff, you'd get beat on some weak, cut-down shit. If you didn't get dead on an overdose, you'd get deader on a long strung-out kick. Everything in the world depended on heroin. You'd go to bed thinking about stuff and wake up in the morning thinking about it. Love and life took second place to it and nothing mattered except where, and how soon. It was like my whole puking system had copped a mind bigger than the one in my head.

I walked toward the roof landing. I was thinking. I was gonna kick for good. "I can do it. I swear ta God and the Virgin. Gonna get me li'l shit and cut down good. *I ain't no fuckin' junkie.*"

I went looking for Waneko. I found him in *El Viejo's* candy store. I put my want to him in fast words. "Help me kick, man?" It was a question. Waneko knew how it was. Even though he was pushing now, he wasn't using, but he'd been through that kicking road *mucho* times. Waneko nodded, "Sure, *panin—sure* I will." We walked into Waneko's place. He explained to his moms what was shaking. She smiled nice-like and said everything was gonna be all right. Waneko followed that assurance up with, "Moms helps most of the cats that want to kick and even some of the chicks. She should be some kind of church worker or something." He laughed. I tried a weak smile.

They put me in a room that just had a bed and chair and a window that had a metal gate across it to keep the crooks out and kicking junkies in. I laid down, and after a while Waneko brought in a small radio so I could dig some music, to take my mind off what was coming. Both he and I knew that the li'l taste of stuff I had shot up on the roof a while ago was gonna wear off and then World War III was gonna break out inside of me. Billie was wailing some sad song. I wailed along with her in a soft hum. Then some kinda time started to go by and my system was better than a clock. And then Judgment Day set in . . .

Man, talk about wantin' to die—everything started off as it should. First like always, the uncomfortable feeling as you knew your system wanted its baby bottle. And nose running ever so gently at first and the slow kind of pain building up not so gently. I tried hard to listen to some wailin' on the radio, but all I could hear was my own. I got up and went to the door. It was locked from the outside. "Hey, Waneko, open the door," I yelled.

"*Quotes?*"

"I feel real bad, like in bad, man."

"Man, lay down, you ain't been in there long enough to work up any kind of sweat. I'll tell you when, and only then I'll give you a li'l taste to ease you off. So cool it, *panin.*"

I don't know how many hours ran crawling by. I just knew I couldn't make it. *But I hadda. I just hadda.* "Lemme out, Waneko—lemme out, you mother-fucker." I swam to the door and hit at it.

"Waneko is not home right now." It was Waneko's moms.

"Let me out, *senora.* I kicked already."

"He said not to let you come out until he comes back, *hijo.*"

"Did he leave something for me?" My voice sounded like tears. I went back to bed and just rolled and moaned all alone.

I don't know how many hours ran crawling by. It was a lot of them. At one time I heard the lock being taken off the door and heard it fall from someone's hand. I felt Waneko's mom's voice—I felt her cool hand on my face and felt her wipe my cold sweating face. I heard sounds of comfort coming from her.

"No te apures, hijo, you weel soon be fine."

I tried to get up and make it, but she was faster. I felt the iron gates on the window. I shook them. I turned and flopped back on the bed. I was shaking. I was in bad pain. I was cold and I couldn't stop my snots from flowing. I was all in cramps and my guts wouldn't obey me. My eyes were overflowing real fast.

"Lemme out, Waneko—lemme out, you mother-fucker." Shit, I was like screaming out of veins. Nobody answered and I just lay there and moaned and groaned all alone and turned that mattress into one big soaking mopful of my sweat.

I don't know how many hours went crawling by. Millions maybe. And then a real scared thought hit me. Waneko wasn't coming back. He was gonna let me make it—cold-turkey—a *la canona.* I kept trembling and my whole swinging soul full of pain would make my body lurch up and tie itself up into one big knot and then ease itself almost straight and then retie itself. I felt like a puke coming afar. I thought, didn't I puke before? I felt it come out of my mouth like a green river of yellow-blue bile. I couldn't control nothing, and all the strength I had was enough just to turn my head away. I think I made some soft ca-ca on myself. I think I made some hard ones too.

Sometimes I think I heard Waneko telling me, "It's almost over, baby, it's almost over—we got it beat." But I couldn't answer. I'd just hold myself together with my arms holding me tight and rockabye baby myself to some kind of vague comfort. In a dream I'd eat mountains and mountains of sweet, sweet candy. I opened my eyes and Waneko had me sitting in a chair and I saw Moms cleaning the toilet I had made out of the room—and then I was back in the bed. I still had all the pain, all the cramps. I still had the whole bad bit, but I knew I was gonna make it. I rocked myself to and fro.

I don't know how many hours ran crawling by. Jillions maybe. At last the pain cut itself down. I felt all dried out. Waneko came into the room and rubbed my body down, like trying to work all the knots to straighten out. Waneko and his moms kept me with them for a week or so putting me into shape with hot pigeon soup, liquids, and later heavier stuff like I mean, rice and beans. They were great, Waneko and Moms. My body was kicked free from H—gone was dogie. They said it takes seventy or so hours to kick a habit. I think it seemed like seventy years. Now all I had to do was kick it outta my mind.

I left Waneko's house after really thanking them from way down. I hit the street thinking, "Wow, dying is easier than this has been. Never— *never—nunca mas.*"

. . . .

THE ALCOHOLIC STUDENT . . . .

The use of alcohol by children and adolescents in the United States has increased alarmingly. It is becoming a more pervasive problem in schools than the use of other drugs and narcotics. Alcohol is easily available to children, although it is illegal for minors to buy or drink it. Youngsters can get liquor from people older than themselves, from illegal sales, through use of false identification cards, and at their own or at friends' homes. Although liquor prices run high, the cost is small compared to the price of illegal drugs. What's more, liquor can be obtained by theft from businesses or homes. Teenagers hold up and loot liquor stores more frequently than any other type of store.

Many children grow up seeing their parents drink, whether socially or heavily. The use of alcohol permeates American culture. A "happy hour" is frequently advertised by restaurants and bars, and liquor stores abound in every village, town, and city. The corner tavern, immortalized in "Cheers," is as much a part of the scenery to children as the gas station or drugstore. It is highly unlikely that a child could grow up today without seeing TV programs or movies depicting drinkers and drunks.

Any child whose family serves or drinks alcoholic beverages can taste wine with dinner, beer with snacks, or hard liquor at parties. Some ethnic groups give children alcohol as a matter of course. Many of these children do not abuse alcohol, but some family practices may instigate its overuse. Although stereotypes are always dangerous, there are clinical observations that, given low-income and low-employment opportunities, some ethnic groups are more susceptible to alcoholism than others. For example, the Irish and the American Indians tend to find alcohol a particularly difficult chemical to handle. However, all ethnic groups are prone to misuse alcohol when their conditions in life appear to be or truly are overwhelming. Children from these families grow up considering alcohol a way to veil misery.

Children who drink too much may start for any reason: to be "one of the gang," or because they have seen their parents reach for drinks under stress, or because they found a bottle on the playground and found that drinking erased their problems temporarily. They may become severe drinkers if their home life is miserable, if they feel imprisoned in untenable situations by dependence on their parents or caretakers, or because they cannot yet fend for themselves in normal activities. Sometimes, a child is neglected or mistreated by one or more drunken parents. In an effort to erase the feelings of being uncared for, he or she proceeds to do what the elders do—opt for escape. In some ways, alcoholism is a contagious disease. It is so difficult to relate to an alcoholic family member that spouses and children may give up and join what they cannot fight. Sexual fears tend to be rampant at adolescence anyway, and they simply contribute to the teenage drinker's primitive neediness and sense of general inadequacy.

Like many drugs, alcohol numbs—it depresses the rigid controls most people live by. For a short while, it permits a child who feels lonely, unhappy, and unsure to feel OK, likable, affectionate, entertained, amusing, strong, and able. Yet, at the very moment liquor makes the child feel in control, he or she is usually most out of control. Illusion is the essence of excessive alcoholic intake. Often, drink gives these children an initial glow of ability to cope, and the numbness that follows momentarily loosens the pressures they feel and makes the world seem rosier, if unreal.

As different as alcoholics are from each other, there are some basic similarities. Whether adults or children, they are fundamentally very dependent, needy, and infantile, while presenting a facade that is often poised, charming, seductive, winning, indirect, and manipulative. They have great expectations of themselves, often because of explicit or implicit parental demands or because they want to prove to neglectful parents that they are worth loving. Their aspirations tend to be grandiose, and they are given to extremes of elation and despair. They are either the most wonderful or the most terrible, or they want to be one or the other, never in between, never ordinary. They must be special or nothing. Their need for reassurance and support is as bottomless as their thirst. Although they make demands for closeness, when push comes to shove they keep a wall or protective distance between themselves and others, because they feel so empty, so needy, so thirsty inside. They fear that others will discover their emptiness, what they see as their fakery or deficiencies, and will despise them. They are therefore filled with self-hate and guilt. This self-hate is exacerbated by drinking, but to drown it they drink more.

For alcoholics of every age, the symbol of a bottle is apt. Inside the alcoholic personality, no matter how sophisticated, is an infant needing the complete nurture one gets only at the breast. Underneath the grandiose goals or the "out-of-it" manner, there hides a fearful, self-critical, and pervasively guilty person who has unendingly voracious needs that are not met by what the world is offering.

Alcohol becomes a poison for a child even more, and sooner, than for an adult. It destroys not only liver and kidneys but also self-esteem, will, and motivation. It ultimately can affect the nervous system and the brain. It feeds on fantasy rather than fact. To drinking children, alcohol represents a return to the nipple or the bottle, a wish for the warm oblivion of infancy before expectations and demands became overwhelming. Often, alcoholism is an unspoken message that a child is not ready to grow up. This is particularly true where a child is under heavy pressure to act grown up or to undertake responsibility that he or she is not ready to bear. The escape from burdens that can't be shouldered is frequently through the bottle, which offers comfort and oblivion for a little while. Such a child often behaves and performs very well for periods, by mysteriously falls apart from time to time. The child has become a secret drinker (and secrecy and shame are part of the essence of alcoholism).

If a child comes to school drunk, it would be helpful for a teacher to know whether the home life is unsatisfying, or whether the parents are modeling drinking behavior. Teachers can observe whether the alcoholic child fears other children in or outside the classroom, or fears being exposed as unprepared, ridiculous, or stupid in school. Both home and school have to be examined. Are the pressures and the rigidity of standards and expectations too great? When a pupil is drunk in school more than once, it is essential to take a good look at the youngster and the family, through interviews and, if possible, home visits. When teachers report that a child is drinking, parents may deny it and refuse to believe the facts until the habit is too far advanced to be easily curtailed. Often, a child is devastated by realizing he or she is addicted and cannot stop drinking. Parents usually need help to acknowledge that, directly or indirectly, their habits, attitudes, pressures, or unrealistic dreams for their children have brought on addictive behavior.

Help can come through appropriate attention and recognition. Training can help the student to be comfortable with honesty and to develop more openness. Realistic expectations can be opened up along with opportunities for the pupil to relax and be childish when he or she needs to be. The family may need guidance in helping the child to order his or her social horizons. Finally, offering group therapy as a mode of treatment can ameliorate the student's drinking problem and the problems underlying it. Alcoholics Anonymous (A.A.) continues to be one of the very best organized groups dealing with both alcoholics and their families (through its auxiliary group Al-Anon). The patient joins an A.A. group, and his or her family joins an Al-Anon group, which can help the families of alcoholics understand the problems of the alcoholic while drinking and while withdrawing from alcohol. It helps family members with their problems as well. Individual, group, or family therapy may also be used.

School personnel need to understand the part they can play in referral and in setting clear limits without overmoralizing or make unrealistic expectations. The parents or family of a drunk child must understand that the teacher attempting to deal with the child will try to furnish basic satisfaction of the youngster's needs while setting firm and clear limits on behavior. For example, the child will not be permitted to disrupt the class by becoming the center of attention. If too drunk to work, he or she may be allowed to sleep at the nurse's office and then be seen by an expert in the field of alcohol abuse. The counselor or other helping person needs to find out what factors in the child's life set off the desire to drink, and then to guide the child and the family to recognition and appropriate treatment of the problem.

ARTICLE 1.8

Interview with a Patient— The Alcoholic Teenager

I began to drink when I was twelve and my parents went out, which they did often. I would raid the liquor cabinet. At first, it burnt and made me sick, but I kept trying—and I don't know why. It made me feel smart when I felt dumb. It made me laugh and made me forget things like bad report cards and the beatings I'd get for them. I made people laugh with me, or maybe at me, but anyway—Only then I couldn't do anything without a drink. It was like punctuation marks: I needed a drink to be with people, a drink to be alone, a drink before homework so I could tackle it, and another after, for reward. I carried vodka with me to school in my milk thermos, I chewed chlorophyll mints to keep away any smell. I'd steal liquor from my parents and put water in the bottles. They fired the maid because they thought she did it.

They found out when I was drunk and stole a guy's car and ran into a pole and I landed in the hospital. The social worker here saw my parents and the A.A. people came to see me. They said I could get well, and they'll help me, and my parents will go to Al-Anon, though I don't believe they'll go to their meeting. But I still want a drink right now so bad. You see when I'm drunk I know I'm good at things. I'm the best car designer. I'm the best basketball player like my father was. The girls are crazy for me instead of turning me down. Anything, everything looks good, and I don't even have to try—it just is there, one drink away . . . maybe.

ARTICLE 1.9

Patient's Reminiscence of the Alcoholic Parent

I never told anyone, you see, that my mother was mostly drunk when I came home from school. Sometimes, she was very drunk and had fallen down in the house or even outside and, though I was little, I had to pull her into the bedroom so no one would find out—not my friends or the neighbors or the teachers who passed by. So, of course, I couldn't have friends over. I didn't have many friends. I tried to buy them things so they'd like me

---

Printed with patient's permission.

and make me feel like other people, but I couldn't invite them in. They would have seen my mother like that.

It was worse when she yelled or ranted. She wanted me with her all the time. The first time I stayed out overnight was in high school at a friend's. My mother got drunk and came and got me, yelling curses at my friend's family. My father left us when I was two, and there was never a man around I could count on. Oh, she'd bring drunk dates home from time to time, but no one lasted and in between she'd rave and rant about men and my father and how awful he was, so I grew up hating men. I still don't trust them. I always felt her drunkenness was his fault for leaving. But now I wonder if he left her because she was a drunk.

The worst was graduation day from the parochial eighth grade school I went to. For weeks, the nuns asked us to get dresses or have them made. My mother promised and promised—weeks went by and nothing happened. I had no money but I took little jobs and saved up and bought the material and my mother promised to sew it. When she was sober she could sew. Dress rehearsal came and went; the Sister was furious at me because I had no dress. I promised I would have it on graduation day and pleaded with my mother to get it done. She began working on it the night before graduation, but then she got very drunk and as usual yelled and screamed at me because I wanted something. In her rage and drunkenness, she tore the dress in ribbons, and threw them at me.

All the long day of graduation the phone rang. My mother passed out and I knew it was one of the Sisters from school. I couldn't answer. I just cried and cried, and I never got to graduation. The one Sister in charge of my class was furious with me because I had spoiled her processional line, and called me to come in. She said I couldn't graduate because I'd been so unreliable. I went myself to see the head Sister—the Mother Superior—and burst into tears and, for the first time ever, told the truth about my mother. She was nice and put her arm around me, and I wept with shame and hurt. My mother couldn't come to explain. She got upset about what she had done, so she went out to a bar and got drunk. I never could think at school since I was busy worrying about what was happening to her and my worst thoughts always happened.

2

The Psychology of Helping: Becoming Important and Useful in Troubled Students' Lives

T his book is devoted to various strategies teachers and others can use to help troubled youngsters both through hands-on efforts and bringing changes to their ecologies. Various chapters focus on specific procedures such as how a teacher can support the family, strategies to use in crises, positive use of group life, designing a reclaiming curriculum, and suggested strategies for particular types of problems. Support for such specific strategies rests on generic attributes of the helping process. Given the poor outcomes of work with troubled children, there are many questions concerning how we help. Is the popular focus on control an adequate strategy? What are the essential ingredients of a helping milieu? Is advocacy of the least restrictive environment through total inclusion the priority placement to help troubled children? What is the role of caring? Does it matter how the teacher conceptualizes the helping? Are there essential ingredients to be sought in all helping processes regardless of the specific medium employed? In short, are there general factors that undergird those more specific helping strategies in subsequent chapters? We bear in mind the assumption that troubled children can be reclaimed to perform within the normal range. They can learn new ways of thinking, feeling, and behaving. Where there is significant biological vulnerability, medical therapies may be an essential corollary.

The method a teacher can best use to assist a particular troubled youngster toward a better quality of life remains ubiquitous. Helping appears in many guises from screaming and hypnosis to talking and drawing, ranging from waiting for development to intense invasions. We are faced with a paradigm: Everything works and everything fails in particular situations. Research on different modes of helping record both success and failures. The spectrum of helping includes adult behaviors that seem to belie a generic consistency.

Helping is so complex it is virtually impossible to make a satisfactory cognitive map of the vicissitudes of what an adult can do to foster a student's new learning. We are often naive even though we are aware that what helps a youngster is not always what we would expect. Some students improve almost in spite of what we do while others make little progress even with the best practice. In response to uncertainty, we develop a set of helping rituals for practice, sometimes applied without thinking of how our acts will benefit a student in a given instance. There are simply too many dimensions to reduce to one comprehensive paradigm. Also, it is not always reasonable to apply approaches coming from adult work to children at various developmental levels. Most students do not come of their own choice to seek help but are coerced by adults who decide they need to change. It is unusual to have a youngster apply for a space in special education or a remedial program. Small wonder that many students initially resist adult efforts to help them.

The typical approach to dealing with the vast array of helping methodologies is to contrast major theories, such as cognitive, behavioristic, ecological, psychoeducational, and dynamic, by compiling an idealized position statement for each. The teacher is expected to select, combine, and integrate them into an effective teaching style. There is no such contrasting theory chapter in this book. The delineating of contrasting models puts the emphasis in the wrong place. The focus of attention shifts to the theory, rather than the unique needs of the individual student in trouble. In this book, we follow the time-honored child study approach: Study the individual child and his or her ecology, then search out the appropriate interventions. This is also in tune with the IEP required for all special students. Before the advocates of various stereotyped approaches, teachers worked with children in a variety of ways rather than trying to help youngsters by inserting them into a particular preselected treatment envelope. Teachers are multimodal, finding uses for a wide variety of helping procedures adapted to their own style and depending on the child and the situation. Unfortunately, the literature indicates that a troubled student is often still subject to an adult's favored methodology with seldom any effort to match the template of helping acts to an individual child's nature or circumstance.

Our knowledge of helping far exceeds our practices in schools. Because of time, skill, and cost limitations, helping efforts seldom match what we know is really needed. A student living in abject poverty is given a school breakfast. Amelioration and surface compliance are accepted in place of more extensive interventions. Reclaiming children and their families is a very complicated and expensive process. Half-way measures seldom work. A teacher or even a school, working in isolation, can rarely marshal the necessary resources. As the African proverb states, "it takes the whole village to raise a child." The idea that a child and an adult conversing in an isolated setting can "fix" most of our troubled children or adolescents is a myth. After exploiting all aspects of schooling, the school must have access to the full range of community services.

The term *helping* best replaces *therapy* in the educational setting. Helping is a more generic concept. Therapy depends on specific processes that are owned by particular professional guilds. Once therapy and education were separated by a wide gulf, but it is now acknowledged that there are many school activities that have therapeutic potentials. Sarason and others now include teachers along with the holy trinity of psychologists, psychiatrists, and social workers as essential members of the mental health enterprise. After all, of the professions, only teachers spend extensive time with youngsters in a wide variety of situations. In some cases, teachers spend more time with the awake youngster than the parents. Since we are concerned with troubled and ineffective youngsters, our work is more complicated, but the essential model is an extension of the good and wise parent. Helping students grow up successfully was never easy and certainly has become even more complex. Unraveling and rebuilding already maligned and mixed up lives is our task. This carries an ethical burden of responsibility since we make judgments concerning what is good for youngsters who constitute a borrowed, captive clientele.

Because of the prestige associated with being a therapist, there has been a proliferation of hybrid therapies: reading therapy, music therapy, dance therapy, art therapy, and on and on to embrace most of the curriculum. There is a national organization of Educational Therapists. When does an activity cease to be education and become a therapy? This is a puzzling question. Does it depend on specialized training, the clientele (problem students become clients), or the use of specialized methodologies? No matter what term is employed, helping or therapy, this chapter focuses on troubled children and youth and the teachers who are dedicated to assisting them in achieving satisfactory lives. Because of the high societal cost, to say nothing of the personal pain, the teacher who redirects even one student a year from failure to success has repaid her salary to society. High-risk youngsters who later become resilient often credit the change to a particular teacher who took an interest and believed in them. For some students, the act of accepting help is admitting a personal failure or weakness: Failure to cope is interpreted as personal weakness.

Before reading on, jot down a few notes as benchmarks of where you are in this complex of being a helper. As a child and adolescent, who and what helped you deal with your problems? Did you follow the common pattern of referring to parents or another adult early on and then move to peers for assistance? Were teachers ever the source of help or were they part of the problem? Did you ever seek help but found none? The last time you had a significant crisis in your life, how did you handle it? What have been your major frustrations in trying to help youngsters? Armed with such reflections, you will be able to challenge the content of this chapter through personal experience.

Helping always involves an interaction between a helper and a helpee, in our case, a teacher and a student. Each brings a unique personal experience to the relationship: a self and role perception embodying needs and goals, values and attitudes, and capabilities. In helping troubled students, two adult qualities are essential in the relationship. One is empathy, the ability to see an event from each individual student's viewpoint. This is also the key to seeing beyond the surface behavior in order to understand the student's affective state and his or her private world of childhood or adolescence. Though we were all once children, then adolescents, we often have forgotten important feelings about living in these developmental stages. It is not a simple operation to empathize. Often a youngster has had a life voyage foreign to our own. Considerable attentive listening is required to fill out the life story. The work of helping requires that we transpose ourselves into the youngster's world, akin to what we did in reading the selections in Chapter 1. We learn what it feels like to walk in another's shoes. But it is not enough to feel empathic: It is necessary for the adult to convincingly communicate the empathy so that the youngster feels understood. Many troubled youngsters take a lot of convincing because they have not experienced empathic adults in their lives.

The second basic quality the adult brings to the helping relationship is caring. Again the process is more complicated than having caring feelings. The helpee must be convinced that we care. One way he or she does this is to test the adult. The youngster requires a persuasive communication of the intent to help. Authenticity appears to facilitate caring, meaning that what we portray is what we really are, not a role we assume from nine to four. As far as possible, we are living examples of what we espouse. This requires emotional honesty and admitting shortcomings. Youngsters say about certain teachers, "You should see him when the principal comes in; he pretends he really cares about us. Otherwise he couldn't care less." Students, especially troubled students, are astute in recognizing facades and personal frauds.

Empathy and caring are transmitted by both verbal and nonverbal communication as well as how we select and conduct the educational activities. Caring by the teacher is critical, but caring goes beyond the individual helper. The total school environment needs to be caring. Teachers find it difficult to create an oasis of care in a desert of rejection. Schools are subject to many obligations and rescuing troubled students is not always high on the agenda in school reform. Thus the school as a helping milieu requires our attention.

Of particular importance in guiding the adult-child relationships are the attributions each holds about both the responsibility for the troubled child's dilemma and the solution. Who is to blame and who can fix things takes up a lot of time in meetings. In general, the younger the student, the more adults are reluctant to blame the student and the more adults feel responsible for supplying a cure. The causes for childhood problems are split between environmental and biological attributions: The young child is usually deemed helpless. As youngsters grow older, especially when they reach adolescence, they are assigned personal blame for their mistakes and are assumed to have the power to change their behavior once given verbal advice by an adult. Misbehavior is then considered willful. The young child's helpless behavior has become the adolescent's defiant behavior. We tell students how to behave and when they don't reform we reveal our attribution theory by such statements as "Well, there you go again. You are your own worst enemy. Why don't you ever listen to what I tell you to do?" Troubled children become willfully bad students as they grow older. The strategies in this book are focused on the many ways in which we can help students learn replacement behavior and cease to depend only on verbal admonitions and punishment.

Youngsters have their own list of attributions for being in trouble: bad luck (getting caught while others did worse but went free); unfair rules enforced by parents or teachers; peer seduction ("We were all doing it" or "They made me do it"); ethnic attitudes; or "because of my disability" (such as having a bad temper or a learning disability). More sophisticated adolescents may practice the self-absolution disease theory: "I was on drugs," "I was drunk and didn't know what I was doing," or perhaps, "I was abused in a terrible family," pleading their case of "not my fault" in the same way that adults do. They expect others to provide a cure without their active participation. Their primary goal is to ward off blame and keep adults off their case ("I'm not responsible, so I don't own my trouble or cure"). Taking responsibility for one's own behavior is out-of-date in this society, as we see in the daily papers. Pupils who do internalize, blame themselves and feel depressed and hopeless about themselves and their prospects. They assume responsibility for the fix they are in. It is their fault, but they are unable to manage a solution.

Everything is instant in this society. Both students and adults want instant solutions to problems. We have had students ask to be hypnotized into goodness; others have volunteered to sign in blood to produce instant reform. We say, "Don't ever do that again. Do you hear?" and they answer, "I won't never. Honest." It is a game we both play. There is considerable magical belief in attributions.

Teachers and students have attributions about cures for dilemmas. Some kids have learned to *say* they will try harder even if they have no belief that trying harder will work. Others have given up. If youngsters have problems, something has to change in how they see things, in their skills, or in the stress put on them. Teachers range in solution attributions from assuming total responsibility ("It's up to me to save this pupil") to hopelessness ("Given his past and present situation, nothing can be done to change this student"). Sometimes, it is easier to remember that every youngster is committed to something, even if only avoiding involvement in our efforts. We have both conscious, expressed attributions and unconscious attributions that leak through in our relationships. Each teacher has a list of the students who are easy to like and those who are hard to like. Such lists should be explored because usually the resistant and unlikable students need us most.

As we examine the essence of the helping process, we face very deeply held personal attitudes concerning human nature, causation, human development, and human learning. One way to think of the IEP meeting is to see it as a forum for various attributions about the problem and about remediation from parents, teachers, various experts, and, sometimes, students. Usually, a public layer and an unspoken layer of assumptions are both at work.

The outcome of empathy and caring is the awakening of a trusting relationship, a condition of being open with another human being without fear of being hurt. This condition enables working through life's problems, considering new modes of behaving, and, eventually, consolidating a personal sense of how the world is and how one relates to it.

In several of his writings, Nick Hobbs, the father of Re-ED, addressed our question of the underlying forces that foster significant changes in human behavior. His list of essential characteristics of movements that change people includes being exposed to a belief system that makes sense of life and provides personal direction. The successful lifestyle is personified by an interpreter-example—in our case, the teacher. Discussion of issues and of new convictions is worked through in a group setting, as a prelude to taking positive action on constructive commitments. All of this activity takes place in the company of a caring community. If we intend to help pupils change, we will have to offer more than surface manipulation. Programs will need to embody the helping elements Hobbs describes. The articles that follow suggest ways of accomplishing this aspiration in our programs.

It is not too complicated to list the resources that should be available to help troubled students wherever they are placed—in a regular classroom or an institution. The birthright of salient services begins with an honest individual educational plan—the IEP for designated special students, which is useful for others as well. In many cases, it would be better to think in terms of a life plan rather than just a school plan. The plan is based on a thorough assessment of the youngster's individual needs and ecological condition. Although all troubled students will require some of the services to be delineated, and specific students will need a unique constellation of support, all services should be available in a program. The list centers around a trained and caring teacher and staff in a school that is hospitable to troubled youngsters. Program elements should reach into the family, offering consultation, counseling, support, and parent education. The teacher should have the same access to community services for the child and family as in a Full Service School that has wraparound services in place. Schooling goes beyond a normal spectrum of curricular and extracurricular activities by emphasizing study skills and social skills training. For some youngsters, alternative education and an emphasis on vocational training will be the choice. Individual counseling at the required depth is combined with group work and peer self-help efforts. Particularly important is crisis intervention to exploit life events for learning. This service is critical when disturbed students are included in the mainstream. The management system, developed jointly by teacher and pupils, should be based on prevention and social learning rather than punishment. The arts and other expressive media should be extensively employed. All programs need a transition provision for moving students to regular education or, later, to the work world. Program evaluation is judged by the quality of present and future life, not just months of gain in academic learning. Each day should include at least a taste of satisfaction for the pupil. (These issues are elaborated in subsequent chapters.)

It is one thing to list necessary program resources and quite another to blend the selected elements into a therapeutic milieu. We speak of the "quality of the experience" provided by the school, but quality is an elusive phenomenon. The youngster lives in a series of ecologies: his or her own internal world, then the family milieu, the classroom bridging to the school at large, the peers, and the neighborhood. Bronfenbrenner has pointed out that there are other overlapping ecological circles such as class and ethnic belonging, religious affiliations, mass media images, and belief systems. The various ecologies seldom speak with one voice. Given the competitive nature of the multiple ecologies, the school has low power for some students and high potency for others.

The difficulties of meshing ecologies to produce coherent restorative surroundings for pupils with problems are obvious. The combination that is receiving the most attention has been unification of the home and the school efforts. With adolescents, we also have to recognize peer power. Students pick up and exploit disparities between what the school or family teaches and what they experience through the mass media. Even in school, there may be a lack of homogeneity—for example, in value differences between the teacher and the administration. Exploitation of adult differences is a youth survival skill. The differences are translated into license for behavior, especially by the adolescent. When we cannot alter life beyond the school, our influence resides in how gratifying and meaningful we can make the classroom. We anticipate that increasing numbers of students will look back and say that it was in school and with the help of a significant teacher that they first began to put their lives together and gain control.

Even as we admit that school is not all-powerful, we remember that the student is in this setting from 9:00 to 3:00, five days a week, accumulating an average total of over 15,000 school hours. School is a place where a wide variety of services can be delivered and where many efforts can be focused on reclaiming. The question is: What makes for a true therapeutic milieu? Fritz Redl spent his career creating curative milieus for distraught children and youth. Here, he details for us the factors, tangible and intangible, that make for a powerful restorative ecology for troubled youngsters. Although Redl speaks of special therapeutic settings, one can easily translate these elements to a school setting. Do the schools you know consider these matters? What changes would you propose to increase the helping quotient of the school environment?

ARTICLE 2.1

The Concept of a Therapeutic Milieu
Fritz Redl

TRAPS FOR THE MILIEU CONCEPT

1. The cry for the therapeutic milieu as a general slogan is futile and in this wide formulation the term doesn't mean a thing. No milieu is "good" or "bad" in itself—it all depends. And it depends on more factors than I want to list, though some of them will turn up as we go along.

2. It won't do to use our own philosophical, ethical, political convictions, or our taste buds, in order to find out what really has or has not "therapeutic effect." Even the most respectable clinical discussions around this theme drift all too easily into A's trying to convince B that his setup is too "autocratic," or that what he called "democratic" group management isn't really good for those youngsters. Whether a ward should have rules, how many and which, must not lead to an argument between those who like rules and those who don't; I have seen many a scientific discussion end up in the same personal taste-bud battle that one otherwise finds acceptable only when people talk about religions or brands of cars.

3. Even a concept of "total milieu therapy" does not imply that all aspects of a given milieu are equally relevant in all moments in clinical life. All games, for instance, have some kind of "social structure" and as part of that, some kind of "pecking order" which determines the power position of the players for the duration of the game. Whether the specific pecking order of the game I let them play today had anything to do with the fact that it blew up in my face after five minutes is a question that can be answered only in empirical terms. I know of cases where the pecking order was clearly it; I have to look no further. I know of others where it was of no *clinical* relevance at the time. The boys blew up because they got too scared playing hide-and-seek with flashlights in the dark. In short, the scientific establishment of a given milieu aspect as a theoretically valid and important one does not substitute for the need for a diagnosis on the spot. It alone can differentiate between potential milieu impacts and actual ones in each case.

4. The idea of the "modern" and therefore social-science-conscious psychiatrist that he has to sell out to the sociologist if he wants to have his "ward milieu" studied properly is the bunk. Of course, any thoughtful ap-

From (1959) "The Concept of a 'Therapeutic Milieu,' " by Fritz Redl, *American Journal of Orthopsychiatry*, XXIX, 721–734. Reprinted by permission.

praisal of a hospital milieu will contain many variables which the mother discipline of a given psychiatrist may never have dreamed about. On the other hand, the thing that counts is not only the description of a variable, but the assessment of the potential impact on the treatment process of a given group of patients. That is basically a *clinical* matter, and it remains the clinician's task. The discipline that merges social science with clinical criteria in a balanced way still has to be invented. There is no short cut to it either by psychiatry's stealing particles of social science concepts or by selling out to the social scientist's domain.

5. The frequently voiced expectation that the discovery of what "milieu" one needs would automatically make it easy to produce that style of milieu in a given place is downright naive. An instrumentology for the creation of "ward atmosphere," of "clinically correct policies of behavioral intervention," etc., has yet to be created, and it will cost blood and sweat to get it. The idea that all it takes to have a "good treatment milieu" is for a milieu-convinced ward boss to make his nurses feel comfortable with him, and to hold a few gripe sessions between patients and staff, is a daydream, the simplicity of which we can no longer afford. . . .

A "MILIEU"—WHAT'S IN IT?

Obviously I am not going to use the term in the nearly global meaning which its theft from the French language originally insinuated. For practical reasons, I am going to talk here only of one sort of milieu concept: of a "milieu" artificially created for the purpose of the treatment of a group of youngsters. Within this confine you can make it somewhat wider if you want, and think of the "Children's Psychiatric Unit" on the fourth, eighth, or ninth floor of a large hospital, or you may hold before your eyes, while I am speaking, a small residential treatment home for children that is not part of a large unit. Of course, I know that the similarity of what I am talking about to other types of setups may be quite great, but I can't cover them all. Hence, anything else you hold before your eyes while I talk, you do strictly at your own risk.

So, here we are on the doorstep of that treatment home or at the keyhole of that hospital ward. And now you ask me: If you could plan things the way you wanted to, which are the most important "items" in your milieu that will sooner or later become terribly relevant for better or for worse? The choice is hard, and only such a tough proposition gets me over the guilt feeling for oversimplifying and listing items out of context.

1. *The social structure.* This is some term, and I have yet to see the psychiatrist that isn't stunned for a moment at its momentum—many would run and hire a sociologist on the spot. Being short on time, I have no choice, but let me hurry and add: this term in itself is as

extendible and collapsible as a balloon. It doesn't mean much without specifications. So, let me just list a few of the things I have in mind:

a. A hospital ward is more like a *harem society than a family,* no matter how motherly or fatherly the particular nurses and doctors may feel toward their youngsters. The place I run at the moment is purposely shaped as much as possible after the model of an American camp, which is the only pattern I could find which children would be familiar with, where a lot of adults walk through children's lives in older brother and parentlike roles without pretending it to be an equivalent to family life.

b. The *role distribution* of the adult figures can be of terrific importance for the amount of clarity with which children perceive what it is all about. Outspokenly or not, sooner or later they must become clear about just who can or cannot be expected to decide what; otherwise, how would one know when one is getting the runaround?

c. The *pecking order* of any outfit does not long remain a secret to an open door neighborhood-wise toughie, no matter how dumb he may be otherwise. He also smells the outspoken "pecking order" among the adults who take care of him, no matter how carefully disguised it may be under professional role titles or Civil Service Classification codes.

d. The *communication network* of any given institution is an integral part of its "social structure." Just who can be approached about listening to what is quite a task to learn; and to figure out the real communication lines that are open and those which are secretly clogged in the adult communication network is usually an insoluble task except for the suspicious outside researcher . . . .

2. *The value system that oozes out of our pores.* Some people subsume that under social structure. I think I have reasons to want a separate place for it here, but let's not waste time on the question why. The fact is, the youngsters not only respond to what we say or put in mimeographed writing; they smell our value-feelings even when we don't notice our own body odor any more. I am not sure how, and I can't wait until I find out. But I do need to find out which value items are there to smell. Does the arrangement of my furniture call me a liar while I make a speech about how much at home I want them to feel, or does that gleam in a counselor's eye tell the child: "You are still wanted," even though he means it if he says he won't let you cut up the tablecloth? By the way, in some value studies I have missed one angle many times: the *clinical convictions* of what is professionally correct handling, which sometimes even questionnaire-clumsy workers on a low salary level may develop, and which become a motivating source for their behavior in its own right, besides their own personal moral convictions or their power drives.

3. *Routines, rituals, and behavioral regulations.* The sequence of events and the conditions under which people undergo certain repetitive maneuvers in their life space can have a strong impact on whether they can keep themselves under control, or whether their impulse-control balance breaks down. Since Bruno Bettelheim's classic description of the events inside a child while he seems engaged in the process of getting up or getting himself to sleep, no more words should have to be said about this. And yet, many "therapeutic milieu" discussions still waste their time on arguments between those who like regularity and those who think the existence of a rule makes life an unimaginative drudge. All groups also have a certain "ritual" by which a member gets back into the graces of the group if he has sinned, and others which the group has to go through when an individual has deviated. Which of those ceremonial rites are going on among my boys, thinly disguised behind squabbles and fights, and which of them do adult staff people indulge in under the even thinner disguise of a discussion on punishment and on the setting of limits? Again—the mere discovery of phenomena fitting into this category is not what I am after. We are still far from having good research data on the *clinical relevance* of whatever specific practice may be in vogue in a specific place.

4. *The impact of the group process.* We had better pause after pronouncing this weighty phrase—it is about as heavy and full of dodges as the phrase "social structure," as previously pointed out. And since this one milieu aspect might well keep us here for a week, let me sink as low as simple word-listing at this point. Items that I think should go somewhere under this name: over-all group atmosphere, processes like scapegoating, mascot-cultivation, subclique formation, group psychological role suction, experiences of exposure to group psychological intoxication, dependency on contagion clusters, leadership tensions, etc. Whatever you have learned from social psychology, group psychology and group dynamics had better be written in right here. The point of all this: These phenomena are *not* just interesting things that happen among patients or staff, to be viewed with a clinical grin, a sociological hurrah, or with the curiosity stare of an anthropological slumming party. These processes are forces to which my child patient is exposed, as real as the oedipus complex of his therapist, the food he eats and the toys he plays with. The forces producing such impacts may be hard to see, or even to make visible through x-ray tricks. They are there and as much of his "surroundings" as the unbreakable room in which he screams off his tantrum.

5. *The trait clusters that other people whirl around within a five-yard stretch.* I first wanted to call this item "the other people as persons," but I know this would only call forth a long harangue about feelings,

attitudes—Isn't it people anyway, who make up a group?—etc. From bitter discussion experience, I am trying to duck these questions by this somewhat off-the-beat phrase. What I have in mind is this: My youngsters live as part of a group, true enough. But they are also individuals. And Bobby who shares a room with John is within striking distance of whatever personal peculiarities John may happen to throw at others. In short, we expect some children to show "shock" at certain colors on a Rorschach card. We expect children to be lured into excited creativity at the mere vision of some fascinating project outline or plane model seductively placed before their eyes. Well, the boy with whom Bobby shares his room is worse than a Rorschach or a plane model. Not only does his presence and the visualization of his personality do something to Bobby, for John not only *has* character traits and neurotic syndromes; he swings them around his body like a wet bathing towel, and it is going to hit whoever gets in its path, innocent or not. In short, personality traits remain psychological entities for the psychologist who watches them in the youngsters. They are *real things that hit and scratch* if you get in their way, for the roommate and all the other people on the ward.

We have learned to respect the impact of certain extremes in pathologies upon each other, but we are still far from inspecting our milieus carefully enough for what they contain in "trait clusters" that children swing around their heads within a five-yard range. Let me add: not all traits and syndromes are "swung"; some stay put and can only be seen or smelled, so they become visible or a nuisance only to the one who shares the same room. Also: we are far from knowing what this all amounts to clinically. For the question of just what "milieu ingredients" my ward contains, in terms of existent trait clusters of the people who live in it, is still far removed from the question of just which *should* coexist with each other, and which others should be carefully kept asunder.

6. *The staff, their attitudes and feelings—but please let's not call it all "transference."* This one I can be short about, for clinicians all know about it; sociologists will grant it to you, though they may question how heavily it counts. In fact, the attitudes and feelings of staff have been drummed up for so long now as "the" most important aspect of a milieu, often even as the only important one, that I am not afraid this item will be forgotten. No argument needed, it is self-evident. Only two issues I would like to battle around: One, while attitudes and feelings are very important indeed, they are not always all that counts, and sometimes other milieu items may gang up on them so much they may obliterate their impact. My other battle cry: Attitudes and feelings of staff are manifold, and spring from many different sources. Let's limit the term "transference" to those for which it was originally invented. If Nurse's Aide A gets too hostile to Bob because he bit him too hard,

let's not throw all of that into the same terminological pot. By the way, if I grant "attitudes and feelings of staff" a place on my list of "powerful milieu ingredients," I mean the attitudes and feelings that really fill the place, that are lived—not those that are only mentioned in research interviews and on questionnaires.

7. *Behavior received.* I tried many other terms, but it won't work. There just isn't one that fits. In a sentence I would say: what people really *do* to each other counts as much as how they feel. This forces me into a two-hour argument in which I have to justify why it isn't unpsychiatric to say such a thing. For, isn't it the underlying feelings that "really" count? That depends on which side of the fence your "really" is. The very fact that you use such a term already means you know there is another side to it, only you don't want to take it as seriously as yours. In short, there are situations where the "underlying feeling" with which the adult punishes a child counts so much that the rather silly form of punishment that was chosen is negligible. But I could quote you hundreds of other examples where this is not the case. No matter what wonderful motive—if you expose child A to an isolation with more panic in it than he can stand, the effect will be obvious. Your excuse that you "meant well and love the boy" may be as futile as that of the mother who would give the child an overdose of arsenic, not knowing its effect.

This item of *behaviors received in a day's time* by each child should make a really interesting line to assess. We would have to look about at "behaviors received" from other boys as well as from staff, and see what the implications of those behaviors received are, even after deducting from them the mitigating influences of "attitudes that really were aiming at the opposite." The same, by the way, should also be taken into consideration for staff to be hired. I have run into people who really love "crazy youngsters" and are quite willing to sacrifice a lot. Only they simply cannot stand more than half a pound of spittle in their face a day, professional attitude or no.

In order to make such an assessment, the clinician would of course be interested especially in the *forms* that are being used by staff for intervention—limit-setting—expression of acceptance and love, etc. The totality of prevalence of certain forms of "behavior received" is not a negligible characteristic of the milieu in which a child patient has to live.

8. *Activity structure and nature of constituent performances.* Part of the impact a hospital or treatment home has on a child lies in the things he is allowed or requested *to do.* Any given activity that is halfway shapeful enough to be described has a certain amount of structure to it—some games, for instance, have a body of rules; demand the splitting up into two opposing sides or staying in a circle; and have certain assessments of roles for the players, at least for the duration. At the same

time, they make youngsters "do certain things" while the game lasts. Paul Gump introduced the term "constituent performances" into our Detroit Game Study, and referred by this term to the performances required within the course of a game as basic. Thus, running and tagging are constituent performances of a tag game, guessing word meanings is a constituent performance in many a charade, etc. We have plenty of evidence by now that—other things being equal—the very exposure of children to a given game, with its structure and demand for certain constituent performances, may have terrific clinical impact on the events at least of that day. Wherever we miscalculate the overwhelming effect which the seductive aspect of certain games may have (flashlight hide-and-seek in the dark just before bedtime) we may ask for trouble, while many a seemingly risky game can safely be played if enough ego-supportive controls are built right into it (the safety zone to which you can withdraw without having to admit you get tired or scared, etc.). In short, while I would hardly relegate the total treatment job of severely disturbed children in a mental hospital ward to that factor alone, I certainly would want to figure on it as seriously as I would calculate the mental hygiene aspects of other factors more traditionally envisioned as being of clinical concern. What I say here about games goes for many other activities patients engage in— arts and crafts, woodwork, outings, overnight trips, cookouts, discussion groups, musical evenings, etc. Which of these things takes place, where, with which feeling tone, and with what structural and activity ingredients is as characteristic of a given "milieu" as the staff that is hired.

9. *Space, equipment, time and props.* What an assortment of names, but I know as yet of no collective noun that would cover them all equally well. Since I have made such a fuss about this for years, I may try to be shorter about it than seems reasonable. Remember what a bunch of boys do when running through a viaduct with an echo effect? Remember what may happen to a small group who are supposed to discuss plans for their next Scout meeting, who have to hold this discussion unexpectedly, in a huge gym with lots of stuff around, instead of in their usual clubroom? Remember what will happen to a baseball that is put on the table prematurely while they are still supposed to sit quietly and listen, and remember what happens to many a well-intended moral lecture to a group of sloppy campers, if you timed it so badly that the swimming bell started ringing before you had finished? Do I still have to prove why I think that what an outfit does with arrangements of time expectations and time distribution, what prop-exposure the youngsters are expected to stand or avoid, what space arrangements are like, and what equipment does to the goals you have set for yourself, should be listed along with the important "properties" of a place where clinical work with children takes

place? So far I have found that in hospitals this item tends to be left out of milieu discussions by psychiatrists and sociologists alike; only the nurses and attendants have learned by bitter experience that it may pay to lend an ear to it.

10. *The seepage from the world outside.* One of the hardest "milieu aspects" to assess in a short visit to any institution is the amount of "impact from the larger universe and the surrounding world" that actually seeps through its walls and finds its way into the lives of the patients. No outfit is airtight, no matter how many keys and taboos are in use. In our own little children's ward-world, for instance, there are the following "seepage ingredients from the world outside" that are as much a part of our "milieu," as it hits the boys, as anything else: Adult visitors and the "past case history" flavor they leave behind. Child visitors and the "sociological body odor" of the old neighborhood, or the new one which they exude. Excursions which we arrange, old haunts from prehospital days, which we happen to drive through unintentionally on our way to our destination. Plenty of purposely pulled-in outside world through movies, television, pictures, and stories we may tell them. And, of course, school is a full-view window hopefully opened wide for many vistas to be seen through it—if we only could get our children to look.

    There is the "hospital impact" of the large building that hits them whenever they leave the ward floor in transit, the physically sick patients they meet on the elevator who stir the question up again in their own mind: "Why am I here?" There are the stories other boys tell, the staff tells, the imputed secrets we may be hiding from them whenever we seem eager to divert attention to something else. As soon as the children move into the open cottage, the word "seepage" isn't quite as correct any more. Suffice it to say: the type and amount of "outside world" particles that are allowed in or even eagerly pulled in constitute a most important part of the lives of the captive population of an institutional setting, and want to be given attention to in an appraisal of just what a given "milieu" holds.

11. *The system of umpiring services and traffic regulations between environment and child.* Those among you who have a sharp nose for methodological speculations may want to object and insist that I am jumping category dimensions in tagging on this item and the next one on my list. I don't want to quarrel about this now. For even though you may be right, it is too late today to start a new chapter, so please let me get away with tagging these two items on here. In some ways they still belong, for whether there are any umpiring services built into an institution, and what they are like, is certainly an important "milieu property" in my estimation. . . .

    In short, it runs somewhat like this: Some "milieu impacts" hit the children directly; nobody needs to interpret or translate. Others hit the child all right, but to have their proper impact someone has to do some explaining. It makes a great difference whether a child who is running away unhappy, after a cruel razzing received from a thoughtless group, is left to deal with this all by himself; or whether the institution provides interpretational or first-aid services for the muddled feelings at the time. Some of our children, for instance, might translate such an experience, which was not intended by the institution, into additional resentment against the world. With sympathy in the predicament offered by a friendly adult who tags along and comforts, this same experience may well be decontaminated or even turned into the opposite.

A similar item is the one I had in mind in using the phrase "traffic regulations." Much give-and-take can follow naturally among the inhabitants of a given place. Depending on the amount of their disturbance, though, some social interactions which normal life leaves to the children's own resources require traffic supervision by an adult. I would like to know whether a given milieu has foreseen this and can guarantee the provision of some help in the bartering custom among the youngsters, or whether that new youngster will be mercilessly exposed to the wildest blackmail with no help from anyone, the moment he enters the doors to my ward. In short, it is like asking what medical first-aid facilities are in a town before one moves into it. Whether this belongs to the concept of what makes up a "town," or whether it should be listed under a separate heading I leave for a later chance to thrash out. All I want to point at now is that the nature of and existence or nonexistence of umpiring services and social traffic regulations is as "real" a property of a setup as its walls, kitchen equipment and clinical beliefs.

12. *The thermostat for the regulation of clinical resilience.* If it is cold in an old cabin somewhere in the midst of "primitive nature," the trouble is obvious: either there isn't any fire going, or something is wrong with the stove and the whole heating system, so it doesn't give off enough heat. If I freeze in a building artificially equipped with all the modern conveniences, such a conclusion might be off the beam. The trouble may simply be that the thermostat isn't working right. This, like the previous item, is a property of a given milieu rather than a "milieu ingredient" in the stricter sense of the word. However, it is of such utmost clinical relevance that it has to go in here somewhere. In fact, I have hardly ever participated in a discussion on the milieu concept without having this item come up somehow or other.

The term under which it is more often referred to is actually that of "flexibility," which most milieu therapy enthusiasts praise as "good" while the bad men in the picture are the ones that think "rigidity" is a virtue. I have more reasons to be tired of this either/or issue than I can list in the remaining time. It seems to me that the "resilience" concept fits better what most of us have so long tried to shoot at with the flexibility label. A milieu certainly needs to be sensitive to the changing needs of the patients during different phases of the treatment process. It needs to "tighten up"—lower the behavioral ceiling when impulse-panic looms on the horizon; and it may have to lift it when self-imposed internal pressures mount. Also, it needs to limit spontaneity and autonomy of the individual patient in early phases of intensive disorder and rampant pathology; it needs to throw in a challenge toward autonomy and even the risking of mistakes, when the patient goes through the later phases of recovery. Especially when severely disturbed children are in the process of going through an intensive phase of "improvement," the resilience of a milieu to make way for its implications is as important as its ability to "shrink back" during a regressive phase.

JUST HOW DOES THE MILIEU DO IT?

Listing these 12 variables of important milieu aspects which can be differentiated as explorable issues in their own right is only part of the story. I hold no brief for this list, and I am well aware of its methodological complications and deficiencies. The major value of listing them at all lies in the insistence that *there are so many of them* and that they *can be separately studied and explored.* This should at least help us to secure ourselves against falling in love with any one of them to the exclusion of the others, and of forcing any discipline that wants to tackle the job, whether it be psychiatry, sociology or what not, to look beyond its traditional scope and directly into the face of uncompromisingly multifaceted facts. . . .

. . . .

All of the elements Redl describes have a parallel in school milieus. Teachers have often reported to us that the elements of the restrictive bureaucratic school cause the most trouble, not the kids or the class.

A milieu of control remains the dominant modicum for working with students with behavior problems in the public school. Because troubled youngsters most often do not or cannot control themselves, the notion is deeply ingrained that we best help them by imposing adult control. Control dominates the field, as recent studies make clear. In some of these programs, the earlier concept of controlling youngsters is being challenged by efforts to develop self-control. But the fear of loss of adult control still consumes many teachers and administrators. Polly Nichols has worked with troubled children in many capacities—teacher, administrator, teacher trainer, and author. But she has never lost her teacher viewpoint. Here, in a balanced discussion of the issues, she addresses the heart of the matter of control. What do we mean when we say a procedure "works"? Works to what end? How would you and your system respond to her arguments? Any teacher could apply the before-and-after self esteem assessment she describes.

ARTICLE 2.2

The Curriculum of Control: Twelve Reasons for It, Some Arguments Against It

Polly Nichols

Classrooms of control—in these words, Jane Knitzer, Zina Steinberg, and Braham Fleisch (1990) characterize the school day world of children with emotional or behavioral disabilities and of their teachers: "For children labelled emotionally or behaviorally handicapped, control is . . . a central part of schooling . . . Too often the dominant curriculum is not the traditional academic curriculum, nor is it about concepts, thinking, and problem solving. Instead the curriculum is about controlling the behaviors of the children. The reward system is alike for teachers and students. A quiet class is highly regarded and few supervisors, administrators or even parents look much beyond this."

Their book, *At the Schoolhouse Door: An examination of programs and policies for children with behavioral and emotional problems,* published in 1990 by New York's Bank Street College of Education, is the report of a major study of programming for students with emotional or behavioral disorders (EBD). The report is exhaustive, the findings disturbing, but in no way more so than in their characterization of the EBD classrooms they studied as being dominated by a "Curriculum of Control."

"The curriculum emphasis is often on behavioral management first" with a central concern upon behavioral point systems. "Yet often, these seem largely designed to help maintain silence in the classroom, not to teach children how better to manage their anger, sadness, or impulses."

When we entered this field—we teachers, administrators, teacher-trainers, consultants—we had other dreams and purposes than to control children. Why do we all, to some degree or another, buy into this "curriculum of control"? The answers are complex and rooted so deeply in our beliefs about what children and grown-ups are about that they are hard to bring into the light for a close look. As someone who has worked in all of these job categories and has thought a good deal about our care of students with EBD. I have worried about a seeming overemphasis on "managing" our students, as though they were accounts or hirelings athletes. At least a dozen reasons for this preoccupation with control occur to me:

- Controls are necessary for an orderly, productive existence. When we lose control, we are at risk for unpleasant or dangerous consequences. As we are grown-ups, we know these facts to be true from our own

From *Beyond Behavior.* (1992). Vol. 3, No. 2. Reprinted by permission.

experience. As we are teachers, we devote our professional lives to the notion that we can teach children what we know that they do not already know, that they will be better off for it, and that they might even thank us for it sometime. So, since we know control is good, and we know EBD children are short of it, we make control the central point of our programming.

- Somewhere in the hearts of most of us is a desire, felt rarely or frequently, to show disobedient, mouthy children and teens just what authority is and who has it. We may genuinely believe that enforcing limits is the best lesson we can teach, or we may react that way only when we sense we are losing—our dignity, a battle, our touch.

- Everybody knows that controlling is what teachers are *supposed* to do. Teachers have known that from the time they were little girls (rarely boys) playing school. Remember the scoldings, the bossy directions, the hands on hips, the recesses denied, the principals sent to? Some teachers, the warmest, most easygoing people in the faculty lounge, are stricken with facial paralysis when they encounter students. They do not smile, they become severe, austere, bent on control. This seems to be a role, one of which they are scarcely aware. Note how much like playing school these descriptions by Knitzer and her colleagues sound:

    "But in many of the classrooms we visited, group work is not allowed, children's comments are squelched, and questions and answer format of the most teacherly kind is the only form allowed. If children talk, they lose points, if they exchange baseball statistics, the cards are taken away. Helping each other is called cheating—genuine excitement is rare."

- From the start, the degree to which boys and girls are or are not presumed to be "in control" is a primary factor in how sympathetically they are viewed and treated and where they are placed. There "lurks an implicit belief that somehow socially maladjusted children are able to control their behavior, while seriously emotionally disturbed or behaviorally disordered children cannot."

- Behavior modification techniques, when poorly understood and improperly applied, may lead the modifiers to rely most heavily upon external control for management. "In most behavior modification programs, obedience predominates over responsibility, punishment over logical consequences. Though children are placed in special (EBD) programs because of their behavioral difficulties, systematic, coherent attempts to help them gain control over their problems is the exception, not the rule."

- Society expects good teachers to have "excellent classroom control," perhaps above all else. When students misbehave, it reflects at least as poorly on their teachers as on themselves, a negative halo effect all EBD teachers have felt at one time or another, if not from their administrators, then probably from a regular education colleague or a faculty lounge clique.

- We think of control as something that can be and should be applied, rather like a behavioral ointment. When children in our care are neither self-controlled nor easily controlled by us, we may attribute their control deficiencies primarily to parents who have not applied enough control at home. Then it follows that the best thing for us to do is to slather on a lot of control at school. We may do this in the purest expectation that it will be helpful, or we may do it with some extra zeal, showing parents just how control can be and should be applied. We may extend this directly to parents themselves by setting up controls over their parenting behavior that can result in front office or social agency sanctions.

- Some published programs such as Assertive Discipline (Canter & Canter, 1976) or the Boys Town Model (Michael, 1987) are tremendously popular perhaps because they offer teachers completely prescribed, ready-to-operate methods of control. The skillful teacher is flexible and encouraging while using them, but their strongest appeal may be to teachers inexperienced or insecure about their ability to cope with students' misbehavior. In such programs, they may find a prescription for control that they sense they lack.

- Teachers fear their students. They are unsure what lengths students will go to if given an inch. If students were allowed free choice or free movement or free time to talk with friends, who knows if teachers would be able to regain control?

- Being controlling may be due to basic traits that are part of some individuals' personalities.

- Additionally, teachers may be struggling, isolated, depressed, or frightened and strong control in silent classrooms the only method they have found for dealing with what they fear otherwise would overwhelm them and be intolerable.

THE EFFECTS OF CONTROL

Control is not merely pepper in the pot, sometime there is enough, too much, or too little of according to one's taste. Neither is it intrinsically related only to harshness. In fact, many controlling behaviors are sweet indeed, from giving praise to giving M & Ms. A body of research has evolved from Edward Deci's cognitive evaluation theory which discriminates between rewards that are given in order to control children's behavior and those that are given in order to impart information to children about their behavior.

Deci and his colleagues (Deci, Nezlek, & Sheinman, 1981) note that most studies on the effects of rewards and constraints indicate that rewards actually work to *decrease* intrinsic motivation, clearly something to think about in a world which Knitzer and her colleagues describe as being preoccupied with the giving of points. Does this mean our behavior management systems are all to no avail? Not at all. "If rewards are administered in a way that does not emphasize control but rather signifies competence, the theory predicts a maintenance or enhancement of intrinsic motivation. The suggestion, therefore, is that rewards will not undermine intrinsic motivation if they are administered in a way that emphasizes positive competence rather than control."

Studying this theory, Deci et al. researchers predicted a correlation between teachers' attitudes toward control versus autonomy and children's feelings about the climate of their classroom. The more positive the students' views of the classroom climate, the greater their intrinsic motivation and the higher their self-esteem levels were likely to be. Teachers were asked to choose among solutions for eight typical school problems—the playground bully, stealing, homework not done and such—which represented the following four basic orientations, two extreme and two moderate:

Highly Controlling: teachers make decisions about what is right and use highly controlling sanctions to produce the desired behavior.

Moderately Controlling: teachers make the decisions and emphasize that the children should perform the desired behaviors for their own good.

Moderately Autonomous: teachers encourage children to compare themselves with others to see how to handle the problem.

Highly Autonomous: teachers encourage children to consider the relevant elements of the situation and to take responsibility for working out a solution to the problem.

The self-esteem of the 610 fourth through sixth graders who participated in the study had their self-esteem measured twice, once at the end of the first six weeks of school, again near the end of the year. The prediction was that students in a classroom all year with either a control- or an autonomy-oriented teacher would change their original perceptions to develop either higher or lower self-esteem as the year went along. Instead, the researchers made a more startling discovery. There were meaningful differences between measures of children's self-esteem over the course of the year—the significant relationship between teachers' orientation toward control versus autonomy and students' self-esteem and intrinsic motivation occurred during the first six weeks of school and did not change markedly thereafter.

Vernon Jones and Louise Jones (1990) preface their book on classroom management with a reminder that in the 1960s, most teacher training went little beyond such simple prescriptions as "don't smile until Christmas" or "don't grin until Thanksgiving," homespun advice still passed along to neophytes. But the research by Deci and his colleagues suggests that in the first six weeks of the school year, the die is cast for development of student self-esteem for the year. Waiting until December to start to smile would be months too late for the affirmation and support youngsters need, sacrificed presumably to show no-nonsense control.

Perhaps many teachers are deliberately taught other aspects of the "curriculum of control" in their training programs. Certainly many administrators seem to have been. More than one principal in our Iowa town has launched his school year with an opening assembly speech which let everyone know the dire consequences that would befall students who did the rotten things that students had done the year before—and they soon had behavior to contend with they had not dreamed of, such as severe vandalism. *Should* that be so? Isn't firm limit setting from the start a maxim of behavior management? It seems reasonable enough an idea, but the results are predictable. As Jones and Jones comment:
"In short, the use of power is often effective at intimidating students who need control least and is seldom effective with students whose behavior is most unproductive."
So, it turns out that the curriculum of control is not only dreary; it is counterproductive. It tends to generate the very behaviors that EBD placement is designed to ameliorate. Even those who are successfully ordered by a classroom climate of quiet control may not be internally convinced it is the way to go. Have you experienced or heard tales of the ever-so-well-regulated classroom that no one can handle but the regular teacher? When his or her back is turned, or worse, when the substitute comes, the place turns upside down.
Even more pernicious are the findings reported by Allen and Greenberger (1980) of laboratory studies on the relation between hostility and defiance and perceptions of control over events. The less control a person has over objective events, the more satisfaction he or she draws from destructive acts; they create feelings of success that are unavailable elsewhere. Students who experience failures in school are more likely to act in deviant ways to increase, at least temporarily, their feelings of power and self-determination. One high schooler reported to an interviewer that each time he passed a locker he had smashed, he thought with pride, "There's my little destruction to this brand new school." He had made his mark of control on his environment.
So why, if the curriculum of control can be so damaging, is it so prevalent in EBD classrooms? In fairness, a twelfth cause of teachers' preference for it must be listed:

• The curriculum of control works. We can make our classrooms quiet—a mark of ourselves as good teachers in virtually everybody's book. But even more striking, we sometimes truly seem to shape up some kids by showing them the bottom line. We convince them that appropriate behavior is the only winning card and change their understanding of how the world works—at least it seems so while they are with us, and some youngsters' new behaviors do generalize to mainstream classes and to other environments very well.

Whether or not we choose to operate our classrooms along strictly behavioristic lines, the fact remains that everyone is subject to principles of operant conditioning. What is the most powerful schedule of reinforcement for maintaining a behavior? As we all learned in our first Intro to EBD courses, it is the intermittent schedule of reinforcement—and that is exactly the schedule we teachers are put on by our successes, no matter how rare, with our control-responsive students. If controlling techniques appear to be effective in changing children's lives for the better or improving our lives in the classroom or heightening our own feelings of competence even just once in a while, we will almost surely persist in using them. We will do so even in the face of irrefutable evidence that those control techniques are not bringing about improvement in the majority of situations with the greater number of our students and are instead causing dreadful confrontations or boredom or just chronic dissatisfaction.

When our controlling techniques—positive through our bestowal of rewards or negative through meting out of penalties—are effective, we attribute those successes to our effectiveness as teachers. When our techniques fail, we are likely to blame one or more factors lying within the students themselves. Failing to do this—and EBD teachers do like and defend most of their students as individuals, pointing out how "wonderful they can be on a one-to-one basis"—teachers next look for causes within their students' families. To look at our own teaching or management practices as blameworthy invites feelings of failure, and they may be intolerable.

IF NOT CONTROL, WHAT?

If studies have revealed such findings to us at least since the 1970s, why have we not all made use of them and created stimulating, effective classrooms that would have been a joy for Knitzer, Steinberg, and Fleisch to behold? Actually, they did find some that were:
    "But both in self-contained classrooms and in separate programs we saw and learned about alternatives that supplement more typical strategies (time-out rooms, point and level behavior management systems) with strategies to help students take responsibility for their own actions."
    They tell of a fairness committee of EBD student representatives who discuss complaints and plan remedies; of a social skills project where students team with adults to discuss, practice, and try out strategies for use in their lunchrooms and playgrounds; of a "Time-In" room where students in difficulty are helped to relax, gain control, and work out solutions to their problems; of a sophisticated model of behavior management used in

a girls' residential treatment facility called a Therapeutic Just Community; of an especially strong extra-curricular activity program involving coaches who teach social skills on the spot.

The common attribute of the programs Knitzer, Steinberg, and Fleisch admire is an innovative approach to designing meaningful, rewarding activities through which students will learn ways to fit into their real worlds with less stress, unhappiness, and conflict. In the academic domain where they generally found even less to admire, they sought alternatives to an impoverished life "defined by dittoed worksheets and isolation" but found few to describe.

A group of well-known theorists, researchers, and teacher trainers in the field of emotional or behavior disorders who call themselves the Peacock Hill Working Group, have recently produced a more encouraging account of the health and well-being of the EBD field in the United States (Cook et al, 1991). Noting that the authors of *At the Schoolhouse Door* have described existing problems "compellingly and comprehensively," they assert that less sweeping reforms than Knitzer and her colleagues call for may be needed:

"Effective school-based approaches for children or youth with emotional or behavioral disorders are presently available, but a lack of commitment to youngsters and families and the scarcity or resources have stymied their implementation. Indeed, much that we know can ameliorate the problems that have been described. To be sure, research is needed to address critical questions in many areas of practice, but current practices would be dramatically improved were the strategies and the programs known to be successful implemented with fidelity."

If so much is known and possible, why are so many teachers having such a difficult time with EBD classes that so much criticism is raining down on them? We know what the outcome of criticism is likely to be—lowered feelings of personal efficacy. It works the same way with adults as with children. With less sense of competence may come a greater need to exert external control over students which will, in turn, be likely to create more rather than fewer problems in the classroom (or on the sneak out of the classroom). Lowered self-esteem in teachers has even been shown to result in smaller academic gains in students over the course of a school year as compared to the progress made by children taught by teachers with high self-esteem (Aspy & Buhler, 1975). With such a discouraging set of outcomes likely, why do any teachers put up with it?

Many do not. The figure given in the Peacock Hill Group paper for teacher burnout is over a third of teachers surveyed saying that they expected to be doing something else within a year. They note one contributing reason to be the low levels of likability and social acceptability of youngsters with EBD. Others reasons are probably related to the unattractive working arrangements EBD teachers have in many schools. In a survey of EBD teachers' working conditions, Mary McManus and James Kauffman

(1991) found that fully one-fourth of self-contained EBD class teachers dealt with disruptive behavior more than 22 times a day, one-fifth were verbally threatened daily, one-fourth were physically threatened monthly, and the mean numbers of physical attacks were nearly 14 per year, 47 per teaching career. And these teachers might well be in conflict with their superiors as well for, as the Peacock Hill writers point out, teachers and administrators tend not to agree about how to handle students whose behavior is extremely distasteful to them.

SKILL TRAINING—AND PERSONALITY TRAINING, TOO?

The Peacock Hill Group states that about 30 percent of teachers currently working in EBD programs are not trained and certified to be doing so; but that means that about 70 percent, a substantial majority, after all, are. We cannot blame the inadequacies that now exist only on a lack of training among the un- or under-certified. We must look at what happens within the actual certification programs. Besides teaching methodology skills, are there positive personality characteristics that can be taught to make a true master?

In a 1971 review of teacher effectiveness studies, Rosenshine and Furst identified 11 teacher variables that had shown the strongest relationships to student gains. The three strongest were clarity, variability, and enthusiasm. Anyone trained to think task-analytically could come up with training strategies to teach students to display these behaviors, even one as seemingly a part of built-in personality as enthusiasm. In fact, Rosenshine (1970) did exactly that. His observations of teachers revealed that components of enthusiasm were rapid speech, frequent movement, gesture, variation in voice, eye contact, appearing relaxed, asking varied questions, and praising frequently. Coleman (1977) comments:

"If the anxieties of teachers, particularly beginning teachers, and the boredom of students can be somewhat relieved by training teachers to be more enthusiastic or energetic, as the research suggests is possible, this could be a most useful contribution to teacher effectiveness."

Experiences I have had suggest to me that such training is possible and useful. Years ago, I taught in a program staffed by our children's psychiatric hospital and operated in a public junior high school. Our students registered typical complaints about the boringness or hardness or unfairness of various mainstream teachers, but one teacher escaped their criticism, the science teacher, Mr. Moeller. They thought he was great. When I looked at the homework they brought from his class, it did not appear to be especially stimulating nor geared to their individual learning abilities, nor did the students express any strong interest in the particular science they were studying. New to that school, I guessed that Mr. Moeller might be especially good-looking, young, with-it, but when I identified who he was I saw him to be middle-aged, balding, neither fit looking nor a snappy dresser. I pressed my questions, got a lot more "I don't know . . . he's just nice" answers, but finally got this description: "Well, whenever I go by him in the hall between classes, he always says 'Hi, Nick.' " So I checked the scene between classes. The rule in that school was that teachers were to be in their doorways between bells, watching students pass. A walk down the halls revealed teachers standing in pairs or alone, arms crossed, faces watchful, true standard bearers of the need for quiet and order in the halls. Mr. Moeller, by contrast, relaxed against his doorjamb and said such things as "Hi" or "How's it going," or he nodded, or he just smiled. As time went on and I spent more time in classes, I never discovered anything more remarkably charismatic or reinforcing about Mr. Moeller than that he was relaxed, looked at kids when they talked, smiled easily, used their names frequently, and spoke pleasantly. From that, I developed my first set of social skills steps for teachers:

- Use eye contact
- Smile
- Say the student's name
- Use pleasant words

I was thrilled with my discovery and taught this magic to good effect in a Methods class I was teaching in the evenings. Later I learned that I had only rediscovered some of Dale Carnegie's basic ingredients for winning friends and influencing people; later still, I recognized the same steps in various social skills curricula published for use with students. But it has never seemed less magic a discovery or less obvious a deficit among teachers who are having trouble with or hating their EBD classes.

It would be simple minded to suggest that all we need to do to help EBD teachers become effective and like their jobs is to teach them to smile more often, look at their kids when they talk to them, and quietly exchange everyday pleasantries. Yet when I consult in a classroom where the teacher is having trouble, these are the behaviors that are immediately conspicuous by their absence. Whether the stern faces, distance from students, and eyes focused on academic materials or point sheets except when surveying to pierce a bad actor with a piercing stare are the results of hard time or the results of having played teacher from the beginning, is impossible to say. Whichever, they are among the most obvious behaviors connected with the troubles at hand.

TRAINING FOR DOING

The most crucial part of teacher-training programs is experience in classrooms with experienced teachers. But what I wonder is this: What happens if a student teacher flunks adaptability or is only so-so on optimism, for instance, or manages only luke-warm relationships with students? It is a sure bet that he won't be flunked out of his program; and it is a sure bet that once alone in an EBD classroom instead of under the supervision and magic spell of a master teacher, those deficiencies will loom larger. It is then, when feeling uncertain and ineffective, that teachers seem to look to increased control for the structure *they* need. The conclusion is easily drawn that warm relationships are possible only after students have learned that the teacher is boss, and they must do what the boss says—don't smile until Christmas! But as efforts go on to establish control, those first crucial weeks during which the foundation for healthy self-esteem and positive personal expectations for the year pass by, and it is a cold and stormy year—for students and their teachers, too.

The key interaction, affect, and attitude variables that are listed as goals for teachers-in-training to acquire first appear as competencies not in course syllabi but on student teaching checklists. Who has taught these skills that are then to be practiced? Do we count on the supervising teachers alone to teach these critical elements of teaching children and teens with emotional or behavioral disorders? But what if the supervising teacher him- or herself lacks these skills? Certainly, one's impression from reading the criticism of EBD classrooms is that master teachers are rare. With many students to place for practice teaching, it seems inevitable that a majority will be placed with supervising teachers who themselves lack key skills and attitudes we urgently desire for our next generation of teachers in the field.

Shouldn't we offer to students in our teacher-training classes opportunities to develop the skills of interpersonal relationships just as we offer the youngsters in our EBD classes social skill training? Wouldn't it be possible to describe and demonstrate just what EBD teachers need to do and say to promote their students' sense of autonomy, control, and personal competence and then have teachers-in-training practice, role play, receive feedback, and try out their new skills in real classrooms until they were truly confident and competent? Do we know how to teach the behaviors associated with enthusiasm or warmth, of giving quiet reprimands, offering instructional praise, assuming non-threatening physical postures, talking an out-of-control student down or a depressed student up, responding to lies, handling anger? What would you say to the oppositional child who would rather argue than agree no matter what? To the anxious child who couldn't handle stress? To the teenager who hated being in special ed? When is it better *not* to talk? Instead of discussing these problems, we might model, role play and practice things to say and do, when and how to say and do them.

We have cast a dubious professional eye on canned programs such as Assertive Discipline (Evans, Evans, Gable, & Kehlhem, 1991). Part of its huge success may be due to the implied control it gives to teachers by its use and even by its name, but part of its success is also undoubtedly due to its accessibility. A one-day workshop, a manual, some materials, and you are off and running. By having it offered as a school-wide program, the teacher not only knows what to do, he knows he has built-in administrative and peer support for doing it.

Teachers are not lazy, but we are often tired. All day teaching the same children, perhaps for years, consumes a lot of materials, and some EBD teachers must plan for students from first through sixth grades daily. Their cry in faculty rooms, at inservices and conferences, is, "Does it have anything in it I can use?" By use, they mean open up a manual, read the directions, copy a worksheet or gather some materials, and have a lesson set to go.

Rather than deploring this behavior, we need to think creatively about it. What can we package this way that will travel the farthest toward our goal of improving academic and behavioral instruction for EBD children and teenagers? An example of one such widely-traveled program is *The Walker Social Skills Curriculum* (1983). Not only does the teacher have "something she can use" ready with little extra planning beyond reading it through first, she actually has entire teaching scripts. Once the teacher has taught the program through according to the scripts, she will find that she has acquired a wonderful set of direct teaching, feedback, and encouragement skills that she can apply throughout her program.

SUPPORT FOR TEACHERS AND
AN END TO ISOLATION

We say we cannot do enough in a one-day workshop to help teachers out substantially, so what can we do? In a world of video everything, surely there are ways to arrange two-way communication with far-off buildings to answer questions, model approaches, and share techniques. Instead of standing before crowds of people and delivering papers, we could lead remedial coping classes, dealing with nothing but the questions that usually are relegated to the last four minutes of a presentation. Perhaps we could convert state and national conferences, where often what one gains is a matter of serendipity, into focused training weeks, offering credit for advanced courses in the manner of a Berlitz blitz. Or remember those lab schools where teachers-in-training could work with real students every day?

What we cannot do is give up on our colleagues already in classrooms around the country. We are off and running, and we do not have the luxury of ordering a recall. But as we deal with the call for new kinds of service delivery to the students in our care, we must consider new means of service delivery to their teachers, too. No one went into teaching because he or she wanted to be boring, controlling, and miserable. We chose the field so that we could do good and change the lives of children—never were their needs greater, or ours.

REFERENCES

Allen, V. L., & Greenberger, D. B. (1980). Destruction and perceived control. In A. Baum & J. E. Singer (Eds.), *Advances in environmental psychology: Vol. 2, Applications of personal control.* (pp. 85–109). Hillsdale, NJ: Erlbaum. Cited in Adelman & Taylor, 1990.

Aspy, D. N., & Buhler, J. H. (1975). The effect of teachers inferred self-concept upon student achievement. *Journal of Educational Research, 68,* 386–389.

Canter, L., & Canter, M. (1976). *Assertive discipline.* Los Angeles: Lee Canter & Associates.

Coleman, P. (1977). The improvement of aggregate teaching effectiveness in a school district. In G. D. Borich, *The appraisal of teaching: Concepts and process.* Reading, MA: Addison-Wesley.

Cook, L., Cullinan, D., Epstein, M. H., Forness, S. R., Hallahan, D. P., Kauffman, J. M., Lloyd, J. W., Nelson, C. M., Polsgrove, L., Sabornie, E. J., Strain, P. S., & Walker, H. M. (1991). Problems and promises in special education and related services for children and youth with emotional or behavioral disorders. *Behavioral Disorders, 16,* 299–313.

Deci, E. L., Nezlek, J., & Sheinman, L. (1981). Characteristics of the rewarder and intrinsic motivation of the reward. *Journal of Personality and Social Psychology, 40,* 1–10.

Evans, W. H., Evans, S. S., Gable, R. A., & Kehlhem, M. A. (1991). Assertive discipline and behavior disorders: Is this a marriage made in heaven? *Beyond Behavior, 2,* 13–16.

Jones, V. F., & Jones, L. S. (1990). *Comprehensive classroom management.* Boston: Allyn & Bacon.

Knitzer, J., Steinberg, Z., & Fleisch, F. (1990). *At the schoolhouse door. An examination of the programs and policies for children with behavioral and emotional problems.* New York: Bank Street College of Education.

McManus, M. E., & Kauffman, J. M. (1991). Working conditions of teachers of students with behavioral disorders: A national study. *Behavioral Disorders, 16,* 247–259.

Michael, A. (1987). A trip to Boys Town. *Behavior in Our Schools, 1* (2–7).

Rosenshine, B. (1970). Enthusiastic teaching: A research review. *School Review, 78,* 499–512.

Rosenshine, B., & Furst, N. (1973). The use of direct observation to study teaching. In R. Travers, Ed., *Second handbook of research on teaching.* Chicago: Rand McNally, Cited in Borich, G. D., 1977.

Walker, H. M., McConnell, S., Holmes, D., Walker, J., & Golden, N. (1983). *The Walker social skills curriculum.* Austin, TX: PRO-ED.

· ·

If you were to list the ten predominant characteristics of troubled children, how many would be assets? The team of Brendtro, an international figure in the field of rescuing high-risk children, and Brokenleg, a counseling psychologist who is bringing the very different view of American Indian ideology to our awareness, shows how we can begin to think quite differently about helping these children. Both authors are on the faculty of Augustana College. Adding to Knitzer et al.'s similar bleak findings of an international study team, these authors propose an alternative to the curriculum of control. They take us back to our roots and reverse the negative preoccupations of our field. As they search for the positive, they suggest we avoid the "D" words. We remember Hobbs's statement that an ideology is a necessary component of helping. What Brendtro and Brokenleg give us is virtually a revolutionary ideology; they reject the belief system based on folk psychology. In restorative work, we are confronted with value differences. We react to troubled pupils as if they were negatively all-powerful, ignoring their available positive potentials. Thus, adult behavior fosters further alienation.

Here, our western culture of individualism is contrasted with the American Indian child-raising assumptions, which teach children to move outside of themselves and contribute to others. We know that failure in our competitive arena results in a sense of powerlessness, hence the reactive aggressiveness that displays one kind of power. These authors describe what a milieu would be like if the Indian concepts replaced rampant individualism. How many current programs have "giving to others" as an essential ingredient in helping kids put their awry lives back together? Are we ready to entertain a new model? Brendtro and Brokenleg give numerous examples of things to start on Monday morning. Cooperation can replace individualistic competition in the classroom, and community service projects can transform the receiver-from-others to a giver-to-others.

ARTICLE 2.3

Beyond the Curriculum of Control

Larry K. Brendtro and Martin Brokenleg
Augustana College

Existing approaches to children with emotional and behavioral problems are often little more than a rigid "curriculum of control," according to a recent study of educational and mental health programs in the United States (Knitzer, Steinberg, & Flesch, 1990). These researchers concluded that the widespread use of simplistic behavioral interventions contributes to a "bleakness" in the daily lives of troubled children.

Similar observations about this preoccupation with control were made by an international group of professionals who completed a year-long fellowship sponsored by ILEX (International Learning Exchange in Professional Youthwork). Reflecting on their experiences in North America, the visiting fellows from Europe, Australia, and Africa shared these poignant criticisms:

> *Control is the word I hear most often here and, to me, it is the opposite of creativity.*

> *I see "crisis intervention" as a reaction to the aggression that these children show, but also as a cause for some children to be aggressive.*

From *The Journal of Emotional and Behavioral Problems*. (1993). Vol. 1, No. 4. Reprinted with permission.

> *How can you teach youngsters to be independent when there is so much control on their behavior? . . . I had a feeling of heaviness and immobility.*

Knitzer and colleagues report that such obedience-training strategies are increasingly being called into question. However, without viable alternative models, many who work with troubled children and youth still assume the curriculum of control to be "necessary." In this discussion, we will examine ways in which traditional "treatments" have actually fostered greater alienation; and we will suggest the foundations for an alternative paradigm rooted in empowerment philosophy rather than obedience.

BEYOND DEVIANCE AND DEFICIT

Our current preoccupation with the management of "deviant" behavior is in stark contrast to the vision of the early pioneers in working with troubled youth. These Pygmalion optimists set out to find positive potentials in the most difficult youth. Pestalozzi gathered street urchins into his castle school, declaring that beneath their coarse exterior, he would find "precious faculties" waiting to be released. "Badness is misdirected energy," asserted Floyd Starr. "What makes delinquents unique," declared Jane Addams, "is their greater spirit of adventure!"

Goldstein (1991) notes that much of recent psychological literature addresses only the negative (disease, crime, psychopathology, aggression, etc.) and how it may be corrected. Rarely is the focus on strength and its facilitation. In fact, most of the terms used to describe emotional and behavioral problems are pejorative and demeaning. Youth are labelled as Disturbed, Disordered, Deprived, Deviant, Disadvantaged, Disruptive, Disrespectful, Dysocial, Disobedient, etc. A similar disparaging mindset is the labelling of parents and families as "Dysfunctional." "D words" focus on the negative. And, those who target what is wrong with a young person are apt to overlook strengths and resources.

Our fixation with deviance and its control is a vestige of a long cultural tradition in which human relationships were organized around dominance and subjugation. This authoritarian mindset has marked the relationship of children to adults in Western civilization, and schools are a product of that tradition. Scholars are just beginning to recognize how deeply our theories of human behavior are influenced by the "folk psychology" of our culture (Rogoff & Morelli, 1989). Each of us drags this belief system behind like a cultural tail a thousand years long.

In our book *Reclaiming Youth At Risk,* (Brendtro, Brokenleg, & Van Bockern, 1990), we proposed a model of youth empowerment based on contemporary developmental research, the heritage of early youth work pioneers, and Native American philosophies of child care. Anthropologists have long known that these tribal peoples reared courageous, respectful

TABLE 2.1

Foundations of Self-Esteem	Native American Empowerment Values	Western Civilizations Patriarchal Values
Significance	Belonging	Individualism
Competence	Mastery	Winning
Power	Independence	Dominance
Virtue	Generosity	Affluence

children without using aversive controls. Nevertheless, Europeans in North America tried to "civilize" indigenous children in punitive boarding schools, unaware that Native Americans were using sophisticated child-care systems that were the product of advanced cultures.

Table 2.1 shows how Coopersmith's (1967) foundations of self-esteem compare with Native American and Western values. In a traditional Native American culture: 1) significance is nurtured in a community that celebrates the universal need for belonging, 2) competence is ensured by guaranteeing all children the opportunity for mastery, 3) power is available to all by cultivating each person's independence, and 4) virtue is embodied in the preeminent value of generosity.

These traditions contrast with Western patriarchal values, where 1) hyper-individualism replaces belonging as the measure of one's importance, 2) competition becomes a zero-sum game where enthroning "winners" ensures an abundance of losers, 3) those who wield power to dominate are depriving others of power, and 4) a society that equates worth with wealth provides its young with a script for selfishness.

Pioneer youth workers like Pestalozzi, Addams, Montessori, and Korczak advocated many ideas similar to traditional Native American philosophy. They were attacking the dominant patriarchal values of a culture that did not respect children. Today, the wisdom of these early educational pioneers and of indigenous tribal cultures are being validated by child research. Drawing on these sources, we propose replacing the "curriculum of control" with a new paradigm rooted in the core values of belonging, mastery, independence and generosity. This model, which we have called "the circle of courage," is portrayed in the medicine wheel, a sacred Native American symbol for the wholeness of life.

FROM ALIENATION TO BELONGING

Psychiatrist Karl Menninger warned that when the family, school, and community fail to meet the need to belong, youth will desperately pursue artificial belongings. Gangs and cults and promiscuous relationships are desperate attempts by some youth to meet the most basic human need—to be related to other human beings. Those most alienated have virtually abandoned the pursuit of belonging and become guarded, lonely, distrustful, and unattached.

Alienation between children and adults has reached massive proportions in modern society. Families are buffeted by a constellation of risk factors that now are converging dramatically to produce what Lisabeth Schorr (1988) calls "rotten outcomes." However, it is simplistic to blame the nuclear family for these problems.

Theologian Martin Marty argues that the core problem is the loss of the "tribe." From earliest times, biological parents were often too young, irresponsible, and overwhelmed; and short life spans made orphans abundant. However, the tribe was always there to carry on the culture. Today, says Marty, we have lost our tribes. Now, schools and youth organizations are being asked to become "new tribes" for our modern psychological orphans. But how do we go about creating such a culture of belonging?

Native American educator and anthropologist, Ella Deloria, noted that the spirit of belonging in Native American culture is expressed in these simple words: "Be related, somehow, to everyone you know." Treating others as kin forged powerful social bonds of community that drew all into relationships of respect. From earliest childhood, tribal youngsters experienced a network of human bonds where every older member of the tribe—adult or youth—felt responsible for the well-being of all younger members of the community. Wherever he or she strayed, a child was always at home, because all claimed relationships. Native American communities believed that all must be part of the circle of relatives. If a stranger entered the tribe, a rite of adoption ensured that he or she would feel part of the circle of relatives. This sense of belonging also extended to nature, in the belief that all of creation must live in harmony as relatives.

In this era of broken belongings, schools and youth organizations are being challenged to reclaim alienated young people. But our child-serving institutions are not always belonging places. The factory-school first comes to mind. These large, impersonal bureaucracies foster estrangement between teacher and child. Attachment theory research is expanding our knowledge of the powerful effects of human bonds. We once were taught that attention-getting behavior should be ignored and it would be extinguished. Now, it appears that at least some of this behavior may be understood better as an attempt to rebuild damaged attachments. Conventional wisdom in the control curriculum dictated "unbelonging" as the basis of discipline—suspend, exclude, isolate, expel. We now have discovered that children are most receptive to human attachment in such times of crisis and difficulty.

A comprehensive therapeutic approach for children with damaged attachments has been articulated by Vera Fahlberg (1991). She describes these children as having poor impulse control and weak conscience development. They often cannot appropriately manage feelings, especially anger, sadness, and frustration. Related cognitive problems include difficulty in understanding cause and effect and in planning ahead. Interpersonal relationships with these children may be marked by superficiality, distrust, hostile dependence, the need to control all situations, and continuous seeking of attention through attachment behavior.

Fahlberg describes three modes of building relationships for preventing and treating attachment problems:

- "Claiming" behaviors to foster inclusion. In any group there are markers that determine who is an insider and who is out, the "we" and "they." Addressing persons by relationship terms (e.g. "son"), claiming physical space with possessions and photographs, engaging in ceremonies and songs, adoption rituals, clothing styles and insignia shared by group members—all serve to include persons in the family, gang, or tribe. Fahlberg puts particular emphasis on claiming activities with children who have been buffeted around by the foster care system.

- Initiating positive interaction cycles. This includes engaging in pleasurable activities, expressing affection, supporting children in pursuing their outside interests and in achieving goals, and participating in fun and joyful living. Increasing positive social interaction has a reciprocal positive effect. The adult bonds to the child, while the young person is emotionally and intellectually stimulated and feels loveable and worthy.

- Support in periods of high arousal. These periods might include a range of crisis situations, such as grief, illness, frustration, being hurt or injured, etc. Even physical restraint in moments of rage can serve to build positive ties. As the adult walks through these storms of life with the child and alleviates psychological or physical discomfort, bonding and attachment are enhanced. The caregiver develops feelings of efficacy for meeting the child's needs, while the child develops trust, security, and attachment to the caregiver.

The life space interview strategies developed by Fritz Redl provide a sophisticated application of support in periods of turbulence (Wood & Long, 1991). Instead of walling off the youth in crisis, the goal is to surround the young person at that opportune moment, using problems to teach new ways of solving life's problems. Another model of attachment building is being developed in Europe by Maria Aarts and colleagues (1990). Their Orion program uses videotapes of natural family interactions to teach parents to spot even those faint initiatives that signal the willingness of children to enter into positive communication with adults.

Two hundred years ago, Pestalozzi declared that the crowning achievement of education is to be able to criticize a young person and, in the same instant, convince the youth of our fervent love. But today, the typical adult response in times of conflict is to avoid youth, preach at or punish them, and, when that fails, kick them out. The professional must learn to view problems as critical moments for teaching. Thus reframed, a crisis becomes a window of opportunity for attachment rather than trouble requiring punishment or exclusion.

FROM INADEQUACY TO MASTERY

Children and adults strive for mastery of their environments. Some psychologists argue that the search for competence is the most basic motivation for all behavior, a phenomenon that Robert White of Harvard referred to as *competence motivation.* When the child's need to be competent is satisfied, motivation for further achievement is enhanced; deprived of opportunities for success, young people express their frustration through troubled behavior or by retreating into helplessness and inferiority.

Today, in the face of such major problems as school failure, dropouts, and dysfunctional, marginally skilled youth, there is a growing belief that we need another educational model for ensuring mastery for all our children. Long ago, traditional Native American culture refined just such a system.

The goal of traditional Native American education is to develop cognitive, physical, social, and spiritual competence in each child. Children are taught that wisdom comes from observing and listening to those with more experience. A person with more skill should not be seen as a rival but as a model for learning. While there is a strong emphasis on achievement, striving is for the attainment of personal goals, not for proving superiority to one's opponent. Adults ensure that each child has some opportunity for success, giving even the smallest child important daily tasks to master. The simple but profound wisdom of Native American culture is that, since all need to feel competent, all must be nourished in competency. One may generously celebrate the achievement of those who are the most skilled, but such honor must be accepted in humility. By sharing in the achievements of others, success becomes a possession of the many, not of the privileged few.

Fostering mastery has been a goal of forward-looking educators from the time of Pestalozzi. One little-recognized pioneer in mastery education was Sylvia Ashton-Warner (1963), who worked with Maori children in New Zealand. Her approach was a bellwether for the whole-language approach which challenges traditional paradigms of learning. She described the mind of the Maori child as "a volcano with two vents, destructiveness and creativeness." They arrive with no other thoughts than to take, break, fight, and be first. Without opportunity for creativity, they develop combat as their ideal of life. "To the extent that we widen the creative channel, we atrophy the destructive one."

Ashton-Warner rejected the tradition of authoritarian, competitive schools as contradictory to the nature of children. The "two worst enemies of teaching" are the children's interest in each other and their desire for expulsion of energy. Schools need to harness these "enemies" by going along with the nature of the child. Instruction in pairs and small groups where children learn from one another mixes learning with relationships and defeats the first enemy. An active, creative, experience-based curriculum outflanks the enemy of explosive energy.

Research synthesized by Nichols (1990) indicates that children in their natural state—not goaded by rivalry—are more preoccupied with learning from others than with trying to beat them. Yet traditional schooling pits students against one another, thwarting the natural tendency toward modeling and cooperative exploration. The result is that "how I measure up to others becomes more important than how I master a task." This is egoistic involvement instead of task involvement. These two orientations are compared below.

Two Competing Models of Motivation for Achievement

Task Involvement	Egoistic Involvement
Fostered by highlighting value of work done, suggestions for future development	Fostered by competitive grades, praise, and comparing students with one another
The belief that school should make one competent fosters greater task involvement for all students	The belief that school should help one gain wealth and prestige fosters academic alienation for many students

Nichols also suggests that the cultural bias toward hyper-competitiveness is even reflected in the measurement of self-esteem. Many psychometric scales are dominated by questions about feelings of competence where children must believe that they are "above average" to score well. He suggests this is just the criterion one might expect from researchers in a competitive, meritocratic society.

Rather than trying to make all feel highly able and good about their ability (which will require delusional thinking by many), research suggests we should shift attention away from ability and toward the task at hand. Children can be taught that the lack of competence is good, because it motivates achievement. Often, we must first recognize our incompetence if we are to learn to do something about it (Sternberg, 1990). We do not advocate teaching failure for therapeutic reasons; however, perhaps we do need to teach children to fail courageously.

The hyper-competitive model of education, which developed from the patriarchal tradition, cannot be defended by scientific data or democratic values. While some youth become winners, a large group are relegated to the status of losers, the "forgotten half" who are placed at risk by schools unresponsive to their needs and life goals (William T. Grant Foundation, 1988). At a time when we are recognizing the immense social cost of "disposable" children, we need a new model for achievement. Carol Gilligan (1989) and colleagues question the kind of education that teaches us to trample others to win. A faculty member says: "To compete against another person, my students felt they needed to separate from that person. To beat you in competition meant that I could not know you or care about you." Competition must be redefined so that one can master skills, celebrate achievement, and enjoy the spirit and company of those with whom we share the quest. As we rediscover a more human and democratic form of competition, we become partners rather than enemies. We compete *with,* rather than *against,* one another. Our pedagogies, games, and grading systems will never be the same again.

FROM IRRESPONSIBILITY TO INDEPENDENCE

Education in a democracy, said Horace Mann, is an apprenticeship in responsibility. Yet too many of our youth are not responsibly independent. Fighting against feelings of powerlessness, some youth assert themselves in rebellious and aggressive ways. Those who believe they are too weak or impotent to manage their own lives become pawns of others. All of these young people need opportunities to develop the skills and confidence to assert positive leadership and self-discipline.

Traditional Native American culture places a high value on individual freedom. In contrast to "obedience" models of discipline, Native American education was designed to build "respect" and to teach inner discipline. From earliest childhood, children were encouraged to make decisions, solve problems, and show personal responsibility. To make a decision for a child was to make the child weak. This autonomy did not involve any lessening of the human attachments with adults. Adults would continue to model, nurture, teach values and provide feedback. But children were given abundant opportunities to make choices without coercion.

Children answered to self-imposed goals, not out of fearful obedience to others. Children were never offered prizes or rewards for doing something well; the achievement itself was the appropriate reward, and to put anything above this was to plant unhealthy ideas. Likewise, harsh punishment was virtually nonexistent; but an errant youth would get many gentle "lectures" from his or her relatives. The focus of these talks was to set expectations and offer feedback on how the behavior was seen by others. Lakota writer Luther Standing Bear stated that he had never heard force with anger behind it until he met white teachers in boarding school. "My father would never say, 'You must do this.' Instead he would say, 'Son, someday when you are a man, this is what you will do.' "

Research by Benson (1987) and colleagues indicates the most dramatic developmental change during the middle years of childhood is an increase in autonomy, but this is not met with significant increases in responsibility. Knitzer (1990) and colleagues noted that the privileges attached to behavior modification systems "were the same for five-year-olds as they were for 14-year-olds." Students are expected to show their responsibility by being obedient. But, as W.E.B. DuBois once observed, only responsibility builds responsibility.

We have learned from research on peer-group processes that empowerment is reciprocal: adults who respect the autonomy of youth find youth more receptive to the legitimate authority of adults. However, adults caught in power struggles with youth only fuel a powerful negative counterculture. Wasmund (1988) researched the treatment climate in residential settings for delinquents. Adults in a control-oriented program believed they were in charge, but the *sub rosa* culture was actually chaotic and disorganized. Programs built on youth empowerment were actually better controlled, since youth shared—rather than sabotaged—the treatment goals of staff.

Summarizing child-development research, Martin Hoffman notes that there are only three ways of disciplining children: 1) power assertion, 2) love withdrawal, and 3) inductive discipline (e.g., learning how your behavior affects others) (1977). North American Indians practiced inductive discipline for thousands of years. The parent managing a small problem would quietly go the child, whisper in Lakota the word "mistake," walk away, then allow the child to ponder the error. With really big problems, parents would talk more gently than usual, explaining that younger brothers and sisters look up to the child or that people who act like that won't have friends. Several grandparents might "gang up" on the most difficult youth, flooding him with these gentle conversations. Encircled by concerned friends—there is no more powerful human discipline system than being told how you are seen by people who deeply care about you. To paraphrase Karl Jung, "When love rules, there will be no will to power."

FROM EGOISM TO GENEROSITY

Unless the natural desire of children to help others is nourished, they fail to develop a sense of their own value and become absorbed in an empty, self-centered existence. Today we see many of these young people desperately pursuing empty pleasures in lifestyles of hedonism and narcissism. In fact, our society does not do a good job of nourishing the spirit of caring: research at the Search Institute on thousands of youth showed that the spirit of justice and concern for others reaches a peak at fifth grade and then declines! (Benson, Williams, & Johnson, 1987). The antidote for this malaise is to create opportunities for young persons to be of value to others.

A central goal in Native American child rearing is to teach the importance of being generous and unselfish. In *The Education of Little Tree*, Forrest Carter (1976) gives an account of his childhood reared in the mountains by Native American grandparents. The philosophy of his grandmother was "when you come on something good, first thing to do is share it with whoever you can find; that way, the good spreads out where no telling it will go." A person who accumulated property for its own sake was distrusted. One of the highest expressions of good values was to give away what one cherished the most. Native American writer Dr. Charles Eastman tells of his grandmother teaching him to give away his puppy so that he would become strong and courageous. Prestige was accorded those who gave unreservedly, while accumulation of property for its own sake was disgraceful.

At the end of the nineteenth century, William James wrote of the need of young people to move outside of themselves and contribute to some important cause. He saw community service as a means of replacing self-seeking behavior with civic discipline. The principles of James were embodied by Kurt Hahn in the Outward Bound programs developed in the 1930s in England. Hahn decried the malaise of youth who suffered from the "misery of unimportance." His prescription was to involve young persons in some "grande passion," allowing them to become committed to a cause outside of themselves.

The search for happiness through materialism and selfish pleasure is at the root of the alienation of many contemporary youth. Diane Hedin (1989) concludes that young people have never been more self-centered and consumed with money, power, and status. She cites research on the positive outcomes of volunteer service, including increased responsibility, self-esteem, moral development, and commitment to democratic values. The Carnegie Foundation has strongly supported the implementation of service-learning as part of the curriculum of all schools in the United States. Students are asked to spend time with the elderly, younger children, the sick, and the lonely. The benefits of such prosocial activity are particularly pronounced with troubled adolescents.

Our own earlier work on peer group treatment is in the tradition of empowering youth to care (Vorrath & Brendtro, 1985). Similar ideas have been used by many public schools in natural peer-helper programs. As youth decenter, they learn to empathize with others. In helping others, they create their own proof of worthiness; they have the power to make a positive contribution to another human life.

CONCLUSION

Maria Montessori said that a teacher must be humble enough to learn from the child. She was challenging a culture where childhood meant inadequacy by the standard of adult power. We still drag this cultural tail behind us. The word "child" is a pejorative in the English language. A racist calls an

African-American man "boy," and a sexist addresses an adult female as "girl." Such words can be only pejorative in a society where children are of lesser value. In the Lakota language, one cannot insult a person by using the word "child," since the literal translation is "sacred being." One does not abuse, dominate, and control sacred beings; but rather, one learns spiritual truths from them.

The First Nations' cultures of North America have developed a wealth of core principles for rearing caring, confident, respectful, and generous children. These concepts are supported by the ideas of the great European youth work pioneers who challenged the authoritarian, patriarchal traditions of Western culture. Now, emerging research is validating this early wisdom.

In our pluralistic, "do your own thing" society, it has not been fashionable to suggest that there may be absolute values unbounded by history, culture, or circumstance. Some hold that this radical moral relativism is one of the great philosophical mistakes of our time. All values are expressions of either "wants" or "needs." Our wants are personal or cultural preferences and thus based on values that are relative. But human needs are universal, and absolute human values are those tied to absolute human needs.

The Native American "circle of courage" would seem to express absolute values. Children in every culture need to belong; therefore, depriving a child of caring is universally evil. Children by their nature are created to strive for mastery; thus, schools that sabotage this motivation to competence are wasting and maltreating children. Children from any background have inalienable rights to self-determination; to block this development of independence is to commit an injustice. Finally, children from the dawn of cooperative civilization have sought to give back to others the concern they have known; if we fail to provide opportunity for caring and generosity, we extinguish the human spirit.

WORKS CITED

Aarts, M., Lammerink, E., & Vostermans, M. (1990). Support by videoanalysis: Orion hometraining and early intervention. In F. Kool (Editor), *The power to change lies within the families*. Rijswijk, Netherlands: Ministry of Welfare, Health and Culture.

Ashton-Warner, S. (1963). *Teacher*. New York: Simon & Schuster.

Benson, P., Williams, D., & Johnson, A. (1987).*The quicksilver years: The hopes and fears of early adolescence*. San Francisco: Harper & Row.

Brendtro, L., Brokenleg, M., & Van Bockern, S. (1990). *Reclaiming youth at risk: Our hope for the future*. Bloomington, IN: National Educational Service.

Carter, F. (1976). *The education of Little Tree*. Albuquerque, NM: University of New Mexico Press.

Coopersmith, S. (1967). *The antecedents of self esteem*. San Francisco: W. H. Freeman.

Fahlberg, V. (1991). *A child's journey through placement*. Indianapolis, IN: Perspective Press.

Gilligan, C., Williams, N., & Hanmer, T. (1989). *Making connections: The relational worlds of adolescent girls at Emma Willard school.* Troy, NY: Emma Willard School.

Goldstein, A. (1991). *Delinquent gangs: A psychological perspective.* Champaign, IL: Research Press.

Hedin, D. (1989). The power of community service. *Proceedings of the Academy of Political Science, 37*(2), 201–212.

Hoffman, M. (1977). Moral internalization: Current theory and research. In L. Berkowitz (Ed.), *Advances in experimental psychology, 10.* New York: Academic Press.

Knitzer J., Steinberg, Z., & Fleisch, B. (1990). *At the schoolhouse door: An examination of programs and policies for children with behavioral and emotional problems.* New York: Bank Street College of Education.

Nichols, J. G. (1990). What is ability and why are we mindful of it? A developmental perspective. In R. Sternberg & J. Kolligan Jr. (Eds.), *Competence considered.* New Haven, CT: Yale University Press.

Rogoff, B., & Morelli, G. (1989). Perspectives on children's development from cultural psychology. *American Psychologist, 44*(2), 343–348.

Schorr, L. (1988). *Within our reach: Breaking the cycle of disadvantage.* New York: Doubleday.

Sternberg, R. (1990). Prototypes of competence and incompetence. In R. Sternberg & J. Kolligan Jr. (Eds.), *Competence considered.* New Haven, CT: Yale University Press.

Vorrath, H., & Brendtro, L. (1985). *Positive peer culture* (2nd ed.). New York: Aldine de Gruyter.

Wasmund, W. (1988). The social climates of peer group and other programs. *Child and Youth Care Quarterly, 17*(3), 146–155.

William T. Grant Foundation Commission on Work, Family, and Citizenship. (1988). *The forgotten half: Non-college youth in America.* Washington, DC: Author.

Wood, M., & Long, N. J. (1991). *Life space intervention: Talking with children and youth in crisis.* New York: PRO-ED.

. . . .

As we have seen, the single most central matter at the core of helping is the act of caring. Many of the changes proposed to improve the helping process require system changes beyond the immediate control of the teacher. It is easy to become discouraged at the magnitude of the task and the slowness of progress toward changing systems; yet we must join with colleagues and persist in such efforts. In caring, we have a vital area of professional potential that is under our personal jurisdiction. It is a personal and professional attribute that each of us can cultivate. Caring has been treated as "a nice thing to do" when feasible, a good but nonessential thing to do. The next article holds that mature caring is a most powerful and essential tool in fostering change in youngsters. Caring is the antidote for punishment and control; it enables the teacher to move beyond symptoms to deeper involvement. Actually, cultivation of caring, especially for the many hard-to-like kids who need us most, is a lifelong professional task for most teachers. Morse suggests things one can do to nurture caring.

ARTICLE 2.4

The Role of Caring in Teaching Children with Behavior Problems

William C. Morse

Little wonder that education of problem children has been described by critics as generally ineffective: Helping these youngsters is a most sophisticated and ecologically involved endeavor. Teaching such pupils saps the very core of teacher being and is a major contributor to professional fatigue. With rapidly spreading practice of inclusion, this stress is felt by all teachers. Further, the number and severity of behavior problems continues to surge, reflecting the increase of poverty and family disintegration. Teachers come to feel impotent to do anything significant for these children in view of the myriad of overwhelming life situations they bring to the classroom. The inability to help these children is doubly frustrating because many teachers were attracted to the profession to do good things for children. We know there should be multiple community services available for troubled children and their families, but this is less and less the reality as services, always in short supply, are drastically reduced. So often the teacher remains the central figure in restorative possibility. Yet little has been done to present a comprehensive picture of the teaching role with behavior problem pupils (Morse, 1985). Because of the acting out which is characteristic of most of these children, the focus has been on management through teacher authority meted out as if this single dimension were a cure all. Teacher exercise of power easily becomes an end in itself. Sarason (1985) considers this an inadequate conceptualization of the teaching role for today's children. He includes teaching in the mental health professions since teachers, for better or worse, must assess and respond to many problem children in the course of a day. Sarason continues that such a view is seldom explicated in training and we know that once on the job the ethos is control. The fear of loss of control permeates the field since the teacher is judged on ability, single-handed, to manage whoever is assigned to the classroom. Just conducting a classroom with such distraught pupils included can be highly taxing. Of course control is necessary but control is not a sufficient reason d'être.

It is sad to note that proposals for school reform or special education inclusion seldom give attention to conditions which would facilitate the school as a setting for continuity of caring for all children. Yet caring is the experience so desperately needed especially by troubled children and those at risk.

From *Contemporary Education*. (1994). Vol. 65, No. 3. Used with permission.

The aim of this brief essay is to explore caring as one relatively neglected aspect of the teaching matrix for children with problems. The impetus came from visiting classrooms for the socioemotionally impaired where the teachers were considered by their supervisors as outstandingly effective. There was great admiration for these teachers ("I don't know how she (or he) does it, but you must see for yourself"). After observing it was easy to agree that real business was going on in these classrooms. Useful things were happening for the children. Of course there were many facets to what went on in each classroom. To me, the striking thing was how different the classrooms were. Each teacher employed a unique mode. One might run a strict behavior modification point system while another concentrated on Life Space Interviews and group work. In some instances there were work sheets done in unison while in others there were individual self-selected projects. All included a wide range of activities and surprises. These classes did not always run smoothly. There were low profile quiet modulated teachers and some approaching manic. At times some of the teachers said and did things which shocked naive me.

What I was looking for were underlying common attributes of these gifted teachers. Usually there was a time the teachers could talk about their kids, and here I found one common thread: They knew their pupils and had a deep empathy for the stress in their youngsters' lives. They faced unacceptable behavior without panic. They were not permissive. They worked out what they considered was best for the child even when it caused pain and resistance. In short, these exemplar teachers all cared deeply about their charges though expressed in different ways. Later, when I talked to the youngsters, sometimes raising questions about certain practices, the answer would come back in one form or another with a yes but, "My teacher cares about us kids." Somehow that message was registered. The youngsters were persuaded that this teacher really was concerned about their welfare: That was the common essence. Such teacher commitment overrides moment by moment tactics. Not every teacher won over every youngster to be sure but for most of the pupils the level ground was teacher caring. Usually there was a sequence of testing which preceded acceptance.

As we explore the essential role of caring in teaching youngsters beset with problematic behavior, it is well to remember that love alone is not enough. Without the presence of order little will be accomplished. A teacher who tolerates chaos will be seen by the students as incompetent and thus uncaring. Children and adolescents lacking adequate internal control require assistance in management in the home and in the school. The issue is, control in what wise and to what end? External control has far too often become the ultimate goal, the sine qua non of the restorative effort. The problem is fixation at this low level of adult interaction, without caring. The raw use of adult authority encourages the youngsters to develop skills in outwitting adults. But even if the pupils win they lose. The system may be bested in a battle but the system eventually wins the war even if victory means exclusion. A few authors such as Jones and Jones (1990) do go beyond management through power and system-based intimidation to management through relationship. They demonstrate how teachers can use pupil feedback to achieve a humanized control. Brendtro and Brokenleg (1993) work from a base of attachment and American Indian ethos to present alternatives to a school culture of control. Nichols (1991, 1992) has faced the issue of compassion and control directly in her work with an inclusive awareness. For most of us the most difficult children to deal with are value deviant delinquents. Even here, recent recovery programs no longer rely on control alone but advocate control awash with caring.

It is imperative to bear in mind that the salient etiological condition most often mentioned in the histories of at risk and problem children is the lack of adequate adult caring. The common state of increasing numbers of school children is that they come to school uncared for, neglected and sometimes abused. Such sequela often are the consequence of family struggles with poverty and dysfunction. Age wise, these youngsters are developmentally unfinished, suffering from the absence of nurturing parenting. An adequate family primary group experience is missing: Thus the children lack a sense of self, suffer low self esteem and have not been taught impulse control. They seek to assuage low self esteem in antisocial ways. They are not ready for school and school is not ready for them. The numbers of inadequately cared for children in some schools reaches epidemic levels. This is not to say that even the special education teacher with a small group can be a replacement parent. Whenever possible the child's family is assisted to become the core source of caring. But this is wishful thinking in a good many situations. The argument is that the school should face up to the need for a curriculum of caring and do whatever is possible to engender what children need. No teacher can be the central caring figure for all the children seen in a day. But perhaps each problem pupil might have at least one school adult as an especially concerned advocate.

It is not enough for a teacher to feel that he or she is a caring professional. Most of us believe we are. The task is to communicate our caring to the youngster so that she or he feels cared about. There is obviously no single way to establish such a bond of trust. Those "exemplar" teachers each achieved this in a unique mode, just as caring parents demonstrate their care in various ways. Perhaps teacher trainees should be selected from those with high profiles in two of Gardner's (1991) seven domains of intelligence. One he defines as *interpersonal intelligence* the capacity to sense and respond properly to the internal states of others. Thus interpersonal interaction functions on understanding the other individual. It is the empathic ability to take the perspective of another and respond appropriately to the moods and motivations of that other. The other intelligence having a direct bearing on caring is what Gardner terms *intrapersonal intelligence,* access and knowledge about one's own feelings to use in guiding one's behavior. This access to one's own feelings, as well as strengths and weakness enables one to conduct honest dialogue. Gardner sees different profiles of intelligence suited to given professions. Noddings (1991, 1992) has a slightly different slant, using the term *interpersonal reasoning,* which embodies an effort to cultivate relationships with engrossment and compassionate attention to the afflictions of others. Caring involves solicitude. The image is of the good responsible parent. Rightly or wrongly, a major pupil complaint is, "The teachers just don't care so why should I follow them?" While this may sometimes be a convenient defense, too often it is an accurate perception of the reality. On the other hand when a teacher offers a convincing demonstration of caring, troubled children frequently respond.

In contrast to the helping professions of child psychiatry, social work and psychology, there is little in the training of teachers to expedite caring. Also, the organization of schools seems designed to frustrate caring activity. Persons drawn to teaching by deep caring for youngsters face culture shock on entering actual practice. The native caring which should have been made more functional through training is destroyed instead. There is also the intriguing possibility that our natural caring potential differs with age of the child. Some can reach out to toddlers more easily and others to adolescents. Do we select or train teachers for given age roles?

Similar to other essential concepts of human intercourse, caring is difficult to define. We know it is the enzyme which makes personal and social growth possible so that the neonate becomes a human being. We recognize caring because we have experienced it at some level from parents, mates, friends and teachers. The closest of human relationships is that between child and parent which is at the same time the most distant relationship because the adult and child live in separate worlds and adults have responsibilities for the immature which cannot be easily met. Goodlad, Soder, and Sirotnik (1990) remind us that caring in schools involves the whole life of the child in the setting. It is not just an atmosphere of being listened to with patience and non-rejection. Every learning task has both a cognitive and affective component. It is meeting the instructional, curriculum and learning needs too, so that school is an exciting and fun place as well as a safe place. Teachers do provide, for some children, the only anchor of security and attachment.

It is obvious that teachers as well as parents must have power to influence youngsters, especially vulnerable and behavior problem children. Normal children are given to testing limits as part of growing up. Problem children make a career of limit pushing and testing which presumably accounts for the adult obsession with control. Yet teaching children, especially those with behavior problems, puts an adult in the center of youngsters' need for caring. The current modus operandi is usually to sell out for devices to get immediate control, not as a stage but as the final end point. Again we emphasize that there is no gainsaying that an effective management plan is a classroom necessity. Deeper than management, teachers hope to change attitudes and even values in the confused and value deficient youngsters. This requires the teacher to be a model, or deeper yet a figure for identification, one who interacts and discusses with children, pointing the way to more successful ways of feeling and acting.

Caring induces identification, a powerful force dominating the long term impact adults can have on children. It is our hope for long term change through incorporation of our behavior into the self of the child. Even how management is conducted can be permeated with caring as Jones and Jones (1990) demonstrate.

There are caveats to recognize when advocating caring as a key teaching process. Some children and adolescents are too damaged to respond to a teacher's caring beyond insatiable testing and minute gains followed by regressions. Adult veracity becomes at stake. As Nodding (1992) explains, it is difficult to keep caring when rejected even though the rejecters are the very youngsters most in need of caring. Our attributions for their behavior slip into volitional and global causes for behavior which put the behavior beyond our influence (Baden & Howe, 1992). Much attention-demanding can be recognized as the child seeking a caring relationship, irritating though the way it is done may be to the adult. Can one care about a person one does not really know through communication and dialogue? Large classes and transient flow of many students certainly are handicaps. Of course we hope for most children the home will be the primary guarantee of caring with the school an important supplement. But there are more and more public school pupils where the teachers become a primary source of nurturing.

How can teachers be persuaded to go beyond lineal bureaucratic authority to foster caring as a source of influence leading to permanent changes in pupils (Noblit, 1993)? If teachers are going to make long standing inroads on behavior problems, they obviously must be convinced they do have a profound source of influence. James Paul (1994) is engaged in research on a method he created to bring home the power of caring to teachers in training or already in the field. He has the teacher write two letters. The first is a letter of thanks as if to send to the teacher who had the greatest positive influence on the person. These are then read in the group and the qualities extruded which made that teacher so important as to leave an indelible mark. These qualities of being cared about include being respected, being listened to, feeling safe, being able to express one's feelings and still be accepted, sharing lives, confirming accomplishments and fostering one's power over his or her life. These helpful teachers shared the feeling that student and teacher were together on life's journey, learning how to cope. The discussions explicate the actions of teachers who cared.

A second letter proposed by Paul is to the teacher who did the most personal damage to the individual. The insensitivity, humiliation and anger generated by these uncaring teachers, are also discussed. Most adults have vivid and penetrating memories of such teachers, even to the point of an abreaction with potent emotional feelings. What this teaching method does is to open up the power in pupil–teacher relationships for pupil good or ill. As with any process, it is Paul's deft working with the contributions which does the convincing. An additional exercise is to have the teachers ask their pupils to write descriptions of teachers or adults who have helped them and those who have hindered to obtain the consumer view. While this does not imply that other management procedures are not also necessary, it does introduce the power of interpersonal processes. I have also had teachers write out episodes of "peak" experiences with youngsters—kids they liked and ones they disliked and why. Another stimulus to use is the recall of episodes of being punished in school. It has been surprising how often there is a pleasure in the punishment, or even glee. It was well worth it. Paul also suggests that teachers write out an account of a student where they feel they have done an outstanding job, and another they would relate to again but in a different way, given a second chance. The accounts emphasize the unique nature of caring exchanges. It becomes evident that there are ways to circumvent an assembly line bureaucratic educational operation even in schools as they are today. I have asked high school teachers to describe situations where they have reached out to a student beyond the call of duty: Examples of such caring are almost universal though admittedly desired results were not always forthcoming.

It is not fair to encourage caring as a central feature unless teachers are given training to deal with the complications which can occur (Rogers & Webb, 1991). There are unwarranted expectations which generate depression if one does not learn protection from futile expectations. Children cannot be "adopted" by their teachers, or even mentally taken home. It is not enough to want to help. The intent must be buttressed with deep knowledge of child development and pathology as well as interpersonal relationships. Training is required to know how to understand and respond to the deep human needs pupils express to caring teachers. Some teachers are given to keeping distance from pupils in order to avoid the feeling that they should respond to what children might spill out when they get close. In company with other helping professions, teachers need to learn how to handle what children produce.

Teachers are primarily group workers (Hobbs, 1982) and have the opportunity to do much of their work though this medium. They function largely in group settings. Since classrooms are saturated in peer culture, teachers need to know group work skills in order to make a classroom a caring culture. New social skills may have to be taught to pupils. Consultation and referral services are crucial. There are times when a child is temporarily unable to function in the classroom group and crisis support is necessary to take over for that period.

Of course, just to have caring teachers is no adequate solution. The overall neglect of our youngsters is too acute. The country has to care about the children who are living in poverty and neglect. All agencies will have to become more caring in their practice, each doing whatever is possible to help families be caring. The school can become the hub of service integration through the Full Service School concept where relevant agencies function right on the campus and work under the monitoring of a case manager to bring appropriate services to the child and family. There is no implication in this essay that caring teachers can do it all. The argument is that teachers can be part of the solution rather than part of the problem.

REFERENCES

Baden, A. D. & Howe, G.W. (1992). Mothers' attributions and expectancies regarding their conduct disordered students. *Journal of Abnormal Child Psychology, 20,* 476–485.

Brendtro, L.K. & Brokenleg, M. (1993). Beyond the curriculum of control. *Journal of Emotional and Behavioral Problems, 2,* 5–11.

Gardner, H. (1991). *The unschooled mind: How children think and schools should teach.* New York: Basic Books.

Goodlad, J.I., Soder, R., & Sirotnik, K.A. (Eds.). (1990). *The moral dimensions of teaching.* San Francisco: Jossey-Bass.

Hobbs, N. (1982). *The troubled and troubling child.* San Francisco: Jossey-Bass.

Jones, Vernon F. & Jones, Louise S. (1990). *Classroom management.* Boston: Allyn & Bacon.

Morse, W.C. (1985). *The education and treatment of socioemotionally impaired children and youth.* Syracuse: Syracuse University Press.

Nichols, Polly. (1991). Through the classroom door: What teachers and students need. *Mountain Plains Information Bulletin,* May. Des Moines, IA: Drake University.

Nichols, Polly. (1992). The curriculum of control: Twelve reasons for it, some arguments against it. *Beyond Behavior, 3,* 5–11.

Noblit, G. W. (1993). Power and caring. *American Educational Research Journal, 30,* 23–38.

Noddings, Nel. (1991). Stories in dialogue: Caring and interpersonal reasoning. In Withrell, C. & Noddings, N. (Eds.) *Narrative in dialogue as a paradigm for teaching and learning.* pp. 157–170. New York: Teachers College Press.

Noddings, Nel. (1992). *The challenge to care in schools.* New York: Teachers College Press.

Rogers, Dwight & Webb, Jaci. (1991). The ethic of caring in teacher education. *Journal of Teacher Education, 42,* 173–181.

Sarason, Seymour B. (1985). *Caring and compassion in clinical practice.* San Francisco: Jossey-Bass.

. . . .

TREAT ME WITH RESPECT . . . .

Students at Our Lady of Lourdes Elementary School on the Pine Ridge Indian Reservation participated in "Child Abuse Awareness Month" with activities that stressed respect for children. Wakiyan Teca, a drum group from the school, performed on radio station KILI, and students worked on posters and essays. Sister Rita Ostrey, counselor at the Porcupine, South Dakota, school, shared these essays by three children.

As I Grow

Echo LeBeaux—Grade 5

Treat me with respect, the way you would to a person who you look up to.

Teach me things from right to wrong.

Understand me and have patience with me when I'm having hard times.

Be proud of me when I do things right.

When something does go wrong, show me the right way without getting mad.

When your anger flares up, put your hands in your pocket and don't use them on me.

Remember, I am a gift to you from God, and you are a gift to me from God, and His love is always there for us to share.

Respect

Jerome His Law—Grade 7

I want to be treated with respect and dignity. If you respect me, I will respect you. If you take pride in me, I will take pride in you. But if you treat me bad I will probably abuse myself by drugs, alcohol, and low self-esteem. This is going to all the parents on earth. If you do not abuse your children—good and don't start. Give us love and attention, listen to us when we have a problem and talk to us when you have a problem. Because when you ignore us it makes us feel stupid and mad.

It doesn't matter if you're white, black, or Indian, we are all human and humans have feelings. And it feels bad when we get hurt by bad names, teasing, taunting, and being ignored. So, talk it over with somebody, and tell your kid you love them and maybe he/she will say she/he loves you.

Article 2.5, 2.6, and 2.7 are from *The Journal of Emotional and Behavioral Problems.* (1993). Vol. 1, No. 4. Used with permission.

ARTICLE 2.7

How Do We Respect the Child?
Missy Kills Right—Grade 6

We can respect the child by not abusing them and taking very good care of them. It is abuse that makes the kids get hurt by their parents, grandmas, grandpas, aunts, uncles, sisters, brothers, and anybody else in their life. When the parents are drinking, they do not respect their children. The children don't have food to eat because the parents spend it on booze and drugs. What can we do to change child abuse? We can change child abuse by banning all beer. We can also set a law where the parents have to buy their kids clothes, food, shoes and school supplies. When I see a child getting abused, I get worried how I'll be with my children. As people say, "Words hit as hard as a fist." And don't give them a fist if they do something wrong! They get embarrassed when they go out in public with their scars, bruises, slap marks, and cuts. They tell their friends lies, because they don't want anybody to know that their parents abuse them. They say they fell off their bike, fell down the stairs, and sometimes they say that they got into a fight. Instead, congratulate them when they do something right.

. . . .

We are in the midst of a huge debate over ecological factors in efforts to help certified special education students. The arguments apply as well to all troubled youngsters. What is the most effective setting for interventions for helping: pull-out programs, or the mainstream? Special education previously meant small classes that allowed more intensive teacher input to each individual pupil; a teacher specially trained for work with children who suffer from the given disability; and the individualized education program (IEP). Critics hope to salvage the IEP. They propose that all teachers be generically trained for all disabilities. The ladder of possible placement options is to be replaced with one—*inclusion*, with all needed services administered in the mainstream. One main argument for inclusion is that it is a youngster's civil right to be educated with normal peers in the local neighborhood school. It is further argued that extruded settings stigmatize and are poor places to provide special assistance. Although the original proposition was based on Dunn's study of mildly retarded students, inclusion has been expanded to include all special children even when an aide is required to help the child negotiate the mainstream. The federal government has fostered inclusion under the Least Restrictive Environment clause, and the courts have in general supported parents who have demanded inclusion under both P. L. 94-142 and P. L. 93-112 (section 504). Parents have rights, and schools have obligations. As a practical matter, the intensity of intervention is typically reduced or eliminated when seriously troubled students are mainstream candidates. Anticipated financial savings (accomplished by reducing services) has become a strong motivation. The cost of separate special education for troubled students is two to four times that for regular students. The dual special education bureaucracy is expected to wither away.

There is one very important caveat to our consideration of inclusion. In this book, we are not speaking in general terms, lumping all special children in a class action. Here, our concern is for emotionally and socially troubled children, their classmates, and their teachers. Many of our "troubled" youngsters became designated as such because they acted out their conflicts and failed to be successfully helped in the regular classrooms with whatever ancillary support was available. In short, they interfered with their own learning and the learning of their classmates, and they absorbed inordinate amounts of teacher time. The reality of this contention is evident when we learn that, of all the handicapped categories, disturbed children are the least likely to be mainstreamed. Recent national figures indicate less than 15% of the 1%–2% certified emotionally and socially disturbed students are in regular classes. A counterargument is that special classes that are saturated with problem children encourage negative contagion. Troubled students need the good peer models who are present in regular classrooms—a view that introduces the question of how optimum the regular class is (or can be made) for special learning needs. For troubled students who do not act out (and thus are often ignored) but are depressed and without hope, the placement decision should also consider not just where they can exist or be tolerated but where their needs can be best addressed. They may have a seat in the regular classroom but not be a part of the academic or social life unless special efforts are implemented. Because troubled youngsters have the potential for changing, the issue is how and where they can be most effectively reclaimed. Many of the successful inclusion examples come from elementary classes with highly gifted teachers. Some parents sue to have their special child included, and others sue to have them kept out.

The inclusion revolution and other changes in special education are taking place in the midst of significant restructuring efforts in regular education, coming in response to widespread criticisms of public education. Usually, these reforms have originated in efforts to raise academic achievement. Very seldom do the changes proposed attend to equity for children with handicaps. A major element in school reform is empowerment of the local school (parents and teachers) to make decisions about the character of the school and thus accommodate to local needs and escape the foot-dragging district bureaucracy. Local school improvement committees vary greatly in accomplishment, from cosmetic changes to reorienting the total structure around new policies. Such variation is to be expected in such a grassroots movement. In general, special educators have not been highly visible in these restructurings. As Long will elaborate in the next article, the history of such school reform movements is not encouraging. In fact, some of the establishment are sitting this one out, expecting it will soon die. Because general education restructuring plans seldom attend to children with problems, state special education departments sponsor their own parallel reform movements. Like politically motivated movements, these are high on image and low on realistic substance.

Even as these reform efforts are taking place, there are deeper educational changes that may end public education as we have known it. In fact, some see the actual survival of public education in doubt. Illustrations include the increasing discouragement with busing; reductions in financial support; and the powerful groups advocating vouchers, open enrollment, and home schooling. Private corporations for profit are already operating a few schools, and the number of independent charter schools is increasing. These far-reaching changes have implications for troubled youngsters. Some forecaster are predicting that public schools, if they survive, will be left for the misfits—our poor who have no alternatives, and, of course, the handicapped. The tragedy of so many urban school systems will become endemic. Amid all this gloom, one can find, here and there, public schools that have changed drastically: they have become caring places for all children, including those at risk.

As we turn to Long's article, we agree that no student should be removed from the mainstream when his or her needs can and will be fully met in that mainstream. The program elements described at the beginning of this chapter should be available. Placement should always be an individual matter based on both the child's needs and the qualities of the receiving ecology. The critical element is the IEP, which outlines what listed services will be needed and where they can be delivered. Successful inclusion will require adjustments in the curriculum, a purification of teacher attitudes for acceptance, and work with the receiving peer group. The fact that many regular classes are already harboring a high number of problem students also needs to be recognized. Teacher support services of the Full Service School will be needed. Crisis intervention can convert untoward classroom events into social learning events. Above all, a continuum of special services should be maintained: some pupils will benefit most from special classes, others will need day schools, and a few will need a period of institutional care.

There is nothing new about inclusion. That was the state of affairs when special education for troubled students began. There was inclusion and, when that failed, there was expulsion. The difference today is that the expulsion option is no longer permitted.

Long's spirited discussion goes into detail about inclusion for troubled students. Whether their particular program espouses inclusion or rejects it, special teachers must be prepared to discuss the matter—if not on the basis of theory, then on the basis of each individual child as the IEP is composed. Because parents have diverse opinions about inclusion, they can be expected to raise the issue if no one else does. Long presents the arguments and counterarguments that serve as guides for examining particular cases of troubled children.

ARTICLE 2.8

Inclusion of Emotionally Disturbed Students: Formula for Failure or Opportunity for New Acceptance

Nicholas J. Long

I have always been impressed by the African proverb, "Never test the depth of a river with both feet." There is a similar American proverb, "Look before you leap." Someone should have reminded "Thelma and Louise" of this proverb before they got into their car. Personally, I do not think it would have mattered because they were operating on the proverb, "She who hesitates is lost." As a society, Americans are conditioned to be impulsive, adventurist, and daring. Developmentally, we have been suckled by the good taste of scientific progress. We have been programmed like a VCR Plus to be thrilled by newness, innovation, and technological novelty. If a new idea, concept, gadget, or diet sounds legitimate, promises excellent results, is marketed well, and has the support and approval of established groups, then it must be another successful example of good old "American Know How." As my friends in South Dakota say, "When something good comes along, you either jump on the Conestoga band wagon, or you get left behind in a cloud of dust on the road of progress."

   I like progress. But after four decades of re-educating emotionally disturbed students, I have lost my rose-tinted glasses. I have lived through several education and mental health reform movements, which erupted with widespread professional support but ended a few years later. For example, Charles Silberman (1970) wrote a provocative book called, *Crisis in the Classroom: The Remaking of American Education.* Silberman was director of a three million dollar grant from The New York Carnegie Study on Education. His book was one of the most significant statements on education since World War II. It was a national best seller, and it received multiple educational, religious, and organizational awards. *Crisis in the Classroom* helped education reform become a national priority. It was the age of Aquarius! The time was right for change, and the public schools responded by engaging in massive innovation and experimentation. New teaching methods were proposed. New curriculums were developed. New grouping and instructional patterns were planned along with new strategies for assessing and evaluating educational change. Even teacher training colleges, administrators, and parent advocacy groups were involved. It seemed like the perfect reform movement. The need for educational change was documented by Silberman, and the new theories of how to "Remake Education" were accepted and as hopeful as *The Sound of Music.* In addition, the marketing of

From *The Journal of Emotional and Behavioral Problems.* (1994). Vol. 3, No. 3. Used with permission.

this reform movement was highly successful and had the political blessings and the financial support of the White House, State Departments of Education, Teacher Unions, and the man on the street. Did it work? What happened? Was it successful? John Goodland (as cited by Silberman, 1970) said it best in his April, 1969, article in the *Saturday Review,*

"We are forced to conclude that the educational reform movement has been blunted on the classroom doors."

This was hardly the expected outcome after all the national and professional excitement, money, and educational innovations. It appears public education, like the resilient termite, is successful in thwarting all attempts to alter its environment. It also means classroom teachers have the final vote power on innovations. When they decided to close their leaded classroom doors to educational reform, not even the most penetrating ideas could enter. Throughout the nation classrooms became CIA safe houses for old ideas.

I would like to support the newest education reform movement, the one calling for inclusion; but my enthusiasm for any national educational change is dampened by my history. I want to reserve judgments until I have more information. I guess I want to look before I leap on the Inclusion band wagon. As I continue to read, study, and discuss the Inclusion Movement, I have the following five concerns:

1. the need to go beyond the rhetoric of Inclusion,
2. the need to bring classroom teachers into the Inclusion process,
3. the naive assumptions about re-educating emotionally disturbed students,
4. the lack of professional support for emotionally disturbed students and staff,
5. the conflicting goals between the rights of emotionally disturbed students and the rights of the school to protect its program must be re-examined at the policy level.

1. A CONCERN ABOUT THE RHETORIC OF THE INCLUSION MOVEMENT

The ideological arguments justifying the need for and the outcomes of the Inclusion Movement are impressive. They are positive and humanistic, but they do not allow much room for open discussion if the debate is to go beyond "politically correct" rhetoric. To be against Inclusion is like being against God, Country, Motherhood, and Elvis. Who can argue against the following published visions of Inclusion:

- Full inclusion of students with disabilities, within a restructured classroom, reflects the belief that diversity strengthens society and should be honored and protected.

- In our vision, communities, parents, teachers, specialists, and administrators work collaboratively to ensure each student's success.
- In our vision, there are no failures, because there is proactive, successful prevention planned at an early age.
- In our vision, all children are seen as capable and able bodied, with strengths waiting to blossom.
- In our vision, no one complains about not having materials because there is an adequate, equitable supply of resources.
- In our vision, adequate professional support is provided by city councils to comment and coordinate the public school with other agencies in the city.
- In our vision, the monies currently assigned to special education, with its costly administrative structure, and to private schools and institutions, with their enormous tuition fees, will be reallocated and used to provide adequate training, personnel, and resources for full inclusion.

After much thought, I concluded the Inclusion Movement was like a sponge. It soaked up all the positive phrases, sentences, and ideas of many of the education reform movements of past decades. The language of Inclusion offers parents and educators, who are upset by the present turmoil of special education, an attractive way of denying the complexity of re-educating emotionally disturbed students. The arguments for Inclusion are filled with soothing language, and the favorable promises of Inclusion have the effect of lulling the public into passive head nodding and dreamlike acceptance loaded with terms like—"There will be . . . adequate . . . appropriate . . . a common vision . . . ample, etc.," is a concern to me. I want someone to tell me what "adequate," "appropriate," and "ample" mean. I want to know what is left after the red hands of reality squeeze this Inclusion sponge dry.

I have no doubt the advocates of the Inclusion Movement believe in the goodness of this reform. They may say that I am not adequately representing the level of professional support they are proposing. For example, classroom teachers will not be alone; rather, they will be assigned additional resources and personnel. They will be a part of a collaborative support team and feel more empowered and less helpless. When life gets rough in the classroom, a crisis team will be available immediately.

It sounds innovative. It sounds very democratic. But this is not a perfect world. Screws drop out; things go wrong; promises are not fulfilled. Budgets get cut, and good intentions end up as empty promises. The Inclusion Movement is an innovative and exciting idea to be explored; it should not be a cult to be followed. What is needed is more national discussion of the professional issues involved in Inclusion. James Kauffman's article, "How We Might Achieve Radical Reform in Special Education," offers an objective presentation of the challenges involved in reforming special education that goes beyond the rhetoric of Inclusion.

2. A CONCERN ABOUT THE STRESS LEVEL OF REGULAR CLASSROOM TEACHERS

The Inclusion Movement did not begin with regular classroom teachers. It was a top-down decision, and many teachers are reeling under the additional pressure. Talk with any urban teacher and they will confirm that ethnic, academic, physical, and social/emotional diversity already dominates their classroom, although it may not be celebrated. They will tell you they are under increasing pressure to improve the academic scores of their class, and if their students are to compete in the international marketplace, they will need to be more competent in mathematics, science and language. The emotional strain for classroom teachers to find more time for instruction is real. This expectation for academic excellence is reinforced when teachers are rated not on how they nurture their students, but on whether the students perform above the school norm in citywide tests.

Whether we like it or not, some teachers still resent taking any time to meet any student needs that are not academic. They view themselves as academic teachers. Their operating assumption is: "I'm here to teach these students and not be their psychologist or social worker." While this extreme attitude represents a very small group of teachers, the thousands of caring teachers express a similar frustration. Teachers are overwhelmed by the demand to find the time and energy to improve their instructional skills while also trying to meet the social/emotional needs of their non-troubled students experiencing normal developmental crises, the increasing number of abused, impoverished high risk students, and the unidentified but active emotionally disturbed students in their classrooms. Perhaps this tension for higher academic achievement and the demanding needs of their students explains why teachers' number one educational concern, (as reported by the NEA yearly survey of teachers), for the past ten years, continues to be classroom discipline or disruptive student behavior. This is understandable since it is difficult to teach when students are acting up and challenging teacher authority. This professional dilemma was stated with unmistakable clarity by an urban sixth-grade teacher who felt she had enough problems in her classroom. When asked to accept one of our emotionally disturbed students from Rose School, she said, "If I have to take Jason into my classroom, this placement will be called Mainscreaming and not Mainstreaming." Clearly, she was not ambivalent about her level of stress.

One approach to supporting classroom teachers is to provide them with additional behavior management skills. Stan Fagen (1986) argues, "Too many teachers have a limited range of techniques for reacting to deviant behavior and quickly escalate the problem to the point of student exclusion." He proposes an inservice program in which teachers learn a continuum of intervention strategies to reduce negative behaviors and to increase positive behaviors. The assumption is: If teachers feel more in control of their class, they will have more instructional time and be more likely to accept a troubled student into their classrooms.

Albert Shanker, president of the American Federation of Teachers, has called for a moratorium on inclusion policies and practices until the promises of providing the additional personnel, released time, and monies for ongoing teacher training to support inclusion is ensured (Gorman & Rose, 1994). Teachers have not been protected from administrative pressures and bureaucratic delays. All too often, innovative public school programs begin and the new students arrive before the new staff are hired and the current staff completes the necessary training. When this happens, the program is guaranteed to fail. Let us remember what Goodland taught us. If classroom teachers do not support the proposed change, if they are not an active part of the planning, and if the promises are not kept, then it does not happen.

Inclusion needs to become a grass roots movement with real teacher input and support if it is going to have a chance to succeed.

3. A CONCERN ABOUT A SIMPLISTIC, NAIVE VIEW OF RE-EDUCATING EMOTIONALLY DISTURBED STUDENTS

When I read articles that suggest any emotionally disturbed student can be taught in the regular classroom if reasonable accommodations are made in instruction and management, I wonder what emotionally disturbed students they are talking about. They are not talking about the students admitted to the Rose School, a day psychoeducational treatment program which I directed for 18 years. The Washington, D.C. Public Schools referred these students to us because of their chronic and pervasive emotional and behavioral problems. These emotionally disturbed students were beyond the benefits of an accepting teacher or an individualized education plan. Frequently, they needed wrap-around educational, mental health and other social services to alleviate their successful self-defeating behaviors. Even in our therapeutic school, these students initially were motivated *to avoid interpersonal closeness, to foster teacher and peer rejections, to reject academic success and to perceive their placement as a form of punishment.* Can they make those "reasonable" accommodations for emotionally disturbed students in their classrooms? Are principals and counseling staff ready to support teachers and to manage these students during crises? For example, if a student who has asthma is admitted to the classroom, is its staff prepared to manage a possible asthma attack? If a student who has cerebral palsy is included, is the staff prepared to manage him when he loses his balance and falls? Likewise, if emotionally disturbed students are included, is the staff prepared to manage them therapeutically when they:

1. carry in a stressful home problem and act it out in the classroom?
2. misperceive and over react to normal classroom disappointments and frustrations by screaming and threatening others?

3. believe any consequences they receive are because the teacher is hostile and rejecting?

4. have immature social skills and show friendship by teasing, hitting, and name calling?

5. feel guilty for some action and then respond in self-abusive behaviors?

6. justify their aggressive behaviors by blaming others while perceiving themselves as the victims and not as the aggressors?

These are examples of disruptive behaviors commonly displayed by emotionally disturbed students. Are we really expecting classroom teachers, who have little understanding of emotional disturbance in children and youth and who are academically oriented, to be the best therapeutic teachers for these students? If special education teachers have difficulty with these students, will classroom teachers with 30 students be more effective? Don't we have enough experience and knowledge about the nature of emotional disturbances to shatter the illusion that re-educating emotionally disturbed students is a simple process of restructuring the classroom by making reasonable accommodations?

4. A CONCERN ABOUT FINANCIAL AND PROFESSIONAL SUPPORT

The history of re-educating emotionally disturbed students in the public schools is filled with examples of professional neglect and minimal support. In the early sixties, teachers who were rejected because they were unfit to teach normal students were assigned to teach emotionally disturbed students. The philosophy seemed to be: You had to be one to teach one. Classrooms for these students were in the basement and out of sight of the public.

You might argue this historical example does not reflect the professional status of teachers of emotionally disturbed students in the nineties. Many of our special education teachers are superbly trained with Master's degrees in the area of emotional disturbances or behavior disorders. However, there also is a significant number of teachers who enter this field by default. For example, in 1991 I was asked to spend two weeks training a group of 20 teachers who were hired to teach emotionally disturbed students in high schools. They turned out to be Peace Corp graduates who had college degrees in content but not in education. They were given temporary teacher certification and a monthly inservice training seminar. They were competent adults and dedicated to take on the challenge of this new position. I met with them for the first time during their November seminar; but by that time, their classrooms were out of control, and these well-motivated teachers were feeling helpless and angry. They said they had little or no administrative support and were blamed for their chaotic classrooms. They were told they were too easy on the students. I wish I could say this is an isolated example. But as I travel across the country and work with a variety of special education programs, I hear this same pattern of lack of professional support repeated again and again.

Let me share a nagging thought. We live in a political society, and emotionally disturbed students do not have any political clout. They have no effective parent groups or community support groups, as do the parents of learning disabled and developmentally delayed students arguing for their children's rights. The only real advocates for emotionally disturbed students have been professional groups and individual educators. Schools are struggling with reduced public funds and parental pressure for better academic results, and administrators are not fighting with each other to win the honor of having more emotionally disturbed students in their buildings. Is it possible that some school systems are supporting the Inclusion Movement not because of a "common vision" but because they believe an integrated program will cost less to fund than the current dual program? If Inclusion fails for emotionally disturbed students, one does not have to feel guilty about it, since it was a good idea that did not work out.

5. A CONCERN ABOUT THE CONFLICTING GOALS OF HAVING SAFER VIOLENCE-FREE SCHOOLS AND INCLUDING MORE EMOTIONALLY DISTURBED STUDENTS IN THE REGULAR CLASSROOM

Stemming the tide of school disorder and violence is a national concern that has attracted the attention of the media, and most national and state educational organizations. Numerous conferences have been held on preventing violence and creating safer school environments, and numerous new conferences on this topic are being planned. Simultaneously, parent groups are demanding that the public schools be less tolerant toward deviant behavior. No one disagrees with the argument that teachers need to protect their students from aggressive peer threats and acts. However, the Inclusion Movement will place more emotionally disturbed students in the regular classroom. With these students will come their growing legal rights. For example, emotionally disturbed students cannot be expelled because of their disability. This means an aggressive student cannot be expelled because he behaves aggressively in the classroom. Also, some parents insist that their troubled children and youth cannot be sent to "Time Out Rooms" or be restrained physically, regardless of their behavior. Even when a student's behavior is too dangerous for his peers, staff, and program, the school has the responsibility to prove that the student's behavior could not have been handled in a more constructive way. When these cases came to court, the civil rights of the individual usually were supported; and the schools lost the cases. Sometime soon, these two different school goals will collide. The rights of an individual student and the rights of a school to protect other students may become a central issue for the Inclusion Movement.

PLACEMENT CRITERIA FOR EMOTIONALLY DISTURBED STUDENTS: AN OPPORTUNITY FOR NEW ACCEPTANCE

If the following five conditions are guaranteed, I will applaud the Inclusion Movement. These five criteria will ensure that troubled students have a level playing field and have an opportunity to be successful in their classrooms. Eliminate any one of these five conditions, and a high rate of failure is predicted. These conditions are:

1. The school staff must meet and agree to participate in the Inclusion Movement. This means a willingness to participate in any ongoing training in this area.

2. An emotionally disturbed student should not be administratively assigned to a classroom teacher. A mutual process should take place to find the best fit between the teacher and the students. The receiving classroom teacher also must be willing to serve as this student's advocate.

3. The support staff, including the principal, must agree to participate in advanced crisis-intervention training in order to have the skills to support the classroom teacher and the student during times of conflict.

4. The classroom group must be open to accepting new students, or at least not scapegoat or reject them.

5. The emotionally disturbed student must function no more than two years below the academic norm of the classroom, be motivated to keep up with the daily academic assignments, use the support staff, and make a personal commitment to this placement.

There are no easy, inexpensive solutions to the complex problem of re-educating emotionally disturbed students. Inclusion can work for some emotionally disturbed students, but I cannot support the concept of full inclusion. The public school cannot be all things to all students. There are some students whose social-emotional and academic needs far exceed the resources and the talents of a public school. Any attempt to force them into a predetermined setting would be a violation of their civil rights. A full continuum of services for these seriously disturbed students needs to be maintained. Anything less would be irresponsible, another example of professional exploitation of emotionally disturbed students and a formula for failure.

REFERENCES

Fagen, Stanley A. (1986). Least intensive intervention for classroom behavior problems. *The Pointer, 31*(1).

Gorman, T., & Rose, R. (1994). Inclusion: Taking a stand. *American Teacher, 78*(1).

Kauffman, James, M. (1993). How we might achieve radical reform of special education. *Exceptional Children, 60*(1).

Silberman, Charles E. (1970). *Crisis in the classroom: The remaking of American education.* NY: Vintage Books Ed., Random House.

. . . .

Whether favored or opposed, inclusion of troubled students is likely to increase. The safeguards Long proposes will be ignored unless teachers bring them into focus. To the degree that inclusion takes place, the special teacher role will change with it. Special classes, dayschools, and institutional schools are already on the decrease. All teachers will be expected to become competent in ways of helping troubled students. More low-cost aids will be employed. Those who are most highly trained will serve more as consultants on curriculum and management than as direct service providers. Being a peer consultant will become essential, but consulting to and training peers is a much different role than direct service to a needy child. The direct use of skills and the personal gratification of helping a special child will be less present. Crisis management will be expected to support regular classrooms. There already are co-teaching arrangements—another possible role change for special reachers. How does a teacher make the regular classroom not only compatible for troubled children but healing as well? That will become the teacher's challenge. Troubled children will still be in the school population in growing numbers, and, after trying various substitutes, the most seriously troubled will need some time in special programs.

This chapter on generic aspects of helping troubled children began with Redl's elements of a therapeutic milieu and now moves to Van Bockern's description of a reclaiming school milieu. It is clear that both authors are concerned with the climate created by particular settings. *The Model Re-Ed Classroom* (page 471) could be considered another example.

Van Bockern brings teaching experience, school administrative experience, and technical expertise to his topic. He is currently on the faculty of Augustana College. A new type of relationship between adult and student is proposed in Van Bockern's paper. It is important to note that making a school "reclaiming" does not require vast new monies. But what it does require is in equally short supply: acceptance of new ideologies and arrangements. How many of the characteristics of the reclaiming school exist now in your setting?

Schools are powerful cultures that transmit core values to the young. Wozner (1985) suggests that educational environments can be classified as either "reclaiming" or "nonreclaiming." Reclaiming schools are organized to meet the needs of both the young person and society. Nonreclaiming schools operate only to perpetuate the system. The distinction is whether one is teaching students or tending school.

Profiles of Reclaiming Schools

Steve Van Bockern

In the hands of a competent and caring staff, schools inspire and challenge students to discover wonders and great possibilities. In "careless" hands, schools become destructive. Sequenced, fragmented, contrived curricula delivered by a teacher who mimics a gumball machine can bore and disenfranchise a child. Such schools swallow students in a sea of purple ink and black-lined worksheets.

What do reclaiming schools look like? The reclaiming school must empower each student to experience belonging, mastery, independence, and generosity (Brendtro, Brokenleg, & Van Bockern, 1990). There is no single mold for such a school, but reclaiming schools challenge any practice that leads to alienation, futility, impotence, or purposelessness among youth. In the following discussion, we spotlight innovative programs of empowering education that redefine the standards for excellence in the reclaiming school.

CELEBRATING OUR SCHOOL COMMUNITIES

It is easy to recognize schools that know the importance of making students feel at home and that invite student success. The hidden curriculum makes itself known when you see teachers greet the students by name at the school or classroom doors. Bulletin boards honoring students of the week can be found. Welcome bags containing paper and pencils, coupons, candy, and other items from community businesses are given to the students. Degrading and demeaning freshman initiation rituals do not exist. The building is clean, attractive, and well lit. Often, in these belonging schools, desks are in circles. Teachers talk about student success stories in the teacher's lounge.

Many of our schools have lost a sense of meaningful ritual. The pledge, school song, homecoming, and other events simply fill up the day, serve as entertainment, or are vestiges of a forgotten tradition. This is not the case at an alternative school in Rapid City, South Dakota. They have "attachment and detachment rituals." Passed from foster home to foster home, school to school, and community to community, the students have had few chances to build any meaningful attachments. The staff understands what

From *The Journal of Emotional and Behavioral Problems*. (1993). Vol. 1, No. 4. Reprinted with permission.

it means for the students to be treated like a ping-pong ball. Consequently, students are encouraged to carve their initials into a log placed at the entrance of the building. When students leave the school, candles are lit, stories of praise are told and songs are sung to signify that the student affected everyone's life in some way.

A major hurdle in the reclaiming process is to help the child build a new kind of relationship with an adult who can be trusted for support, guidance, and affection. Research by Gary Wehlage (1989) and colleagues demonstrated that effective schools for at-risk youth have markedly different teacher-student relationships than conventional schools. In successful programs, teachers assume the roles of counselor, confidante, and friend, strengthening the attachment of students to the school, to teaching staff, and to peers. This social bonding is associated with increases in academic concept, responsibility, and achievement.

The emphasis on fostering attachments is also prominent in the middle school movement. Typically, schedules are designed so that frequent and sustained contact between students and teachers is possible. Maeroff (1990) describes one such program where a small team of four to five adults, including teachers, administrators, and counselors, serve 45 students. Each adult meets twice daily with a smaller advisory group of 8 to 10 students. In another middle school, teachers greet their students as the buses arrive. Bells are eliminated, team-teaching is used, award assemblies are held, and F's have been changed to U's (Raebuck, 1990).

At the Jefferson County High School in Louisville, Kentucky, success with at-risk youth is a result of flexible schedules (school is open from 8:00 A.M. to 9:30 P.M., 12 months a year), promise of success, treating students with respect, and awarding a regular high school diploma. The director of this alternative school, Buell Snyder, says, "I hire only teachers who agree to treat students with respect at all times and I discard those who, despite their good intentions, infantilize or ridicule students" (Gross, 1990).

Teachers in North American schools have traditionally been attached to grade levels or subjects, not to cohorts of students. In contrast, Norwegian elementary school teachers often progress through the grades, remaining with one group of students for several years. In like manner, Holweide, a comprehensive secondary school in Cologne, Germany, assigns teachers in teams of six or eight to follow the same 120 students over the course of six years. In this structure, the beginning and year-end rituals are eliminated, freeing more time for instruction. These teachers come to know their students in ways that tests can never approach (Shanker, 1990).

Some schools add a child's autobiography to the cumulative records. The autobiography is reworked each year as students write about their hobbies, relationships, work and interests. These schools understand that it is difficult to know a child only through numbers and "objective" reports from adults. When a teacher knows a child's story, the teacher understands. Understanding is the beginning of a meaningful relationship. The Cities in

Schools program (ASCD, 1991) acknowledges this premise. Now found in 50 cities, including Atlanta, Houston, and New York, the ultimate goal of CIS is to get caring adults in positive relationships with young people. Their adage is that programs don't turn people around; relationships do.

THE CONNECTING AND CAPTIVATING CURRICULUM

Teaching and learning too often center on competition instead of cooperation. Even in physical education classes, countless teachers eliminate students from practicing and developing skills. Novice ball-dribblers and rope-skippers, those that need the practice the most, often are the first to sit down when the teacher is bent on finding the "best." Terry Orlick, in his *Cooperative Sports and Games Book* (1982), points out the "King of the Mountain" type games that permeate our schools keep all but one from achieving. Competition can create unnecessary stress, destructive behavior, and depression. When the outcome in competition is made to seem important, young people will cheat, hurt, and deceive to get to the top.

Increasingly, the sterile, traditional curriculum is being challenged by innovations in experiential education. In Shoreham-Wading River Middle School on Long Island, seventh-grade students spend as much as four weeks at seashore or mountainside locations. Other students spend part of the year working on a farm, conducting experiments in a greenhouse, and running a school store (Maeroff, 1990).

In Grand Rapids, Michigan, the Environmental Education Program operates alternative schools at a nature center and a zoo. Activities include nature studies, winter camping, entrepreneurship on a small farm, and operating a computer lab to carry out experiments. Extensive use is made of community resource persons, including astronomers, ornithologists, Native American artisans, and parents with unique skills (Young, 1990).

The Illinois River Project (Williams, 1992) has as its ultimate goal scientific literacy. To achieve that end, the project actively engages students in meaningful and authentic work. Students from more than 150 schools in six states analyze water samples from various test sites along rivers. The study also includes the historical, social, and economic implications of the status of these rivers. Integration of curriculum is key; students from science, social studies, and English classes are involved. The traditional 50-minute class periods, unrelated and uneventful, lose significance in the river schools. A telecommunications network links all of the participating schools with each other and the Project headquarters. The students contribute to a publication called *Meanderings* and the Project newsletter, *River Watcher's Log.* The project holds a Student Congress meeting each year. Ideas and experiences are shared. Topics range from the scientific to the historic to the creative, including original "river music" and puppet shows. Through a National Science Foundation grant, a River Curriculum in the areas of chemistry, biology, geology, geography, and language arts has been developed that can be applied to any river in the world.

There are other science and math curricula, such as Activities in Math and Science (AIMS), Project Wild, and Math Your Way, that get students actively involved in meaningful learning without leaving the school. For example, in one AIMS activity small groups of elementary students compare the mass of a banana peel with the part that is eaten. Students measure, chart, and report, confirming that we eat only about 70% of a banana. In Math Your Way, students count, add, and subtract real objects before they ever put pencil to paper.

Just as unconnected curricula are outdated, so, too, are the teacher-dominated instructional techniques of lecture and recitation. The whole-language movement recognized the value of an integrated curriculum that immerses students in story and social exchange of ideas. Now, more teachers are using the techniques of story telling and true discussion, which have served to transmit culture since the beginning of humanity. Educators are rediscovering the lost art of using story and metaphor as a medium for higher-order learning (Barton & Booth, 1990). True discussion, unlike recitation, engages the mind in a process of active learning.

The curricula designed for gifted students has much to offer those who work with regular and at-risk students. George Betts (1985) developed a model of learning for gifted and talented students that could serve as the foundation for all children's education. Student responsibility, skill development, and active learning are the cornerstones of the model. Students learn about themselves by writing biographical sketches, role-playing the part of an important person, and interviewing adults about their jobs. Students are taught problem-solving and organizational skills, photography, computer use, study, and goal-setting. They learn about appropriate behavior, creative lifestyles, and the psychology of a healthy person. Time is spent learning interpersonal skills. Each student develops and studies what Betts calls the "passion content," that which the student is motivated to devour. Students attend cultural activities, museums, plays, concerts, speeches, and debates. There is a service and adventure component in the model. As students gain skills and understand themselves and their interests, they form small groups to select and research a suitable topic. They are given time to prepare a seminar and then present the seminar to members of the community.

One early intervention program called Success for All (ASCD, 1991) accelerates learning instead of focusing on remediation. Remediation often is slow and repetitious, and it only increases the likelihood that students will fall further behind their peers. The Higher Order Thinking Program is designed to teach thinking skills to remedial students. The program affirms that even remedial students need the opportunity to go beyond memorization. In one computer simulation, students land a hot air balloon on a designated spot by manipulating such variables as altitude and wind speed. By doing so, they learn to identify patterns and develop thoughtful strategies.

EMPOWERING RESPONSIBILITY

Service learning can give meaning to the lives of children. Evidence suggests that when youth are involved with helping, positive results happen. Diane Hedin (1989) summarizes various research that supports the positive results of volunteer service, including increased responsibility, self-esteem, moral development, and commitment to democratic values. In addition, she cites a series of findings that identity intellectual gains that accrue from helping others.

Maryland has become the first state to incorporate volunteerism as part of the curriculum. It has produced curricula for high schools, special education, and middle schools. Maryland has defined student service as "actions of caring for others through personal contact, indirect service, or civic action, either in the school or in the community, with preparation and reflection." Stories of success already can be found. Students at Suitland High School in Prince George's County were 87.5% successful in reducing suspensions due to absences and tardiness. Students in Howard County proposed and got passed a bicycle helmet law. The student government organization in Baltimore City opened and runs a food pantry in a poor neighborhood. Allegany County students produced and distributed a booklet dealing with child abuse.

Integrating service learning into the curriculum can happen at three levels. First, it can be extracurricular volunteer work. Students do not receive credit nor are they given time in school to participate. All over the country in alternative and some traditional settings, examples of extracurricular service learning can be found. At Chadwick School in Los Angeles, privileged students run a soup kitchen, help the mentally ill put on plays, work with disturbed children, and campaign for environmental protection. At Rice High School in New York, students work with the sick and needy. In Connecticut, students serve as the professional rescue squad for a semi-rural area. In all of these programs, young people's abilities to participate and help are valued (Lewis, 1990).

On another level, a unit is offered in a regular class that complements the traditional content. In a home economics class, students might sew clothes for the homeless, or an English class might publish a newsletter for the local neighborhood watch organization. Teachers may assign independent study outside of class, as was done by two high school teachers in Sioux Falls, South Dakota. Susan Lee and Carla Middlen assigned 81 students in their American studies classes to do volunteer work, with the hope that they would learn the value of giving. The assignment came after the students read Ralph Waldo Emerson's essay, "Gift's," which says a gift must be necessary, chosen especially for an individual, and given from the heart. The students were asked to put the words into action. Some worked at the food pantry, others went caroling at nursing homes. One group volunteered to help the Children's Inn, a shelter for abused women and children, move into its new building. Some offered time to the Humane Society, while tour students spent hours at the zoo feeding penguins or cleaning out the buffalo pens.

When asked why more students weren't involved in volunteer projects, Lee said, "I don't think they have been asked."

Elective or mandatory volunteer courses may be offered, often in a social studies class. The class is provided information and skills to assist students. Blocks of time are structured into the school day for two to four days each week so that students can work on site. For six to eight weeks in Shoreham Wading River, students spend a double period twice a week in some community service activity. For example, students may work with elderly or handicapped individuals (Maeroff, 1990). Students in Petaluma, California, worked hard to clean up the endangered Adobe Creek. Twenty truckloads of junk were hauled out, including washing machines, sofas, two beds, and 36 old tires. Willow trees were planted. Now the group is trying to raise $200,000 for a fish hatchery. At least 25 of the students in this program who graduated went on to study natural resources and wildlife at Humboldt State University in northern California. Three others are majoring in environmental law at other schools (Sims, 1990).

Another kind of service can be found in such programs as the Peer Assistance Leadership Program (PALS), a joint project of the Orange County Department of Education and Orange County Drug Abuse Services in California. Students help students change their attitudes about drug use. Supported by business and community agencies, schools in this county live the African proverb, "It takes a village to raise a child." Students, as natural helpers, reach other students with the message that "it is OK to be drug free." School has become the primary setting for many students to learn about social relationships and responsibilities. During leadership summer camps, elementary students attend such workshops as "Make Your School a Safe Place," "Being Responsible," or "Listening Skills."

Responsible independence is not just a goal for adolescents. Those who work with even the youngest children can be encouraged by Robert Fulghum (1988), who suggests that wisdom is not to be found at the top of the graduate school mountain but in the sandbox at nursery school. In early childhood education, there is recognition that young children need to be trusted to make sensible decisions concerning not only themselves but also others. For Joanne Hendrick (1992), trusting children translates into transferring power to them whenever possible. She suggests giving children the power to choose, to try, and to do. When we wait patiently for a two-year-old to pour his own milk or for a three-year-old to struggle into her coat or we allow a six-year-old to take a message to the office, we are building reclaim.

REFERENCES

Association for Supervision and Curriculum Development. (1991). *Curriculum update.* Alexandria, VA: ASCD.

Barton, B., & Booth, D. (1990). *Stories in the classroom.* Portsmouth, NH: Heinemann Educational Books.

Betts, G. (1985). *Autonomous learner model: For the gifted and talented.* Greeley, CO: Autonomous Learning Publications.

Brendtro, L., Brokenleg, M., & Van Bockern, S. (1990). *Reclaiming youth at risk: Our hope for the future.* Indianapolis, IN: National Educational Service.

Fulghum, R. (1988). *All I really needed to know I learned in kindergarten.* New York: Villard.

Gross, B. (1990). Here dropouts drop in—And stay! *Phi Delta Kappan, 71*(8), 625–627.

Hedin, D. (1989). The power of community service. *Proceedings of the Academy of Political Science, 31*(2), 201–213.

Hendrick, J. (1992). Where does it all begin? Teaching the principles of democracy in the early years. *Young Children, 47*(3), 51–53.

Lewis, A. (1990). In valuing young people. *Phi Delta Kappan, 71*(6), 420–421.

Maeroff, G. (1990). Getting to know a good middle school: Shoreham-Wading River. *Phi Delta Kappan, 71*(7), 5.

Orlick, T. (1982). *Cooperative sports and games book.* New York: Pantheon.

Raebuck, B. (1990). Transformation of a middle school. *Educational Leadership, 47*(7), 18–21.

Shanker, (1990). The end of the traditional model of schooling and a proposal for using incentives to restructure our public schools. *Phi Delta Kappan, 71*(5), 345.

Sims, C. (1990). Teens mop up. *Outdoors, 5*(2), 23–24.

Thomas, M., Sabatino, D., & Sarri, R. (1982). *Alternative programs for disruptive youth.* Reston, VA: The Council for Exceptional Children.

Wehlage, G., Rutter, R., Smith, G., Lesko, N., & Fernandez, R. (1989). *Reducing the risk: Schools as communities of support.* London: Falmer Press.

Williams, R. (1992). *The rivers curriculum: The Illinois river project.* Edwardsville. IL: Southern Illinois University.

Wozner, Y. (1985). Institution as community. *Child and Youth Services, 7,* 71–90.

Young, T. (1990). *Public alternative education: Options and choices for today's schools.* New York: Columbia University Teacher College.

. . . .

The needs of most troubled children extend beyond even the most gifted teacher and hygienically planned classroom. As new insights and new patterns for helping special children become accepted, the role of the teacher changes. Ideologically, teaching still implies a direct, hands-on interaction with a small group of students. But the future format of both regular and special education may bring drastic alterations.

A major change advocated in education for troubled students is a more active collaboration between special education teachers and mental health personnel (evidence of the growing recognition that education is a community affair). A major strategy of helping has become collaborative problem solving in which our children and their families, school teams, and community service teams all share. Traditionally, teaching has been an activity of a solitary teacher laboring in an isolated room. Now, teachers and mental health workers will have to learn new skills for collaboration.

Collaboration is logical and looks easy until one tries to make it work. Theory and reality are different worlds.

The nature of the education–mental health collaboration is presented in depth in the following paper by Morse. We must make collaboration effective. This paper offers some ways this can be accomplished.

ARTICLE 2.10

Mental Health Professionals and Teachers: How Do the Twain Meet?

William C. Morse

EDUCATION–MENTAL HEALTH INTERPLAY, PAST AND PRESENT

The need for mental health-education liaison is not just a recent concern. Ekstein and Motto (1969) report that the history of such collaboration begins with teachers and analysts in the 1920s. A few teachers, Fritz Redl being our prime example, were provided a personal analyst. Their subsequent synthesis of the two fields made them the first educational therapists. A small group of teachers and analysts became committed to collaboration based on mutual respect, with each open to learning from the other since both disciplines utilized learning by repetition, by insight and identification. Prevention was an underlying goal. The early analysts respected the difficulties of teaching, even suggesting education was the impossible profession, more difficult than psychoanalysis. Sarason (1985) makes a strong case for including teaching in the clinical professions, saying that, after parents, teachers have the prime contact with children. He says that we expect more from teachers than any other professional and subject them to considerable unrealistic, inadequate and ultimately disillusioning training. So what is old is also new.

We have yet to resolve how the twain shall meet. The matter has become increasingly complex. We are especially interested in teachers of the behaviorally disordered, but there are other specialists, the regular class teachers and the school milieu to consider as well. Teachers may work in a wide variety of public or private settings. In addition, there are several mental health disciplines and each may reside in the school, community mental health or private practice.

But why the present intensification of concern about this relationship? It may stem from the state of recent studies from both education and mental health advocates which suggest that Behavior Disorders is the least

From *Beyond Behavior*. (1992). Vol. 3, No. 2. Reprinted with permission.

effective area of special education. Parenthetically, there is not similar scrutiny of possible limitations in child mental health programs, perhaps because mental health is under no legal mandate to provide service for all children. The major papers on school collaboration focus mainly on the lack of and the need for symbiotic education-mental health collaboration. Students with behavioral disorders have access to mental health services in less than half of the educational programs serving such students, a percentage similar to the situation for the 6 to 8 million other children in the country who need such care. When mental health service is provided, little is known of the intensity or quality of such services. We are dealing with disturbed youngsters and yet our monitor, the Individualized Educational Program (IEP), often ignores pupils' emotional needs.

The National Needs Analysis in Behavioral Disorders (Grosenick et al., 1987) found a lack of mental health services among the program inadequacies commonly found in such programs. Forness (1989), in the mental health-special education coalition report, recommended increased liaison between such fields, a recommendation which found its way into P. L. 101-476. The law now makes social work related services generic (no longer prefixed by school), and provides grants to enhance education-mental health integration. While many current critics of BD special education see the better program solution in education and mental health collaboration, we best look beyond this shot gun marriage to the concept of an array of all service agencies from the various sources in working collaboratively on the school campus. It becomes clear that our goal must go beyond education-mental health to family centered, total community agency collaboration in the Full Service School if we hope to succeed with BD pupils.

No one denies that many education programs for BD youngsters are inadequate in various ways. We do have many successes and there are "points of light" but the drop out rate and concomitant employment histories as well as the quality of young adult lives depicts a shortfall. Whether the addition of mental health magic to special education magic will provide the solution remains to be seen. Interagency cooperation includes both formal agencies and natural support systems under the guidance of a case advocate. While the education-mental health combination is being emphasized, what is required is an integrated community service for these children, monitored by a case manager-advocate. Collaboration with law enforcement, health, social service, and recreation agencies or religious groups may be, in particular cases, more crucial than mental health services. Or the first need may be to generate new community services or augment particular services.

To accomplish community integration, a personally individualized service must replace categorical agency service. It reminds one of what we hoped for with the IEP! As a practical matter, children's mental health services have always been in short supply and are currently in stringent retrenchment.

That increased education and mental health cooperation will benefit our children is not a question, but there are several conditions ignored in the vision of a quick fix by liaison. First, regardless of professional input, it is extremely difficult to change the life course of many of our children with their multitudinous and severe problems. Fatigue rates in child helping professions, especially teaching, attest to the stress. The second obstacle is that both disciplines remain by and large still tied to notions of education and therapy not tailored to BD school programming. We are all in a common business of child upbringing regardless of labels and roles. Neither education nor mental health has adequately reconceptualized the generic aspects of helping let alone applied such concepts to programs for individual youngsters. There is still a great deal of yesterday's business as usual.

The third condition which limits effectiveness is the belated and limited recognition of the power of ecological factors as determinants in children's lives. The difficulty of altering negative ecological factors in communities, families or schools results in undue concentration on child change since the child is the only part of the total ecology easily available. There are ecological tactics which might be employed (Hobbs, 1982; Morse, 1991; Munger, 1991). Our "restorative oasis" programs still face the problem of sending the youngster back to the desert where he or she failed because of inability to cope.

Given the difficulties of the task and scarcity of resources, special teachers and mental health workers have a right to be proud of their considerable success. When things work out, we can expect to find at the center a very competent and dedicated teacher with creative mental health support. Very few disagree that improved collaboration with mental health will increase effectiveness, but it is fantasy to expect collaboration by itself will solve our many problems, especially if both parties are glued to traditional practice.

Pfeiffer (1982) has studied the value of collaborative team decision making. He points out that interdisciplinary evaluation and placement procedures are mandated in special education and his findings indicate that team decisions are less variant and more accurate than individual decisions, although it is difficult to understand the accuracy criterion. While many advocate team work, Pfeiffer (1980) does list several experts who see teams as increasing confusion, duplication, cost, territorial problems and ambiguous decisions. Stone (1988) holds that we cling to teams when all the necessary skills and experience may be possessed by a single member. After the reductionist operation of dividing the child into segments, meeting time is required to reconstruct the total child, if indeed that can be accomplished. Group decisions can also serve to diffuse responsibility. While the decisions are made jointly, execution is often left to a single member, usually the teacher.

Who actually collaborates in the most critical meeting of all for the special child, the needs at which the individualized education program is designed? Cruickshank, Morse, and Grant (1990) examined this team composition in over 600 such meetings. Mandated are a parent, a person from the diagnostic team, an administrator, and a teacher of the child. A parent attended 95% of the time. The average number of professionals attending was five, with two as the low and occasionally over seven the high. School mental health professionals attended 93% of the meetings (School Psychologist 93%, School Social Worker 47%, and School Counselor 18%), a special teacher 72%, and a regular teacher 30%. Non-school mental health personnel were not indicated. The school psychologist's diagnostic data generally carries considerable influence in these meetings.

It would be comforting if there were a simple answer to the enigma of how the twain shall meet—meet, that is, "to the maximum benefit for BD pupils." The fact is, almost every collaborative design works sometimes and almost every design fails sometimes. There are non-overt variables which enter in. We still dream of finding *the model* solution. While examples help, one still must work out how a given individual collaborative functions or malfunctions. To become informed participants in this cooperative team process, the areas to explore range from contracts to group dynamics.

Not parenthetically, mental health is a related service for BD pupils. Special education has the legal mandate to supply the services contained in the IEP contract. Mental health involvement is often left out because, as I was told again the other day by a social worker, it is often not politically wise to include this need. If included and yet not provided by an outside service, the IEP committee is to be reconvened to discover alternative means to provide the service. The right to psychotherapy or counseling for our clientele has not been adequately clarified by the courts. The result is wide variation from district to district. Osborn (1984) holds that the only BD related services expressly excluded are medical: social work and psychological counseling are clearly options, and psychotherapy when states permit the practice by disciplines other than the medical. But such mental health intervention can be required only if it is necessary in the effort to educate, a perplexing situation with considerable room for indiscretion. While both education and community mental health are public tax grant agencies, there is no universal right to mental health as there is to special education. With the rapid privatization of mental health, schools may have to contract with insurance agencies. How mental health participation can be considered ancillary for our clientele is a mystery.

COLLABORATION BY CONTRACT

As indicated above, there is a strong belief that liaison with mental health is the *sine qua non* for BD program improvement. This leads us to both interprofessional agreements and interagency contracts. There is the "one roof illusion" that when both professionals are under one budget or one administrator, there will be automatic collaboration. Unfortunately, this is often not the case under either mental health controlled with education ancillary or education controlled with mental health the foreign body. When budgets tighten, whichever agency is in charge tries to expurgate responsibility for the other. The first order is for intra-agency professional understandings. In mental health agencies the subspecialities may have trouble collaborating and in schools there can be conflicts between administrators, regular teachers, special teachers and school mental health workers. In-house agreements clarifying exchange of services and responsibilities precede interagency contracts. For example, where does the teacher get help in a crisis?

Each contract between mental health and education is unique. Some are brief memoranda of understanding while others are legal documents. I know of one over two years still in the making, now approaching book size. Perhaps this is a clue to the reluctance of one or both parties to integrate services. The old battles over turf have been replaced by strategies to avoid responsibility. Skrtic (1991) provides understanding as to why many interagency contracts end up impotent. By and large these are bureaucratic instruments, labored over pieces of paper. Both education and mental health are what he terms "machine bureaucracies" where technocrats rationalize and formalize rules and do task analysis—the 200 skills which make a BD teacher for example. Division of labor is central, dispersing ownership, prescribing specific worker task, and thus avoiding total responsibility. Contracts may come laden with red tape accountability forms to keep everyone honest. Interagency contracts negotiated in bureaucratic havens of national, state or county offices are usually brought about by external edict. In place of the past expanding turf efforts, now, to meet budget cuts, agencies try to avoid involvement as they are forced unwillingly to the bargaining table.

Skrtic holds that special education is not simple work and does not fit the mass production reductionist task analysis paradigm which dominates our contract agencies. Because of the complexity and individualistic nature of special education, what is required is not piece work but active problem solving by coupled service-providing workers. It is not the contract but how team members work together that becomes the focus. Such collaboration is required under P. L. 99-457 where intervention is organized around a lead agency and where a family plan replaces the IEP.

Interagency contracts are necessary for permission to collaborate. There are several patterns including merged budgets, and merged administration. Sometimes mental health and education contribute funds or stipulate personnel time to a new separate entity. Then, who has ultimate authority over the various personnel becomes critical: too many bosses can be an accerbation. In the long run budget control equals power.

What does this analysis suggest concerning effective contracts? We have learned that a good contract is only point zero and should not be taken as an actual cooperative program. A contract is permissive legislation. The test is the collaborative synergy at the work station level. The best way to insure either intra- or inter-professional cooperation is to give the personnel who are to be responsible for the delivery of integrated services a dominant role in contract development. Work from the bottom up rather than from the top down. We note too that there is not equality in the bargaining between mental health and education agencies. Special educators are in weaker position since there is no legal requirement for mental health to provide services. For special teachers, this may mean "Don't include in the IEP services not available in schools, lest, the school will have to pay." In spite of difficulties, many contracts do work out and enhance the programs for BD children. Failures can usually be traced to money, power disagreement, lack of clarity on responsibilities or interpersonal dissonance on the line. It would be interesting to give each BD teacher a time or money budget to purchase those mental health services on an open market which the teacher deemed most needed by the students.

RITUALS AND RITUALISM WHEN THE TWAIN MEET

We have the contract: Now how do the two professionals actually function in collaboration efforts? The answer requires attention to the nature of professionalism. Just as agencies follow the idiom of machine bureaucracies, so do professions. Both school mental health and special education are derived subspecialties and inherit much of their training and liturgy from very strong and different parent disciplines. As Erikson informed us, rituals are necessary to organize behavior lest every act become a complicated new decision. The danger comes when rituals ossify into ritualism so encapsulating that it stymies flexibility. Becoming a professional means becoming socialized into a given liturgy, part explicitly taught and part unconsciously absorbed. When rituals are diverse, team dissonance can result and team meetings become contests of these beliefs rather than problem solving. To work above these habits of thought requires training. Mental health workers usually get training only in working with other clinicians, while special educators are seldom trained in interdisciplinary work.

The pecking hierarchy between and within professions can produce contention. Like Orwell's animals, some are more equal than others. Professional prestige is an illusive phenomenon. One of our colleagues, seeking to elevate teacher status in a psychiatric setting, arranged for teachers to have white coat training and supervision in psychotherapy. While teachers at first anticipated the one-to-one engagement, many found they missed the group activity and did not prefer the "higher" calling. Paraprofessionals tell me how powerless they feel and we know they may sometimes be as effective as the certified personnel. Psychology and psychiatry are engaged in a nation-wide battle over prerogatives. In general, the time spent directly interacting with children is in reverse order of the amount of training required and pay scale. School mental health workers and school special teachers often suffer rejection from their parental disciplines. Thus the team dance is choreographed to some extent by prestige factors and defensive ritualism.

Sometimes our two professions forget their common cause because of role differences even though the professional codes of practice are quite similar. Both are anxious to do everything possible to rehabilitate the disturbed child. But they have been socialized into different professions, see the same youngster differently, have different concepts of helping and have different roles. Not only are there two disciplines but the fact is that each discipline within itself is not unitary in psychological orientation. The diversification of practice and ideology within a profession has become so great that stereotyping differences is misleading: Within-profession variation may be greater than between-profession variation when it comes to interventions. For example, educators generally put a high priority on external control of behavior while mental health personnel are more attentive to internal states. But in one instance the out-of-school mental health collaborators became so possessed with the need for external control that they violated pupil and parent rights. The contract was canceled in an acrimonious divorce. It is not an abstract matter of mental health and education collaboration: It is what brand of each profession is to collaborate. We must study the attitudes of the members of each specific team.

To appreciate what could go on in good and poor teaming it is helpful to examine general differences in professional socialization. When mental health workers leave the interview for the milieu (and especially the educational milieu), they experience a new set of demands often at odds with their training. The same is true of BD teachers who find themselves at odds with the dominating educational ethos of their school. What follows is, as they say, a story. It is a stereotype of professional dissimilarities and as such does not fit well. But it can serve as a check list to apply to local situations. Mental health professions have *clients* while teachers have *pupils*. In truth, both have *children*. Teachers focus on control and academic achievement by necessity. Traditionally, mental health emphasis has been concerned with the affective domain and inner control. Educators are mandated to take all comers, while mental health implies client initiation. Of course with children client initiation is not the case, it is coerced therapy vs. consensual. Both therapy in school and special education are coercive. Children can only "object" by being mute or acting out: Parents can directly refuse help or become no shows. The implications of coercion for school mental heath have largely been ignored. While both the classroom and the clinic are nonchoice, professionals often operate on the basis that the children should want my services and beyond their defenses really do. Thus neither discipline does well with the fundamentally alienated youngster.

Usually teachers are group workers regardless of the individualized IEP. They serve many roles in a day while mental health workers are usually single role and one-to-one. Generic education is designed to serve so-called "normals" in large, prepackaged, age level groups in public view. Mental health attends to the atypical who is having trouble meeting normal expectations, with provisions of confidentially. Teachers spend long, consecutive hours with numbers of children. Mental health interacts episodically, usually on a single case basis. This contract makes for a significant difference in orientation, with BD teachers caught in the middle. Schools expect change on the basis of punishment and simple praise which produces complex systems of positive and negative contingencies. Teachers must remain on the line unless a substitute is provided, and thus are not free until the bus leaves. Criteria for progress may differ, teachers watching academics and manifest behavior and mental health workers watching for increased self-esteem and general coping capacity. BD teachers are more professionally isolated than the typical mental health person who uses cross-discipline consultation. These statements contrasting the two disciplines are true and untrue and serve only as points to consider in a specific team operation and as an aid for reflection on one's individual professional heritage. Better yet, one can compile a list of the differences between external and in-school mental health work, between BD teaching and other special education and regular teaching, and use these lists for sophisticated comparisons.

There is a sidebar to all of this. Youngsters often do not respect the assigned roles. They may not be moved at "interview" hour. Because of our definitions of therapy, the fact that the classroom can be a therapeutic place is often ignored. In helping distraught children there is really no division of labor. A mental health person may function more effectively in the classroom milieu, especially with young children. After being trained atomistically, the most effective professional may be those who cross over the lines of staid roles (Nichols, 1984). There are joint efforts in group counseling where both disciplines join together (Anderson & Marrone, 1977). Unfortunately "group" is too often institutionalized, becoming a mini course with a set time and agenda. Thus schoolized it has all the problems of the traditional curriculum.

There are signs of change in both professions which would make liaison more sibling-like, rather than of distant cousins. Mental health workers in schools are increasingly concerned with early intervention. Screening for vulnerability and preventive intervention (Hughs & Hurth, 1984) replaces preoccupation with certification for special education services. Mental health personnel are training themselves for crisis intervention. Test kits are matched with observation, interviews and curriculum based assessment. Parent education and support groups supplement parent therapy. New styles of cooperative consultation (Friend & Cook, 1992) and active consultation (Newman, 1991) are making inroads on didactic interactions. Developmental considerations are countering method-driven intervention. Even old style social work reaching out in the community and homes has seen some return.

Cognitive skill learning is being advocated, especially for the value deficient kids. Finding figures for identification in the community is recognized as essential. The mental health journals are as replete with "break out" articles as are journals in special education, so both professions are changing.

Generally speaking, special education for BD children seems to have a harder time moving from traditional academics and control to new patterns. But there is change here, too. I was once informed that teachers could do therapeutic things but never therapy. I have never figured this out, except to understand that "therapy" reflects a definitional guild matter and rights of practice. Woods (1986) strains to clarify the boundary between psychotherapy and therapeutic teaching, the teacher being tuned to the ego level and not to the unconscious, presuming the layers are discrete. Nichols (1984) has shown the limitations of this view. The role of educational therapist has been developed by Ungerlighter (1991) and Sapir (1985) to clarify the training and practice of a different BD teaching role. The Educateur is a different model, especially as practiced in parts of Canada (Hobbs, 1982; Linton, 1973; and Mitchell & Nicolaou, 1984). Nickerson and O'Laughlin (1982) show how teachers contribute through action oriented therapies in the curriculum. When Rhodes' pupil empowerment curriculum becomes available we will have another example of the merger of education and therapy. In short, both BD education and school mental health work show the potential for melting artificial boundaries. When we think of liaison, it should be in terms of new models.

TRAINING, SPECIALIZATION AND COLLABORATION

Just as agencies are structured along the idiom of machine bureaucracies, so are professions. Skrtic (1991) holds that the division of labor shapes the interdependencies and coupling of workers. Professional guilds are interesting entities. Each has to have some defined, unique specialization. A specific training curriculum may provide the rites of passage, but often there are also state or national exams. Legal status becomes registered in licensing. Then rights are jealously guarded and fought over. This a BD teacher can do, this only a psychiatrist, this a social worker. Teachers are not in the guilds permitted to provide psychotherapy and so on. Who can give individual intelligence and other psychological tests, take a family history and work with families, assess academic achievement? In special education does intervention dealing with the learning disability of a BD pupil require a different teacher? In this quagmire the strong professions lobby to maintain their identity and expand their roles. In general the longer and more exclusive the training, the greater the guild prestige. The more the guilds divide up the child, the more the need for collaboration and the more excruciating that collaboration. All of this aside, the studies show that so often the student has only the BD teacher who must serve all roles.

The fact is, while upbringers have common cause and often considerable shared knowledge base there is not common training. Even if we end up with common knowledge or skills, these must be learned in separate enclaves to perpetuate separate mystiques. Professions develop private languages and in-group code words. Krueger et al. (1987) have proposed a generic team approach which plays up the common functions. One special director explained that his psychologists, social workers and special teachers were taught through inservice the basic skills of all three. They could not afford the cost of shuttling children from one to the other and the time spent in subsequent integration. The higher the prestige of the specialization, the less willingness to engage in cross-disciplinary training and give away secrets, even if there are no secrets. Training institutions set up parallel courses for co-practicing professions rather than combining resources.

There are many who see conjoint multidisciplinary training as the road to improved collaboration. McCall (1990) holds that interdisciplinary training requires a broader integrating base than found in any present discipline. He proposes "children, youth and families." Bloom and Parad (1976) discuss this matter as well as interdisciplinary functioning in community mental health. In common with others, except for Sarason (1985), they do not include educators and see only membership of the Holy Trinity. Since all child upbringers have considerable common cause, they should by and large learn together in common curriculum. Actually, with increased specialization and certification structures, the trend is in the opposite direction except where personnel are in short supply and then anything goes, particularly in teacher accreditation.

It will not be enough to learn together: There will have to be joint practica together in settings where collaboration is active. There are settings where there is a meltdown of non-essential professional differences.

We can take measures to counteract training separatism for professionals engaged in a common task. We can lobby for joint training programs. Inservice and continuing education credits can be combined. Mental health workers can spend time helping in the classroom to see first hand the issues confronting the teacher. Teachers can participate in three-way conversations with the child and therapist to appreciate that mode of helping. This is with the goal of developing empathy and appreciation of the diverse contributions. Fenton et al. (1977) have discussed the implication of role expectations on interdisciplinary work in schools. All disciplines need to become familiar with emerging new concepts in other disciplines.

THE DYNAMICS OF COLLABORATION

Not all mental health special education collaboration is in team meetings. Often the interaction is in a consultative relationship where the mental health representative, on request or on schedule, meets with the BD teacher. Since many BD youngsters are in the regular classroom, consultation may be to apply the mental health approach in the mainstream least restrictive environment (Hughes & Hurth, 1984). Both system and individual consultation take place in a multitude of styles, which cannot be discussed here. Sufficient to say, professional role playing should be out. Consultation is a matter of co-equal status mutuality, to the end of problem solving. There are significant differences between one shot collaboration in an IEP versus sustained shared obligation on an on-going basis.

There is considerable slippery talk about teams and teaming the equality of disciplines. Understanding how teams really function takes us into the world of small group dynamics. There are roles to be played out that sometimes are like the dance of the wolves. Professional rituals may replace mutual problem solving as elaborated in Friend and Cook (1992).

But there is also a personal layer which can frustrate the efforts at problem solving. Beyond the professionalized role relationships are individual personal styles. One can find, in the same setting, mental health-education teams which flourish while others are perfunctory, meeting only to follow the rule. Incompatible personality styles can breed mistrust and disrespect, usually pasted over with a thin paper of civility. How a given member feels about the contribution of colleagues may stem from preordained stereotyped views carried into the "collaborative." "Teachers are rigid and do not understand therapeutic goals" or "Therapists don't make any real contribution: they just talk to kids." Which job is the more taxing? Who bleeds more profusely at day's end? It is particularly important for high status professions to function without arrogance. Reactions to team member participation get a going over with peers after the meeting but are seldom dealt with directly as team malfunctions. Also considerable interaction of the mental health and teaching professions takes place in a setting with parents, administrators and other disciplines. In such a mixed bag of lay and professionals, strange things may happen. In effective meetings expression is in basic English rather than professional lingo. While there are recognized role differences there is ideological similarity in both philosophy and psychology. Members all see the same youngster.

The study of team member roles is a fascinating and worthwhile exercise: Sometimes we learn to predict member roles and biases before they speak. Other team meetings are acts in the theater of the absurd, with each talking past the other. Small teams are usually the most effective. The gist of this is, collaboration at the service providing level is not simple. And yet we know that there are many examples of highly effective professional teaming. What does the literature say about effective teams and problem teams? Giangreco et al. (1991) review common practices which interfere with integrated delivery of services. Interfering processes include decisions made before consensus and from independent disciplinary perspectives, both major violations of proper team functioning. Larson and LaFasto (1989) found that successful teams had a clear and elevated goal, were driven by results, had competent team members, held a common commitment, produced a collaborative climate, enjoyed principled leadership and were given external support. Fenton et al. (1979) suggest trouble results from the fact that members do not agree on team goals and responsibilities.

Pfeiffer (1980) reviews four major conditions facing school-based professional teams: increasing parental and regular teacher involvement, selecting team relevant diagnostic information, getting the most meaningful decision and facilitating collaboration. Among his strategies for improving effectiveness we find: shared responsibility, rather than delegation to a single discipline; continuous support to the implementers; including a regular classroom teacher on the team; if necessary bringing in a process consultant to clear the air; and making provisions for program evaluation. He decries the current insular approach to training.

TACTICS FOR TEAM PROCESS IMPROVEMENT

There are times when the predominate issue to be solved is lost in ineffective group or two-person consultation. Implicit in the discussion above are many procedures for improving group effectiveness, both items of self-awareness and team involvement.

Because so many collaborations succeed or fail at the fusion point of group process, all of us must be students of how groups work and how to improve productivity. Few are comfortable in dealing with team conflict even when the child is ill-served by what goes on. Certain team members may be intimidating or hold power over others. Members not responsible for an intervention may propose actions alien to the one responsible for conducting the program. There is scapegoating—"He has been seen twice already and the little bastard is still impossible" or "We had it all worked out until the teacher got on his case again." Sometimes antagonists are open but frequently they are stifled until after the meeting when discussing the meeting with a friendly colleague. How can we introduce more honesty into group process without becoming hostile? Useful tactics follow analysis of the particular group dilemma. Post-meeting reaction blanks can help. Rotating chairmanship may be tried. In some instances the quality of collaboration can only be improved by the services of an outside "neutral" consultant. Specific training in collaboration may be necessary. The short of it is to face the necessity of working directly on ineffective collaboration. A personnel change may be the solution since frequently the team members are thoughtlessly assigned to work with each other.

The work of Friend and Cook (1991) is indispensable for dealing with team collaborative problems. While embedded in group process theory, there are concrete examples which identify various malfunctions followed by specific remedial actions. Particularly pertinent are sections on conflict and resistance in groups. This manual can be used by individuals or teams for training in the processes of collaboration.

The place for concentration is generally acknowledged to be common goal setting. If there is not agreement on goals, other problems are impossible to resolve. Often common goals are taken for granted when they need to be hammered out and prioritized. Participating in goal setting is the key to subsequent effort and commitment. Our division of labor requires not just cooperation: it requires *integration* of our work guided by the child and ecology. This is why the child study team is so important. Intensive child study takes the focus from disciplines back to the child and needs. The team members come to see the same child, albeit there are different facets.

Sometimes confounding differences of philosophy, psychology or methodology can only be resolved by substantive seminars. For example, cooperative learning or emergent teaching may be new to mental health workers. The role of cognitive therapies may need clarification for educators. Both disciplines may need to study pertinent new books and articles together. Given the diversity of training, we should not underestimate the time and energy that must be put into team exchange to reach a meeting of the minds. Worker divergency presents the same problem for our struggling pupils as does parental dissonance.

Speaking of promoting interdisciplinary work, McCall (1990) says that "the reputation, abilities, respect, sensitivity, selflessness, and energy of the staff are the ingredients which produce professional collaboration and hold them together during the process." It is such an overwhelming task that we might give up were there not so many examples demonstrating the possibilities of success.

REFERENCES

Anderson, N., & Marrone, T. (1977). Group therapy for emotionally disturbed children. *American Journal of Orthopsychiatry, 47,* 97–103.

Bloom, B. L., & Parad, H. J. (1976). Interdisciplinary training and interdisciplinary functioning: A survey of attitudes and practices in community mental health. *American Journal of Orthopsychiatry, 46,* 669–677.

Bray, N. M., Coleman, J. M., & Gotts, E. A. (1981). The interdisciplinary team: Challenges to effective functioning. *Teacher Education and Special Education, 4,* 44–49.

Cruickshank, W. M., Morse, W. C., & Grant, J. 0. (1990). *The individual education planning committee: A step in the history of special education.* Ann Arbor: University of Michigan Press.

Ekstein, R., & Motto, R. L. (1969). *From learning for love to love of learning.* New York: Brunner/Mazel.

Fenton, K. S. et al. (1977). *Role expectations: Implications for multidisciplinary pupil programming.* Washington: U.S. Dept. of Education.

Forness, S. R. (1989). *Statement of The National Mental Health and Special Education Coalition to Senate Subcommittee on the Handicapped.* Mimeographed Committee Report.

Friend, M. P., & Cook, L. (1992). *Interactions: Collaboration skills for school professionals.* New York: Longman.

Garner, H. (1982). *Teamwork in programs for children and youth.* Springfield, IL: Charles Thomas.

Giangreco, M. F., Edelman, S., & Dennis, R. (1991). Common professional practices that interfere with integrated delivery of related services. *RACE: Remedial and Special Education, 12,* 16–24.

Grosenick, J., George, M. P., & George, N. L. (1987). A profile of school programs for the behaviorally disordered: Twenty years after Morse, Cutler and Fink. *Behavioral Disorders, 12,* 159–168.

Hobbs, N. (1982). *The troubled and troubling child.* San Francisco: Jossey-Bass.

Hughes, J. M., & Hurth, J. L. (1984). *Handicapped children and mainstreaming: A mental health perspective.* U.S. Dept. of Health and Human Services.

Kauffman, J. M., & Wong, K. L. H. (1991). Effective teachers of students with behavioral disorders: Are generic teaching skills enough? *Behavioral Disorders, 16,* 225–237.

Krueger, M. A., et al. (1987). The generic team approach. *Child and Youth Care Quarterly, 16,* 131–144.

Larson, C. E., & LaFasto, F. M. J. (1989). *Teamwork: What must go right/what can go wrong.* Beverly Hills, CA: Sage.

Linton, T. (Ed.). (1973). The educateur: A European model for the care of 'problem' children. *International Journal of Mental Health, 2,* 1–88.

McCall, R. B. (1990). Promotion of interdisciplinary and faculty-service-provider relations. *American Psychologist, 45,* 1319–1324.

Mitchell, M. L., & Nicolaou, A. (1984). *From multidisciplinary to interdisciplinary: Training the educateur generalist.* Paper presented at 62nd Annual C.E.C. Convention, Washington, DC.

Morse, W. C. (1991). Ecological approaches. In T. R. Kratochwill & R. Morris (Eds.) *Handbook of psychotherapy with children.* Boston: Allyn and Bacon.

Munger, R. L. (1991). *Child mental health practice from the ecological perspective.* Lanham, MD: University Press of America, Inc.

Nichols, P. (1984). Down the up staircase: The teacher as therapist. In Grosenick et. al. (Ed.) *Social/affective interventions in behavioral disorders.* pp. 43–68. Des Moines, IA: Iowa Dept. of Public Instruction.

Nickerson, E. T., & O'Laughlin, K. S. (Eds.). (1982). *Helping through action-oriented therapies.* Amerherst, MA: Human Resources Development Press.

Osborn, A. G. (1984). How the courts have interpreted the related services mandate. *Exceptional Children, 51,* 29–252.

Pfeiffer, S. I. (1980). The school-based interprofessional team: Recurring problems and some possible solutions. *Journal of School Psychology, 18,* 388–393.

Pfeiffer, S. I. (1982). The superiority of team decision making. *Exceptional Children, 49,* 68–69.

Sapir, S. (1985). *The clinical teaching model.* New York: Brunner/Mazel.

Sarason, S. B. (1985). *Caring and compassion in clinical practice.* San Francisco: Jossey-Bass.

Skrtic, T. M. (1991). The special education paradox: Equity as the way to excellence. *Harvard Educational Review, 61,* 148–206.

Stone, F. H. (1988). Reflections on multidisciplinary teams. *Maladjustment and Therapeutic Education, 6,* 93–97.

Ungerleider, D. (1991). An educational therapist is . . . *The Educational Therapist, 12,* 2–8.

Wellins, R. S., Byham, W. C., & Wilson, J. M. (1991). *Empowered teams.* San Francisco, CA: Jossey-Bass.

Woods, J. (1986). The boundary between psychotherapy and therapeutic teaching. *Journal of Child Psychotherapy, 12,* 67–78.

· ·

Mental health–education collaboration is not the only professional change in the offing. More services are likely to be delivered in tandem with colleagues. Because special teaching has historically been a teacher and a class of students, co-teaching requires new skills. It can be great for the adults and the students, or it can be a disaster. Teaching teams are like marriages: not all turn out to be compatible, and divorce is difficult. Relationships have to be worked out rather than ignored. Students will work two teachers similar to the way they work parents. Also, special teachers will become responsible for a variety of subject matters, adaptation of the curriculum, differential grading, and discipline processes. The descriptive "my kids" becomes "our kids," and "my class" becomes "our class."

There are impending roles where the specially trained teacher will serve as consultant to others who are doing the hands-on interventions—peers, parents, aides, teacher colleagues, and, perhaps, other disciplines. Old-style authoritarian consultation is no longer acceptable.

This chapter has expanded the perception of how teachers help troubled students. We turn now to chapters detailing specific teacher methodologies, starting with how to better know our students and their families, the nature of the school as an institution, and our personal relationship to our work.

3

The Challenge of Reeducating Troubled Students: Understanding the Interaction Between a Student and His Community, Family, and Staff

The knowledge base required for teaching troubled students is extensive. To be effective, a teacher should know the students and their families, how educational and mental health systems function, and his or her own nature. As a case in point, teachers frequently report that their biggest problem is not in helping the students but in dealing with the regular and special education systems. Although a system may be theoretically designed for teacher and student support, in reality it can become a bureaucratic nightmare of frustration. How often one hears that a youngster would be no problem were it not for the unworkable family. The troubled student area of education is known for wearing out the tolerance of teachers faster than any other.

Information does not necessarily produce understanding or empathy for a troubled student. An inch-thick file on a youngster may contain reams of data, little of which becomes functional in the teacher–pupil relationship. Such information is usually collected by third-party professionals, each of whom presents an independent piece of a jigsaw puzzle which, when completed, may not make a recognizable picture. In contrast, for the teacher there is firsthand shared information coming directly from personal interaction with the student or parent. The sharing of information generates an interpersonal dynamic. For example, only that material discussed together by the teacher and student becomes part of their common public domain. In the process of making a hundred decisions a day, the teacher has little opportunity to consult the records and usually relies primarily on the firsthand knowledge accumulated in interpersonal exchanges.

The first article in this chapter presents a strategy for learning school-relevant information about a troubled student by initiating what becomes an ongoing dialogue. Through the process described, traditional teacher authority, delegated by the system, is acknowledged and augmented by building a collaborative relationship. The content of the resulting dialogue differs from typical case history reports, though material from that source is included. There is a dual focus: building teacher understanding of the student and, at the same time, fostering student understanding of his or her past and potential. The information in the file is a stimulus for getting pupil perceptions of past life events and current situations. The areas for joint teacher–pupil exploration are extensive, usually too numerous for a single session. As with any procedure, individual adaptations by the teacher are necessary to fit each child. Many of the items can be explored later as classroom exercises and, to the extent each pupil is willing, responses can be shared in the class—a way of developing the class as a support group. Troubled students are often surprised to find how much their lives have in common with their troubled peers. It is important to be alert for positive experiences and attributes that might offset the painful ones. Reversing common interpretations of certain behaviors is a case in point. For example, the youngster reports fighting when called a name. The positive side is the concern to protect one's integrity: "That means you have not given up, and in this class we will find other, better ways to defend your self-image." Interpretation of the self-salvation effort inherent in much of what the student does opens the option of finding better solutions as one goal of the class.

ARTICLE 3.1

Knowing Your Students: The Initial and Ongoing Dialogue

William C. Morse

The one theme which dominates educational programs for troubled students is the issue of control. Control is a major topic in training programs and fear of losing control is a common source of anxiety for both new and experienced teachers. Since control is erroneously considered solely a teacher function rather than a product of how the total system functions, administrative evaluation of a teacher usually begins (and even sometimes ends) with how well that teacher controls the students. While there are differences in what various professionals consider adequate control in given circumstances, certainly no one advocates chaos. According to many recent studies, the problem is, a singular goal of control has become the be all and end all of many programs.

Of course the teacher must have authority in the classroom, but the day of the adult being given automatic authority by virtue of being a teacher has long since disappeared. There is no free ride, especially with troubled students. In fact many pupils become special problems primarily because of their incessant resistance to authority, including that of the teacher. While there are many subtle aspects to the way an individual teacher achieves and uses power, the following discussion covers the two central sources of adult power, bureaucratic and personal. Both are essential in classrooms.

The most common, and unfortunately often the only, student control effort is through the application of bureaucratic power. Bureaucratic power is exemplified by the common behavior management systems of imposed rules of order and standards of acceptable behavior with contingencies attached. Often the rules are posted in large print as commandments in front of the class as constant reminders. These are the rules which the system is ready to enforce with sanctions ranging from verbal reprimands, point losses, time outs, referral to higher authority in the chain of command, exclusions and in very rare instances court action.

Since troubled students are usually characterized by previous violations of such standards, enforcement becomes the critical issue. Restrictions and punishments often have to be increased to make an impression and even then may fail to produce student compliance. As in the society at large, the codified law has to be enforced by a judicial system: the teacher often operates as judge, jury and police enforcer. Most teachers try to reward desirable behavior rather than punish undesirable behavior, thereby avoiding control by a stream of negatives. In many cases such effort is an ideal rather than a reality in the student's perception.

Arbitrary authority by teacher or parent is not easily accepted these days and arguing about the justice of the rule or its application only whets the student appetite for contest and legalistic wrangling from our student lawyers. Teachers are sometimes advised not to get too friendly less the students try to take advantage of them when teachers have to sanction their behavior. Since many of our troubled students are already struggling against feelings of powerlessness, the battle is on to prove "you can't make me." Talking about rules in contrast to arguing is important as part of planned social learning.

Several alternative strategies have been used to make the use of bureaucratic power more palatable. Teachers may invite the students to help make the rules, incorporate rules that are based on basic human rights and not just convenience for the adult or just because that's the way we do things in school. We explain the "why" of regulations to reduce the arbitrariness. Social learning programs are designed to teach youngsters the necessary skills for compliance. But, as Bandura has pointed out, it is not enough for any of society, be it classroom or nation, to depend only on internal willingness to comply: There must be enforcement of external standards as well.

The underlying purpose of any discipline should be more than the mere management of behavior. The goal of discipline is to help the student develop reasonable standards of behavior and the necessary skills to comply.

We now turn to the other very potent source of influence beyond the use of bureaucratic power. We recall, those who have had the deepest positive influence on us have usually been those who cared about us, as described in the paper on caring, page 106. Thus, fostering modeling and identification through personal concern provides another powerful source of influence for the teacher working with troubled students. Through knowledge about the pupil, followed by expressed and validated concern for that pupil, we are able to foster modeling and identification as one essential way to transmit values.

Caring provides an alternative source of control in contrast to exclusive use of bureaucratic management. Of course as in any human relationship, it is not a simple matter to build trust and the adult must be prepared for considerable testing. There are some students so damaged by prior adult deceit and rejection that they can go no deeper than to eventually recognize that the teacher does try to be "fair." For other students the first time trust in the teacher may come to represent a deep bonding. When youngsters come back to visit their significant teachers they talk about their struggles and the teacher's caring, often stating they don't see how the teacher ever stood them back then. To utilize the relationship channel the adult must be involved and accept the responsibility for helping which some teachers cannot or will not risk doing, feeling they have done their duty by remaining psychologically at an arms length from the student.

The question is, how can the teacher begin to tap a relationship which will result in teacher influence with pupils? The process recommended here is to open an ongoing dialogue between the teacher and student, starting with the initial interview and continuing intermittently during their many hours together. Both teacher knowledge of the student and self knowledge by the student are cultivated. First hand exchange produces a quality of information which is more functional than reported data which has not been personally shared. Both parties are influenced by the exchange. Most students are gratified by the interest the teacher takes in their life story. Youngsters have had lots of experience of adults talking *at* them; this is an adult talking *with* them. Listening to the student's perception of life begets adult empathy.

Why is it essential to have the initial individual interview before the student joins the first class? This interview sets the format of the teacher-pupil relationship. Once the student is in a group setting a totally different set of forces are activated, so the teacher begins with a one-on-one to establish the relationship before the peer group influences are activated. Admittedly it may take some arranging and be foreign to the usual onslaught of facing the whole group at once, but it pays off well for the effort. The teacher is in charge and demonstrates that he/she means business. The interview also personalizes the work with those having an IEP. It is a time of sensing each other out in private with no audience to play to. Meeting all the students for the first time en mass at the first class can be a trying undertaking. The interviews provide the teacher with a prior starting position worked out with each student. Some teachers later use bits of the nonsensitive and positive information in the first round of class peer introductions and to activate group counseling sessions. The knowledge bank regarding each pupil signifies the teacher is concerned and at the same time means serious business in this classroom.

Before the interview with the student, the teacher is primed by reading the records to get a sense of the student's life and school experiences. The teacher is in charge at this point, benefiting from whatever authority "newness" provides. The intent is to get as much relevant information out on the table as possible. The significance of being listened to by a sympathetic adult is not lost on most students. At times use of background file information may be necessary for prompts as well as to demonstrate that the teacher is not naive concerning the seriousness of the student's problems. Frankness about prior events is essential. The records may cover important life events, but they seldom provide information on how the youngster feels about an event. Many of our students have failed so often that they have no real hope of success in managing their lives. The teacher has a chance to explain how, together, they are going to work on the problems in the class. It will require hard work but this is a new opportunity. Information on the pupil's assets are interspersed along the way even when it takes ingenuity to uncover them. No student should be left with a recital of negatives. The goal is to cultivate realistic common goals and reactivate hope of a better life.

The interview uncovers the *meaning of significant life events* to the student. The outline of possible interview content which follows is not to be construed as arbitrary. Certainly the total list of suggested items is usually too much to cover in a single session. Productive dialogue cannot be prescribed and must be thought of in dynamic terms, always adjusted to the particular child. Non verbal students give brief responses, or sometimes block completely. But getting some substance from the student is important to start a sharing relationship. Perhaps a drawing will be more effective: the student draws his/her last school and teacher or house, room and related persons or family. Certain very hesitant students may respond to "Was it like this vignettes" by the teacher. It is critical to get whatever is possible to start the student's portfolio, which is the repository for important events and, hopefully, progress throughout the year. As teachers have considered the possible dialogue topics, they have sometimes decided that certain items would make useful class exercises rather than the first interview, or they may see some areas as productive for periodic repeats.

Not only does the initial interview begin to define the student: It also begins the explication of the teacher's role. "I need to come to understand you and your life. We are in this together and I want to be helpful to you. Sad things sometimes happen to students. I am not upset by knowing the truth, no matter what." Teachers face the fact that the personal histories are often painful and sense some topics are for later. For example, sexual abuse or sexual acting out are usually too private to share initially. On the other hand, there is a charade here regarding things known from the records but ignored. Most children know they have records although few have explicit knowledge of what is written there. Possible upsetting information can be managed by treating the information only in gross generalization, "I know there was trouble in that foster home" which cues the student in to teacher awareness without demanding a response. Children handle private events in very different ways. Some share easily with a sincere teacher. In fact some are so preoccupied by past traumas that they blurt out everything. Others withhold, realizing that information delegates power to the teacher which they are not ready to give. There are also distorters, fabricators, and once in a while a young Baron Munchausen. How a student presents himself gives cues as to the self.

With experience, each teacher evolves a personal interview schedule and methodology which can be adjusted to the individual context. The teacher's knowledge of developmental psychology cues in the talk at an appropriate age level. Some items are not appropriate for young children, and some are expanded with adolescents. Often young students and some LD students will be concrete and will need a lot of help to fill out the picture. Every exchange with a child is a challenge to adult ingenuity. Incidentally, while an adult does not share life intimacies, there is no reason not to share relevant memories and experiences in discourse with students, including mistakes the adult has made. While the points covered below are stated as a series of questions, they should be incorporated as items in conversations and not a sequence of interrogations. The student is frequently encouraged to ask questions. Many items can be depersonalized by using "kids your age," or "what do the kids say about this" to reduce the personal focus.

The following interview content has been put together from items initially suggested by teachers in seminars where they were working to perfect their initial interviewing skills. The series includes the things the teachers want eventually to know about their students, but that does not mean that all items can be used in the initial dialogue. Some teachers plan individual time built into the program when various topics can be covered. The central goal is to know the student's life through student eyes. Time lines and diagrams have been found useful in obtaining child perceptions. Somehow the diagrams make it easier for most students to express themselves, and it is made clear at the start that the original diagrams are for the child to keep. The teacher makes a file copy. When feasible, the pupil actually makes out the chart after seeing an example.

1. *Developing the personal time line.* The interview discourse begins with a time line. After drawing a long line on a piece of paper, the student is asked to describe his or her earliest memories which are then located by age and date on the time line. Often the early years are unknown by the student; then the adult fills in the information from the records, including the caretaker, and what the pupil's earliest life period was like. Then there is movement up the time line weaving the student's recollections with

information from the record. Important and critical life events are discussed. What were the living situations, placements, family constellation, good and bad events, etc.? At various times the question is where and with whom the child has lived, what it was like then? Was it a happy or sad time? Not only is the life saga important but the reflections on the saga are even more so. The current ecology is clarified but gets detailed scrutiny in Part 3, with The Stress Diagram.

The time line dialogue ends with the expectation for the next few years and then the eventual adult future. Anticipations reveal the youngster's hope index. What will your life be like next year at this time, in five years, when you are grown up? What do you expect adult life will be? What do you wish it to be? What will likely make things turn out one way or another? This provides insight regarding the child's attributions, the balance of personal power vs. fate and helplessness. A point might be, "When you think about your life, what is the best/worst thing? What would you like to change?" A nice item to end this section is "What is the best age to be and why?" to which both pupil and teacher can contribute.

2. *The education time line.* Because of the central importance of school in our work, the child's school experience deserves its own time line. The line goes back to what is known of nonfamily preschool care and then on though school to the present including the placement before the present one. Memories of school successes and problems and what they meant are especially germane. Prompts may be required about some of the painful times, especially the conditions before the present placement. Teachers have used such questions as: Who was your best teacher? Worst? How can teachers help kids? What subjects did you like/dislike? What were the kids like in these classes? Any friends you miss? Is school a good thing for you? Is school important? Why? Did you take any special tests? How did they come out? [Here the teacher supplies information from the file, stressing any assets.] How should schools be changed to be better for kids? The search is for any school satisfactions which the teacher can use. The school time line closes with projections about future schooling, next year and long term. The teacher contributes why he/she has chosen this profession.

There are two school areas that need attention before the first class meeting: one is how the student became special and the second is school discipline. A crucial aspect is the student's perception of how he or she came to be in special education, or be considered in need of special help. How did it happen? What does your family think about special education? How long do you think you will be in this program? What are the good and bad things about it? What have you heard about this program?

School discipline is so important that the student's perceptions of this area are essential to prepare for the current setting. What things get kids in trouble in school? What should be done about such behavior? How can I respond to such events that will be helpful? Then there is a brief discussion of bureaucratic control and the rules to be used (with a copy supplied), and what sanctions are invoked. Do these seem fair? Alternatives? Notes are kept on the discussions for both pupil and teacher to use as necessary in the future.

3. *Creating the current stress-support diagram.* Because the current ecology is so important in assessing a student's behavior, the present life milieu is elaborated though constructing a stress support diagram (see below) depicting the self and conditions and persons who are positive and negative in current life space. Who is helpful, and who produces stress?

First is the *me* where the youngster is asked to list several adjectives that could be used in self description, and also to describe one's role in groups. What are your strong and weak points? What about yourself would you most like to change? How are you like or unlike other family members? What might be your ideal self? What are the best and worst things about being your age? An alternative would be to use the Harter self efficacy scale, the results which can then be discussed. How one is, is then contrasted with how one would like to be.

The diagram is filled in, enumerating the situations/people in the student's life space, starting with the most intense relationship, then the less powerful. The stress side includes those with whom the subject has hassles, including for what reasons. On the support side are friends, relatives and peers (and situations) on the positive side. Each individual is described along with what they do to or for the youngster. When the student likes a person, the question is, what is there about the person that you like (or dislike)? Do you have similar characteristics?

4. *One student's day.* Were it possible, as a teacher you would like to shadow each student though a typical day, witnessing the hundreds of contacts with people and things, the hassles and joys which are the daily emotional diet. The next best thing is to go through a typical day with the student, starting with sleeping arrangements, getting up, who gets breakfast, any chores, and possible hassles. Getting to school (usually on a bus) which often sets off the day. How long a ride? Any scraps? And how goes the long school day if not covered previously. Then comes the trip home, activities until dinner, who is home, TV, chores, peers, games. Who prepares dinner, cleans up? Evening activities. Bed times rules. Sleep setting. Dreams, nightmares? Fears for personal or loved one's safety? If medications are taken, what does the student see as the purpose, and do they work. Who do you talk to when you have a problem? Punishments used in the home. Your recent best and worst day. What would you like to change about your life? What would have to happen to make these changes?

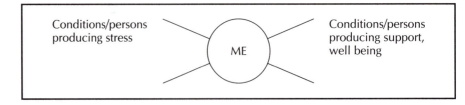

5. *The concluding individualized contract or understanding.* The information is now at hand to draw up an agreement of how we shall live and work together, reflecting the IEP and new information. A mutually understood and hopefully agreed upon contract will go in the student portfolio and a copy in the teacher's records. As matters develop over time, there may be many mutually made modifications.

Academics. The required academics are discussed with rationale as related to the student's future. Methods to be used to achieve the goals are reviewed and related to achievement test data and prior information on school subjects as available. Individual topics and hobbies of personal interest to the student are included in the academic plan. Usually no one has discussed personal attributes indicated by test data such as academic ability or what LD really means. Attention is given to sports, art, music, and drama. Using anticipated possible problems, areas are reviewed with indications of how the teacher might help the pupil learn. Clarification of educational goals and special activities planned for the class close this area. Self selected games or activities of choice indicate to the teacher possible rewards for each student. We have found that Gardner's paradigm helps a student appreciate individual patterns of possible talent when academics are not the forte (see page 509).

Behavioral. Interpersonal problems in the prior school are reviewed. How was discipline managed? Was it helpful? What you would like to accomplish in this area? When something goes wrong, what should the teacher do to help you? Available resources are listed such as individual and group counseling, social learning, LSI and crisis support. A thorough airing of rules and management design is included. Contributions are elicited from pupil concerning fairness. The culmination is an agreement on plans as an essential part of the contract.

After making a copy for the teacher file, the original contract is given to the student for the student portfolio. The portfolio is explained as a method used to chart our course. When there is an issue such as a satisfying or exciting event, or a disciplinary incident, the student writes his/her view of the happening. The teacher responds when germane. The writing exercise becomes part of both language learning and the continuing dialogue with the teacher, but it is the student's possession.

Neither the contract nor the ongoing dialogue are expected to eliminate problems, but they do provide a solid start so the teacher can make more judicious and caring decisions on the basis of shared information. The relationship channel has been opened. The knowledge the teacher has about the pupil can be a source of potential influence. It is not knowledge alone that matters. Rather it is the shared, first-hand information that counts. When the interview is completed, the teacher has started a basic human relationship which may remain perfunctory or become profound. Teacher and pupil each know where the other stands and what is expected.

Of course some students are reluctant to share very much and a teacher does not over demand. The dialogue is never over. In fact students may come out with significant information at the oddest moments when something touches off a memory. The teacher's professional stance is made clear through the initial exchange. If I am going to spend all of these hours with you trying to be helpful, I need to understand your life, your expectations and your goals. A teacher has a right to know in confidence; no other professional spends as much face to face time with troubled students. Who else lives this much together in such diverse situations and makes 100 decisions a day intended to help?

It is true that many teachers have not been given training in how to talk productively with troubled students and yet this is a survival skill for the professional. Some teachers do very well using their natural inclinations while others will need extensive training. Then the start must be gradual and listening to one's efforts can be self corrective if no training is available. Conducting such dialogue is an extension of the LSI, for talking effectively with students out of crisis is a parallel to the ability to talk with them in crises. Above all, any personal information revealed in the exchanges remains strictly confidential.

As the student enters the ongoing events of his/her life in a journal for the portfolio, it is not only a language exercise: It is at the same time a self understanding exercise. There is also the opportunity for the teacher to comment. For many students, especially adolescents, this relating of the personal life story, rereading and commenting on the contents, has therapeutic implications in itself.

· ·

STRATEGIES FOR UNDERSTANDING FAMILIES · · · · · · · · ·

A family is not necessarily the same entity to the professional, the parents, or the children. It is important to see all the different "families" embodied under the rubric of the single family. Often, a teacher's perception of a family changes with ongoing contact and as new information is added. Long scapegoated as the sole cause of the child's problems, the family is our best resource according to the wisdom of today.

A description of a family does not necessarily tell us the *dynamics* of that family—the nature of the interactions, including the feelings, favorites, aspirations, power dimensions, competitions, manipulations, support "agreements," secrets, and hidden agendas. Families have a public and a private family. Not all family members like each other. In the family resides the potential for the strongest support and, simultaneously, the greatest pain. A teacher can unwittingly enter a maelstrom.

A useful device to get families to work out problems is the Moos Family Scale: each member independently fills out a scale of the family as it is now and as they wish to have it. Then they come together and exchange their results. This process has been particularly helpful for teachers dealing with adolescent–parent arguments. Because the family is a primary group, it abounds with strong emotional currents that foster both nurture and conflict. Indelible marks remain visible on all of us from our family experiences, whatever their nature.

The Positive Education Program (PEP) in Cleveland, Ohio, is a combined educational and mental health program for over 600 troubled and troubling students. The program is notable for carrying on the traditions and insights of Nick Hobbs, and maintaining the essence of ReEd. As the next selection, *An Ecological Form* signifies, in ReEd the child is seen as a member of a family complex—a generic family, a reconstituted family, a fluid family with ever-changing membership, or whatever. We now recognize that, being dependent, the youngster forms the most fundamental attachment (positive or negative) to the family. Children are family anthropologists; they compare their families with others. Cultural lore prints out the image of what a family should be and what it should provide. The deepest self-feelings and emotions are born of the family as it is perceived to be. The best way to become familiar with the Family Form is to fill it out as if you were being interviewed (or better still, interview your parents). This accomplishes two things. First, we realize how parents feel when confronted with family forms, and how judicious we must be as teachers in collecting information. Second, when we contrast our own family with what the families of many troubled students face, we can more easily bridge probable gaps in understanding.

As teachers use this form with parents, it will become obvious that not every item is needed for every student. Eventually, the teachers will compose a list of essential issues. Also, much information can be obtained from the records and then just checked out with the parents. Not all issues have to be raised in a single meeting. Usually, the mother provides the family connection, and there are families that refuse to interact at all. One helpful way to get started is to ask to see family snapshots. The teacher might also inquire how many places the family has lived and what serious incidents have happened. It will be noted that many items parallel the prior study of the child's day.

ARTICLE 3.2

An Ecological Form for Assessing Child and Family Information

The Positive Education Program Staff

See pages 160–171.

The Pointer. (1989). Summer Vol. 33, No. 4.

Person(s) providing information: _____

Date: _____/_____/ _____   Supplemented/Updated: _____/_____ /____
(updated information in different ink/type)

Child Demographics

Child's full legal name: _____
Date of birth: _____/_____/ _____   C.A. _____   Sex: _____ M _____ F
Preferred nickname: _____   HGT: _____WGT: _____
Hair color: _____   Eye color: _____
Birthplace: _____
Racial identification: _____   Current grade: _____
Child's current residence with: ☐ Parents ☐ Other: _____
  Address: _____
  City: _____   Phone: _____

Parent's Residence

Father's name: _____ D.O.B.: _____
  Natural parent? ☐ Yes ☐ No: _____
  Address: _____
  City, State, Zip: _____
  Home phone: _____
Mother's name: _____   D.O.B.: _____
  Natural parent? ☐ Yes ☐ No: _____
  Address: _____
  City, State, Zip: _____
  Home phone: _____

Alternate Contacts

If no home phone, how can parent(s) be reached? _____
Whom to contact in case of emergency: _____
  Phone: _____ Relationship: _____

Alternate Transportation

If your child misses his/her regular assigned transportation, indicate preferred method of transport: _____

Custody and Legal School District of Residence

Who has legal custody of the child?_____

☐Temporary Name:_____
         Address:_____
☐Permanent
        _____
         County:_____
         Phone:_____

I

*If the Department of Human Services (Welfare) has custody (i.e., foster parent placement), indicate the address of the parents at the time that the department took custody.

Parent's name: _____

Address: _____

County: _____

School district: _____

Parents' Occupation

Father's occupation: _____

Employed by: _____

  Shift: _____   Business phone: _____

Can you be called at work for nonemergencies? ☐ Yes ☐ No

Business address: _____

_____

Mother's occupation: _____

Employed by: _____

  Shift: _____   Business phone: _____

Can you be called at work for nonemergencies? ☐ Yes ☐ No

Business address: _____

_____

Parents' Marital History/Current Status

Married: _____/_____/_____   To: _____

Separated: _____/_____/_____   From: _____

Divorced: _____/_____/_____   From: _____

Remarried: _____/_____/_____   To: _____

Other: _____

Income Data Form

Total number in household: _____

Please check income range that applies to your family:

a. _____ Employment   e. _____ Pension, Retirement,
b. _____ Unemployment   Disability
c. _____ Aid to Dependent   f. _____ Public assistance, Welfare
         Children   g. _____ Support
d. _____ Social Security Income   h. _____ None
                              i. _____ Other (Specify)

2

Please check all sources of income that apply to your family:

a. _____ Under $5,000   f. _____ $25,000–$29,999
b. _____ $5,000–$9,999   g. _____ $30,000–$34,999
c. _____ $10,000–$14,999   h. _____ $35,000–$39,999
d. _____ $15,000–$19,999   i. _____ $40,000 and over
e. _____ $20,000–24,999

Please list family social security numbers:

Father: _____-_____-_____
Mother: _____-_____-_____
Children: _____   _____-_____-_____

_____   _____-_____-_____

_____   _____-_____-_____

_____   _____-_____-_____

Please list children's ADC numbers:

_____   _____

_____   _____

_____   _____

_____   _____

_____   _____

_____   _____

Family and Home Information

1. All persons currently living in the household:

Name	DOB	Sex	Highest grade	Relationship to child
_____	__/__/__	_____	_____	_____
_____	__/__/__	_____	_____	_____
_____	__/__/__	_____	_____	_____
_____	__/__/__	_____	_____	_____
_____	__/__/__	_____	_____	_____
_____	__/__/__	_____	_____	_____
_____	__/__/__	_____	_____	_____

2. Natural parents or siblings who do not live in the household:

_____	__/__/__	_____	_____	_____
_____	__/__/__	_____	_____	_____
_____	__/__/__	_____	_____	_____

3

3. Has the child lived with both parents since birth? ☐ Yes ☐ No
   If no, list changes chronologically (include residential placements).

   From   **To**   **Child lived with**
   (dates preferred, or child's ages)

   _____   _____   _____
   _____   _____   _____
   _____   _____   _____
   _____   _____   _____

4. If the child does not live with both parents, why?

   ☐ Parents separated
   ☐ Parents divorced
   ☐ Parent deceased
   ☐ Other: _____

5. If the child has a parent not living with him or her, are there visitations?

   ☐ Yes   How frequently? _____
   ☐ No   Reason: _____

6. If there are other children in the family:

   A. Do any of them have physical or emotional problems?

      ☐ No   ☐ Yes: _____
      _____

   B. Have they received or have you tried to obtain special help for them?

      ☐ No   ☐ Yes: _____

7. Are there any guns in the household? ☐ No ☐ Yes

   If yes,
   How many? _____
   What kind(s)? _____
   Are they stored loaded? _____
   Are they kept locked? _____
   Who has access? _____
   Would your child have access to guns from any other source? If so,
   where or who? _____

8. Are there prescription drugs in the household? _____

   If so,
   What type(s)? _____
   Where are they kept? _____
   Does your child have access? _____

4

9. Is your household troubled by domestic violence? _____

_____

_____

_____

Child's Developmental and Medical History

1. Any problems during pregnancy?
   (bleeding, fever, high blood pressure, diabetes, medication, etc.)

_____

_____

_____

_____

2. Any problems during delivery?
   (length of labor, Caesarian, breech birth, etc.)

_____

_____

_____

_____

3. Birth weight?

_____

_____

4. Infancy:
   a. Were there any feeding problems?

_____

_____

_____

_____

   b. Did your child sleep well?

_____

_____

_____

_____

   c. At what age was your child toilet trained?

_____

_____

_____

_____

   d. Was toilet training difficult?

_____

_____

_____

_____

5

5. Milestones—at what age did/was your child:
　　_____ weaned　　　　　　　　_____ walk
　　_____ sit up alone　　　　　　_____ talk
　　Were there any difficulties with the above? _____
　　　If so, explain: _____
　　_____
　　_____

6. Are there problems with bedwetting/accidents?
　　_____ night　　　　　　　　frequency: _____
　　_____ daytime accidents　　frequency: _____

7. Please indicate age of child at time of illness/problem:
　　_____ Chicken pox
　　_____ Mumps
　　_____ Diphtheria
　　_____ German measles (3 day)
　　_____ Red measles (14 day)
　　_____ Poliomyelitis
　　_____ Rheumatic fever
　　_____ Scarlet fever
　　_____ Tuberculosis
　　_____ Whooping cough
　　_____ Pneumonia
　　_____ Other: _____

Does/did your child have frequent or severe ear infections?
　□ No □ Yes: _____

Does/did your child have allergies?
　□ No □ Yes: To what? _____
　　　　　　　How severe are the reactions? _____
　　　　　　　Special precautions? _____

Does/did your child have lead poisoning?
　□ No □ Yes: _____

Does your child have any dietary restrictions?
　□ No □ Yes: _____

Does your child have any special health/physical limitations?

_____

8. Please detail any of your child's hospitalizations:

Dates	Age	Hospital	Reason	Length of stay
_____	_____	_____	_____	_____
_____	_____	_____	_____	_____
_____	_____	_____	_____	_____
_____	_____	_____	_____	_____

6

9. Detail medication history (prescription and nonprescription)
   *Asterisk *current* medications

Dates	Age	Drug	Reason	Physician
_____	_____	_____	_____	_____
_____	_____	_____	_____	_____
_____	_____	_____	_____	_____
_____	_____	_____	_____	_____

10. Please initial if your child can be administered any of the following nonprescription medications at school.

_____ Aspirin   _____ Tylenol (acetaminophen)
_____ Antacid (liquid)   _____ Throat lozenge
_____ Antacid (tablet)

Family Medical History

Is there a history of any of the following in the family?
Use M for mother's side; F for father's side.

_____ TB   _____ Vision problems
_____ Birth defects   _____ Hearing problems
_____ Emotional problems   _____ Drugs
_____ Behavior problems   _____ Alcohol
_____ Mental retardation   _____ Diabetes
_____ Goiter (thyroid)   _____ Other: _____
_____ Convulsions/seizures

Other comments: _____ _____
_____
_____

Child's School History

School Attendance

	When	Where	Problems	Reasons for leaving
Nursery/Preschool	_____	_____	_____	_____
Kindergarten	_____	_____	_____	_____
Grade 1	_____	_____	_____	_____
Grade 2	_____	_____	_____	_____
Grade 3	_____	_____	_____	_____
Grade 4	_____	_____	_____	_____
Grade 5	_____	_____	_____	_____
Grade 6	_____	_____	_____	_____
Grade 7	_____	_____	_____	_____
Grade 8	_____	_____	_____	_____
Grade 9	_____	_____	_____	_____
Grade 10	_____	_____	_____	_____
Grade 11	_____	_____	_____	_____
Grade 12	_____	_____	_____	_____

7

Were you informed of any behavioral, emotional, or academic problems from school personnel? If so, detail: _____

_____

_____

_____

_____

Have the schools provided special help/attention of any sort? If yes, detail: _____

_____

_____

_____

_____

Agency Involvement/Service Treatment History

Please include (chronologically, if possible) as complete a history as possible. Include agencies, physicians, counselors, institutions, therapists, etc. Provide dates, if possible, as well as contact person.

Dates	Age of child	Name/Contact person	Service provided	Length of involvement
___	___	___	___	___
___	___	___	___	___
___	___	___	___	___
___	___	___	___	___
___	___	___	___	___

Is or has your child been court involved? If yes, detail:_____

_____

_____

_____

_____

Comments/Notes:

_____

_____

_____

_____

Typical Day Descriptions

1. Describe your child's behavior during a usual day.
   (Use reverse side, if necessary.) _____

   _____

   _____

   _____

   _____

8

2. Describe your child and the family activities during a usual weekend. (Use reverse side, if necessary.) _____
   _____
   _____
   _____
   _____
   _____

3. A. On a school day, how does your child awaken? (i.e., Does the child awaken by himself?) _____
   ___ _____

   B. How does your child prepare himself for the day? (i.e., Who selects the clothing, etc.?) _____
   _____

   C. Does your child get ready quickly or does he/she require continual reminding? _____
   _____

   D. Does your child eat breakfast? _____ Who prepares breakfast? _____
   Any problems at this time? _____

   E. Does your child watch the time and leave promptly, or do you have to remind him frequently? _____
   Has your child ever refused to go to school? _____

   F. Does your child come home for lunch? _____ Who prepares lunch? _____ Any problems at this time? _____
   _____ Does your child watch the time and leave promptly, or do you have to remind him frequently? _____
   _____

   G. What happens after school? (i.e., What does your child do first?) _____
   _____
   Next? _____

   H. What occurs at dinner time? _____
   1. Does the family eat together? _____
   2. Is your child on time? _____
   3. Any problems during dinner? _____
   4. Does he/she participate in family conversations during meals? _____
   _____

   I. What happens after dinner? _____

9

J. What happens at bedtime? _____
    Does he/she get ready for bed and go to bed when requested? _____
    _____

K. What does your child do on weekends? (You may need to break the weekend
    into specific days and periods of time.) _____ _____
    _____

L. Does the family have a chance to do many things together? (i.e., shopping,
    movies, etc.) _____
    _____

M. What activity do you enjoy doing most with your child? _____
    How often? _____ Do problems arise during
    this time? _____
    How do you handle them? _____

N. Does your child spend time with friends? _____
    1. How much time? _____
    2. How many friends? _____ _____
    3. How do you feel about your child's friends? _____
    _____

O. Does your child belong to any groups or organizations? (i.e., Scouts, Y,
    afterschool activities, sports) _____
    _____

P. Does your child have any particular interests or hobbies? _____
    _____

Q. Does your child get an allowance? _____
    1. Is the allowance earned, or does he ever earn money? _____
    _____
    2. How does your child manage the money? _____
    _____

R. Does your child have specific chores? _____
    1. What? _____
    2. How often? _____
    3. Any problems about chores? _____ How does your child
    avoid chores (i.e., refuses, argues, disappears, etc.) _____
    _____

S. How do you generally discipline your child? _____
    1. How often? _____
    2. Does it work? _____

Behavior Checklist (current problems/concerns)

Check those behaviors listed below that apply to your child within the last 6 months.

_____ makes no sounds
_____ makes sounds but no words

10

_____ says a few words (Specify _____)
_____ speaks well but was slow in developing speech
_____ repeats words over and over
_____ did talk but does not anymore
_____ is clumsy and awkward
_____ is often drowsy
_____ displays stereotypic behaviors (for example, waves hands in front of face, stares blankly) (Specify _____)
_____ engages in self-destructive behavior
          _____ hair pulling _____ self-biting _____ self-pinching
          _____ head banging _____ other (Specify _____)
_____ has tantrums frequently
_____ is hyperactive
_____ seldom makes eye contact
_____ demands too much attention
_____ is often sluggish or slow moving
_____ often has physical complaints, for example, headaches, stomachaches
_____ usually plays alone
_____ is disobedient, difficult with disciplinary control
_____ asks for help when not needed
_____ gives up easily
_____ does not interact appropriately with:
          _____ parents _____ siblings _____ peers _____ others
_____ physically abuses:
          _____ parents _____ siblings _____ peers _____ pets
          _____ toys, furniture, other objects
          _____ other (Specify _____)
_____ cries, whines, or pouts frequently
_____ makes unreasonable noise, yells
_____ does not play with toys
_____ rarely obeys requests, commands, etc.
_____ talks back to parents, other authority figures
_____ overreacts when on the losing end in competitive situations
_____ has unreasonable fears (i.e., darkness, height, animals)
          Please specify _____
_____ does not recognize danger
_____ runs away frequently
_____ does not observe curfew
_____ will not play alone
_____ has problems at mealtimes, __ disruptive, __ selective about foods
_____ has a sleeping problem
_____ cannot feed self
_____ cannot dress self
_____ is not toilet trained
_____ is toilet trained but ____ wets bed, ____ wets pants, __ soils pants
_____ lies frequently
_____ has been known to set fires
_____ steals repeatedly
_____ seems to have a hearing problem
_____ seems to have a vision problem

11

_____ has other physical handicap (Specify _____)
_____ makes negative comments to:
    _____ parents _____ siblings _____ peers _____ others
_____ teases:
    _____ parents _____ siblings _____ peers _____ others
_____ exhibits irritability
_____ wanders off
_____ exhibits sadness
_____ complains
_____ has had police contact
_____ has had school contact
_____ has had complaints from neighbors

Please describe other problems:

_____

_____

_____

Circle the one behavior from the previous checklist that distresses you the most.

What does your child do well?

_____

_____

_____

What do you like about your child?

_____

_____

_____

Did anyone advise you to bring your child to the Positive Education Program?

☐ Yes ☐ No If yes, who? _____
                why? _____

How do you feel about a placement at PEP for your child?

_____

_____

_____

Has the parent involvement commitment been thoroughly explained?

☐ Yes ☐ No If yes, by whom? _____

What do you believe your commitment to be?_____

_____

_____

_____   _____
Date   Parent

_____   _____
Date   School Psychologist
                           12

STRATEGIES FOR STUDYING THE SYSTEMS . . . .

Before taking a new job, a wise teacher would want to confer not only with the administrator but with the prior teacher as well. Organizational charts give little information on what the working conditions are like. There are matters of collegiality, access to consultation, expectations that may be highly unrealistic, and processes of evaluation that deserve attention. Who controls immigration and emigration for the classroom? Nowadays, some systems are driven by cost cutting and fear of lawsuits. As remarked earlier, all special programs start with the goal of serving children but end up with more prosaic and expedient operating goals. Some programs use collaborative problem solving; others, rule-bound, cling to the way things were done in the past. Some systems have a rule for every exigency, or make one when an issue arises. There are hierarchical systems that require climbing many steps to get a decision, because power resides at the top. Colleagues may be turf holders or true collaborators. When questions are raised about seemingly obtuse rules, the irrationality may be undiscussable. Managing to survive in the system may be a bigger task than surviving with troubled students.

The author of the next paper pulls no punches in assessing the impact of institutional formats. Fimian is an Assistant Professor in the Department of Special Education at Appalachian State University in North Carolina. His paper examines the system from the teacher's main concern: What is the impact of the system on the teacher's workstation. He recognizes that although one-person programs do exist, programs are characteristically system products. Given today's high level of teacher fatigue and turnover in the field of helping troubled children, we had best address system issues. This presentation is significant because it goes beyond diagnosis to remediation. Fimian deals with ways to improve the situation.

ARTICLE 3.3

Social Support, Stress, and Special Education Teachers: Improving the Work Situation

Michael J. Fimian

In a broad sense, any school can be characterized as a complex social system consisting of many interrelated and interacting parts. The degree to

The Pointer. (1985). Vol. 31, No. 1, 49–52.

which the social milieu keeps these parts "oiled" will often determine the degree to and fashion in which these parts continue operating in a smooth, efficient, and relatively frictionless manner. When the school's social system becomes impaired, however, or when it does not function as it should, the "wear and tear" on the human components of this complex assembly becomes evident. It has often been argued that the degree of wear and tear that school personnel experience is strongly related to the social aspect of working with people.

Interest in the wear and tear on teachers has increased dramatically since the late 1970s. Numerous studies have identified both the school- and/or profession-related factors that are manifestations of stress. The "social aspects" of functioning within a school can be defined by various dimensions, including worker morale, school climate, social interactions, social support, personnel satisfaction, and needs satisfaction. Two levels of one such factor—social support, specifically the presence or absence of on-the-job peer and administrative/supervisory support—are the focus of this article.

Although rarely addressed in the education literature as a means of improving one's work life, the concept of support has been investigated in other fields, particularly those dealing with adaptation to illness (e.g., medicine) or crisis (e.g., counseling).

Numerous terms have been used to characterize such supports: adjustive resources, social networks, psychosocial assets, and more recently, social support. These terms stem from one key concept: the recipient of support comes to believe that he or she is recognized, esteemed, valued, and is part of a network of mutual communication and obligation by peers, subordinates, and superordinates. The most enduring notion related to this concept is that, in the process of receiving social support, recipients experience significantly less stress than do nonrecipients. The presence or absence of such support, therefore, can be a powerful moderator of life or occupational stress.

SUPPORT AND STRESS

The search for a clearer understanding of the relationship between social support and stress in the schools is a relatively recent enterprise. Generalizations such as "overstressed and undersupported teachers care less now than they once did about their profession, jobs, and students," or that teachers feel uneasy about their work and themselves, or that experience deteriorates performance, productivity, and morale level have led to many comments, articles, workshops, and books. Unfortunately, most of these attempt to resolve poorly defined problems without benefit of an empirical base.

Inadequate financial remuneration is no longer the sole reason for decreasing teacher numbers; the quality of professional interactions has also become suspect. The resulting loss of teacher control, lack of support during the first years of teaching, altered roles for both administrators and teachers, misconceptions inherent in such change, and increased formalization of special education have dramatically increased the stressful aspects of teaching over the last two decades.

Researchers have clarified the relationship between support and stress since the late 1970s, however. They have begun to confirm the relationships between administrator/supervisor behavior and teacher perceptions of stress and burnout.

Several have found that the leading cause of teacher resignations was the fatigue resulting from "hassles" with their administrators. Minner and Beane (1983) established that acting as a student advocate, an essential element of any teaching role, placed four of ten special education teachers in danger of being verbally reprimanded or even fired.

Such dilemmas have prompted teachers to report that administrators' and supervisors' incompetence, unavailability, lack of support, and poor communication skills increased their stress and burnout levels. Lack of administrative support, poor quality of feedback, lack of professional guidance, poor supervision, and other administrative issues were some of the most frequently reported sources of stress, poor job morale, and teacher recidivism. Farber (1981) discovered that almost nine in every ten teachers thought their administrators did not help solve problems or provide support, while Arreenich's (1982) teachers perceived more problems in their relationships with their supervisors and administrators than with their students. One of the earlier surveys determined that six out of ten teachers felt their principals do not take an active role in promoting teacher mental health. Similarly, in a survey of three different special education teacher samples (1,107 teachers from two states), Fimian (1984) determined that half were supported by peers but not supervisors, one-third received support from both sources, one-tenth reported support from neither, and only two in a hundred received supervisory but not peer support. Only three to four out of ten teachers reported receiving supervisory support. Finally, it was established that those teachers not receiving supervisory support reported significantly stronger personal/professional stressors, professional distress, discipline and motivation problems, emotional, biobehavioral, and physiological-fatigue manifestations, and more overall stress than did the recipients of such support.

Peer support as a stress moderator has also been recognized in the empirical literature, although not as thoroughly as has administrative/supervisory support. Thomas (1984) and McKnab and Mehring (1984) found that conflicts with other staff members and lack of support from faculty colleagues partially influenced on-the-job stress and teacher recidivism. Fimian and Santoro (1983) found that feelings of frustration due to poor attitudes and behaviors on the part of administration were the third strongest and fourth most frequently occurring sources of stress of the twenty-five they investigated. Finally, Fimian (1984) found that many more teachers were supported by peers than by supervisors; over 90% typically are supported by peers, whereas only 25–40% are supported by supervisors. Those not receiving support also reported significantly stronger professional distress, emotional manifestations, and total stress in comparison to recipients.

On a more positive note, there is evidence that such support from administrators and/or peers can moderate stress levels. Those respondents to the *Instructor* survey who reported receiving principal support functioned "much better" physically and mentally than did their nonsupported peers (*Instructor,* 1977) . Thompson (1980) found strong positive correlations for men and women instructors' stress levels and the quantity and quality of the administrative support they received. In another investigation, "low-stress" teachers reported significantly more support than did their "high-stress" counterparts (Fimian & Santoro, 1983). Needle, Griffin, and Svendson (1981) reported that teachers who found their principals competent and supportive also tended to report greater well-being and fewer stress symptoms than those who did not. Finally, in studies of teacher coping behaviors, Burke and Belcourt (1974) and Dewe, Guest, and Williams (1979) found that the most frequently cited "coping mechanisms" reported by teachers under stress were characterized by verbal and nonverbal support from superordinates, peers, and friends. In summary, there is growing evidence that teacher stress levels are strongly related to the degree to which the teachers receive on-the-job administrative, supervisory, and peer support. The greater the support, the lower the stress and burnout levels.

FIRST STEPS

It would appear, therefore, that one key area of preservice and in-service training, organizational analysis, and further study would be an examination of supports that could be realistically provided to teachers, and how these supports may or may not be related to supervisory styles and resources. With respect to peer support, it would be advisable to study further the types of support that teachers currently and informally provide to other teachers, and how the quantity and quality of such supports can be varied in both informal and formal ways to moderate stress levels. The purposes of such activities are:

1. to define the administrators', supervisors', and teachers' resources that would help them respond to stress on a proactive or before-the-fact basis;

2. to help teachers manage their overall stress levels in their teaching and work environments; and

3. to support the teacher faced with difficult personal or professional situations (Taylor & Salend, 1983).

Although numerous extra-professional and extra-school solutions to the problems of stress and burnout have been proposed, few have been verified empirically (Gallery, Eisenbach, & Holman, 1981). Increasingly, therefore, professionals are looking less to the fad type of solutions and more to themselves, their peers, administrators, and colleagues for these solutions (McCabe, 1984). Jogging five miles a day may make teachers feel better about themselves by reducing the frequency and/or strength of their stress manifestations, but it will probably do little to resolve the sources of stress encountered in a teacher's daily routines. We must look more closely at these routines to more clearly understand the problem.

The first steps toward improving the support base in any school need not be complex or extravagant, and they need not use any more resources than presently exist. Werner (1980) suggests starting small and on a human level: acknowledging, accepting, and sanctioning the feelings of one's colleagues; providing a means of "drawing off" pressures; helping all personnel clarify and organize their values, attitudes, and feelings; helping one's peers and supervisors maintain realistic orientations; providing opportunities to increase knowledge and skill bases; and making attempts at boosting morale and increasing job satisfaction levels are all realistic first steps. Lemley (1981) proposes that educators begin by proactively exercising some degree of control over the little things in the school environment that, left unattended, can later function as significant stressors. Organizing and efficiently using one's time, improving one's positive interpersonal influence, and coping with or modifying some of the less desirable aspects of working in today's schools (e.g., rules, regulations, and paperwork) are all areas for positive change (Gmelch & Swent, 1981). In many cases, attending to a number of methods of recognition and modifying one's behavior accordingly, as outlined in Figure 3.1, can significantly enhance the working environment. None of these informal methods requires financial or material resources, but all require time and a degree of honest commitment to change and improvement (Bauer, 1982–83).

Establishing more formal, yet low cost, interventions can also improve support levels. Learning how to use positive and constructive feedback with others (Houten, 1980) or how to implement organizational development interventions for organizational development and renewal (Fullan, Miles, & Taylor, 1980) can be important first steps. Some have suggested the use of journal or log writing, two-day seminars on improving relations or managing stress, or weekly or monthly support meetings (Fimian, 1980; Greenberg & Valletutti, 1980). "Mutual aid," "selfhelp," or "support" groups have been used successfully in the counseling profession to expand opportunities for selfcare, to obtain new insights, and to strengthen feelings of being supported (Taylor & Salend, 1983; Spicuzza & DeVoe, 1982). Generalizing these techniques to special education should not be too difficult, particularly if the issues in Figure 3.2 are addressed as the group develops. As in the case of the informal interventions, the more formal need not be time consuming or expensive, but all would require a commitment to change and

FIGURE 3.1 Methods of recognition operationally defined by supportive administrator/supervisor/peer behaviors.

1. Smile.
2. Put up suggestion boxes.
3. Treat to a soda/beer/wine.
4. Quickly reimburse school-related expenses.
5. Ask for a verbal report.
6. Send a birthday card.
7. Arrange for discounts with local merchants.
8. Establish and maintain a coffee club.
9. Plan annual/periodic ceremonial occasions.
10. Be honest and straightforward with the staff.
11. Recognize and accommodate personal needs and problems.
12. Be pleasant.
13. Use in emergency situations.
14. Act as a good role model.
15. Post "Honor Roll" in recreation area.
16. Respect wishes.
17. Give informal teas or wine-and-cheese parties.
18. Keep challenging staff while providing support.
19. Send a Thanksgiving card to the teacher's family.
20. Say "Good morning."
21. Do not reward good work with more work.
22. Provide quality preservice and in-service training.
23. Help foster and develop self-confidence.
24. Award plaques/certificates.
25. Take time to explain fully.
26. Be verbal.
27. Hold rap sessions and/or support group meetings.
28. Give additional responsibility.
29. Encourage participation in team planning.
30. Respect sensitivities.
31. Enable to grow on the job.
32. Enable to grow out of the job.
33. Send newsworthy information to the local media.
34. Ask teachers to evaluate their work service.
35. Say "Good afternoon."
36. Honor teacher preferences.
37. Create and maintain pleasant work surroundings.
38. Welcome to coffee breaks.
39. Have a public reception.
40. Take time to talk.
41. Defend against hostile or negative staff.
42. Make quality well-articulated plans.
43. Comment to supervisory staff.
44. Send valentines.
45. Recommend to prospective employers.
46. Provide scholarships to conferences and workshops.

(Continued)

FIGURE 3.1 *(Continued)*

47. Offer advocacy roles.
48. Utilize in areas of expertise.
49. Write them "thank you" notes.
50. Invite participation in policy formulations.
51. Surprise with coffee and cake.
52. Celebrate outstanding projects and achievements.
53. Nominate for awards or other recognitions.
54. Carefully match professional with job.
55. Praise teachers to their friends and colleagues.
56. Provide good working conditions.
57. Say "Good night."
58. Plan staff social events.
59. Rent billboard space for public praise.
60. Accept individuality.
61. Provide opportunities for positive evaluation.
62. Plan occasional extravaganzas.
63. Institute student-planned surprises.
64. Use purchased newspaper space.
65. Promote a "teacher-of-the-month" program.
66. Place letter of appreciation in personnel file.
67. Plan a "recognition edition" of the school newsletter.
68. Send commendatory letters to prominent public figures.
69. Obtain and maintain teaching supplies.
70. Identify, recognize, and use personal motivators.
71. Distinguish between groups and individuals in the group.
72. Visit classrooms occasionally.
73. Maintain safe working conditions.
74. Orient adequately.
75. Award special citations for extraordinary achievements.
76. Ask "How's everything?" every so often.
77. Send Christmas cards.
78. Be familiar with the details of assignments and lesson plans.
79. Conduct school-wide cooperative events.
80. Plan a theater party.
81. Attend a sports event.
82. Have a picnic.
83. Say "Thank you" occasionally.
84. Say "Good job" occasionally.
85. Keep on smiling.

FIGURE 3.2   Six aspects of establishing and maintaining a professional support group.

1. *What is a support group?* A support group is an informal group of coworkers who meet on a regular basis to provide an opportunity for unstructured communication or socialization, discussion of business, and constructive praise or criticism of the topics raised within the group. It also provides an opportunity to vent emotions and frustrations and to develop strategies to improve work situations.

2. *Why is the group being formed?*
   a. personal needs—to discover or reassess one's sense of self.
   b. professional needs—to diminish feelings of solitude within the school and to search for one's own personal meaning within the school.
   c. time—to provide the opportunity to discuss ideas and topics with each other in a casual, relaxed atmosphere.
   d. lines of communication—to open and expand upon the communication within the school.
   e. roles—to clarify roles and clear up ambiguity and misinterpretation associated with them.
   f. support—to facilitate feelings of being recognized and appreciated.

3. *Who should be involved?* Anyone who is experiencing work-related stress at any level within the school.

4. *How often will the group meet?* Ideally, once a week.

5. *What are some of the group's goals/topics?*
   a. policies and philosophies of the school.
   b. suggestions to improve situations.
   c. coping with problems.
   d. meeting needs.
   e. improving lines of communication.
   f. clarifying roles.
   g. resolving hassles with the job.
   h. establishing or improving upward mobility within the profession.

6. *What are the general principles of the support group?*
   a. Do not "bitch."
   b. Operationalize problems.
   c. Identify a range of options to meet the problems, including solutions and plans of action.
   d. Assign responsibilities/tasks/timelines.
   e. Make no distinction between administrators, supervisors, teachers, and paraprofessionals—everyone is equal and mutually supportive.
   f. Give each member equal time to present self, if he/she chooses, without interruptions.
   g. Provide a relaxed, nonthreatening, productive atmosphere.
   h. Compromise, accept suggestions, understand why some things are the way they are, and be willing to accept that some things cannot change.
   i. Do not make anyone feel that the content or the way he or she says something will jeopardize his/her position or relationship with others.
   j. Do not let someone's presence or absence affect someone else's commitment or lack of interest.
   k. Share matters in a constructive and supportive way (not "so and so" did this or said this, etc.).
   l. People should not feel they have to say anything.
   m. No one should feel it is mandatory to join or attend.
   n. Welcome and appreciate everyone's participation.

consuming or expensive, but all would require a commitment to change and improvement.

The present professional *zeitgeist,* although initially appearing somewhat negative, actually offers positive suggestions for resolving some of today's education problems. Simple solutions to very complex problems no longer suffice. For example, salary raises may help, but improved salaries are not sufficient in themselves. The Council for Exceptional Children's Ad Hoc Committee to Study and Respond to the 1983 Report of the National Commission on Excellence in Education noted, "educators also require environments which are supportive, provide sufficient teaching resources, recognize and strengthen professionalism, and encourage and support continuing professional development" (CEC, 1984, p. 490). The message of the Commission is clear: if we are to improve education as a profession and ourselves as professionals, we must do so based on our own abilities, skills, and commitment in an atmosphere of positive and productive support.

REFERENCES

Arreenich, T. (1982). A study of factors influencing the burnout syndrome as perceived by North Dakota Public School classroom teachers. (Doctoral dissertation, University of North Dakota, 1981). *Dissertation Abstracts International, 42* (University Microfilms No. DA 8207354)

Bauer, R. W. (1982–83). Our own self-esteem. *Today's Education, 71,* 37–38.

Burke, R. J., & Belcourt, M. L. (1974). Managerial role stress and coping responses. *Journal of Business Administration, 5,* 44–68.

CEC Ad Hoc Committee to Study and Respond to the 1983 Report of the National Commission on Excellence in Education. (1984). *Exceptional Children, 50,* 484–492.

Dewe, P., Guest, D., & Williams, R. (1979). Methods of coping with work-related stress. In C. Mackay & T. Cox (eds.). *Response to stress: Occupational aspects.* Guildford: IPC Science and Technology Press.

Farber, B. (1981). *Teacher burnout: Summary of first phase of research done in academic year 1980–81.* Unpublished report. Teachers College, Columbia University, New York, NY.

Fimian, M. J. (1980). Stress reduction techniques for teachers. *The Pointer, 1*(2), 64–70.

Fimian, M. J. (1984). *Social support and occupational stress among special education teachers.* Paper submitted for publication. Department of Special Education, Appalachian State University, Boone, NC.

Fimian, M. J., & Santoro, T. M. (1983). Sources and manifestations of occupational stress as reported by full-time special education teachers. *Exceptional Children, 49,* 540–543.

Fullan, M., Miles, B. M., & Taylor, C. (1980). Organization development in the schools: The state of the art. *Review of Educational Research, 50,* 121–183.

Gallery, M. E., Eisenbach, J. J., & Holman, J. (1981). *Burnout: A critical appraisal and proposed intervention strategies.* Unpublished manuscript. Department of Special Education, Western Michigan University, Kalamazoo.

Gmelch, W. H., & Swent, B. (1981). Stress and the principalship: Strategies for self-improvement and growth. *NASSP Bulletin, 65,* 16–19.

Greenberg, S. F., & Valletutti, R. J. (1980). *Stress and the helping professions.* Baltimore, MD: Paul Brooks, Inc.

Houten, R. V. (1980). *How to motivate others through feedback.* Lawrence, KS: H & H Enterprises, Inc.

Instructor survey. (1977). *Instructor, 86,* 12.

Lemley, R. E. (1981). Where does one begin? An "up close and personal" look. *NASSP Bulletin, 65,* 20–23.

McCabe, M. (1984). Still tense? Maybe work makes you sick. *The Charlotte Observer.* Sunday, May 6, 5E.

McKnab, P. A., & Mehring, T. A. (1984, April). *Attrition in special education: Rates and reasons.* Paper presented to the Council for Exceptional Children, Washington, D.C.

Minner, S., & Beane, A. (1983). Professional dilemmas for teachers of mentally retarded children. *Education and Training of the Mentally Retarded, 18,* 131–133.

Needle R. H., Griffin, T., & Svendson, R. (1981). Occupational stress: Coping and health problems of teachers. *The Journal of School Health, 51,* 175–181.

Spicuzza, F. J., & DeVoe, M. W. (1982). Burnout in the helping professions: Mutual aid groups as self-help. *The Personnel and Guidance Journal, 61,* 95–98.

Taylor, L., & Salend, J. S. (1983). Reducing stress-related burnout through a network support system. *The Pointer, 27*(4), 5–9.

Thomas, W. R. (1984, April). *Occupational stress among exceptional education teachers.* Paper presented to the Council for Exceptional Children, Washington, D.C.

Thompson, J. W. (1980). "Burnout" in group home house parents. *American Journal of Psychiatry, 137,* 713–714.

Werner, A. (1980). The principal's role: Support for teachers in stress. *The Pointer, 24,* 54–60.

. . . .

STRATEGIES FOR SELF-UNDERSTANDING

Logically, self-understanding comes before attempting to understand others. Through an awareness of our own life experience, we appreciate the life experiences of others. Self-insight provides an understanding of our own behavior and enables us to moderate useless social relationships. Many troubled students have not been accepted because of their behaviors. Our task is to be accepting, though not permissive. There is always a relationship of a teacher self to a student self, even when a teacher attempts to be objective or nonrelating. Students soon learn how to push our sensitivity buttons, and if we react on their level we are not being helpful. This is a part of the Conflict Cycle discussed on page 244. One of the common reasons for caring and enthusiastic teachers' departure from the field is that the behavior pupils induce in them is foreign to their teaching self-image. They become depressed at yelling or punishing their students in futile efforts to get control. Yet one can observe a teacher who appears completely oblivious to the impact of the self on students and of students on the teaching self. Signals are sent by both verbal and nonverbal communication, regardless of our efforts to be antiseptic.

Teaching is the only interpersonal relationship profession that eschews self-understanding. In one way or another, often as an integral part of the training, social workers, psychiatrists, and clinical psychologists are expected to undergo a cursory, or even a thorough, self-awareness experience. When one teaches troubled students, their behavior encourages resonance with one's own past or present life. Personal unfinished business can interfere with the ability to help by calling forth denial or overidentification with the student's situation. For example, a teacher who has experienced an unresolved divorce custody battle should recognize how this may affect counseling a student who is facing the same dilemma. Suppose a teacher feels unsuccessful in life or in raising his or her own offspring. When a student then says, "You can't help me; nobody can help me," how will that affect the teacher–student relationship? It takes both courage and skill to create a common bond by seeing the situation as one that is commonly shared during our life journeys.

A well-known admonition is to "know thyself and thy profession." It is interesting that educators are quick to recommend counseling for others and are the last to engage in it themselves, even when their work becomes an emotional burden. Freud has said that the most difficult task anyone faces is self-understanding, which he saw as the basis of becoming truly human. To gain self-insight, there are many simple things to do, in addition to formal counseling. Personality scales are available for "normal" individuals. A most useful technique is to write an autobiography and analyze the impact of family and subsequent significant events on your development. Are you by nature more of a rebel than a conformist? How much risk capital do you have for investment in new activities? As previously suggested, one can do a time line and a family interview and apply them to one's own life. Frank discussions with trusted colleagues concerning the handling of problematic situations open the door to self-reflections. In this work, one has to learn to take disappointments and failures and not just attribute them to inadequacy.

All too frequently, we inflict our unfinished business on those under our charge. "No more of that. If there is anything I can't stand, it's foul language [or whatever gets to us]." Such statements put students in control by advertising what will upset us. One of the exercises that produces self-awareness requires a description of the kids or situations least liked and a comparison with those that are rewarding. The next step is to consider the *why* beyond the responses. Do the most liked become class favorites while the disliked get indifference or extra restrictions? We are highly differential in our acceptance of youngsters, often in reverse order of their need for our help. Self-awareness can blunt the impact of our personal hang-ups on relationships with children, families, or the system. This is not to imply that we must be perfect ourselves, but we do have to be in control of our sensitivities. Teacher mental health does not demand that teachers must mold into a pattern of the always smiling, calm, and patient adult. But teachers can view their own successes and failures with some objectivity. They can feel hopeful enough to put zest into their teaching and to continue to learn and grow. They can feel the gamut of human emotions. No human is always cheerful, patient, and carefree. A teacher who knows he or she has acted crabby all morning, because of a squabble at home, can still pull things together for a more normal afternoon. The first person in every face-off is one's self.

Personal aspects blend with professional requirements. One place to start professional self-examination is to study professional codes produced by local systems and by national organizations such as the Council for Exceptional Children. Does your personal practice follow the code? Do you have arguments with some code items? Does your system follow the code? There is much to be gained by discussing some of the following items with a colleague confidant. What are your motivations for entering and staying in the difficult profession of teaching troubled students? Are your goals realistic? Are psychological or physical fears generated in your work? How long do you expect to be in this role? Do you take the students' problems home with you at night? Are there certain pupils who depress you and make you feel hopeless? How do you deal with such feelings? Do you dread meeting certain parents? What do your friends and relatives think about your profession?

One of the best sources of information about the professional self of a teacher is the pupils, but the teacher must be willing to encourage feedback from them. They can tell us how we are helpful and how we are not. Some systems provide consultation that reflects on both personal and professional growth. No matter the years of experience, all systems should provide realistic consultation on responding to difficult cases.

This chapter began with the saga of understanding the student self, and it concludes with these comments on the saga of the teacher self, the alpha and omega of our business. Even as each of us is a fascinating and complex adult, so is each new pupil an exciting individual conundrum to be solved. Our profession is a continual quest to comprehend life journeys.

4

The Power of Group Forces in the Classroom: Strategies and Skills of Promoting Positive Group Behavior

Groups are ubiquitous. Except for the rare hermit, humans are immersed in group life of one kind or another. Many times, we need the stimulation of a group; at other times, we seek escape to nourish our individuality. In their pursuit of group contact, students range from virtual addiction to a take-it-or-leave-it attitude. For growing youngsters, group life is a laboratory for exploring the fundamental nature of self, the sense of belonging, and the newness of becoming. Group membership has highly individual values for particular participants. A teacher may think of the classroom group as a place for academic learning; some pupils may see that same class as a convenient site for making social contacts. Teachers usually find that dealing with a troubled student on an individual basis is simple compared to dealing with that student in a peer setting. Students who are amenable as individuals may join the enemy when they are in a group. It is important to remember that the teacher is a minority of one in a classroom, and the assumed power of the teacher can sometimes be an illusion.

Simply stated, a group is an aggregate of persons who are related in some way, and who are joined by a social structure. A family is a group. So are a half-dozen teenagers independently watching their favorite TV show, all preparing to participate in tomorrow's peer group exegesis at school. Schools themselves are group agencies; they harbor a myriad of formal and informal peer groups. Teachers direct their instruction to the individual, but most of this teaching takes place in group settings; nevertheless, most instruction is targeted to the group average. Incidentally, much educational research on learning yields little benefit for classroom teachers because results are confounded by powerful group currents that are not factored in.

Group membership presents a dilemma. To affiliate as a group member can provide rewards, but belonging usually requires some compromise of individuality. Yet the pull for social participation, response, and verification is strong. Even temporarily uncoupling a youngster from social contact constitutes strong medicine. Forced isolation is a punishment most of us would avoid. Group phenomena described in this chapter commingle with other content of this book, especially the chapters on curriculum, crisis, and helping.

To appreciate the impact of groups in our lives, each of us can do an interesting accounting. (This activity is also appropriate for our students as an introduction to their understanding of groups in their lives.) First, list all group involvements for the past week, including telephone conversations, and indicate the time spent. What benefits were derived from each group? Did you attend any groups where you felt like an alien rather than a participant? What roles did you play in each group? How many ways could you classify these groups (age, purpose, elected or required, etc.)? Some groups are fortuitous and others are scheduled. Exploring one's own group life is the best preparation for this chapter.

Group life is a consuming quest for most students of all ages. It does not await adolescence, as some have opined. If students are working in booths, they will peer out or sometimes make holes to see how their neighbors are doing. In classrooms, students conduct surveillance scans to see who is doing something they need to appraise. Any noise is a signal for alert. Schools devise classroom groups for academic learning; at the same time, the give-and-take of group life is the setting for social learning. Feedback from the group reaffirms identity. So powerful is group involvement to adolescents that some mental health personnel consider group work necessary to reach this age.

Of the many types of groups serving different functions for members, a major distinction is made between primary and secondary groups. The most significant imprinting takes place in primary groups. The prototype is the family, which ideally is relatively permanent, intimate, and safe. Because the child is dependent, the family is expected to provide for basic physical and psychological needs. Family interaction is the transition channel for developing and sustaining values, nurturing the emergence of a healthy self-concept, and enforcing social behavior standards. Where the child is loved and cared for, such adaptations are possible. The obvious problem today is that many of our troubled students come to school unfinished or distorted because they have never had a satisfactory primary family experience. The school, expecting to use and expand the socialization gained in the family, instead finds itself in the business of creating the moral substrata, a most difficult and consuming task for which most school settings are ill equipped. We all benefit from the sustaining support of a primary group throughout life. Even as adults, we mourn the loss of a family member. For a child, the breakup of the family primary group has traumatic implications. The pull of the gang mores is decisive for some youngsters because the gang becomes a substitute familylike primary group that fulfills deep affiliation needs. A caring classroom for troubled children can become a surrogate primary group that will have a deep and lasting impact on students.

A youngster who has incorporated the lessons of the family primary group is ready for secondary group participation. This expanded group life is exciting, though not always easy to negotiate. The usual classroom, with peers, activities, and an adult leader dedicated to helping, is an excellent example of a secondary group. Young children often have a difficult time sorting it all out; sometimes, they call a teacher "Mother." There are all those siblinglike peers to get along with, and children hope some will become their friends. But there are also the school tasks the child is supposed to stick with, even when they seem impossible or boring. Year after year, a school group can be heaven or hell. A multitude of dimensions intermix in a classroom group, and any generalizations are hazardous. One class may be a sharing, interdependent place for learning. Another may be competitive and individualistic. Teachers differ in style and in their use of power in the classroom. Nevertheless, membership is mandated, particularly for special classes. A major motivation of many special students is to get out of the separated group and rejoin regular peers, even when past experience there has ended in failure. Schools offer many group affiliations beyond the classroom: playground, lunchroom, hall hangout, ethnic groups, the jocks, the brains, and street gangs. Most schools develop an "in" and "out" group stratification well known to the students. Amid all the hustle and activity of a large middle or high school, it is hard to remember that many of our troubled children are lonely and miss out on healthy peer associations.

In spite of the fact that schools are group agencies and teachers are group leaders, group dynamics is shortchanged in professional education. Teachers have two vital interests in classroom group dynamics: (a) to understand what transpires in groups and assess the impact on individual youngsters, and (b) to change unhealthy group conditions and create classes that are caring places. A class can become the most stable "primarylike" group the pupil experiences, if the teacher develops trust through seeing the students as they could be—their promise rather than their present shortcomings. In a rare quiet moment, one special-class student spoke out as follows: "This class is like a family. We spends lots of time here. Teach, you are like a parent trying to help us. And all of these brothers and sisters. We do lots of things together. We eat here. We have parties, and we go on trips together. Only we don't sleep here." No one added anything more, and the group went back to its work.

It is instructive for both teachers and pupils to consider the variety of teacher and student roles enacted in school classes. Role analysis allows us to observe both actual and wished-for identities. In general, troubled children have ineffective classroom roles though they may be successful in peer groups outside of class. Often, special classrooms are saturated with negative peer roles such as clowns, bullies, negative instigators, and seekers of attention-at-any-cost. As we know, these students are generally referred because of their negative effect on their own and the class's learning. One class finally explained why they could not have successful group sessions. The "hard gels" (the tough antisocial and delinquent members) would have nothing to do with the "soft gels" (the anxious, nervous youngsters). The hard gels did not consider themselves to be in the same class psychologically, regardless of their physical placement.

Sadist–scapegoat pairs enjoy each other. Idea youngsters introduce creativity, though not necessarily in the desired direction. Feuding clans may bring an outside conflict into the classroom. The class group may have a conflict generator or a conflict resolver, a magpie or a silent and isolated watcher. Sometimes, a junior cleric announces the sins of others, earning their considerable consternation. Peers often assume co-teaching roles. We would appreciate a group of interested learners who take delight in legitimate new school experiences. It would make a teacher's life simpler if school groups were internally balanced with complementary roles that led to harmony and productive enterprise but, in a group of troubled children, there are seldom enough positive roles to balance the negative ones. Most of our youngsters crave affiliation even in the face of negative feedback. One role we can be sure of for pupils is that of cultural anthropologist—someone who compares and evaluates how various teachers conduct their roles, in order to exploit any discrepancies. Life in children's play groups and adolescent peer groups can be cruel. Finding ways to empower youngsters in positive roles is a large part of the helping task.

A teacher necessarily plays many roles in a day, or even in an hour: listener, dispenser of information, giver of caring, advisor, lawgiver, limit setter, police officer, jurist, and judge. The teacher is continually modeling values and behavior. Difficult teaching roles include protector of the weak and even-tempered responder to misplaced hostility and anger. Some teachers are freedom misers; others conduct more laissez-faire classes. All the while, the teacher–counselor role is supposed to be operating to accomplish academics and personal support.

Group dynamics and teacher leadership styles are seldom considered in pupil placements. We do know that group interactions are such a major concern that teachers often class them as interfering with the main goal of teaching the curriculum. The fact is, group problems are outcroppings of students' personal and social problems, and working with these problems is a significant part of the curriculum for troubled children. Methodologies are offered in many of the chapters in this book, especially Chapter 5 on discipline. A good understanding of group processes can lead to design of helpful rather than hurtful group life for youngsters.

We all recognize how group power impinges on us. Peer power is especially obvious in the lives of children and adolescents. What is the nature of this power? Groups have overt and covert ways of giving or withholding affiliation. A student group can accept or reject a potential member, regardless of the fact that the student is physically assigned to a given cooperative learning pod. Groups impose roles and give uncomplimentary names to hapless low-power members. As gang members realize, there is safety and protection in membership. Groups dispense belongingness as well as rejection. Redl pointed out that groups also provide behavior insurance. "We was all doing it" is like saying "None of us is accountable." Groups provide an audience and a response source, and they empower members. Members are defended against external threats, a major consideration in the lives of many pupils. The more sophisticated members become behavior models for emulation for the next stage in development. Groups provide potential friends and associates to do things with. Groups have power because they are the source for filling many psychological needs.

The more cohesive the group, the greater the group power. Cohesion refers to the intensity of the members' identification with the group life. In a worst-case scenario, a class may become cohesive through common dislike of a teacher. Some groups send messages to the student who doesn't join in: Shape up to the group mores or be cast out. Initiation rights of some nature usually precede membership, as is evident when a new pupil is introduced. If the "just passing" mode is accepted as the group academic standard, those who outperform are labeled "teacher's pet" or "smart ass," and are expected to dumb down or suffer isolation, which presents a conflict for high-performing students. While adults are praising diversity, the group is espousing modal behavior.

It is useful to know the history of the group one is teaching. Groups develop self-perceptions. One group might consider itself the "retard" group or the "trouble maker" group that has a reputation to uphold. Groups develop their own code of rights and misdemeanors; Sarason calls it their local constitution and bill of rights. This code is often quite different from the teacher-imposed code posted in a conspicuous place in the classroom. There are expectations of how one should be treated by authorities, and what punishments are fit for breaking what rules. A teacher who tries to trace an incident is often stymied by the article in the bill of rights that reads "No squealing on a member." Both by observation and group discussion, a teacher can learn about the peer code and open up issues for consideration.

Several common group phenomena are often seen in classes with troubled youngsters. Redl introduced contagion, where a guiltless provoker juices up the group by acting out behavior far beyond the usual limits. Group members join and become intoxicated with the ascending activity, which might involve defying the teacher or riding the scapegoat as school lets out. The behavior spirals up until it reaches an intensity that shocks some of the perpetrators. They then call a halt, turning on the stimulator. The provoker loses power and becomes "the bad guy," and the others take refuge in their newfound holiness. It's "all his fault" and they are guiltless.

There is another type of instantaneous contagion where a subgroup of students with the same pathologies (siblings under the psychological skin) behave as a unit. A teacher addresses one, and it is as if all four were directly chided to get on-task. The three who escaped censure cannot restrain their enjoyment of the one caught while they escaped, and a disruption occurs. In this unique instance of a ripple effect, a teacher addresses one student but the impact ripples differentially throughout the class.

We have also witnessed what we call the "pie process." Nobody does "nothing," yet chaos results. Each member does his or her own thing with no feeling of guilt, but the cumulative activity beckons other members to add their bit, and so the chaos spreads. Each contributor acts within the confines of his or her own conscience and thus feels blameless. One is "the idea man": "I know where we could steal some stuff." The second produces the strategy for an escapade. The third is the lookout, and two others help out with the act. No one feels guilty, having played only a partial role in what was proposed by someone else, an act the member wouldn't ever have thought of were it not for the seductive idea man. Groups also develop rituals or games that can go on sub rosa in the midst of a class. Playing the Dozens, to be described in the next chapter, is such a game. First, the players signify they are in, then the teasing starts. Knowing vulnerabilities, the taunters can hit hurting spots. The words may only be mouthed and not spoken, or gestures may be used (the finger), but the players know what is meant. Everyone tries to "stay cool" but finally someone can't stand it any longer. Losing one's cool is a sign for all players to have a free hit on the loser. Then they may start a new round. Because the rules allow for a free punch, no player minds the social disruption resulting from collecting the winnings. After the hits, the players usually subside as if nothing had happened. There are often intimidators in a group who collect possessions given by peers. The motivation for giving has been fear. It takes a lot of work to unravel group behavior, and it requires ingenuity to propose acceptable alternatives. Groups of troubled youngsters often join the battle of the generations. To upset the teacher, someone starts the "You're not fair" game, or the "Our other teacher doesn't make us" game. Every substitute teacher knows these games for what they are and develops countertactics. Adults can be a vulnerable minority to the peer culture.

If the peer group is not to be the enemy, teachers of troubled children have to apply strategies to convert group life to positive ends. Instructional groups may be cooperative or competitive, congenial or hostile, and the actual leadership may reside in a student rather than the teacher. Didactic lectures are seldom effective. Interventions can be divided into the indirect and direct. The indirect change strategies employ such arrangements as cooperative learning (Chapter 8), selection of particular members for group projects, and use of games with particular interaction properties. Direct interventions are group work and counseling focused on the particular problems. Both will be discussed in the papers that follow.

A teacher's first task is to know the social relationships in the class. Through observation, teachers usually have a reasonable perception of pupils' likes and dislikes. The stars and isolates may be evident, but there are usually some surprises in the youngsters' actual reports. A teacher prediction chart can be compared with the pupil responses on the variables that Popieil, Hollinger, Loschi, and Crawford suggest in the first article. These authors are properly cautious concerning the impact of asking for negative choices: one does not request any information unless there is a hygienic plan to digest possible consequences, especially with already troubled youngsters. Knowing the social structure opens the door for possible alterations. The authors go beyond discovery to examples of how one rectifies unsavory conditions. In some cases, individual and group counseling will be required. In other cases, the teacher utilizes indirect methods such as specific assignments to cooperative work groups.

The important thing is to go beyond likes and dislikes to the *why* of the choices. This requires an analysis of the nature of the individuals chosen and rejected and the implications for healthy group life. Some classes distribute as much as 90% of their liking to only 10% of the group. Other classes are more widespread in their distribution of positive targets. Studies report that, in general, our pupils are more likely to be rejectees, either as victims or as victimizers. Some classes are very different places when just one student is absent. Rearrangement of liking–disliking patterns is very difficult, especially with insecure youngsters. Both the choice givers and receivers are potential candidates for change. Even the rejectees have a desperate attachment to what they consider their rightful group membership—another illustration of the power of belonging. It is also important to recognize that some students have quite another set of social relationships, and perhaps a very different role, outside of the classroom.

The use of a sociometric approach to understanding classroom relationships is presented by Popeil et al. The authors are all graduates of the Rose School training program as developed by Nicholas Long while at the American University. They provide easy-to-follow directions for conducting a class sociometric, help on analyzing the information, and recommendations for change.

ARTICLE 4.1

A Sociometric Approach to Understanding Interpersonal Relationships in a Classroom for Emotionally Disturbed Pupils

Pamela S. Popeil, J. Daniel Hollinger, Grace A. Loschi, and Donna R. Crawford

Just as groups can act as a primary force for reinforcing deviant behavior, they also can become a powerful force for promoting the mental health of group members. Groups have the potential to provide a sense of acceptance

From *The Pointer*. (1983). Vol. 27, No. 3. Reprinted with permission.

and status, to protect from threats of other groups or individuals, and to internalize the group norms, values, and standards of its members. Most important, groups provide a network of friendships and the opportunity to develop new social skills.

All too often special classes of emotionally disturbed pupils develop their own peer counter-culture in which the social structure and interpersonal relationships are designed to resist the reeducation program. Unfortunately, too little professional time has been directed to this problem. Also, the emphasis on the IEP has diluted and denied the importance of understanding group dynamics and those select pupils who have the attributed social power to influence and control other pupils in the classroom.

Unless the teacher is aware of these social forces, behavior management and group instructional decisions cannot be made with any precision or accuracy. Consequently, it is the practice at Rose School to collect sociometric data from each classroom.

ADMINISTERING THE L-J SOCIOMETRIC TEST (NOTE #1)

The L-J Sociometric Test (Long, 1966) is best administered by the classroom teacher at least four weeks after a group is formed. An interval of at least six weeks is recommended before readministering the test.

The variables that the L-J test measure are *liking, like the least,* and *fear.* A few teachers and principals have strong feelings about collecting data on "like the least" and "fear" because it appears that they would be creating and/or solidifying social rejection. Long's research in this area documents that these variables do not create any new ideals or attitudes in pupils. They know, with great clarity, whom they like and dislike. The group members know it but usually do not use the information therapeutically. The only person in the class who may not know it but is in a position to take corrective measures is the classroom teacher. If the teacher stresses the confidentiality of the information, the small risk of collecting personal data is significantly outweighed by the benefits this information can have for the group and individual pupils.

DATA COLLECTION

If class size is smaller than twelve, the students are asked to give a first and second choice to the following three questions:

1. Who do you like most in this class?
2. Who do you like least in this class?
3. What students in this class can make others afraid of them?

The last question is important since certain pupils have social power in the classroom not because the pupils like them but because they fear them. This negative power needs to be identified early in the school year.

After the data are collected, the information is recorded on a matrix table which shows how the students rate each other. Two types of data are derived. First, each row represents the rater's two choices; and second, each column represents each pupil's frequency of choice and weighted score. A weighted score is obtained by assigning three points for each first choice and two points for each second choice.

The weighted score is used to assign each pupil to an appropriate band on the sociometric target.

> *Band 1* is the outer band of the target and represents those pupils whose weighted score is zero or "Significantly Below Expected Base Score."
>
> *Band 2* is the "Below Expected Score" and represents weighted scores between 1–4.
>
> *Band 3* is the "Expected Base Score" and represents a weighted score of five (5).
>
> *Band 4* is the "Above Expected Score" and represents weighted scores between 6–10.
>
> *Band 5* is the inner band of the target and represents weighted scores of 11+ which are "Significantly Above the Expected Base Score."

Once each pupil is assigned to his proper band, based on his weighted score, a line is drawn from each pupil to his first choice. The result is a graphic picture of the social structure of the classroom.

For example, on Matrix Table 1: *Liking* (on page 194), Andy (No. 1) selects Harold (No. 8) as his first choice and Frank (No. 6) as his second choice (Row Analysis). Andy in turn was selected twice, once by Ed (No. 5) as his first choice and by Frank (No. 6) as his second choice. Therefore, Andy's frequency score is 2 and his weighted score is 5. (Three points for a first choice plus 2 points for a second choice).

To transfer Andy's weighted score of 5 to the sociometric target on "Liking," he would be placed in Band 3 (Expected Base Score) and a line connecting Andy to his first choice Harold (No. 8) would be drawn. This is repeated until all pupils are placed in their appropriate band and connecting preferences are drawn.

GROUP INTERPRETATION OF THE SOCIOMETRIC TARGET

The complex social structure in the classroom requires careful analysis in order to understand accurately significant group roles.

MATRIX TABLE 1: Liked the Most

Group:
Date:

CHOICES

	1 (Andy)	2 (Bob)	3 (Carl)	4 (Don)	5 (Ed)	6 (Frank)	7 (Gary)	8 (Harold)	9 (Ian)	10 (Jon)
1 (Andy)						2		1		
2 (Bob)						2		1		
3 (Carl)						1		2		
4 (Don)					1	2				
5 (Ed)	1			2						
6 (Frank)	2				1					
7 (Gary)		2						1		
8 (Harold)		1			2					
9 (Ian)		1			2					
10 (Jon)				2	1					
No. of times selected	2	3	0	2	5	4	0	4	0	0
Weighted score	5	8	0	4	13	9	0	11	0	0

ANALYSIS OF LIKED THE MOST: MATRIX AND TARGET I

Ed (No. 5) and Harold (No. 8) were chosen as the most liked students with weighted scores of 13 and 11 respectively. Frank (No. 6) was chosen the same amount of times as Harold but received a lower weighted score. These three students share similar characteristics. They tend to be withdrawn and avoid confrontation with other students. Their passive approach to social interaction does not promote active use of the social power ascribed to them by their peers. As a result they are underusers of attributed social power.

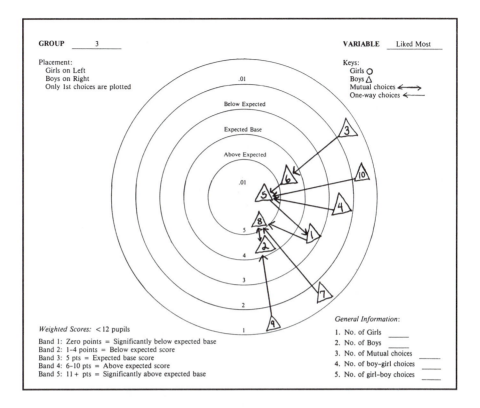

GROUP ____3____   VARIABLE ___Liked Most___

Placement:
Girls on Left
Boys on Right
Only 1st choices are plotted

Keys:
Girls ○
Boys △
Mutual choices ←——→
One-way choices ←———

.01

Below Expected

Expected Base

Above Expected

.01

5

4

3

2

1

Weighted Scores: <12 pupils

Band 1: Zero points = Significantly below expected base
Band 2: 1–4 points = Below expected score
Band 3: 5 pts = Expected base score
Band 4: 6–10 pts = Above expected score
Band 5: 11+ pts = Significantly above expected base

General Information:

1. No. of Girls ____
2. No. of Boys ____
3. No. of Mutual choices ____
4. No. of boy-girl choices ____
5. No. of girl-boy choices ____

The distinction between attributed assigned power and manifest actual power is a crucial factor in the analysis of this group. Although Ed, Harold, and Frank were chosen as the most liked students, they are passive in the group. Their potential positive influence is thwarted by strong negative influences of several other students and a lack of cohesion among the three of them.

A close look at the dynamics among Ed, Harold, and Frank reveals that Ed is the recipient of friendship from Harold and Frank. However, Ed expresses no preference for either Harold or Frank. This lack of cohesion among the most preferred students diminishes the potential for this group to be positive and active. It is important to note that Carl (No. 3), Gary (No. 7), Ian (No. 9), and Jon (No. 10) received no positive choices. This finding highlighted the lack of peer acceptance in this classroom. Consequently, the classroom teacher needs to fill this gap in leadership by reinforcing and encouraging positive attempts these three pupils make.

ANALYSIS OF LIKED THE LEAST: MATRIX AND TARGET II

The sociometric target illustrates a real subgap around rejection in this group. For example, Ian (No. 9) chose Don (No. 4), who chose Carl (No. 3), and Carl completed the triangle by choosing Ian. The rest of the group split their rejection between Carl and Ian.

MATRIX TABLE 2: Liked the Least

Group:
Date:

CHOICES

	1 (Andy)	2 (Bob)	3 (Carl)	4 (Don)	5 (Ed)	6 (Frank)	7 (Gary)	8 (Harold)	9 (Ian)	10 (Jon)
1 (Andy)		2							1	
2 (Bob)							2		1	
3 (Carl)				2					1	
4 (Don)			1						2	
5 (Ed)			1							2
6 (Frank)			1						2	
7 (Gary)			2						1	
8 (Harold)	2						1			
9 (Ian)				1			2			
10 (Jon)							2		1	
No. of times selected	1	1	4	2	0	0	4	0	7	1
Weighted score	2	2	11	5	0	0	9	0	19	2

This interconnection is interesting. In the classroom, as the targets indicate, Carl is the scapegoat, Ian is the most aggressive, Gary is the most powerful, and Don *tries* to be the most aggressive.

In the interpretation of significant group roles, Carl and Ian are the "significantly rejected" pupils. This correlates with actual patterns in the classroom. Carl bears the brunt of jokes, teasing, and embarrassment from other students. Carl is the clear example of a scapegoat. He is a person with little status in the classroom, and the group has given him a name— "Fat Carl." It is amazing to see the entire "cycle" unfold daily. Carl will

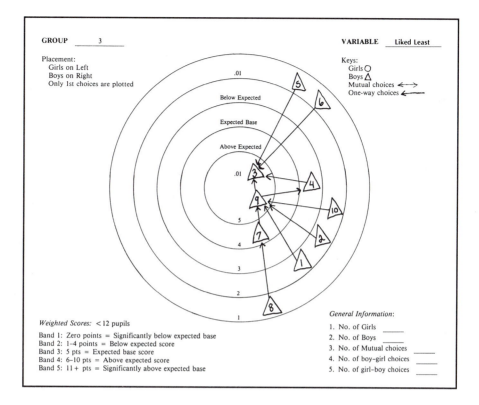

GROUP   3   VARIABLE   Liked Least

Placement: Keys:
  Girls on Left   Girls ○
  Boys on Right   Boys △
  Only 1st choices are plotted   Mutual choices ⟵⟶
                                                                One-way choices ⟵

Below Expected

Expected Base

Above Expected

Weighted Scores: < 12 pupils

Band 1: Zero points = Significantly below expected base
Band 2: 1–4 points = Below expected score
Band 3: 5 pts = Expected base score
Band 4: 6–10 pts = Above expected score
Band 5: 11+ pts = Significantly above expected base

General Information:
1. No. of Girls _____
2. No. of Boys _____
3. No. of Mutual choices _____
4. No. of boy–girl choices _____
5. No. of girl–boy choices _____

make attempts to get "in" with the group, and the group rejects him. Carl, not liking the rejection, will act out, which then gives the rest of the group the opportunity to be hostile towards him without feeling guilty. The entire cycle applies perfectly to this on-going situation within the classroom. Ian, on the other hand, scores in both significantly rejected and feared. As opposed to Carl, Ian holds this position because he is feared rather than scapegoated.

The group appears centered around rejection. In one sense, Ian controls the class through physical aggression. Five of the ten students chose Ian as the first choice for least liked and three students chose Carl. The students who are "liked the least" were chosen for different reasons. Nonetheless, the group's patterns of behavior are governed by peer rejection.

ANALYSIS OF FEAR: MATRIX AND TARGET III

Gary (No. 7) and Ian (No. 9) are identified most feared pupils in the group. Gary and Ian also fear each other. Gary is feared because of his physical stature and sheer strength. Occasionally, his propensity to tease other students results in aggression and anger. When the "playful bear" Gary loses control, he becomes a serious threat despite his initial playful intentions. Ian presents a different type of threatening behavior. His aggression is impulsive and primitive in nature without the element of playfulness. He intimidates the group with his language and body.

The differences between Gary and Ian affect their roles in the group significantly. Gary occasionally uses his strength for helpful purposes. He is also able to interact appropriately and maintain friendships. Ian's influence is limited to destructive forces and intimidation. This is supported by the difference between their "liked least" weighted scores.

INDIVIDUAL ANALYSIS OF SIGNIFICANT GROUP ROLES

Significantly Preferred Pupil: (SPP)

A Significantly Preferred Pupil is defined as any pupil who has a weighted score of 11+ on "like the most" and a weighted score of zero on "like the least." In this class there are two SPP—Edward (No. 5) and Harold (No. 8).

Edward has responded to his reeducation program quite successfully. He participates in a mainstreaming program one hour per day which gives him special status. He also is considerably more articulate than his peers, and he shares personal property without complaint or reluctance. Psychodynamically, Edward is quite a reflective person and avoids any group responsibility. Social skills and academic success contribute to Edward's status as a preferred pupil although he does not use the status in an active leadership role.

Harold (No. 8) is also significantly preferred. Except for a recent mutual friendship with Bob (No. 2), Harold functions in his own world generally avoiding both negative and positive interaction with peers. He prefers the security of an isolated, accommodating approach to life rather than an involved, aggressive approach. Harold's nonthreatening, friendly personality makes him the recipient of preferences, but he lacks any desire for any active group leadership roles.

Significantly Rejected Pupil: (SRP)

A Significantly Rejected Pupil is defined as any pupil who has a weighted score of zero on "like the most" and a weighted score 11+ on "like the least." In this group there are two SRP: Ian (No. 9) and Carl (No. 3).

Ian's weighted score of 19 on the "least liked" question reflects intense rejection by the group. He is a socialized aggressive child with poor impulse control. The impulsive aggression behavior frequently threatens and frightens other students. The rejection he experiences results from both dislike and fear. Ian has the potential to relate affectionately and supportively with other students. However, that aspect of his social behavior is overshadowed by his intimidating behavior. Ian provides an excellent

MATRIX TABLE 3: Feared the Most

Group:
Date:

CHOICES

	1 (Andy)	2 (Bob)	3 (Carl)	4 (Don)	5 (Ed)	6 (Frank)	7 (Gary)	8 (Harold)	9 (Ian)	10 (Jon)
1 (Andy)							1		2	
2 (Bob)							1			
3 (Carl)							1		2	
4 (Don)		2							1	
5 (Ed)		1							2	
6 (Frank)									2	1
7 (Gary)		2							1	
8 (Harold)							1		2	
9 (Ian)		2					1			
10 (Jon)							2		1	
No. of times selected	0	4	0	0	0	0	6	0	8	1
Weighted score	0	9	0	0	0	0	17	0	19	3

example of a student who is rejected because of his aggression, despite his ability to interact appropriately at times.

Carl received no friendship choices and four negative choices equivalent to a weighted score of 11. The group uses Carl as a scapegoat. The group's open and negative behavior causes Carl to respond with aggressive and defensive language which the group uses to reject him. Carl then turns to the adults for intervention for protection. The group responds to his helplessness and vulnerability with more scapegoating thus continuing the unhealthy pattern.

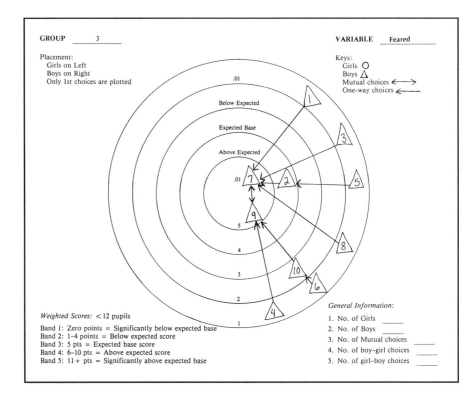

Significantly Ignored Pupil: (SIP)

A Significantly Ignored Pupil is defined as any pupil who receives a weighted score of zero on both "like the most" and "like the least" variables. This pupil is neither rejected nor liked within the group. The pupil promotes a group experience of isolation and uninvolvement.

This class fails to identify a significantly ignored pupil although Jon's (No. 10) weighted scores of zero and 2 indicate he is very close. Jon was only chosen once by Ed as a second choice, on the "like the least" question. Psychologically he has no influence in the group.

The basic social skills necessary to risk making friends have not been mastered by Jon (No. 10). He is easily frustrated by circumstances and responds with empty threats. Jon's behavior is more defeating to himself than to other students as he is easily manipulated into acting out.

Significantly Split Pupil: (SSP)

The SSP experiences significant rejection and friendship simultaneously (11+ on both variables). While there is no SSP in the class, his dual group role in the classroom can be very powerful. Teacher awareness of this group role can avoid unnecessary pairing of pupils that would lead to disruptive behavior.

Significantly Feared Pupil (SFP)

Fear is often a powerful force in social groups. Intimidating classmates with threats and physical aggression gains the aggressor a destructive position of power.

Gary (No. 7) and Ian (No. 9) were identified as the most feared students, with weighted scores of 17 and 19 respectively. However, Ian was also significantly rejected by the group. As the most feared and rejected student, Ian clearly is a negative force in the classroom. He engages other students in disruptive behavior by involving them in power struggles instigated by threats of physical aggression. Fortunately he is inept at using his social power, for his behavior is not modeled by his peers. Occasionally, a pupil who is significantly feared also is significantly preferred. When this is the case, the group has identified with the aggressor and will support his acting out behavior in the classroom.

RECOMMENDATIONS

The following recommendations are based upon the group dynamics presented in this sociometric analysis. These recommendations should enhance the gaining of respect and power by positive means as opposed to negative, i.e., aggression and intimidation. Status through positive means needs to be fostered so that the "most liked" but most passive students will not learn that social power or leadership is gained through aggression or intimidation. This can be done by:

1) *Actually teaching social skills and insights* by using a self-control curriculum, classroom meetings, and Life Space Interviewing.

2) *Placing emphasis on cooperation* rather than competition. The highly aggressive, most feared students also excel in sports. In such situations these students tend to overpower and outshine the more passive and better liked students. Positive group interaction can be encouraged by deemphasizing these competitive sports and introducing cooperative games.

3) *Promoting individual students' academic qualities.* The more passive students tend to excel in academic and artistic areas. Two of the most liked students are excellent readers while one is highly accomplished at piano. More emphasis in these areas might affect the status of these group members. Using small learning groups to help each other work through problem areas is another means of providing a more cooperative, positive atmosphere.

4) *Creating opportunities for students to be seen in a "new light."* There are times when the most aggressive and feared pupils in the classroom overflow with kindness. This kindness can be exploited

to provide opportunities for others to view and accept these students in a more positive manner.

SUMMARY

The group lacks positive cohesion but is organized around rejection. The powerful pupils in the classroom gain their power through aggression and use of fear tactics. In this kind of situation teachers spend much time and energy intervening in crisis situations making group management difficult. Management tends to be reactive rather than supportive because the most active pupils are disruptive.

The most liked and least disruptive students are also the most passive. Ed (No. 5) is susceptible to pressure from disruptive students and will occasionally participate in aggressive and inappropriate behavior in order to gain respect. Frank (No. 6) and Harold (No. 8) lack leadership qualities, limiting the possibilities for group cohesion around their positive social qualities.

Other pupils have the potential to be positive leaders within the group. In order for group cohesion to be developed, the students with leadership qualities need to channel their energy into creative and appropriate behavior rather than disruptive behavior. This can be done through strategically grouping individuals together for specific tasks, emphasizing individual talents, interest-boosting in academic areas, and providing opportunities for *all* students to be seen in a "new light."

NOTE

1. L-J Sociometric Test stands for Long and Jones who developed this test of analyzing social choices based on statistical criteria of probability.

REFERENCE

Long, N. *Direct help to the classroom teacher,* chapter 2. L-J Sociometric Test. School Research Program. The Washington School of Psychiatry. Washington, D.C., 1966.

. . . .

There is seldom homogeneity in group sociometrics. There are reciprocal choices, chains of influence, and sometimes fractures of the whole into distinct halves or thirds that resent being placed with aliens in work groups. In such cases, a teacher can explain the values of having close friends but at the same time work toward a common classroom citizenship identity. One of the most important ways to build a positive group identity is to have exciting "fun events" together, to create good memories. Treats and trips are two examples. Games that intrinsically require cooperation can be selected over individually competitive ones. Vigorous games can provide tension discharge. As we know, many at-risk youngsters would have never made it through school without team athletics. A class project involving doing something for others can also enhance positive togetherness. Selecting a class name, flag, or insignia, and posting individual pictures may foster positive belonging. Teaching problem solving to reduce conflicts can mitigate abrasions. Action-oriented therapies can foster a positive feeling about the class as a group. Camping trips (with snapshots) can start a storehouse of common positive memories. Birthday celebrations are opportunities to build positive cohesion. Teachers have found that feedback to the group about how they are learning to get along together is essential. However, any of these strategies can backfire unless the teacher is an effective group leader.

Another group analysis is the power-influence-dominance chart. Placed at the top are the most powerful members with their major characteristics, group role, and chains of influence. We need to discover why individuals have differential power, and whether the power as used is healthy for the individual and his or her peers. One way of working with a bully is to use "it" games where the "it" is low power (such as the person in the middle in dodge), or put a low-power person in a high power "it" game (Simon says), thus temporarily transforming roles. Converting negative leaders into positive ones usually requires counseling, situational alterations, and good luck. Taking negative power away from a youngster before facilitating a positive exercise of power is devaluing. Sometimes, a feisty student who is unthreatening by reason of size and prowess is taken on in a mascot or "baby brother" type of role.

Most groups require a new member initiation fee of some nature before belonging. In aggressive groups, it may be fighting for status; in gangs, it could be doing an act of external violence. Classroom groups can be taught more positive ways of welcome than a reworking of the pecking hierarchy. As friendships are building, a teacher can ask who phones or visits another class member. Peer friendship is necessary to achieve and maintain self-esteem. Team projects, when properly monitored, can encourage friendships, but we should not expect troubled students to create mature friendships without help. The instructional class climate may be cooperative or competitive, congenial or hostile, and the real leader may be the teacher or a student. There are many indirect ways to influence the quality of group life after we appreciate what is taking place, not the least of which is feedback to confront the group with its workings.

The next article by Steve Parese demonstrates the value of cohesion in groups. Parese is a master counselor at Eckerd Family Youth Alternative. This program makes extensive use of camping as a therapeutic medium.

An Example of Promoting Group Cohesion and Positive Group Behavior in an Emotionally Disturbed Classroom

Steve Parese

In a one-on-one, individualized treatment program for emotionally disturbed (ED) students, special educators sometimes overlook the potential of the classroom group itself as a motivator and a behavior management tool. The same elements that can influence a group of ED students toward inappropriate, undesirable behaviors can, when properly focused, be used to help establish and maintain desirable behaviors.

Emotionally disturbed students are often described as self-centered, impulsive, unable to interact successfully with others, and lacking in social competence. The groups they form are often transitory, incohesive, and competitive rather than cooperative. At times, these classroom groups come together or become cohesive by resisting the authority or source of help, the teacher. The purpose of this article is to describe one method used within an already-existing behavior modification program to increase the cohesiveness of just such a group, focusing their strength upon a common goal rather than a common enemy.

At The Rose School, a psychoeducational program of the D.C. Department of Mental Health: Children and Youth Services, the behavior management program integrates strategies based on psychodynamics, behavioral, and social learning theories. The behavior modification program includes a level system. As a result, daily point sheets are used to record appropriate behaviors on a half-hourly basis. Expected standards are clearly and operationally defined, and each student earns points based upon his or her behavior. At the end of each school day the points are tallied to determine which of four levels the students achieved. For instance, the highest level, Level 4, requires 300 points; Level 3, only 275; and so on. The reinforcement of this individual achievement is reflected in the color of the next day's point sheet and in the placement of the student's name in a prominently displayed achievement board. Students must earn new levels each day, so the opportunity for improvement and recognition always exists. Higher levels are rewarded both daily and at week's end with various privileges and activities.

Although this system provides for individual reinforcement of appropriate behaviors, it does little for the development of group cohesion or

The Pointer. (1989). Vol. 33, No. 3.

individual cooperation. However, it does lend itself easily to the implementation of a program designed with that purpose.

To reinforce positive behavior and encourage group cohesion, it was necessary first to identify effective group reinforcers. A class meeting was held in which the students generated a list of tangible and social rewards that they would be willing to work toward, ranging from a root beer float party to a hamster for a class pet. The teachers selected the options most feasible and described the system through which the students would have the opportunity to earn these rewards *as a group.*

Daily behavior levels were assigned a direct exchange value: Level 4 was worth 4 points, Level 3 was worth 3, and so on. Individuals having a difficult day, or choosing not to cooperate with the system, could still contribute at least 1 point; *everyone's* involvement counted. With 10 students in the class, the group might earn as many as 40 points in a day or as few as 10. These points were recorded at the end of each school day on a 3-foot "thermometer" displayed in the front of the room; as group points were added in, the "mercury" rose steadily each day. The highest scoring student for each day had the privilege of filling in that day's progress.

Rewards were scheduled into the chart for reinforcement. The group earned the root beer float party after earning 100 points, and immediately they became more enthusiastic about progressing toward the next goal. Discussions at class meetings centered around the group's present level and ways to move the mercury even faster. Students soon discovered that encouraging one another's positive behavior resulted in higher individual levels and thus greater group progress toward the next reward. Even the group scapegoat made valuable contributions and thus improved his status.

The daily charting became a focus of group attention and conversation and continued until the end of the marking period, about 6 weeks after its inception, when the class had earned a trip to the pet store to choose their new pet—a golden hamster they dubbed Fuzzy!

During this 6-week trial, teachers noticed an increase in the class's cooperative, prosocial behavior and a small corresponding improvement in individual achievement. Most important, the students felt that they had earned their rewards as a group and so enjoyed them with less selfishness than with individual rewards. Although by no means an objective measure, the encouraging results of this method indicate a strategy through which common motivating goals might be used within an already existing behavior modification system to promote group cohesion, which, in turn, may help to establish and maintain desirable, prosocial behavior.

. . . .

Cohesion is the social glue that holds a group together. A highly cohesive group exists when the members are welded together by a common identity and attraction to the group. It is not enough to be cohesive. For our work, cohesion should be combined with positive cooperation. An essential process is to have rewards earned as a group rather than by individuals.

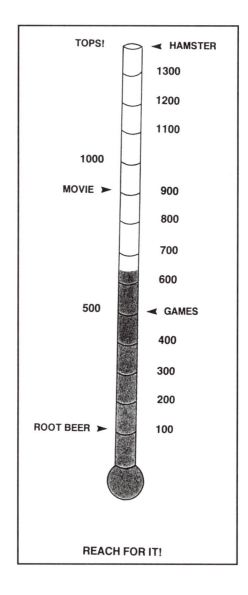

Sometimes, the most cohesive groups are anything but placid: strong opinions are voiced, and disgruntled members threaten to leave. When a member of a truly cohesive group threatens to leave, a re-inclusion effort is launched to induce an unhappy soul back. One caution should be recognized when employing Parese's methodology of total group awards. With so much depending on the group performance, any member automatically becomes empowered to sabotage a group effort. In a few cases, a student does just that. The group then turns on this member in consternation. The use of tactics other than total group performance to foster cohesion should be considered when saboteurs are prevalent.

A direct approach to bringing help to troubled children is available through group work or group therapy. Usually on a regular basis, though sometimes only as an issue arises, members discuss various classroom and personal problems. The goal is to employ problem solving to devise solutions. Proposed behavioral changes are tried out and reassessed at subsequent sessions. A youngster learns that he or she is not alone in troubles and gets help on solutions from peers as well as adults. Often, the recognition of another's plight increases interpersonal acceptance. Hobbs (1982), the father of ReED programs, incorporates group "pow wows" as an essential element in treatment.

Group crises represent a special case for group life-space interviews (Chapter 7). Leadership in such helping groups is usually shared by a teacher and mental health specialist, or a teacher and aide who have been trained in group process. Training and consultation are essential. The intent of group work is to foster mutual empathy and to enhance group cohesion. Here, spoken and unspoken group codes can be explored. In many instances, peers are more effective than adults at suggesting resolutions for conflicts and giving age-relevant advice about problems. In effect, youth become realistic co-counselors.

Group work is not a simple matter and has different parameters than the academic class. Unfortunately, few teachers receive formal training in group counseling. In addition to reading and attending training seminars, beginners typically start with a co-leader. Anderson and Marrone (1979) advocate a few simple rules such as the freedom to speak on any topic the student wishes. Confidentiality is stressed. No one is forced to contribute on a topic, and the content stays in the room. Over many years, these authors have conducted thousands of groups for troubled children in the public school and would not consider a helping program without including "cost effective . . . therapeutic discussion groups in the classroom." It has been our experience that both in crises life-space interviews and in scheduled discussion groups, the group process often induces, for the first time, significant ideation related to behavior of the youngster. Because some material revealed is of such a nature as to require subsequent individual attention, group counseling must be collated with individual counseling.

Resistance to accepting help in groups is as real as resistance in individual counseling. We should not forget that the members did not choose enrollment. The reasons and values of group work and group goals must be explained at the initial session. A minimum of simple rules suffices, such as: no one is forced to contribute on a topic; what we talk about does not go outside this room; everyone gets a chance to contribute while others listen without interrupting; each person tells his or her story.

Group work is a specific way in which the school can provide personalized social learning for troubled kids. Three themes are often obvious: (a) "Others have my same problem so I am not alone in my pain," (b) "I get ideas about what to try from my peers," and (c) "Our group is a place of helping." Hobbs encourages the members to subsequently bring back to the group the successes and failures of proposed solutions.

Unfortunately, programs for troubled students sometimes include "group" but in a regressed state resembling an academic class. Programs may even consist of didactic moral lectures. For nonverbal groups, where getting students to talk about personal problems resembles dental extraction, an introductory activity can be mutual peer interviews following a schedule the group devises. Sometimes, the place to start affiliation is through a selected activity such as art, drama, crafts, or selected games, followed by discussion about "how we are getting along." At the very least, group discussion can deal with solving group problems and listing ideas of how to make the class a more satisfying place.

There are times when the group becomes the whole school and even extends to the neighborhood and broader community. Some school happenings can send shock waves with a wide radius. An automobile wreck that takes the lives of teenagers, the murder of a teacher or principal, destructive assaults on the school, a suicide, or a gang battle can raise demands for a severe and instant fix. Unfortunately, catastrophic events are more and more common in schools and require sophisticated handling. "Stay put" cases are making exclusion and alternative education much more difficult even for dangerous students. A minor incident is sometimes blown up by poor handling, as Long's Conflict Cycle describes (page 244).

 In the article below, Long presents a positive prototype for responding to catastrophic whole-school group events.

ARTICLE 4.3

Managing a Shooting Incident in School

Nicholas J. Long

On Thursday, January 26, 1989, at about 2:30 P.M., as hundreds of students were leaving the building, a shooting occurred at Wilson High School in Washington, DC. An 18-year-old youth opened fire with a 9mm. semiautomatic pistol and wounded four students while also precipitating group fear and hysteria. This senseless shooting shocked the high school staff, enraged the community, mobilized city officials, and attracted the attention of the nation as it was reported on network television and by *Time* and *Newsweek* magazines.

At one time, most parents believed that if their children and adolescents were in school, they would be safe from the unpredictable violence of street crimes. Public schools were viewed as the safety zones in the community . . . a sanctioned place where students are protected by adults and secure

From *The Journal of Emotional and Behavioral Problems*. (1992). Vol. 1, No. 1.

from the fears of extortion, assault, and shootings by other students and outsiders. This belief has been shattered by the unparalleled increase in school violence over the past five years.

For example, in one academic year, 2.4 million students had some property stolen from them at school. Four hundred thousand students were victims of assaults; one out of twenty students reported that they were frightened they would be intimidated by a bully during the day, and in 1991, *Time* magazine reported that 20 percent of teenagers carried a weapon to school at least once a month for self-protection or because they might need it in a fight. One newspaper headline captured this concern among adolescents by stating, "Gun fights are replacing fist fights in schools!"

These acts of violence are not restricted to urban schools or to minority groups. To believe that school violence is a ghetto problem is to delude oneself. School violence is a national problem which affects all schools, social classes, and regions of our country. School administrators no longer can say this type of problem will never happen in their schools. The painful realities of the 90s demand that every principal with his staff develop and test contingency plans for any school emergency including guns, gangs, and shootings.

The purpose of this article is to describe one school-related shooting and highlight the complexity and confusion that occur during a school-wide emergency. It illustrates the intensity of the feelings and reactions of the students, staff, parents, and community to the shooting, the double-edged sword of TV coverage, and the intervention strategies the school used to de-escalate and control this crisis.

THE UNIQUENESS OF WILSON HIGH SCHOOL

Washington, DC, is not noted for its outstanding public schools; but there are real exceptions, and Wilson High School is one of them. Located in affluent northwest Washington, DC, in a primarily white community, Wilson High School has the reputation of being one of DC's finest academic schools and is noted for its many Merit Scholar finalists. Wilson High School also is unusual because its 1,600 students come from over seventy different countries. This is a school that celebrates cultural differences among its students and has a student body which identifies and supports the school behavioral norms and academic goals. While 80 percent of the students are minority group members representing all socio-economic levels, 75 percent of the students who graduate go on to college. Wilson High School in many ways represents the very best of urban education.

The principal of Wilson at this time was Mr. Michael Durso, an exceptionally strong and clear principal who had no difficulties expressing his behavioral and academic expectations to his students, staff, parents, and supervisors. He was highly valued by the community and was seen as a man of action. He was the type of leader who would not become conflicted or ambivalent during a school crisis.

THE INCIDENT

Like many peer conflicts which began in school, the initial incident was a minor reality frustration. The conflict involved Jermal, a 17-year-old special education student who played on the Wilson basketball team, and Rodney, an 18-year-old outsider who was a non-student. Jermal was having lunch in the cafeteria with several of his teammates. After getting up to get a drink, he returned to find Rodney sitting in his chair talking to his exgirlfriend. Rodney also had two other non-Wilson friends standing nearby. Jermal asked Rodney to move and Rodney refused. The situation was ripe for a predictable adolescent power struggle. Jermal, needing to assert his masculinity in front of his peers, wanted his chair back, and Rodney, finding himself in a similar psychological situation, became oppositional. Additional words were exchanged. Finally, Rodney got up and said, "I'll see you again. We'll meet again!" What followed next is confusing. The police reported that Jermal agreed to meet Rodney after school, but Jermal denied any planned group action. However, around 2:30 P.M., Jermal and three of his friends were leaving the school entrance when a jeep pulled up to the school entrance. Jermal saw Rodney and started walking towards him. Rodney and his friend jumped out of the jeep, and Rodney pulled out a gun and fired eleven shots into the crowd wounding Jermal and three other male students. What happened next was a classic example of group panic and chaos.

INITIAL REACTIONS TO THE SHOOTING

As hundreds of students were screaming, hiding, or darting back into the building, Rodney and friends fled the area. Several students helped the walking wounded back into school while Jermal laid on the ground with a serious bullet wound in the right leg. As the principal and staff rushed outdoors to assist the wounded students and to calm the crowd, the police, ambulances, and rescue squads were called. At this time, no one knew what had happened and the explanations were confusing, conflicting, and contagious.

What added to this disorder was the rapid appearance of TV cameramen. Channel 9 (CBS) is located directly across from the entrance of Wilson High School, and within minutes, cameramen were filming the confusion and reactions to the shooting by interviewing any willing student or staff. Ten minutes later, other TV personalities and cameramen from NBC and

ABC, along with reporters from local radio stations and newspapers arrived. They flooded the scene seeking out their competitive share of the fragmented and rumored information. By this time, the police cars and ambulances arrived with screaming sirens. As the officers and rescue squad members tried to sort through the wounded students, the crying students, concerned staff, and the prying TV cameras and reporters, the situation looked more like a circus event than a school tragedy.

TV coverage is not inherently bad, but it can add to the confusion of the immediate situation if it is not organized. Reporters want information, especially if it involves the safety of students, and they will get this information any way they can. Jermal was rushed to Children's Hospital for immediate surgery and the other three wounded students were taken to Georgetown University Hospital. One student had a bullet pass through his upper lip and needed plastic surgery. Another student had a superficial wound in his leg, and the third student was shot in both legs. By 3:30, all the TV networks had interrupted their regular programs to announce their "news bulletin." Unfortunately, all this brief bulletin did was to raise the anxiety level in the parents of students at Wilson High School. The school received hundreds of phone calls from anxious parents and concerned city officials about the shooting. As a result, all the school's telephone lines were tied up which made it difficult for the school to communicate with the outside world.

When accurate information is not available to the public during a crisis, then rumors and speculations run wild. While there was no deliberate attempt to magnify this crisis, the initial TV reporting added to the confusion to the point where it was difficult to separate facts from rumors. For example, one rumor was that this shooting was drug related. Another speculation was that this shooting was a continuation of a fight that occurred the previous week during a Wilson basketball game at another school. Another rumor was that the shooting was a drive-by shooting in a white community. Fortunately, cooler heads prevailed, and the principal, his staff, and the police took charge of the situation. The parents of the wounded students were notified, all the appropriate DC officials were called, and an official press conference was scheduled. Later in the afternoon, the principal met with the remaining members of his staff to provide them with additional information and to develop a school-wide plan for the returning students. Around 5:30 P.M., the superintendent of the school arrived and met with Mr. Durso to review the shooting and the proposed school intervention plans. Meanwhile, the TV networks were actively interviewing school officials, school board members, and city councilmen to get their views on the shooting for their evening news program. The majority of the civic leaders wanted to make a statement about the shooting, but unfortunately, the brief sequences that were reported or shown on TV were mostly negative and discouraging. The superintendent was reported as saying, "I don't think our schools are safe, but neither are any other places in the city." The Assistant DC Police Chief was quoted, "If kids can't go to school, what is this world coming to?" The city councilmen in the Wilson area endorsed student run peer-mediation programs, while the school board president and other vocal citizens recommended using metal detectors, keeping the students in during lunch hour, and closing all the school doors. Even the mayor of the city responded to the shooting by meeting with the parents of the three victims at Georgetown University Hospital. Afterwards, he made an appeal for any information leading to the arrest and conviction of these gunmen.

In summary, the initial reaction to the shooting was emotional, upsetting, and contagious. The TV coverage and news reporting added to the escalation of the incident by reporting the speculations of students and staff that were most involved in the shooting but had myopic information. It was a school crisis which nearly got out of hand.

THE NEXT DAY—PLANNED INTERVENTION

On Friday, the school staff was prepared to deal with the aftermath of the crisis. Additional security measures were implemented. Supportive groups and individual services were planned for the students, staff, and parents. A command center was organized and staffed to manage communication problems and all relationships with the news media. Friday was a day of coping with, rather than reacting to, the shooting.

ADDITIONAL SECURITY MEASURES

The first goal of the staff was to ensure the safety of all students and school personnel. There needed to be visual evidence that the school had the manpower and the resources to manage any future emergencies. Therefore, four additional school security guards were transferred to Wilson High School, creating a task force of six full-time security specialists. The opposite problem the staff wanted to avoid was having too many security guards in the building. The staff did not want to create the atmosphere that Wilson was under siege.

This concern was magnified when twenty members of the Nation of Islam, directed by their spiritual leader, Abdul Alin Muhammad, were assigned to patrol the sidewalks around Wilson High School. Muhammad said, "We were concerned about what happened Thursday, and we wanted to show the student body that we are willing to help. . . ." School officials arranged an immediate meeting with Mr. Muhammad and his advisers to thank them for their show of support. However, the school officials stated the situation at Wilson was under control, and that additional volunteer guards were not needed. The meeting ended amicably.

SUPPORTIVE SERVICES TO STUDENTS

At 10:30, Mr. Durso held a school-wide assembly in the school auditorium which lasted 1 1/2 hours. For the first 25 minutes, he gave a blunt, clear, and honest presentation of the incident. He said, "We could very easily be talking about planning four funerals today. It's nearly miraculous the four young people were not killed." His presentation captured the total attention of the students and was effective in clarifying many of the current rumors about the shooting. What happened next was most therapeutic. He invited all students to share their concerns and questions with the group. Frequently, school principals forget to listen to their students and to drain off their feelings after a crisis, but this was not the case at Wilson. For example, several of the students arrived in the auditorium carrying large posters expressing their concerns about the shooting such as, "We demand a SAFE SCHOOL NOW!" "If being shot at school dismissal is being at the WRONG PLACE at the WRONG TIME, then something is WRONG!" "ONE SHOT FIRED AT SCHOOL IS ONE SHOT TOO MANY."

Many of the students took advantage of his offer and expressed their shock, asked pertinent questions, and even offered some solutions. Their participation during the assembly cannot be over-evaluated. Mr. Durso summarized the discussion by telling them that this was their school, their reputation, and their responsibility to get involved. It is a problem both students and staff share. He then asked them to pledge their support to fight school violence, to report any outsiders they see to any staff and to focus on the large issue of "where they go as a school now and where they go as a generation."

The assembly was very successful not only in draining off the students' feelings and clarifying the misinformation about the shooting, but also in developing a group focus and a renewed pride in the school. The intense feeling of personal helplessness was replaced by a group feeling of school unity.

INDIVIDUAL STUDENT SUPPORT SERVICES

Any shooting involving adolescents will stir up strong feelings in them. With a school population of 1,600 students, it is predictable that a small percentage of these students will be troubled by this event and will need some personal counseling. Anticipating this problem, the Superintendent assigned more than twenty plus psychologists and social workers to be available at Wilson High School during the day and to meet with any students who wanted to discuss their feelings of anxiety, fear, loss, helplessness, etc. While the primary target for this help was directed to the students, the service also was made available to any staff member. After all, until the staff are comfortable with their feelings about the shooting, they will not be psychologically ready to accept and manage the feelings of their students when the staff talk about this incident in class. No data were collected on the number of students and staff that were seen, but the availability of psychological counseling was another clear way the school was saying we care about you and you are important to us!

PEER INITIATED SUPPORT SERVICE

In every high school there will be student leaders who will respond to the crisis by initiating student-directed activities. At Wilson High School, a female student spread the word that school violence had to be discussed among the students, and a meeting was being organized to take place during the lunch hour on the lawn next to the flagpole. Dozens of students appeared, and they spoke with anger for 50 minutes.

They talked about their feelings of powerlessness and wondered who they could talk to "down town." After much discussion, one suggestion was to make a joint statement to the press. Another idea was to form a city-wide council of student leaders on school violence to work on prevention programs. This suggestion was presented to the staff for their input and discussion. While this student-initiated peer program was small, it played a significant role in moving students from feelings of powerlessness to empowerment.

SUPPORTIVE SERVICES FOR PARENTS

On Friday afternoon, Mr. Durso met with twenty members of the executive board of the Wilson PTA. The meeting provided the parents with an opportunity to express the full range of their concerns about the shooting and the school's reactions. Once again, Mr. Durso sanctioned the parents' feelings of concern, clarified the realities of the shooting, and explained what steps were being taken to assure the safety of all students. If an emotional split had happened between the executive members of the PTA and the principal, the crisis at Wilson would have been exacerbated. The parents would have focused on the issues of personal blame, lack of trust in the school, threatened transfers of students, and a movement to replace the principal. Fortunately, none of these issues had any real support. Instead, a feeling of parent-school unity was reestablished.

SUPPORTIVE SERVICES TO THE PARENTS AND PUBLIC

The Assistant Superintendent of Senior High Schools and the Director of School Security held an open meeting in the evening at Wilson to meet with parents, citizens, and community leaders to discuss the shooting and security measures. While this type of meeting is never pleasant, it is essential if the goal is to de-escalate any current crisis.

Parents have the right to react if they feel the safety of their children is threatened. The most predictable reactions of parents at this time are expressions of fear, followed by anger, blame, and open hostility. In an upper middleclass community like Wilson, the parents are not passive, and they have the skills to organize action groups like petitioning the DC school board, city council, filing law suits, and demanding changes in personnel. Parents also have the potential to be supportive, understanding, and an active part of the solution.

This evening meeting drew hundreds of parents whose feelings ranged from personal concern to open disgust regarding how and why the shooting occurred, what the school did or didn't do to protect their adolescents, and why was the outsider allowed to be in the cafeteria. The school officials appeared to be ready for this initial blast of anger, and they quietly listened to the criticism without overreacting or becoming defensive. They were able to accept what the parents were saying and feeling as legitimate statements of concerns. Once the parents felt they were heard, they were better able to listen to what the school was proposing to improve security measures at Wilson High School and to develop more effective emergency plans.

Once again this meeting was successful in listening to the parents' concerns, clarifying upsetting rumors, and demonstrating that the school will be prepared to handle all future emergencies.

ESTABLISHING A COMMAND CENTER

When a crisis like this one happens in schools, the community expects the school to know what is happening, to make appropriate decisions, and to provide them with accurate information. The principal has the responsibility to direct these activities and to set up a decision-making process that is clear and effective. All information needs to be directed through one source so that it doesn't get lost or distorted. Significant staff need to have two-way radios so they can stay in touch with the command center at all times. By Thursday night, the principal had organized his command center. One school counselor was put in charge of all incoming telephone calls to assign them to appropriate staff to answer. On Friday, over 100 telephone calls about the shooting were recorded. Many of these calls were from newspaper and radio stations from other states. One call even came from Australia.

A DC official from the central office was assigned to Wilson High School to serve as the public relations officer. Her duties included managing all the news media and scheduling regular news conferences. Teachers were informed that all information to TV and news reporters must come from the public relations officer and not from individuals. This administrative decision was met with mixed feelings by the teachers. The TV cameras and interviews had to be controlled, but a few teachers felt this decision was censoring their rights of freedom of speech. This conflict highlights how new issues will arise during a crisis that no one had thought about previously.

By Monday, January 30, the intensity of the crisis had diminished. Jermal had a successful operation, and the three outsiders were identified and charged with assault with the intent to commit murder. A school counselor reported that it took another six weeks before the school atmosphere was back to normal.

SUMMARY

This school-related shooting at Wilson High School was an example of a senseless and spontaneous adolescent power struggle between two youths representing two different subgroups (students versus nonstudents). The outcome was not a fist fight, but a shooting that involved hundreds of innocent students. The shooting illustrated the confusion and complexity of a schoolwide crisis, the intensity of student, staff, and parents' feelings, the power of rumors, the double-edged sword of TV coverage, and the need for specific intervention strategies to manage any school crisis.

Acts of violence in our schools will continue to happen and every principal needs to develop a crisis management plan for his school. The adage, "Forewarned is forearmed" is our battle cry since planning can make a significant difference in determining whether the school crisis will become a school disaster or an opportunity to understand and cope with the many new problems facing our schools.

. . . .

The challenge Long presents is: What can we learn from such a case? How can we convert our understandings to prevention? And what procedures should be in place when prevention fails?

Gangs used to be considered a big-city problem. Now, gangs can be found even in outwardly placid communities. A gang differs from the informal group associations of adolescents who gather at favorite haunts to commune with each other. Not all formal gangs are delinquent, but many are associated with crime, violence, drugs, and intimidation. The early gangs were friendship groups of adolescents with kindred interests—say sports. Today, the power of gangs can produce ethnic empowerment, turf ownership, a way of getting money, and membership in a primary-type family substitute group. Consensual and violent sex may be involved. Membership provides protection, behavior insurance, and friendship. Youth who do not fit in school or school groups are good candidates to fit in a gang. Mathews, of the Toronto Youth Services, points out that how we frame the problem indicates how we will focus interventions. We can check out our own perceptions and those of our local community against his categories.

ARTICLE 4.4

Re-Framing Gang Violence: A Pro-Youth Strategy

Frederick Mathews

The explosion of youth violence in Toronto this spring was a watershed event. Many members of our society, especially the young and visible minorities, are holding up a mirror and showing us that they, and we as a society, are in crisis. The events of this spring were, if anything, a sign of what is to come if we do not change our thinking. To believe otherwise is a serious mistake and a reflection of the same denial and apathy that led us to this flashpoint in the first place.

This disturbing public spectacle was a convergence point for a number of deep and troubling social currents. However, at issue is more than just finding solutions for things that upset the public. It is about choosing a new path and a new vision to address the serious, complex, and increasing problem of youth violence.

In public and private discussions and in stories in the media, people have tried to come to terms with this apparent sudden downturn in our collective social well-being. Some believe the violence was caused by opportunistic "hooligans." Others feel it was a sign of racial tension or venting on the part of bored, frustrated, and disenfranchised youth. All are likely right. One thing is certain: the actions we take now to understand and address the rising problem of youth violence will affect the social environment of our city for many years to come. Our challenge is to respond from a place of reason and compassion and not to simply react out of fear.

FRAMING THE "PROBLEM" OF YOUTH GANGS/GROUPS

This paper will focus on one aspect of contemporary youth violence—youth gangs/groups. The intended purpose is to open a broad discussion of youth gangs/groups and frame the process of developing a comprehensive prevention/intervention strategy in a pro-youth way.

This paper is a beginning to the process of naming problems and solutions and raises more questions than it answers. Asking more and better

From *The Journal of Emotional and Behavioral Problems*. (1992). Vol. 1, No. 3. Reprinted with permission.

questions at the outset of the process may help avoid making costly mistakes later on. Poorly conceived and hastily implemented plans to respond to youth gangs/groups could make matters worse. Simply throwing money at the problem, in the absence of real understanding, could result in an expensive disaster.

The essence of the paper can be distilled down to the following two statements:

- How we define or frame the problem will shape our solutions.
- The process of developing a comprehensive pro-youth prevention/intervention strategy will be the message of the strategy.

What is meant by "framing"? Basically, framing implies that the "problem" is in the eye of the beholder. Our culture, attitudes, values, beliefs, education, and training, or the opinions of family, friends, or peers determines or influences the way we see or interpret otherwise neutral events in the world. Our thoughts and beliefs are like eyeglasses we look through into a sea of human interactions. These glasses are invisible and, with or without our awareness, organize the outside world into "events" or "intelligible wholes." The lenses in these glasses focus our attention and literally "construct" otherwise neutral phenomenon into "events" or "problems" or "nonproblems" and help us assign meaning to the situations and actions of others we encounter in our daily lives.

Simply stated, three people looking at the same phenomenon may see it in totally different ways. Depending on one's age, gender, life experiences, cultural background, or socioeconomic status, a social problem may look quite different. When people's perspectives on a problem differ or appear to be irreconcilable, core issues can become lost or clouded in rhetoric and blaming. In these circumstances, the original problem can become explosive or escalate. Framing helps us prepare for the challenge of engaging in real dialogue on controversial subjects.

Let's look at three different ways of framing the youth gang/group phenomenon and see how complicated the problem definition and solution generating process is. We will examine youth violence from the perspectives of racism, alienation, and law enforcement.

YOUTH VIOLENCE AS RACISM

Framed as a racial issue, youth gang/group activity is difficult to define with any precision. There is a small number of racially-based gangs/groups involved in organized criminal activities. These gangs/groups tend to focus their activities on people from their own cultural group and do not generally see themselves in competition with other cultural groups. Conflicts between racially homogeneous gangs/groups in Toronto appear to be small in number and most gangs/groups are racially mixed to varying degrees.

However, racial conflict between gangs/groups does exist and may in fact be on the increase.

There are other racial dimensions to the phenomenon which need to be taken very seriously and confronted strongly: systemic and structural ethnocentricism and racism. Basically, "structural and systemic" ethnocentricism and racism refers to assumptions or behaviors that are an unconscious part of everyday personal interactions or professional and institutional practices. These assumptions and behaviors are often detrimental to people of other cultural backgrounds because they are grounded in our own version of history, and the values, attitudes, and beliefs of our own cultural reference group.

People who do not otherwise think of themselves as racist might focus only on visible minority youths in a media account of a racially mixed gang's/group's activities. Others might cross the road when faced with having to walk past a group of minority youths on a sidewalk. Think of the kind of suspicion aroused in some people when they see a minority youth in everyday dress simply running down a street. Negative attitudes can quickly form about minority youths as a result of this "biased" way of viewing the world.

Systemic and structural ethnocentricism and racism is often invisible as it plays out in institutional and professional practices, but it can influence the way we understand social problems, define solutions, and deliver support services. For example, many recent immigrants come from countries where authority figures are feared and avoided because contact with them means peril. Without sensitivity to this, social service professionals, police, or other authority figures could easily misunderstand these people's mistrust and reluctance to provide information or seek assistance.

Structural racism influences how we understand why a youth decides to join in a willfully criminal gang/group activity. It is easy to "blame the victim" when assessing another person's motivation. What is construed as "criminally motivated" behavior could actually be desperation. Deprived of opportunities, discriminated against in employment, education, housing, or living on the margin of mainstream society, a young person may find other, nonsanctioned means to achieve the "good life" that is the mark of success in our society.

Solutions for a race-based view of gang/group activity would have to address both macro- and micro-social levels. Including minority representation in all aspects of social life is imperative. It is important as an enlightened society to ensure that positive and affirming images of minorities appear in the media and in popular culture mediums such as film, television, and commercials. Communities "at risk" or in crisis need to be given adequate resources and services in a culture and language sensitive way. Language skills and literacy, problems in adjustment to life in Canada, and access to employment and housing also need to be addressed. Public and professional education programs about the harmful effects of racism need to be implemented.

YOUTH VIOLENCE AS ALIENATION

Framing the problem as a youth alienation and "disempowerment" issue brings us face to face with inequities in the distribution of social power. However, disempowerment is a relative term. While youth as a group share a common experience of having far less power than adults, not all youth are affected equally. Visible minority youth, young women, children, and teens living in poverty are far more "disenfranchised" and disempowered than their male peers from middle and upper class family backgrounds. However, youth as a group have little control over their lives, and seldom are given a voice when it comes to making policy decisions about important things such as education or social services. If government tries to impose a plan of action to confront youth violence on communities and schools without consulting young people and all the stakeholders involved, few will have an interest in supporting what is offered.

Young people are giving us a clear message. They feel powerless and left out. Involving them in the planning process will convey a message that we as a society value their opinions and are prepared to tap their energy and creativity in the struggle to find solutions together in community. To do otherwise is to replicate the paternalistic patterns of social relations in bureaucracies that young people face every day of their lives, patterns that disempower youth and create many of the problems of youth unrest and violence in the first place.

Empowering youth would involve adding their voices to the decision-making process of community and government institutions. Creating youth employment would require a direct intervention in the economy by government or business. It would also require government to make children and youth a higher priority in terms of policy and to better resource "at-risk" communities and families in order to help them provide more optimal care for their young.

YOUTH VIOLENCE AS CRIMINALITY

Framed as a law enforcement issue, the problem of youth gangs/groups appears deceptively easy to solve. This is a criminogenic view that defines the problem as being in the individual; in effect, gang/group members are deviant or delinquent and their behavior in need of punishment. Interventions based on this conceptualization of the problem are fear-based, reactive, and short-sighted. Policy formulated along these lines would direct resources to the criminal justice system instead of where it is more desperately needed—to "at-risk" families and communities. Using a criminal justice response, the investment of resources may appear smaller, at least in the beginning, but the social costs over time will be staggering.

There is no preventative aspect to this strategy and no social empowerment for anyone except professionals in the criminal justice system.

This approach risks encouraging some youth to remain in a life of crime, stigmatizes others, and removes any accountability on the part of government to youth, families, and communities "at risk" or in crisis. We need to understand that criminal charges will not help young people who become involved in crime because they perceive they have no other choice.

In Toronto, a criminal justice response has been our only response to the phenomenon of youth gangs/groups. We have relied on the police alone to deal with our rising concern about youth violence. The police already have a difficult and demanding enough job without putting on their shoulders the responsibility for being social workers and youth counsellors. However, the police can play an important role as part of a broader community response.

Because the police are out in the community 24 hours a day, they often come into contact with "at-risk" youth before any social service agency. With a backup system of integrated community resources, police would have an option to divert many young people to the kind of support services that could help prevent them from having further difficulties with the law. However, we are far from having this kind of comprehensive community involvement. Mobilizing resources to meet the needs of "at-risk" youth, families, and communities will have a more permanent impact on the problem of youth gang/group violence than simply a punishment-focused criminal justice response.

THE PROCESS IS THE MESSAGE

Engaging in open, honest dialogue is rarely a straightforward or simple process because it requires suspension of one's own frame of reference (literally taking off one's eyeglasses) and looking at or listening to others with a more objective or detached point of view. Yet, difficult as the process of dialogue may be, the consequences of not listening are tragic—for all sides. Winning an argument rarely leaves people with anything more than their limitations. If we are to come to terms with and solve complex and difficult social problems, we will have to move past "identity politics" and personal bias and toward real dialogue and an attitude of right thinking and action. The future well-being of our young people—and thus of our cities and nation—will depend on our success in this process.

The foregoing discussion on framing demonstrates how complex and hard to define the problem of youth gangs/groups is. Gang/group activities range from overzealous teen pranks to acts that are organized, often violent and willfully criminal (for a typology of different gangs/groups see Mathews, 1990). We also need to be realistic about what we can hope to accomplish as we move through the long and tedious process of defining the problem and struggling to find solutions. Some problems will be easier to define and solve in a short period of time. Others will take a lot longer and require fundamental changes in the way we organize our society and share power and resources.

HOW DID WE GET HERE IN THE FIRST PLACE?

By examining media reports and soliciting the views of school officials, the police, and the other professionals who deal with this issue, it is possible to draw up a list of "signals" indicating there is a "problem" with young people and violence today. The following list covers the behaviors most often reported:

1. Youth gangs/groups commit many insensitive acts of gratuitous violence.
2. Kids involved in gangs/groups are getting younger in age.
3. There has been a rise in the number of girls involved in gang/group activity.
4. Guns are replacing the use of knives or other weapons.
5. Actions are bolder, with little apparent regard for authority or legal consequences.
6. Some violence has racial overtones and is organized along ethnic lines.
7. Gang/group activities have become a public spectacle and are more visible.
8. Activities are becoming more organized.
9. Male gender role hype and macho posturing [are] prevalent.
10. Victims are typically other young persons.

Gang/group activities are usually characterized by various words or expressions such as "insensitive," "gratuitous violence," "power and control," "indifference to feelings of others," "objectification of others," "use of force," "spontaneous sexual assaults," "extortion," and "disrespect for authority." People exposed to media accounts of youth gang/group violence are often shocked at some of the behaviors they see portrayed. But how did we get here in the first place? What has happened over the past few years that has brought us to a point where our young people are increasingly resorting to violence to deal with their problems, achieve status, or to feel powerful and efficacious as persons?

Our children are socialized as they internalize the direct and subtle messages they receive from adults, friends, peers, school, and the media and popular culture. Young people are, in effect, what they have learned from us and what we have taught them to think about themselves.

At a time when our communications technology allows us to phone anyone at any time virtually anywhere, we have never been so isolated from one another in terms of true intimacy and connection. This isolation places us in smaller and smaller circles of influence and breeds "enemy thinking," mistrust of others who are different in any way, and a tendency to irrationally lash out against whoever or whatever challenges our increasingly narrow worldview.

The move towards a global economy and the resulting unemployment caused by displaced industries and workers is seriously affecting the lives of young people and their families. Canada is losing its political and cultural sovereignty to market forces. Decisions affecting young people's present and future lives are being made in circles of influence far removed from their lived reality. Kids now not only have to compete against their neighbor in the next desk or across the street, but with strangers halfway around the world in the Pacific Rim or in Europe or South America. Economic tough times are especially hard on minorities, single parents, and children and youth.

Much of the world's young people live in is in turmoil. High youth unemployment, the perceived irrelevance of their education (it is only about getting a job), and the pressure to be a full consumer participant in the expensive (and adult created) youth subculture adds great stress to lives of young people. Governments are struggling to reduce expenditures and are being forced to cut back significantly on what used to be "basic" services such as child welfare, social services, education, and health care.

We give our young little reason to trust adults. Children and youth are neglected or abused physically and sexually at home or in care in such numbers that it is impossible for the average person to comprehend. Some have no choice but to flee their abusive home environment. They typically end up on the street and some are forced to work in prostitution or become involved in illegal activity to survive when there are no resources available to help them in their communities.

Parents, struggling to pay mortgages and keep up with the bills, often have little energy left to give their offspring. Young people today are faced with a bewildering array of choices, stresses, and conflicting messages and often have nowhere to turn for support. Peers can help but are often confused and scared themselves. It is an absolute tragedy that the bond—call it love, mutual trust, respect, intimacy, reciprocity, whatever you choose—that is singularly the most important anchor point in a young person's life, perhaps in all our lives, is often missing these days. Without that connection life in a fast-changing and uncertain world can be scary.

Finally, we have created for our children an environment with contaminated soil, air, and water and sunshine that can now cause life-threatening cancers. Our garbage is piling up faster than we can safely dispose of it. And we dare to ask what is wrong with young people today? It is an affront to the concept of justice that we deprive our young of information about sex, abuse them in unimaginable numbers, leave them out of important decisions affecting their lives, compromise their environmental heritage, then presume to have the right to simply punish them when they act out.

Returning to the question of how we got to this point in the first place, adults should be seeing something very familiar in the behavior of young people. They are reflecting back to us who and what we are as a society.

ASKING MORE AND BETTER QUESTIONS

The phenomenon of youth gangs/groups in Canada is evolving and we are only in the early stages of trying to understand all its complexities. Having more questions than answers is far from comforting but it should not keep us from acting. However, it should force us to pause and thoughtfully consider our next steps. At this point in time we have an opportunity a "teachable moment, to reflect on the events of this spring and decide where we are going as a society and the message we wish to send to our young. Saying "we do not know" is the first step on a path to knowledge. Acting as if we know—and we don't—is a path to calamity. This is a time for us to ask more and better questions.

What is happening to relationships among young people? Why are they targeting each other for violence, sexual assault, theft, or extortion? Can it be that young people as a disenfranchised group may be turning on each other because another youth is a safer target? Is it misplaced aggression? Are young people lashing out at just any target because they cannot identify the source of their frustration and anger?

Are frightened, underparented youth testing the boundaries only to find them soft with indifference? Is the gang/group activity of some youths a desperate call for limits, real intimacy, and connection?

What is the appeal of gangs/groups? What needs do they meet that aren't being met elsewhere? Young people, by nature, tend to gather in groups. Peers are important confidants, models, supporters, and comrades in the developmental transition to adulthood. Gangs/groups give opportunities to try out new roles, get support, form an identity, and obtain security and a sense of connectedness and belonging. This latter point is especially true for abused, abandoned, or neglected youth. Gangs/groups provide instant access to power, self-esteem, and personal efficacy.

Are gang/group members more vulnerable to influence or open to intervention at different ages and stages of their adolescent development? Are all youths equally at risk of becoming involved in gang/group activity?

Media and popular culture images often portray gang/group members as outlaws with mythical and romantic dimensions. Males with poor self-esteem and a desire to be macho can get caught up in this glamorized fiction about gangs/groups. But if gangs are about macho male hype, why are so many young girls now targeting other girls for acts of violence?

Is much of the behavior we see in Canada motivated by a desire to copy the American gang scene? What accounts for the overwhelming involvement of middle-class youth? What moved the gang/group phenomenon from a street-based problem three and a half years ago to one more centered around schools?

The above questions represent only a beginning to the process of moving towards a more comprehensive understanding of this troubling phenomenon. As we move as a community into the process of searching for answers, we will need to be mindful of the message our work is conveying to youth and all members of our society.

The following first principles are intended for use as a guide in the search for a pro-youth strategy:

FIRST PRINCIPLES FOR DEVELOPING A COMPREHENSIVE PRO-YOUTH STRATEGY

Recognize that the process of development is the message of the strategy.

Recognize the power and creativity of youth.

Validate the creativity, power, and knowledge of youth by involving them directly in the process of naming the problem and in the search for solutions.

Recognize that most young people are law-abiding, honest, caring, and responsible.

Recognize and respect that the process of empowering youth will be painful and fear provoking for some adults because it means letting go of control.

Involve all stakeholders in the search for solutions, including gang/group members.

Recognize that young people learn responsibility by having responsibility. Youth need to have a voice with respect to their schools and education, social services, community programs, and in government policy and planning directed towards them.

Recognize that the well-being of children and youth will continue to be compromised until they become a first priority in the policy of all government.

Encourage peer self-help for gang/group members.

Recognize the need for community-driven solutions.

Recognize that there is a link between the economy and families, communities, minorities, and youth at risk.

Recognize the need to address the risk, not the youth, as the problem.

Recognize that young people caught committing willfully criminal acts should be held accountable for their behavior using alternatives to the criminal justice system wherever possible.

Recognize that we need to closely examine our institutions and professional practices and confront any and all structural and systemic paternalism, ethnocentrism, racism, homophobia, and sexism.

Recognize that paternalism, ethnocentrism, racism, homophobia, and sexism contribute to youth violence.

Recognize that youth violence is a community problem and that solutions must be found in the community.

Recognize the centrality of the school in the lives of young people, and link educational institutions to community resources that can

support youth and address the risk or vulnerability factors that motivate young people toward involvement in gang/group activity.

Recognize the need for schools to offer or link up with services for
victims of gang/group activity.

Recognize the need for government policy to give resources to families
(however defined) to provide optimal care to children and youth.

Recognize that a pro-youth strategy is a pro-social strategy and a vision of hope and optimism that can heal our young, our communities, and ourselves.

. . . .

A specific problem occurs for schools when gang activity begins to permeate the school culture, even at times becoming the dominant culture. As
Mathews points out, the response is to be found in many school and community interventions, not just in a get-tough regime, although the school
code must be explicit and enforced. What is needed is a pro-youth strategy
including youth-sensitive processes, cooperative problem solving, and the
generation of community resources. Because the proliferation of gangs is a
societal phenomenon, the response must be societal. Mathews' principles,
designed for a comprehensive effort, imply a role for each of us, including
youth. Troubled students are at special risk for gang participation or vic-
timization, so prophylactic efforts are our responsibility.

Linda Lantieri is the national director of the Resolving Conflict Creatively
Program. She decries the school climate of violence, which has appalled and
made hopeless so many of us. Linda does not propose a quick or easy fix. But
she does provide hope, buttressed by evidence to substantiate her position. It
is convincing because she has been in areas where the violence is most acute.
We need courageous and creative leadership to give us heart. Her forthcoming book will be on piecing our schools back together.

ARTICLE 4.5

Waging Peace in Our Schools: Beginning with the Children

Linda Lantieri

If we are to reach real peace in this world . . . we shall have to begin with
the children. —Mahatma Gandhi

Recent events in our country have shaken us as never before. We have
come to the realization that we as a society are in the midst of an epidemic

From *The Journal of Emotional and Behavioral Problems.* (1995). Vol. 4, No. 1. Reprinted with
permission.

of violence. Homicide has become the third leading cause of death for children 5 to 14 years old and the leading cause of death for young African-American men. Counting suicides, a gun takes the life of an American child every two hours.

In the last few years, we have witnessed the killing of several students in the hallways of what was once a sacred place—the school. At Thomas Jefferson High School in New York City, my alma mater, one student shot and killed another and critically wounded a teacher. This kind of incident has been repeated in other schools throughout the country. The U.S. Department of Justice estimates that each day 100,000 children carry guns to school. Each hour, over 2,000 students are physically attacked on school grounds. Teachers suffer, too. Each hour, approximately 900 teachers are threatened and nearly 40 are physically attacked.

NO school seems immune. A 1993 Harris poll of students in grades 6–12 found a widespread fear of violence at school. This fear is not unreasonable. More than 400,000 violent crimes are reported in and around our nation's schools each year, with still far more crimes going unreported.

The toll this violence takes on our children's psyche is clear. More than one-third of the students in the Harris poll said they believe their lives will be cut short by violence. Miguel Sanchez, a student from New York City, described his fear during 1993 National Hearings on Violence and the Child in Washington, DC; "When I wake up in the morning, I ask myself, am I going to survive this day? So everyday I try to make it seem as if it is my last day on this earth. So far I've been lucky. I don't know when my luck is going to run out."

According to Carol Beck, former principal of Thomas Jefferson High School, over 50% of the young people in her school have puncture wounds on their bodies. Many of our children in large cities are covering their ears to muffle the sound of gunshots in the night. They exhibit the same signs of post-traumatic stress syndrome we observe in children who grow up in war-torn areas.

Why is this violence taking place? Deborah Prothrow-Stith, Assistant Dean at Harvard School of Public Health, has addressed that question, and her response is hard for us to swallow: Why are our children killing each other? *Because we are teaching them to.* Our society glamorizes violence (Prothrow-Stith, 1991). Indeed, the media often portray the hero as one who chooses violence to get what he or she wants and needs.

"They say we are the future," observes 11-year-old Jessica, a student mediator at PS 261 in Brooklyn, NY, "but they treat us like we're nothing. On TV, it's sex, drugs and violence—they're projecting that to kids. Practically all cartoons have something to do with guns or destruction."

The students at Thomas Jefferson High School went home after the shootings that left one student dead and a teacher wounded and on their television sets a few nights later they saw *Saturday Night Live* portray the scenes at their school in a comedy skit. For the producers of the program, there were no tears, funerals or images of kids crying in teachers' arms. Yet we as adults are confused and appalled when we see young people commit violent acts with no apparent remorse. That's the bad news.

The good news is that, as big as the problem of violence is, we have the power to change it. Ten years ago, I co-founded the Resolving Conflict Creatively Program (RCCP) in New York City, and today I serve as the program's National Director. In our work at RCCP, we have found that violence is not inevitable but preventable. I visited Brooklyn's Thomas Jefferson High School after the incident and had an intense discussion with 14 young people, several of whom had actually witnessed their schoolmate dying. In the first hour, I learned a lot from them about the futility of the violence that surrounds them and the hopelessness they feel. They knew that violence was destroying them but saw no alternatives.

Then I began asking them whether, from the beginning to the end of this fatal dispute, there was anything anyone could have done differently. They began to identify eight or nine things—mainly done by bystanders—that had actually escalated the conflict in the hallway. What I was helping them to see was that the dispute that culminated in tragedy had escalated by the accumulation of many small acts. Young people often think these are things that no one has any control over, and that makes them feel helpless. When they step back and reflect, they begin to feel empowered.

Although the problems facing our young people are complicated, immense, and horrifying we do know a great deal about what causes violence, and this knowledge can help direct our search for solutions. First, we need to teach our children values that emphasize respect and concern for others, principles that are universally acknowledged as the basis for any communitarian society. Second, young people need concrete skills to deal with their potentially disruptive emotions as well as the everyday conflict they will face in their lives. In short, we must teach our children ethical and emotional literacy.

A NEW WAY OF FIGHTING

"Mom," says 8-year-old Wayne, "the fifth graders are learning a new way of fighting.
"Oh? What do you mean?"
"Well, when kids get mad, they don't hit each other.
Other kids help them talk out the fight instead."

Wayne is referring to the student mediation process being established in his school as part of the Resolving Conflict Creatively Program. RCCP began in 1985 as a collaboration of the New York City Public Schools and Educators for Social Responsibility's New York City chapter (ESR Metro). Now in its tenth year, RCCP educates for intergroup understanding, alternatives to violence, and creative conflict resolution among students, teachers, parents, and administrators in five school systems in the country: the New York City Public Schools, the Anchorage School District, Alaska, the New Orleans Public Schools, Louisiana; the Vista Unified School District in Southern California; and the South Orange-Maplewood School District in New Jersey.

Participants in RCCP during the 1993–94 school year included 120,000 young people in over 300 schools from a variety of communities nationwide. RCCP is now the largest school-based program of it's kind in the country. RCCP National established the RCCP National Center in September 1993 to support national replication efforts already begun and to provide technical assistance to additional school systems in developing and implementing conflict resolution programs.

The world yearns for "a new way of fighting," one in which people are strong without being mean. Conflict is part of life. We would not want to eliminate it even if we could. But we are urgently looking for ways to end the violence between diverse groups of people that causes so much unnecessary pain and suffering. At RCCP, we are giving young people an important message—that the Rambos of the world, far from being heroes, are pathetic because they can think of only one response to conflict. Young people in our program are beginning to see that the highest form of heroism is the passionate search for creative, nonviolent solutions to the problems of our pluralistic society. They are beginning to incorporate these ideas into their everyday lives, as in the following scene:

> With tears streaming down her face, seven-year-old Veronica picks herself up from the asphalt of the playground and charges toward her friend Jasmine.
>
> "Why'd you trip me?" she screams.
>
> "I didn't trip you."
>
> "Yes, you did and I'm gonna trip you right back on your face."
>
> "Try it and see what happens!"
>
> Suddenly two fifth graders appear, wearing bright blue T-shirts with the word *mediator* emblazoned on front and back.
>
> "Excuse me!" says one. "My name is Jessica."
>
> "I'm Angel," says the other. "We're mediators. Would you like us to help solve this problem?"
>
> "I guess so," the girls say grudgingly. Jessica and Angel get agreement to some ground rules (including no name calling and no interrupting), and suggest they all move to a quieter area of the playground to talk things out.
>
> "You'll speak first, Veronica," says Jessica. "But don't worry, Jasmine, you'll get your chance. Okay, Veronica, tell us what happened."
>
> Within two minutes, the girls solve their problem. Jasmine acknowledges that she tripped Veronica by accident as she was trying to tag her. She says she is sorry. Veronica agrees to accept the apology and to be Jasmine's friend again. After being congratulated by Angel and Jessica for solving their problem, the girls resume their game.

THE RCCP MODEL

RCCP is based on a relatively simple idea that is often hard to carry out: that people should listen to one another when there are problems and work toward peaceable solutions. RCCP encourages open discussion in a supportive atmosphere to help children and adults better understand conflict and its roots. Most importantly, RCCP teaches students, as well as teachers, parents, and administrators, practical skills that enable them to find creative solutions to conflicts as they happen. RCCP helps young people realize that they have many choices for dealing with conflict besides passivity or aggression. They learn the skills needed to make these choices in their own lives, and they increase their understanding and appreciation of their own and other cultures.

By creating a "peaceable school"—a safe environment where students are encouraged to experiment with peaceful ways of resolving conflict—RCCP teachers strive to give their students a new image of what their world can be. For this to happen, however, the teachers themselves must change. They must learn, and then apply, a new set of skills for heading off and resolving conflict. Even more difficult, they must adopt a new style of classroom management, one that fundamentally involves a sharing of power with students so that they can learn to deal with their own disputes.

To this end, RCCP's comprehensive approach includes the following components:

1) *A K-12 classroom curriculum.* The curriculum concentrates on teaching several key component skills: active listening, assertiveness (as opposed to aggressiveness or passivity), expressing feelings in appropriate ways, perspective-taking, cooperation, negotiation, appreciating diversity, and countering bias. Learning these skills requires weekly practice. Teachers are encouraged to do at least one "peace lesson" a week, to use "teachable moments" that arise from what is happening in the classroom or the world at large, and to "infuse" conflict resolution lessons into the regular academic program.

RCCP lessons involve role-playing, interviewing, group discussion, brainstorming, and other experiential learning strategies, all of which require a high degree of student participation and interaction.

2) *Professional training and ongoing technical assistance and support for teachers.* RCCP first provides 24 hours of introductory training in a series of after-school or full-day sessions. The training introduces the RCCP philosophy and the curriculum; teaches communication, conflict resolution, and intergroup relations skills; and demonstrates "infusion" strategies for integrating these concepts and skills into social studies, language arts, and other academic subjects.

A key to RCCP's success is the follow-up support that teachers receive. Each new teacher is assigned to an RCCP staff developer who visits between six and ten times a year, giving demonstration lessons, helping the teacher prepare, observing classes, giving feedback, and sustaining the teacher's motivation. In addition, the staff developer convenes bimonthly follow-up meetings after school so that the teachers can receive additional training, share their experiences, discuss concerns, and plan schoolwide events.

3) *A student-led mediation program.* A key component of RCCP's plan for school change, the student mediation program provides a strong peer model for nonviolent conflict resolution and reinforces students' emerging skills in working out their own problems. Ultimately, by reducing the number of fights between students, the mediation component can contribute to a more peaceful school climate. Student mediation is not a substitute for an effective school disciplinary policy, for if strictly enforced sanctions against fighting are not in place, students are unlikely to turn to the mediators for help. RCCP initiates the mediation component only in schools that have been participating in RCCP for at least a year and have a group of teachers who regularly use the curriculum. As explained by ESR's philosophy, school mediation programs are best implemented as part of a larger effort to train staff and students in conflict resolution. This is a significant strength over mediation-only approaches elsewhere in the country.

4) *Parent training.* No one would disagree that parents and teachers should work together to teach children how to resolve conflict nonviolently. The reason is clear: If students are to use their emerging conflict resolution and intergroup relations skills outside of school, they must have family support.

In the last five years, parent education has become a top priority for RCCP. Staff recently launched a Parent Involvement Program that was piloted in New York and is being disseminated to other RCCP sites nationwide. A team of two or three parents per school is trained for 60 hours to lead four 2½ hour workshops for other parents on intergroup relations, family communication, and conflict resolution. During the 1993–94 school year, teams from several schools subsequently led workshops for other parents. To date, nearly 2,500 parents have received training nationwide.

5) *Administrator training.* This component of RCCP introduces school administrators to the concepts and skills of conflict resolution and bias awareness and shows them how they can use their leadership to achieve effective implementation of the program. RCCP's primary aim is to encourage administrators to embrace and model the humane and creative approaches to dealing with conflict and diversity that teachers are implementing through the classroom curriculum. RCCP has also learned that the more principals understand and "buy into" the program, the more willing they are to provide the flexibility and administrative support needed to make RCCP work at the school level.

The price tag for RCCP comes to just over $33 per student per year. To educators accustomed to buying packaged curricula that sell for a few hundred dollars, this might seem expensive. It should be remembered, however, that RCCP is much more than a curriculum. Rather, it is an intensive effort at school reform, with a strong emphasis on teacher training and professional development.

AN OBSERVABLE IMPACT

From the beginning, teachers have reported positive changes in their students and themselves as a result of introducing RCCP in their schools. Tony Soll, a sixth grade teacher at the Brooklyn New School, related one of his experiences with the program:

We had been discussing news articles, and I asked the students in my class to find stories in the newspapers about people solving conflicts. There were two boys in the class who were buddies, and at least five times during the day became enemies. The fighting would go on and on, and it was driving everybody crazy. One day they decided, on their own, to go out in the hall and write a peace treaty. They were afraid to get into an argument about the peace treaty, so they picked four other kids—not necessarily their best friends, but definitely people who would be dependable. They all went out into the hall and signed the peace treaty. (At that time, we hadn't even used the word *mediation*.) The treaty is still up on the wall. It belongs to the whole class now, and serves as a reminder that you don't always have to fight.

A formal evaluation of RCCP conducted in 1989–90 confirmed the teachers' impressions. Metis Associates, an independent evaluator, concluded in its report that the program had "an observable and quantifiable positive impact on students, participating staff, and classroom climate." The teachers reported that they devoted an average of seven periods per month to specific lessons in conflict resolution and that they were also infusing conflict resolution concepts into other aspects of the curriculum. They noted less physical violence in their classrooms, a decreased use of verbal put-downs in favor of more supportive comments, spontaneous student use of conflict resolution skills, and an increase in their students' self-esteem, leadership skills and initiative. They also reported positive effects in themselves, particularly in their ability to handle angry students and to deal with conflict in general.

RCCP-New York is currently involved in an in-depth, three-year evaluation of the program funded by a grant from the Federal Centers for Disease Control and Prevention.

A WAY OF LIFE

Learning conflict resolution skills is only one way to address the epidemic of violence in our society. Violence has many sources, as Ted Quant, Co-Director of RCCP-New Orleans, points out: "I look at the violence and see that it is rooted in fear, rooted in injustice, rooted in poverty, racism, sexism, ageism, homophobia—all of these are examples of violence because all of them deny the basic humanity of our brothers and sisters and the children in this village we call Earth." Conflict resolution can help, but it will be most effective as part of a larger strategy. As one of our teachers put it, "RCCP is more than a curriculum, it's a way life."

Those interested in replicating RCCP's approach should keep two points in mind. First, RCCP and other violence prevention programs cannot be "parachuted" into a school. Building an effective program takes time. Although teacher training, staff development, and other resources provided by outside agencies are necessary, the process of developing an effective program must ultimately be driven by leadership from within. Only the school's principal, teachers, students, and parents can create a sustainable program that will have strong impact on the learning environment. Second, while RCCP has demonstrated that principals, teachers, students, and parents can work together to create "peaceable schools," this work must eventually be carried outside the schools to create "peaceable neighborhoods." An African proverb teaches us that "it takes a whole village to raise a child." Likewise, we are convinced that it will take the "whole village" working together to rescue our children from the epidemic of violence.

Conflict resolution is not a quick fix. We have learned that it takes time for adults to integrate conflict resolution concepts and a multicultural perspective into their own lives, it takes time for them to learn how to translate those concepts for students, and it takes time for even the most effective classroom instruction to have a significant impact. Some of the most effective teachers in RCCP have observed that it sometimes takes months for youngsters to begin integrating concepts and skills in such a way that their behavior begins to change.

But we are seeing the change. We are seeing adults change first. We are seeing individual students change second, and then we are seeing whole schools change for the better. More than anything, we are demonstrating the power of nonviolence and showing that the right kind of intervention can turn us and our schools around. Our focus is on changing the total school environment, thereby creating a safe community that lives by a credo of nonviolence. It takes the words of Gandhi to heart: "It is possible to live in peace." Unlike most school-based programs, RCCP is institutionalized within the school and its message of nonviolence is seen as part of the school's central mission. RCCP's hope is that the lessons of peace and intercultural understanding will eventually become a basic part of every school's curriculum, with as much emphasis devoted to teaching negotiation and other conflict resolution skills as is given to other academic subjects. We can create violence-free growing zones in our nation's schools.

Imagine a child being born today who enters kindergarten in 2000 and begins to learn "another way of fighting." Imagine that, from that first day of school, this child experiences an atmosphere in which differences are accepted and nonviolent approaches to conflict are the norm. Imagine that, by the time the student reaches fifth grade, he or she is chosen by peers to be a mediator to settle disputes among classmates. And imagine that, by the time this young person enters high school, all students are walking through doors without metal detectors and are taking required classes in conflict resolution and intergroup relations. Finally, imagine that this young person will, for the rest of his or her life, have the courage to be a hero or shero for peace and justice.

This imagined scenario is already taking place in the lives of thousands of young people across the nation. We have the preventive tools to begin to turn back the tide of bigotry and violence. Now we must put them to good use. Our children deserve a future in which their right to safety is reclaimed and their cultural diversity is celebrated.

REFERENCES

DeJong, W. (1993). *Learning Peace, The Resolving Conflict Creatively Program in the New York City Schools.* Report prepared for the National Institute of Justice, New York.

Lantieri, L., & Roderick, T. (Jan., 1990). A new way of fighting. *RCCP News 1,* 4–5.

Prothrow-Stith, D., & Weissman, M. (1991). *Deadly Consequences: How Violence Is Destroying Our Teenage Population and A Plan to Begin Solving the Problem.* New York: HarperCollins.

. . . .

Matthews and Lantieri move us in the same direction: Don't give in to a culture of violence. Although violence is a total community problem, there are things we can do, and the school has a critical role. If there is a primary thing our disturbed pupils need, it is an accepting and inviting school environment that insulates them from the pull of gangs.

There is a continual cry about the very real shortage of professional help to meet the needs of high-risk children and those already in trouble. Not even the most optimistic observer expects that adequate professional help will be provided in this time of reduced budgets. When looking at all the services children need, observers are impressed by how many of these supports are already supplied by volunteers at no cost to taxpayers. The most obvious support is parenting: Providing a substitute for family requires a very expensive social investment. Thus, efforts at reconstituting effective families are both psychologically and financially a first call.

One source for adding to the resource pool is through training both children and adolescents in helping skills, as Lantieri does. By and large, even adolescents are not thought of as a resource, except for fast-food service. There are often professional prejudices against giving power to youth. Although not all youngsters would or should volunteer, even kids with serious problems can undergo role reversals and tutor younger pupils. Youngsters "figure out" their charges about as well as adults, even though they lack the professional vocabulary. They can directly express things to peers when an adult would hesitate. There is a veracity to peer advice that is hard for adults to duplicate. Kids need training, adult consultation, and supervision, especially when they man crisis lines. Such service can become a therapy for the helper. The volunteer moves from being a part of the problem to being part of the solution.

Several youth self-help groups, such as Delinquents Anonymous, along with youth associations and newsletters for disturbed youth, illustrate the many ways in which the group process can utilize indigenous helpers. One skill that transfers for these youth is advocacy. They learn how to negotiate for themselves, even designing special courses to meet their needs. It is interesting how many "why-peer-helping-won't-work" excuses authorities can generate until they actually try a program. It is hard to accept that not everything resides in professional credentials.

Groups with many profiles will be with us as long as we have schools, even with the proliferation of computers, which are now spawning their own network groups. Teachers should think of themselves as group leaders. Even individual tutoring is a group of two. Students develop in groups as ecological creatures, interacting with various groups most of their waking day. Even when there is no visible group, children respond as if from a group position. They leave a session with the principal, or an important event, considering how they will stage the situation when they narrate the encounter to friends in their peer group. No man is an island, and the same can be said even more strongly for youngsters.

REFERENCES . . . .

Anderson, N., & Marrone, R. T. (1979). Therapeutic discussion groups in public school classes. *Focus on Exceptional Children, 12*(1), 1–15.

Hobbs, N. (1982). *The troubled and troubling child.* San Francisco: Jossey-Bass.

5

Promoting Responsible Student Behavior: Essential Concepts and Skills for Effective Classroom Discipline

No other topic in education receives greater attention or causes more concerns for teachers and parents and students than classroom discipline. This is not a new problem for public schools or to classroom teachers. The lack of effective classroom discipline or behavior management skills is the major stumbling block to a successful career in teaching. For example, a study of first year teachers reported 65% of this group were anxious about their ability to maintain classroom order and wondered if their students viewed them as competent authority figures. A similar finding was reported by the National Education Association in their annual survey of teacher concerns. For the past ten years, teachers ranked classroom discipline as their number one problem and, as teachers experienced more disruptive student behavior, they felt their classrooms were more difficult to manage. Students who disregarded classroom rules, challenged their authority, interfered with the instructional program, used obscene language, were apathetic to learning, and were verbally and physically threatening to the staff and peers caused teachers to feel less safe in their classrooms than they did in the past.

Students also are concerned about their physical and psychological safety. The majority of students want a safer and more secure school and classroom and become anxious when a few students act up in a frightening way. The majority of students are not ambivalent about the need for adult protection and the importance of clear, reasonable, and enforceable rules. However, in select schools, students are questioning the staff's ability to protect them against peer bullying and assaults. Perhaps this is one reason why some students bring weapons to school, not as an aggressive act, but as a last resort of self protection. As one student reported, "I spend more time watching my back than planning for my educational future."

237

Parent groups, PTAs, and community leaders are voicing the same concern as teachers and students. These groups are alarmed by the growing reports of school violence, drugs, gangs, guns, and shootings. They are demanding their school board members restore safety, order, and discipline to public schools and to stop the trend of having public schools reflect the destructive values of, "Life on the Streets." Parents also want the school principal to be in charge of the students and the staff. They want stricter student rules and want the staff to be less tolerant of the rights of deviant students. They believe the prerequisite to classroom learning is classroom order and classroom order can only be achieved by classroom discipline.

When schools have chronic disciplinary problems and the staff seem helpless to resolve them, staff competence emerge as the central issue in subsequent discussions. More principals and teachers are dismissed or leave public education because of their ineffective disciplinary skills than for any other reason. If this trend continues, teachers and administrators will become our new educational "drop outs."

Why has there been so little improvement in this area when there is a consensus among school board members, administrators, teachers, students, and parents that classroom discipline needs to be more effective? One explanation is because there are no easy or simple solutions to this complex problem. A school based classroom discipline program does not function in the vacuum of college textbooks nor can it be divorced from the social, ethnic, economic, political, professional, and personal values of the community, the school board, principals, teachers, and students. Each of these groups frequently holds different, and at times conflicting, views, values, beliefs, and expectations regarding what are appropriate school policies, rules, behaviors, and consequences. In our consultation with public schools, the following five interrelated reasons have contributed to this dilemma.

1. The Multiple Meaning of Classroom Discipline . . . .

Classroom discipline is a sponge-like word which soaks up a variety of different meanings and attitudes. For some educators, discipline means the power of the teacher to control the behavior of their students. It is a set of skills which makes students obedient to their authority. The "locus of control" is external and the goal is to maintain a strict code of law and order. Teachers who operate on this definition frequently have students who perceive discipline as an act of punishment they receive for breaking school rules.

For other educators, discipline means an opportunity to teach students a set of values about how people can live together in a democratic society. This would include the values of honesty, fair play, the rights of others to learn, respect for property, respect of multicultural differences, and so on. Discipline is perceived as the process of helping students internalize these values and to develop self-control over their drives and feelings. The "locus of control" is internal and not external and the goal is to help students learn responsible behavior. For these students, discipline is perceived as a chance to learn self-control or self-discipline from their personal experiences based on the natural consequences of their behavior. This definition fosters a developmental view of discipline in which students learn how to behave responsibly in various situations over time.

When staff meet to discuss ways of improving classroom discipline, they rarely pause to acknowledge and work out the different beliefs they attach to this term. As a result, these group deliberations frequently end up creating more staff frustration and confusion than staff consensus and direction.

2. The Growing Social/Emotional Needs of High Risk Students . . . .

More students are entering public schools without the benefits of ongoing, positive parental bonding and attachment. Many of these students already have been damaged emotionally by the debilitating effects of poverty, neglect, abuse, divorce, drugs, and rejection. They have not internalized a sense of trust in other adults or developed the necessary pro-social skills necessary for group instruction and personal learning. Consequently, the students have low frustration tolerance, misperceive social interactions, limited attention spans, and low self-esteem. Their social/emotional needs dominate their behavior and disrupt the learning process. Teachers who are motivated by the cognitive process of teaching may not be prepared to recognize and meet the social/emotional needs of these students. A few of these teachers defend their educational position by saying, "I have an excellent program, but the wrong students come to my class."

3. The Needs of Multicultural Students . . . .

The public schools are serving an increasing number of multicultural students, resulting in significant and different racial, religious, sexual, gender, and socioeconomic issues, values, and norms to exist in the classroom. Teachers brought up on middle-class values may have little direct experience or knowledge of the importance these multicultural values have and can inadvertently deny or misread the behavior of their students. For example, a student's particular style of dress, language, and manners can become an on-going cultural battleground for some teachers. This is particularly true when the cultural norms and values of the community are different from the social/academic norms and values of the school. Under these conditions, the issue of school discipline can spark powerful, multicultural school/community conflicts.

4. The Top Down Administrative Solutions to Classroom Discipline . . . .

When school violence erupts, the community puts pressure on the local school board to implement new and more restrictive policies on deviant behavior. Occasionally, these policies are rigid, absolute statements that become unrealistic to implement with any degree of fairness. While the intentions of these school board policies may be honorable, the actual enforcement of these policies becomes self-defeating. For example, murder in our society is viewed in three degrees. Let's assume for a moment the government decided to get tough on murder and have a zero tolerance towards killing others. The new policy immediately collapses the three degrees of murder to just one inclusive degree of murder. Murder is murder and is an unacceptable act regardless of the circumstances. How long would this new policy last before it would be contested legally? However, a local board of education expects their administrators and teachers to carry out their policies or risk losing their jobs. For example, some city school systems have initiated a policy of zero tolerance toward any student who brings a weapon to school. This policy includes an automatic five-day suspension and an immediate transfer to a different school. In order to guarantee a city wide standard of objectivity, the policy listed all the objects defined as weapons from hat pins, scissors, and knives to guns. If any of these weapons were found on a student, there would be no further discussion of this incident. The principal must file a report to the superintendent, and the student is automatically suspended without exceptions. No one can disagree with the goal of keeping weapons out of school. This goal is uncontestable! However, a rigid policy which operates in a robotic fashion and does not involve any meaningful student discussion only succeeds in depersonalizing any respect for the student. For example, the following school incident was reported in the *Herald Mail* newspaper. A five-year-old boy found a razor blade at his bus stop. He picked it up and showed it to the bus driver, who in turn reported it to the principal. Since the razor blade was on the list of weapons, the principal was obligated to suspend the student and file the appropriate forms to transfer him out of his community school. It is this type of nonthinking, automatic policies that cause some teachers and administrators difficulty in supporting top-down discipline policies regarding student crimes and punishments.

5. The Limitations of Pre-Service Teacher Education Skills in Classroom Management ....

A survey of first-year teachers documented that 70% of the teachers felt their pre-service training in classroom management was naive and ineffective. The psychological concepts and marginal skills they learned were restricted to a part of a course in Educational Psychology or Student Teaching. Often they were taught only one theoretical approach to behavior management with little or no training in group management. The assumption seems to be that classroom management is an interaction which takes place only between a student and the teacher independent of group forces. However, many classroom teachers must manage groups of 35 to 40 students with limited space and little administrative support. One first-year teacher summarized her pre-service training as follows:

I was not prepared to survive in the real world of classroom life. It was like learning to dive without ever going into the water. I was long on theory but short on skills. The first time I tried to manage a class on my own, it was a disaster. I almost drowned!

Our experience with teachers confirms this fact that many first-year teachers are not adequately prepared to manage student behavior successfully.

When these five reasons interact, it is understandable why there is so much confusion and frustration in developing and agreeing on the concepts and skills of promoting effective classroom discipline.

OUR DEFINITION OF EFFECTIVE CLASSROOM DISCIPLINE . . . .

Our definition of effective classroom discipline involves four interrelated concepts and skills.

1. Classroom Discipline Begins with the Teacher and Not the Students . . . . .

The teacher's level of self-awareness and the quality of her relationships with her students directly influence the effectiveness of her behavior management skills. This important and least understood concept of classroom discipline is rarely appreciated, but it is the basis of our belief that all significant student learning involves and revolves around the personality of the teacher. No teacher enters the classroom with a symptom free history or has a perfect psychological fit to work successfully with all the students assigned to the classroom. This fact can be used to motivate teachers to gain greater insights into helping troubled students. The journey begins by digging through one's developmental past and uncovering those powerful and buried life events that have affected the teacher's attitudes and behaviors toward select students. The question she needs to answer is, why is she compassionate and caring toward some students, tolerant and tactful toward others, and rejecting and renouncing toward still others? The image of the "Perfect or Great Teacher" is an education myth. The only reason the characteristics of the "ideal teacher" flies is because it is filled with hot air. In reality, each teacher carries their personal history, like a locked briefcase, into the classroom every day. Unfortunately, a few of the students have discovered they have the key to the teacher's psychological briefcase and they take some pleasure in exposing the teacher's unfinished business to the class. The nature of the teacher's unfinished psychological business explains why some teachers can help troubled students, like a clinging, helpless, infantile behavior of a dependent student, while other teachers would react to this same student with anger and repulsion. If these two groups of teachers used the same behavior management skills on the same dependent student, the results would probably be significantly different. Effective classroom discipline cannot be successful when a teacher is stirred up emotionally. What a teacher can handle intellectually far exceeds what she can tolerate emotionally. This is why the first cornerstone of classroom discipline begins with the teacher's level of self-awareness and interpersonal skills, and not the behavior of the students.

2. Classroom Discipline Involves Long-Term Goals . . . .

The long-term goals of effective discipline is to teach students the basic democratic values and standards of our society, such as equality, work, fairness, and honesty, which lead to self control and personal accountability. This is a gradual and on-going learning experience for students based on their internal locus of control. The teacher can play a meaningful role in promoting long-term goals by providing their students with opportunities (a) to move students from a point in time where adults make most of their decisions to a point in time where students make most of their decisions (b) to move students who have little responsibility for their behaviors to a point in time where they have maximum responsibility for their behaviors; and (c) to move students who are motivated by immediate and narcissistic goals to a point in time where they are motivated by long-range altruistic goals. These three examples of long term goals reflect how a teacher can advance the second cornerstone of effective classroom discipline by facilitating students to become responsible, self directed, and productive members of our society.

3. Classroom Discipline also Involves a Multitude of Short-Term Skills That Maintain Classroom Order and Effective Student Instruction and Learning . . . .

A teacher needs a variety of daily intervention skills to maintain the ongoing educational program. These "on the spot" teacher skills are used for three different reasons.

One set of skills is targeted to prevent problem behaviors from developing by increasing desirable student behaviors. This would include such techniques as rewarding positive behavior, using descriptive praise, and developing cooperative group norms and standards of appropriate behavior. The second set of short-term skills is aimed at teaching students the necessary pro-social skills they will need in order to cope with a stressful school incident. This would include such topics as, How to Enter a Group, How to Develop Friendship Skills, How to Manage Frustration, How to Manage Peer Rejection, and so on. The third set of skills is intended to decrease inappropriate student behavior by direct teacher intervention. This would involve using a variety of surface management skills from "planned ignoring" to "physical restraint." The goal of these short-term skills is to deter any minor student problem from becoming a major school crisis.

These three subsets of skills are necessary, learnable and represent the third cornerstone of effective classroom discipline.

4. Classroom Discipline Is Not a Bag of Tricks or Gimmicks a Teacher Uses During a Crisis . . . .

Our definition of classroom discipline is a thoughtful and purposeful way of interacting with students on a daily basis. It is a style and a philosophy of relating to others, and not a switch to be turned on and off in times of need. It is a professional way of modelling the values and the behaviors a teacher wants students to learn. It flourishes in an atmosphere where a teacher respects the dignity and self-esteem of the students and has the maturity and skill to set realistic expectations and limits on student behaviors. This is the fourth and final cornerstone of our definition of effective classroom discipline. We will use it throughout this chapter.

All of the articles selected for this chapter have been classroom-tested. They demonstrate successful ways of translating psychological theory into effective teacher practices. The first selection deals with the fascinating concept of how troubled students can get reasonable teachers to behave inappropriately during a student–teacher conflict.

For years, teachers have been told how their behavior influences the behavior of their students. While the statement is true, the corollary is also true. Troubled students can greatly influence the behavior of their teachers. Troubled students are proficient at provoking and pushing the "emotional buttons" of concerned, dedicated, warmhearted teachers, who can end up feeling and behaving in hostile and rejecting ways toward selected students. When this happens, many of these teachers feel surprised and guilty by their reactions. One mild-mannered junior high school teacher expressed this problem in an open and honest way. "Each night I promise myself I will not lose my temper with Gary; but by 11 A.M., after he has fallen out of his seat, teased a girl about being overweight, talked out loud during instruction time, and given the finger sign to a quick tempered peer, I want to strangle the little S.O.B."

To understand why and how competent teachers find themselves in such self-defeating struggles, Long developed the Conflict Cycle Paradigm. This model describes how the interaction between a student and teacher follows a circular process in which the attitudes, feelings, and behaviors of the teacher are influenced and, in turn, influence the attitudes, feelings, and behaviors of the student. During a stressful incident, this circular process becomes a Conflict Cycle, creating additional problems for the student and the teacher. Once in operation, this negative interplay between a student and teacher is extremely difficult to interrupt. For example, we know students under stress behave emotionally rather than rationally. They are controlled more by feelings than by logic. They protect themselves from physical and psychological pain by becoming defensive, primitive, and regressive. When a teacher reacts to these inappropriate behaviors impulsively or with righteous indignation, a "power struggle" develops in which understanding and helping disappear and "winning" becomes the only acceptable outcome for the teacher. When teachers react emotionally, they deny the issues and feelings behind the students' behavior and become part of the problem.

The purpose of the Conflict Cycle is to help teachers (a) become aware of how their personal beliefs and values are challenged when helping troubled students, and (b) develop effective strategies to prevent students from pushing their "emotional panic buttons." Teachers do not have complete control over student behavior, but they do have complete control over how they react to student behavior. The Conflict Cycle is an essential tool for teachers' success in helping troubled students.

ARTICLE 5.1

The Conflict Cycle Paradigm on How Troubled Students Get Teachers Out of Control

Nicholas J. Long

The Conflict Cycle is a paradigm that describes the circular and escalating nature of student/teacher conflict. Figure 5.1 presents the student's Conflict Cycle and its five interacting steps: The Student's Self Concept

- Stressful Incident
- Feelings
- Observable Behavior
- Adult/Peer Reactions

To understand the dynamic nature of the Conflict Cycle Paradigm, Figure 5.2 presents an overview of the circular sequence of the Conflict Cycle in action.

To give the sequence of the Conflict Cycle more meaning, each of the five steps are described in greater detail.

STEP 1: THE STUDENT'S SELF CONCEPT

The student's self concept plays a central role in determining how he thinks about himself, how he relates to others and what he believes will happen to him in the future (i.e., his self-fulfilling prophecy).

FIGURE 5.1   The Student's Conflict Cycle

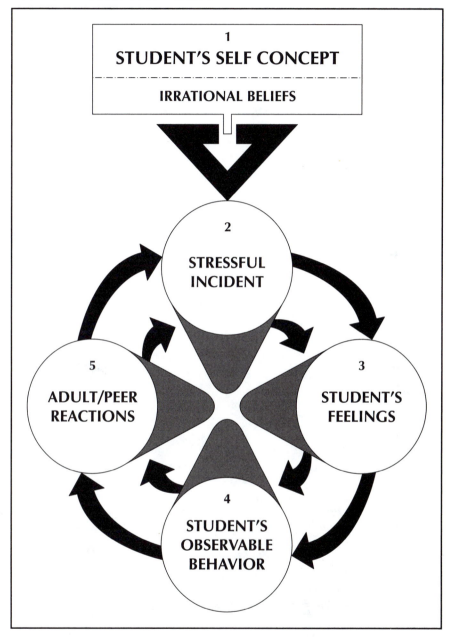

Developmentally, a child's self concept is formed by the repetitive reinforcement of significant adults and peers in his life who give him daily and on-going feedback about his behavior and character. If a child receives clear and positive reinforcements, such as he is lovable, curious, happy, smart, attractive, and strong, he will internalize these experiences and statements and slowly begin to attribute these characteristics to himself.

FIGURE 5.2   The Conflict Cycle Paradigm

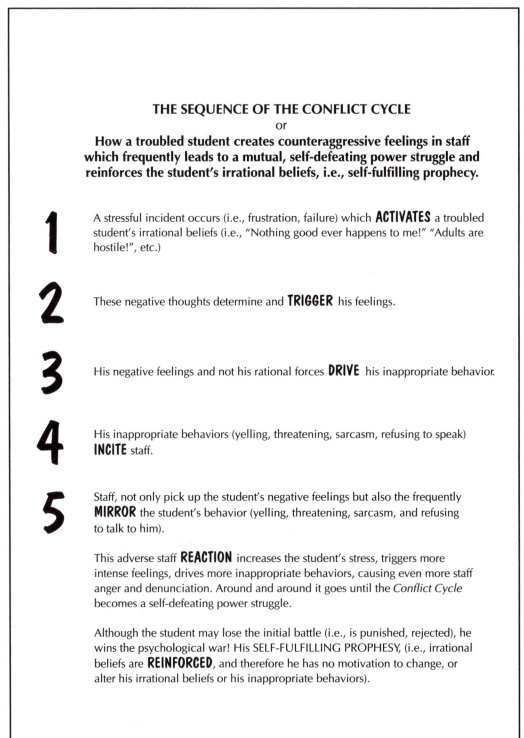

THE SEQUENCE OF THE CONFLICT CYCLE
or
How a troubled student creates counteraggressive feelings in staff which frequently leads to a mutual, self-defeating power struggle and reinforces the student's irrational beliefs, i.e., self-fulfilling prophecy.

1 A stressful incident occurs (i.e., frustration, failure) which **ACTIVATES** a troubled student's irrational beliefs (i.e., "Nothing good ever happens to me!" "Adults are hostile!", etc.)

2 These negative thoughts determine and **TRIGGER** his feelings.

3 His negative feelings and not his rational forces **DRIVE** his inappropriate behavior.

4 His inappropriate behaviors (yelling, threatening, sarcasm, refusing to speak) **INCITE** staff.

5 Staff, not only pick up the student's negative feelings but also the frequently **MIRROR** the student's behavior (yelling, threatening, sarcasm, and refusing to talk to him).

This adverse staff **REACTION** increases the student's stress, triggers more intense feelings, drives more inappropriate behaviors, causing even more staff anger and denunciation. Around and around it goes until the *Conflict Cycle* becomes a self-defeating power struggle.

Although the student may lose the initial battle (i.e., is punished, rejected), he wins the psychological war! His SELF-FULFILLING PROPHESY, (i.e., irrational beliefs are **REINFORCED**, and therefore he has no motivation to change, or alter his irrational beliefs or his inappropriate behaviors).

If, however, he receives negative feedback and is told he is a fearful, diffi-cult, sad, stupid, ugly, and weak child, over time, he will internalize a de-preciating view of himself. As a result, how a child learns to think about himself is more important in determining his feelings and behavior than any objective professional evaluation. For example, a student may score in the average range of intelligence, but if he thinks he is not smart, then his be-havior will be consistent with his thoughts about himself regardless of the test results.

Irrational Beliefs

In addition to developing a unique set of beliefs about himself, the child concurrently develops a personal set of beliefs about his world and the peo-ple in it. If the adults in his life are hostile, rejecting, negligent, depressed, helpless, ambivalent, perfectionistic, or inconsistent, the child probably will learn to be suspicious of all new situations, to mistrust adults, and to avoid interpersonal closeness. These negative beliefs about others in his world and whether the world is a safe place become the second active part of his self concept. By early elementary school age, his beliefs about himself and his beliefs about others merge and become the major motivating force of his emerging personality. This solidification of his self concept results in the de-velopment of a characteristic way of perceiving, thinking, feeling, and be-having. Now the child has a consistent and stable way of responding to most current and future life events, although most of these forces function outside of his personal awareness.

Just as a primitive tribe can explain a tidal wave or an exploding vol-cano as something the tribe had done to offend the Gods, troubled chil-dren need to explain why they were abused, neglected, given away, or rejected. The search for an explanation does not take place in their reality, but in their irrational beliefs about their painful life experiences. This means all life events are filtered and evaluated by an individual's thoughts about these events activated by his belief system.

Rational versus Irrational Beliefs

What are the differences between rational and irrational beliefs? Irrational beliefs are not based on true conditions, and usually operate to the detri-ment of the mental health of the student. The distinction between rational and irrational beliefs becomes vague for troubled children who have been abused, neglected, and rejected. Initially, their negative beliefs about oth-ers are an accurate reflection of their life experiences.

What causes these reality-based beliefs to become irrational is the psychological process of *overgeneralization.* This is a specific way of think-ing, which allows a traumatic event to be perceived by a troubled student as an on-going pattern of defeat. This thinking is achieved by using the words, *always* and *never* whenever an individual thinks about this event. For example, a troubled student who was neglected by his parents would say: "My parents neglected me" (fact). "I can't count on my parents to meet my needs" (fact). "Therefore, I think all adults I meet in the future will always neglect my needs" (irrational belief).

The following lists describe some of the irrational beliefs commonly held by troubled students.

1. *Irrational Beliefs about Self*
   - I should never express my anger openly and if I do I will be punished.
   - I should be perfect at everything I do.
   - I am stupid if I make mistakes.
   - I am a terrible person.
   - I am unworthy of love.
   - I never have to listen to anyone except me.
   - I have to be in control to survive.

2. *Irrational Beliefs about Others*
   - Never depend on adults to meet your needs. They will always let you down.
   - This world is filled with dangerous people and situations.
   - People are too helpless and depressed to care about me.
   - People will take advantage of me every time they can.

The Advantages of Irrational Beliefs

Since irrational beliefs interfere with everyday, interpersonal relationships and psychological comfort, why are they maintained? What are the intricate rewards for holding on to irrational beliefs that are pathological and self-defeating? Irrational beliefs provide troubled students with a sense of security and control. Irrational beliefs brings order to an unstable and chaotic world. Irrational beliefs make their world predictable and manageable. Irrational beliefs allow students to know in advance what will happen to them in new relationships. Such beliefs protect students from moving beyond their feelings and becoming responsible for their behavior. Most important, irrational beliefs protects them from experiencing the dreaded and underlying feeling of helplessness and rage. As a result, students feel there is no reason to change.

These irrational beliefs are maintained as troubled students project their internal world view on others by engaging adults and peers in endless and absurd power struggles. This psychological process of getting others to confirm their irrational beliefs is called the student's Self-Fulfilling Prophecy.

The Self-Fulfilling Prophecy of the Student's Self Concept

The self-fulfilling prophecy is the student's way of validating irrational beliefs by getting staff/peers to act them out. Most staff and peers are unaware of this covert goal of a troubled student and end up fulfilling the student's prophecy about life. The following three illustrations demonstrate the effectiveness of the students' self-fulfilling prophecies.

The Self-Fulfilling Prophecy of an Aggressive Student   This student believes he has the right to meet his needs regardless of the rights of others and to get back at others who interfere with his pleasures. Concurrently he believes adults are hostile and ultimately will reject and punish him. The question is: How can he maintain these irrational beliefs about all adults when his new teacher is kind, compassionate, skilled, and caring? Like a director of a play, his solution is to cast her into the role of a hostile adult, regardless of her personality, and to look for an opportunity when he can accuse her of being unfair, and rejecting. The following classroom observation clearly highlights this process.

> Earl, a large, 12-year-old boy, is sitting at his desk, completing his morning work. He raises his hand and asks for permission to get a drink of water. The teacher approves. Earl stands up, but instead of leaving the classroom, he walks over to Carl's desk and starts talking to him. Carl responds and Earl pats Carl on the head, laughs, and grabs his paper. Carl grabs it back and shouts, "Your sister!"
>
> The teacher intervenes and says, "Earl, you are more interested in causing trouble than getting a drink, so just forget it and return to your desk."
>
> Earl reacts as if he had been slapped, shouting, "What a gyp! You can't even get a damn drink in this school. This is not a school. It is a prison. I could die of thirst and you wouldn't care!" He walks back to his desk, slams a book closed, and looks sullen, expecting his teacher will fight with him.

The Self-Fulfilling Prophecy of a Passive Aggressive Student   This student believes the direct expression of anger is dangerous so he must always hide and disguise his aggressive feelings and thoughts. If adults ever found out how he really felt about them, "terrible things would happen." Consequently, he learns to express his normal anger in passive aggressive or indirect ways. He doesn't hear, see, or remember anything the teacher asks him to do. If he has to do something that he doesn't want to do, he does it in a way that disappoints and frustrates the teacher. If he is really angry at the teacher, he will get back at her by deliberately stealing her keys, hiding some objects she needs, or messing up the room without her knowledge. Kevin's indirect and subtle "drip by drip frustrations" begin to add up for the teacher. Over time she gets to the point where she is emotionally loaded, but psychologically unaware of her accumulated anger toward

Kevin. At the end of a difficult classroom lesson, Kevin falls out of his chair, makes the teacher ask him three times before acknowledging her, and accidentally rips her newly designed bulletin board. This is the straw that breaks the camel's back, the spark that lights the fuse. The teacher explodes, yells, and threatens Kevin. She has a 20-second intense temper tantrum.

Kevin appears shocked, "Gee, it was an accident. I didn't really mean to do it." The teacher is also shocked by the amount of anger she expressed. She begins to think—perhaps it was an accident. Perhaps I did overreact. This is not like me. After all, Kevin is not the most difficult student in my class. I guess I owe him an apology. "Kevin," she says, "I'm sorry that I yelled at you." Kevin replies, "It's okay" but thinks: Wow! Look at how crazy people get when they express their anger, it's a good thing I don't express my anger. My teacher needs to change, but I don't.

The Self-Fulfilling Prophecy of a Withdrawn Abused Student   This 13-year-old student believes she is a terrible person, unworthy of anyone's love. Her family consists of an alcoholic, abusive father, a subservient mother, and two younger sisters. Mary has been sexually abused since age seven. Her mother knew about it, but never said anything or did anything to stop it. It was a family secret never to be told. Mary believes if she were a better person, these sexual assaults would not have happened. Her irrational beliefs include: I deserve what happened to me, and if others found out what I was really like, they would know how terrible I am and reject me. Mary's self-fulfilling prophecy is to avoid all meaningful relationships and attachments since they would only cause her more pain, shame, and rejection. Mary's classroom teacher reports Mary has no friends, and appears to be uninterested and unresponsive to her peers and teachers. She is a loner and if there was one word to describe her relationship with others, it would be "ignored." Clearly Mary has created a social reality in school that maintains her irrational beliefs.

The self-fulfilling prophecy of a troubled student is an important concept to know when staff decide to help this student.

STEP 2: STUDENT STRESS OF THE CONFLICT CYCLE

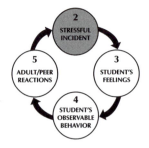

The second step of the Conflict Cycle is student stress. Not all events in life are stressful. A stressful incident is defined as an external event which threatens the well being of a student or activates his irrational beliefs. A teacher may ask two students to come to the front of the class and to read from the textbook. Gary thinks this request is a wonderful opportunity to demonstrate his reading skills and dramatic voice, believing it will improve his social status among his peers. Jason, however, thinks this same request is a disaster. He thinks he will mispronounce the words, stutter, and make a fool of himself in front of his peers. In these examples, the process for deciding whether the incident was stressful or not was due to the specific meaning each student gave to the request to read aloud. In Jason's case, it prompted his irrational belief that "nothing ever works out for me," so it became a stressful incident for him.

The Physiology of Stress

There are four types of student stress, Developmental Stress, Economic/ Physical Stress, Psychological Stress, and Reality Stress.

Once a life event is thought of as a stressful incident, a natural biological reaction follows: This response is automatic, unconscious, and very predictable. Stress prepares the body for action. It does this by releasing a series of hormones into the bloodstream that activate the autonomic nervous system. This system controls the involuntary muscles that alter the blood pressure, respiration, and digestive systems. Anthropologically, stress has functioned as a personal alarm system enabling a person to survive an attack. During this stress state, all bodily senses are intensified. The person has an abundance of energy, creating increased levels of strength, agility, and endurance. The person can either attack a foe with new ferocity or escape by running great distances without tiring. In either case, for primitive humans, stress served a very useful, specific, and important purpose. In many cases, it was the basis of their survival.

However, in today's complex society there are many rules against attacking others or running away. Students must learn to control what their bodies are urging them to express. Students must learn how to cope with this state of stress instead of acting it out. Since self-control takes considerable skill and maturity and is a difficult task even for adults, we can expect that even "normal" students will break down at times.

1. Developmental Stress   *Developmental stress* refers to the normal developmental stages we all go through from birth to death. For example, to be born is stressful. To be weaned from the breast or bottle is stressful. To be toilet-trained is stressful. To leave parents and home for teacher and school is stressful. Learning to read can be stressful. Learning to understand sex differences between boys and girls can be stressful. Learning to be part of a group can be stressful. For adolescents, there are numerous developmental stresses: watching one's body change, becoming independent, developing personal values as opposed to group values, understanding the excitement and confusion of one's own and others' sexuality, developing career courses, graduating from high school, and so on. Each of these developmental events can be stressful for all students regardless of race, color, creed, or socioeconomic level.

2. Economic/Physical Stress   *Economic/physical stress* is felt by millions of families in our society who are living on the brink of economic disaster. Not all of these families come from the slums, ghettos, or disadvantaged groups. Many striving middle-class families are living beyond their financial resources and have extended their credit lines to the breaking point.

For the chronically poor, economic stress shows itself in poor diet and food; poor health habits; greater susceptibility of illness; lack of acceptable clothes; lack of privacy; lack of sleep; lack of opportunity to participate in social and school-related activities; greater parent exhaustion; parent models of joblessness and helplessness; social isolation from the mainstream of society; and a sense of being different from the group.

3. Psychological Stress   *Psychological stress* consists of an unconscious or deliberate attempt by individuals, groups, and institutions to destroy the self-concept of a student. For example, many students are told they are a burden and the primary source of their parents' problems. Life would be better if they were not around. They spoil the family and neighborhood because of their demands and behaviors. They are told they are stupid, inconsiderate, ungrateful, and useless to themselves and others. For some students, the stress does not come from open rejection but from trying to meet unrealistic standards. Students are told they must be perfect to be loved. Whatever they do is not good enough. For other students, the psychological stress is related to specific adults who are emotionally troubled. For example, the seductive parent who stimulates excessive sexual awareness and fantasy by showing unusual interest in sexual topics. The psychotic parent, who is suffering from a major mental illness, and is not capable of carrying out adult responsibilities. The alcoholic or drug-abusing parent who creates a home where there is little consistency. In these settings children never know if the parent will care and relate to them or whether the parent will expose them to shame or terror. Other students must cope with the overprotective or the depressed parent. Moreover, any parent, sibling, relative, or significant friend who is emotionally disturbed and interacts with these students will have a profound impact on their ability to focus his remaining energies on classroom learning.

4. Reality Stress   *Reality stress* arises from all the unplanned events that frustrate the personal goals of a student. These frustrations happen spontaneously, rather than from an organized attempt to frustrate the student.

The reality stresses happen with such frequency for a few students that the students begin to believe the world and all the people in it are against them. For example: (1) A boy looks forward to wearing his favorite sweater only to discover that his brother wore it yesterday and spilled syrup on it; (2) A girl lends her algebra book to a friend who forgets to bring it to school the next day; (3) Two classmates are fooling around in class. One pushes the other into a third girl's desk tearing her English composition, which is due in a few minutes. (4) A teacher warns the class that the next pupil who talks will be given a detention. The pupil next to one boy whispers to a friend and the teacher points to the boy as the offender. (5) A teenage boy's dad lets him use the car to go to a basketball game. The boy goes to pick up his friends only to discover on the way to the game that the gas tank is empty. In other words, things go wrong that should not go wrong. It is not anyone's fault, but the stress is very real, frequent, and intense.

For most of our students, stress comes not from one source but from multiple sources. For example, a student may have the normal developmental stress of a final exam. That evening his parents have a violent argument, and he is unable to study or sleep. On the way to school he is scapegoated by a hostile group who call him various racial and ethnic names. As he enters the classroom a friend greets him by slapping him on the back, causing his glasses to fall off and break. Finally, the teacher announces a new school policy that no exam can be taken over, regardless of the circumstances.

It is important for adults to understand that a student in a crisis needs to talk. Through mutual conversation rather than punishment, a greater appreciation of the students' stresses and a broader perspective on his behavior can be achieved. When teachers understand these multiple cycles of stress, they are more willing to help students rather than *blame them for their misfortunes.*

The following list represents some of the common stressful classroom incidents.

I. Developmental Stress
   - Student experiences group pressure to conform to their norms.
   - Student experiences sexual attraction to a classmate.
   - Student wasn't called on or selected for a group game.
   - Student is jeered by his peers.

II. Physical Stress
   - Student is too tired to concentrate on the assignment.
   - Student is too sick to concentrate on the assignment.
   - Student is too hungry to concentrate on the assignment.
   - Student has a handicapping condition that prevents him from competing with his peers.

III. Psychological Stress

- Student fails an examination.
- Student is racially depreciated.
- Student believes others have a higher expectation of his performance than he does.
- Student is deliberately rejected or scapegoated by his peers.
- Student is too conflicted by his home problems to concentrate on his assignment.

IV. Reality Stress

- Student is blamed for something he didn't do.
- Student doesn't have the appropriate textbook, notebooks, etc.
- Student doesn't understand the content of the assignment.
- Student doesn't understand the teacher's directions.
- Student cannot get his locker to open which contains a report which is due next period.
- A friend accidentally tears his favorite shirt.

STEP 3: THE STUDENT'S FEELINGS IN THE CONFLICT CYCLE

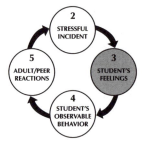

There is considerable confusion among teachers and other helping professionals concerning the origin, the awareness, the accuracy, and the expression of student feelings. The following questions reflect the quandary many helping professionals have in defining how to work with the feelings of troubled students. What is the relationship between thinking and feeling? Are they independent of each other? Isn't it healthy for students to express their feelings; to get them out in the open so they can be understood? Is it accurate to describe feelings as "good feelings" and "bad feelings?" What about negative feelings, shouldn't they be controlled? If feelings are swallowed or blocked, don't they come back as psychosomatic illnesses. Since feelings are real, are they an accurate assessment of the precipitating incident or are they an assessment of the student's current emotional state? Is there a difference between acknowledging feelings and expressing them? If the same feeling can be expressed in different ways are some expressions healthier than others? These questions corroborate the uncertainty, ambivalence, and fogginess that has developed around the concept of understanding and managing student feelings.

Biologically, feelings are spontaneous, temporary physiological states of pleasure and displeasure, sparked by thoughts.

Thinking Creates Feeling

David Burns, a cognitive therapist writes "you feel the way you think." The source of feelings starts with thoughts and not with personal frustrations. It is how one thinks about an external event, and not the event itself which triggers feelings. Positive thoughts about an event trigger positive feelings and negative thoughts about an event trigger negative feelings like the example of the two students who were asked to read aloud. The process of thinking and feeling does not follow an independent path, but is a continuous circular process. Thoughts trigger feelings and negative feelings influence the way a person thinks about an event creating a new cycle of negative feelings.

If the same external event happens frequently, i.e., a child is harshly yelled at by an adult, and if this event is perceived as a stressful incident, the child not only will have negative feelings such as anger or fear, but also the child will be conditioned to respond automatically to all future acts of yelling, without being aware of his thinking. For example, I entered the crisis room at Rose School to listen to a new student talk about a fight he just had with a classmate. Without saying a word, I sat in the corner to observe the process.

> After 10 minutes I decided to stand up and take off my jacket since the room was too warm. Simultaneously, the student looked at me and dove under the desk. The student was convinced that when the principal of the school, the man of authority, took off his jacket he was going to be hit.

This reaction is called automatic thinking and explains the rapid response many troubled students have during conflict.

The Usefulness of Feelings

All feelings are real, powerful, and give excitement to life, but they are not always an accurate assessment of a situation. Emotions are not facts, they are feelings that are triggered by rational and irrational thoughts. If the feelings are triggered by irrational thoughts, then the subsequent feelings are real but are self-defeating. When students act on these feelings, their behavior only makes the situation worse. However, if the feelings are triggered by rational thoughts, then the feelings are an accurate assessment of the situation and need to be accepted. This involves a developmental process of distinguishing between acknowledging one's feelings and learning to express them in proper behavior. For example, it is healthy to feel upset and angry when one has been psychologically depreciated or discriminated against, but it is not acceptable to assault the offender. It is healthy to experience fear when someone threatens to hurt or abuse you, but it is not helpful to encourage it to happen. It is healthy to experience intense feelings of sadness when someone you love dies or moves away, but it is not healthy to withdraw from all relationships. It is healthy to feel guilty when you behave in a way that you know is unacceptable, but it is not useful to behave so others will punish you. It is normal to experience anxiety when you are anticipating a new experience or a new relationship, but it is not healthy to handle this anxiety by drinking or drug abuse. It is normal to feel happiness when you are in love, but it is not helpful to express blatant sexual feelings in front of others. The existence and importance of accepting one's feelings are irrefutable. The question is, how do students learn to express these feelings?

Three Ways of Expressing Feelings

The three ways children learn to express their feelings are (1) to act them out, (2) to defend against them, and (3) to accept and own them.

1. Act Them Out   Many immature, impulsive, and unsocialized children express their feelings directly. There is no attempt to modify the direct expression of their feelings in behavior. If they are angry, they hit. If they are sad, they cry. If they are frightened, they run, and if they are happy, they giggle and laugh. There is an obvious one to one relationship between their feelings and behaviors. When students express their feelings directly in spontaneous classroom behavior, they almost always create more problems for themselves since they lack the skills of "self-control." Some students cannot distinguish between feeling angry and smashing a chair. For these students, the feeling and behavior are one response and not two.

2. To Defend Against Them   Many children are socialized to believe certain feelings are unacceptable to them, like anger, sadness, or jealousy. When these feelings occur they create such anxiety, discomfort, and inner conflict, the children learn to develop ways of avoiding them. At these times, their primary motivating goal is to reduce or block the tension of anxiety that originated from their unpleasant and unacceptable feelings.

Anna Freud, in 1946, described these strategies of avoiding the pain of personal anxiety as Defense Mechanisms. This psychodynamic concept provided "helpers" with valuable and insightful knowledge on how children avoid anxiety by denying the unacceptable feeling by escaping from the unacceptable feeling and by shifting or substituting the unacceptable feeling to another person or object. The most common defense mechanisms using Denial are: *repression, projection,* and *rationalization.* The most common defense mechanisms using Escape are: *withdrawal,* and *regression* and the most common defense mechanisms using Substitution are: *displacement, compensation,* and *sublimation.* While defense mechanisms are successful in diminishing anxiety, they also use up psychological energy, deny the real problem, and usually create new interpersonal problems with adults, peers, learning, and rules. Psychologically, a student solves one problem by using defense mechanisms, but usually ends up by creating a new problem. This is like the adolescent driver who is concerned about running out of gas. His solution is to drive to the nearest gas station as quickly as possible, but in the process, he gets a speeding ticket and also runs out of gas.

3. To Accept and Own Them   Students who have learned to accept and own their feelings can use them to enrich their lives and to develop coping skills to manage the inevitable frustrations in their lives. These students have learned to distinguish between having the full range of feelings and being had by their feelings. When students are flooded by their feelings, their behavior is driven by their emotions and not by their rational thought. If this pattern happens often, these students are labelled "emotionally disturbed" because their emotions drive their behavior. However, when students learn to own their feelings and think about them rationally, then the resulting behaviors usually are appropriate, logical, and realistic. Accepting one's feelings and learning how to be friends with them, including the feelings we don't enjoy, like sadness, anger, jealousy, envy, and rejection, is one goal of mental health.

STEP 4: OBSERVABLE BEHAVIOR OF THE CONFLICT CYCLE

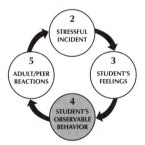

When students express their feelings directly or by defending against them, they usually create additional problems for themselves in their school. Behaviors such as hitting, running away, becoming ill, stealing, teasing, lying, becoming hyperactive, fighting, using drugs, inattention, and withdrawal, cause students to have difficulty with teachers, peers, learning, and school rules. For example, when a student displaces his feelings of hostility he has for his father on his teacher, an inevitable teacher–student conflict develops. When a student becomes depressed because his mother is ill or battered, the student may not be able to complete his assignments, and a learning problem emerges. When this interpretation of behavior is accepted, one grasps the concept that the problems students cause in school are not always the causes of their problems. More accurately, the problems students cause in school are the result of the way they have learned to express their feelings.

Inappropriate student behavior can be analyzed in the following four categories:

1. Difficulty with staff.
2. Difficulty with peers.
3. Difficulty with learning.
4. Difficulty with institutional rules.

For staff living with inappropriate behaviors, the professional task is to avoid describing the student's behavior in general terms like: "Jason hit Sam," or "Jason tore up his assignment," but to pinpoint the significance of his behavior by describing: Where did it happen? When did it happen? Who or what was the target of this behavior? What was the duration of the behavior? What was the intensity of the behavior? What was the frequency of the behavior?

Notice the difference in meaning between a teacher's statement: "Jason spit on Sam" and the statement, "Jason and Sam were on the playground during lunch recess playing tag. Sam tagged Jason by hitting him on the side of his face. Jason reacted by spitting in Sam's face, chest, and hands at least three times over a period of two minutes. The spits were intense and involved large amounts of saliva. This is the third time Jason has spit on another peer this week." This full description gives us a much clearer sense of the hostility Jason is expressing by spitting. The incident was not a simple, spontaneous act, but part of a destructive pattern of behavior he is using.

STEP 5: TEACHER/PEER REACTION OF THE CONFLICT CYCLE

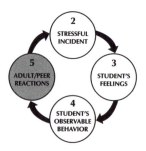

How staff reacts to inappropriate student behavior is the most critical step in the Conflict Cycle. While staff do not have control over the student's thinking, feelings and behaviors, they do have complete control over how they react to the student's behavior. Unfortunately, too many student/staff conflicts become escalated by the staff when they respond emotionally, impulsively, and in counteraggressive ways. An analysis of over 600 student/staff Conflict Cycles revealed at least four different categories of inappropriate staff responses to student behavior. They are: Reacting in Counteraggressive Ways; Rigid and Unrealistic Teacher Expectations; Caught in a Bad Mood; and Prejudging a Troubled Student.

1. Programmed to React in Counteraggressive Ways   One of the most important insights of the Conflict Cycle is how a troubled student can create in staff his negative feelings and, if the staff are not trained to accept these feelings, they will act on them and mirror the troubled student's behavior. For example, when a student yells at a teacher and shouts, "I'm not going to do it," the normal impulse is to react by shouting back, "Yes you will." Once the teacher behaves like the student, the Conflict Cycle is fueled for extensive travel. This means an aggressive student will always create *counteraggressive feelings* in others. A depressed student will always cause others to feel sad and helpless. A hyperactive student will always create feelings of impulsivity in others, and so on.

The staff didn't start the Conflict Cycle, they only reacted to it inappropriately. Initially the staff had no thoughts or intentions of yelling, threatening, or hitting the troubled student. But, once the cycle of counteraggression begins, it is extremely difficult for the staff to stop or to acknowledge their role in escalating the conflict. They feel unjustly attacked and become flooded by their feelings of righteous rage. This feeling justifies their *retaliatory reaction* or counteraggression and accounts for 68% of school-based Conflict Cycles in our sample.

2. Rigid and Unrealistic Teacher Expectations Regarding Normal Developmental Student Behavior   There are a few teachers who are not well-adjusted. They are mean spirited, rigid, narrow-minded, critical, and exacting about what kinds of behavior they tolerate in their classrooms. These teachers believe students should be obedient to authorities, attentive to instruction, motivated to excel, and use proper language and manners at all times. Problem behavior is defined as discrepancy between what they expect and what they observe in their classrooms based on their personal histories. If there is a difference, it is because the student has the problem and needs to be disciplined. These teachers are unaware of how their forked tongues can become instruments of pain and how this contributes to escalating the crisis.

Over time, even the "normal students" react to the autocratic and repressive classroom atmosphere and begin to get back by "acting up" or becoming passive aggressive toward the teacher. Troubled students in the classroom have even more difficulties. These students react to demeaning and critical verbal style by picking up the teacher's negative feelings and by mirroring the teacher's behavior. For example, the teacher may threaten a troubled student sternly and say, "you better stop whispering or else!" only to hear him say, "you better stop talking or else!" After the class stops laughing, the student is labeled defiant and is sent out of the room. However, if the student refuses to leave the classroom, swears, or slams the door on the way out, the problem behavior escalates into a student/staff crisis. The behavior of rigid teachers accounts for 7% of our sample of student/staff Conflict Cycles.

3. Caught in a Bad Mood   School staff are not robots. They have the same stresses as all adults. Occasionally their personal and/or family life takes a dip. When their level of stress increases they become emotionally overwhelmed and exhausted, such as when their parents are ill and need special care, their children are having academic and interpersonal problems and need additional support, and they are having financial difficulties, and are angry with their mate or friends.

These teachers usually are competent, dedicated, and supportive of their students, but today they feel rotten. They have a bad taste in their mouth and a bitter attitude toward life. They cannot stomach the acid irritation of the normal and annoying developmental behavior of their students and are ready to spew out their exasperation on any student who upsets them.

Then Jason decides it would be clever and fun if he added a little excitement to the classroom by making "burping sounds" with his armpits. From the teacher's perception, it was an ugly sound that was heard around the world. The teacher *overreacts* to Jason's attention getting sounds, becomes punitive, and a crisis develops. Afterwards, these teachers usually can acknowledge their role in the crisis and respond positively to benign confrontation. Teacher stress due to personal life situations account for approximately 20% of our sample of student/staff Conflict Cycles.

4. Caught in Prejudging a Troubled Student in a Crisis   In every school, a peer social structure exists in which students are assigned and assume specific group roles such as the leader, jock, nerd, mascot, lawyer, as described in the chapter on Groups. One group role is the instigator or *trouble maker.* Everyone knows who this student is. His reputation is acknowledged by the staff and peers and follows him around like a shadow on a summer day.

If this student is involved in a crisis, and the sounds of trouble are all around him, there is a high probability this student will be prejudged, as the instigator, before all the relevant information is obtained. The staff, who intervenes, is likely to say, "I knew it would be you!" If this staff were playing the mystery game Clue, he would conclude after receiving his first card; It's the butler with the knife in the library!

Call this process faulty clairvoyance or defective conclusions, but it happens to the nicest of people. Judgments are made that are not true and the targeted student is accused of some act he did not do. In this sequence, the student becomes upset and the staff is convinced the student is lying to protect himself. The result is an unfortunate incident that escalates into an ugly crisis. This process of prejudging a troubled student before all the facts are obtained account for 5% of our sample of student/staff Conflict Cycles.

These four categories of inappropriate staff reactions during a student/staff Conflict Cycle are helpful in identifying what additional skills adults need in order to break their own pattern of self-defeating behavior. While the most frequent response category was "Being Programmed to React in Counter Aggressive Ways," further analysis of our sample student/staff Conflict Cycles revealed all staff used "You Messages" which escalated the Conflict Cycle.

The Destructive Use of "You Messages" That Fuel the Conflict Cycle

The following list of "You Messages" were recorded during a student/staff Conflict Cycle which escalated the students' Conflict Cycle.

- Can't you do anything right?
- You apologize immediately!
- Don't you dare use that language with me!
- You better start acting your age!
- You think you know everything. Should I call you Einstein!
- You have no respect for anyone or anything!
- You don't listen to anyone, do you?
- You better shape up because I have had it with you.
- You just never use your head.

Around and Around It Goes Until a No-Win Power Struggle Develops

The blaming "You Messages" a student receives from the staff frequently supports the student's view of himself and confirms his self-fulfilling prophecy. This creates more student stress, causing the student to feel and behave in more unacceptable ways. As the student's behavior deteriorates, the staff becomes even more angry and disgusted with him. As the staff reacts in a negative, punitive way, this intensifies his stress, creating more negative feelings and primitive behaviors. The Conflict Cycle continues around and around until it escalates into a no win *power struggle*. Logic, caring, and compassion are lost, and the only goal is to win the power struggle. For staff, the student is seen as the source of the problem. He is told to "shape up" and to improve his attitude and behavior. If he doesn't, the staff labels him as disturbed, delinquent, dangerous, and disgusting. The student is usually suspended, transferred, or referred to a more restrictive, special education setting.

What is important to remember is that there are no winners when the Conflict Cycle reaches the level of the power struggle. This cycle cannot be broken by asking immature students to act maturely during intense states of stress. If change is going to occur, the staff must accept the responsibility for acting in a mature, professional manner. This means understanding how students in conflict can provoke concerned, reasonable, and dedicated teachers to act in impulsive, dispassionate, and rejecting ways.

In summary, the Conflict Cycle follows this self-defeating sequence for a troubled student.

- External events arouse thoughts.
- Thoughts, irrational beliefs, trigger negative feelings.
- Feelings drive behavior.
- Inappropriate behavior incites others.
- Others create additional stress for the student.

An Illustration of How an Aggressive Student Successfully Creates Counteraggressive Behavior in a Female Student Teacher (Ms. Sarah Drue)

I did my student teaching at a city junior high and I was told there were specific rules and regulations that needed to be followed.

This incident occurred because of the "tardy policy." When students are late for school without a legitimate written excuse, they must first report to the office to pick up a sign in sheet, which is carried to homeroom. After the homeroom teachers sign this sheet, the students are required to stay in Tardy Hall at 3:00 to 4:00 P.M. Brian, a 16-year-old learning disabled student came in to my homeroom without his "sign in sheet" at approximately 9:30. I had already filled his name in as absent for the day but he requested that I change it immediately. He did not want to go to the office because he did not want to stay after school. This was my first day of student teaching the class. The regular teacher was in the class, but I was being observed. Therefore, everything I did was being evaluated.

Of course, Brian insisted I change his name on my sheet from being "tardy" to "present." "Come on Ms. Drue, it won't hurt anything. I want to go to the game this afternoon and I can't stay in Tardy Hall."

"Well Brian, if I did this for you I would have to do it for everyone else. Isn't that right class?" Of course, the entire class agreed with me and began approaching my desk. One of my students had already been to the office because of being late, therefore, she insisted that if he was changed, then so should hers. I replied that I was not going to change anyone's and that Brian had better hurry to the main office before he's late for his first period class.

Brian replied, "You're not my teacher anyway. I don't have to talk to you. Ms. Shell will do it for me." Ms. Shell was the "real" teacher for the Learning Center and she told Brian it was up to me since I was teaching for the rest of the semester. I had already decided not to make any changes. As much as I wanted to, I just could not.

Brian began raising "hell" after I had made my final decision and threatened he was going to "kick my ass" after school. Of course, I was scared. Brian stands at least 6 feet tall and is huge! Little ole' me was not used to this sort of outrage. He called me all sorts of "bitches" and "MF's" so I told him to wait in the office until I came down. Ms. Shell said I was to report this incident because this behavior cannot be tolerated. Brian again threatened me and Ms. Shell got up angrily, grabbed Brian by his collar and escorted him to the main office. "Bitch, you just wait" he continued to holler. "I'm going to flatten your tires along with your face." Well, I was in hysterics by now, but Ms. Shell told me to continue with the class.

By 10:30 A.M., Ms. Shell returned to the classroom without Brian. She informed me he had been sent home and could not return without his parents. I was very upset but she informed me there wasn't more that could be done. "You did well!" "You didn't lose your temper." "I'm used to seeing Brian going into these rages every now and then, why, I am practically the only teacher who can do anything with him."

I tried to make my day go on as usual, but my mind kept thinking about what Brian said. I had already made up my mind to stay after school, so I could get away "scot free." I thought I would be safe. By the time I checked my name out in the principal's office, sweat was over my face. I was scared! I proceeded down the hallway and out comes Brian! I should have turned around and gone back to the office, but if he knew I was afraid of him he would probably provoke me for the rest of the semester. No way, I had to stand up to this kid. If I show him that I am not afraid, maybe he won't bother with me.

"Yea Bitch, I told you not to send my name to the office. Wait until you see your tires," Brian says.

"Aren't you supposed to be home by now? I thought you were sent home until your parents arrived back to school with you."

"Yea Bitch, I can tell, you ole' whoe!"

"Okay, I'm a whore and you're a faggot. Now we're even." I continued toward my car.

"Faggot! Does this look like a faggots' dick?"

I wanted to faint. I hope he didn't actually pull his penis out! I surely wasn't going to turn around to find out either. "Brian, I am surprised at you. You have really disappointed me. I thought you were one of my better students. Say what you will, just make sure that you don't touch me. I am here to teach you, not to beat you."

Why did I say that? Brian then began throwing rocks and sticks at me outside of the school. I still didn't turn around, but I did warn him that if any of them hit me, I was going to forget about being his teacher and actually "KICK HIS ASS!" "Bang," a rock hit me in the back of my leg. I stopped and turned around to look at him. He began saying "Kick my ass, come on, kick my ass." I proceeded toward my car but began telling him that I was going to call his parents tonight. "Bang" this rock hit the middle of my back and I turned around and began walking toward him with full force. By now I had forgotten I was a teacher and I was aiming to kick his tail. When I got to him he looked so much larger than I but I was not going to back down. I began hollering and pointing my finger in his face, telling him that my brothers would love kicking his tail if he hurt me. He kept breathing real hard down on my face, just trying to provoke me even more. By now the Assistant Principal and two other teachers came running out and grabbed Brian, dragging him to the office. I began crying and they questioned me about the entire incident. They wanted me to press charges. The school security guard stayed with Brian until his parents picked him up from the police precinct.

This student/staff conflict between Brian and Sara Drue demonstrates, with startling clarity, how quickly a Conflict Cycle can escalate into a no-win Power Struggle. The incident began with Brian experiencing a reality disappointment (being tardy) moved on to verbal threats, finally on to physical threats—throwing stones at Ms. Drue. This pattern of Brian's self-defeating behavior was not new to his regular teacher, Ms. Shell, who said, "I'm used to seeing Brian's rages," but it was a new and upsetting experience for Ms. Drue, even though she was commended by Ms. Shell as "doing well" and "not loosing her temper."

The more Ms. Drue "thought" about Brian's threats the more anxious and fearful she became. When she inadvertently saw Brian, she had two thoughts: "I'll show him I'm not afraid of him," and "I need to walk back to the office and avoid this confrontation." She selected the first thought and decided to take him on head to head, one to one, teacher against student. Brian started this new cycle by using verbal/sexual language, "Yea Bitch, I can tell, you ole' whoe!" and discovered Ms. Drue's emotional panic button. She reacted by using similar counter verbal/sexual language, "Okay, I'm a whore and you're a faggot!" This remark only succeeded in escalating the situation. Brian retorted and started to throw stones at her. This triggered her feelings of righteous rage and when he urged her to "kick his ass," she couldn't refuse. She threw away her professional skills and started toward him with aggressive intentions! If her colleagues had not arrived in time to rescue her, this situation could have resulted in serious injuries. The outcomes were predictable. Ms. Drue fulfilled her prophecy that Brian was a dangerous student. Brian fulfilled his prophecy that Ms. Drue was a hostile woman, and Brian ended up being totally responsible for this incident and was suspended with no insight into his pattern of self-defeating behavior.

Could this second student/staff incident been avoided? If Ms. Drue understood the goal of the Conflict Cycle and was aware Brian was trying to push her emotional buttons and to get her to act in unprofessional and counteraggressive ways, she would have selected her second thought: "Perhaps I need to avoid Brian at this time and walk back to the office." With this rational decision, Ms. Drue could have prevented the second cycle of craziness.

SUMMARY

The Conflict Cycle is a paradigm that explains why the management of student behavior begins with the staff and not the student. Unless the staff can control their reactions to inappropriate student behavior, and have an awareness of their "emotional buttons," staff will escalate the incident and only succeed in making it worse. It would be like trying to put out a small fire by throwing gasoline on it. The dynamics of the Conflict Cycle not only helps staff understand their role in acting out the feelings of students, but also opens an array of new alternatives to school punishment. The skills involved in avoiding a "Power Struggle" with students helps staff identify and address the important, underlying issues in a student's life rather than simply react to his annoying surface behavior. It allows staff the freedom of talking with troubled students and learning more about their lives, their struggles, and their beliefs about themselves and others. In this process, staff have an opportunity of teaching troubled students better ways of behaving, being accepted, and becoming empowered.

. . . .

Once teachers are knowledgeable about how troubled students can push their emotional buttons and create counteraggressive feelings in them, teachers can use this insight to accept these feelings. A conscious choice can be made to *not* engage these students in a power struggle. Regarding these feelings, the necessary skill is to express them by using "*I* messages" instead of "*You* messages." A teacher who is aware of counteraggressive feelings could express them by saying, "I get angry when you walk into my room, kick over a chair, and yell in my face. I hear and can see you are upset, but that kind of behavior doesn't help me understand why you are so angry."

When teachers use *I* messages to talk about their anger, they substitute descriptive words for destructive acts. *I* messages reduce a teacher's impulse to get back at students, and they help the teacher to focus on what the students need to get themselves under control rather than on what he or she is feeling. *I* messages also are less likely to provoke anger, do not imply a sense of "right" and "wrong," open up communication, and model the use of verbal control over angry feelings. The most important reason for using *I* messages is that they release the teacher's counteraggressive feelings in a healthy and appropriate way.

In the next article, Long and Newman have adapted Fritz Redl's (1959) four-notched scale of responding to student behavior to one of the essential concepts of effective discipline. This concept offers teachers specific guidelines for deciding when to *permit*, to *tolerate*, or to *stop* student behavior or when to *prevent* inappropriate behavior by reorganizing the classroom design or curriculum. The article also proposes eight reasons why teachers should intervene when inappropriate student behavior occurs.

ARTICLE 5.2

The Four Choices of Managing Surface Behavior of Students

Nicholas J. Long
Ruth G. Newman

There are four major alternatives to handling student behavior. They are: permitting, tolerating, interfering, and preventive planning. Redl emphasizes that no one of these alternatives is better than any of the others. The task is to make the right choice for each student.

PERMITTING BEHAVIOR

Most rules in a school are made to inhibit and regulate the impulsive behavior of students. During the day, they are told in many ways to stop, slow down, and control their behavior. No one would argue against the importance of these rules in a group setting. If it is important for students to know what they cannot do, it is equally important for students to know what they can do. For example, students should be told that it is permissible to be messy when they are fingerpainting, to have some degree of movement within the classroom, to go to the lavatory when necessary, to show freedom of expression in their creative works, and to express an opposing view without being ridiculed or chastised. Students are reassured when they know in advance that their activities will not meet with adult frowns, shouts, or physical interference. More important, the sanctioning of behavior by teachers eliminates much of the students' unnecessary testing of limits. A teacher who permits students to leave their desks and go to the book corner after they have finished the assignment should make this privilege clear. Then a student does not have to sneak a book and feel guilty or feel victorious about squeezing more freedom from the teacher than the student thinks he would expect. Teachers need to be clear and active in listing what behaviors they will applaud!

TOLERATING BEHAVIOR

A lot of classroom behavior must be tolerated, but students should have no reason to believe that teachers approve or sanction it. The more common

Abridged from Nicholas J. Long and Ruth G. Newman, "A Differential Approach to the Management of Surface Behavior of Children in School," *Teachers' Handling of Children in Conflict*, Bulletin of the School of Education, Indiana University, XXXVII (July 1961), 47–61. Reprinted by permission.

basic assumptions behind tolerating behavior are (1) learner's leeway, (2) behavior that reflects a developmental stage, and (3) behavior that is symptomatic of a disease.

1. Learner's leeway. Whenever a student is learning a new skill, experimenting with new ideas, or trying to win status in the group, the teacher should expect that the student will make mistakes. The teacher should not expect that the student will do it correctly the first time. For example, many sensitive teachers tell their class they are not going to be upset when students err in trying to master new academic and social skills. With some teachers, the more mistakes students make, i.e., on an arithmetic assignment, the easier it is for the teacher to help them clarify and correct their misunderstandings. This was found to be true in the following incident:

> I have noticed that Carole (third grader) became very upset if she made a mistake on an assignment. The children were writing to a railroad company for some free material, but they did not know how to address the envelope. I went to the board and showed them the proper form and asked them to practice. In a little while I noticed that Carole had her head on her desk. When I asked her what was the matter, she said that she couldn't do it and that she already had made three mistakes. I asked her to show me her work. (She has misspelled one word, did not capitalize one of the words, and had the return address crowded up on the upper left-hand corner.) I told Carole that these are the kinds of mistakes that many students make and that I did not expect her or any of the other children to do it perfectly the first three or four times that they tried. With this encouragement, she started again.

Sometimes it is helpful to talk about "good mistakes" versus "poor mistakes." A good mistake is made when a student's answer reflects some personal logic. A poor mistake is one which rests on impulsive behavior with no semblance of logic.

2. Behavior that reflects a developmental stage. Some behavior is age typical and will change as the student becomes more mature. Any attempt on the part of the teacher to alter or inhibit this behavior results in such negligible changes it usually is not worth the inevitable fight. For example, students in the early grades are impulse-ridden and motor-oriented. Every kindergarten teacher knows this level of activity needs to be tolerated and channeled into activities. This concept of tolerance should not be confused with sanctioning it or permitting wild behavior. Another example is that students in the late third or early fourth grade, caught between group pressure and allegiance to the teacher, are notorious for tattling; e.g., "Miss Jones, Johnny hit Mary," or "Johnny pulled a leaf off your flower when you were in the hall." Other illustrations of age-typical behavior are the unscrubbed, unhygienic appearance of the pre-adolescent boy, the primping of sixth-grade girls, the secrets of preadolescent girls, and the sex language and behavior of adolescent boys. A classroom example of age-typical behavior is presented below.

At noon, several third-grade girls came bursting into the room relating a story about the third-grade boys. The boys had discovered several pictures of nude women which were hidden in a bush on the playground. In small groups, they were examining the pictures in detail when a few of the third-grade girls "worked their way in" to see what was taking place. The girls screamed and found their way to my room. They related the story; then the bell rang.

The boys entered (without pictures), as though nothing had happened. Silence prevailed. They knew that I knew. Finally, I asked one of the boys where the pictures were. He explained that they had hidden them in the bathroom and planned to secure them after school for more detailed study. I asked another of the boys to bring the pictures into the room. This he did and I, *without looking,* threw them into the wastebasket.

The pictures remained in the wastebasket until after school. Several students sought me out at the teacher's desk, casting glances at the wastebasket all the while. Others, whom I had never seen before, entered the room and quickly left upon finding me there.

Next morning the wastebasket was empty; the pictures were gone. I didn't see them again until I entered the boiler room, where they were on the wall—property of the school janitor.

3. Behavior that is symptomatic of an underlying illness. When a child has a respiratory infection, the chances are he will cough in class and that the symptom (coughing) will continue until the child is well. This cause and effect relationship between an infection and a cough is accepted among teachers. However, when a student who is emotionally disturbed shows the symptoms of his illness, such as recurring temper tantrums, fights, and irrational fears, the student is likely to be rejected by his classmates, his teacher, and even himself. A psychologically trained teacher realizes that, when a student suffers from emotional problems, the symptoms are rarely conscious forms of meanness but are simply a self defeating way of expressing his feelings. For example:

Some of the things that Martha did were fighting, tearing up other children's property, walking the floor constantly, tearing pages out of her book, name calling, and spitting. Although Martha makes me angry and caused all of us many problems, I feel we have grown a little in understanding that we all have problems and that the class is simply not divided into good and bad, accepted and unaccepted. Martha's behavior has improved during the year and, if I did anything to help it, I was doing it with kindness, firmness, and accepting her as an individual, rather than judging her on the basis of her actions.

Again, let's not confuse tolerating behavior with sanctioning it. This teacher's attitude towards Martha was more accepting because she didn't blame and punish Martha for her behavior.

INTERFERING WITH BEHAVIOR

While a psychologically trained teacher is aware of long-range goals, the teacher still has to handle the spontaneous behavior that occurs in the classroom. Some behavior has to be stopped if the classroom learning is to take place. A student cannot continue to act out his feelings. The task is to find ways of interfering with any inappropriate behavior so that it does not disrupt the group, but still is helpful to the particular student. Redl and Wineman in *The Aggressive Child* have listed 21 specific influence techniques that they have been able to identify in their work with aggressive boys.

Before suggesting ways of intervening, the question of when a teacher should intervene needs to be considered. While this question cannot be settled without considering many variables, school psychologists have observed that too many teachers never set limits or intervene until they are choked with counter-aggressive feelings. When this happens, the teacher is likely to intervene in a way which is inappropriate and too severe. To remedy this situation teachers need to be given clear guidelines to help them with this difficult problem. Once again Redl gives us the direction and suggests the following criteria for teacher intervention.

1. *Reality dangers.* Adults are usually more reality-oriented than children and have had more practice predicting the consequences of certain acts. If students are playing some dangerous game, fighting, or playing with matches so it looks as if they might injure themselves or others, then the teacher must move in and stop the behavior.

2. *Psychological protection.* Just as the adult protects the student from being physically hurt, he also should protect the student from psychological injury. If a group of boys is ganging up on a student, or scapegoating him, then the teacher should intervene. The teacher does not support or condone this type of behavior.

3. *Protection against too much excitement.* Sometimes a teacher intervenes in order to avoid the development of too much excitement, anxiety, and guilt in children. For example, if a game such as dodge ball is getting out of hand and if it continues another 10 minutes, the students may lose control, mess up, and feel very unhappy about their behavior later. Once again, the teacher should intervene to protect students from this consequence.

4. *Protection of property.* This is almost too obvious to mention, but sometimes it is easy to overlook. Students are not allowed to destroy or damage the school property, equipment, or building. When the teacher sees this, he moves in quickly and stops it. But at no time does he give the impression so common in our society that property is more important than people. Protecting property protects people.

5. *Protection of an on-going program.* Once a class is involved in learning and the students have an investment in its outcome, it is not fair to have it ruined by one student who is having some difficulty. In this case, the teacher intervenes and asks this student to take a time out or to move next to her in order to insure that the enjoyment, satisfaction, and learning of the group are maintained.

6. *Protection against negative contagion.* When a teacher is aware that tension is mounting in the classroom and a student with high social power begins tapping his desk with his pencil, the teacher might ask him to stop in order to prevent this behavior from spreading to the other students and disrupting the entire lesson.

7. *Highlighting a value area or school policy.* There are times when a teacher interferes in some behavior not because it is dangerous or disturbing but because she wishes to illustrate a school policy or rule which may lie slightly below the surface of the behavior. For example, the teacher might want to demonstrate why it is impossible for everyone to be first in line, or to point out how a misunderstanding develops when there is no intent to lie or to distort a situation.

8. *Avoiding conflict with the outside world.* The outside world in school can mean neighboring classrooms or the public. It is certainly justifiable to expect more control on the part of your children when they are attending an assembly or are on a trip than when they are in their classroom.

What are some of the counter indications against interfering with a student's behavior when the behavior is not dangerous? (1) The fuss that it would create at this time is not worth it! For example, the group is going on a trip, is about to have lunch, etc. The groups reaction might disguise the real purpose of the teacher's intervention. In such a case it is better to wait for another incident. There is a written guaranty that it will come. (2) The teacher decides to wait until the behavior deviates to the point where it is obvious not only to the student but also to the entire group. This way the student's typical defenses, such as projection, i.e., "You're always picking on me," or "I never get a fair deal," are clearly inappropriate. (3) The teacher is in too good a mood today. He cannot work up enough genuine concern to impress the student and/or the group with the seriousness of the student's behavior. While this feeling is a common one, it should not be the barometer for teacher intervention.

PREVENTIVE PLANNING

Redl's fourth alternative is preventive planning. Preventive planning should be considered whenever a chronic classroom problem exists. Sometimes this problem can be prevented by reorganizing the classroom, the curriculum, or the daily schedule. For example:

The staff of an alternative school for troubled elementary students noticed an increase of "off task" behavior around 11:30 A.M. A ten day study was initiated and the findings confirmed the initial impressions. Three out of the four classrooms showed a significant increase in inappropriate behavior between 11:15 A.M. and 11:45 A.M. A staff meeting was called to discuss the findings and to propose ways of solving this problem. Staff suggestions included: (a) providing more structured assignments, (b) increasing reinforcers to these students who were "on task," (c) developing more appealing lessons, (d) using more audio visual aides, (e) setting up a new contingency program which ties student recess to completed classroom assignments between 11:30 A.M. and noon. One staff member asked if they knew what time the students got up in the morning, if they had breakfast, what time the special education bus picked them up, and how long they were on the bus? Much to everyone's surprise, the staff learned most of their students had to get up between 6:15 A.M. and 6:30 A.M., only 60 percent of them had a sit down breakfast, they were picked up between 7:00 A.M. and 7:15 A.M. and had a bus ride that lasted between 40 minutes to 1 hour and 15 minutes. The staff decided the "off task" behaviors at 11:30 A.M. may be due to physical fatigue so they moved the lunch period from noon to 11:30 A.M.

The results of this simple change of schedule was most rewarding. The problem was not due to the teachers' personality, the type of assignment, the instructional method or the reinforcers available to the students. The basic problem was physical stress. The students were exhausted by 11:30 A.M. By moving the lunch period 30 minutes earlier, this school wide problem was prevented and everyone was happier.

Managing student behavior becomes an intellectual challenge for classroom teachers when they use this concept. Teachers need to ask themselves: Do I permit this behavior?, Do I tolerate this behavior?, Do I stop this behavior?, or do I prevent this behavior from occurring. Remember, teachers have the choice over how they respond to student behavior.

. . . .

Direct intervention is the third of four choices of responding to student behavior. We want to emphasize the importance of pairing teacher intervention with school values. This association between teacher intervention and school values is often neglected when behavior management skills are being taught, but it is a skill that enhances the teacher's effectiveness. For example, Mrs. Conner, a fifth-grade teacher, observes Brian making a racial comment in her classroom. She decides to intervene so she walks up to Brian, gets his attention, and says, "Brian, your comment is inappropriate and needs to stop!" Brian looks at her and replies, "Why?" Mrs. Conner doesn't respond with a "control statement" such as, "I'm the adult or the boss in this class and you must be obedient to my authority," or, "If you don't, you will lose your points." Instead, she uses this intervention as an opportunity to teach Brian an important value about how students in this school treat each other. Mrs. Conner is aware that whenever she stops student behavior she is saying there is a different and more rewarding way of living together. All direct teacher intervention can have three positive outcomes: (a) it interferes with undesirable student behavior, (b) it teaches an important school value, and (c) it models that teacher intervention is an act of professional protection and support and not an act of personal hostility and punishment. This third reason confronts a predictable problem between troubled students and teachers. Many of these students have been socialized by parents who were volatile, hostile, and out of control. Like Pavlov's dogs, the students have been conditioned to associate adult intervention with adult aggression and hostility. Frequently, these students' initial reaction to any teacher intervention is to misinterpret it as a function of the teacher's personality (i.e., "She hates me," "She enjoys putting me down," "She's against me"), rather than recognizing it as a realistic adult response to inappropriate behavior. This type of thinking reinforces the students' resistance toward the teacher and can escalate the problem into a no-win Conflict Cycle. The teacher needs to counteract this distortion by removing his or her personality from the act of intervention. This removal can be accomplished by explaining the decision to interfere with the students' behaviors. Here are some examples of how this skill can be realized:

> Brian, the reason I'm stopping your racial comments is that, in this school, we believe students have a right *to be protected* from verbal and psychological abuse. Whenever I hear any verbal abuse, it is my professional job to stop it.

> Brian, the reason I'm asking you to take another seat [take a time out, etc.] is that, in this school, we believe students have a right to learn without being disrupted. It is my job *to protect and maintain* the ongoing instructional program. Whenever I see or hear any student behaving in a manner that interferes with group learning, it is my professional job to stop this behavior.

> Brian, the reason I want you to stop writing on the desk [wall, etc.] is that, in this school, we believe we should protect our learning environment. This is where we live and we need to make it as attractive and as comfortable as possible. Whenever I see anyone defacing or destroying our cared-for setting, it is my professional job to intervene and stop this behavior.

This skill of explaining teacher intervention as an act of *protection* is an effective way of confronting the students' belief that the teacher is hostile and rejecting. The teacher makes it abundantly clear that his or her actions have nothing to do with a student's personality or with liking or disliking the student. The teacher's response is a function of the student's behavior. Intervention is part of a professional commitment to enforce the school values by protecting the rights and responsibilities of all the students. Over time, this skill will promote teacher trust and respect among the students.

The skill of pairing teacher intervention with teacher protection of school values can be used for all circumstances in which teachers need to stop disruptive behavior.

The pairing defines the teacher's role in stopping student behavior, identifies appropriate and inappropriate behaviors, provides an atmosphere of consistency and fairness, helps curb impulsive behavior, promotes a safer environment, and reinforces the rights of all the students. These rights can be translated into effective classroom rules. We make these suggestions for the development of classroom rules:

- Students should be involved in the writing of classroom rules.
- The rules should be short, precise, easy to understand, and written as a positive statement.
- Classroom rules should be posted, throughout the year, in a prominent location where they cannot be overlooked or forgotten.
- Classroom rules should be reviewed frequently, especially after long holidays or absences.
- Classroom rules should be discussed by teachers and students when a new student joins the class.
- Different situations (cafeteria, gym, music, assemblies) may require a different set of rules.
- Classroom rules need to be reviewed with students to determine their effectiveness.
- Teachers must be sensitive to different cultural and family values when establishing class rules.

In the next article, Fagen presents a comprehensive and functional list of teacher skills for managing the surface behaviors of students. These short-term, on-the-spot skills are essential if a teacher is to maintain classroom order and learning. There are eight specific skills for reducing undesirable student behavior, and seven specific skills for increasing desirable student behavior. All of these skills should be practiced until they become an automatic part of the teacher's professional behavior. The focus remains on effective practices rather than on intellectual awareness of these skills.

ARTICLE 5.3

Fifteen Teacher Intervention Skills for Managing Classroom Behavior Problems

Stanley A. Fagen

Unfortunately, too many teachers have a limited range of techniques for reacting to deviant student behavior and quickly escalate problems to the point of exclusion. A common nightmare for special educators is when Billy returns to a regular class after a year of painful limit setting, contingency

From *Pointer*. (1980). Vol. 31, No. 1. Abridged from "Least Intensive Interventions for Classroom Behavior Problems."

TABLE 5.1   CONTINUUM OF CLASSROOM BEHAVIOR INTERVENTION STRATEGIES

Intensity	For Reducing Undesirable Behavior	For Increasing Desirable Behavior
Least Intensive	1. Planned Ignoring	1. Stating Expectations
	2. Stating Expectations	2. Modeling
	3. Signaling	3. Structuring
	4. Restructuring	4. Positive Reinforcement
	5. Conferencing	5. Regulated Permission
	6. Warning	6. Contracting
	7. Enforcement of Consequence	7. Token Systems
Most Intensive	8. Life Space Crisis Intervention	

management, behavior rehearsal, and self-recording. The bad dream shows Billy muttering an obscenity upon being criticized by Mr. Meticulous, after which the teacher loses his temper and yells at Billy. This, of course, results in an exciting and nasty exchange of insults and the predictable banishment to the principal's office. Or, even worse, there is a dramatic suspension to emphasize the seriousness of Billy's "loss of control."

Disruptive student behavior should be dealt with in the simplest way possible to achieve the desirable outcome. The general rule is to use the least intensive strategy necessary to reduce or stop negative behavior and to increase positive behavior. This same point of view has been advocated by Glasser in his "10 steps to good discipline" (1977).

Table 5.1 presents a continuum of intervention strategies from least to most intensive in relation to undesirable and desirable behavior. This continuum of intervention strategies is applicable to elementary and secondary levels. In view of the large scale concern about behavior in our secondary schools, however, specific illustrations and examples will focus on problems presented by adolescents. Before discussing the intervention strategies, it is important to recognize that instruction in behavior requires careful planning in the same way that is true for academic instruction. Behavior planning involves four key steps: (1) establishing individual classroom behavior expectations, (2) identifying behavior deviations, (3) identifying incompatible desirable behaviors, and (4) selecting behavior intervention strategies.

ESTABLISHING INDIVIDUAL CLASSROOM BEHAVIOR EXPECTATIONS

An individual classroom teacher's efforts to reduce problem behavior will be greatly enhanced if basic values have been defined in terms of *schoolwide behavior standards and limits* (i.e., expectations for behavior). It is widely recognized that consistency in stated expectations for behavior promotes adherence to those expectations, while ambiguity or inconsistency perpetuates disorder and limit testing. Desirable student behavior is directly related to the consistency of support of school-wide standards and limits by all staff (e.g., counselors, cafeteria workers, maintenance personnel, arts teachers). If, however, adults turn their backs when a student scribbles his name on a wall or curses out another student, then instruction in discipline is undermined. There is a place for differing expectations by staff, and for students to learn to respect differences between teachers. However, such differences should not exist in relation to agreed upon school-wide standards and limits. Examples of behaviors that are usually considered unacceptable by all school staff, as well as parents and students, are: physical attack on staff and students, verbal abuse, extortion, possessing dangerous weapons, vandalism, drug abuse, truancy, tardiness, profanity, overt disruptiveness. These are all obvious examples of acting out. Examples of staff differences that are typically not school-wide expectations are teacher preferences for being called by first or last names, amount of noise and movement in the classroom, and allowing questions about instructions or rules.

Thus, individual classroom expectations are established on the basis of school-wide standards and limits plus additional personal values that do not conflict with total school norms.

IDENTIFYING BEHAVIOR DEVIATIONS

Before any problem behavior can be reduced or eliminated, the teacher must be sure that it is indeed a significant problem. Given thirty students in a class, the teacher can ill afford to spend time dealing with behaviors that reflect momentary deviations or minor irritations. Laughter at an inappropriate time or inattentiveness to a presentation may be very annoying but not worth serious intervention in comparison to physical aggression, verbal hostility, or loud interruptions. Two guidelines should be kept in mind in setting priorities for dealing with behavior problems: (1) *flagrant violations must be prioritized above other possible concerns* (e.g., threatening someone with a knife has to be addressed before modifying failure to complete assignments); (2) *management of the disruptive behavior of several class members must precede attention to unique individual problems* (assuming the individual problems are **not** dangerous to self or others). It would be foolish to discuss the needs of one learning disabled student for increased group participation when many members of the class shout out and walk around the room at will.

IDENTIFYING INCOMPATIBLE DESIRABLE BEHAVIORS

Once the teacher is clear on the undesirable individual or group behaviors which require priority attention, the next step is to specify desirable goals

FIGURE 5.3

Undesirable Behavior	Incompatible Desirable Behavior(s)
Making fun of others	• Cooperation with others • Helping others • Ignoring others who are not liked • Respectfully stating own feelings toward others
Fighting	• Expressing differences in words • Avoiding fighting while stating the negative consequences ("Hey man, I'm not gonna get in big trouble") • Avoiding antagonistic situations • Releasing physical energy in permissible ways • Taking a break to "cool off"
Loud, unrestrained talking	• Whispering or soft talking • Talking when permitted • Listening to others • Working independently
Disregarding rules	• Following an instruction • Expressing a difference of opinion or asking a question • Offering an alternative method • Restating rules before acting • Explaining rules to others

and objectives. A major weakness in many attempts to overcome behavior problems is the lack of positive or desirable behaviors to replace the negatives. Undesirable and desirable behavior should be seen as "two sides of a coin"—for every problem situation there are one or more desirable behaviors which are both preferable to and incompatible with the undesirable behavior. Finding incompatible desirable behaviors stems from asking oneself the question: "what can I teach the student to do instead of - - - - - - ?" In other words, the undesirable behavior cannot be occurring at the same time as the new desirable behaviors. An incompatible relationship can be depicted as a seesaw—when the desirable behavior goes up, the undesirable goes down. Consider Figure 5.3.

SELECTING CLASSROOM BEHAVIOR INTERVENTION STRATEGIES

As shown in Table 5.1, a variety of behavioral intervention strategies are available to the classroom teacher. However, the teacher should be sure that these strategies are sanctioned by the local board of education, the school principal, and the parent community before using them. It should be noted that the severity of the undesirable behavior will greatly influence the level of intervention required, particularly in regard to acting-out behaviors. For example, a student who starts throwing objects around the room must be stopped immediately and removed from the program until the disturbance can be understood and resolved. In this case, a less intensive intervention like planned ignoring would be totally inappropriate.

EIGHT TEACHER SKILLS FOR REDUCING UNDESIRABLE BEHAVIOR

1. *The Skill of Planned Ignoring.* Many students engage in negative behavior to receive attention from the teacher or peer group. For some, even this negative attention is preferable to being ignored. The decision to ignore or tolerate undesirable behavior so that it will drop out or be extinguished is planned ignoring. Part of the planfulness also includes giving positive attention (e.g., praise, privileges, recognition) to the incompatible desirable behavior. An example would be not attending to a student's daydreaming and facial grimaces, while complimenting him when he is working.

Planned ignoring is not as easy as it appears since it requires the teacher to withhold his usual response to a distraction and cope with some feelings of anxiety or frustration (Caldwell, 1979). It has the advantage of avoiding power struggles and suggesting confidence in the student's self-control. On the other hand, planned ignoring should not be used when the behavior is potentially dangerous to physical or psychological well-being, or when the group becomes confused or disorganized by the violation of limits.

2. *The Skill of Stating Expectations.* As noted earlier, individual classroom behavior expectations must be clearly established, preferably with student input and agreement. Most secondary schools publish a student handbook which contains rules and disciplinary actions. Each teacher is responsible to maintain these school-wide rules in their *[sic]* own classrooms. The teacher should develop a list of any additional standards or limits that will be emphasized in her [/his] own classroom. These expectations should be discussed with the class and posted conspicuously on a bulletin board.

It is best to keep stated expectations to a minimum and to word them positively. One classroom had the following standards mounted on poster board: Thou shalt listen to one another; Thou shalt ask permission for changes; Thou shalt let others learn; Thou shalt start and stop on time. With this common understanding, the teacher could effectively use direct reminders such as "too much noise," "*we* need to listen," "time to get to work," "we're supposed to be seated now," "people are trying to work."

3. *The Skill of Signaling.* Many nonverbal signals may be used to curb negative behavior, thus avoiding the pitfall of nagging or constantly naming particular students. *Three major types of signals are available:* (a) *facial expressions,* including eye contact, (b) *body movement,* sounds and gestures, and (c) *mechanical devices.* A well-fixed glare or frown can be a relatively private and gentle way of redirecting behavior. Body movement, sounds, and gestures include rising from a seat, emphatically clearing one's throat, snapping the fingers, motioning with the hand, shaking the head, and using various postures. Mechanical aids are helpful for gaining attention of the class. With prior notification, switching the lights on and off, ringing a bell, or playing a note on the piano can provide the group with a clear message to "desist" (Kounin, 1970).

A somewhat different but related form of signaling is called proximity control (Long & Newman, 1980). Five levels of proximity control may be employed: (a) orienting one's body toward a student, (b) walking toward a student, (c) putting one's hand on the student's desk, (d) touching or removing the object used by a student to create distraction, (e) putting one's hand gently on a student's shoulder or arm. In the latter instance, caution is advised, since some students resent being touched.

The essence of proximity control is the offer of teacher support for self-control without verbal reprimand or reminder. Teachers who are adept in the use of their physical presence can often reduce unacceptable behavior in an unobtrusive and humane manner.

4. *The Skill of Restructuring the Situation.* Undesirable behavior does not happen in a vacuum. The classroom is an extremely complex environment with many precipitating conditions for disruptiveness. A sensitive teacher can regulate the level of classroom disruption by restructuring or modifying the situation to bolster behavior control and attenuate stress. Modifications are possible in such areas as seating, grouping, degree of teacher assistance, nature of the task, format and complexity of the material, physical movement, degree of involvement, amount of recognition, extent of decision making, and personal feelings.

Examples of restructuring are numerous: separating two boys who are continually fooling around *(seating change)*: placing an immature, distractible student in a small group of responsible learners *(grouping change);* moving next to a student to offer assistance when the work becomes frustrating *(teacher assistance change);* modifying the assignment from completion of 20 problems to attempting 15 minutes worth of problems *(changing nature of task);* substituting a colorful, well-spaced workbook for an advanced textbook *(changing format and complexity of material);* asking a student who is angry at having been tripped to return a film to the school library *(physical movement change);* requesting that class members paraphrase another person's remarks before giving their own when there is a lack of group attentiveness *(change in degree of involvement);* providing opportunities for students who seek attention negatively (e.g., clowning, throwing paper, seat hopping) to take leadership roles (e.g., reading a part in a play, putting on a skit, giving a report) *(change in amount of recognition);* offering rebellious students a mixture of optional, required, and creative learning activities or centers *(change in extent of decision making);* reassuring students who are nervous about a test that it is OK to be anxious and to just relax and try their best *(change in personal feelings).*

5. *The Skill of Conferencing.* Arranging for a private conference with a problem student is a useful strategy for two reasons. First, it permits an exchange of views in a confidential manner. On occasion, both teacher and student gain in awareness of each other's interests, needs, and feelings. Second, it helps the student see that the teacher is concerned with him [/her] as an individual, despite the fact that classroom standards and limits must be protected.

The teacher should not be surprised, however, when the student repeats his [/her] unacceptable behavior upon returning to the classroom after a "successful" conference. The dynamics of a class group create considerable pressure on the student to maintain his [/her] autonomy, particularly if it might appear that he [/she] submitted to teacher "sermonizing." Furthermore, student conferences can become rewarding to some students and thereby perpetuate undesirable classroom behavior.

6. *The Skill of Warning.* Consequences for undesirable behavior should be established in advance of any enforcement. For example, constant talking during a lesson results in being sent to a time-out area; cursing the teacher necessitates a conference with the principal and parent notification; lateness to class causes an after-school detention. This does not require that all students receive identical consequences for similar behavior, since flexibility is important to meet learner differences. However, all students need to have a definite understanding that their negative behaviors *cause* unwanted consequences.

Many students lack a true realization that their own actions predictably determine what happens to them. Adolescents, in particular, greatly resent arbitrary or irrational treatment. Fair and direct consequences are important for the development of character and decision making. By providing a "warning"—that is, a reminder or restatement that a choice of continued unacceptable behavior will cause a negative outcome—the student has a clear and responsible decision to make. It should be recognized that by choosing to misbehave following a warning, a teenager may be saying "I don't believe you will follow through." On the other hand, the student is indicating that he [/she] is ready to accept the consequences that have been stated. One warning is preferred since more than that one usually results in more limit testing.

7. *The Skill of Enforcement of Consequences.* Follow through on announced consequences for unacceptable behavior is critical to effective discipline. The consistent use of warnings and enforcement of consequences enhances cause and effect learning, and establishes a structure for teacher authority. As long as consequences are considered fair by the group, enforcement is expected and psychologically appreciated. A teacher should remember that unacceptable behavior can spread rapidly and that the class (as well as the community) holds the teacher accountable for preserving basic behavior values, even if that requires punishment.

In enforcing consequences, the teacher should strive to be (a) immediate, (b) non-punitive, and (c) consistent. Immediacy means trying to implement the consequence as close in time to the misbehavior as possible. In some situations (e.g., field trips, auditorium programs) it will be necessary to delay enforcement until a more opportune moment. Non-punitiveness is often difficult to accomplish, especially when the student's behavior has been flagrantly disrespectful. It is human to feel counter-hostility towards our pupils. At such times, the teacher would do best to count to ten and then enforce a consequence in a tough, but not vindictive, manner.

The challenge of multiple misbehaviors, varying in intensity and frequency for different students, requires that all teachers have a range of negative consequences available at any time. Consequences will vary from those which can be administered in-class to those which involve others in-school and out-of-school. *Some common consequences which are available to the teacher and have been found to be effective are:* (a) use of soft reprimands, (b) in-class time-outs (e.g., sending to corner of room or outside door of room), (c) changing a preferred seat location, (d) taking away privileges (e.g., free time, class helper status), (e) taking away points or tokens (which may have been earned towards a grade or reward), (f) during-school detentions (e.g., during activity or elective periods), (g) before- or after-school detentions, (h) restitution activities (e.g., repaint the room, repair a chair, replace a pen), (i) parent telephone calls or conferences, (j) time-outs or conferences with principal, (k) recording a poor score on behavior for grading class participation and/or work habits (Kerr & Nelson, 1983). In addition, the teacher can refer the child for further evaluation and recommend another replacement.

Major infractions of school rules will usually result in an out-of-class consequence. For example, drug abuse may involve police notification and short suspension; verbal attack on staff may require a parent conference and a one-day suspension. Penalties for infractions of this magnitude are typically set forth in the Board of Education discipline policy. The classroom teacher is responsible for accurately reporting such incidents so that out-of-class consequences may be properly enforced.

It is important to recognize that while many negative consequences may be enforced by the classroom teacher, their use should be carefully reviewed in the light of student progress. The teacher should keep in mind the strengths of the student and look for opportunities to praise or reward desirable behavior. *Where enforcement of consequences does not appear to be improving matters, the teacher should ask for help.* Resource or special class teachers, counselors, school administrators, and other teachers can be emotionally supportive while helping to develop new approaches. These people may also assist in the implementation of alternative management strategies.

8. *The Skill of Life Space Crisis Intervention.* On occasion, a student will lose complete control and become a threat to himself or others. Intervention must be rapid to protect the student and the group from harm and to avert major escalation of the crisis. At these times, the goal is to reestablish order and control as soon as possible without hurting the student in crisis. Incidents such as a student threatening to commit suicide or attack another student with scissors, or smashing furniture and other property require quick backup for the classroom teacher. Specific staff roles and procedures should be defined in advance to provide for such crisis intervention, and the teacher should send an urgent message that assistance is needed. At such times the message can be delivered to the main office by another student. Wood and Long have developed a training program for teachers in this area.

In handling a crisis situation, the teacher must make every effort to appear outwardly calm. Signs of panic or hysteria will create more instability in an already tenuous situation.

An empathic appeal to the student's core values and inner strengths is most likely to prevent further breakdown of controls: "*I* know you're very upset but you're too important to hurt yourself"; "Tom, stop! Hold that knife. You're furious but you can't stab him." The teacher can also use her relationship to halt dangerous or destructive actions, for example, "Betty, I don't want you to rip up your drawings."

The teacher may be able to position herself so as to prevent the dangerous action. Physical restraint may be possible and should be carried out if it can successfully prevent attack or destructiveness. However, physical holding should only be attempted when a "clear and present danger" to person or property exists.

STRATEGIES FOR INCREASING DESIRABLE BEHAVIOR

1. *The Skill of Stating Positive Expectations.* Expectations for positive behavior (standards) should be specified for group and individual behavior, in the same way that limits are stated. Teachers need to highlight their list of Incompatible Desirable Behavior. See Figure 5.1.

2. *The Skill of Modeling.* This is a relatively easy and efficient way to promote positive behavior (O'Leary & O'Leary, 1977). To model desired behavior, the teacher should consistently display the behavior others are expected to exhibit, both in words and actions. Some examples are acting in a friendly and respectful manner to demonstrate a stated norm of "getting along with each other," allowing students to challenge [their] own ideas when advocating freedom of thought, listening attentively to students to exemplify respect.

As simple as modeling appears to be, it is predicated on a congruence of teacher word and deed. One teacher was very surprised when a student refused to participate because "you don't want to hear what I have to say." The student was reading the teacher's nonverbal behavior (frowns, side glances, etc.) even though the class was being encouraged to speak freely.

Peer modeling can also be used. Thus, a teacher may have one student perform a certain behavior and then ask another student to try it. Or, the teacher may draw attention to the positive behaviors of some members of the class so that they may serve as positive models for others. For example, "*I'm* really pleased that some people are talking quietly, and not shouting." Another option is to group students so that a person needing improvement is placed with others who typically display the desirable behavior.

3. *The Skill of Structuring the Situation.* In contrast to restructuring to reduce negative behavior (see strategy #4 under "reducing undesirable behavior"), structuring the situation entails arranging classroom conditions to produce desired behaviors. As with restructuring, arrangements are possible in such areas as seating, grouping, degree of teacher assistance, nature of the task, format and complexity of the material, physical movement, degree of involvement, amount of recognition, extent of decision making, and personal feelings.

Some examples of structuring the situation are placing chairs in a circle for group discussion, setting up private cubicles to support concentrated seat-work, planning brief periods of work for students with a short attention span, pairing students with liked classmates to promote positive relationships, providing locker or cubby space to assure respect for property rights, and permitting verbal expression of emotions to foster self-awareness and responsibility.

4. *The Skill of Positive Reinforcements.* No strategy is more powerful or necessary than positive reinforcement for desirable behavior. Teachers and parents tend to take a child's achievements for granted and to focus on faults or needs for improvement (Swift & Spivack, 1975). Amount of wealth, status, or education seems to matter little when one considers the lack of appreciation shown children for their sincere efforts. In fact, in upward striving communities it is quite probable that offspring are less likely to satisfy parental expectations for success. By reinforcing desirable behavior, the classroom becomes a more positive environment—one in which accomplishments (behavioral and academic) are appropriately recognized and personal esteem is strengthened.

Positive reinforcement is defined as "a stimulus that, when presented as a consequence of a response, results in an increase or maintenance of that response" (Madsen & Madsen, 1974, p. 208). In other words, a stimulus becomes a positive reinforcer when it is valued or appreciated by the learner. However, the teacher cannot really know in advance what will be valued by a particular student.

As the student's interests, likes, and desires become known to the teacher, more positive reinforcers emerge. Whenever feasible, the teacher should try to find out from the student what would be rewarding or offer a choice of rewards, that is, positive reinforcers.

Several types of positive reinforcers are readily available to the classroom teacher, including activities and privileges, materials, food, parent recognition, leadership or prestige roles, physical proximity, awards, verbal approval, and nonverbal approval. Illustrations of these types of rewards for secondary students are shown in Table 5.2.

TABLE 5.2   ILLUSTRATIVE REINFORCERS FOR SECONDARY STUDENTS

Activities and Privileges
Operate equipment
Listen to records
Free time
Do a special project
Go on field trip
Help custodian, secretary,
    principal, teacher, etc.
Use typewriter
Play musical instrument
Choose own seat
Have work displayed
Exemption from a test
Exemption from an assignment
Doing errands

Leadership/Prestige Roles
Tutoring others
Peer counseling
Representing group in some activity
Help teach class
Get materials ready for class
Lead opening exercises
Lead discussion groups or panel
Passing out exams
Helping grade papers
Present own hobby or collection

Awards
"Most improved"
"Teacher for a day"
Certificate of merit
Letter of commendation
"Super student"

Parent Recognition
Telephone call to parent
Take home letter
"We're proud" note,
    signed by parents

Nonverbal Approval
Smiling
Nodding
Laughing
Signaling O.K.
Saluting
Waving
Cheering
Winking

Materials
Books and magazines
Book markers
Bookcovers
Pencils with own name
Plants
Buttons
Address books
Stationery
Playing cards
Money
Records
Posters
Craft kits
Stamps

Food/Drinks
Soda
Potato chips
Ice cream
French fries
Peanuts/Raisins
Fruit juice
Celery with spread
Flavored ice cubes
Sucking candy
Gum
Jaw breakers

Physical Proximity
Patting a shoulder
Sitting on desk near student
Walking alongside student
Special handshakes
Standing alongside student

Verbal and Written Approval
Good job
Super!
Outstanding
First rate
I'm proud of you
You did it
Real progress
Written compliments
Written comments on assigned work
Feedback stamps or stickers

5. *The Skill of Regulated Permission.* This strategy capitalizes on the momentum underlying a student's negative, unacceptable behaviors and calls for ingenuity on the part of the teacher. The goal is to channel basic impulses which are expressed disruptively into socially acceptable expressions. To implement this strategy, the teacher must first identify the likely impulse or motive behind the student's undesirable behavior. The next step is to find acceptable classroom alternatives for expression of this drive.

In many cases, the student can verify the motive behind his [/her] disruptive behavior, as might occur in a conference during which the teacher seeks to understand the student's feelings and perceptions of the class. For example, when asked how come she always called out answers to questions, Maria replied, "cause those dummies think I don't know anything." Hearing this, the teacher was able to think of ways for Maria to display her intelligence which did not interfere with her classmates' desire to answer questions. This process of regulating permission is shown in Figure 5.4.

Other examples of regulated permission are: allowing an angry student to flatten clay, punch a boxing bag, or bang a blackboard eraser; enabling a dependent child to serve as a teacher aide; organizing a controlled debate when students want to assert their power toward one another, permitting structured small group discussion to meet needs for social contact during class.

6. *The Skill of Contracting.* Contracting is a process for establishing a written and/or verbal agreement with one or more students to provide a particular service, reward, or outcome in return for a particular behavior or performance. Contracting often involves reinforcing desirable behavior, but adds a component of mutual goal-setting and negotiation. For example, Mrs. Smith and Robert agree that he can show his stamp collection if he first completes a class assignment.

FIGURE 5.4   Changing Undesirable to Desirable Behavior

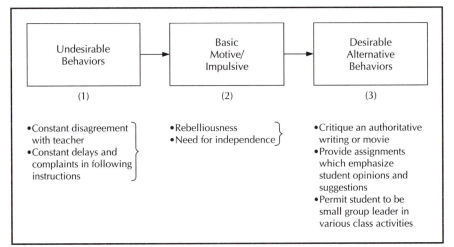

The process for teacher–student contracting has four main steps (Fagen & Hill, 1977):

> **Step 1—*Planning for the student conference.*** Here the teacher selects a priority concern and considers a respectful way of communicating this concern to the student.

> **Step 2—*Exploration with student.*** During this step, the teacher shares her [/his] concern and listens to the student's reactions and views. Areas of agreement are identified for priority desirable behaviors, incentives for student effort, and responsibilities of student and teacher.

> **Step 3—*Establish contract.*** At this point, the actual terms of the contract are specified, including: (a) desirable behaviors, (b) people involved and time period, (c) criteria for attainment, (d) responsibilities of people involved, and (e) consequences of behavior. Agreement is marked by a handshake or signatures.

> **Step 4—*Review and revise contract.*** This is a follow-up phase, at which time progress is checked and necessary adjustments are made.

A sample contract is shown in Figure 5.5. Some important guidelines for contracting are as follows:

(a) When other people have to be involved, let the student know that agreements are tentative and subject to others' approval.

(b) Use language the student can understand; use the student's words as much as possible.

(c) Written contracts offer the advantage of greater commitment; verbal contracts are quicker and more comfortable.

(d) Strive for as few objectives as possible; make them important and short-term.

(e) Build in some items which have high probability for success.

(f) State objectives in positive terms, wherever possible. Negative phrases may be necessary, however, to assure specific understanding. For example, "*Carl* will not fight when mad but will count to ten, walk away, or ask teacher permission to use the typewriter" (which helps him cool off).

7. *Token Systems.* Tokens are tangible objects or symbols which can be exchanged for a privilege, activity, or reward. They may include such things as points, chips, special cards, or homemade bills. Token systems usually include three features: (a) instructions to the class regarding behaviors that will be reinforced, (b) how tokens are earned as a result of

FIGURE 5.5   Sample Contract

CONTRACT FOR: _____
(name of student)

I have decided to work on <u>"Staying on task."</u>
(desirable behavior)

This will not always be easy, because I would often rather <u>talk or play with</u>

<u>friends than concentrate on my school work.</u> However, I also know that I will
(undesirable behavior to be replaced by desirable behavior)

earn the respect of teachers, parents, and friends by being a good student. There

will always be a place for fun, too, at the right times.

Each day the teachers will rate me according to the following scale: (indicate

evaluation criteria)

    5—stayed on task all the time
    4—stayed on task most of the time
    3—stayed on task some of the time
    2—seldom on task
    1—off task all the time

When I achieve <u>5 contracts that average 4.0 or higher,</u> I will then earn
(indicate criteria for specific reinforcement)

<u>a free interest period on Friday.</u> This contract will be in effect for the period
(indicate specific reinfocement earned)

of _____ .

Signed: _____   Signed: _____
          (student signature)   (teacher signature)

Date: _____   Date: _____

---

producing desired behaviors, and (c) rules for exchanging the tokens for the back-up reinforcers (Gallagher, 1979).

Token systems offer the following advantages:

(a) whereas all students cannot receive the teacher's attention, they can all be involved with tokens,

(b) positive reinforcement can be given quickly and consistently (through supplying tokens),

(c) students can benefit from their responsibilities in record keeping,

(d) there is flexibility to vary items and costs for token exchange so that students begin to save for more expensive rewards. This results in longer periods of desirable behavior and greater ability to delay gratification (Kerr & Nelson, 1983).

REFERENCES

Caldwell, J. (1979). Basic techniques for early classroom intervention. *The Pointer, 24,* 53–60.

Canter, L., with Canter, M. (1976). *Assertive discipline: A take-charge approach for today's educator.* Santa Monica, CA: Canter & Associates.

Fagen, S., & Hill, J. (1977). *Behavior management: A competency-based manual for in-service training.* Washington, DC: Psycho-educational Resources.

Gallagher, P. (1979). *Teaching students with behavior disorders: Techniques for classroom instruction.* Denver, CO: Love.

Glasser, W. (1977, November–December). 10 steps to good discipline. *Today's Education, 61*–63.

Kerr, M., & Nelson, C. M. (1983). *Strategies for managing behavior problems in the classroom.* Columbus, OH: Merrill.

Kounin, J. (1970). *Discipline and group management in classrooms.* New York: Holt, Rinehart and Winston.

Long, N., & Newman, R. (1980). Managing surface behavior of children in school. In N. J. Long, W. C. Morse, & R. G. Newman (Eds.), *Conflict in the classroom: The education of children with problems* (4th ed.), 233–241. Belmont, CA: Wadsworth.

Madsen, C. H., & Madsen, C. (1974). *Teaching/discipline: A positive approach for educational development.* Boston: Allyn & Bacon.

O'Leary, K., & O'Leary, S. (1977). *Classroom management: The successful use of behavior modification.* New York: Pergamon.

Sabatino, D., Sabatino, A., & Mann, L. (1983). *Discipline and behavioral management.* Rockville, MD: Aspen.

Swift, M., & Spivack, G. (1975). *Alternative teaching strategies: Helping behaviorally troubled children achieve.* Champaign, IL: Research Press.

Wimberly, L. (1985). Guidelines for crisis management. *The Pointer, 29*(2), 22–26.

Wood, P., & Long, N. (1991). *Life space crisis intervention.* Austin, TX: PRO-ED.

· ·

In addition to the skills Fagen has described, teachers must master several other specific skills: descriptive praise, decoding student behavior, therapeutic humor, and physical restraint.

THE SKILL OF DESCRIPTIVE PRAISE · · · · · · · · · · · · · · · · · · ·

Behaviorists have taught us that all behavior is learned and can be strengthened or weakened by the consequences that follow it. Positive reinforcers accelerate the behavior, and negative reinforcers decelerate the behavior.

The use of teacher praise is heralded as a positive way of building up or promoting a student's self-esteem and confidence. Teachers frequently use words such as *terrific, wonderful, excellent, outstanding, fantastic, perfect, very good, kind,* and *considerate* as positive reinforcers. When they use these terms to praise a student's conduct, they believe they are behaving as positive and effective teachers. *Unfortunately, this is not true when working with high-risk and troubled students.* Just as too much sunlight makes a desert and not an oasis, too much praise will "hothouse" troubled students' personalities and can have effects opposite to those intended. If a teacher tells one of these students he or she is "terrific," "wonderful," and "the best," the student may feel that the comments are not an accurate assessment. Instead of making the student feel better, they introduce additional pressure and cause feelings of guilt.

The student might conclude:

1. My teacher is a poor judge of character and is lying to me.
2. I had a lucky day. I happened to hit the bulls-eye today, but it will never happen again.
3. I am unworthy of such glorious praises and I find it troublesome to own them.
4. I will have to show you I don't deserve such praise.

Descriptive praise is the skill of describing a student's motivation and accomplishments and not his or her personality. It addresses what is left over after the teacher pinpoints what the students were heard and seen to do today. Descriptive praise deals with only the students' efforts and behaviors, without interpreting them as "good," "better," or "best." The effect of the praise is the silent or verbal positive message a student self-delivers after evaluating the teacher's comments. If the student declares, "I am good," "terrific," "on task," or "considerate," then the teacher can reinforce it by saying, "I agree with you" or "I was just about to say the same thing."

Here are some actual classroom examples of effective (descriptive) and ineffective (personality) praise:

1. *Descriptive praise:* This room was a mess a few minutes ago and now I look around and see everything is picked up and put away. What am I going to say to this class? (Answer: We are good at cleaning up our classroom.)

   Personality praise: You are priceless for cleaning up my classroom. What could I do without you! (Answer: I don't believe you. I am not priceless, I'm worth about a nickel; or, I could get along without you.)

2. *Descriptive praise:* Jerome, I noticed you worked at your desk for 15 minutes, and when you needed some help you raised your hand and waited until I could assist you. (Answer: I showed a lot of self-control today and I'm learning to follow the rules—good for me!)

   Personality praise: Jerome, you were wonderful to wait for me to come help you. You showed amazing self-control. This was the best day you had in weeks! (Good thing you got here when you did. I was about to yell at you for taking so long, and tomorrow I may end my one-day streak of goodness.)

3. *Descriptive praise:* I can tell Susan is thinking by what she just said. (Answer: I am a competent thinker—I'm smart.)

   Personality praise: I can tell Susan is a terrific, smart student by what she just said. (Answer: Yes, but I'm not as smart as Taylor.)

4. *Descriptive praise:* Stan, I noticed how you picked up all your resource materials, walked quietly to your desk, and started to work immediately. (Answer: I am a capable student—cheers for me.)

   Personality praise: Stan, you were super today. You did everything perfectly. You are one of my best students. (Answer: I can't always be super or perfect. It is too much strain on me. I hope I won't mess up tomorrow.)

Remember, when a teacher tells students they are wonderful or terrific, it is not helpful praise. When students tell themselves they are resourceful, talented, and competent, the positive comments promote self-esteem and investment in learning.

THE SKILL OF DECODING STUDENT BEHAVIOR . . . .

Frequently, students in stress do not talk about their feelings; they act them out. They yell, run, cry, and withdraw, or they deny their feelings by saying, "I don't care" or "It doesn't matter to me." The skill is to learn how to decode their words, actions, and body language so they are connected to the students' feelings and initial source of stress. This skill is difficult to learn because it involves reading students' nonverbal behavior and reflecting what they are communicating in a clear and sympathetic way: "When I see you close your eyes and put your head on your desk, and I listen to you say, 'Nothing's wrong,' I get a different feeling. (wait for reaction) Perhaps you wish your problems would disappear, but you seem upset. (wait for reaction) A part of you knows that problems don't go away until you solve them. This is a difficult time for you. (wait for reaction) It is difficult and upsetting to talk about it, but perhaps in a few minutes you can begin to tell me what is troubling you."

Until students can accept their feelings and understand how feelings drive their behavior, they will never be able to accept the full responsibility for their behavior. Decoding skills (a) let students know their teachers are sensitive to their internal struggles, and (b) offer them an invitation to talk about what is troubling them. This is an act of compassion and not a form of confrontation.

THE SKILL OF THERAPEUTIC HUMOR . . . .

There is nothing new about this skill. Everyone is aware of how a humorous comment is able to penetrate a tense and anxiety-producing situation.

It clears the air and makes everyone feel more comfortable. The example below shows how one teacher used this technique to her advantage.

> I walked into my room after lunch period to find several pictures on the chalk board with "teacher" written under each one. I went to the board and picked up a piece of chalk, first looking at the pictures and then at the class. You could have heard a pin drop! Then I walked over to one of the pictures and said that this one looked the most like me but needed some more hair, which I added. Then I went to the next one and said that they had forgotten my glasses so I added them, on the next one I suggested adding a big nose, and on the last one a longer neck. By this time the class started to smile and then laugh. After a few seconds I said it was time to return to our lesson.

This example illustrates the phenomenon of group testing. The pictures were put on the board to test the vulnerability of the teacher. Some teachers could have reacted with sarcasm. They might have said that this was infantile behavior and not becoming of a fifth-grade class. Other teachers might have given the class extra work or administered a group punishment, such as denial of recess or free time. However, this teacher demonstrated she was secure, and a drawing could not cause her to regress or to become counteraggressive. She turned a challenging moment into a therapeutic event and validated that she could be counted on during a stressful incident. She also was cognizant that therapeutic humor is a two-way experience in which both parties enjoy the situation. One-way humor is sarcasm, a put down, a way of humiliating others, a form of social interaction in which one person has pleasure while the other person experiences psychological pain.

A common example of one-way humor is called "Playing the Dozens" (Foster). This verbal game of peer insults probably has caused more fights in city schools than any other activity. The dozens has been called various names—*crackin'*, *ribbin'*, *dis-ing*, *rankin'*, *mamma talk*, and *snaps*. The basic purpose is to deliver verbal abuse to a point where a peer gets out of control in front of the group. This form of verbal aggression depreciates the peer's family, mother, sister, or girlfriend. Its taunting has a clever twist and usually succeeds in winning group laughter and approval. Don't confuse it with two-way humor. Here are two examples: "Your mamma is so dumb she failed her urine test," and "Your sister works at a gas station because she likes to get pumped." This is a form of cruelty, not therapeutic humor.

THE SKILL OF PHYSICAL RESTRAINT . . . .

Once in a while, students will lose complete control and threaten to injure themselves or others. In such emergencies, these students need to be restrained physically by being held firmly but not roughly. Once again, there is not an indication of punishment, but only a sincere concern to protect the students from hurting anyone. If a feeling of protection is to be communicated, such techniques as shaking, hitting, or threatening only make it harder for the students to believe the teacher really wants to offer protection. Some teachers believe a student should be punished for such inappropriate behavior. However, if teachers with this opinion were given a chance to observe a student who has lost control over his or her impulses, they would soon realize how frightening and fearful this experience is for the student. These teachers would see the suffering and anguish that are part of this experience. Loss of control is no game; it strikes at basic feelings of helplessness.

In the preferred physical hold, the teacher crosses the student's arms, draws them around the student's ribs, and stands behind the student while holding on to the student's wrists. Occasionally, it is necessary to hold a child face-down on the floor in this position. If held correctly in this position, there is no danger that the student can inflict self-injury, although the student might scream that the teacher is causing hurt or considerable physical pain. A student who needs this physical restraint usually goes through four different phases.

First, the student fights being held and controlled, becomes enraged, and says and does things that are fed by feelings of frustration, hate, and desperation. The student may swear, bite, and carry on in other primitive ways. Teachers who are not used to dealing with intense feelings may find it difficult to absorb this degree of aggression without becoming frightened and/or counteraggressive. If this is the case, additional adult help should be summoned. The teacher has the responsibility to provide the nonaggressive handling that a student needs during a crisis. A professional nurse doesn't take away a patient's antibiotics because the patient happens to vomit on her. Likewise, a teacher does not reject a student when adult control is most needed. The teacher's self-control system must take over until the student's controls are operating again.

During the first stage, it is sometimes helpful to say softly, "You are all right," "In a little while, you will get over your angry feelings," and "I am going to take care of you and not let anyone or anything hurt you." Once the student realizes he or she cannot break away and the protection is a shield against his or her own impulses, the rage usually turns to tears. This begins phase two.

The student's defenses are down in the second phase. The coat of toughness has vanished, and inadequacy and immaturity become evident. After a period of time, the student usually becomes silent or asks to be let go. This begins phase three.

If the teacher thinks the student has regained control and is not going to start an aggressive cycle all over again, the teacher should release the physical hold on the student. One point must be emphasized: the *teacher, not the child*, makes this decision. One indication that the student is regaining control over his or her impulses is that expressions of language become more coherent and logical. If the student gives correct answers to "Who are you?" "Where are you?" and "What has happened?" the student is usually on the way up the ladder of reason. As self-control returns, the student has to save face, usually by pulling away from the teacher or making a sly remark. This ends phase three and usually is a good sign the student is ready to assume control.

In phase four, the teacher may ask the student to go to the bathroom and clean up. Once the student is comfortable, the first question a teacher needs to ask is: "Why did I have to hold you?" or "What would have happened if I had not held you?" The purpose is to clarify any distortions regarding why the student was held. The purpose of this follow-up conversation is to help the student realize the teacher gave protection against even greater problems by using physical restraint.

Occasionally, a student may have to be held in the classroom, but this should be avoided whenever possible. If it cannot be avoided, one of the other students should get the principal immediately so that the student can be removed from the class. Later, the teacher *must* explain to the class and to the student exactly what has happened in order to counter any misinterpretations of the teacher's behavior.

An important point to remember is that whenever a teacher holds a student and is able to control the student's personal feelings of anxiety and aggression, the chances are that the relationship with this student will improve significantly. The message the student receives is: "I care enough about you to protect you from your own frightening impulses. The fact you had to be held is no point against you. I'm not angry, but pleased that you are feeling more comfortable and are in control of your emotions." This kind of support can only foster the student's feeling that the teacher is a person who can be trusted.

In the following article, Fagen demonstrates the second set of short-term teacher intervention skills. Included is how to teach students the social skills necessary to function successfully in a stressful school situation. Fagen elaborates on how teachers can instruct troubled students in managing personal frustration by modifying their goals, trying new alternatives, and identifying positives in themselves. This article is an excellent example of how a general psychological concept—in this case, managing frustration—can be broken down into understandable and instructional skills.

ARTICLE 5.4

Teaching Frustration Management

Stanley A. Fagen

Teaching frustration management can be characterized as having three major facets: (1) attitudes and perceptions associated with the goal-thwarting or

Excerpted from a paper published in *Proceedings of a Conference on Preparing Teachers to Foster Personal Growth in Emotionally Disturbed Students*. Advanced Institute for Trainers of Teachers for Seriously Emotionally Disturbed Children: University of Minnesota, May 29–31, 1977. Used here by permission of the author.

FIGURE 5.6   Three Facets of Adaptive Frustration Management

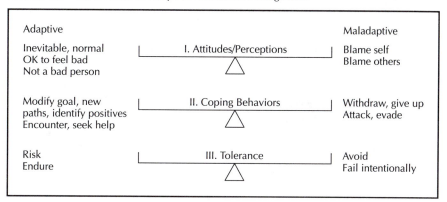

frustrating experience, (2) coping behaviors available to the student, following the frustration, and, (3) tolerance for experiencing frustration. Figure 5.6 depicts the three facets of adaptive frustration management.

ATTITUDES AND PERCEPTIONS

A primary frustration reaction for many young children is either rage or helplessness. As children grow older, they learn to attach words and ideas to their experience with the result that others or self are seen as at fault. The perception of blaming others is often a correlate of aggressive, acting out behavior, whereas blaming self is associated with inhibited, withdrawn behavior.

Blaming self or blaming others are not necessarily mutually exclusive. To the contrary, the two perceptions or attitudes are frequently related to one another, as when hating others is used as a defense against the pain of hating one-self. Such a relationship is depicted by Sanford and Comstock:

> The disposition of destructiveness is not inborn but is generated out of experience and learning in a social environment . . . Fundamentally, its source is inner conflict, which leads to a need to get rid of what is all too human in oneself. If this badness is felt to be located in the self, a person may become self-destructive; but, often, he may ascribe the badness to other people . . . (p. 331).

Unfortunately, much of our social learning and modeling emphasizes placing blame for not achieving goals. Parents and teachers constantly criticize children for "not trying," "being careless," "being stupid," etc. Or, parents blame teachers, teacher blame parents, and so on. Children are taught that someone *must* be at fault when frustration occurs, and, of course, they become experts in blaming by the time they reach 2nd and 3rd grade.

It is possible, however, to reeducate youngsters so as to promote new perceptions of frustration. This can be accomplished by teaching students to acknowledge their upset feelings without reinforcing faultfinding. Helpful comments might be: "I know you're really upset about it," "Things like this happen a lot. I got angry when all those PA announcements came on when I was talking," "Look, you tried darn hard and have a right to feel bad. But you're all right." Positive teaching points are those which (a) share or empathize with the student's feelings, (b) confirm the normalcy of feeling bad, (c) support the worth of the student despite the failure to reach the goal, and (d) foster appreciation for the necessity or inevitability of frustration. As students begin to regard thwarting of their wants as acceptable, rather than as a time for depreciating someone, they are able to assimilate the experience into their lives and move on to further efforts.

COPING BEHAVIORS

Students with emotional problems are usually woefully lacking in skills for coping with stress. Perceiving themselves as incapable, defective, or victimized, there is little left to do but escape from the situation as quickly as possible. Escape routes may take the attacking-evading form of loud outbursts, throwing things, cursing, or running away. Or, they may follow withdrawal–defeat behaviors, such as giving up, sobbing, staring into space, shrinking into a corner, or refusing to talk. Each frustration can precipitate a crisis in self-esteem, trust, and peer relations, since emotional controls are likely to be marginal and perceptual distortions are prevalent.

To teach students coping behaviors, the teacher must first have a firm hold on coping resources within self. The abruptness and explosiveness of the students present a tremendous challenge to the teacher's own capacity to maintain self-control. It is natural for the teacher to experience intense counter-aggression feeling. In other words, positive coping behaviors must first be internalized on the part of the teacher if the student is to be successfully taught new alternatives.

Given that frustration happens, the question becomes how to cope with it effectively. Effective coping is defined as "behavior which promotes positive change in self or environment, i.e., change which maintains or heightens self-esteem, prospects for successful striving towards constructive goals, or understanding and helpfulness between self and others" (Fagen and Hill).

Two major strategies are available for teaching coping with frustration experiences: (1) self or internal change, and (2) environmental or external change. That is, the frustration may be managed by modifying one's own personal behavior or by seeking assistance from another person.

1. Self (Internal) Change

Three basic classes of behavior are available within the self (internal) change strategy, namely: (a) modifying goals, (b) trying new paths to the goal, and, (c) identifying positives in self.

A. Modifying Goals   It is not possible or desirable to set goals in advance for which success is assured. Sensitive teachers strive to prescribe learner goals or objectives which represent a "reasonable challenge," necessitating a "stretch" upwards for the student. Often, the student attains the desired objective and consequently gains in personal satisfaction and esteem. Just as often, however, the student falls short of the goal as a result of ability limitations or uncontrollable natural obstacles (e.g., space, time, physical, or communication). The exact same factors pertain to the teacher's own goal setting for self. In fact, when one considers the teacher–student relationship, it becomes evident that, for the conscientious teacher, any student frustration is in some way a teacher frustration, as well.

In falling short of an initial goal, a person may choose to modify this goal in one of several ways: (a) *select a partial* or *sub-goal* and recognize that progress has occurred. For example, a student is striving to obtain an A by answering 10 problems correctly. After a good try, he correctly answers only 7 and earns a C. The student can revise his goal of 10, bring it to 7, and reflect on the fact that 7 correct was better than he had done previously; (b) *clarify and prioritize the goal importance.* The student could decide that getting an A was not as important as improving in a different subject. Conversely, the student might be helped to recognize that achieving an A means a great deal to him and, therefore, that additional time and effort may be necessary to accomplish the goal. Developing a plan for attaining this end would follow as a next step toward positively coping with the initial frustration; (c) *postpone or cancel the goal.* It is important to understand that some goals may need to be postponed or canceled. Teachers, like students, usually are simultaneously engaged in multiple goal seeking. At any given point in time a teacher may be struggling to accomplish a host of tasks, such as: formulating a lesson plan, arranging the room, doing some reading on a particular subject, consulting with a colleague, calling a parent, completing some forms, preparing for a PTA meeting, grading class papers, etc. To the extent that all goals are given equal importance within a narrow time span, futility and frustration must result.

B. Trying New Paths to the Goal   Another technique for coping with frustration is to maintain the desired goal but alter the method used to reach the goal, i.e., find a new way around the obstacle. This coping mechanism requires an openness to alternative and unfamiliar actions. Emotionally handicapped youth are known, however, for their lack of behavioral freedom and for their tendency to employ a restricted and inflexible range of reactions, particularly in times of stress. Introduction of possibilities for new paths to a goal must occur in the context of an empathetic and trusting relationship. In addition, students must know the potential risks or gains from using a new path.

For example, John constantly sought to achieve a prominent place in his peer group. To accomplish this he yelled out, came late, interrupted others, and boasted about his deeds. Through conferencing with John, it became evident that new paths were available. John agreed to try gaining group importance by praising others and offering help to the group if it were requested. He was surprised to learn that other students came to notice and accept him far more when he was supportive than aggressive.

New paths can be explored and tried through various supportive strategies such as life space interviewing, e.g., "new tool-salesmanship" (Redl), training in behavior principles to increase acceptance by others (Graubard and Rosenberg), and peer group counseling (Berg and Johnson). Regardless of the strategy used for identifying a new path, it is important to create a relaxed optimism about trying out something new. Follow-up support will be necessary to provide for further adjustments or modifications to the new paths.

Identifying Positives in Self.   Reactions to the experience of frustration frequently include temporary declines in self-evaluation (cf. Diggory). For example, the student who wants to read aloud but cannot has an immediate feeling of stupidity; the teenager who asks a girl for a date and is turned down has an immediate feeling of unattractiveness; the teacher who wants to command class respect but finds noise, disorder, and back talk has an immediate feeling of impotence.

Frustration experiences signal times when one's own real self is apt to be lower than one's ideal self, and thus represent low points in self-esteem. The more important the goal that is thwarted, the greater the blow to self-esteem. Adaptive coping requires that these blows to self-esteem be absorbed and shaken off so that renewal of esteem can take place. On the other hand, maladaptive coping means a prolonged focussing on preoccupation with one's deficiencies, making it extremely difficult to strive or risk again.

Identifying positives in self may enable one to break free of negative self-messages and get back in touch with the "OK" core of one's existence. To reexperience own positives, exercises or activities may be employed which: (a) focus on existing strengths and sources of pride, (b) demonstrate that failure in one goal does not mean total inadequacy, (c) strengthen appreciation for own best efforts, and (d) reaffirm interests and desires for enjoyment in other life areas.

Students may be helped to see positives despite the wound to self-esteem through such means as how others view their strengths ("strength bombardment"), having the opportunity to use a strong skill, hearing appreciation for the real effort, and encouragement to enjoy a satisfying personal interest or pursuit.

2. Environmental (External) Change

In addition to the possibilities for coping by self-change, frustration can be effectively resolved by seeking to effect change or help from the environment. Two basic classes of coping behavior may promote environmental change: (1) encountering the frustration source, and (2) seeking help and assistance.

Encountering the Source. The term "encountering" is intended to mean the direct sharing of one's own thoughts and feelings with the person viewed as responsible for presenting an obstacle to reaching one's goal. Encountering requires that the student experiencing frustration must first take ownership of his or her own feelings by accepting and identifying these feelings and then must encode these feelings by sending a clear "I message" to the intended receiver (Gordon). In its purest form the encountering "I message" describes both a strong existing feeling and the reason for this feeling. For example, "I am mad because you did not call on me." "I feel like quitting because the work is too hard for me." These "I messages" are in marked contrast to communications which blame others for the discomfort one feels. Examples of "you-blaming" messages are: "You are being unfair," "You're always telling us what to do," "I'm disgusted because you're so dumb."

Encountering the source of frustration is the first step in creating a meaningful and constructive dialogue, which hopefully can lead to a more mutual fulfillment of wants and goals. Preparing a student or staff member to effectively execute the first step, however, does not assure a constructive resolution of differences. All too often we have seen how receivers are unable to accept the genuineness or forcefulness of the "I message" and become threatened. Many times, staff have laced the communication skills to constructively respond to students. In effect, encountering the source of frustration may result in additional frustration which then needs to be handled through seeking help, or self-change strategies.

Troubled students have a great deal of difficulty encountering others constructively. Some may attack with very clear expressions of emotion, verbal or otherwise. Others may be totally unable to acknowledge their own feelings. Almost all such students will be reluctant to risk learning to encounter other due to their anxiety about possible harm from emotional release (whether that potential harm is attributed to own explosiveness or to another's reaction).

A gradual, continuous process of emotional reeducation is essential for these students. Teachers with excellent communications and counseling skills can, through patient and trusting relationships, promote the development of encountering skills for students with emotional problems (Fagen and Guedalia). We have found that the model of sending effective "I messages" can, to a large extent, be regarded as a criterion for emotional growth and development. That is, as students learn to encounter others constructively they are also overcoming their social problems.

Seeking Help and Assistance. As obvious as this method of coping appears to be, far too many youngsters avoid it's use. Invariably, in every classroom there are a few students who create disruptions as a behavior equivalent for getting help. For example, the student who bothers others when he cannot understand the task directions; the student who destroys or damages objects when the fine motor demands exceed his tolerance level; the student who daydreams when she's not sure what to do next. The sensitive teacher can spot these students. Through caring inquiry into their concerns or feelings, the teacher can usually identify the point at which a student needs help. As long as the teacher does not make the child feel infantile or inadequate for needing help, it is usually a simple matter to arrange a means for the child to signal the need for help or assistance. Signals have included such things as: raising one's hand, clasping hands on desk and looking up, tugging at an ear, sitting in a rocking chair, and going to a "help station."

Class norms will greatly influence the ease with which students seek help. One very successful program has a motto: "It is dumb not to get help."

TOLERANCE

Once students believe they have resources for accepting and coping with frustration, it is possible to build their tolerance level for frustration by promoting awareness of the multiple, natural obstacles which occur during their daily experiences. Everyday obstacles may be *physical* (e.g., a wall, a person in the way, a desk), *temporal* (e.g., lack of time to finish a task), *interpersonal or communications* (e.g., speaking too low, not listening), or *cognitive* (e.g., complex instructions, high level vocabulary words).

Teachers need not feel guilty about the presence of such obstacles in the classroom since it is impossible to create an obstacle-free environment. However, the teacher should be alert for these obstacles and be ready to positively reinforce students for their willingness to endure or persist in the face of these obstacles. The opportunities for such reinforcement are unlimited. A few illustrations are: "Good Sally. You were able to wait until they got out of your way"; "I'm pleased that you did not get upset when Roger bumped into your desk"; "Thank you for repeating your question. I was distracted"; "Children, you were so good about stopping your drawings this morning that we will have a special game this afternoon."

Mastery activities can be conducted in the classroom to demonstrate the students' ability to tolerate frustrating situations. Thus, activities can be arranged which expose the students to a variety of obstacles. The shared aspect of facing common frustrations, as well as a game-like format, promote an atmosphere in which children can feel challenged without being threatened.

SUMMARY

This paper is based on the fact that stress is a fundamental aspect of living. As Selye has found, "wear and tear" of the body is constantly occurring and determines the rate of aging. As long as people continue to strive towards fulfillment of goals, we are vulnerable to experiences of frustration and concomitant emotional drain. Teaching the management of frustration can minimize emotional wear and tear and thus prolong the quality and enjoyment of life. On the other hand, maladaptive responses to frustration will prolong emotional agitation and the maintenance of self-defeating reactions of helplessness/self-blame and rage/blaming others.

Frustration management can be taught and learned—to teacher trainers first, next to teachers, and then to children. Three major facets of frustration management have been sequentially presented: (1) attitudes/perceptions, (2) coping behaviors, and (3) tolerance. Concepts and general teaching strategies have been described with the hope that a total perspective for managing frustration will facilitate teacher development.

REFERENCES

Berg, Robert, and Johnson, James. *Group Counseling: A Sourcebook of Theory and Practice.* Fort Worth, Texas: American Continental, 1971.

Diggory, James. *Self-Evaluation: Concepts and Studies.* New York: John Wiley, 1966.

Fagen, Stanley, and Guedalia, Leonard. *Individual and Group Counseling: A Competency-Based Manual for In-Service Training.* Washington, D.C.: Psychoeducational Resources, 1977.

Fagen, Stanley, and Hill, Jeffery. *Behavior Management: A Competency-Based Manual for In-Service Training.* Washington, D.C.: Psychoeducation Resources, 1977.

Fagen, Stanley; Long, Nicholas; and Stevens, Donald. *Teaching Children Self-Control: Preventing Emotional and Learning Problems in the Elementary School.* Columbus, Ohio: Charles Merrill, 1975.

Gordon, Thomas. *Parent Effectiveness Training.* New York: Peter Wyden, 1971.

Graubard, Paul, and Rosenberg, Harry. *Classrooms that Work: Prescriptions for Change.* New York: Dutton, 1974.

Redl, Fritz, "The Concept of the Life Space Interview." *American Journal of Orthopsychiatry, 29,* 1959, 1–18.

Sanford, Nevitt, and Comstock, Craig. *Sanctions for Evil: Sources of Social Destructiveness.* San Francisco: Jossey-Bass, 1971.

Selye, Hans. "The Stress of Life." In *Human Life Cycle,* edited by W. C. Sze, pp. 589–598. New York: Jason Aronson, 1975.

. . . .

In the final article, Powell and Powell explore the use and abuse of time-out intervention. Time-out is a major and useful technique for reducing inappropriate student behavior, but there is a growing legal and professional challenge to this procedure. We feel time-out is one of many necessary behavior management procedures that should be available to classroom teachers. To assist in properly planning and using time-out procedures, a precise set of guidelines is presented to ensure that students receive proper help with their behavior and at the same time are protected from possible abuse.

ARTICLE 5.5

Using Time-Out Procedures with Disruptive Students

M. Catherine Grayson, John Kiraly, Jr., and Archie J. McKinnon

Increasingly, educators have been expected to deal with disruptive behavior in schools and to do so without hostile or punitive retaliation. As a result, a great need has developed for disciplinary techniques that interrupt unacceptable behavior yet maintain student–teacher relationships. Time-out is one such technique which has gained considerable popularity in many school districts. Unfortunately, when educators discuss time-out, there is often confusion over the meaning of the item. From review of the literature, it is evident that two different approaches to time-out have been implemented in schools.

1. *Behavioral Approach.* Time-out is viewed as a procedure to reduce undesirable behaviors by withdrawing the student from opportunities for reinforcement of the undesirable behavior (Bostow & Bailey, 1969; Endres & Goke, 1973; Madsen, 1974; O'Leary & O'Leary, 1977; Patterson & Guillion, 1971; Pendergrass, 1972; Tyler & Brown, 1967).

2. *Cooling-Off Approach.* Time-out spent either alone or with a "helping adult" such as a teacher, counselor, or psychologist, is used to help a student cope with problems during an intense period of stress (Bassin, Bratter, & Rachin, 1976; Caplan, 1963; Glasser, 1974; Long, Morse, & Newman, 1976; Redl, 1959; Redl & Wattenberg, 1959).

3. *Modified Approaches.* Time-out is used as a combination of withdrawal of reinforcement and cooling-off methods (Drabman & Spitalnik, 1973; Morris, 1976; Ramp, Ulrich, & Dulaney, 1971).

BEHAVIORAL APPROACH

Time-out is based on the idea that if an individual is in a motivating environment, whether it is one that provides intrinsic motivation or one that

M. Catherine Grayson is a learning disabilities resource teacher in the Mechanicsville Elementary School, Mechanicsville, Iowa (NCTL). John Kiraly, Jr., is an associate professor in the College of Education, Division of Special Education, at the University of Iowa, Iowa City. Archie J. McKinnon is an associate professor in the College of Education, Division of Special Education, at the University of Iowa, Iowa City.

provides external rewards, he will want to remain in that environment. Removal from that environment will cause the individual to exhibit behaviors which allow him to return and will cause him to avoid engaging in those behaviors which created the original removal. Thus, *time-out is a procedure in which the occurrence of inappropriate behavior is followed by a period of time during which reinforcers are no longer available.* An example of steps used to initiate and maintain this procedure is described in the following incident.

> Chris, a ten-year-old boy in the fifth grade, disturbs others in the classroom, does not complete his assigned work, and must have directions repeated over and over. He exhibits many behaviors his teacher would like to see eliminated, but two behaviors are particularly disturbing to the class and the teacher: (1) hitting other children and adults; and (2) having tantrums when asked to do something he does not want to do.

The teacher took the following steps to initiate and maintain a time-out program for Chris:

1. *Baseline data.* Before any changes were made, Chris was observed in a variety of settings and a frequency count was made of how often he engaged in the two target behaviors: hitting others and having tantrums. The baseline data were needed to note decreases or increases in the occurrence of the two target behaviors. The baseline data also provided an evaluation guide for the teacher. After the time-out procedure had been in use for a week or two, she was able to compare the frequency counts and note differences.

2. *The program is carefully explained to Chris.* He is shown the time-out room and told, "Whenever you hit another child or adult, or whenever you have a tantrum, you will immediately be put in the time-out room for _____ minutes. (Time should be as short as possible—three to five minutes seems to be chosen most often.) After the time period is up, you will be returned to the classroom." The teacher makes sure Chris understands her because she will have no verbal exchange with him when he is being placed in time-out. She knows that time-out is effective because it provides a neutral situation that withdraws all reinforcement, and she realizes that talking to Chris may be reinforcing. The teacher makes all aspects of the situation clear and even writes some of them out for him. The conditions will be reviewed daily but never when Chris is acting out. For instance, a condition for removal from time-out is that Chris must stop his tantrum. His teacher tells him, "After _____ minutes, if you are still in a tantrum, you must remain in time-out until you stop."

3. *Time-out will be applied immediately and consistently* after each occurrence of the target behavior(s), and the time limits will always be held constant.

4. *Concurrent with the initiation of the time-out procedure, a positive reinforcement program will begin.* When Chris is not hitting others or having tantrums, he will be rewarded. Rewards (e.g., praise, free time, points) will vary based on the child's needs and on those of the educational setting.

The actual time-out area will vary depending on physical limitations of the school setting. Not all teachers have an acceptable free room close by. The time-out area should be secluded and designated only for this purpose (many people use simple arrangements such as refrigerator shipping containers, storage areas, or space surrounded by screens), devoid of all distractions and contact with others. Ideally, there should be a small one-way window or unobtrusive peephole so the student can be seen by the teacher. The time-out area should not arouse fear in the student, cause physical discomfort, or have the potential to cause injury. Instead, it should be a neutral area where reinforcers are removed and social isolation results.

After completing steps 1 through 4 and designating the time-out area, Chris' teacher is prepared to implement a time-out procedure. Later when Chris hits Tom, his teacher immediately escorts Chris to the time-out room, avoiding eye contact and without any conversation. When the specified time period is up, she opens the door and simply says, "You may return to your work." Nothing else is said about the situation and he is treated normally when he returns to the classroom. If he hits or has a tantrum within thirty seconds, or after ten minutes, or two hours later, the same procedure will be repeated.

In order to evaluate the effectiveness of the time-out procedure, Chris' teacher can count the frequency of tantrums and/or hitting behaviors or she can just count the frequency of time-outs. If the procedure is effective, there should be a steady decrease in frequency of time-outs and a decrease in hitting and tantrum behaviors.

Time-out from the behavioral approach can be used with individuals of any age and with a variety of populations (normal, retarded, autistic, emotionally disabled, etc.). It is most effective for decreasing specific inappropriate behaviors and is not designed to discover the underlying causes of these behaviors.

COOLING-OFF APPROACH

The cooling-off approach emphasizes two features of time-out: (1) to decrease specific inappropriate behaviors; and (2) to provide an opportunity to understand the underlying emotions or feelings which cause the inappropriate behaviors. The frequency of an inappropriate behavior is decreased by working directly on the behavior and by exploring associated feelings while that behavior is occurring.

The cooling-off approach may require definition and observation of the specific target behaviors, but these functions are not essential. In the cooling-off approach, the student can voluntarily use time-out when he wants or needs a less stimulating environment or has an emotional outburst. This is in contrast to the behavioral approach, where time-out is reserved for one or two specific behaviors whose frequency and duration are carefully recorded.

Another difference is that, in the cooling-off approach, a large part of the management in the situation is shared because the pupil is involved in the decision making with the teacher. In contrast, the teacher makes all decisions, without student input, from the behavioral approach.

This approach is used almost exclusively with acting-out behaviors and my be referred to as "crisis intervention" or "cooling-off."

- Crisis intervention occurs when the pupil acts out. At that time the pupil is upset and more available to some assistance. This may be the time to sit with the pupil and try to discuss his concerns.

- Cooling-off is needed when a pupil acts out because there is too much stress present in his environment. The pupil cannot cope with the stimulation in his surroundings and needs a separation. Placement in a time-out room, where pressures and excessive stimulation are not present, can assist him to manage his behavior. An illustration of this approach is shown in the following description of Bob, an eight-year-old student in the third grade.

Bob has reading problems and is usually frustrated during the part of each day set aside for reading. Peer relations are also difficult for him, and, when he is having a conflict with a peer, he is likely to explode (i.e., yelling, throwing books). Bob's explosions occur two to three times a week and disrupt part of his and his classmates' school day. His teacher uses the time-out room as (1) a place where Bob can go before an explosion occurs and continue his work until he feels able to handle the classroom situation again or (2) a place where he can go during an explosion so the classroom disruption can be brief. When he explodes, he is immediately removed from the classroom and remains in time-out until he feels able to handle the classroom situation. His teacher or a school staff member is available to Bob at these times to help him sort out problems and develop ways of coping with the problem situations. The teacher and other school personnel who work with Bob are continually evaluating their availability to him so that the attention they provide does not become a reinforcement for the explosion behavior.

Use of relationships is one of the basic differences between the behavioral and cooling-off definitions of time-out. Behaviorists avoid all contact with a pupil when he is engaging in inappropriate behaviors they believe any contact may be reinforcing. Supporters of the cooling-off approach feel it is a time when contact should be made because the pupil is more open to assistance.

The teacher has taken the following steps to initiate and maintain this type of time-out program for Bob.

1. *A room is available which can provide a pressure-free environment for Bob.* It is a place where Bob can continue his work or work with other more neutral items: for example, puzzles, individual worksheets, or learning games.

2. *An adult should be available when Bob is in time-out.* An aide is on hand to take over the class so Bob's teacher can be with him to help him sort out problems and develop ways of coping with problem situations. The availability of an adult to stay with the pupil at these times is a significant feature in this approach. If an adult is available, the time may be used for crisis intervention, and efforts are made to discuss the causes of the explosion. If an adult is not available, the time is used for cooling-off, and a few words from an adult ("Bob, I want you to think about why you did that") provide the impetus for self-examination on the child's part. The cooling-off procedure can be used most effectively with students who have an adequate level of language understanding and who have social relationships.

3. *The time-out area is made available to the pupil, and its purpose is explained.* The teacher may say something like, "Bob, when things get too confusing in class and you feel like you are going to explode, you can take a time-out and continue your work there until you are ready to return. When you explode in the classroom, I will ask you to take a time-out until you calm down. I will be there to help you sort out the reasons for the explosion, and we can discuss ways to prevent future ones."

The behavioral approach to time-out requires complete control by the teacher of placement terms and placement termination. The "cooling-off" approach gives the teacher and/or pupil permission to use the time-out process and to determine time-out termination.

CRITICAL STEPS FOR TIME-OUT PROCEDURES

Despite the fact that alternative approaches to time-out are available, it is essential to recognize that students do exhibit seriously disruptive and inappropriate behaviors that are best managed by using a time-out procedure. *Regardless of which overall approach is adopted, the following critical steps are required for implementing any time-out procedure.*

- Identifying the serious behavior(s)
- Designating a specific area for time-out purposes

- Immediately placing or providing for placement of the pupil in the designated time-out area
- Monitoring the actual time in time-out
- Conducting an appropriate procedure for returning the pupil to the usual class routine as soon as possible
- Evaluating the effect of the time-out procedure, including maintenance of records showing frequency and duration of time-out

REFERENCES

1. Basin, A., Bratter, T. E., & Rachin, R. (eds.) *The Reality therapy reader.* New York: Harper and Row, 1976.

2. Bostow, D. E., & Bailey, J. B. Modification of severe disruptive and aggressive behavior using brief time-out and reinforcement procedures. *Journal of Applied Behavior Analysis,* 1969, 2, 31–37.

3. Caplan, G. Opportunities for school psychologists in primary prevention. *Mental Hygiene,* 1963, 47 (4), 525–539.

4. Drabman, R., & Spitalnik, R. Social isolation as a punishment procedure: A controlled study. *Journal of Experimental Child Psychology,* 1973, 16, 236–249.

5. Endres, V. J., & Goke, D. H. Time-out rooms in residential treatment centers. *Child Welfare,* 1973, 52, 359–366.

6. Glasser, W. A new look at discipline. *Learning,* 1974, December, 6–11.

7. *Guidelines on behavior management.* Report by the Florida Task Force on Retardation, Florida Division of Retardation, 1975.

8. Long, N. J., Morse, W. C., & Newman, R. G. *Conflict in the classroom: The education of emotionally disturbed children* (3rd ed.). Belmont, Calif.: Wadsworth, 1976.

9. Madsen, C. H., & Madsen, C. K. *Teaching discipline: A positive approach for education development.* Boston: Allyn & Bacon, 1974.

10. Morris, R. J. *Behavior modification with children: A systematic guide.* Englewood Cliffs, New Jersey: Winthrop Publishers, Inc., 1976.

11. O'Leary, K. D., & O'Leary, S. G. *Classroom management: The successful use of behavior modification.* New York: Pergamon, 1977.

12. Patterson, G., & Guillion, M. E. *Living with children.* Champaign, Ill.: Research Press, 1971.

13. Pendergrass, V. E. Time-out from positive reinforcement following persistent, high-rate behavior in retardates. *Journal of Applied Behavior Analysis,* 1972, 5, 85–91.

14. Ramp, E., Ulrigh, R., & Dulaney, S. Delayed time-out as a procedure for reducing disruptive behavior: A case study. *Journal of Applied Behavior Analysis,* 1971, 4, 235–239.

15. Redl, F. The concept of the life space interview. *American Journal of Orthopsychiatry,* 1959, XXIX, 1–18.

16. Redl, F., & Wattenberg, W. *Mental hygiene in teaching* (2nd ed.). New York: Harcourt, Brace and World, Inc., 1959.

17. Tyler, V. O., & Brown, G. D. The use of swift, brief isolation as a group control device for institutionalized delinquents. *Behavior Research and Therapy,* 1967, 5, 1–9.

. . . .

SUMMARY . . . .

This chapter has presented the essential concepts and skills of effective classroom discipline. Current definitions represent opposite points of view and describe the goal of classroom discipline as either maintaining student order or teaching students to be self-directed. Our definition is more inclusive and integrates the following four concepts and skills:

1. Effective classroom discipline begins with teacher self-awareness and self-control, not with the students.

2. Effective classroom discipline teaches the democratic values of our society by providing students with opportunities to choose, regulate, and be accountable for their behavior. This long-range goal of discipline develops an internal locus of control.

3. Effective classroom discipline consists of a variety of short-range, on-the-spot, direct interventions based on school values and rules. These interventions either increase positive behaviors or decrease negative behaviors.

4. Effective classroom discipline is viewed as a professional philosophy of relating, teaching, and empowering students, and as a positive way of perceiving, thinking, feeling, and behaving toward students. It is not a bag of unrelated tricks.

6

Beyond Student Behavior: Strategies and Skills Helping Students Who Come with Personality and Chronic Behavioral Problems

This chapter looks beyond students' behavior in order to make their personal problems more understandable and less mysterious. Personal problems are not temporary reactions to frustration; they are definable personality problems that are chronic and perplexing to teachers. As professional problem solvers, teachers are comfortable making decisions about how to help their students academically. However, when asked to help these same students deal with their personality problems, teachers seem reluctant to assume this responsibility. Their ambivalence often is reinforced by administrators, who may inform them that helping troubled students is not their area of professional competence and may instruct them to refer those students to the school counselor, psychologist, or social worker. This sounds like reasonable professional advice and a sensible division of labor. In fact, staff collaboration can result in an effective "team approach" to helping troubled students when adequate psychological staff and resources are available. When it works, it represents the best of interdisciplinary cooperation. Unfortunately, in the majority of public schools, including special and alternative schools, the psychological staff frequently are referred to as the "hidden faculty": they are rarely seen, are overloaded with cases and reports, and usually are not available when teachers need them. Meanwhile, the referring teacher continues to have the responsibility of providing the troubled students and their classmates with a safe, secure, and appropriate learning environment. Given this situation, what are the teacher's options and responsibilities? What should the teacher be doing to help these students and the class until professional help arrives? What if professional help never arrives? Should the teacher suffer through this frustration by saying, "That's life!" or "There is nothing I can do about this situation"?

Our recommendation is a resounding "No." Just as teachers are trained medically to administer CPR to a student who is not breathing and to perform the Heimlich Maneuver when a student is choking, teachers need to integrate their instructional skills with specific mental health practices. This does not change a teacher into a psychologist any more than performing CPR turns a teacher into a physician. These additional skills simply acknowledge that the current conditions in many classrooms create a need for deeper and more effective understanding of the social–emotional problems of troubled students.

LOOKING FOR CAUSES . . . .

A basic principle of Gestalt psychology is: The whole or "personality" of a person is greater than the sum of its parts. Similarly, a student is more complex and psychologically more elaborate than the sum of his or her behaviors. Inappropriate behavior needs to be managed, but it is important to look beyond the behavioral deeds of troubled students and to consider their unmet psychological needs. As professionals, teachers are naturally interested in understanding the underlying or causative reasons of chronic student problems. For example, teachers are aware something is psychologically awry when a high-achieving student begins to fail exams, when a student becomes enraged and explodes when asked to carry out a routine classroom request, when a student enjoys bullying peers, or when a student becomes overstimulated and hyperactive during nonstructured times. Teachers also understand there are underlying problems when a student escapes into silence and looks depressed; when a student is anxious, fearful, and helpless in normal situations; and when a student comes to school under the influence of alcohol and drugs or talks about ending his or her life. Rather than determining which students have chronic social–emotional problems, teachers are concerned with what insights and skills they can bring to these problems.

One way of learning about the underlying causes of personal problems is to review the various Psychological Need Theories of Personality Development. A word of caution is offered at this time. When they study the needs of children and youth, teachers can become acutely troubled by the severity of a student's unmet psychological needs. It is important to emphasize that understanding a student's needs does not mean the teacher excuses the student's disruptive behaviors. An awareness of the emotional pain of a student's life can elicit a ground swell of teacher compassion, but this compassion must not be confused with sympathy. Teacher sympathy sends a message, "Oh you poor child! I understand your emotional pain so I will not add to it by expecting the same standards for you. You have been treated unfairly by life and have deep and justifiable reasons for being angry, confused, fearful, dependent, or depressed." Teacher sympathy reinforces a student's belief that he or she has been psychologically gypped and encourages more irresponsible student behavior. Any message of sympathy is a clear misuse of the concept of psychological acceptance. Compassion, however, sends a different message. It says, "Thank you for sharing some of your psychological struggles and feelings with me. They helped me better appreciate and understand you. Now let's plan how we can use these difficult times to figure out what specific support and skills you need if you are to be emotionally strong, independent, and competent." Compassion emphasizes students' strengths rather than their weaknesses and promotes the beginning source of trust for the students while becoming a positive source of motivation for the teacher.

MASLOW'S HIERARCHY OF NEEDS . . . .

In 1943, Abraham Maslow published an article entitled "A Theory of Human Motivation." He proposed the existence of a hierarchy of five human needs that motivate behavior. He believed the lowest level of need must be satisfied at a minimum level before the individual is motivated to seek out the next higher level of need.

Maslow's hierarchy is:

Level 1: *Physiological needs.* All the biological drives for survival and development—food, water, sleep, protection from heat/cold, and so on.

Level 2: *Safety needs.* All activities that protect the individual, such as physical and psychological security and personal safety.

Level 3: *Belongingness and love needs.* All activities that promote psychological attachment, trust, acceptance, and emotional security from others.

Level 4: *Esteem needs.* All activities that enhance the worth, recognition, achievements, and competitiveness of the individual.

Level 5: *Self-actualizing need.* The highest level of development—all activities that involve self-directed intellectual and aesthetic appreciation of life.

Maslow writes that the first four needs can only be satisfied by others (i.e., family, school, community): the individual is dependent on the skills of adult caregivers. Their quality of nurturing, attitudes, expectations, rules, and punishments govern and determine the extent to which the individual's needs are met. In contrast, the self-directed individual functioning on level 5 has had the other four levels of needs met, is less dependent on others for approval, and can be more directed by inner capacities, talents, and goals.

Maslow's hierarchy of needs has been very instructional to educators. His theory represents a positive view of personality development. He describes what needs must be met to foster the development of a well-adjusted individual. The theory also is useful in understanding the behavior of high-risk and troubled students. When students are deprived of their basic needs of food, shelter, sleep, and health, when students are frightened about their physical and psychological safety, when students are rejected and neglected, when students are feeling worthless and inadequate, they will be driven to meet these unmet needs before they have the motivation and energy to achieve the higher level skills of education.

GLASSER'S CONTROL THEORY

William Glasser is a child psychiatrist who has committed himself to finding more effective strategies of helping troubled students in school. In 1986, in *Control Theory in the Classroom*, he presented the fundamental needs critical to a student's psychological welfare:

1. The need of survival
2. The need of belonging and love
3. The need for power
4. The need for fun
5. The need for freedom

The first two needs are similar to Maslow's needs. The need for power means a student is motivated to assert control over life and the immediate environment. The need for freedom means the choice to choose, to be free from autocratic control, and to be self-directed without violating the rights of others.

Glasser believes that educators who are teaching alienated and troubled students must be aware of these needs and must develop specific learning opportunities to meet these needs when designing school activities and programs for these youth.

BRENDTRO, BROKENLEG, AND VAN BOCKERN: THE CIRCLE OF COURAGE

In 1990, Brendtro, Brokenleg, and Van Bockern wrote an inspiring book entitled *Reclaiming Youth at Risk*. Building on the history of traditional Native American child-rearing philosophies, they proposed a positive culture of caring to meet the four essential needs of developing children. Their model is based on a holistic concept characterized by the symbol of the Indian medical wheel or Circle of Courage and not a hierarchical system like Maslow's. They believe all children, regardless of their culture, will become healthy adults if the needs or "spirits" of belonging, mastery, independence, and generosity are met.

1. *The Spirit of Belonging.* All infants need nurturing parents, but all infants need to belong to the tribe, to have many mothers with many honored relationships and relatives. Children need to live in an extended family and, over time, the children become a part of a shared community with a clear identity and sense of trust regarding their cultural roots and feelings of belongingness.

2. *The Spirit of Mastery.* Children are taught the importance of competency by observing and listening to the wisdom of their elders, and in participating in tribal games, stories, and work. Each of these activities reflects the importance of mastering a skill, based on the value of cooperative achievement, personal persistence, creativity, and problem solving. This process of learning by doing becomes the basic educational experience of fostering the spirit of mastery in Indian youth.

3. *The Spirit of Independence.* To survive, to become brave, children are taught the importance of being autonomous, responsible, assertive, and self-disciplined. They are encouraged to hunt and trap on their own, to be accountable for their actions, and to take some risks by adventuring into the unknown. These expectations result in a sense of empowerment and is similar to Glasser's need for power and control over one's immediate environment.

4. *The Spirit of Generosity.* The spirit of generosity is a vital force in the socialization of Indian youth. They are taught the importance of giving and sharing their resources instead of accumulating and increasing their material wealth. Personal acts of generosity are a significant way of building the importance of helping others and in defining the quality of one's character. The emphasis on seeking intrinsic rather than extrinsic rewards is another way to enhance the spirit of generosity.

Using this theory, the authors advocate how special schools and treatment agencies can restructure their daily program and activities to reclaim troubled students by promoting their need to belong, to be competent, to be independent, and to be generous. This is the most positive model of helping troubled students, and it has an exciting future as these concepts become translated into specific psychoeducational strategies.

All three of the previous theories describe the underlying needs and the environmental conditions required to promote the development of a well-adjusted student. The next logical question is: "What happens to children and youth when these psychological needs are not met by the adults in their environment?" How do children and youth behave when they have been neglected, rejected, and depreciated? All of the previous three theories would predict that the unmet needs of these students for adult attention, approval, and acceptance would be greater and more difficult to meet in the classroom than the needs of other students. To make matters more frustrating, these troubled students have learned a variety of protective behaviors that are offensive to teachers and are less likely to result in a response of respect and approval. Like the adage, the rich get richer and the poor get poorer, the students having the greatest need for teacher acceptance and approval usually end up getting the least, and the students having the least needs in these areas usually end up receiving the majority of teacher acceptance and approval. Dreikurs was one of the first child psychiatrists to write about this concept and to help teachers understand the meaning of student misbehavior.

DREIKURS' FOUR GOALS OF MISBEHAVIOR . . . .

In 1971, Dreikurs, Grunwold, and Pepper published an innovative textbook entitled *Maintaining Sanity in the Classroom*. It was an immediate success. They proposed an original concept regarding student misbehavior. They believed misbehavior was motivated by four identifiable and underlying goals that teachers must learn before they attempt to correct or stop inappropriate student behavior. The four goals of misbehavior are motivated by the students' belief that these behaviors are in their best interests.

1. *Attention-getting mechanism (A.G.M.)*. Dreikurs documented that some troubled students believe they do not have any chance of being recognized by constructive behaviors so they take up a variety of attention-getting behaviors or mechanisms to engage the teacher's attention. The mechanisms of misbehavior include showing off in class, interrupting others, clowning around, becoming silly, and bullying others. For these students, it is more important to be noticed by the teacher and to tolerate his or her anger than to be ignored, forgotten, and excluded by the teacher. Behaviorists have acknowledged these same attention-getting behaviors and have taught teachers to ignore them while actively reinforcing any of the students' positive behavior.

2. *The need for power seeking*. Some students try to get their needs met by becoming rebels with a cause. They try to master or control their immediate environment by being disobedient and stubborn, and by engaging the adults in power struggles (the Conflict Cycle, page 244). Their false beliefs are: "If I win this power struggle, I am in control of my life." "If I am successful, I am in charge of this situation and if I'm in charge, I have real power in this group and have earned the respect of my peers."

   To maintain their feelings of power or self-worth, their goal is to outsmart the adults by knowing how to push their emotional panic buttons. Unfortunately, there are no winners in a "power struggle," and this goal of misbehavior ultimately becomes self-defeating for the student.

3. *To compensate for feeling rejected and emotionally hurt by seeking revenge.* This goal of misbehavior is limited to a few very troubled students who have been damaged by their traumatic life experiences. They have given up trusting adults and are motivated by the desire for revenge. These students are so filled with hate at what has happened to them, they are controlled by the active thought: "You have hurt me, so I will find a way of hurting you!" They have lost their ability to discriminate between adults who care and adults who are exploitative. Consequently, during stressful times, they end up treating all adults alike. These students will need special education programs and perhaps an alternative school in order to provide them with an appropriate education.

4. *To express feelings of discouragement and hopelessness.* The goal of this misbehavior also is limited to a few students who have internalized their traumatic life experiences and have concluded it is their fault. They do not seek revenge but have come to the conclusion that, because life is so overwhelmingly painful, they cannot manage the daily emotional stress. They have internalized a belief that they have failed, and they have given up the struggle to succeed. They don't want to try anymore. Their goals are to be left alone and to be able to turn to the nonrealities of drugs, alcohol, and passivity for relief and satisfaction.

Dreikurs states that these four goals of misbehavior are not rigid categories; instead, they are general diagnostic classifications that will help teachers understand the multiple meaning of troubled students' behavior.

WOOD'S DEVELOPMENTAL ANXIETIES ....

Another important advocate of understanding the needs of students is Mary Wood. She has taken a developmental view of troubled students and believes *anxiety* is a private, persistent reaction to unmet emotional needs.

In 1986, she described her theory in a creative textbook entitled *Developmental Therapy in the Classroom*. She states that all children experience five developmental anxieties from birth through adolescence. These intrapsychic anxieties are: feelings of *abandonment, inadequacy, guilt, conflict,* and *identity*. If a developmental anxiety is not resolved at the age-appropriate time, it will be carried into the next developmental stage and will create even more unmet emotional needs in the future. Like Maslow, Wood believes many unresolved developmental anxieties will become the primary motivational force of the student at the next level and will interfere with all future relationships.

1. *The anxiety of abandonment.* Feelings of abandonment occur as a normal developmental crisis in infants and young children under the age of two. If a young child bonds with the parents or a significant adult and receives consistent love, care, and security, the feelings of abandonment will be resolved and a growing sense of trust will develop. However, if the child experiences early and prolonged physical or psychological neglect, the feelings of abandonment will become real and the child will likely develop superficial relationships, hoard objects, and have a gnawing desire to be accepted by others. This developmental anxiety is the other side of Brendtros' spirit of belongingness.

2. *The anxiety of inadequacy.* Feelings of inadequacy become a normal developmental crisis of preschool children as they understand the needs and expectations of the important adults in their life. This developmental change generates additional feelings of self-doubt: Can I meet their expectations? Will I get it right? If the preschool child experiences chronic failure or is repetitively told that his or her behavior doesn't meet adult standards, the child will learn to deny or justify mistakes by blaming others, lying, or by projecting feelings on others.

3. *The anxiety of guilt.* Wood writes that feelings of guilt become a developmental crisis for children between six and nine years of age. If these children have not resolved the previous developmental anxiety of inadequacy and think they are "no good" and "unworthy," they will actively put themselves down emotionally for not meeting *their own standards.* When this occurs, the merging of their feelings of inadequacy and guilt can result in such intense guilt that they actually seek out punishment. Troubled students have been observed stealing objects and breaking school rules so openly that they are guaranteeing they will be caught and punished. These students also can end up as group scapegoats and willing victims of exploitation. During stressful times, their behaviors are frequently examples of self-abuse due to personal guilt.

4. *The anxiety of conflict.* This developmental anxiety, which takes place between the ages of nine and twelve, emerges when the need for budding independence conflicts with the will of authorities. If this crisis is resolved, the preadolescent develops a new feeling of self-confidence and social flexibility. One of the significant outcomes of this developmental anxiety is the insight that with independence and freedom comes personal accountability for one's decisions and behaviors.

   If this developmental crisis is not resolved, the preadolescent is likely to enter the adolescent years ill prepared to cope with the normal additional adolescent stresses. Fights with authority figures will continue and will ensure negative teacher reactions. A student may begin to believe there is status and power in being the "bad kid" in the classroom. This is very similar to Dreikurs' *need for power seeking.*

5. *The anxiety of identity.* Developmental anxiety for adolescents is illustrated by the psychological questions: "Who am I?" and "Will I be able to handle this crisis?" These questions reflect the dynamic interplay between new feelings of independence and residual feelings of dependency. This struggle increases as the adolescent's maturing body creates concerns about sexuality, attractiveness, and group acceptance. During this stage, adolescents experiment with new attitudes, appetites, and behaviors with the same interest as if they were buying a new pair of jeans. "Does it look right? Does it feel right? Am I comfortable wearing it?" As this anxiety about their identity is resolved and they feel more comfortable about themselves, they solidify their social and emotional skills and develop a direction for life after high school.

Wood's developmental therapy highlights the importance of understanding these five normal and predictable developmental anxieties in children and youth. She believes this awareness can aid teachers in helping troubled students to identify their underlying anxieties and to recognize how they trigger their feelings, behaviors, and resulting teacher reactions.

LONG'S CONCEPT OF HOW NORMAL DEVELOPMENTAL NEEDS OF VERY TROUBLED STUDENTS GET TURNED INTO SELF-DEFEATING FEARS . . . .

Long's (1993) study of reeducating seriously troubled students has provided teachers of emotionally disturbed students with additional insights into the dynamics of unmet needs. He states that because these students have experienced such early, intense, and prolonged neglect, abuse, and rejection, they no longer are motivated by personal trust or the spirit of human kindness. By the time they are placed in special programs or alternative schools, they come to the classroom not only with a chip on their shoulders, but also with an intent to avoid interpersonal closeness and academic learning, and to view any therapeutic program as an intrusive and hostile life sentence. Their initial behaviors are centered on psychologically biting any hand that tries to feed them. Their negative attitudes and rejecting behaviors are difficult to accept, particularly if the teachers are reaching out to them in a friendly way. Most caring teachers believe that if a student is cold, hungry, and tired, and if the adult provides that student a hot meal, warm clothes, and a good night's sleep, these caring conditions should improve the student's condition and disposition. Likewise, if a student has not experienced a nurturing adult, positive learning opportunities, and a chance to be empowered, and if these essential psychological needs are provided by a caring teacher, the student should respond with new hope, appreciation, and more appropriate behaviors. Long reports this rarely happens with seriously troubled students. He has observed that emotionally disturbed students initially do not respond positively to interpersonal relationships or special programs. They seem to have developed psychological antibodies against the warmth of healthy relationships and supportive programs. They appear to have been conditioned to consider close relationships as toxic rather than enriching experiences. Interpersonal closeness does not mean love, trust, and bonding, but a new cycle of rejection and abandonment. Interpersonal closeness is not something to seek and attain; it is a condition to avoid and fear. This reaction is particularly true when teachers begin to have some emotional meaning to them. Their defense against adult closeness is to react with renewed resistance and teacher rejection. Similarly, academic competence for these students does not create a sense of mastery, but only a belief that adults will demand a greater and higher level of performance. These students are not motivated by success, but by a fear of academic success, which they think will only end up as failure. Likewise, becoming independent does not lead to freedom of control, but to a quagmire of new and overwhelming responsibilities. It appears much safer psychologically to become dependent and manipulate others rather than to take charge of one's life. Independence is something to fear and not a role to realize. Finally, generosity is not something that leads to altruism and sharing, but another experience of personal deprivation. To give something away means that one has less of it for oneself. The goal is to hold on to whatever one has and protect it. Generosity is something to avoid.

Long has documented how these students have turned their healthy developmental needs into a fear of these needs. As infants, they were seriously abused, neglected, or rejected. As children, they still were motivated toward having their emotional needs met, but they frequently used a variety of inappropriate behaviors that resulted in more adult abuse. If this cycle of psychological and physical rejection continues into early adolescence, many of these seriously troubled students learned to fear their own healthy psychological needs, and conclude it is safer to avoid or deny them than to try again and suffer the pain of rejection. These seriously troubled students are not going to be helped in the regular classroom unless the teacher has many skills in seeing beyond the defensive behaviors. Many of them will need comprehensive and intensive therapeutic services and programs such as the one Fecser describes in his article (see page 471).

This chapter is organized for a better understanding of the needs of troubled students with specific psychological problems. The collection of articles represents the best and the latest psychoeducational insights into how to understand and help students who are struggling with the specific problems of low self-esteem, selective speaking, aggression, passive aggression, alcoholism, attention deficit and hyperactivity disorder, suicide, and grieving.

BIBLIOGRAPHY . . . .

Brendtro, L. K., Brokenleg, M., & Van Bockern, S. (1990). *Reclaiming youth at risk*. Bloomington, IN: National Educational Service.

Dreikurs, R., Grunwold, B. B., & Pepper, F. C. (1971). *Maintaining sanity in the classroom: Illustrated teaching techniques*. New York: Harper & Row.

Gallagher, P. A. (1988). *Teaching students with behavior disorders* (2nd ed.). Denver, CO: Love.

Glasser, W. (1965). *Reality therapy: A new approach to psychiatry*. New York: Harper & Row.

Glasser, W. (1990). *Quality school: Managing students without coercion*. New York: Harper & Row.

Kerr, M. M., Nelson, C. M., & Lambert, D. L. (1987). *Helping adolescents with learning and behavior problems*. Columbus, OH: Merrill.

Long, N. J. (1993, Spring). Stages of helping emotionally disturbed students through the reeducation process. *The Pointer, 30*(1).

Walker, H. M., Colvin, G., & Ramsey E. *Antisocial behavior in school: Strategies and best practices*.

Wood, Mary. (1986). *Developmental theory in the classroom*. Austin, TX: PRO-ED.

HOW TO UNDERSTAND AND HELP STUDENTS WITH LOW SELF-CONCEPTS AND FEELINGS OF FAILURE . . . .

The first article, *Masking the Feelings of Being Stupid*, was written by Sally Smith, the founder and director of the Lab School of Washington, DC, and a professor of the graduate program in Learning Disabilities at American University. The Lab School is recognized as a national model center for learning disabled students. This is a one-of-a-kind, innovative school in which the creative arts play a central role in the reeducation process. Smith's writings not only describe the needs and strategies of helping these special needs students, but also they have implications for all students who have academic problems and low self-esteem.

Self-esteem, defined here as the student's feeling of self-worth, is an internal source of motivation that guides and directs behavior. Students with high self-esteem, in general, are confident, optimistic, and active; have little anxiety; and enjoy new challenges. Students with low self-esteem, in general, are fearful of angering others, dependent, anxious, and resistant to new challenges. Students with special needs are more likely to have low self-esteem and to develop ways of hiding their feelings of inadequacies.

This article was selected because it provides important insights into student behaviors. One concept to remember is: *The same underlying problem among students—in this case, the feelings of low self-esteem or the feelings of stupidity—can be expressed in many different behaviors*. There is rarely a one-to-one relationship between the cause of the student's behavior and its expression in behavior. The corollary statement of this concept is also true: *Different problem behaviors among students can all be motivated by the same underlying cause*.

Smith describes 18 different masks or behaviors that learning disabled students use to defend against their feelings of stupidity and peer embarrassment. An awareness of these different protective masks may enable a teacher to see beyond these false images and to respond to these students by discovering the meaning behind their masks. When this connection is made and the teacher acknowledges their feelings, the possibility of genuine teacher support and help can develop.

ARTICLE 6.1

Masking the Feeling of Being Stupid
Sally L. Smith

I run a seminar with learning disabled adults every Tuesday evening at the Lab School of Washington. This is my current research. Learning disabled adults can tell you what our learning disabled children cannot. Through these seminars, I have been able to improve the teaching of our students and the training of special education teachers! The most important message they have given me is that the biggest battle of all with dyslexics is for their self esteem. They feel stupid. They have been treated as stupid. School stands for mastery of academic disciplines. All through school for many years, they have felt defeated, worthless, dumb. They learned to mask their hurts.

One adult stated, "I learned to act a certain way so I couldn't be teased. I would appear bored, tired, eager to be of help, all knowing or funny, depending upon what was going on. In other words, I would do anything but let them know I couldn't read the material." Another adult shared that "I faked my way all through school. I had the gift of gab and an excellent memory."

"I masked my handicaps and saved my job."

"My ex-husband never knew."

"I masked my inability to write and used my wife to do all the correspondence and the billing."

"I don't want my own child to think I'm a dummy, so I hide it from him."

"When you don't know something or cannot read something and you feel you should be able to, then don't you mask this disability in front of people you respect? I do!"

Unfortunately, many of these learning disabled adults reported they started developing masks in first or second grade, when they could not

From *Pointer.* (1988). Vol. 32, No. 3. Reprinted with permission of The Helen Dwight Reid Educational Foundation.

read what others could. Few of our students ever received special education. They were not identified as learning disabled or dyslexic; their teachers usually identified them as lazy, when they were trying their hearts out. They were called "retarded" if they had any speech or language problems and "disturbed" if they were hyperactive, impulsive or had any of the behavioral manifestation of a learning disabled child. Often they were gifted, surely above average in intelligence, and could not bear their inability to accomplish the simplest of academic tasks. Here are some of the masks they wore:

THE MASK OF SUPER-COMPETENCE

"Easy!" "Oh, sure." "Everyone knows that." "I know, I know, I know . . ." With a great deal of bravado, everything is made to look simple. This person knows he can talk his way through anything. His logic is impeccable. He's good with people, with numbers, with problem-solving, trouble shooting. General George S. Patton assured his daughter that Napoleon couldn't spell either and he quoted Jefferson Davis as saying, "A man must have a pretty poor mind not to be able to think of several ways to spell a word."

THE MASK OF HELPLESSNESS

"I don't know." "I don't understand." "I can't do anything." "I'm such a failure." "I'm dyslexic." Through pity, this person gets everyone around him to help him, do his work, take on his responsibilities, so that he never fails; he refuses to risk any failure. However, he feels even worse inside because he knows he didn't do any of the work.

THE MASK OF INVISIBILITY

"I would hide in my shell, hold my neck like a turtle, my eyes bulging out, almost pleading with the teacher not to call upon me." Through looking frightened, whispering to teachers, acting terrified with peers, this person too has everyone else doing his work for him. "You can get through school by not talking, just repeating when necessary, and taking a low profile, no waves!" With head down, sitting quietly for a long time, nobody bothers this person. He has the talent of sitting in the back of the room, melting into the crowd, into nothingness . . . Teachers and supervisors realize they never got to know him; they barely know he was there.

THE MASK OF THE CLOWN

"Isn't that a riot!" "Ha, ha, ha . . ." "What a joke!" Everything is funny when this guy is around. Laughter will obfuscate the issue. The well known singer-actress Cher admits she was "the class clown" because she could not read, write, or do arithmetic at school even though she was exceedingly verbal and outstanding in all the arts. Her teacher proclaimed that she was not working hard enough. She felt dumb. She dropped out of school at 16 and wasn't tested for her learning disabilities until she was over 30. Another "class clown," for the same reasons, was Henry Winkler, The Fonz, who didn't discover his learning disabilities until his stepson was diagnosed as dyslexic.

THE MASK OF THE VICTIM

"It's not fair." "Everyone picks on me." "Why me?" "Look, she's not calling on the others, just me!" "There's no justice anywhere." Injustice collecting is a basic theme with this person. Often called "a jailhouse lawyer" because there's an argument for everything with this person, he truly feels victimized and takes on a "poor me" attitude. He assumes no responsibility for anything. He angers everyone around him.

THE MASK OF NOT CARING

"I don't care." "It doesn't matter." "Nothing matters." "Nobody cares about me. Who cares?" "Whatever you do, I don't care." With this mask, the person is never vulnerable. The person risks no failure. If he tries to succeed and fails, he says he never tried and it doesn't matter. It is a way of keeping others as distanced as possible from him and it makes them feel woefully inadequate. If nothing matters, then it's impossible to motivate somebody or get him to change.

THE MASK OF BOREDOM

"This is boring!" Yawn. "It certainly is not interesting." Yawn, yawn. "Boy, this is dull!" Yawn, yawn. "Can I go to the bathroom?" "What time is it now?" Yawn, yawn, yawn. With big yawns, loud sighs, tapping fingers and toes, this person lets his teacher, boss, supervisor, know how bored he is, which puts the other person on the defensive. Usually he is not bored, but frustrated, and can't do what he's been asked to do. Thomas Edison was kicked out of schools for not following instructions (he probably did not understand them because of his auditory problems and his severe learning disabilities prevented him from being able to write what he was told to). Often, the learning disabled make teachers feel terrible about themselves; feelings of inadequacy are catching.

THE MASK OF ACTIVITY

"Gotta run." "Have to make a call now." "Sorry, I'm in a hurry, can't talk now." "I'm late; I'm busy now; I'll do what ever you want later." "Later, later . . . no time now." This person is always on the move. Standing still may bring him close to others and he precludes any intimacy. Constant activity wards away others and keeps him from having to perform. This person frustrates everyone around him.

THE MASK OF OUTRAGEOUSNESS

"I'm way out." "I don't like conformists." "I believe in individualism to the extreme . . ." Through a wild choice of clothes, the color of hair, wigs, extraordinary glasses, stockings, boots, neckpieces, this person projects eccentricity and hides what he is worried about. Cher, extraordinarily talented as singer, dancer, actress, has drawn attention to herself through her bizarre clothing and incredible wigs. Robert Rauschenberg, the artist whose works are treasured all over the world and in virtually every important international collection of contemporary art, did outrageous, unheard of things. Many artists feel he expanded the definition of art for a generation of Americans by daring to innovate.

THE MASK OF THE GOOD SAMARITAN

"Let me help you." "Let me carry it for you." "What can I do for you?" "Where can I be of most help?" "Let me run your errands. Let me take care of your needs." This person wants to please at any cost. Frequently, he is too nice and too accommodating. He will echo what you say, work longer hours and be obsequiously helpful to get out of doing what he can't do or to achieve his goals. One Night School student spent 10th, 11th, and 12th grade in choir even though he detested it, because in his high school the choir teacher decided who graduated.

THE MASK OF CONTEMPT AND, CUTTING EVERYTHING DOWN

"They don't know how to teach." "My glasses aren't right." "This whole place sucks." "I get all my information from TV—it's better." "Why go to church when I've been allowed to live with this much difficulty? They haven't helped me." Negativity encompasses this mask. This joyless person has a negative word for everything. If it's sunny out, it could be sunnier. This person wears out the people around him because nothing is ever good enough and he takes no pleasure in his small successes. He's angry at the whole world for making him feel stupid, and feels the world owes him something. He puts everybody else on the defensive.

THE MASK OF THE STRONG SILENT TYPE

"I'm Joe Cool." "Nobody comes too close to me but they follow me everywhere." "Get out of my face. Nobody moves on me." "Every sport is for me. I live for sports." "Life is like getting psyched for a wrestling match."

Personified by a sleek body and incredible prowess at sports, this person is revered by many and endowed, in their minds, with every fine feature. Bruce Jenner, Olympic Decathlon Champion, said that sports gave him his self esteem and that reading aloud in the classroom was much more frightening and harder for him than the decathlon. Tom Cruise, today's hot movie star, poured all his energies into sports because he suffered so from learning disabilities and needed to shine in an area. It was only when he became hurt, he auditioned for a school play, got the lead, ended up on Broadway and then in the movies, becoming a top star at age 23. Olympic gold medalist diver Greg Louganis said he turned to diving to show the world he was worth something since he was called "dumb and retarded" all through school. Ann Bancroft, one of the six explorers to reach the North Pole last year, found the grueling trip to the North Pole easier than getting through the University of Oregon in six years.

Sometimes The Strong Silent Type aches to open up and share his feelings, but can't. There is a wall that he creates often between him and those close to him.

THE MASK OF PERFECTION

"If they don't recognize my talents, it's their problem." "I have everything going for me." "If the world is a bunch of conformists, let them know I'm unique!" "Good artists don't have to read anyhow." "I'm doing fine, really well!"

Proclaiming loudly that there are machines to spell and write, secretaries to take dictation and lawyers to read for him, this person presents himself as perfection. He tolerates no mistakes in himself or others. Often carrying an impressive book or magazine he cannot read, he saunters into rooms looking completely pleased with life. He makes everyone around him feel miserable.

THE MASK OF ILLNESS, FRAIL HEALTH, VULNERABILITY

"My head." "My stomach." "My side." "My bladder." "My back." "My migraine." "My eyes." "My illness." "I'm weak in the knees."

To receive extra attention and to get out of the work he cannot do, this person calls in sick, leaves sick, constantly pretends to be sick and talks about his frailties. Given something to read, he uses his illnesses or fatigue as an excuse, or he cries if necessary. Expecting special attention, special privileges, while avoiding what he cannot do, this person confuses everyone around him and usually gets by with it.

THE MASK OF SEDUCTION

"Hey female, write this down for me. Men don't write." "Math is male stuff, baby doll can't do it." "Big man can."

This doll baby asks "Big Daddy" to do what she can't do and uses her feminine wile to make it all appear sexy. She hides behind the female mask while the macho chauvinist hides behind his mask in order for her to do for him what he can't do.

THE MASK OF BEING BAD

"Don't mess with me. You'll be sorry." "I don't care if she wants me to sit down, I won't." "I threw the book at him, so what?" "I'd rather be thought of as bad than dumb!"

Losers at school often become winners on the street. This person feels stupid, powerless, useless at school and often his frustration and anger get directed towards his teachers. His peers often enjoy his acting out and encourage more of it. Dallas real estate magnate, Rick Strauss, tells how he rode a cart down the school halls, played tricks on everyone, sold his Mom's good jewelry to neighborhood children for twenty-five cents apiece. He changed schools several times, always suffering the humiliation of not learning to read or write. He compounded his problems by cutting up, but at least he succeeded in getting the attention of the teachers off his poor work. Not until his last year at high school did he learn that his inability to read and write were due to his learning disabilities.

THE MASK OF "THE CON"

"My smarts got me by. I could sweet talk any teacher and be absent for all tests." "I could convince a teacher of any excuse—my dog died, my brother had my homework, my mother brutalized me, the hand that I wrote with had been operated on twice." "I learned to lie looking you straight in the face." "Hey, I'm a personality guy: I can out talk a salesman and make people like me."

This wheeler-dealer uses moxie. He negotiates how much work he will do and what the teacher will do for him. G. Chris Andersen, Managing Director of the Finance Department of one of Wall Street's biggest firms used his gift of gab to talk himself into or out of almost anything. He, who traveled through 38 states and 12 countries before he was eighteen years old, used every line and talent he had, to get through school. Even though he didn't know his left hand from his right and couldn't spell, he graduated from the University of Colorado and won a scholarship to obtain his MBA in finance from Northwestern University. Harry Anderson, TV's Judge Stone on "Night Court" each week, grew up on the streets learning card games and magic. He then conned and charmed his way through school. He was called brilliant in his early school years when large pictures accompany schoolbook texts. At age 16 he was Valedictorian at a Hollywood high school and only he knew that he could barely read!

THE MASK OF FANTASY

"I'm going to be a millionaire by 30! . . . The world will understand me soon." "I'll have a Ph.D. once I learn to read."

Characterized by a fertile imagination and, often, a great deal of creativity, this person tends to live more in his hopes and fantasies than with the daily frustrations. Hans Christian Anderson failed to learn to read and write even with the help of ten royal tutors of the Danish Court. He dictated his wonderful fairy tales to a scribe. His suffering came through in stories like "The Ugly Duckling." His mask protected him from continual pain. It is said that even at age 66 he woke up with nightmares of a schoolmaster trying to teach him to read.

Think of the energy spent on hiding, on masking the feeling of being stupid. It's an elaborate subterfuge that ends up making the person feel even worse about himself. The mask protects but, also it isolates a person from others. Often, it interferes with being able to learn.

The masks can be reduced or dropped when a certain comfort level has been achieved, when a person realizes he is not unintelligent, but learning disabled. There is enormous relief that comes from knowing what you know, knowing what you don't know and understanding why you don't know it.

In my mind, the purpose of research is to improve the quality of human life. What learning disabled adults have to say about their masks, heightens the need for all educators to reach children in the early years, identify those having trouble learning before they need to put on the masks, and teach them in ways they can succeed! This is my mission in teacher education!

· ·

HOW TO UNDERSTAND AND HELP STUDENTS WHO ARE SILENT AND DO NOT TALK IN SCHOOL · · · · · · · · · ·

Teachers have been telling their students to be quiet and stop talking since the days of the one-room schoolhouse. Silence is still honored in many classrooms because talking is correlated with disruption and classroom disruption is correlated with low academic achievement. Historically, students who sat at their desks quietly and completed their lessons were rated as the "good students," the ones to be emulated. At the extreme end of these "good students" is a small group of students who are mute or rarely talk in school. They come to class, never volunteer, complete their assignments, have no friends, are lonely, and are troubled by the demands in their life. A closer look at these students reveals that their decision to be silent is not a healthy response to classroom life, but a symptom of an underlying problem. A word of warning: not all children who are quiet or shy are troubled. There is a difference between being alone and being lonely. A characteristic of a healthy student is his or her ability to enjoy peaceful, quiet times without feeling lonely. The troubled student can feel lonely even when surrounded by peers. The difference between these two students lies in the content of their thoughts. Both students can be observed to be silent, but this does not mean they are not thinking. The stream of consciousness is bombarding each of them with endless thoughts and messages. For the troubled student, listening to the thoughts and messages frequently causes feelings of anxiety, fearfulness, and preoccupation with upsetting fantasies. Withdrawal from social interaction and nonverbal behavior are not functions of developmental shyness; they reflect feelings of being unacceptable and worthless to significant adults.

The next article, *Understanding and Helping Children Who Do Not Talk in School*, was written by Ralph Gemelli, a child psychiatrist who trained at Rose School, a psychoeducational day treatment center. Most of the students attending this school were aggressive, street-wise, and verbal. A few students were withdrawn, reluctant to talk, or selectively mute in school. Dr. Gemelli found these students fascinating and decided to study them.

His article provides teachers with helpful information regarding the developmental stages of speech, four underlying reasons why students do not talk, and four specific recommendations to help these nonverbal students. This article also highlights another important concept: *The same student behavior, silence, can be caused by different, underlying problems.* The corollary statement is also true: *Different, underlying causes can be expressed in the same behavior.* Once again, the complexity of student behavior is identified and the need for greater understanding is validated.

ARTICLE 6.2

Understanding and Helping Children Who Do Not Talk in School

Ralph J. Gemelli

A DEVELOPMENTAL APPROACH TO UNDERSTANDING THE MEANINGS OF SPEECH

Speech Brings Love and a Sense of Being Valued

When a toddler begins his first vocalizations, all of his language is initially the language of others, most commonly the toddler's parents. In one view, every toddler is given the gift of speech by his parents and, in time, learns that to "give back" the words he has learned brings love and admiration from them.

Through his parents' speech, the child is responded to in a unique way, and hence through speech *his unique sense of self begins to develop.* In time, the developing child learns that speech is one of the *principal socially accepted ways of both receiving feedback about his uniqueness and his performances and of exhibiting his newly developing sense of being a separate self.* He learns that his words are valued and that they are responded to by his parents with love and support. As Helen Ross (1977) stated, "In the loved and responded to child, verbal communication and love begin to become synonymous."

Speech Brings Relief from Frustration Which Facilitates a Sense of Mastery of the Environment

The developing child, in responding to his inner world (e.g., hunger) or his outer world (e.g., a stranger), reaches out through speech to relieve anxiety. When these signals are answered by an empathetic mother and/or father, the child begins to equate the *activity of verbal communications with both a method of achieving relief from distress and a way of mastering his body as well as the environment. Speaking becomes a way of signaling distress* that the child learns will produce results; speech will produce responses from his parents that will take the distress away or at least lessen

---

it significantly. When speech brings positive responses from his parents, the child begins to believe in the power, importance, and value of his words in influencing others and asking others to help him with his daily struggles and worries.

Speech Becomes a Facilitator of Developing Independence

When the child's first words and initial sentences are being spoken around age two, the child is in the midst of developing an internal image of his parents as basically good and protective. He "uses" this image, calls on it, for example, when he is left with the baby-sitter. He waits without overwhelming anxiety, remembers his parents as "good," and begins to listen to and trust their words that told him "We will be back later." *Words,* for the developing child, function in one sense then *as a means of tolerating separations and assist the individuation process.* As Eveloff (1971) hypothesizes, "the process of individuation both stimulates language development and reflects it." In other words, the individuating and separating child is encouraged to speak, to talk about his experiences and verbalize the worries he has about exploring and being away from his parents. At the same time, however, the degree of individuation and development of a sense of separateness in the child is reflected in the child's ability to produce speech to verbalize his needs, worries, and frustrations.

Speech Becomes a Means to Control and Understand Feelings

As speech develops, the child desires to verbalize what he perceives with his senses. When the child perceives and experiences feelings within himself, before he can verbalize the correct word for a feeling, his parents must correctly perceive the specific feeling state in the child. When they decode their child's behavior as sad and tell the child "You are sad right now," the child not only is given the correct word label for his inner feeling state but also is given permission to verbalize this word label—sad.

In order for speech to help the child control and modulate his feelings, Furman (1978) outlines a process in which feelings are initially dominated by action expression. That is, when angry, the child hits or runs, etc. *Dominance of action gives way to dominance of speech* when the child learns that he can control his feelings by putting them into words. He is told "You can say you are angry at your brother but you can't hit him." With increasing ability to verbalize feelings, the child slowly develops his ability to delay immediate gratification of a feeling. For example, a seven year old boy who was developing dominance of speech over action told his teacher he was angry at another boy and wanted to hit him. The teacher reminded him he couldn't hit in school. By the time recess arrived, the boy had used the time to think and subsequently decided on racing instead of hitting him. In delaying action (hitting) he was able to consider different options, that is, more socially acceptable ways of expressing angry feelings.

Ability to verbalize feelings also helps the child to develop the capacity to figure out why he is feeling a certain way in a particular situation. For example, a seven year old girl sat alone at a picnic. Her mother sensed her sadness and encouraged her to talk about her sad feelings by saying, "You look sad, tell me why?" The girl responded, "Because I want to play with my friends and Dad told me this morning that this is a new big park and that I should watch you and take care of you at the picnic." Mother smiled and explained to her that Dad was only encouraging her to be a big girl and help Mom if she needed help. She didn't have to worry about Mom, and she could go play with her friends. Her daughter smiled, looked relieved, and went to play with her friends.

FOUR REASONS WHY CHILDREN DON'T SPEAK IN SCHOOL

The Unloved and Unvalued Child

The child who has parents who do not value him in any significant way enters the world of peers and school with excessive worry about offering or presenting himself to others. He is afraid that what he offers of himself will not be valued. Eric Erikson (1959) spoke of the developmental psychosocial task of the child of about six or seven. When grade school begins, the child struggles to attain *a sense of industry*. This is the ability *to produce among his peers,* and the child's words are his major production. When the unloved and unvalued child is asked by his teacher to produce words, he becomes *anxious* because he expects his words will not be welcomed, bring approval, or be seen as valued. He then will hide this anxiety by developing an outer shell in the form of shyness, or dumbness, or disinterest. In some children, stuttering will develop as the child's outer shell or defense to hide his anxiety about producing for others (Gemelli, 1982). In a graphic manner, stuttering becomes a visible expression of his conflict of wanting to give his words and, at the same time, wanting to hold them back. He wants the love and admiration of his teacher but is afraid his teacher will not value the words he produces. As a result, these children withdraw from any lesson or activity that involves talking.

The Anxious and/or Shocked Child

Every child has a threshold of how much tension and anxiety the child can tolerate *and still be able to speak.* The normal child learns that signaling his parents through speech brings responses from them that reduce his level of stress. Consequently, once speech has become a trusted signal of distress, the child will use words to communicate what is making him anxious, what is or has scared him, and what he wants his parents or his teacher to do at the moment. However, even the child who uses words as a distress signal has a limit to how much tension and anxiety he can tolerate. When he reaches his limit, he may regress to an earlier stage of development. As a result, speech is given up, and the child communicates his anxiety in other ways. For example, an eight year old girl used speech when anxious and communicated well to her teacher. Her father was killed suddenly when she was five years old. She adjusted reasonably well after his death and could speak about her father with fond memories. One day she arrived at school to find that the gerbils she cared for had been smothered under a towel and had died. She cried and told her teacher how sad and frightened she was that someone would kill her gerbils. That afternoon while she waited for her mother at her usual place outside school, the principal took her to her office to tell her that her mother had a car accident and was in the hospital but that she was doing fine. This day now had become too filled with loss, both real death (the gerbils) and the threat of possible death (her mother). She couldn't speak when the principal and her teacher told her it was okay to talk about how she felt. She could only cry for her favorite doll at home and whimpered that she wanted to be with her mother. Otherwise she refused to talk. She was too afraid to continue to be an eight year old; she was too afraid to put into words, to hear herself say what she was most afraid of, i.e., that her mother might really die just like her father had suddenly died 3 years before.

The Overprotected or Abused Child

The child's gradual development of a sense of autonomy (Erikson, 1959) and separateness is mediated and fueled by the child's development of speech. Separations from mother and father and other caretakers gradually are associated with less separation anxiety when the child is able, for example, to tell mother where he is going and what he will do, and mother tells him it's all right and that she will listen to what he tells her when he returns.

The parent who reacts with tension or sadness when the child says he wants to play at a friend's house communicates to her child that she needs to overprotect him, and that something bad might happen if he leaves her. Subsequently, this child's *words of wanting to leave mother* are sensed by the child as *an attack on mother.* After some time, this child may equate *speaking in general as a non-gratifying activity,* as an activity that causes mother and others to become upset, anxious, or depressed.

Similarly, the parent who is physically and/or emotionally abusive to a child produces in this child a beginning mental image of the parent as someone who is not to be trusted and not available to soothe if a sudden danger arises. This child will not view speaking as a way of announcing and sharing his explorations of the world away from his parent. To speak up could result in physical harm.

The child with an overprotective or abusive parent amazingly does not avoid the parents but tends to cling to them in an intense manner. This child cannot tolerate a mental image of his parents as being bad because this creates unbearable anxiety. A "bad" parent is never available, etc. Instead, the child takes the badness onto himself and thinks of himself as bad and unlovable and consequently clings fiercely to his "good" parents. Such a child will abandon speech because he feels valueless and unlovable, and therefore expects that his speech—his verbal productions—will be ignored and unvalued (which often in reality they have been by his parents) or reacted to in a hostile way.

The Angry or Sad Child

All children when excessively angry or very sad may withhold their speech. The angry child wants to retaliate in some way, and if he senses that people want him to talk, he may refuse to speak as one manifestation of an "inner" temper tantrum. The child, however, who has just experienced the loss of someone or something of value will experience sad feelings. If the sadness is excessive, the child needs to withdraw and will not have the energy to engage in speaking with his teacher or his friends. He will often want to remain in school, but his energy level is low and he asks to be allowed to be quiet.

There are, however, other children who almost never talk when they are angry or sad. These children must be given the correct word labels for their different feelings, and permission by their parents to talk about these feelings. The parents can only do this when they can tolerate the same feelings in themselves and talk about them. For example, what if a mother says she is sad, then withdraws into a chair for hours? What if a mother looks sad but verbally denies she is sad while criticizing and nagging her child. For example, in an interview with the parents of a seven year old boy, I was asked to evaluate psychiatrically this child's listlessness in class, poor motivation, and unwillingness to talk in school. In the child psychiatry playroom he denied any feelings of sadness. In the interview with his parents, I stated that his mother looked sad. Father suddenly stated harshly, with much anger, "In my family no one gets sad, there is no time for sadness, it's just not allowed!" He then roughly grabbed his wife's arm and led her out of the room. He stated that he would only return if I called to apologize for "encouraging my wife to become sad and feel sorry for herself."

When the son of these parents stated that he was never sad, he believed it. *He had stopped perceiving within himself his sad feelings,* because to become aware of his sadness left him with a feeling that brought an angry attack from his father, and now also his mother. Incredibly his teacher could emphatically sense this boy's sadness, but when she told him he looked sad he reacted, much like his father had, as if he were being attacked by the teacher. On one occasion when his teacher said "You look sad, why don't you tell me about it," he responded with, "I don't get sad, it's wrong to be sad, I'm not sad, I don't feel sad, you say I'm sad when you want to say I'm bad."

WHAT THE TEACHER CAN DO FOR THE STUDENT WHO IS NOT TALKING

Four recommendations are offered which may help the teacher formulate a helping plan for these children. The child who periodically does not talk is somewhat easier to help than the child who is almost continually unwilling or unable to speak. For this latter group, an evaluation by a speech-language pathologist and a child psychiatrist should be arranged. Regardless of the diagnosis, if the child remains in class, the following recommendations will help these silent children to talk more in school.

Recommendation No. 1. Suggest to the child that he has good reasons of his own, from his own point of view, for not wanting to talk. Tell the child that if he can talk about his reasons for not wanting to talk, he might learn what is frightening him about talking. He might then reveal his fear that his words are "not smart enough," or that the teacher will not like him despite what he says, etc.

For example, the child who has grown up in a family where his words have never received much attention or positive feedback initially will not believe his teacher when she tells him, "*I'd* like to hear what you have to say about what just happened in the school yard." The teacher must convey the message that she realizes the child wants to talk, but doesn't want to talk because he expects the teacher not to be interested. The child, however, in time will sense the teacher's empathy for his conflict. On the teacher's side is the developmental force present in all children to interact and engage with new people. With time, children are people seekers. This is a major reason why some children with unloving, abusing, or hateful parents will nevertheless develop good self-esteem through their emotional interaction with teachers, coaches, relatives, and other adults. Once this process is set into motion, the teacher provides the conditions that permit the child to have the gift of speech. The child will accept this gift slowly and hesitantly because once before the child, after being given "the gift of speech" by his parents, discovered that his use of this gift was fraught with anxiety, conflict, and shame.

Recommendation No. 2. Allow yourself to empathize with the child. Allow yourself to observe how you feel in the child's presence in order to become aware of the feeling(s) the child is experiencing but unable or unwilling to put into words. For example, the sad non-talking child will produce a similar feeling of sadness in the empathic teacher.

Once the teacher senses a feeling the child is not talking about, it is useful for the teacher to tell the child, "*I* know you think it won't help or make you feel better if you tell me how sad you feel, but you'll have to take a chance to see what happens. If you give talking a try, you'll feel better and the feelings you have inside won't feel so scary or make you feel you are not a nice boy." When the teacher speaks in this manner to a child, she must be prepared to be suddenly perceived by the child as a "reincarnation" of one of the child's parents. The child may say, for example, "*I* don't believe you; I know you'll yell at me if I tell you I'm sad." At that moment the child is mis-perceiving the teacher as being the reincarnation of his mother. His mother did indeed yell at him when he spoke of being sad. If the teacher is aware of the "transference" of fears and feelings associated with mother onto the teacher, the teacher will not respond to the child's view of the teacher as a personal attack. In time, the child may indeed take a chance and talk to the teacher despite his fear that the teacher will yell at him the way his mother often did.

Recommendation No. 3. Encourage and suggest to the child that she can communicate in other ways other than through speech. A child not speaking can be asked to "draw a picture that tells a story about children at school," etc. Another useful technique is to engage the child in some form of play. While playing with the teacher, some children will feel less pressure to produce speech. In play, the child will often communicate a message about what conflict the child is experiencing about talking.

For example, a seven year old girl came to school looking upset and angry. She would not talk about what was wrong or how she felt. Her teacher at recess spent a quiet time with the child encouraging her to play in the corner of the classroom where dolls and puppets were kept. While holding a doll the little girl stated, "My baby had a hard time making up her mind; if she could make up her mind she would be happier. I want her to talk to me, but she can't make up her mind to talk to me or not talk to me." The teacher later found out from the child's mother that the girl had been recently nagging and clinging to her mother because her mother was spending a great deal of time with this little girl's new baby sister. Her mother admitted that she had not been able to give her seven year old much time lately and didn't find talking to her a joy but more of a chore and responsibility.

Recommendation No. 4. Ask yourself, and then decide, if you are able and/or willing to give to the non-talking child a little more attention, patience, feed-back, and kindness. This recommendation is listed to emphasize what observational data from child research tells us. Speech unfolding follows, more or less, a maturational sequence, but speech blossoms through the child's loving interaction with his caretakers. When the child's caretakers, usually the child's parents, fail the child in all the functions listed earlier in this paper, the child's speech is in great jeopardy. A recrudescence of speech development can often only take place through the child's close interaction with an empathic and admiring adult who can accept the child's productions, of which speech is only one, but a very crucial, production of childhood. Perhaps one of the most gratifying experiences for a teacher is helping a non-talking child to talk. When this occurs, the child begins to blossom in many other areas of development because speech is not only very highly valued in our culture, but through speech children learn, adapt, and build positive self-esteem.

SUMMARY

Children need and want to talk. It is their way of reaching out and relating to others. With some children their feelings are so intense that they retreat into a world of silence. Teachers can play a significant role in identifying these students, developing trusting relationships, referring them to helping professionals, and supporting their team program.

REFERENCES

Erikson, E. Identity and the life cycle. *Psycho-logical Issues,* 1959, 1, 101–172.

Eveloff, H. Some cognitive and affectlye affects of early language development. *Child Development,* 1971, 1895–1907.

Furman, R. Some developmental aspects of the verbalization of affects. *Psychoanalytic Study of the Child,* 1978, 187–213.

Gemelli, R. Classification of child stuttering: Part I. Transient developmental, neuro-genic acquired, and persistent child stuttering. *Child Psychiatry and Human Development,* 1982, *12* (4), 220–253.

Richmond, M. Personal communication, 1976.

Ross, Helen. Personal communication, 1977.

. . . .

HOW TO UNDERSTAND AND HELP THE ANTISOCIAL OR AGGRESSIVE STUDENT . . . .

Antisocial or aggressive behavior among students has increased significantly over the past ten years. The frequency and intensity of student aggression have led to popular use of the phrase "school violence," which is a generic and not a diagnostic term. School violence also continues to be a popular and appealing topic for special television shows, radio talk shows, endless newspaper articles, and national conferences. Most of these media programs are advertised as Violence Prevention Programs, but their underlying intent is to shock the audience with the latest and most frightening statistics about school violence. Schools are portrayed as intimidating Blackboard jungles populated with roaming street-wise delinquents organized in gangs, armed with guns, and confronted by naive and ineffective teachers. John Wayne-like principals might be wielding a baseball bat and using a cellular communication system as they walk through dimly lighted halls.

These media messages rarely provide in-depth understanding of the nature of anger in students, but they do succeed in stirring up strong adult feelings of helplessness and counteraggression. They describe spontaneous fights between students as a potential life-threatening school event. "Fights no longer consist of name calling, verbal threats, and shoving, but quickly escalate into physical assault and the use of lethal weapons, and the switchblade has been replaced by the 9mm gun as the weapon of choice."

A recent media study of the New York City public schools reported a 35% increase in the number of reported student assaults over a five-year period, and identified junior high school students as the most likely targets of a peer assault. During this same period of time, acts of larceny against other students increased 24%, and the number of reported attempted and actual school rapes escalated. As if these figures were not shocking enough to upset law-abiding citizens, the study also reported a substantial increase in the number of teacher assaults by students and circulated a new diagnostic term: "battered teacher syndrome." This syndrome was described as being similar to battered spouse syndrome because of its concomitant feelings of anxiety, sleep problems, physical ailments, and depression. This medical condition was viewed as a painful example of the deteriorating role of teacher authority and the impulsive behavior of angry students. Undeserved teacher assaults do happen, but we have observed some battered teachers who clearly lacked the skills to deescalate an angry student and inadvertently fueled the attack.

Another way of dramatizing school violence is to document the national increase in school vandalism. Broken windows; damaged lockers, walls, and ceilings; trashed classrooms and bathrooms; and destroyed school equipment are all examples of malicious vandalism and expressions of students' anger. The economic costs to taxpayers of repairing and replacing damaged or destroyed school property has reached multimillion-dollar figures. This money could have been used to build more effective educational programs; instead, it was needed to repair and replace school buildings and equipment. School vandalism is used as a powerful illustration of how angry students displace their hostility toward schools in a blatant and destructive way.

We do not deny that antisocial student behaviors have increased in select schools and are a concern of students, staff, and parents. If one's only source of information is TV talk shows or the tabloid news stories, it appears America is preoccupied with school violence. However, we do not believe antisocial student behaviors are out of control, unmanageable, or unsolvable. Aggressive behaviors toward students, staff, and property can be stopped, controlled, and prevented. Contrary to media hype, American schools are basically a normal civilized place.

The problem of student violence is complicated and distorted by lack of accurate and useful information regarding the nature and expression of student anger and staff counteraggression. When students behave aggressively, teachers can spend too much time trying to decide *who* is right in this conflict instead of judging *what* is the right thing to do professionally.

Teachers are not to be blamed or to be made the professional scapegoats for the rise of aggression in schools. Most teachers have not received adequate training in anger management and, without it, teachers are forced to act like firefighters trying to put out a blaze without having an adequate water supply. To be successful in a volatile situation, teachers need many resources and intervention skills.

We believe teachers need to understand the nature of anger, the difference between angry feelings and antisocial behaviors, how their counteraggressive feelings can escalate an aggressive student incident, what short- and long-term teaching strategies are effective in deescalating antisocial behaviors, and how to help students learn more appropriate ways of expressing their anger. To begin this discussion, a brief summary of basic terms, concepts, and strategies is presented.

WHAT ARE THE DIFFERENCES AMONG FEELINGS OF ANGER, HATE, AND RAGE?

Anger is a temporary internal neurophysiological feeling or an emotional state triggered by how one thinks about life events that are perceived as frustrating, painful, and fearful. Anger can have a rational or irrational base. It can be triggered by an accurate perception or a misperception of a life event. The feeling of anger exists in all persons as an automatic survival response, as a learned habit, and as a personal choice. Anger is always a feeling and should not be confused with aggression. Aggression is a behavior and is only one of several ways anger can be expressed.

Hate is an internal neurophysiological feeling and is a more intense and focused state of anger. Hate is like frozen anger that rarely melts. Hate usually has a specific target and develops when love has become bitter or when one is betrayed by a friend or group. Unfortunately, hate is contagious and easy to pass on from one generation to the next or from one group to another. Religious, racial, ethnic, and national conflicts and wars are examples of what can happen when hate is taught to others, and how others can internalize a feeling of hatred toward another group without ever having any reality experiences with that group. Hate is deliberate, identifiable, and unresponsive to logic or rational thinking. Hate is a feeling and should not be confused with hostility, which is a behavior.

Rage is an explosive feeling of uncontrollable anger or hate. It is a final response to overwhelming frustrations and feelings of helplessness. Rage hides behind the feelings of helplessness and is the biological beast or primitive feeling that exists in all of us. Rage is mindless, runaway anger. It serves as the high-octane fuel for violent and destructive behaviors.

Anger, hate, and rage are all internal feelings and should be distinguished from their corresponding behaviors of aggression, hostility, and violence.

WHAT TRIGGERS FEELINGS OF ANGER IN STUDENTS? . . .

Anger in students is triggered by the way they have learned to think about specific life events and by the subsequent negative thoughts they have. If they fail an exam, are rejected or criticized, or lose an object, they might send themselves negative messages such as: "This is unfair! I have been gypped! No one should treat me like this! I will never let anyone know about my limitations! This is hopeless! I will get back at you! People are making fun of me!" When these negative messages occur, students end up feeling the way they think.

The following 12 conditions, emotional needs, fears, events, and re-actions have been documented to trigger in students negative thoughts that result in angry feelings.

1. Student anger can be triggered by altered states. The use of alcohol, marijuana, amphetamines, barbiturates, heroin, and opium has the physiological effect of dissolving the rational part of the mind and causing altered states of reality. The student's ability to misperceive a normal event as a threatening one or to have a delusional experience can create angry feelings.

2. Student anger can be triggered by mental illnesses such as psychotic conditions that result in altered perceptions of reality, active negative thoughts, and angry feelings.

3. Student anger can be triggered by brain trauma and dysfunction. Only an intact and sober brain can perceive and think rationally and sort out the differences between real and imaginary threats. Dr. Hunt, a research psychiatrist, observed that in children who have prefrontal cortical deficits, the slightest irritation can cause intense feelings of anger or rage.

4. Student anger can be triggered by personal frustration ranging in de-gree and intensity from dropping a pencil to experiencing over-whelming and multiple physical, psychological, and reality stresses that bring on feelings of helplessness, anger, and rage. Personal frus-trations are probably the most frequent triggering events that result in negative thoughts and angry feelings.

5. Student anger can be triggered by a need for attention. As Dreikur pointed out in his concept of A.G.M. (attention-getting mechanisms), some students decide it is more effective to act up and receive nega-tive attention than to be ignored or neglected.

6. Student anger can be triggered by a need to maintain group power and status or to respond to group pressure. Some students' anger is triggered more often by their group role and the dynamics of the group, such as a group contagion or group scapegoating, than by in-dividual forces.

7. Student anger can be triggered by a need to be punished. Students who are abused, deprived, and abandoned commonly have blamed themselves for their emotional plight. They may use emotional reasoning that says, "Bad things happen to me because I'm a bad person. Bad people need to be punished. When I do bad things, I need to be punished." These students will almost always succeed in being punished if they act aggressively and violate class rules by cheating, stealing, and fighting.

8. Student anger can be triggered as a defense against failure. A psychological defense is one way a student can protect against experiencing a painful feeling. Some of our troubled students will become angry and disrupt the learning process or argue with the teacher as a way of avoiding their fear of impending failure. The article by Sally Smith (p. 318) describes how this feeling of failure can be acted out in various ways, including antisocial behavior.

9. Student anger can be triggered as a defense against closeness. Some of our troubled students have been so traumatized by their primary adult relationships that any new nurturing adult relationship triggers their fear of closeness. To trust someone means they will become vulnerable to more rejection. The solution is to respond to interpersonal acceptance by becoming angry and oppositional.

10. Student anger can be triggered as a defense against sadness and depression. Many children find it difficult to acknowledge their sad or depressed feelings. They have discovered that they can mask their feelings of depression by becoming angry and aggressive. In a study of incarcerated delinquent youth, one-third of the sample group were diagnosed as having an underlying diagnosis of depression and all of them were involved in antisocial behaviors. Acting out one's angry feelings is easier than talking about one's feelings of sadness.

11. Student anger can be triggered as a reaction to watching violent movies, television shows, and sporting events. The visual stimulation of observing violent acts of vandalism, extortion, torture, sexual perversion, murder, and the excitement of the home team's winning or losing a game can create vicarious experiences and overstimulation that trigger angry feelings and riotous behavior.

12. Student anger can be triggered by feelings of revenge. This anger, triggered by a conscious choice to get back at the hated person or group, probably represents the most heinous expression of hate.

These twelve conditions, needs, psychological defenses, reactions to frustration and overstimulating events represent the most common motivations of angry feelings in students.

HOW ARE THE FEELINGS OF ANGER, HATE, AND RAGE EXPRESSED IN BEHAVIOR? . . . .

Feelings of anger can be expressed in three different ways: (a) as overt behavior in the forms of aggression, (b) as covert behavior, for example, passive aggression, in which the feelings of anger are masked and indirect, or (c) as a reaction to be swallowed and turned inward, resulting in psychosomatic illnesses, pain, rashes, and so on.

For our purposes, it is important to understand the differences among aggressive behavior, hostile behavior, and violent behavior.

Aggressive Behavior . . . .

Aggressive behavior, an unplanned spontaneous expression of anger, is most frequently triggered by stressful life events or personal frustrations. Aggressive behavior is usually the result of a sudden impulse breakthrough or a loss of self-control skills. Often, students are not aware of their aggressive behavior until they hear themselves shout, swear, slam a book down, run out of a room, or hit someone. After an aggressive outburst, some students feel guilty about their behavior and redirect their anger into self-punishment. Other students find ways of rationalizing or justifying their aggressive behavior by saying, "He started it," or "I was only defending myself." Student aggression is the most frequent expression of anger and is the easiest to modify and prevent.

Hostile Behavior . . . .

Hostile behavior is characterized as a deliberate expression of hate. It is evidenced in conscious, calculated acts of revenge that are thoughtfully planned to intimidate, injure, or hurt a person or to take, steal, or destroy specific properties. Hostile behavior is not a function of an impulse breakthrough or a loss of self-control. It is cruel behavior directed at a particular person, group, or country. The bombing of the federal building in Oklahoma City is an example of hostile behavior. Gang wars and targeted killings are all forms of hostility, not aggression. War is always an act of hostility, not an act of aggression.

Violence . . . .

Violent behavior is anger and hate that have gone out of control and turned into rage. All expressions of rage are violent and mindless. Violence is like a volcano that has erupted. Everyone in its path will be hurt. Violent behavior does not discriminate between friends or foes and it often results in hurting, injuring, or killing everyone in the target area.

This section has described the differences among aggressive, hostile, and violent behavior. These differences are diagnostically important because certain intervention strategies that are effective in controlling student aggression are not effective in controlling hostile or violent behaviors.

UNDERSTANDING THE DYNAMICS OF
STUDENT AGGRESSION

Although aggressive behavior is driven by anger and triggered by many different causes, the dynamics of aggression are predictable. An aggressive student has never learned to tolerate normal amounts of frustration, disappointment, or anxiety. Instead of owning these feelings, the student gives them away by attacking or depreciating everyone in sight. The student knows how to engage staff by using provocative words and/or actions that upset them. While the aggressive behavior reduces the internal level of anxiety, the impulsive behavior simultaneously creates normal counteraggressive feelings among the staff. If the staff are not trained to understand the dynamics of aggression, they not only will pick up the student's aggressive feelings but will match them with similar counteraggressive reactions, thus escalating the aggressive conflict. For example, when a student shouts, "I'm not going to do it! Don't you hear me?!" and a staff member shouts back, "Yeah, you will! Do you hear me?!" the response is counteraggressive. By mirroring the student's behavior, the response creates more psychological stress for the student. The student's angry feelings become more intense, and his or her behavior becomes more primitive. At this point, the staff member and student become locked in a power struggle, and the problem escalates. What is surprising about the dynamics of aggression is that, even if the student loses the power struggle and is suspended or physically restrained, the aggressive student's basic assumptions that adults are hostile and that he or she has a right to be angry or "to get even" are reinforced. There are no winners in a power struggle with aggressive students.

The staff's psychological position, however, is complicated by the fact that staff anger seems entirely justified, and this seems like an ideal time to teach this arrogant, aggressive student a "lesson."

If the staff acts out these feelings, does what comes naturally, and decides "to take the student on" by returning a verbal attack, then the staff will perpetuate the aggressive cycle. The statement "Aggression elicits counteraggression" becomes true, and the aggressive student has been successful in controlling the staff's behavior.

Insight occurs when the staff begins to understand the nature of this aggressive cycle and realizes that an aggressive response by staff is only going to make a bad situation worse. To continue any counteraggressive behavior with an aggressive student is self-defeating. To break this cycle, the staff must make a conscious decision to break off the fight, disconnect from the struggle, and abandon feelings of righteous rage, primitive revenge, and an infantile wish to win.

BASIC CONCEPTS ESSENTIAL TO MANAGING AGGRESSIVE STUDENT BEHAVIOR . . . .

The following list describes important concepts that are basic to managing aggressive student behavior.

1. A knowledge of the dynamics of aggression raises staff consciousness about conflict; staff will know in advance that a student in stress will create in them normal counteraggressive feelings. "To be forewarned is to be forearmed."

2. A knowledge of the dynamics of aggression enables staff to accept and "own" their counteraggressive feelings toward a student and to use them as useful information regarding the student's feelings.

3. A knowledge of the dynamics of aggression enables staff not to act on their counteraggressive feelings. Personal insight comes when staff can say "yes" to acknowledging their angry feelings and "no" to the expression of their counteraggressive feelings in behaviors. Thus, both parts of their life (the intrapsychic and emotional part, and the behavioral, rational, and overt part) can live in harmony.

4. A knowledge of the dynamics of aggression helps staff to choose not to join in a power struggle with a student. (A conscious choice is made: "I will not fight with you.")

5. A knowledge of the dynamics of aggression helps staff to stop all "you" messages, which escalate the aggressive cycle (i.e., "You apologize" "You'd better use your head").

6. A knowledge of the dynamics of aggression helps staff to use "I" messages as a way of expressing their feelings while reducing the pressure of a "double struggle" (controlling one's own feelings and avoiding loss of self-control while simultaneously trying to manage the aggressive student's inappropriate behaviors).

7. A knowledge of the dynamics of aggression helps staff to focus their energies on what a student needs instead of on what staff members are feeling.

8. A knowledge of the dynamics of aggression helps staff remember that although feelings are real and powerful, they may not reflect an accurate assessment of any aggressive conflict. Feelings are not rational functions and should not be used to determine what is helpful to a student at a particular time.

9. A knowledge of the dynamics of aggression enables staff to decode aggressive behavior into the student's angry feelings.

10. A knowledge of the dynamics of aggression enables staff to help an aggressive student connect the inappropriate behavior and angry feelings with the original stressful incident or life event.

SPECIFIC GUIDELINES FOR MANAGING AGGRESSIVE STUDENT BEHAVIOR . . . .

Once a staff member has successfully controlled his or her counteraggressive behaviors and has substituted "I" messages for "you" messages, the staff can focus on the student's needs by responding to the aggressive behavior as an opportunity to protect, model, and teach.

- Begin by using the various strategies for reducing inappropriate behaviors (see Fagen's article, page 273).
- State clearly and firmly the positive, expected behaviors.
- Accept the student's angry feelings but not the aggressive behavior.
- Refer to specific classroom rules that are appropriate for aggressive behavior.
- Encourage the student to make a good decision to solve this problem.
- Make sure the student, not the staff, is responsible for the choice of behavior.
- If the student's behavior improves, affirm the efforts made (e.g., "That was a difficult choice to make, but you made the right decision this time!").
- If the aggressive behavior does not improve, intervene quickly with a time-out or a stated logical consequence for the aggressive behavior.
- Explain the reasons (or values) why the staff had to stop the behavior (e.g., "My job is to protect the learning process. Your behavior was interfering with classroom learning so I had to stop it.").
- If possible, set up with the student a behavioral contract that reinforces the expected behavior. Make the conflict a learning experience.

These guidelines are offered as immediate strategies for managing aggressive behavior. The long-term goal is to teach students acceptable ways of expressing their angry feelings using appropriate social skills.

Eggert and Nicholas (1996) have developed a Personal Growth Class Program that includes teaching troubled students and staff a cognitive self-talk strategy for controlling their anger. A brief excerpt of this approach is included here to demonstrate this important skill.

A STRATEGY OF USING SELF-TALK AS A WAY OF CONTROLLING STAFF ANGER . . . .

Preparing for Anger Triggers: Things That Push My Button . . . .

This is going to be upsetting, but I can handle it. This doesn't have to be a catastrophe. Stop! Figure out what I have to do . . . work out a plan. I can manage this. I know how to control my anger. I'll know what to do if I find myself getting upset . . . relax, take a deep breath, remember my plan. Don't overreact. Don't blow this out of proportion. This could be a sticky situation, but I believe in myself. . . . Feel comfortable, relaxed, at ease. Easy does it. Remember to keep your sense of humor. Easy does it. Remember your lines.

When Confronted: When My Button Is Pushed . . . .

Stop! Stay calm. Think! Don't jump to conclusions. . . . Count to ten. Don't blow things out of proportion. So it hurts! There's no use stretching it into an AWFUL, DREADFUL, TERRIBLE situation. As long as I keep my cool, I'm in control. Don't get bent out of shape. Stick with the plan. You don't need to prove yourself. You know you're OK. There is no point in getting out of control. Don't make more of this than you have to. Look for the positives. Don't assume the worst. If I start to get mad, I'll just be banging my head against the wall. So I might as well just relax. There is no need to doubt myself. I can handle this! I'm on top of the situation and it's under control.

Coping When I'm Already Angry or Starting to Fume . . . .

My muscles are starting to tense. . . . Slow things down. "Catastrophizing" won't help. Think straight! I'm angry . . . that's a signal of what I need to do. Time to instruct myself. Lower the tone, lower the volume, speak slower. Getting upset won't help. It gets me into trouble. Negatives lead to more negatives. Work constructively. Reason it out. Take the issue point by point. Try the cooperative approach. Maybe we're both right. Ask that we treat each other with respect. I can't expect people to act the way I want them to. Take it easy, don't get pushy! Negotiate.

Reflecting: After the Event . . . .

When Conflict Is Unresolved

Forget about it. Thinking about it makes you more upset . . . at a minimum, don't stretch the situation into AWFUL! This is a difficult situation that will take time to heal. Try to shake it off. Don't let it outweigh the positives. Remember relaxation, exercise. It's better than depression. Can you laugh about it? It's probably not so serious! Don't take it personally. You did the best you could . . . better than last time! It takes two to resolve things. You did your part! I'll get better at this with more practice.

When Conflict Is Resolved or Coping Is Successful

I handled that pretty well. It worked! That wasn't as hard as I thought. It could have been a lot worse. Nice going! I could have gotten more upset than it was worth. I actually got through that without "losing my cool!" My pride gets me into trouble, but when I don't "blow it," I'm better off. I guess I've been getting upset for too long when it wasn't even necessary. I'm getting better at this all the time.

WHAT CURRICULUM RESOURCES ARE AVAILABLE TO TEACH ANGER MANAGEMENT, ANGER REPLACEMENT, OR SELF-CONTROL SKILLS TO AGGRESSIVE STUDENTS? . . . .

This curriculum area has attracted our interest and we have reviewed and used the following five curriculum resources:

1. *The Walker Social Skills Curriculum*
   - The ACCEPTS Program: A Curriculum for Children's Effective Peer and Teacher Skills (K–6).
   - The ACCESS Program: Adolescent Curriculum for Communication and Effective Social Skills (Secondary).
   - Walker–McConnell Scale of Social Competence and School Adjustment: A Social Skills Rating Scale for Teachers (K–6).

   Order from: PRO-ED, 8700 Shoal Creek Blvd., Austin, TX 78758-6897.

2. *Della the Dinosaur Talks About Violence and Anger Management* (for elementary students). This curriculum teaches healthy ways of expressing anger and how to contact people to help.

   Order from: Performance Resource Press, 1863 Technology Drive, Troy, MI 48043-4244.

3. *Aggression Replacement Training: A Comprehensive Intervention for Aggressive Youth*, by Arnold P. Goldstein and Barry Glick.

   Order from: Research Press, 2612 North Mattis Avenue, Champaign, IL 61821.

4. *The Self Control Inventory.* This is a positive social skills program organized around five goals: (a) to control impulses, (b) to follow school routines, (c) to manage group situations, (d) to manage stress, (e) to solve social problems. Developed by Martin Henley.

   Order from: Pegasus Center for Enabling Education, P.O. Box 1472, Westfield, MA 01086-1472.

5. *Anger Management for Youth: Stemming Aggression and Violence 1995.* Developed by Leona Eggert. This is an award-winning cognitive

model of teaching anger management in a well-structured small group. The activities are realistic and appealing to small groups of troubled adolescents.

   Order from: National Educational Service, P.O. Box 55, Bloomington, IN 47402.

6. *Personal Growth Class: A Group Approach for Youth 1996.* Developed by Leona Eggert and Lula Nicholas. This personal growth class is a therapeutic program designed to help students reconnect with school and with particular skills to decrease drug involvement, depression, anger, and suicidal risk.

   Order from: National Educational Service, P.O. Box 55, Bloomington, IN 47402.

The goals of these curricula are to help students learn to manage their anger by allowing them to be assertive, to stand up for their beliefs, to resist peer and adult pressure, and to become independent and responsible for their decisions and behaviors without becoming aggressive, hostile, or violent.

In the next article, Hill Walker describes the dramatic rise in aggressive and antisocial student behavior in public schools. He summarizes ten years of continuous observational studies of aggressive and nonaggressive students and provides educators with a comprehensive and accurate understanding of the causal influences, behavioral characteristics, long-term developmental outcomes, and promising intervention with these aggressive and antisocial students.

ARTICLE 6.3

Anti-Social Behavior in School

Hill M. Walker

Antisocial behavior is defined as the persistent violation of social norms and consists of two major types: overt and covert (Patterson, 1982; Kazdin, 1985). Overt forms of antisocial behavior are characterized by antisocial, aggressive acts directed against persons and include verbal or physical assault, oppositional-defiant behavior, use of coercive tactics and humiliation of others. Covert antisocial behavior involves acts committed against property or directed toward the self. These acts, characterized by stealth, involve stealing, lying, drug abuse, and a range of delinquent acts that are difficult to detect.

From *The Journal of Emotional and Behavioral Problems.* (1993). Vol. 2, No. 1. Reprinted with permission.

A relatively small proportion of the antisocial population is considered *versatile* in that, by adolescence, they engage in *both* forms of antisocial behavior. Versatile antisocial children and youth are generally at another level of deviance beyond those who display primarily *overt* or *covert* patterns.

CAUSAL INFLUENCES

Numerous theories exist concerning the exact factors that cause young children to go from antisocial behavior to juvenile delinquency and, finally, to adult criminality (Kazdin, 1985). Patterson and his colleagues have conducted some of the basic work on identifying and validating the family antecedents and correlates of this pattern. They have constructed a social learning theory that persuasively argues that: a) Families that produce antisocial children are characterized by powerful stressors, including divorce, physical abuse, psychological and or sexual abuse, poverty, alcohol and drug abuse, and unemployment. b) These stressors have the effect of disrupting normal parenting practices and family support processes. And c) parents under severe stress do not discipline fairly, consistently, or appropriately; they do not monitor their children's activities, whereabouts, or affiliations; they do not use positive behavior-management techniques of support, encouragement, and praise; they do not spend adequate amounts of time involved in their child's lives; and their problem-solving and conflict resolution skills often are highly ineffective. Further, such parents do not model and teach positive, prosocial forms of behavior to their children. Attitudes toward schooling in such families often are very negative. Most ominously, very antisocial acts committed in the parents' presence are sometimes ignored, thus communicating a message of legitimacy.

These conditions provide a fertile breeding ground for the development and strengthening of antisocial behavior patterns. Discipline in these families is chaotic and often random, which encourages children to play "Russian Roulette" by committing deviant acts that may or may not have consequences. The unsupervised and weakly monitored behavior patterns of these children set the stage for the formation of deviant peer associations within and outside school.

Children whose antisocial behavior occurs at *high rates* across *multiple settings* and who engage in a *diversity* of antisocial acts are extremely vulnerable to rejection by teachers and peers, school failure, and association with deviant peers in middle school. These outcomes greatly increase the student's risk for delinquency and adult criminality.

BEHAVIORAL CHARACTERISTICS

The vast majority of children currently being identified as antisocial are boys. These children, from the first day of school, appear to base their behavior on the aversive control of others. They frequently defy teachers and engage them in escalated interactions that often become explosive. They are masters at provoking adults into fits of anger and rage.

Antisocial children display a singular disinclination to be cooperative; their level of participation in group activities is often low as a result. They usually have below-average profiles on the adaptive, social behavioral competencies that teachers prefer (that is, compliance with teacher instructions, working independently, appropriately making needs for assistance known, and so forth). Instead, they frequently use maladaptive behaviors that are *extremely* upsetting to most teachers (that is, tantrums, defiance, stealing, aggression, and so forth) (see Hersh & Walker, 1983; Walker & Rankin, 1983). Such students are among the least liked by teachers and would be among the first to be referred out of the classroom.

Adults frequently blame antisocial students for their inappropriate behavior patterns. School officials view these students as making a deliberate choice to behave as they do, an assumption many experts strongly question. Consequently, these children and youth often are denied access to needed services and interventions. They are truly the public school system's "homeless street people" in that school professionals avoid assuming responsibility for dealing proactively with the problems they present.

In many instances, great efforts are expended by school systems to ensure that such students do not receive special handicapped certifications and thus do not receive the accompanying legal protections. This denial of certification not only controls costs, but also gives schools more freedom to punish and exclude these students who are not certified. In fact, Slenkovich (1992) has developed a profitable cottage industry around teaching school officials how to use P.L. 94-142 regulations and the diagnostic classification criteria to *decertify* severely, emotionally disturbed students who are suspected of having either conduct disorders or antisocial behavior patterns. With the loss of certification comes a corresponding loss of access to needed support services and interventions which could have substantial benefit for these students.

However, a substantial number of students with antisocial behavior patterns end up being referred and certified anyway, because it is one way to remove them from the educational mainstream. Another convenient avenue for such removal is through placement in home tutoring regimens; SED students represent 9% of the total handicapped population in schools but account for 40% of those receiving home tutoring. As a general rule, antisocial students are likely to be controlled, punished, excluded, and contained through their schooling experiences. While these strategies clearly do not address the students' problems in either an effective or proactive manner, they continue to be practiced.

The peer relationships of antisocial children and youth are equally problematic. They often use coercive tactics in their peer interactions to force the submission of others. They frequently are verbally, and sometimes physically, abusive of peers: they often tease others, but they react very provocatively and angrily to similar taunts by peers. While they tend to have relatively weak interactions with normal peers, they often find a much stronger support system among deviant peers.

Students who are both aggressive *and* rejected by peers are among the most aggressive and least liked in the school setting. Dodge (1983) discovered that when an aggressive, peer-rejected student is placed into a play group with students who have had no previous contact with each other, the play group members show clear signs of rejecting and excluding the antisocial student within less than an hour. These same results were duplicated by Coie and Kupersmidt (1983) in a separate study.

Essentially, these aggressive students encourage peers to reject them and then complain about being victims, even though they are the ultimate victimizers of others. Antisocial students tend to be very sensitive to the operation of social consequences within the school, but they are relatively insensitive to the impact of their own behavior on others. At times, their descriptions of their own behavior can be astonishingly unrealistic. Once, when the author asked an aggressive second-grade boy why he was choking a kindergartner on the playground, the boy was surprised by the question and said, "Well, it was recess!"

It is estimated that 80% percent of criminal acts are committed by youth and adults who have dropped out of school. Antisocial students have highly elevated profiles on the variables that predict subsequent school dropout. These include low achievement, weak school attendance, enrollment in a number of different elementary and middle schools, negative narrative comments by teachers in their school folders, behavioral referrals within and outside school, and discipline contacts with the principal's office (Walker, Block-Pedego, Todis, & Severson, 1991).

LONG-TERM DEVELOPMENTAL OUTCOMES AND PROCESSES

The developmental progression and long-term outcomes associated with antisocial behavior are extremely problematic and negative. They include: *school failure, school dropout, teacher and peer rejection, delinquency, low self-esteem, bad conduct discharges from the military, relationship difficulties, vocational adjustment problems, appearance on community psychiatric registers,* and *higher hospitalization and mortality rates* (Kazdin, 1985). The path through this sequence of outcomes is highly predictable and driven powerfully and directly by a well-established pattern of antisocial behavior.

Standardized measures of intelligence are considered to be among the most stable of human traits, with correlations over a ten-year period ranging consistently in the .60 to .70 range. Highly aggressive, antisocial behavior is approximately as stable as intelligence over a decade, with correlations of approximately .60 to .80 (Quay & Werry, 1986; Reid, 1992). Thus, very aggressive patterns observed early in a child's development are very likely to be in evidence later in their school careers and beyond. This finding is a testament to the difficulties involved in successfully changing aggressive behavior patterns.

The life experiences and causal influences to which such at-risk children are exposed, especially within home and school settings, produce a *very* maladaptive behavior pattern that sets them up for failure in school and, ultimately, in life. These conditions are normative for antisocial children but are very atypical for children who are not at risk. Eventually, antisocial behavior often leads to extremely costly consequences for the individual, their friends, their associates, as well as the larger society.

As a rule, antisocial students list as their best friends other antisocial students in their age/grade cohorts. Beginning in fourth or fifth grade, these children band together and form a deviant peer group that a) provides a strong support system for antisocial behavior and b) teaches skills in committing delinquent acts through modelling and demonstration, coaching, and social approval from deviant peers. Patterson and his associates find that, following acceptance of membership in this peer group, about 60 to 70 percent of antisocial youth experiences at least one felony arrest within two years (Loeber, 1982; 1985; Patterson, Reid, & Dishion, 1992). It is estimated that one arrest occurs for every ten arrestable offenses committed.

Unfortunately, our society's deteriorating social and economic conditions seem to be exacerbating the problem of antisocial behavior. The number of students displaying these behavior patterns is increasing. In some urban settings, antisocial forms of behavior have created police states within school buildings. For example, it recently was noted that 35% of fifth-grade students brought weapons to school in one elementary school in North Carolina (Reid, 1992).

Beginning in 1984, the author began collaborating with Patterson and his associates at the Oregon Social Learning Center in a long-term longitudinal study of boys at risk for antisocial behavior. Two hundred boys who resided in neighborhoods with high rates of police contacts were initially identified. The study then focused on two groups of 40 boys each. Group One had moderate to very high levels of antisocial behavior when selected for participation in the study; Group Two students manifested no or only very minimal levels of antisocial behavior at selection. Both groups were in the fifth grade when selected. The study sought to determine 1) the possibility of predicting which of the antisocial boys would be arrested during adolescence, and 2) the factors that led to their antisocial behavior. Currently, the two groups are completing their high school careers.

Dramatic differences between the two groups, in terms of their school behavior, have emerged over the past eight years. School data, collected on all subjects during the fall and spring, include 1) teacher ratings of social skills, 2) behavioral observations recorded in classroom and free play settings, and 3) analysis of archival school records. Police and court records also are examined annually for all the boys in our sample.

By the seventh grade, 21 of the 40 most antisocial boys in our sample had been arrested a total of 68 times for their criminal behavior; in contrast, only three boys in the at-risk control group had been arrested, for a total of three arrests. As a general rule, the adjustment patterns of the antisocial students have tended to deteriorate across school years, while the adjustment status of the at-risk control students has remained relatively adaptive and stable (Walker, Stieber, & O'Neill, 1990).

Our longitudinal data suggest that three relatively easily obtained measures, recorded in the fifth grade, can accurately predict the arrest records of approximately 80% of these youth when they are in tenth grade, five years later. These measures are: (1) teacher ratings of social skills, (2) total negative playground behavior recorded on the target student and his peers during recess periods, and (3) discipline contacts with the principal's office as measured by written file records.

We also find strong differences in the parenting skills to which the two groups of boys are exposed. Parents of the highly antisocial boys were ineffective and inconsistent in their disciplinary practices, often ignoring an infraction on one occasion and then harshly punishing it on another. These parents tended to be only minimally involved in their children's lives, if involved at all. Further, they did not encourage their children and tended to have negative, often hostile social exchanges with them. Finally, they tended to be weak in their display of the problem solving skills expected of parents that are so essential to meeting the challenges of daily life.

The existing knowledge base on antisocial behavior identifies the family conditions that develop this behavior pattern. It is well established that antisocial behavior tends to flow through generations, much like child abuse (Wahler & Dumas, 1986). It frequently is noted in the media that more than 80% of prison inmates suffered abuse in their childhoods. Antisocial behavior is transmitted as reliably across generations as is child abuse.

We have the ability to predict the developmental course of this behavior pattern very accurately. We can identify at-risk children early in their school careers, which enables us to intervene before this behavior pattern moves beyond our ability to remediate or attenuate it. The next section describes some of the promising practices that currently exist in this regard.

PROMISING INTERVENTIONS

Kazdin (1985) argues that unless the antisocial behavior pattern has been affected significantly by age nine (end of third grade), it is unlikely to be changed and should be viewed thereafter as a chronic condition, much like diabetes. However, like diabetes, antisocial behavior after this point can be controlled with a well designed regimen of monitoring, management, and intervention.

We can identify at-risk children early in their school careers, which enables us to intervene before this behavior pattern moves beyond our ability to remediate or attenuate it.

Reid (1990) and his colleagues have developed a universal intervention procedure designed to prevent the development of antisocial behavior patterns within intact classrooms. Every student is exposed to this universal intervention, which consists of social skills training, homework assignments and intensive monitoring, academic tutoring, teacher support, parent training and careful communications between home and school. The intervention currently is being tested on first and fifth-grade students. Preliminary results indicate this to be a highly effective intervention for first-grade students but much less so for fifth-graders. The primary intervention lasts about a year, but follow-up interventions that are less intensive can continue for several years, until a student's problems are stabilized. This longitudinal study eventually will develop a complete package of specific assessment and remediation programs for each of its major intervention components. A relatively strong consensus is emerging among experts that a successful, comprehensive intervention program for antisocial behavior should contain the following elements (see Walker & Sylwester, 1991):

1. Schools should take the lead in setting up and coordinating a home, school, and community agency intervention program.

2. The school should monitor student behavior carefully so that it can begin the intervention process as soon as a student's antisocial behavior indicators emerge.

3. A brief parent training program should focus on five basic parenting practices: a) how to closely monitor a child's whereabouts, activities, and friends; b) how to participate actively in a child's life; c) how to use such positive techniques as encouragement, praise, and approval to manage a child's home behavior; d) how to ensure that discipline is fair, timely, and appropriate to the offense; and e) how to use effective conflict-resolution and problem-solving strategies. The program should assist parents in setting up reward systems in the home that provide incentives for the child to achieve academic success and to behave appropriately at school, and it also should help parents to encourage their child to develop a positive attitude toward school.

4. A tracking-monitoring system for school and home should provide daily, two-way communication about the student's performance at school and parental acknowledgement of that performance.

5. The school program should teach the personal, academic, and social skills that the at-risk student needs for school success. This instructional program should be accompanied by unobtrusive but sensitive school monitoring systems that measure progress.

6. The school should establish a program of peer and teacher mentors who take an active interest in the antisocial, at-risk student's school success.

CONCLUDING REMARKS

The problem of antisocial behavior should be viewed as a national emergency. The magnitude of this problem, the alarming rate with which we are producing antisocial children, and the reliable association of antisocial behavior with a host of very costly and debilitating outcomes (especially adolescent and adult criminality) require the investment of considerable resources and expertise.

To have a chance of success, our collective efforts *must* systematically involve the three classes of social agents that are most important in the antisocial child's life, that is, their teachers, parents, and peers. In addition, we must address this problem from a therapeutic, rather than punitive, vantage point and begin our interventions in preschool and kindergarten settings.

REFERENCES

Coie, J., & Kupersmidt, J. (1983). A behavioral analysis of emerging social status in boys' groups. *Child Development, 54,* 1400–1416.

Dodge, K. (1983). Promoting social competence in school children. *Schools and Teaching, 1*(2).

Hersh, R., & Walker, H. M. (1983). Great expectations: Making schools effective for all students. *Policy Studies Review, 2,* 147–188.

Kazdin, A. (1985). *Treatment of antisocial social behavior.* Homewood, IL: Dorsey Press.

Loeber, R. (1982). The stability of antisocial child behavior: A review. *Child Development, 53,* 1431–1446.

Loeber, R. (1985). Patterns and development of antisocial child behavior. *Annals of Child Development, 2,* 77–116.

Patterson, G. R. (1982). *Coercive family processes.* Eugene, OR: Castalia Press.

Patterson, G. R., & Bank, L. (1986). Bootstrapping your way in the nomological thicket. *Behavioral Assessment, 8,* 49–73.

Patterson, G. R., Reid, J., & Dishion, T. (1992). *Antisocial boys.* Eugene, OR: Castalia Press.

Quay, H., & Werry, J. (1986). *Psychological pathological disorders of childhood.* New York: Wiley & Sons.

Reid, J. (1992). Personal communication.

Reid, J. (1990). *Center for the prevention of conduct disorders:* Core grant application. Oregon Social Learning Center, Eugene, Oregon.

Slenkovich, J. (1992). Can the language "social maladjustment" in the SED definition be ignored? The final words. *School Psychology Review, 21*(1), 43–45.

Walker, H. M., & Sylwester, R. (1991, September). Where is school along the path to prison? *Educational Leadership,* 14–16.

Walker, H. M., Stieber, S., & O'Neill, R. E. (1990). Middle school behavioral profiles of antisocial and at-risk control boys: Descriptive and predictive outcomes. *Exceptionality, 1,* 61–77.

Walker, H. M., Block-Pedego, A., Todis, A., & Severson, H. (1991). *The school archival records search (SARS).* Longmont, CO: Sopris West.

Walker, H. M., & Rankin, R. (1983). Assessing the behavioral demands and expectations of less restrictive settings. *School Psychology Review, 12,* 274–284.

· ·

HOW TO UNDERSTAND AND HELP THE PASSIVE AGGRESSIVE STUDENT ·

The passive aggressive student is rarely studied or understood although he or she is most skilled in frustrating teachers in subtle ways. In the next article, *Understanding and Managing a Passive Aggressive Student,* Jody and Nicholas Long present a dynamic overview of this student with new insights into behavior and specific recommendations for management. This enjoyable and helpful article will make a difference to all teachers who work with passive aggressive students, colleagues, and parents.

ARTICLE 6.4

Understanding and Managing the Passive Aggressive Student

Jody Long and Nicholas Long

Passive aggressive behavior exists in all cultures and passive aggressive students and staff exist in every school. Passive aggressive behavior is an indirect and socialized form of aggression, but it is equally as destructive as aggressive behavior. Passive aggressive behavior successfully has escaped the scrutiny of professional study, perhaps for the same reason a passive aggressive student has escaped being detected by a classroom teacher. Teachers know when an aggressive student is mad at them, but they may not be aware of the indirect "drip by drip" water torture skills of a passive aggressive student.

For example, do you have a student in your classroom who irritates and annoys you in endless and insignificant ways; and over time you have had the impulse to raise your hands around his neck? If you answer, "Yes" to this question, the chances are you have identified a passive aggressive student. What is surprising is that you are not alone in having this urge. In a survey of 300 special educators, over 75 percent said they would prefer to work with an aggressive student than a passive aggressive student. A typical comment from this group was, "When we work with an aggressive student, at least we know where the anger is coming from. It's out in the open and we can deal with it. It is not like those sneaky, arrogant, sulky, passive aggressive students." It also is clear passive aggressive students stir up strong feelings in some staff.

This article will describe the five major questions teachers have about understanding and helping a passive aggressive student.

1. How does a student become a passive aggressive personality?
2. What are the dynamic beliefs of a passive aggressive student?
3. What are the passive aggressive behaviors which frustrate teachers?
4. How does the staff react to a passive aggressive student?
5. What concepts and skills are needed to alter a passive aggressive student's dysfunctional ways of relating to others?

HOW DOES A STUDENT BECOME A PASSIVE AGGRESSIVE PERSONALITY?

Two very different early socializing experiences appear to promote the development of a passive aggressive student. The first developmental pattern involves a child's psychological reaction to early and prolonged verbal and physical parental aggression. For thousands of children, their homes are not secure, protected environments, but an emotional nightmare. Their parents are intermittently out of control and/or under the destructive influence of drugs, alcohol, mental illness, sadism, or hell bent on making their children obedient to their authority and wishes. These children are threatened, intimidated, hit, punished, and made to feel guilty over normal developmental issues. They are frightened and in a chronic state of anxiety. If these children continue to be exposed to their hostile, explosive and unpredictable parents, the children frequently either identify with their aggressive parents and become *aggressive students,* or they learn to survive in their volatile world and become *passive aggressive students.* Just like a child learns not to put his hands on a hot stove, these children learn not to express their angry feelings out loud. Instead, they learn to express their feelings under their breath and in their thoughts. They fantasize, "I will get back at you; not now, but I will find a way. And when I do, you won't even know about it." Nothing grows stronger or becomes more powerful than an unexpressed hostile thought. Over time these abused and exploited students often grow up learning a passive aggressive way of relating to hostile adults. Unfortunately, this indirect or insidious way of expressing personal anger can spill over to any adult who makes demands on them regardless of whether the adult demand is reasonable or irrational.

The second developmental pattern leading to the development of a passive aggressive personality seems paradoxical. It involves nurturing parents who love their children and want them to be socially and professionally successful. These parents have worked hard for what they achieved and want their children to be well liked and accepted because social approval will enhance their children's chances for success, such as making good grades, winning scholarships, finding a professional career, or attracting useful friends. These parents also believe their children are an extension of their values and goals. If their children turn out to be "good children" then they can take pride in their parenting skills. To achieve this, these parents systematically teach their children that "good children" are not angry children. Good children are never hostile or sarcastic. Good children have pleasant thoughts and pleasant behaviors. Good children never think or speak in negative terms. The socialization forces of these parents are effective not only in controlling their children's aggressive behaviors, but also in teaching them negative thoughts and angry feelings must be suppressed. Inadvertently, the goal of developing "proper and well behaved children" ends up as a grievous form of mind control. In the process their children learn they must not express their angry thoughts even though they feel guilty for having them. For example, Susan, age eight, tells her mother she was angry at her friend Nancy at school and told Nancy she hated her. The mother's reaction is predictable.

> "Susan, I'm surprised you said that. It is not nice to hate your friends! I want you to stop all those hateful words. There is too much hate in this world! Everybody seems to be hating someone and the only way to prevent all this hate is to stop those hateful thoughts in our head. I want you to think about yourself like an artesian well which bubbles up only pure, good and nice thoughts and behaviors. So today, no more hate, only love, joy and happiness."

What Susan learns, however, is to experience personal anger as an enemy to be conquered and not as a feeling to be accepted as a normal and natural part of one's life.

These two socializing patterns of promoting a passive aggressive personality are significantly different from each other, but they have a similar outcome. Anger is evil and must be hidden.

THE DYNAMIC BELIEFS OF A PASSIVE AGGRESSIVE STUDENT

The passive aggressive student believes the direct expression of anger is both dangerous and destructive. As a result, he has had to learn to hide, conceal, or mask his anger behind a facade of socially approved behavior. Like the tip of an iceberg, the real size and power of his anger is out of sight. For a passive aggressive student, the expression of anger is not a misdemeanor, but a felony. Here are some statements passive aggressive students told us.

- Angry feelings are upsetting. When people are angry they yell, scream, and are scary.
- When people get angry, terrible things can happen.
- I don't let people know when I am angry. If they knew what I was thinking, they would want to kill me.
- Thinking about anger is wrong, but exciting.
- When I'm treated unfairly by my teacher, I'm smart enough to know how to upset her so she can suffer like she made me suffer.

These statements express the intensity and strength of some of their internalized beliefs about anger and aggression. Once a student has internalized a passive aggressive way of perceiving, thinking, feeling, and behaving, then he will maintain his beliefs about anger by creating a self fulfilling prophecy as he relates to other adults. The following sequence has been documented by numerous clinical observations during a student/staff Conflict Cycle.

1. The passive aggressive student is upset at the teacher.
2. The passive aggressive student behaves in indirect and subtle ways which frustrates the teacher.
3. Over time, the teacher is unaware of the amount of accumulated anger she has absorbed from the passive aggressive student.
4. During a stressful classroom incident, the passive aggressive student falls out of his seat, burps, or malingers. This small incident becomes the straw that breaks the camel's back, the spark that lights the fuse, the pin that pops the balloon, or the final incident which causes the teacher to explode.
5. The teacher has a 30-second temper tantrum, or, in clinical terms, has a brief impulse breakthrough.
6. The passive aggressive student responds with alarm and says to himself, "Wow! Look how crazy people get when they express their anger. Isn't it wonderful I don't express my anger directly."
7. Afterwards, the teacher usually feels guilty for overreacting to such a minor event. She feels sorry for losing her self-control and in some cases, actually apologizes to the passive aggressive student.

The self-fulfilling prophecy of the passive aggressive student has been achieved. The teacher/adult got out of control, acted improperly, and reinforced the passive aggressive student's belief that anger is dangerous and there is no need to change his way of thinking or his behavior.

HOW PASSIVE AGGRESSIVE STUDENTS GET BACK AT STAFF: FROM NORMAL TO PATHOLOGICAL BEHAVIORS

Our observations of passive aggressive students have identified four levels or patterns of behavior, ranging from normal or "age appropriate" behaviors to pathological behaviors.

Level One. The teacher makes a request, and the student agrees to do it, but then doesn't do it. This is the most common of all passive aggressive behaviors. The student does not want to comply with the teacher's request, because of other interests, boredom, fatigue, frustration, etc. Unlike the aggressive student, this student agrees to do it, but then develops selective vision, "I can't find it;" selective deafness, "Oh, I'm sorry, I didn't hear you;" selective memory, "Oh, I forgot, but I will do it in a minute;" and a slow down tactic, "I'm coming!" These passive aggressive behaviors inevitably frustrate the teacher who frequently completes the requested task with resentment. To some degree, all students use these tactics as a way of reacting to authority figures.

Level Two. This is a little more sophisticated form of passive aggressive behavior. The teacher makes a request and the passive aggressive student doesn't want to do it, but decides to do it in a way that will upset the teacher. This is also called "intentional efficiency." Observations of this level of behavior includes:

- cleaning up by making a mess.
- turns in an assignment that is difficult to read or is incomplete.
- asks for help but doesn't listen, looks at the ceiling or makes tapping or clicking sounds.
- during music class, sings too loud or off key.
- during science class, follows the wrong procedures.
- during remedial reading class, student decides to read with one eye closed.
- talks so softly teacher can't hear what the student said.
- over waters the teacher's plants.
- greets his teacher by playfully punching him in the arm. When confronted replies, "Oh, I'm sorry, I was just trying to be friendly."

This level of reacting to authority figures is conscious and more characteristic of a passive aggressive personality.

Level Three. This level of passive aggressive behavior is more problematic because the passive aggressive student has hostile feelings towards the teacher and decides to get back at her at a later time and/or without her awareness. This is a conscious decision and a damaging way of expressing hostile feelings toward the teacher. This is a form of indirect revenge. Our observation of passive aggressive behavior at this level includes:

- giving the teacher the "finger sign," "sticking out one's tongue, or making sexual gestures behind her back."
- hiding the teacher's belongings and resources such as the grade book, keys, erasers, science equipment, etc.
- to be aware of a crisis, but let it happen, i.e., the overhead projector has an electrical short and the teacher is about to use it. An insect has dropped onto the teacher's water glass at lunch and the student doesn't tell her.
- teacher receives an important call and student forgets to tell her.
- the passive aggressive student makes an innocuous comment to a student who is upset, causing him to blow up and cause a new teacher/student conflict.

This level of passive aggressive behavior is inappropriate but is intrinsically reinforcing so the passive aggressive student is not motivated to learn other ways of expressing anger.

Level Four. This is a pathological form of passive aggression in which a student becomes self destructive, unattractive, and repulsive, in exchange for the pleasure of getting back at selected adults, usually involving the parents.

Our observations include passive aggressive students who are very intelligent and frequently come from professional upward mobile families:

- dressing weirdly, or in a cult fashion.
- refusing to turn in a final report because it is stupid and receives a failing grade.
- eating in a gross manner.
- refusing to bathe or brush teeth.
- soiling himself in class, creating a stink with a smile.

Levels three and four are examples of passive aggressive behaviors which are dysfunctional to healthy interpersonal relationships, and they need to be confronted therapeutically.

HOW DO STAFF REACT TO A PASSIVE AGGRESSIVE STUDENT?

The typical staff reaction to a passive aggressive student is to become counter passive aggressive. This reaction is a basic principle of the Conflict Cycle. A student in stress, in this scenario, a passive aggressive student, will create in a staff his feelings and if the staff is not trained, the staff will mirror the student's passive aggressive behavior. Our observations of classroom teachers, who are not passive aggressive personality but are teaching passive aggressive students, verify this principle. These teachers initially respond to passive aggressive students by demonstrating selective hearing, memory, and visual problems. They forget to return a passive aggressive student's paper or they grade it vigorously.

SPECIFIC CONCEPTS AND SKILLS TO HELP
PASSIVE AGGRESSIVE STUDENTS

The following concepts and skills are necessary and effective when helping a passive aggressive student. This student is not going to change over night, but staff will not be participating or reinforcing his inappropriate behaviors.

1. To know in advance that passive aggressive students will create counter passive aggressive feelings in staff with the goal of getting the staff to blow up, lose control, and fulfill his prophecy that the expression of anger is dangerous. To be forewarned is to be forearmed.

2. Understand that all passive aggressive behaviors are inappropriate ways of expressing anger. Never empower a passive aggressive student by saying, the entire class will remain seated, cannot have lunch, or start their project, etc., until Pat (the passive aggressive student) gets off the floor, cleans up his desk, stops talking, etc. The passive aggressive will be pleased if you give him the power to control the class and all the attention.

3. Decode the passive aggressive student's behavior by using the Detective Columbo technique of wondering out loud why the student is using this passive aggressive tactic. A monologue might be as follows: "Hmm. I just don't understand this. William has good hearing. I mean, he can hear all the way across the playing field when I call him to come and take a turn at bat. And he seems to be able to hear without any problems when he talks with his friends. So I wonder why it is that he doesn't hear me when I ask him to start cleaning up. Hmm . . . . this is very strange. I'll bet that he really doesn't want to hear me and is only pretending not to hear. Maybe he's angry at me for some reason, and this is his way of trying to make me angry and frustrated. Let me think about this." Because most passive aggressives believe staff are not aware of their passive aggressive behavior, they usually shape up spontaneously after hearing this monologue.

4. Decode the passive aggressive student's behavior by using Benign Confrontation. The teacher can meet with the student and share her concerns about his passive aggressive behavior. Since the student will

deny his anger, the teacher can arrange for a personal signal such as pointing to her ear when she feels he is being passive aggressive and then hold the student responsible for his behavior.

5. Hold a group discussion in which the teacher gets his peers to talk about how they handle their feelings of anger. It is important to emphasize how normal and acceptable it is to have these feelings and how satisfying it is to talk about them rather than act them out. The goal is to learn to say "yes" to having angry feelings and to say "no" to expressing them in indirect or aggressive ways.

6. If a student uses level 3 or 4 as primary ways of relating to adults refer him to your school psychologist or counselor.

7. Finally, evaluate your style of showing anger to make sure you are not modeling passive aggressive strategies.

SUMMARY

Passive aggressive behavior exists in all cultures and classrooms, but is less understood, examined, or researched professionally than other less subtle types of behavior. Commonly, the passive aggressive student irritates and annoys the teacher (and others) in endless, insignificant ways. The teacher, unaware of her increasing anger over these accumulated irritants, "drip by drip," suddenly blows up over a seemingly minor incident. Quite often the teacher feels guilty over her overreaction, because she does not understand the dynamics of this type of subtle behavior. This article has examined the socializing influences which promote the development of passive aggression, the destructive nature of passive aggressive behavior, as well as specific concepts and skills to help passive aggressive students.

REFERENCES

Berries, M. & Long, N. (1979). "The Passive Aggressive Child." *Pointer, 24*(1), 27–31.

HOW TO UNDERSTAND AND HELP STUDENTS WHO HAVE ATTENTION DEFICITS AND HYPERACTIVITY DISORDERS AND/OR LEARNING DISABILITIES . . . .

Every teacher has struggled with intelligent well-motivated students who seem incapable of maintaining their attention, organizing their materials, remembering instructions, and completing their assignments. Their disorganization and confusion frustrate not only them but everyone around them. We like to represent these students by using the analogy of a driver sitting in a car stuck in a ditch on a country road miles from the closest tow truck. Isolated, anxious, and concerned, the driver's answer to the dilemma is to walk around the car, assess the situation, jump back into the driver's seat, start the engine, and floor the gas pedal. This impulsive decision causes the engine to roar, the rear wheels to spin, and large quantities of dirt, stone, and mud to be thrown onto the road. Considerable energy has been spent, but the situation has not improved. In fact, all this activity has only made the situation worse. The car has sunk deeper into the ditch and is splattered with mud; and the driver is frustrated, angry, and baffled by the lack of forward progress. ADHD/LD students, like the driver of this car, find themselves in a similar situation.

They are aware they have a problem in school, but they seem unable to do anything to better their situation.

The following letter was written by an 11-year-old boy to his teacher as an attempt to explain his frustrations and confusion when he is unable to listen to or remember his classroom assignments. This is an honest, painful, from-the-heart letter that depicts the psychological suffering many of these misunderstood students experience.

> I try to tell the truth and not lie, but my problem is that I can't seem to remember anything or that I'm just not listening. I understand that already but I don't know why I just start listening or just start remembering. Most people think that sounds easy to do, but I wonder why I can't start doing that. Not listening and not remembering has just about got me in trouble every time. I've been in trouble since I've been alive (and take my word for it, I've been in a lot of trouble!) I don't mean I've only been in trouble at school, but at home too. When I was in first grade I got strait A's and I've gotten worse every year until now *unexceptable!* I think I would be happier if I could finish my work and relax. I wish I could just dump every paper out of my binder and start out fresh and see the change. I bet it would be a good one chances are they'd be good changes (90% to 10!). I'd have better holiday's weekends and even in and out of school.

This student was diagnosed later as having an attention deficit disorder with specific learning disabilities.

Recent studies have found that between 10% and 20% of all school-age children have learning disabilities. Of those with LD, about 20% to 25% also have attention deficit hyperactivity. LD and ADHD are two separate problems; however, because they occur together so frequently, it is useful to consider them related. In addition, most children and adolescents with LD and/or ADHD develop emotional, social, and family difficulties. These result from frustrations and failures experienced with family and peers and at school. They are the *consequence* of the academic problems, not the cause.

A BRIEF OVERVIEW OF THE CHANGING
DIAGNOSTIC NAMES . . . .

As these students were recognized and studied, different diagnostic names were applied to describe their condition. Many of these terms are still used by different professionals, causing professional confusion.

Prior to the 1940s, students who had difficulty learning or paying attention were considered mentally retarded, emotionally disturbed, or culturally disadvantaged. The research of the 1940s identified a fourth group of children, those who had difficulty because of the way their nervous system worked. Their problems were described as "neurologically based." Initially, this disorder was called *Minimal Brain Damage*; later, the name was changed to *Minimal Brain Dysfunction*. These terms described students with neurologically based academic problems, hyperactivity, a short attention span, impulsivity, and emotional problems.

Since the 1940s, this group of problems has been a separate focus of study. First, the neurologically based academic problems were identified and named to reflect the primary area of skill difficulty: *dyslexia* for reading problems, *dysgraphia* for writing problems, and *dyscalculia* for math problems. Later, the term *Learning Disability* was applied to the types of learning difficulties that underlie the skill problems.

Hyperactivity, distractibility, and impulsivity were initially called *Hyperkinetic Disorder of Childhood* (thus, the "hyperactive child"). By 1980, the name had been changed to *Attention Deficit Disorder* (ADD) to emphasize that the attentional problem was the major issue, not hyperactivity. In 1987, the name was changed again to reflect the reality that all of the problems were significant. The newest term is *Attention Deficit Hyperactivity Disorder* (ADHD).

The latest terms, therefore, are ADHD and LD. If colleagues use other terms, do not be confused. They are not seeing a different problem; they are merely using older terms to describe it.

If a student in your classroom has ADHD and/or LD, he or she will probably have emotional problems (anger, sadness, anxiety, or disruptive behavior), social problems (immaturity, poor relationships with same-age children), and/or family problems.

To understand this student, you must evaluate these difficulties from all angles to see how they affect every aspect of life—not just in school but with other children and with the family. Learning disabilities do not just interfere with reading, writing, and math. They affect, for example, recess and physical education—baseball, basketball, and hopscotch. They also may interfere with art, music, or related activities. Likewise, ADHD does not interfere with only classroom behavior; it affects peer-related behavior and family life as well. Teachers must become knowledgeable about these students so that they can help them inside and outside the classroom.

The next article, *Helping the Student with Attention Deficit Hyperactivity Disorder in the Regular Classroom*, was written by Larry Silver, a child and adolescent psychiatrist who has specialized in studying students with ADHD and LD problems. His article represents the latest and most comprehensive overview of ADHD and gives specific and realistic recommendations regarding how classroom teachers can accommodate their teaching and managing skills to help a hyperactive, inattentive, and impulsive student.*

ARTICLE 6.5

Helping the Student with Attention Deficit Hyperactivity Disorder in the Regular Classroom

Larry B. Silver, M.D.

WHAT IS ADHD?

ADHD is a neurologically-based disorder manifested by hyperactivity, inattention (distractibility), and impulsivity. Individuals with this disorder might have one, two, or all three of these behaviors. They need not have all three. ADHD is usually apparent by age six and is estimated to be present in about one to three percent of school-aged individuals. About 50 percent appear to mature out of their ADHD by puberty; 50 percent will continue into adolescents. Approximately 30 percent of children will continue past adolescence into adulthood.

Hyperactivity refers to an increased activity level, often reflective in fidgety behavior. That is, he or she is not wild, running around the room but is more likely to be tapping fingers, playing with something, swinging legs, wiggling, or up and down out of the seat. Inattention or distractibility refers to an inability to block out unimportant stimuli, resulting in difficulty staying on task and a short attention span. This distractibility might be with auditory stimuli (reacting to subtle sounds or noises others ignore), with visual stimuli (reacting to movement or items others ignore), or could be with both types of stimuli. Starting with older adolescents and continuing into adulthood, another form of inattention might be noted. The student has difficulty blocking out his or her own thoughts in order to focus on what is important. This student

---

* These introductory remarks have included excerpts from Larry B. Silver, *ADHD*, pp. 1–2, Ch. ADD 1990 (pamphlet).

will daydream or tune out in class. Impulsivity refers to an inability to stop and think before speaking and/or acting. This individual might interrupt or call out in class without raising his or her hand, interrupt parents, act without thinking of the consequences, answer work tasks before thinking through the problem.

Current research strongly supports the understanding that ADHD is caused by a deficiency of a particular neurotransmitter (norepinephrine) in specific pathways within the lower brain stem area (the Ascending Reticular Activating System).

HOW IS ADHD DIAGNOSED?

At this time there are no formal tests or evaluations that establish the diagnosis of ADHD. The formal criteria are noted in the *Diagnostic and Statistical Manual of Mental Disorders,* Fourth Edition (see Appendix). These criteria are descriptive and, thus, it is the collection of these difficulties that distinguishes ADHD from other disorders. Behaviors are listed that describe hyperactivity, inattention, and impulsivity. Professionals are to document a certain percent of these criteria to establish that one or more of the three behaviors exists. Several types of behavioral rating scales are available and often used by school systems to document these behaviors. Once the behavior(s) are documented, it is necessary to show that the behaviors are *chronic* and *pervasive.* Many other difficulties may result in a student being hyperactive, inattentive, and/or impulsive. Thus, as will be explained, the only way we have of establishing the diagnosis is by the clinical history.

Anxiety or depression can result in a student being restless, not on task, or irritable. So, too, certain Learning Disabilities can result in a student appearing to be off task or unable to complete assignments. The hyperactivity, inattention, and/or impulsivity observed in these situations would not be considered to be ADHD.

It is the clinical history of the problems that clarify the diagnosis. If the behavior(s) observed occurred after a certain time in the person's life or occur in certain situations, one must think of an emotional problem or a Learning Disability. ADHD is a neurological disorder, probably present from birth. Thus, if the behavior(s) have been present since early childhood (chronic) and are present during all parts of the student's life, at school, home, and activities, (pervasive) the diagnosis of ADHD is made.

If the classroom teacher suspects that a student has ADHD, she or he should discuss this concern with the parents who should then discuss the concerns with the student's family physician. Members of the special education professional team can participate in finalizing the diagnosis of ADHD. In most areas, the diagnosis is not considered official until diagnosed by a physician (family practitioner, pediatrician, child and adolescent psychiatrist).

HOW IS ADHD ADDRESSED WITHIN SCHOOL SYSTEMS?

If a child or adolescent has ADHD, the public school system can recognize and service the student under education law or under civil law. The education law is the **Individuals with Disabilities Education Act** (IDEA), P.L. 101-476, passed by Congress in 1990 as the reauthorization of P.L. 94-142, the Education for all Handicapped Children's Act. The civil law used is **Section 504 of the Rehabilitation Act of 1973,** P.L. 93-112.

Part B of IDEA defines the categories of disability recognized for special education by the U.S. Department of Education. ADHD is not identified as a separate disability. Thus, in 1991 the U.S. Department of Education issued a memorandum clarifying how students with ADHD could be eligible for special education services. If the student with ADHD also has a Learning Disability, he or she could be identified as having this disability. If the student also has a significant emotional problem, she or he could be identified as Seriously Emotionally Disturbed. Or, if the student does not meet the criteria for these two disabilities, he or she could be identified under the Other Health Impaired category. Any of these three classifications would make the student with ADHD eligible for special education services.

This same U.S. Department of Education memorandum clarifies that students with ADHD can also be served under Section 504 of the Rehabilitation Act of 1973 if their condition is severe enough to be considered a handicap. In this Law, a disorder is considered a handicap if the disability "substantially limits a major life activity," such as learning. Thus, under Section 504, children and adolescents with ADHD may be eligible for accommodations in the regular classroom to meet their educational needs.

Many students with ADHD may not qualify for services within a school district's severe eligibility specifications for Learning Disabilities but can meet the criteria to be serviced under Section 504. Eligible students under Section 504, like students receiving services under IDEA, are entitled to reasonable accommodations in order to benefit from the educational process. These accommodations are to be made by the teacher within the regular classroom.

HEALTH/MENTAL HEALTH TREATMENTS FOR ADHD

ADHD is a neurological disorder resulting from a deficiency of a specific neurotransmitter in a specific area of the brain. The primary approach to treatment focuses on the use of specific medications that increase the amount of this neurotransmitter in this area of the brain. Once the level is where it should be, the student becomes significantly less hyperactive, inattentive, and/or impulsive. The most frequently used medications are methylphenidate (Ritalin), dextroamphetamine (Dexedrine), pemoline (Cylert), and imipramine (Tofranil).

In addition to the use of medications, other services might be needed depending on the remaining problems once the medication is working. Some children or adolescents may need individual therapy or counseling. Parents might need help addressing behavioral or family issues. Social skill training might also be helpful.

With all aspects of this treatment plan, it is essential that the health and mental health professionals work closely with the special education team and the classroom teacher. When a student is on medication, feedback from teachers is critical to learning how the medication is working or what adjustments are needed. Behavioral programs may have to be integrated into a school-based program to have the best impact.

The focus of this chapter is the role of the classroom teacher in addressing the special needs of the student with ADHD. There are two such needs: (1) the ability to adjust the classroom, curriculum, and teaching approaches to accommodate to the needs of this student; and, (2) the need to understand the effects and side effects of the medications needed in order to report the progress or lack of progress of a student as medications are started and doses are adjusted and to recognize side effects so that this information can be forwarded to the physician managing the medication.

The general role of the school in addressing the needs of the student with ADHD will be reviewed first. Then the role of the regular classroom teacher will be discussed.

THE GENERAL ROLE OF THE SCHOOL IN ADDRESSING ADHD

When planning for the placement, curriculum, and classroom strategies needed for a student with ADHD, two important factors must be considered. Each influences the individualized plan developed. The first factor is whether the student also has a Learning Disability. Studies show that between 50% and 70% of students with ADHD also have a Learning Disability; thus, whenever the diagnosis of ADHD is made it is essential that the possibility of a Learning Disability be explored. The second factor is whether this student is successfully on medication or not.

If the student has a Learning Disability, these processing problems must be addressed through appropriate special education services as well as accommodations provided within the regular classroom. For some students with ADHD, no Learning Disability is found; however, the student might have areas of deficit in specific skills or less than grade-appropriate knowledge in certain areas because he or she may not have been available for learning during the years in school before the diagnosis was made and treatment started.

If on appropriate medications at the correct dose, about 85% of students with ADHD will no longer be hyperactive, inattentive, and/or impulsive in the classroom. Thus, no special interventions may be needed. If parents refuse medication, the physician does not recommend medication, or the use and dosage of the medication is not optimum, interventions must be designed to address the specific behaviors that the student has in the school settings.

If the Learning Disabilities result in the student needing more services than can be provided in the regular classroom, the possibility of a special education program to address these needs may have to be considered. If the student is not on medication and the resulting hyperactivity, inattention and/or impulsivity result in behaviors that make the student unavailable for learning in the regular classroom or result in behaviors that make the classroom unavailable for the other students to learn, the child or adolescent might need a special education program for students with serious emotional problems.

The regular classroom teacher should be able to accommodate to the general educational needs of the student with ADHD. He or she should not be expected to address the full special educational needs for the student with ADHD who also has significant Learning Disabilities or serious emotional problems.

THE ROLE OF THE REGULAR CLASSROOM TEACHER

The teacher should be prepared to address two major issues in the regular classroom: (1) adjusting the classroom, curriculum, and teaching strategy to address the behaviors of ADHD; and, (2) recognize the side effects of the different medications used to treat ADHD so that this information can be forwarded to the prescribing physician. The behaviors will be addressed first.

Addressing the Behaviors of ADHD

It is not possible to "cookbook" a list of things to do in the classroom. Each student is different and each needs a specially designed approach. It is important to understand which of the many behaviors of ADHD a specific student has and to accommodate for his or her specific needs.

The list of possible behaviors would include:

1. Hyperactivity (fidgety behaviors)
2. Inattention (distractibility)
   (a) auditory distractibility
   (b) visual distractibility
   (c) internal distractibility
3. Impulsivity
   (a) does not stop to think before speaking
   (b) does not stop to think before acting

In addition to addressing the specific behaviors, it is important to know where the student is academically. If knowledge or skills that should have been learned in an earlier grade are weak or absent because the student was not available for learning at that time, these areas will need to be addressed. Often, once the student is diagnosed and treated with medication, he or she will be available to catch up in these areas.

To successfully work with students who have ADHD in the regular classroom requires a competent teacher who has a positive attitude toward mainstreaming and inclusion. In addition, this teacher needs to have the ability to collaborate as part of an interdisciplinary team and to have knowledge of behavioral management techniques. Teachers who work well with special needs students in the regular classroom are fair, firm, warm, and responsive. They have patience and a sense of humor and are able to establish a rapport with students.

Accommodations for Hyperactivity

These students are most challenging. They have difficulty sitting in their seat for prolonged periods. They may get up to sharpen their pencils frequently. They fidget with pencils, pens, or paper clips, appearing never to be calm and relaxed. This student's need for physical movement and activity must be taken into account in planning classroom accommodations. Try to channel this excessive activity into acceptable activities. Simply telling the child or adolescent to stop her or his disruptive hyperactive behaviors will not work. This student needs to find ways of channeling this excessive activity into acceptable behaviors. The other students will have to be told why this student will be permitted to do some things that the class in general will not. Examples are:

1. Allow nondisruptive, directed movement in the classroom.
2. Allow standing during seat work if the student wishes to do so.
3. Use activity as a reward. Permit specific activities (running an errand, cleaning the board, organizing materials) as an individual reward for improvement.
4. Use teaching activities that encourage active responding (talking, moving, working at the board).
5. Encourage diary writing, note taking, painting, and other meaningful work-related activities.
6. Consider having this student sit near the teacher. If he or she begins to fidget with objects on the desk, tap feet, rock the chair, or do other disruptive behaviors, the teacher can reach over and remind the student what is happening. Perhaps a hand signal could be developed that says "You are too hyper. Relax." Since the student may not be aware of the behaviors, this signal might be all that is needed to stop.

Accommodations for Inattention/Distractibility

These students will have a short attention span and frequently not complete assignments. There are some accommodations that help with all forms of this problem and others that are most appropriate for a specific type of distractibility.

General accommodations to prolong concentration on tasks might include:

1. Shorten the task.
   (a) Break one task into smaller parts to be completed at different times.
   (b) Give two tasks, with the task the student prefers to be completed after the less preferred task.
   (c) Assign fewer problems (spelling words, math problems).
   (d) For rote tasks, set up more short, spaced practice sessions rather than fewer but longer and more concentrated sessions.
   (e) Give fewer and shorter homework assignments.
2. Make tasks more interesting.
   (a) When possible, encourage this student to work with partners in small groups.
   (b) Alternate highly interesting and less interesting tasks.
   (c) Try to create novel ways of teaching a task.
3. Improve the student's ability to focus and listen.
   (a) Be sure to have the student's attention before speaking. Ask for the class' attention and watch for eye contact from this student.
   (b) Give clues that it is important to attend. Use key phrases ("This is important" or "Listen carefully").
   (c) Use short, simple sentences.
   (d) Give one instruction at a time.
   (e) Prompt the student to repeat instructions after listening to them.
   (f) Write a short outline or summary of the directions on the board.
   (g) Use visual aids (charts, pictures, graphs).
4. Have the student sit next to the teacher's desk. When instructions are to be given, the teacher might walk over to his or her desk or reach out and touch the desk. If the student appears not to be focused or to be distracted, the teacher can reach out and help her or him attend. Again, a hand signal might work well as a reminder that the student is distracted and needs to refocus.

Specific accommodations for students who have *auditory distractibility* would start with all of the above ideas. In addition, the student should be working in the quietest place in the room, away from the door, window, air conditioner, and high traffic areas. For some assignments or tests, it might be helpful if this student went to the library or another quiet place to work.

Specific accommodations for students who have *visual distractibility* also include the general interventions. In addition, this student might do best in the least visually active part of the room, away from doors, windows, traffic, posters and pictures. Sometimes a cubicle can be placed on the desk. She or he might be asked to work in a corner facing the wall. If this is done, the student and the others in the class need to understand that this place is not being used as a punishment. This student might do best sitting in the front row. By doing this, much of the possible visual distraction caused by the other students will be decreased. (Do not use this idea for the student with auditory distractibility. He or she will continually turn around to see what the activity or noise is about.) Try to keep the desk top free of clutter. If only the task to be done is visible, the student is less likely to be distracted.

Specific accommodations for students who are *distracted by their own thoughts* include having their desk near the teacher. When they appear to be daydreaming or starring off, a gentle touch or word can bring them back. Once the student looks at the teacher, a hand signal might be used to remind the student what was happening.

Accommodations for Students Who Are Impulsive

These students will call out answers without raising their hand or waiting to be called on. Comments might be made that are inappropriate or that hurt feelings because the student does not think before speaking. They might act before they think, resulting in pushing, yelling, or hitting. Or, they might turn to do something so fast that they bump into other students or knock things over. Some may rush through assignments and tests, putting down the first thought or answer that enters their head. Younger children may have difficulty learning to wait (for their turn to do something, for a toy, for attention).

Behavioral approaches for helping the student become aware of her or his impulsivity should be combined with both accommodating the teaching style and activities and teaching the student techniques for delaying responses or actions. It might be helpful to consult with the school psychologist or other mental health professional when designing specific strategies for helping these students.

Accommodations for helping this student learn to wait would include:

1. Teaching substitute verbal or motor responses to use while waiting.
2. Instruct the child on how to continue on easier parts of tasks while waiting for the teacher's help.
3. Allow this student to doodle or play with clay, paper clips, or other items while waiting or listening to instructions.
4. Let the child participate in setting the pace for activities when possible.

Accommodations for helping the student who calls out or interrupts would include:

1. Suggest and reinforce alternative ways for getting attention (being a line leader or paper passer).
2. Teach these children to recognize pauses in conversations so that they can learn when to speak and how to hold onto ideas while listening for these pauses.
3. Let the child know about upcoming transitions or difficult times or tasks for which he or she will need extra control.
4. Teach and practice social routines (saying hello, goodbye, please).

Medication Management in the Classroom

Two groups of medications are used to treat ADHD. The most frequently used medications in each group will be discussed. The first group consists of methylphenidate (Ritalin), dextroamphetamine (Dexedrine), and pemoline (Cylert). Each increases the production of the deficient neurotransmitter in the lower brain stem area. The second group of medications consists of imipramine (Tofranil), desipramine (Norpramine), and Clonidine. Each increases the level of the deficient neurotransmitter not by producing more but by slowing down the breakdown of the existing amount.

Ritalin, Dexedrine, and Cylert are safe and effective medications. There are few side effects. The most frequent ones are loss of appetite and difficulty falling asleep at night. Less frequent side effects are complaints of headaches or stomachaches. A very uncommon side effect is the development of motor tics (twitching of eyelids, facial muscles, shoulder muscles). If the muscles in the back of the throat develop tics, the teacher will hear sniffing, snorting, or coughing sounds. If other difficulties are observed and the teacher is not sure what these mean, the physician should be called.

Tofranil and Norpramine can make a student sleepy and tired. In addition, less common side effects are constipation, dry mouth, or blurred vision. Clonidine can make the student very tired, sometimes resulting in falling asleep in the classroom.

If any of these side effects are noted, they should be told to parents who should inform the prescribing physician. As with the other medications, if any behaviors are noted that are of concern, the teacher should err on the side of being overcautious and inform the physician.

IN CLOSING

Most, if not more than most children and adolescents with ADHD can be educated in the regular classroom setting. There are some with significant

Learning Disabilities or significant emotional problems who may need supplemental services within the classroom or placement in a special education program. And, there will be some who are not on medication and the hyperactivity, inattention, and/or impulsivity result in this student being unavailable for learning in the regular classroom or in being so disruptive in the classroom that the other students are not able to learn. This student may need a special education placement not necessarily because of the ADHD but because the ADHD is not being treated.

Students with ADHD do not want to be hyperactive, inattentive, and/or impulsive. They do not want to be bad or get into trouble. They do want to learn. By providing the appropriate accommodations in the classroom, with the curriculum, and with teaching strategies, this child or adolescent can be a happy, productive, successful student in the regular classroom.

SUGGESTED READING

1. *Attention Deficit Disorders. Assessment and Teaching,* by J. W. Lerner, B. Lowenthal, and S. R. Lerner. Brooks/Cole Publishing Company, Pacific Grove, California, 1995. (This is an excellent handbook for the regular classroom teacher with a lot of information and practical suggestions.)

2. *Dr. Larry Silver's Advise to Parents on Attention Deficit Hyperactivity Disorder,* by L. B. Silver. American Psychiatric Press, Incorporated, Washington, D.C., 1994. (This book is written for parents but is equally helpful for classroom teachers. Details on diagnosis, and the nonmedication therapies are discussed. Specific information is provided on each medication used, including how the dose is established and side effects.)

TEACHING MATERIALS

1. *Educators Manual,* by M. Fowler in collaboration with R. Barkley, R. Reeve, and S. Zentall. (available through CH.A.D.D., see below)

2. *The Educators Inservice Program on Attention Deficit Disorders,* prepared by R. Barkley, R. Reeve, and S. Zentall. (This is a comprehensive multimedia presentation designed to inform educators about attention deficit disorders. Each program includes a complete script, 47 full-color transparencies, and the above noted *Educators Manual.* It is available through CH.A.D.D.)

HELPFUL ORGANIZATIONS

1. Children and Adults with Attention Deficit Disorders (CH.A.D.D.)
   499 N.W. 70th Avenue
   Suite 308
   Plantation, Florida 33317
   (305) 587-4599

2. Learning Disabilities Association of America (LDA)
    4256 Library Road
    Pittsburgh, Pennsylvania 15234
    (412) 341-1515

DIAGNOSTIC CRITERIA FOR ATTENTION DEFICIT/HYPERACTIVITY DISORDER

A. Either (1) or (2)

(1) Six (or more) of the following symptoms of **inattention** have persisted for at least 6 months to a degree that is maladaptive and inconsistent with developmental level:

Inattention

(a) often fails to give close attention to details or makes careless mistakes in schoolwork, work, or other activities

(b) often has difficulty sustaining attention in tasks or play activities

(c) often does not seem to listen when spoken to directly

(d) often does not follow through on instructions and fails to finish schoolwork, chores, or duties in the workplace (not due to oppositional behavior or failure to understand instructions)

(e) often has difficulty organizing tasks and activities

(f) often avoids, dislikes, or is reluctant to engage in tasks that require sustained mental effort (such as schoolwork or homework)

(g) often loses things necessary for tasks or activities (e.g., toys, school assignments, pencils, books, or tools)

(h) is often easily distracted by extraneous stimuli

(i) is often forgetful in daily activities

(2) six (or more) of the following symptoms of **hyperactivity-impulsivity** have persisted for at least 6 months to a degree that is maladaptive and inconsistent with developmental level:

Hyperactivity

(a) often fidgets with hands or feet or squirms in seat

(b) often leaves seat in classroom or in other situations in which remaining seated is expected

(c) often runs about or climbs excessively in situations in which it is inappropriate (in adolescents or adults, may be limited to subjective feelings of restlessness)

(d) often has difficulty playing or engaging in leisure activities quietly

(e) is often "on the go" or often acts as if "driven by a motor"

(f) often talks excessively

Impulsivity

(g) often blurts out answers before questions have been completed

(h) often has difficulty awaiting turn

(i) often interrupts or intrudes on others (e.g., butts into conversations or games)

B. Some hyperactive-impulsive or inattentive symptoms that causes impairment were present before age 7 years.

C. Some impairment from the symptoms is present in two or more settings (e.g., at school (or work) and at home).

D. There must be clear evidence of clinically significant impairment social, academic, or occupational functioning.

E. The symptoms do not occur exclusively during the course of a Pervasive Developmental Disorder, Schizophrenia, or other Psychotic Disorder and are not better accounted for by another mental disorder (Mood Disorder, Anxiety Disorder, Dissociative Disorder, or a Personality Disorder).

Code Is Based on Type

314.01:   Attention-Deficit/Hyperactivity Disorder, Combined Type

314.00:   Attention-Deficit/Hyperactivity Disorder, Predominantly Inattentive Type

314.07:   Attention-Deficit/Hyperactivity Disorder, Predominantly Hyperactive-Impulsive Type

314.09:   Attention-Deficit/Hyperactivity Disorder Not Otherwise Specified (This category is for disorders with prominent symptoms of inattention or hyperactivity-impulsivity that do not meet criteria for Attention-Deficit/Hyperactivity Disorder.)

HOW TO UNDERSTAND AND HELP STUDENTS WHO HAVE ALCOHOL PROBLEMS

Alcohol use by children and youth is much more than a "gateway" to other drug abuse. Alcohol is inexorably intertwined with a myriad of serious emotional, behavioral, and learning difficulties confronting young persons today. In a recent poll by the National Association of Student Councils, 46% of respondents ranked alcohol as today's most serious school problem. By tenth grade, 90% of youth have tried alcohol; of these, 69% report first use by the eighth grade. One-third of twelfth-grade students engage in binge drinking at least semiweekly. Drinking is strongly related to promiscuous sexual activity and date rape; among sexually active teens, those averaging five or more drinks daily were three times less likely to use condoms, thus placing them at risk for HIV (OSAP, 1991). Such statistics cause pollster George Gallup, Jr. to conclude that America does not have a crime problem, a teenage pregnancy problem, a worker productivity problem, or a problem of broken homes. Instead, says Gallup, America has an alcohol and drug problem.

CHEERS TO THE DRUG OF CHOICE . . . .

Fueling the alcohol crisis among modern youth is a virtual alcohol immersion campaign waged by the media. "Cheers," the corner bar of the long-running television series, has become as familiar to children as the neighborhood supermarket. A multibillion-dollar "beverage" industry feigns responsibility by counseling teens to "wait until you are mature," while simultaneously crafting commercials that tantalize youth. Advertisers employ a deceptive Orwellian "Newspeak," where beer drinking is paired with all the "good things in life." Drinking is associated with images of wild stallions running free (masculinity), a rugby or touch football game (fellowship), an exciting sports event (athletic prowess), a beach party, a volleyball game, or a bar scene involving beautiful women (sexuality). In this make-believe world, real men and women hurry off after a hard day's work—not to meet their families but to reward themselves with a drink. The adolescent readily reaches the intended conclusion: "I can't wait for the Happy Hour."

Contrary to popular opinion, the misuse of alcohol by children and youth is a more serious and pervasive problem in our society than the use of other drugs. Although alcohol is illegal for children and youth to purchase, it is cheap and easily obtained from home and from older peers, through falsified ID cards, and through the complicity of merchants. Even parents often wink at youthful binges: "Thank heavens it is only alcohol and not drugs!" they exclaim, blinded by a culture in which alcohol is the drug of choice. Research by the Search Institute shows this curious inconsistency in parental expectations about alcohol compared to other drugs.

Drinking is deeply rooted in our cultural traditions. In the days of small frontier towns, the mark of moral safety was achieved when the number of churches equaled or exceeded the number of bars. Because spirits are not a recent invention, it is not surprising that the abuse of alcohol was widespread among Europeans who first settled in North America. Many imbibing pioneers could outdrink their modern barroom counterparts. Alcoholics among the poor squandered their weekly wages on liquor, ignoring the needs of their starving families. But this was also the time of Calvinistic revivalism in America. The immorality of alcohol was clear—good was warring against evil, and there was no confusion between them. A dipsomaniac was a tool in the hands of the Prince of Darkness.

A popular Currier lithograph of the time offered vivid and painful images of the nine stages of alcoholism:

> *The Drunkard Progresses from the First Drink to the Grave*
>
> Step 1. A glass with a friend.
>
> Step 2. A glass to keep the cold out.
>
> Step 3. A glass too much.
>
> Step 4. Drunk and riotous.
>
> Step 5. The summit attained: jolly companions—a certified drunk.
>
> Step 6. Poverty and disease.
>
> Step 7. Forsaken by friends.
>
> Step 8. Depression and crime.
>
> Step 9. Death by suicide.

The 12-Step Program of Alcoholics Anonymous (AA) might well have had its origins as a restorative alternative to the ruinous steps of Currier's lithograph.

Ideally, language is designed to clarify ideas and thoughts and to communicate the core values of a civilization. However, when describing alcohol use in Western culture, language is used to *deny, minimize, and rationalize* the destructive effects of this drug. Notice, for example, how very few words in the English language are available to describe sobriety, and how stiff and lifeless they sound: abstinence, prohibition, temperance, and teetotalism. However, when it comes to describing drinking or drunkenness, the dictionary offers a virtual frolic of light-hearted euphemisms; for example, binge, smashed, inebriated, boozer, lush, plastered, pickled, crocked, polluted, stewed, soused, soaked, ranked, bombed, loaded, in the bag, stinko, skunk drunk, blind drunk, three sheets to the wind, high, tipsy, having a drop, a spot, a jigger, a snort, a round, an eye-opener, one for the road, hooch, rotgut, wetting one's whistle, raising one's elbow, or becoming mellow, giddy, or relaxed.

FACING OUR ALCOHOL PROBLEM . . . .

Alcohol is the most consumed drug among children and youth. Adolescents who drink frequently believe that alcohol will not affect their lives. They convince themselves they drink only to relax and loosen up for social activities. They rationalize that drinking beer and wine is not as destructive as drinking hard liquor. However, beer can lead to binge drinking, addiction, lowered academic motivation, sexual promiscuity, dangerous driving, violence, and self-destruction. Alcohol has an insidious effect on a young person's mood, thinking, judgment, and behaviors. It floods the self-control system, rendering intoxicated children victims of their own impulses.

Alcohol is a principal cause of physical and sexual abuse of children and the burgeoning rates of youth suicide. Twenty years ago, the term "fetal alcohol syndrome" (FAS) was first introduced to describe a pattern of birth defects observed in children born to alcoholic mothers (NIAAA, 1991). FAS children are subjected to chemical abuse *in utero*, which leads to severe impairments in learning, human attachment, and social functioning. Between the ages of 6 and 33, traffic crashes are the leading cause of death—and almost half of these are alcohol-related. A recent report to Congress tied alcohol to 49% of murders, 68% of manslaughters, 62% of assaults, and 52% of rapes. In fact, the correlation between alcohol and a host of other antisocial behaviors is so strong that prevention programs often use indexes of disordered behavior to screen for possible alcohol abuse.

Drinking also can be used to deny serious family problems, peer problems, and school problems. Drinking is an immature and unsuccessful way of dealing with feelings of frustration, humiliation, and depression. Unfortunately, drinking can help children or youth believe that relief is easy to attain. When they drink, they feel they can overcome their feelings of unhappiness. Alcohol creates a pattern of thinking errors in which youth delude themselves into believing that they are in control, likable, and competent, when in reality they are out of control, disgusting, and dysfunctional.

As we confront our massive problems with alcohol in contemporary society, every educator needs to reflect deeply on these issues, at both the personal and academic levels, and to develop realistic intervention to take the thrills, the sex, and the feelings of comfort out of adolescent drinking.

REFERENCES . . . .

NIAAA (1991). *Fetal alcohol syndrome. Alcohol Alert. No. 13, PH 297.* Rockville, MD: The National Institute on Alcohol Abuse and Alcoholism.

OSAP (1991). *Too many young people drink and know too little about the consequences.* Rockville, MD: Office of Substance Abuse Prevention.

 The next article, *Growing Up in an Alcoholic Family*, was written by Stephanie Abbot, director of the National Association for Children of Alcoholics. This incisive article for educators, describes the emotional turmoil of students who live in alcoholic homes, the importance of the children of alcoholics movement, and specific ways teachers can help these students.

This introduction has been adapted from *Journal of Emotional and Behavioral Problems* Vol. 2, Issue 3, Fall 1993 by Nicholas Long, Larry Brendtro, and John Johnson. Reprinted by permission.

Growing Up in an Alcoholic Family
Stephanie Abbott

Fifty percent of today's alcoholics are the children of alcoholics. In a typical class of 25 students, four to six children live in alcoholic homes. Children and youth of alcoholic parents are two to four times more likely to develop alcoholism than their peers, are at a higher risk to use other drugs, and are more likely to marry into alcoholic families.

The Joint Commission of the National Council on Alcoholism and Drug Dependence and the American Society of Addiction Medicine recently developed this definition stressing the heterogeneous nature of alcoholism:

Alcoholism is a primary, chronic disease with genetic, psychosocial, and environmental factors influencing its development and manifestations. Often progressive and fatal, the disease is characterized by impaired control over drinking, by preoccupation with this drug, by its use despite adverse consequences, and by distortions in thinking, most notably, denial. Each of these symptoms may be continuous or periodic.

The foregoing definition highlights the psychological maneuvers of denial, which decrease awareness of alcohol as the cause of a person's problems.

A DISEASE OF DENIAL

Denial is not just an individual defense mechanism. Our society is in massive denial about the destructive effects of alcoholism, including the impact that parental alcoholism has on children. The media frequently reinforce this blindness by writing of the "whining" of adult children of alcoholics and by emphasizing the role "codependency" plays in maintaining alcoholism.

Ideally, each member of a family system is respected, cherished, and allowed normal differences in feelings and behaviors. Addiction makes this goal impossible. Because the alcoholic parent is frequently out of control, the family develops a variety of reactive tactics to survive.

The codependent parent teaches by example that survival entails suppressing personal feelings and not talking about the drinking. The overriding principle is: "Let's not upset Dad." These are attempts to deny and contain the addiction and to keep the family stabilized as symptoms escalate. Even in "polite," financially stable families, alcoholism creates a destructive climate of anxiety and stress in children and youth. Overwhelmed by coping with the addiction of one's spouse, the sober parent blocks out what is happening to his or her children.

Historically, school personnel also have participated in denial about the scope and impact of alcoholism on students. However, research indicates that children of substance-abusing parents have decreased cognitive and verbal abilities, particularly as preschool children, as well as increased academic, behavioral, and learning problems in school. In one study of alcoholic families, 48% of the COAs aged 4 to 12 were identified by their teachers as likely to be "problem children," compared to 10% of the control children. There also is a significant relationship between parental alcoholism and child abuse, including incest, since parental self-control and reason disappear during drunken states. The problem is somewhat obscured because a few children respond to parental alcoholism by becoming "successful students." They use their leadership and academic achievement to over compensate for the lack of approval in their home life.

SURVIVAL ROLES OF CHILDREN OF ALCOHOLICS

Studies of the dynamics of alcoholic families suggest that children often become locked into rigid patterns of behavior that serve as "survival roles." Among these childhood roles that often persist into adulthood are the following:

Super-coper. The child who becomes the super-coper or a family hero has learned to feel totally responsible for the problems of others. Such children need to become free to meet their own needs and to seek help when it is needed. They must be encouraged to understand and learn from mistakes, rather than to be overly fearful of failure.

Scapegoat. The child who may be scapegoated needs help in channeling negative attention-seeking into positive constructive behavior. This can sometimes be done by enlisting the child's help in meaningful assignments, by giving responsibilities whenever possible, and by praising for positive talents and abilities.

The Lost Child. The child who may be lost and withdrawn needs help in responding to others rather than hiding from them. This child should be encouraged to find rewards in self-expression, to socialize and take part in class activities, and to differentiate fantasy from reality.

The Family Mascot. The child who may be a family mascot (or class clown) needs help in learning to take himself seriously and in differentiating appropriate from inappropriate humor as an attention-getting device. The child needs to identify feelings that lie beneath the mask of silliness, learning how to express feelings of discomfort and anxiety.

Source: Wegsheider, S., cited by R. Davis, T. Allen and J. Sherman (1989) in *Meeting the Needs of High Risk Youth in the School Setting.* Rockville, MD: National Association for Children of Alcoholics.

THE CHILDREN OF ALCOHOLICS MOVEMENT

Just as Alcoholics Anonymous was begun by alcoholics who were sober, adult children of alcoholics (ACOAs) began a grassroots movement in the early 1980s to become advocates for children of alcoholics (COA). Many professionals who were not children of alcoholics themselves also have added their expertise to the early identification, education, and treatment of these children.

The National Association for Children of Alcoholics (NACoA) was founded in 1983 and currently is the only national, non-profit, membership organization working on behalf of children of alcoholics. NACoA defines children of alcoholics as those people who have been affected by the alcoholism or drug dependence of a parent or other adult filling the parental role. This results in a recognizable, diagnosable, and treatable condition, which can be transmitted from one generation to the next. The mission of the organization is to raise public awareness, to provide leadership in public policy, and to inform and educate academic and other community systems.

One of the major activities of NACoA is to produce educational materials to enable adults to help children of alcoholics. Resources available through NACoA include a variety of curricular packages, including videos, posters, comic books, and guides for teachers and other school staff.

Regional and national conferences have provided another on-going and effective way to train teachers, therapists, and other professionals. NACoA's goal is to reach everyone in the field of education, human services, mental health, medicine, religion, and law enforcement. NACoA also has formed partnerships with other organizations and agencies to enhance public awareness, such as the Center for Substance Abuse Prevention, the National Committee for Prevention of Child Abuse, and the National Coalition for COA Education.

Two position statements by NACoA were published recently. The first, "Perinatal Addiction," expresses the organization's concerns about rights of women, as well as children, and the results of such punitive measures as jailing alcoholic women instead of mandating treatment. The second position statement focused on "Children of Alcoholics and Other Addicts in the Foster Care System." NACoA has recommended paying for relative or "kinship care," rather than multiple placements of children in foster homes. Both policy statements are available from the national office.

Not all COAs become alcoholic. In fact, many ACOAs function well in the world. There is growing evidence that there are environmental and individual resiliency factors in children that protect them from serious interpersonal dysfunction. Also, troubled families who have maintained their family rituals, such as holidays, seem to have lower risk factors for their children.

Alcoholism is a primary and chronic disease that families are ashamed about and deny. COAs frequently are victims of this denial and do not receive the help and support they need. COAs did not choose to be in a troubled family. Over time they may show their pain by antisocial behavior, rage, or withdrawal. Too often, professionals have viewed these problems as pathology in children, ignoring the parental addiction that drives it. Children of alcoholics deserve better from us.

Meeting the Needs of Children of Alcoholics, children of alcoholics have a host of special needs and problems. Here are some ways concerned teachers can be of help:

- Learn as much as you can about alcohol use, its effect on the family, and why COAs are at risk.
- Examine your own attitudes and personal biases toward alcohol.
- Explore facts about alcohol and alcoholism with young people. Show them it's all right to discuss alcohol problems openly.
- Help students develop the life and interpersonal skills that can help them cope better.
- Reassure COAs that they are not alone and that they did not cause, nor can they control or cure, their parents' alcoholism.
- Be alert to behavior that indicates a need for intervention; know that resources are available in your school or community and be willing to use them.
- Recognize that there are limits to the help you can give, and be willing to refer children to trained professionals for further help.

BIBLIOGRAPHY

Behling, D. W. (1979). Alcohol abuse as encountered in 51 instances of reported child abuse. *Clinical Pediatrics, 18*(2), 87–91.

Goodwin, D. W. (1985). Alcoholism and genetics: The sins of the fathers. *Archives of General Psychiatry, 6* (171–174).

Kumpfer, K. L. (1987). Special populations: Etiology and prevention of vulnerability to chemical dependency in children of substance abusers. In Brown, B. S., and Mills, A. R., eds. *Youth at High Risk for Substance Abuse.* National Institute on Drug Abuse, DHHS Pub. No. (ADM) 87-1537. Washington, DC: Supt. of Does., US. Govt. Print. Off.

Miller, D., and Jang, M. (1977). Children of alcoholics: A 20 year longitudinal study. *Social Work Research Abstracts, 13* (4): 23–29.

Morse, Robert, and Flavin, Daniel. (1992). The definition of alcoholism. *Journal of the American Medical Association,* Aug. 26, 1992, p. 1012.

Nylander, I. (1960). Children of alcoholic fathers. *Acta Paediatrica Scandinavia, 49,* (Supplement 121): 1–134.

Werner, E. E. (1986). Resilient offspring of alcoholics: A longitudinal study from birth to age 18. *Journal of Studies on Alcohol, 47*(1), 34–40.

Wolin, S. J., Bennett, L. A., Noonan, D. L. and Teitelbaum, M. A. (1980). Disrupted family rituals: A factor in the intergenerational transmission of alcoholism. *Journal of Studies on Alcohol, 4#*(3), 199–214.

RESOURCES

The following curriculum packages are available from NACoA, 11426 Rockville Pike, Suite 100, Rockville, MD 20852.

The General Education Package contains the educational video, "Poor Jennifer, She's Always Losing Her Hat," which comes with a teaching guide and lesson plans; a pamphlet, "It's Elementary: Meeting the Needs of High-Risk Youth in the School Setting"; and two audio cassettes, a comic book about alcoholism, and Marvel comic book posters.

The Elementary School Package includes a Resource Folder, the posters and the comic book, and two booklets: "COAs: Meeting the Needs of the Young COA in the School Setting"; and "It's Elementary: Meeting the Needs of High-Risk Youth in the School Setting," with a guidebook for the elementary school principal, the teacher, and the counselor or school staff member.

NACoA also made significant contributions to the development of the "Discovery Kit, Positive Connections for Kids," which was designed for community use with 10- to 15-year-olds and was released by the Center for Substance Abuse Prevention. This kit includes video and audio cassettes, illustrated books, poster guides, activity worksheets, and support materials for group leaders. It is available through the National Clearinghouse for Alcohol and Drug Information, PO Box 2345, Rockville, MD 20847, and is free.

For additional resources on Children of Alcoholics, contact:

Al-Anon/Alateen
Box 862
Midtown Station
New York, NY 10018-0862
(800) 356-9996

Children of Alcoholics Foundation
PO Box 4185
Grand Central Station
New York, NY 10165-4185
(800) 359-COAF

National Association for Native American Children of Alcoholics
1402 3rd Ave., Suite 1110
Seattle, WA 98101
(800) 322-5601

National Black Alcoholism/Addictions Council
1629 K Street, NW Suite 802
Washington, DC 20006
(202) 296-2696

National Council on Alcoholism & Drug Dependence
12 West 21st Street
New York, NY 10010
(800) NCA-CALL

. . . .

HOW TO UNDERSTAND AND HELP STUDENTS WHO ARE DEPRESSED . . . .

Depression is a complex term that can be used to describe a fleeting feeling of sadness, the blues, or a chronic state of withdrawal from the everyday activities of life. Depression can be characterized as a feeling, a mood, a negative state of mind, or a severe form of psychopathology. Prior to 1970, most psychiatrists believed depression was only an adult disease and children were immune to this form of mental illness. Currently, depression in children and youth is recognized as a valid diagnosis by the American Psychiatric Association's DSM-III-R and has two classifications: A Major Depressive Disorder and a Dysthymic Disorder. It is estimated that 20% of adolescents in treatment centers have one of these two diagnoses.

Depression has been called the wordless scream for help and is the precipitative cause of suicide. Cognitive therapists believe that most depressed students have internalized a negative way of thinking about themselves. Their irrational thoughts trigger pervasive feelings of guilt, grief, pessimism, and worthlessness, which are expressed in behaviors that have debilitating effects on their academic, social, and personal skills. Psychologically, they are like a flower trying to return to a seed. They block out all the sunlight in their lives and are drawn to the dark magnetism of their thoughts. Their negative statements, such as, "Nothing ever is going to get better or change," "I hate life," "I'm too tired to do anything—just let me rest," "No one really cares about me . . . I don't really care what happens to me," "There is nothing you can do to help me; this is the way it will always be and I only want to be left alone," make it extremely difficult for staff to be motivated to help them.

Another problem for staff is that depression can be as contagious as a noxious virus. Even the healthiest of staff can be affected and will then reflect the students' feelings of irritability, negativism, and hopelessness. This sequence is a supreme example of the dynamics of the Conflict Cycle in action (see page 244): "[A] student in a depression will create in the staff his feelings and if the staff is not adequately trained, the staff will end up behaving like the depressed student." A more direct way of stating this principle is to say: A depressed student will create counterdepression in the staff.

Once the staff begins to feel uncomfortable and frustrated by lack of progress, a common reaction is to withdraw and to accommodate the student's wish "to be left alone." If this happens, the depressed student will be successful in taking another step backward into his or her inner world of sadness.

Another variation of depression occurs when a student is able to mask feelings of depression by becoming irritable, anxious, and aggressive. Not all depressed students are withdrawn and tearful. A few find it more comfortable to direct their anger at people than to talk about their sad feelings. One student at Rose School, who had tears rolling down his cheeks, quickly said to the crisis teacher, "I'm not sad—that's just water!"

Historically, depressed students have been seen as the professional responsibility of psychiatry. Now, educators have a professional responsibility to work with these students—ideally, in a collaborative team model. Unfortunately, teachers (even teachers of emotionally disturbed students) have little or no training or experience in this area. Despite the popular use of the term *depression* in television shows, magazines, and everyday language, there are more myths about depression in children and youth than there are facts about this personality problem.

The next article, *Despair At Any Age,* was written by Norman Alessi, a child and adolescent psychiatrist and director of the Children and Adolescent Mood Clinic at the University of Michigan, Department of Psychiatry. Dr. Alessi exposes ten myths regarding depression among children and youth. Dr. Alessi represents the new breed of psychiatrists who are willing and able to leave the security of a medical center to speak out and address the multiple social and emotional problems of living with and helping depressed students at home, in schools, and in the community.

ARTICLE 6.7

Despair at Any Age
Norman Alessi

MYTHS ABOUT DEPRESSED CHILDREN AND ADOLESCENTS

It has been only 23 years since the publication of the first papers identifying depression in children. Since that time, we have made significant progress in understanding the scope of this problem. Nevertheless, childhood and adolescent depression often goes unrecognized. Frequently teachers who have daily contact with children and adolescents often either fail to recognize this serious disturbance, or mislabel the youth as having a behavioral problem. Possibly, the greatest sources of confusion about childhood and adolescent depression are various "myths" we maintain about childhood that, ultimately, determine our perceptions and actions. What are these myths, and what are the facts about child and adolescent depression?

Myth 1: Childhood Is a Happy Time

Fact: Everyone experiences difficulties in childhood and adolescence that can have lifelong impact: loss, failure, an inability to live up to one's own or others' expectations. But the plight of our children and adolescents is much worse. Child abuse, poverty, and homelessness are only a few factors that make the lives of a growing portion of our children miserable at best and chronically impaired at worst. No longer can or should we harbor the notion of childhood as being pristine, without pain and suffering.

Myth 2: Children and Adolescents Are Unable to Talk About Their Feelings

Fact: Children as young as three and four have been shown to demonstrate an understanding of their affective states. The ability to identify one's affect

From *The Journal of Emotional and Behavioral Problems.* (1993). Vol. 2, No. 2. Reprinted with permission.

and communicate about it has less to do with age than with innate ability. Not surprisingly, there are some children who are far better able to discuss their feelings than are most adults. When approaching a child or adolescent, one should assume that they can express their feelings and communicate with you.

An important source of difficulty is the potential presence of speech and language disorders among children and adolescents with psychopathology. This is not a rare phenomenon, but a rarely noted phenomenon. Studies clearly have noted that up to 75% of inpatient populations and 45% of outpatient populations have some form of communication disturbance, with the majority never being identified.

Myth 3: Prepubertal Children Are too Young to Be Depressed

Fact: Toddlers as young as four years old have been identified as being depressed, though at a rate less than among adults and adolescents. These children are not just unhappy or sad; they have major depressive disorders. This should not come as a surprise, given the early work of Spitz and his identification of "anaclitic depression" among infants. The limiting factor is not the age of the child, but the ability of the observer to identify the depression.

When depression is seen in such a young child, it is often asked, "What could a child that young have experienced that would make him or her depressed?" There are three answers: First, even extremely young children can experience severe trauma, the consequence of which is depression. Second, because of genetic disposition, some children will be more sensitive to stress than other children; and even the normal stresses of life can result in depression for these children. Third, with enough loading, these children may have a spontaneous onset of depression.

Myth 4: Depression in Children and Adolescents Is Always Due to Something

Fact: This idea presupposes that a trauma or conflict in an individual's life is the "factor" that leads to depression. The problem with this assumption is that not all children, adolescents, or, for that matter, even adults will experience depression as a consequence of a "trauma." Also, there are those who will not experience relief even if a "trauma" is identified. This often is seen when patients are in psychotherapy or family therapy for protracted periods of time without progress.

Myth 5: Expressed Sadness Always Accompanies Depression

Fact: One would assume that a depressed person should look sad or "depressed." Nothing could be further from the truth, especially in children and adolescents. A number of studies have demonstrated that "depression" in children and adolescents often is seen as anxiety (especially separation anxiety in younger children), phobias (often of school), opposition, aggression, or irritability, which then is labeled as either an oppositional disorder or a conduct disorder. These symptoms, not the depression, then become the main target for treatment.

One may ask, "Isn't this masked depression?" No! If the depression is not identified, then it is an unidentified depression, not a masked depression. The mislabeling of aggression or other symptoms leads one to apply a "therapy" that does not deal specifically with the problem of depression. Given the new diagnostic procedures, there is no reason to assume that a child, regardless of his or her symptoms, cannot be diagnosed, if depression exists.

Myth 6: Depressed and Sad Feelings Are Short-Lived

Fact: For some, they are. But for those with a mood disorder, they are not. Often, children and adolescents will describe having been depressed for a number of years, with extremely severe periods and extended times of boredom, poor concentration, and irritability. Yet they are repeatedly told, "This will pass with time." It is often this statement that makes the child or adolescent feel embittered and hopeless; it can and does lead these youths to question the value of life and to desire that life come to an end.

Myth 7: They Will Outgrow the Depression. It's Nothing to Worry About

Fact: Several longitudinal studies have shown that if a child has a major depressive disorder, the likelihood is greater than 60% that they will have a recurrence within five years. And if a dysthymic disorder is present, the child is more than 75% likely to have a Major Depressive Disorder within 5 years. If a child or adolescent has either of these depressive conditions, they should be monitored closely for either recurrence or relapses. For some children, adolescents, and their families, depression is a way of life, not a passing phase.

Myth 8: Withdrawal Is Just a Part of Being an Adolescent

Fact: At one time, it was thought that all adolescents experienced "adolescent turmoil" and, as a consequence, were not able to be diagnosed as having a major psychiatric disorder. Whether called "adolescent turmoil" or "adolescent crazies," this undermines the ability to adequately assess adolescents, and when necessary, administer needed care. Social withdrawal is an issue of significance, and to mislabel it as a matter of normal development will unquestionably have lifelong impact.

When a child becomes withdrawn, it is important to assess why. Following a traumatic event, the adolescent may have the onset of a major depressive disorder, a psychotic disorder, or a substance abuse disorder. It is important to not turn your back on them or ignore them.

Myth 9: Mad Versus Sad

Fact: Irritability is one of the most frequent symptoms seen in this population. It is most disconcerting when it is expressed as overt aggression, such as verbal outbursts, the destruction of property, or in extreme situations, physical aggression toward self or others.

Children and adolescents with depressive disorders often have "conduct disorders" or "oppositional defiant disorders" as well. The presence of diagnostic disorders occurring together is referred to as "comorbid disorders." Research has shown several disorders occurring frequently in children and adolescents with depression. In their order of frequency of co-occurrence are anxiety disorders (separation anxiety, phobias, panic attacks, and general anxiety), then disruptive behavioral disorders (attention deficit hyperactive disorders, oppositional defiant disorders, or conduct disorders).

Certainly, the hallmark of the disruptive behavioral disorder is the presence of aggressive symptoms that are extremely bothersome to those professionals who interact with depressed children and youth. One of the most difficult features of this complex illness is the ability to empathize with a chronically angry person who is depressed. Therefore, the therapist, rather than providing a bridge for children and youth to return from their depression, can get caught up in the chronic anger and end up also alienating them.

Myth 10: All It Takes to Make a Depressed Child or Adolescent Better Is Kindness

Fact: This myth may be rephrased as "love will make it all better" or, when medications are suggested, "Hugs not drugs." One should not assume that these children will respond to kindness, nor should therapists be disappointed when their kindness is not rewarded. Many of these patients are unable to respond to the attempts of the therapist to be empathic. In fact, being with these children often can produce within their caregivers enormous feelings of pain, lethargy, and actual fatigue. Until a therapist becomes acutely aware that these conditions exist in himself, he will unconsciously withdraw from the patient, causing the patient to sense rejection.

The ability to make oneself aware of these myths and their consequences is of utmost importance if one wishes to be of help to these children and adolescents. We all harbor myths. It is the ability to rise above these myths in the pursuit of truth that determines the true worth of any profession and its professionals.

DIAGNOSTIC CRITERIA—DSM-IV

The most frequently used diagnostic criteria, developed by the American Psychiatric Association, are published in the Diagnostic Statistical Manual, Fourth Edition *(DSM-IV)*. These diagnostic criteria, a group of signs and symptoms used to identify the syndrome of depression, have proven invaluable in the identification and treatment of depressed children, adolescents, and adults. A significant feature of the *DSM-IV* is the classification of several types of depressive disorders. This classification allows for the study of patients in groups, rather than as individuals, thereby allowing the testing of hypotheses to determine the validity of our treatments. When a treatment is of "proven" value for a group of patients, there is some confidence in putting it to use. The two most frequently identified depressive disorders in children and adolescents are major depressive disorder and dysthymic disorder.

The following is the DSM-IV diagnostic criteria for a Major Depressive Disorder:

- The presence of at least 5 of the following symptoms during a two-week period, at least one of which is symptom 1 or 2 listed below.
  1. Depressed mood or, in some cases, irritable mood.
  2. Diminished interest or pleasure in all or almost all activities.
  3. Significant weight gain or weight loss (when not dieting), increase or decrease in appetite, or failure to make expected weight gain in children.
  4. Insomnia or hypersomnia.
  5. Psychomotor retardation or agitation.
  6. Fatigue or loss of energy.
  7. Feelings of worthlessness or excessive guilt.
  8. Diminished ability to think or concentrate; indecisiveness.
  9. Morbid ideation, suicidal ideation, or a specific plan or attempt at suicide.
- Exclusion criteria. These symptoms and signs, if present, would exclude the diagnosis of a depressive disorder:
  1. Not initiated or maintained by an organic factor. If a medical disorder has been identified, or if the person is taking drugs, using alcohol, or taking prescription medications, a depressive disorder cannot be identified.
  2. A nonnormal reaction to death of a loved one.
  3. At no time have there been delusions or hallucinations for as long as two weeks in the absence of depressive symptoms. This is meant to exclude those with a primary "psychotic" disorder, such as schizophrenia.

4. Not superimposed on schizophrenia, a delusion disorder, or other forms of psychotic disorder. Modifications of this criterion, such as the presence of the symptoms for prolonged periods, make the diagnosis one of a depressive disorder, recurrent or chronic. Also, there are degrees of major depressive disorders and noted seasonal variability.

Following is the DSM-III-R diagnostic criteria for a Dysthymic Disorder:

- Depressed mood (can be an irritable mood in children and adolescents) for most of the day, more days than not, as indicated either by subjective account or observation by others, for at least two years (one year for children and adolescents).
- Presence, while depressed, of at least two of the following:
  —Poor appetite or overeating.
  —Insomnia or hypersomnia.
  —Low energy or fatigue.
  —Low self-esteem.
  —Poor concentration or difficulty making decisions.
  —Feelings of hopelessness.
- No evidence of an unequivocal major depressive episode during the first year of the disturbance. Never had a manic episode or hypermanic episode.
- Not superimposed on a chronic psychotic disorder, such as schizophrenia.
- Organic factor is not the basis of the disturbance, such as a chronic illness or a reaction to a medication.

One of the most challenging difficulties is identifying the presence of a depressive disorder when it occurs in a child or adolescent with possibly numerous emotional, behavioral, or cognitive disturbances. But, after the identification of a depressive disorder and after the child or adolescent receives treatment, some of these comorbid disturbances, such as separation anxiety or attention deficit disorders, may be seen as secondary. Others, such as learning disabilities or conduct disorders, may demand further case conceptualization and therapeutic intervention.

ARE DEPRESSIVE DISORDERS IN CHILDREN AND ADOLESCENTS THE SAME AS IN ADULTS?

One of the hotly debated questions in this area has been: "Are depressive disorders in children and adolescents the same as in adults?" This question arose, in part, from a predominantly psychodynamic perspective that placed a higher value on theory than phenomenology. In contradicting this psychodynamic perspective, many critics failed to acknowledge any difference between these age groups.

Obviously, there are differences. Within the last several years, these differences have been studied. The following table gives a general overview of these differences. However, the reader should be warned that the table is a simplification of a very complex issue. There are many variables that make this issue even more complex, such as mental retardation, developmental disorders, psychosis, or personality disorders, to name just a few.

Several of the most important differences are those in the areas that are sensitive to development—in particular, those reflective of self-development, social-skill acquisition, and language development. These areas are the most vulnerable to the effects of the depressive disorder itself. Several questions reflective of this effect are: Will the loss of social skills be recoverable? Is a self-concept damaged during a severe depressive episode recoverable or reparable? Are the communication skills that are not gained, lost forever? Dramatic in statement, these are the questions that clinicians often must answer after dealing with these children and adolescents.

HOW FREQUENT ARE THESE DISORDERS?

There have been numerous studies attempting to determine the frequency of these disorders in children and adolescents. There are no broad epidemiological studies; this will have to await the completion of the Epidemiological Child Investigation recently begun by the National Institute of Mental Health. Most of the studies that have been completed have involved those who have been identified as having psychiatric difficulties, such as psychiatrically hospitalized children and adolescents. The exceptions have been the studies by Kashani, which focused on the identification of depression in those with physical or presumed physical illnesses. These have demonstrated that between 2% and 10% of children may have major depressive disorders, and this number increases significantly at adolescence to greater than 20%.

CONCLUSIONS

They are frequent, disabling, affect development, and possibly have irreversible consequences; yet depressive disorders among children and adolescents go unnoticed. They are true silent killers, potentially of the body, certainly of the human spirit.

Too often, these children and adolescents are mislabeled and rejected by the people to whom they come for help. Before presuming to care for these children and adolescents, we must admit our own myths about child-hood and depression. Then, and only then, will the care for these youths be improved.

REFERENCES

American Psychiatric Association. (1987). *Diagnostic and statistical manual of mental disorders (3rd ed., rev.).* Washington, D.C.: American Psychiatric Association.

Bromberger, J.T., & Costello, E.J. (1992). Epidemiology of depression for clinicians. *Social Work, 37*(2), 120–126.

Burke, P. (1991). Depression in pediatric illness. *Behavior Modification,* #5(4), 486–500.

Carlson G.A., & Kashani, J.H. (1988). Phenomenology of major depression from childhood through adulthood: Analysis of three studies. *American Journal of Psychiatry 145,* 1222–1225.

Keller, M.B., Lavori, P.W., Beardslee, W.R. et al. (1991). Depression in children and adolescents: New data on "undertreatment" and a literature review on the efficacy of available treatments. *Journal of Affective Disorders, 21,* 163–171.

Kovacs, M., Feinberg, T.L., Crouse-Novak, M.A. et al. (1984). Depressive disorders in childhood, I: A longitudinal prospective study of characteristics and recovery. *Archives of General Psychiatry, 41,* 229–237.

Kovacs, M., Feinberg, T.L., Crouse-Novak, M.A. et al. (1984). Depressive disorders in childhood II: A longitudinal study of the risk for a subsequent major depression. *Archives of General Psychiatry, 41,* 643–649.

Ryan, N.D., Puig-Antich, J., Ambrosini, P. et al. (1987). The clinical picture of major depression in children and adolescents. *Archives of General Psychiatry,* 44(10), 854–861.

Spitz, R. & Wolf, K.M. (1946). Anaclitic depression: An inquiry into the genesis of psychiatric conditions in early childhood. *Psychoanalytic Study of the Child, 2,* 3 13–342.

Weissman, M.M., Gammon, D, John, K. et al. (1987). Children of depressed parents. *Archives of General Psychiatry, 44,* 847–853.

. . . .

The previous article was successful in correcting many of the myths and mis-information about depressed children and youth. The next article, Psychoeducation Strategies for Depressed Students, was written by Sandra Burak-Maholik, a special educator/consultant who has taught depressed students at the University of Michigan Psychiatric Hospital for over nine years. Dr. Burak-Maholik's article translates the theories and knowledge of depression into an effective psychoeducation program for teachers. She advocates the importance of a student study team, describes successful individual and group intervention, and emphasizes the effectiveness of using the creative arts as a teaching strategy.

This psychoeducational approach is one way in which teachers can be active in the reeducation process. Too many of our students are suffering from depression and will never see a professional unless a teacher has the awareness and the confidence to make the initial referral.

Psychoeducational Strategies for Depressed Students

Sandra Burak-Maholik

"You're the meanest teacher in the world!" Jason yells as he stomps back to his desk. His teacher, angry and perplexed, wonders what to do. Jason is a ten-year-old fifth-grader. Just as the teacher had quieted the group down and was beginning a lesson, Jason had walked up to her and begun a personal conversation. She had asked him nicely to sit down. Now he is sitting at his desk, tears rolling down his cheeks, furiously beginning his math assignment. Once again, a simple request turned into a major problem and disruption. It doesn't seem to matter how many times the teacher explains to Jason that sometimes she can not talk to him immediately. It doesn't matter how much extra attention she gives him, he still needs more.

John has gotten the attention of his teacher and is pointing to Anita. Anita has her head down and is clearly upset, but the teacher is in the middle of giving directions for a spelling test. The teacher signals an "I know" look to John and finishes giving the instructions. As the test begins, the classroom is quiet and the teacher approaches Anita. Anita cannot explain why she is upset. The teacher guesses two or three reasons, but Anita shakes her head no. This event is not unusual. Anita is sad almost every day and frequently sobs for no apparent reason. In frustration, the teacher retreats to help students who have a hand raised.

Jason and Anita both suffer from depressive disorders. Jason tends to display an angry outward facade, which can then turn into sobbing episodes. Anita fits a more classical depressive picture. She looks sad most of the time and cries often. Jason has an event in his childhood that helps to understand his behavior, whereas Anita does not. Jason's mother died when he was two, and his father has since re-married. One gets the sense that the loss is ever-present and there will never be enough love or attention for Jason. Anita's parents are loving and caring. They always have given Anita lots of attention, and there have been no apparent traumas. However, the etiology of the disorders becomes relatively unimportant when thinking about strategies for a school setting. Both children need special strategies and an understanding of their disorder.

The rest of this article will be divided into three sections. The first section will deal with student study teams as a means to increase understanding and mobilize cooperation and commitment for both in special education and regular classrooms. The second section will outline a number of different strategies for individuals and groups within the classroom. The third section will discuss the use of art, dance, music, gym, and other special activities.

STUDENT STUDY TEAMS

Student study teams traditionally are used only for special education students. However, this concept can be used for any student who is experiencing emotional/behavioral difficulties and is functioning at or near grade level. For special education, a team of teachers, psychologists, social workers, etc., identify and test students. However, such a process needs to occur for all students who are not functioning within the classroom setting, regardless of special education status. Some districts already provide social workers, psychologists, and psychiatrists for students who do not qualify for special education.

Special education students are provided with the IEPC (Individual Education Planning Committee) process. Non-special-education students deserve a similar process; it is critical for developing a working relationship between parents, teachers, administrators, and all personnel who have contact with the student. Everyone needs to be involved at some level, including day-care staff, custodians, hall monitors, etc. Every student can succeed if everyone is focused and works together.

The team must be prepared to use a blameless approach. It really does not matter how the situation arose. The plan must be to address interventions to implement in the future. Teachers must step forward and identify the students who are not benefiting from their approach or who do not seem to be functioning well. Everyone involved, including the student, needs to be open to suggestions and ideas and, when they do not work, admit that something is wrong.

The team meets as often as is necessary to address the concerns of teachers or other school personnel. Anyone who has contact with the student is then invited to attend the team meeting. In order to have the best attendance, meetings usually occur at lunch or after school. Some teams meet at a regular time during the school day, and substitutes are provided for key personnel. Each member of the team reports observations, and the team outlines a plan for interacting with and helping the student.

Suggestions for different strategies are outlined below. They are organized into two areas: one-on-one interventions and group interventions.

STRATEGIES

Individualized Interventions

Students who are depressed need reassurance that they are not alone. They want to know that they are understood and that the staff truly care. They need to be able to trust in people.

- Meet the student at the door in the morning or say hello as soon as he or she walks in. Make contact, ask how their evening was, show you care.

- When a student is under stress, let him or her talk. If time does not permit it, arrange another time.

- Some students can "talk" better into a journal. Begin by writing in your journal and letting them read it. Include a particularly difficult time for you and how you finally resolved it. Try to be open about something that demonstrates to the student your willingness to share. Then encourage the student to write back. Sometimes a starter phrase is needed, such as, "I am happiest when . . ." or "I am loneliest when . . ."

- Encourage drawings or poems. These can be part of a journal or added to other assignments. Many students enjoy using spelling words in a poem or picture rather than doing the traditional assignment. Think of other assignments that could be adapted.

- Allow the student to help in planning for a future event. What can be done differently? What response would he or she like to see done differently?

- Use the team to plan whom the student can go to when in turmoil and cannot wait to talk. Use custodians, lunch staff, office help, teacher consultants, anyone to whom the student may escape.

- Give the student special jobs that she or he likes. Let the student pass out papers, erase the board, or take care of the class pets.

- Arrange a code with the student so you know when the student needs help or needs to leave the room. Simple statements like, "I need to go" or "It's time" work well. Hand signs also can be used, such as pointing to the door or waving goodbye. The code is pre-arranged to give the student certain options.

- Assign the student a "buddy," someone who has shown an interest in the student's welfare, is considerate, and wants to help. Allow the depressed student to access his or her buddy on an as-needed basis, leaving the class-room if necessary.

- Do not be afraid to try different groupings or different seating arrangements. Seat the student next to his or her "buddy."

- Find out what the student is interested in or likes. Find time to allow the student this outlet. Sometimes the depressed student has no apparent interests; ask the "buddy" to get the student involved in an activity, even if they only watch. Help the "buddy" to try different activities each week. Some teachers plan an option or enrichment time so that all students get this opportunity. These plans include ideas that are somewhat unorthodox, but they work. The key is to plan ahead with the team, so that everyone knows what options the student has available. Parents of other students who are helping need to be informed of plans and asked for consent when necessary. As students feel that their support network is really there and consistent, their trust increases. Their sense of control and self-esteem rises. This trust also allows for more verbal communication with both staff and peers, further increasing understanding.

GROUP INTERVENTIONS

Any deviant behavior causes stress in a classroom. If students do not understand each other, they are less likely to help one another. Classroom groups are mini-families and need time to express their thoughts and fears. When each student feels they are an integral part of this family, not only will they help, they will protect each other. The strategies below are aimed at group interventions.

- A group technique used for students with severe handicapping conditions who have been integrated into classrooms is called "A Circle of Friends." Specific interventions are used to increase understanding of the student's disabilities, and activities are planned to help classmates interact appropriately with the handicapped students. A similar program can be used for any student experiencing difficulties in the classroom.

- Daily class meetings help to bring up issues before they turn into problems. There needs to be a commitment by all students that what is said is confidential and does not leave the classroom. Students are then more willing to raise concerns. Teachers need to be open to suggestions and involve students in problem-solving and decision-making efforts.

- Continually point out that everyone is different. Some of us are good at math, others at reading. Some can play basketball, others like to play Monopoly. Some of us cry when hurt, others bite our lip. When students begin to realize that it is OK to be different, the depressed student no longer has to explain his existence.

- There are a number of visual/perceptual images that illustrate that people have different perceptions of the same event. A favorite is the figure ground perceptual image of the young woman/old woman, which is found in most beginning psychology textbooks.

- Frequently, a problem will arise between the depressed student and one or more other students. A consistent conflict management approach needs to be followed. One method begins with each student agreeing not to interrupt or name-call. Each student then expresses his or her viewpoint. Usually, just having the students express their viewpoints alleviates the problem; however, sometimes students need to be encouraged to come up with a solution with which everyone can live. Sometimes several meetings are necessary. Many teachers and other school personnel have "lunch chats" with groups of students on a regular basis. In that way, when a problem arises, it is not unusual to meet with the teacher, social worker, principal, etc.

All of the strategies mentioned have one underlying theme, group cohesiveness. Helping all students understand and trust one another provides each student, including those who are depressed, a sense of belonging and well-being. The last section of this article discusses the use of art, dance, music, gym, and other "specials" to help increase self-expression and self-esteem.

The Use of Specials: Art, Dance, Music, Gym

- Determine if your district has consultants for art therapy, dance therapy, music therapy, and recreational therapy. Many community programs have these services, and personnel may be willing to give the team some suggestions.
- Include the "special" (art, music, gym, etc.) teachers on the team. Help them to see how self-expression can build the student's self-esteem.
- Help each "special" teacher think of one strategy to try. Examples might include

  Art: Ask students to draw themself as they see themselves now and how they want to see themselves in the future. Each month, take out the drawings and see if positive details can be added.

  Music/Dance: Allow the student to pick out a song they like. Use the "buddy" and the class to help develop the song or dance. Lip-synching is fun for everyone.

  Gym: Encourage the physical education teacher to try non-competitive games where everyone wins.

Everyone needs to feel supported and goal-oriented. Schoolwide student study teams provide support to all students and staff, so the stigma of requesting help can be reduced. We need to support each other and to empower ourselves to prove that every student can succeed!

· ·

HOW TO UNDERSTAND AND HELP STUDENTS WITH SUICIDAL THOUGHTS AND ACTIONS . . . .

Suicide is deadly and suicidal attempts are risky. The only way to prevent a suicide is to prevent a suicidal attempt. This statement implies that teachers can be taught the risk factors of suicidal students and the accompanying life events that precipitate their behaviors. Research studies have confirmed that suicidal behavior is more often observed in troubled students who have been abused, traumatized, or abandoned, or are depressed or on drugs. These high-risk students may be experiencing unbearable emotional stress and may think of suicide as a way out of a painful world.

In the past, educators didn't have a mandate to intervene. Now, a growing number of states have passed comprehensive laws regarding attempted suicidal behaviors. Florida legislators have mandated training for all high school teachers in the areas of suicide detection, interventions, and referral skills. Although the schools are not totally responsible for suicidal acts or behaviors, they can serve as the first line of defense in recognizing and supporting these at-risk students. McGee and Guetzloe have summarized the relevant research findings in this area and have made the following recommendations to teachers:*

1. Be ready to take drastic action if you think a student is in danger. Let the student know you care. It is far better to err in the direction of doing too much than too little.

2. Be ready to talk about suicidal behavior without being shocked. There are no inconvenient times to talk about suicidal thoughts and plans.

3. Never take a suicidal threat or gesture casually. Do something. Mobilize your available resources.

4. Don't be afraid to bring up the topic and question the student closely and carefully about any possible suicidal plan.

5. Encourage the student to talk (i.e., "You seem troubled. Tell me what you are thinking and I might understand how difficult it is for you at this time.").

6. Don't leave a suicidal student alone. Stay with the student until another adult arrives.

7. Get rid of any object in the immediate environment which the student could use in a hurtful manner.

8. Do not promise to keep a student's suicidal behavior secret.

9. Try to get a commitment from the student not to inflict self-harm. If possible, get the student to sign a contract with you. The following wording can be modified as necessary:

    1. I, _____ , agree not to kill myself, attempt to kill myself, or bring any harm to myself during the period from _____ to _____ (dates).
    2. I agree to get enough sleep and to eat regularly and well.
    3. I agree to get rid of things I could use to kill myself.
    4. I agree that if I have a bad time and feel that I might hurt myself, I will call _____ at _____ (telephone number) or the Suicide and Crisis Center at _____ (telephone number).

    > Signed _____
    > Witness _____
    > Date _____

---

* From McGee, K., and Guetzloe, E. Suicidal Emotionally Handicapped Students: Tips for Teachers. *Pointer*. (1988). Vol. 32, No. 4, pp. 7–10.

10. Be sure to connect the student with a crisis counselor or suicide prevention worker.

The next article was written by Eleanor Guetzloe, a professor of special education at the University of Southern Florida and a national expert in suicide prevention training. Dr. Guetzloe presents an extensive and thorough overview of the risk factors, precipitating events, and interventions to use with suicidal students. This article should be read periodically, as a reminder of the seriousness of this widespread problem.

ARTICLE 6.9

Answering the Cry for Help—Suicidal Thoughts and Actions

Eleanor C. Guetzloe

Suicide accounts for the deaths of more than 5,000 young people each year in the United States alone. Authorities estimate that for every completed suicide, there are probably from 100 to 350 attempts and many more threats and thoughts. Estimates of attempts among children and adolescents usually range from 50,000 to 500,000 per year (Allen, 1987).

According to the results of a recent Gallup Poll, one-third of American 15- to 19-year-olds had thought about suicide, 15% had seriously considered killing themselves, and 6% had made actual attempts (Peterson, 1991). In other studies, 8% to 9% of high school students admitted to one or more attempts, and up to 63% reported some degree of suicidal ideation (Harkavy-Friedman et al., 1987; Smith & Crawford, 1986).

Suicidal behavior also has been noted in very young children. In a sample of 16 preschoolers who had been referred to a child psychiatry outpatient clinic after seriously injuring themselves or attempting to do so, 13 had made multiple suicide attempts and expressed specific reasons for wanting to die (Rosenthai & Rosenthai, 1984).

Suicide attempts lead to the hospitalization of an estimated 12,000 youngsters ages 14 and under in the United States each year (Berman, 1986; Matter & Matter, 1984). Many other attempts (as many as 7 out of 8 in this age group) do not require medical treatment and are therefore not included in this estimate (Berman, 1986).

Among high-school-age youngsters, approximately one-fourth of attempts require emergency treatment. However, most suicide attempts by children and adolescents are never reported to mental health professionals or school personnel. Hospital personnel often learn of previous attempts only when a more serious attempt requires hospitalization.

From *The Journal of Emotional and Behavioral Problems*. (1993). Vol. 2, No. 3. Reprinted with permission.

RISK FACTORS FOR SUICIDAL BEHAVIOR

Risk factors specifically associated with completed suicide in young people include the following (Kupfer, 1991):

- Psychiatric disorders, including affective disorder (particularly depression), schizophrenia, borderline personality disorder, conduct disorder, and substance abuse.
- Parental loss and family disruption.
- Familial characteristics, such as predisposition to affective illness or being the biological relative of a suicide victim.
- Biological correlates, such as low concentrations of a serotonin metabolite and a dopamine metabolite in the cerebrospinal fluid.
- Certain personality traits, including impulsivity, aggressivity, cognitive rigidity, excessive perfectionism, and hopelessness.
- Other factors, including homosexuality, being a friend of a suicide victim, access to lethal weapons, and previous suicidal behavior.

Among children and adolescents who have been treated in emergency rooms for suicide attempts, the following individual and family factors, similar to those listed above, have been noted: (a) past history of psychotherapy; (b) aggressiveness and hostility; and (c) current psychiatric diagnosis. The families of these youngsters had histories of mental illness, suicide, drug and alcohol abuse, group or foster placement, unemployment of father, and father absence (Kovacs & Puig-Antich, 1991).

PRECIPITATING EVENTS

The presence of a situational crisis is an important warning sign of potential suicide in a child or adolescent. Among the most common events that precipitate suicide attempts are losses resulting from disruptions of relationships with girl-friends or boyfriends, problems at school or in the community, and conflicts within the family. Among younger children, precipitating events include (a) severe punishment (or fear of punishment), (b) a desire to join a dead relative (or pet), (c) feeling guilty over parents' divorce, and (d) modeling of media events. Any event that contributes to feelings of stress, depression, helplessness, hopelessness, and low self-esteem may in turn lead to suicidal behavior in young people.

EXAMPLES OF SUICIDAL THOUGHTS, THREATS, AND ATTEMPTS

The following actual cases illustrate the suicidal verbalizations and behaviors of children ages 5 to 17 who were hospitalized in the same facility because of suicidal attempts, threats, or thoughts. Each of these youngsters suffered from loss, humiliation, real or perceived rejection or neglect, physical or sexual abuse, or psychiatric disorders. All of them expressed very specific reasons for their suicidal behavior, as follows (Guetzloe, 1993):

- A five-year-old explained that he sees cars and guns on the walls and the ceiling. "The cars tell me to hurt myself—dead." The child tried to jump from a balcony.

- A six-year-old, who had been abandoned by both his parents and foster parents, said that he was "sick and tired of everyone leaving" him. He tried to drown himself in the bathtub.

- A seven-year-old was angry with his mother for remarrying. He stated, "I'm going to kill my mom and then me so Dad won't see her with that man."

- An eight-year-old "felt sad" because his grandfather had died and wanted to join him in Heaven.

- A nine-year-old, who had been sexually abused for years, expressed sadness "about all the bad people in the world who hurt children." She threatened suicide by pointing a knife at her stomach. Her mother took the knife away.

- A nine-year-old was angry because his mother would not let him go to the movies with his friend. He put the entire contents of a bottle of Tylenol in his mouth. He then spit it out and asked, "Can I go now?"

- "I was feeling depressed and like there was no way out. Last resort is how I felt at the time . . . either raise my grades or kill myself. I decided to raise my grades. Other things also was upsetting. I have many girl problems. Sometimes I feel like an outcast. I don't want to be gay. People should give other people a chance to prove themselves so if you ever feel the last resort, think about it hard first. People say that I'm different. Maybe they are mad because they're not like me, but they talk about me every day about something. Just be yourself. Something very good will happen to you."

- A ten-year-old, who had been sexually abused, said that she hated herself and tried to strangle herself with a shoestring while in the psychiatric unit.

- A 13-year-old female tried to hang herself with a bed-sheet. Her mother found her while she was still breathing. "I see Beth and hear her voice telling me to kill myself." Beth is the girl's invisible friend.

- "I want to feel the pain because I can't feel anything anymore." The 13-year-old, a victim of abuse, attempted to asphyxiate herself with carbon monoxide emitted by an automobile.

- "I wish my life was over!" The 15-year-old's identity as a lesbian had "leaked out" at her high school. She attempted suicide by cutting her wrist and swallowing her prescription pills.

- A 17-year-old was driving while drinking and ran his car into a tree. He suffered severe head injuries but lived to tell of his anger over his parents' divorce.
- A 17-year-old swallowed "a few pills" (not a lethal dose) to "get back at Mom" for not letting her date a 30-year-old man.

ASSESSMENT OF SUICIDE RISK

The assessment of suicidal risk in young people consists of an evaluation of the degree to which the various risk factors and/or precipitating events listed above are present in their lives at that specific time. It should be noted that it is not the type of loss that is critical, but rather how much the specific loss means to the individual. For example, many children are not concerned about grades, but a child with a high grade point average may agonize over a B.

Informal assessment of risk may be carried out in the school or other facility by an internal team of professionals, but only a trained professional should conduct a formal assessment and make judgments regarding the seriousness of suicidal behavior. It is important that nonprofessionals (a) recognize the limits of their competence and (b) make appropriate referrals to professionals with skills and experience in working with young people and with knowledge about suicide.

RESPONSIBILITIES OF PERSONNEL IN SCHOOL AND TREATMENT FACILITIES

The primary responsibilities of teachers, counselors, and other staff include:

- To be aware of the risk factors for suicide.
- To detect the signs of potential suicide, including suicidal threats and ideation.
- To report such behavior to the contact person or crisis team within the facility or program.
- To secure emergency medical services, if necessary.
- To make immediate referrals to child study teams or other personnel for further assessment.
- To provide immediate and continuing emotional support and supervision for the suicidal youngster.
- To report to parents and/or other appropriate individuals and agencies (and to document these reports).
- To help parents in securing assistance from school and community resources.

• To provide long-term follow-up services within the program (Guetzloe, 1989; 1991).

PROVIDING EMOTIONAL SUPPORT AND SUPERVISION

All members of the staff in the school or treatment facility who come in contact with a suicidal child or adolescent should be informed of a suicide threat so they can help provide supervision and support. It is important to have the youngster understand that the adults in the setting are deeply concerned about his or her welfare, and staff should be prepared to respond quickly to verbalizations of suicidal intent. Youngsters who are depressed or suicidal may misinterpret uncertainty or failure to respond to be lack of caring. Staff should practice (in role play) what they would say to a student who expresses thoughts of worthlessness, despair, or suicide, so they will be prepared when the situation presents itself.

The most commonly cited warning signs of potential suicide include (a) extreme changes in behavior, (b) signs of depression, (c) making final arrangements or "saying good-bye," and (d) procuring the means (for example, a gun or pills). Most crucial of all is the presence of a detailed, feasible, and lethal plan. Any staff member should not be afraid to ask a youngster directly about a suicide plan, using such questions as: "Are you planning to hurt yourself? How do you plan to do this? Do you have a gun or pills? When do you plan to do this?" In addition to the questions, the staff member should express his or her concern and caring, continue to listen, and indicate his or her willingness to help in any way possible. The young person should be kept under close supervision and must not be left alone.

SUGGESTED INTERVENTIONS BY SCHOOL AND TREATMENT STAFF

Some positive change in the youngster's life, no matter how small, should be affirmed immediately to prove that the situation is not hopeless. Schneidman (1985), who recommends such action for therapists, has called this a "J. N. D." or "Just Noticeable Difference." The major stresses that led to the suicidal behavior should be identified, and steps should be taken to reduce those stresses. For example, dropping a class, changing a schedule, providing a tutor, or removing a threat of punishment may provide hope for a student who is experiencing problems at school.

The 17-year-old youth was a good student, but he had been placed (through "computer error") in a class in which he was failing. His grade point average would be ruined, and his choices for college would be limited. He had become increasingly despondent and had told his counselor he would rather die than lose his chances for the college he wanted. When the counselor requested a schedule change, the principal's response was, "If we changed one student's schedule, we'd have another hundred requests. One failing grade won't hurt him."

This story had a happy ending. Upon receipt of a written memorandum from the counselor outlining the student's symptoms, the risk of suicide, and the principal's responsibility in this regard, the principal reversed her position. The obvious point is that it was possible to make the change (Guetzloe, 1989).

Berman and Jobes (1991) have discussed the themes of escape, relief, control, and power that appear during therapy with suicidal youth. They suggest that the intended goals of suicidal behavior involve attempts to replace pain, helplessness, hopelessness, or powerlessness, feelings and cognitions that are common to the suicidal state. The immediate tasks of a teacher, counselor, or therapist are to provide hope and to instill in the youngster some feeling of being in control. However, it is important not to promise any change that cannot be accomplished; a suicidal child should not be subjected to further disappointment. The focus of the changes, therefore, is on provisions that are under the control of the staff in that setting— whether school or treatment facility.

WORKING WITH THE FAMILY

One of the primary responsibilities of the school or treatment facility is to maintain communication with parents or guardians. Parents may not be aware of problems with school, peers, or community. They must be notified immediately of any signs of suicidal behavior so they can provide support and seek assistance.

Parents also should be advised of their responsibility for securing emergency evaluation, treatment, or other intervention for a suicidal child. It is crucial that they understand that all suicidal behavior must be taken seriously.

A 15-year-old girl shot herself in the abdomen during an agriculture class at a junior high school. Police said that she had brought the 22-caliber handgun from home. The girl was transported to a local hospital, where she was listed in stable condition. The girl's stepfather said that she was upset about problems with her boyfriend. Her mother said that the shooting "wasn't really a suicide attempt . . . she just wanted attention."

Ignoring or belittling suicidal verbalizations or actions may be misinterpreted by a young person as an invitation to die.

Further attempts may occur. Without the desired "attention," the child may try again—and succeed (Guetzloe, 1989).

REFERRALS TO OTHER PROFESSIONALS

Within the school, internal referrals can be made to counselors, school psychologists, and special education assessment teams. Berman and Jobes (1991) have suggested that schools should maintain lists of therapists who are skilled in working with suicidal youth, so that this information can be available quickly to parents and guardians.

Intervention in the home, school, and community requires considerable interagency cooperation. To ensure that services have been sought and are being furnished, a designated member of the staff in the school or treatment facility should maintain contact with the other individuals, organizations, and institutions that are working with the suicidal youngster and the family.

FOLLOW-UP WITH A SUICIDAL YOUNGSTER

After the immediate crisis has been resolved, a suicidal youngster still requires supervision and support for an extended period of time. An intervention plan should be developed for a suicidal child that includes the following (Guetzloe, 1989):

- Some immediate and positive change in the young person's life—at home, in school, and in the community.
- Provision of therapy, counseling, and contact with supportive individuals.
- Continuing supervision and support.
- Delivery of whatever has been promised.

SUMMARY

This discussion has focused on (a) the risk factors associated with suicide attempts, threats, and ideation in children and adolescents and (b) suggested interventions for faculty and staff of schools and treatment facilities. Other information regarding the problem of suicide in young people is available from the resources listed below.

ORGANIZATIONS

American Academy of Child and Adolescent Psychiatry
Public Information Office
3615 Wisconsin Avenue, N. W.
Washington, DC 20016
(202) 966-7300

American Association of Suicidology
2459 South Ash Street
Denver, CO 80222
(303) 692-0985

American Orthopsychiatric Association
19 West 44th Street, Suite 1616
New York, NY 10036
(212) 354-5770

American Psychological Association
750 1st. Street N. E.
Washington, DC 20002
(202) 955-7660, (202) 336-5500

National Alliance for the Mentally Ill
2101 Wilson Blvd., Suite 302
Arlington, VA 22201
(800) 950-NAMI (recorded message) (703) 524-7600

National Depressive and Manic Depressive Association
730 North Franklin, Suite 501
Chicago, IL 60610
(312) 642-0049
(312) 908-8100 (crisis hotline)

National Institute of Mental Health Suicide Research Unit
5600 Fishers Lane, Room 10-85
Rockville, MD 20857
(301) 443-2403

National Mental Health Association
1021 Prince Street
Alexandria, VA 22314-2971
(800) 969-6977

Suicide Information and Education Center
1615 10th Avenue S.W., Suite 201
Calgary, Alberta, Canada T3C O J7
(403) 245-3900

Suicide Prevention Center, Inc.
184 Salem Avenue
Dayton, Ohio 45406

RECENT PUBLICATIONS

Berman, A. L., & Jobes, D. A. (1991). *Adolescent suicide assessment and intervention.* Washington, DC: American Psychological Association.

Blumenthal, S. J., & Kupfer, D. J. (Eds.). (1990). *Suicide over the life cycle: Risk factors, assessment, and treatment of suicidal patients.* Washington, DC: American Psychiatric Association.

Guetzloe, E. (1991). *Depression and suicide: Special education students at risk.* Reston, VA: The Council for Exceptional Children.

Guetzloe, E. C. (1989). *Youth suicide: What the educator should know.* Reston, VA: The Council for Exceptional Children.

Matson, J. L. (1989). *Treating depression in children and adolescents.* New York: Pergamon Press, Inc.

Muse, N. J. (1990). *Depression and suicide in children and adolescents.* Austin, TX: PRO-ED.

Pfeffer, C. R. (1986). *The suicidal child.* New York: The Guilford Press.

Poland, S. (1989). *Suicide intervention in the schools.* New York: The Guilford Press.

Rutter, M., Izard, C. E., & Read, P. B. (1986). *Depression in young people.* New York: The Guilford Press.

Stark, K. (1990). *Childhood depression: School-based intervention.* New York: The Guilford Press.

REFERENCES

Allen, B. (1987). Youth suicide. *Adolescence, 22,* 271–290.

Berman, A. L. (1986). *Epidemiology of youth suicide.* Unpublished manuscript.

Berman, A. L., & Jobes, D. A. (1991). *Adolescent suicide assessment and intervention.* Washington, DC: American Psychological Association.

Cohen-Sandler, R., Berman, A. L., & King, R. A. (1982). A follow-up study of hospitalized suicidal children. *Journal of the American Academy of Child Psychiatry, 21,* 398–403.

Garfinkel, B. D., Froese, A., & Hood, J. (1972). Suicide attempts in children and adolescents. *American Journal of Psychiatry, 139,* 1257–1261.

Guetzloe, E. (1991). *Depression and suicide: Special education students at risk.* Reston, VA: The Council for Exceptional Children.

Guetzloe, E. C. (1989). *Youth suicide: What the educator should know.* Reston, VA: The Council for Exceptional Children.

Harkavy-Friedman, J. M., Asnis, G. M., Boeck, M., & DiFiore, J. (1987). Prevalence of specific suicidal behaviors in a high school sample. *American Journal of Psychiatry, 16,* 313–325.

Kovacs, M., & Puig-Antich, J. (1991). Major psychiatric disorders as risk factors in youth suicide. In L. Davidson & M. Linnoila (Eds.), *Risk factors for youth suicide* (pp. 27–143). New York: Hemisphere Publishing Corporation.

Kupfer, D. J. (1991). Summary of the national conference on risk factors for youth suicide. In L. Davidson & M. Linnoila (Eds.), *Risk factors for youth suicide* (pp. xv–xxii). New York: Hemisphere Publishing Corporation.

Matter, D., & Matter, R. (1984). Suicide among elementary school children: A serious concern for counselors. *Elementary School Guidance and Counseling, 18,* 260–267.

Otto, U. (1972). Suicidal acts by children and adolescents, a follow-up study. *Acta Psychiatrica Scandinavia.* Supplement 233, 7–123. (see p. 141,#31).

Peterson, K. S. (1991, April 2). Suicide by older teens on upswing. *USA Today, p. 1.*

Pfeffer, C. R. (1986). *The suicidal child.* New York: The Guilford Press.

Rosenthai, P. A., & Rosenthai, S. (1984). Suicidal behavior by preschool children. *American Journal of Psychiatry, 141,* 520–525.

Shneidman, E. S. (1985). *Definition of suicide.* New York: Wiley.

Smith, K., & Crawford, S. (1986). Suicidal behavior among "normal" high school students. *Suicide and Life-Threatening Behavior, 16,* 313–325.

Stanley, E. J., & Barter, J. T. (1970). Adolescent suicidal behavior. *American Journal of Orthopsychiatry, 40,* 87–96.

. . . .

HOW TO UNDERSTAND AND HELP STUDENTS WHO HAVE EXPERIENCED THE DEATH OF A PEER, FRIEND, OR STAFF ·

When the first edition of *Conflict in the Classroom* was written in 1965, we never even thought of including an article describing how staff could facilitate the grieving process of students. There would have been no interest in such an article; it would have appeared unusual and quirky. School was then no place to talk about death. But times have changed over the past 30 years, and society is more volatile. Crime continues to increase, and guns are now available to teenagers. In 1990, the Children's Defense Fund reported that 10 children die from gunshot wounds and 30 students are wounded each day. In urban areas, there appear to be daily instances of adolescent shootings in and outside of schools.

Death is no stranger for many students. They have witnessed random shootings, murders, and accidental deaths. Some deaths are unexpected and shocking. For example, a 13-year-old boy was told by Crips Gang members not to wear their symbolic blue baseball cap to school. When he ignored their threats, the gang retaliated by spraying his home with 26 rounds from an automatic rifle, killing his father and six-year-old sister.

Sometimes, a shootout between two students or rival gang members is planned (see page 208, *Managing a Shooting Incident*). Regardless of the motivation, the aftermath of a shooting or death is devastating to all involved parties.

The next article, *Responding to Death and Grief in a School*, was written by Sheldon and Barbara Braaten. They offer teachers a complete and detailed review of the psychological stages of the grieving process, the importance of developing a precrisis school plan for the staff, and specific interventions to use with terminally ill students. This article should be included in pre- or inservice training programs for teachers, because few educators have any training in how to respond to school-related deaths in a humane and caring manner.

ARTICLE 6.10

Responding to Death and Grief in a School

Sheldon Braaten and Barbara Braaten

Death can happen at any time, in many ways. A high school senior, starting for the first time at a home field football game, suffered a head injury and died a few days later. A teacher, committed to working with special needs students, felt ill one day while teaching, walked out of the classroom, and died in the hall. A despondent high school junior hanged himself in a classroom where he was discovered by his coach. A popular counselor, in his early fifties, left his junior high school Friday afternoon and unexpectedly died of a heart attack that evening. A senior stepped into a hallway altercation to defend a friend and was beaten to death just outside the principal's office. Another senior, who had had adjustment problems, committed suicide following a prolonged period of ridicule from classmates after she had accused a group of varsity hockey players of sexually molesting her. In another school, a group of students formed a suicide pact, influenced by a satanic cult, and two of them succeeded in completing the act. These deaths all occurred within one year, affecting students and school staff in one midwestern metropolitan area. Deaths such as these occur daily throughout the country. An incident in Illinois, where a woman walked into an elementary school and began shooting at children, killing one, is still another kind of tragedy that can occur. There are other examples that could be included, but these illustrate that the impact of a death is no stranger to schools.

Whether the death of a student of staff member is the result of accident, disease, suicide, or murder, it temporarily alters the priorities of a school, and some people will require support during their period of mourning. Unfortunately, teachers, administrators, and support-staff team members receive little, if any, preparation for dealing with this kind of tragedy, and seldom do staff manuals include specific procedures and guidelines to implement when responding to death. Sensitivity to the resulting emotional needs of both students and staff dictates that some training be provided, along with a postvention plan that can be promptly implemented for attending to those affected by a death. Our purpose is to describe a school plan that provides support to students and staff and that respects the deceased, the family, and friends.

THE GRIEVING PROCESS

Before any need to implement a crisis plan arises, staff members should receive some basic training on dealing with death. This information can assist teachers to identify students needing support and enable them to respond appropriately to their feelings and the situation caused by a death. Students need and appreciate an open, honest approach to the realities and mysteries that surround death. According to Segerberg (1976), the constellation of emotions that can follow a death include yearning, dejection, depression, nervousness, agitation, despair, hopelessness, depression, shock, denial, numbness, relief, and emptiness, as well as anger and resentment. Responses will vary, depending on one's relationship with the deceased, the circumstances of the death, and individual personalities. Age or maturity is also a factor in how individuals respond. Young children, according to Watts (1975), have not learned to understand or express their inner feelings very well, and so they act them out. Adults are more likely to express grief through emotional responses, whereas older people often grieve physically. All of these responses to death are normal and may occur, in varying degrees, in anyone.

In her book *On Death and Dying,* Elizabeth Kübler-Ross (1969) describes the five stages of the grieving process: denial, anger, bargaining, depression, and acceptance. Although these stages have been identified within terminally ill patients, Kübler-Ross asserts that corresponding stages also occur among grieving family members and friends. The initial stage of denial seems to stem from fear and is a temporary state of shock expressed in statements such as "It can't be true." The goal of denial is to feel safe. Anger, the second stage, is expressed in many ways and may include statements like "Why me?" or "It isn't fair." The anger will often cause the concerned person to get into "crazy behavior." Bargaining, usually a brief stage, is an attempt to postpone accepting death. It is expressed in a childlike plea, along with a promise of good behavior. It is a response to powerlessness in the form of "There must be something I can do." Depression occurs when anger no longer seems to help, and bargaining appears futile. It may be one of two different types: reactive, following a death, or preparatory, in the case of a lingering illness. Acceptance occurs when some peace of mind is available and is described as being neither angry nor depressed—"The struggle is over."

The death of a child is particularly hard to deal with. Siblings and other closely affiliated children have a hard time with grieving and, according to Kübler-Ross (1983), are often forgotten as adults deal with their own feelings. They may have nightmares. Their behavior may include acting out, such as hitting or kicking things. They may be unable to concentrate or stay with any activity, including homework. They may become moody and behave in ways that friends do not understand. At this time they need a friend, extra patience, tutoring, and support.

Children mourn, according to Donnelley, "almost always only when permission has been given" (1987, p. 109). Because they do not have the same inner resources that an adult does, children mourn sporadically and take longer to complete the mourning process. Usually, the child tries desperately to remain in tune with a peer group and needs to be treated as normally as possible. Being set apart can threaten acceptance in the peer group and cause irreparable damage. At the time of a death, educators need to provide support, to calm fears, and to eliminate or minimize overreaction and rumor. They can help students learn how to respond to their feelings appropriately by acknowledging the feelings, maintaining the routine as normally as possible, and involving students in determining what kind of support they need or want.

Staff members must also deal with their own feelings and take time together to discuss the situation. Kübler-Ross states, "Only if we as caretaking persons have been able to sort out our feelings are we able to help the family" (1974, p. 65). She believes that a staff person not directly involved with the deceased is in the best position to help others who are closely affiliated.

SCHOOL INTERVENTION AND POSTVENTION PROCEDURES

Circumstances under which death can affect a school include the anticipated or unanticipated death of a student and the anticipated or unanticipated death of a staff member. Intervention and postvention strategies will vary depending on the specific circumstances. Anticipated deaths of a student or staff member, which would result from a lingering illness or severe injuries, provide an opportunity for carefully considered interventions and postventions, whereas unanticipated deaths require prompt postventions.

School staff members need to be prepared and provided with procedures to deal with the concerns that accompany the death of a fellow employee or student. These procedures should reflect consideration for the emotional needs of all of the people in the school as well as accomplish the essential tasks during the period following a death. Above all, the procedures should assure an emotionally stable environment for students and staff and should do so in a way that will respect the deceased, the family, and friends. Although each case would be treated individually, the procedures and guidelines should accommodate responses to anticipated or unanticipated deaths of students or staff members.

PRECRISIS STEPS

Preparation for a crisis is vital to responding effectively. The following steps will facilitate a reasoned response:

1. Provide a safe environment. Whereas the principal may shoulder the ultimate burden of responsibility, every member of the staff must be committed to reporting and eliminating hazardous conditions of the physical plant, as well as dangerous behaviors.

2. Organize and identify the individual members of a crisis team. This team will include the building administrator(s) and support-staff members such as the counselor, social worker, and nurse. If the school is small and does not have a support staff, experienced teachers or those with relevant skills should be selected.

3. Identify each person in the building who has had first aid and cardiopulmonary resuscitation (CPR) training and post their names in a convenient location.

4. Identify school district crisis support people including psychologists, social workers, and health personnel. In small or rural districts, these may be community resource people, including clergy.

5. Develop written crisis intervention procedures and include them in the staff manual. These should be reviewed at least annually, at the beginning of each school term.

6. Decide on an emergency code word or system, such as the "code blue" used in hospitals.

7. Provide staff in-service meetings and resource materials on topics including suicide warning signs, first aid and CPR, symptoms of drug overdose, crisis management of behavior, and death.

8. Develop a list of names and phone numbers of emergency hospitals and crisis support agencies in the community and include it in the staff manual.

INTERVENTION WITH THE TERMINALLY ILL

Teachers frequently work with terminally ill children. Schools serve an important role in helping such children maintain a normal routine. Although teachers are accustomed to accommodating the physical needs of seriously ill students, they often need support in dealing with the emotional needs of the young person who is aware of impending death. Children are usually quite adept at sensing when adults cannot deal with their needs. In parents, particularly, an overwhelming feeling of sadness is easily detected by the child. The child is naturally protective of the parent and often avoids the subject of dying to spare the parent as much pain as possible. Yet, the child needs to talk to an adult about fears and questions. It is sometimes a teacher who is the listening person for the dying child. Although we are never quite sure what to say, there are specific ways to be comforting and helpful to an ill child. Teachers placed in this position usually have not volunteered; they have been chosen because they have earned a high level of trust from the child. The trust is often there because the adult has listened to the child. According to Donnelley, "*If* you can do no more than actively listen to your friend who is dying, you very probably will have done the thing that matters most" (1987, p. 134). It is important not to respond too quickly, not to tell "I remember when . . ." stories, and not to state that you know *exactly* how the child is feeling.

Talking is the second thing we can do for the dying, according to Donnelley (1987). The student may want to talk about things he can no longer do but is still interested in or about things in the future that he will never do or see. Terminally ill people can fear increasing isolation almost as much as they fear increasing pain, so it is important to feel comfortable talking about things that interest them. Most dying children are very aware of their situation and see through inaccurate statements even if they are intended to be comforting. A teacher should answer questions directly but be careful about offering more information than is requested. For example, the question "Do you think people will come to my funeral?" could simply be answered with a "yes." An explanation of who would attend and what would happen may not be needed unless the child pursues the topic. Suicide is a topic that may also come up. It is important to ask questions before responding to be sure of what the student may be thinking. If pressed for an opinion, the teacher can express personal beliefs without being judgmental about whatever the student may be thinking, as long as the teacher's response does not give permission to commit suicide.

Doing and touching are two other important elements in a relationship with terminally ill people, according to Donnelley (1987). Continuing to do routine activities as long as possible or being invited to come along with other students, if feasible, even if unable to participate, helps the student feel part of the peer group and know that he/she is *wanted.* This activity may also be helpful to classmates in preparing for their responses to the death when it occurs. Touching tells the dying person that he/she is not frightening and is valuable. Except in rare instances where contagion is a problem, a sensitive person can help the student feel better about himself by not being afraid to touch him. Caution about touching should reflect a concern for the student's physical and emotional comfort and one's relationship with the person.

Being available, listening, talking, doing things, and touching are things that one can do for the terminally ill. However, the friend or teacher may become closer to the dying student than was previously expected, Donnelley says, and going through the stages of death can often be an intensely painful act. Consideration should be given to any support that the teacher may need.

Other circumstances that allow time for some interventions include sudden injuries or illnesses. In these instances, procedures should provide for the careful monitoring and support for the people directly affected. When appropriate, and with parent permission, a communication system for current and accurate information, such as a published daily bulletin or announcements over the public address system, can be helpful to inform students and staff about the current status of the victim.

FIRST DAY

- Begin and end day with faculty meeting.
- Assign roles.
- Set up crisis center.
- First hour teacher explains facts to students.
- Counselor visits each of the deceased's classes.
- Gather the deceased's personal property to be returned later.
- Provide individual interventions.
- Notify community support agencies.

SECOND DAY

- Begin with faculty meeting to review the situation, including feelings of students and staff, determine contents of first-period announcements, stress normalizing routine, review procedures for excused absences, and discuss questions regarding a memorial and the funeral.
- Continue crisis center support.
- If possible, schedule an in-service meeting for the staff to review skills for working through grief, and if the death was the result of a suicide, review risk factors, help diffuse and alleviate guilt, and provide information on how to respond to questions and feelings about suicide.
- Review list of crisis services and phone numbers.

THIRD DAY

- Building administration and crisis team meet.
- Provide written announcement to be read by teachers concerning wake and funeral arrangements.
- Principal or chosen staff member(s) visit and/or communicate expressions of sympathy to the family.
- Monitor "at-risk" students and, if appropriate, begin referrals for continued support.
- If the death resulted in a high level of community awareness or media coverage, schedule an evening meeting to answer questions.

FOLLOW-UP

- Arrange for return of the deceased's personal property to the family.
- Develop referral system for those who question the spiritual aspect of death.
- Provide a list of emergency agencies and phone numbers to the parents of the student body.
- Schedule a staff meeting to discuss the interventions that took place, and remind people to continue to monitor the behavior of students.

POSTVENTION

When a death has occurred, the first priority is the notification of key personnel. If the death is discovered within the school, the immediate response must be to call the emergency number (911), then the principal, who should be responsible for notifying the superintendent. Any staff member who becomes aware of a death outside of the school should notify the principal as soon as possible so that he/she can initiate the postvention process. After being notified, the principal should implement the following steps:

1. Initiate a communication tree, beginning with support staff, and then department or grade level leaders who will call other team members. Clerks, lunchroom staff members, and building engineers should be included. The notification will include instructions for a staff meeting to be held prior to the students' arrival the next school day. If a teacher anticipates being absent, he should report that fact so plans can be made to assist a substitute.

2. Notify central office administrators and the district (city) crisis intervention team if one exists. The crisis team should be invited to the staff meeting.

3. Notify students and provide factual information by making an announcement during the first period in the morning. When the announcement concerns the death of a student, prior permission should be received from the surviving parents. Teachers will have received instruction during their preparation meeting about what further information to provide.

ASSIGNMENT OF ROLES

The building principal (or assistant principal in the principal's absence) is responsible for all communication with the media or other callers. All questions should be directed to him/her. The principal will conduct the staff meeting at which specific roles will be assigned to individuals. In larger schools with a support staff, responsibilities might be defined as follows:

Assistant principal(s)—Work to maintain the school routine, respond to an incidents that may happen, and be available for assistance if any particular staff member needs support.

Social worker—Focus on the needs of siblings and close friends of the deceased and contact any community agency people who have been working with the individual.

Counselor—Visit each of the deceased person's classes and assist the teachers in answering any questions.

Classroom teachers—Hold classes as usual. During the first hour, follow the procedures, including sharing information, that were decided on during the faculty meeting, deal with the subject of death if it is brought up during any hour, be alert for any students who appear to be having difficulty, and refer those students to a member of the crisis team.

Psychologist—Meet with students individually or in small groups to listen and provide support.

Truancy worker/attendance clerk—Review the absence list, and, if necessary, call parents to inform them that a student has died.

Other staff—Nurse, chemical dependency counselors, hall monitors, or any other staff members who are not assigned to classroom schedules will be accessible to the crisis team and provide assistance when called on.

District/community crisis intervention team—Contact community resources and inform agency personnel of the death and possible referrals for individuals seeking help, work with building staff to provide individual interventions, call parents of students identified as particularly distraught or "high risk" and advise them how to support their child, and carry out other activities decided on at the faculty meeting.

Postvention procedures require an immediate plan and follow-up activities. The days preceding and including the funeral are the most critical. Some students, however, may require support for an extended period of time.

GUIDELINES FOR STAFF

The essential element of a school plan for responding to a death is to maintain as much of a normal routine as possible, while being alert and sensitive to the needs of grieving persons. The following statements are intended to guide staff member responses.

Before discussing the situation, wait for announcements from the principal, and report information completely and accurately. Any person should respond to students' questions. Be truthful and direct, but do not dramatize. Remind students to deal with facts and be skeptical of rumor. Observe the verbal and nonverbal behaviors of the students. Be careful not to hassle students about their behavioral responses during the first day or two. Be prepared to discuss and offer suggestions for appropriate ways to talk to friends and relatives. Excuse students to go home only if a parent will be there. If the funeral is during school time, excuse only students with written permission from parents. If individuals wish to contribute to a memorial, make information concerning the family's preferences available.

CONCLUSION

A death can occur at any time and in most instances may have little impact on the routine activities of a school, except for those of family members and close friends. In some cases, where the individual is well known and/or is highly thought of, or when a death gets a lot of attention, such as a suicide, the impact on a school can be more pervasive. Our belief is that few educators have any training or guidance in how to respond to a death, and our purpose has been to share some thoughts that may be helpful.

ACKNOWLEDGMENT

The authors wish to thank the administration and staff of Anwatin Junior High School in Minneapolis, Minnesota, for providing the model of a school plan for dealing with death, and Dr. B. J. Bromenschenkel, assistant principal of Mounds View High School in Arden Hills, Minnesota, for sharing the procedures used following both an accidental death and a suicidal death of students at that school.

REFERENCES

Donnelley, N. (1987). *I never know what to say: How to help your family and friends cope with tragedy.* New York: Ballantine Books.

Kübler-Ross, E. (1969). *On death and dying: What the dying have to teach doctors, nurses, clergy and their own families.* New York: Macmillan

Kübler-Ross, E. (1974). *Questions and answers on death and dying.* New York: Macmillan.

Kübler-Ross, E. (1983). *On children and death.* New York: Macmillan.

Segerberg, O., Jr. (1976). *Living with death.* New York: E. P. Dutton.

Watts, R. (1975). *Straight talk about death with young people.* Philadelphia: Westminster.

SUMMARY . . . .

This chapter was written to take the mystery out of helping students with specific personality problems such as: low self-esteem, selective speaking, aggression, passive aggression, alcoholism, attention deficit and hyperactivity disorders, depression, suicide, and grieving. To understand the behavior of these students, the teacher must look beyond the students' deeds to discover his or her unmet needs. Each of these personality problems reveals possible underlying causative reasons. Specific recommendations about how to help these students in the classroom have been offered. The purpose is not to turn a teacher into a psychologist, but to acknowledge that these student personality problems exist. Teachers need as much information and guidance as possible to manage these students until they can be referred to the psychological staff or included in the interdisciplinary study team.

7

Classroom Crisis as an Opportunity: Strategies and Skills of Life-Space Crises Intervention

During NASA's Apollo 13 flight, the equipment in the space capsule malfunctioned and caused severe damage to the navigational and life support systems: Staff members at the Houston Command Center were alarmed by the magnitude of these technical problems and feared for the ultimate safety of the three astronauts. After assessing the damage, the mission engineers reported they were unable to predict the outcome of the space flight. They were concerned that the damaged heat shield of the space capsule would not protect the astronauts from being burned up during the reentry stage, that the three parachutes would not open to protect them from crashing into the sea and drowning, and that the supply of oxygen would not be sufficient to protect them from suffocating. A senior administrator, hearing these statements and reacting to his feelings of panic and doom, said, "This could be the darkest day in the history of NASA." The Command Flight Director turned to him and replied, "This also could be our finest hour, so let's focus on solutions."

These different reactions to an emergency were expressed centuries ago by the Chinese. The word "crisis" is written with two characters that mean an opportunity for change and disaster or destruction.

We believe a student crisis is a unique opportunity for adults to teach and for students to experience some insight into their pattern of self-defeating behaviors, learn more effective social skills to manage volatile emotional situations, and improve their trust in the teaching staff.

This chapter describes the essential concepts and skills of managing a student crisis with particular attention to life-space crisis intervention (LSCI) strategies.

THE NEED FOR CRISIS INTERVENTION . . . .

Student crises do not happen by appointment, nor are they scheduled into the school day. Student crises seem to happen at the most inconvenient

417

times for the staff—at the beginning of the school day, during transitional periods, and between peers when staff are not available or didn't see the precipitating events. During these crises, tempers flare and behaviors become more primitive, disruptive, and dangerous. Something needs to be done immediately, and the staff cannot postpone intervening until they can understand the underlying causes of the crisis. Like firefighters, staff must act quickly to put out the blaze, to protect the endangered, and to save property. Later, they will use their professional skills to identify the source and reasons for the fire. Although the need for staff action is important, it does not justify impulsive and unprofessional staff behaviors. During a crisis, it is common for staff to be quick to speak and slow to listen. With training, staff can learn to be quick to listen; and when they talk, it should be in a nonthreatening way that is intended to deescalate the student crisis as well as provide the student with protection, support, and respect.

In the first article, Crisis Intervention in Schools, William Morse details the changing conditions in the public schools and the need to use a student crisis as a positive and powerful medium for understanding and modifying the behavior of troubled students.

Morse believes that school staff members are slowly recognizing that their authority base has eroded and they no longer can make students change their behavior or conform to school rules. Staff cannot maintain their authority and use fear of failure, transfer, or exclusion to enforce their decisions. These threats are not effective with troubled students. Morse senses that society has moved away from the divine rights of institution to a new base of persuasion based on values. The old power of authority in schools has vanished, and the new theory of crisis intervention provides schools with a significant opportunity to view crises not as a disaster to be avoided, but as another chance to have a positive and profound impact on the students' way of thinking, feeling, and behaving. Crises are an essential part of student life. If used therapeutically, they can result in new coping skills, an improved ability to adapt, and a better student–staff relationship.

ARTICLE 7.1

Crisis Intervention in Schools
William C. Morse

The currently popular concept of crisis intervention has been espoused as an innovation and a central core in the new mental health movement.

Crises are not new, nor is the concept of intervention. Schools have used many different interventions. The problem is, they are usually of a reflexive and haphazard resource. Since they usually lack an awareness of the underlying conditions, they are reactions to symptoms, often with a curbing intention. For example, a student who skipped a day of school is excluded for several days as a corrective intervention, and the more he skips the longer become the exclusions, the further behind he gets, and the more escape becomes necessary. Frequently a teacher-student confrontation is born of a long gestation period of marginal aggravations. Suddenly a minor incident appears catastrophic and there is a reaction. These confrontations are usually quite one-sided, with no attempt to explore the genesis of the situation or the meaning to the particular student. Why do these interventions tend to be so primitive? Are we still seeking instant change devices at a cut-rate counter? Sometimes a passage of time serves as a huge sponge absorbing the true nature of the incident and we have only a charade in the after school appointment. In the past there has been considerable support for cooling-off periods, which is the opposite of crisis intervention or confrontation, and the cooling-off may extend to the point where usable psychological material has been completely dissipated. Often the person with power to determine the intervention is remote from the circumstances which generated the problem. Rather than reality—which is the essential ingredient of crisis intervention—the once or twice removed person deals with second-hand, frequently distorted perceptions of what really happened. The teacher is so often group bound that leaving the class to participate in the necessary discussion would require a new federal grant. When they do desert the classroom for a quick discussion, they are anxious over what may be developing back in the classroom. Time again makes the decision. Frequently the student crisis centers around a teacher who is responsible for the classroom and yet a third party, the principal, many times controls the outcome of the crisis.

The principal is in a very awkward situation. Not knowing exactly what happened, and having past experience or a perception regarding the teacher as well as the student involved, he may make certain judgments about the depth of the problem. He is also by role a "fixer" person. This role demands that he *do something* about the incident. As the superior in the command chain and given the obligation by the teacher for some corrective influence, he is, in fact, often without the resources needed to obtain a change. But this does not allow an escape from the reality problem of doing *something* about the situation. Usually after a dressing down which may be done politely or more vigorously, the student is returned to the original setting, often with the realization he will be back soon for more of the same. Of course the teacher who sent him out does not know what has happened with the authority person either.

The importance of all of this for contemporary mental health ideology is as follows. Studies of life histories of those making successful adjustments differ from those who make unsuccessful adjustments less in the amount of stress they have faced in their lives than in how well they learned to cope with the stress. Thus, we can have two "identical" case histories as far as the supposed genesis of pathology is concerned, but one turns out to be reasonably well-adjusted while the other does not. Corrective influence and good mental health is the result of satisfactory solutions to crises rather than a simple sentence passed upon a person by his life experience. Some turn out well under very poor odds: others had little to sustain them but managed. While the more life adversity the more risk, it is not a simple arithmetic addition. Some learn to cope much more effectively than others.

Thus it follows, we teach how to cope by providing the proper intervention at the time of a crisis, while the student is in the process of learning how to cope. This is not to say that people are always particularly "teachable" at a time of their crises, in the sense that they stand there awaiting help in learning how to cope with a particular situation in a socially acceptable fashion. It merely means that at the point of crisis a person is in turmoil and seeking some resolution. The object of crisis intervention is to provide coping styles which will have long-term utility. In this way it becomes clear that the typical reflective response as now practiced in schools frequently "teaches" coping which is of a nature we do not wish at all. But we cannot avoid teaching something at the time of crisis because the student is always learning some means. The Harvard group which dealt with this problem has been interested in studying overwhelming crisis situations such as accidents, bereavement, and other catastrophic life events. Caplan states that during such a period a person is more susceptible to being influenced by others than in times of relative psychological equilibrium. A particular insight we could gain from their studies of major crises is to avoid conceiving every event in a student's life as catastrophic.

One of the first questions which teachers ask is a definition of a crisis. The reason is obvious. So much happens in certain classes of normal or disturbed students that almost everything could be considered a crisis. An event which may have a great deal of explosiveness in it is not necessarily a significant crisis if it is unrelated to the nature of the group's or individual's abiding problem.

His research points out a very interesting kind of dilemma: Is the crisis in the eye of the "crises" or in the eye of others around him, particularly the teacher? Thus many crisis situations may have no meaning as far as the individual primarily involved is concerned. It is a crisis to the teacher who is the consumer of the behavior. Parenthetically, the type of crisis consultation which many of us attempt takes this into consideration: the teacher is most eager to engage in a problem-solving effort at such a time. The issue of "when a crisis" is of great importance and many interventions fail because they are poised with an inadequate awareness of the fact that the one being helped must sense a crisis. Many events which are crises to us are satisfying, ego building, and gratifying to the student. Hence, there is no crisis except to ward off any effort to make it one. Stated in simple terms, a crisis is precipitated by overloading the student's capacity to cope. It may be generated by external demands in the environment such as the academic or behavioral tasks he is given. Or it may be in consequence of internal perceptions, distorted or accurate. The student's coping failure is of such an intensity that he cannot be supported by the typical supporting tactics which teachers use day in and day out. The crises take many forms. For example a student acts out and becomes a critical management problem. A teacher may recognize a peak of depression sometimes under the guise of clowning. A sharp and noticeable erosion of self-esteem can be the basis of an approach. It may be generated by academic failure or frustration. Frequently, crises are a consequence of contaging social stimulations. Often evaluation experience such as an examination coming up or grades being given precipitates a crisis. Thus, a crisis is a psychological condition of duress which may be accompanied by overt signs but may not. In another article, Gerald Caplan states that a crisis is a relatively sudden onset of disequilibrium in a student where previous functioning was known to be stable. These are states of turmoil. Caplan points out that many students who are facing an identity crisis will have a period of this type but are not necessarily emotionally disturbed unless this develops into a chronic negative pattern.

Caplan also differentiates between developmental and accidental crises. Developmental crises are the transitional periods one anticipates in both normal and disturbed students. For example, the onset of adolescence constitutes a developmental crisis period. We usually think of the third grade and beginning of school as significant periods. The accidental crises are like accidents in general. You can predict there will be a certain number in a population but not when they are liable to occur. These are conditions precipitated by loss of basic support or some threat or challenge which puts heightened demands on an individual. Caplan sees both of these as pathways leading to increased or decreased capacity to cope with one's environment. In his own experience these people are ready for increased help and are more easily influenced.

The important point, from Caplan's point of view, is that the critically correct small force acting for a short time during the period of acute crisis can produce drastic changes which would otherwise be impossible. This is the most central concept of the whole procedure. From my own point of view it becomes important to recognize that interventions must be thought of not only as verbal but as consideration of all aspects of the external environment as well. But the idea remains: an effective solving of today's problem is a most promising way of neurolizing the impact of an unfortunate past. This immediacy with which one attempts to deal with issues is in contrast to the traditional "cool down" theory. Many institutions use a quiet room or have a student quiet down before anyone will talk to him. This is not to say that one would never want some reduction of intensity, but the essential nature of crisis intervention is to use the emotional potency of the contemporary charged situation to help the youngster understand what he is feeling and what can be done. When you let a student "cool down," he has lost the impetus for change. It is particularly amusing to think of expecting a student in a crisis to have his problem ready for discussion when he comes in for his therapy hour the next day. As a matter of fact, if one examines counseling with students, after the precipitating event has passed, it will be clear that a good deal of time is spent in rationalizing the problem to be discussed. One of the reasons so much of the student-teacher interaction is nothing more than hollow moralizing is because the student at that point in time has no feeling of an issue about which he has to do something. A teacher working with a student who has a reading difficulty but who denies it may get him to actually read and thus demonstrate an issue in order to be able to work with him.

The use of the crisis implies keen understanding of the appropriate interventions. This means knowledge in depth—psychological, sociological, and educational—applied at the correct point in time. Actually it requires more rather than less insight in these domains. Inappropriate interventions result in faulty learning rather than real help.

In our own experience there are four places the crisis concept has changed procedures rather radically. One is in consultation, which has changed from supervisory or case analysis of a historical nature to strategic planning for the student. Roles cease to determine function when solutions are sought. No one knows enough to resolve all difficulties. Second is the use of the crisis or helping teacher who is available to operate at the time of severe difficulty and breakdown by handling disturbed students taken from the regular class at the time when they flounder. This teacher works with both emotional and academic aspects in teaching the student to cope. The third major use in working with disturbed students is in the style of interviewing developed by Redl and others entitled Life Space Interviewing. This presumes that working with a student through interviews around the particular difficulty he faces in the contemporary life scene is an effective way to help him learn long-term coping. The last is as conceptual system to handle the confrontation situations which are more and more frequent in secondary education today. If these are seen as crises resulting from a failure to meet situational demands, there will be less repressive action, which solves little.

We are a long way from really understanding how to make constructive use of severe trouble points, but at least we have a theory to explore. One hopes that it will be taken seriously and not as another verbal gimmick with a catchy sound. We need to school ourselves relative to the theory involved and train ourselves in practice.

REFERENCES

Bernard L. Bloom, "Definitional aspects of a crisis concept," *Journal of Consulting Psychology,* 1963, Vol. 27, #6, 498–502.

Gerald Caplan, *Prevention of Mental Disorders in Children,* New York: Basic Books, 1961.

Gerald Caplan "Opportunities for School Psychologists in the Primary Prevention," *Mental Hygiene,* Vol. 47, #4, Oct. 1963, pp. 525–539.

Harold Renaud and Floyd Estess, "Life History Interviews with One Hundred Normal American Males: Pathogenicity of Childhood," *American Journal of Orthopsychiatry.* October 1961, Vol. XXXI, No. 4, 786–803.

. . . .

HOW ARE STUDENT CRISES CONCEPTUALIZED? . . . .

Morse (1971) documented the need for more precise theory about student crises and now there are two generic ways of understanding a student crisis. One model is conceptualized by Wood and Long (1991) as the result of student stress kept alive by the negative reactions of others. The second model is proposed by the Positive Education Program (PEP) in its *Crisis Prevention/Intervention Training Manual* (1995), where a student crisis is portrayed as a predictable and sequential five-phase process.

WOOD AND LONG'S CRISIS CYCLE MODEL . . . .

The Wood–Long model is based on the Conflict Cycle (p. 35), which becomes the Crisis Cycle when the needs of a student clash against the expectations of others. Figure 7.1 illustrates the circular nature of the Conflict Cycle and how, if it is uninterrupted, it will unleash intense feelings and oppositional behaviors, and will incite staff anger. Most student crises begin with a minor event, move into a problem incident, and expand into a personal crisis for the student and a schoolwide crisis for staff.

FIGURE 7.1   If left unbroken, the Conflict Cycle spirals into crisis: the Wood–Long Model.

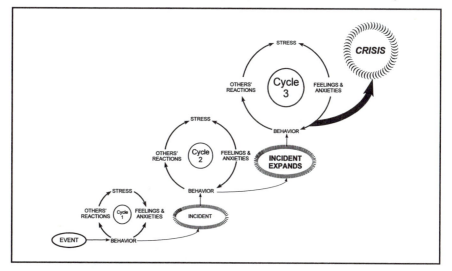

THE POSITIVE EDUCATION PROGRAM'S (PEP) STRESS MODEL OF CRISIS . . . .

The PEP model analyzes a crisis as having five predictable phases (see Figure 7.2).

Phase I: Calm to Triggering Event . . . .

As this phase begins, the student is behaving in an appropriate way. An upsetting event—internal or external—occurs, causing the student to become agitated. The triggering event may be linked to something very obvious and observable, like being teased, or it may be spontaneous and without warning, like a troubling thought. The specific behaviors vary from student to student, but Phase I is marked by feelings of anxiety and agitation.

Phase II: Escalating Behavior . . . .

During the escalation phase, the student becomes more agitated and resistant, and begins to disrupt the setting. At this point, some obvious evidence of increased anxiety appears. As the intensity of these behaviors increases, the likelihood of the student's responding to interventions decreases. During Phase II, the student shows signs of beginning to lose control, such as talking louder, verbally threatening others, or withdrawing.

Other students in the group may be easily influenced during Phase II. "Group contagion" may become a concern. The classroom setting may be overstimulating to the troubled student.

FIGURE 7.2   The five predictable phases of a crisis: the PEP Models.

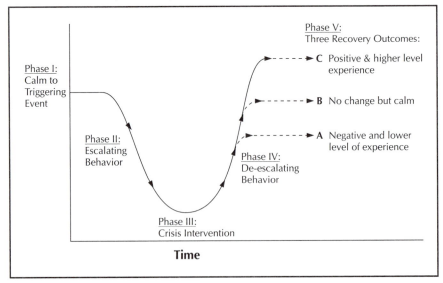

Phase III: Crisis Intervention . . . .

> During this phase, the student acts in a manner that is disruptive to the
> safety of the student and the ongoing program. Staff must intervene and
> take control of the situation. Until the start of this phase, staff intervention
> has appealed to the student's ability to respond rationally. Intervention now
> must provide for the safety and protection of the student and the environ-
> ment. The crisis phase occurs when the student loses control and is no
> longer able to make rational decisions. Behaviors may include abusive lan-
> guage, threatening gestures, open defiance with intense anxiety, and phys-
> iological arousal. Because violent behavior appears imminent, it becomes
> necessary to take control of the student and the situation until the student
> regains self-control. Appropriate action might involve removing the stu-
> dent from the setting or using physical restraint to prevent the student from
> injuring others or self, or from destroying property.

Phase IV: Deescalating Behavior . . . .

> This phase involves draining off the student's anger, panic, or fear; active
> listening, affirming, and decoding skills; and hearing out the entire story
> and accepting the student's feelings from his or her point of view. During
> this phase, the student becomes more rational and attuned to understand-
> ing the sequence of the crisis.

Phase V: Three Recovery Outcomes . . . .

> The goal of crisis intervention is to act or react in a way that is beneficial
> to the student. The recovery phase is staff's opportunity to help the
> student learn and grow from the crisis experience. There are three pos-
> sible outcomes in all crisis situations: (a) a negative, lower-level experi-
> ence, (b) a no-change/no-growth experience, or (c) a positive, higher-level
> experience.
>
> **A. Lower-Level Outcome**   The student is marred by the crisis or the
> way it was handled. Perhaps there was no intervention or the student was in-
> jured. Perhaps the staff who intervened lost control, became counterag-
> gressive, and behaved in unprofessional ways. As a result, the student has
> more hostile feelings toward the staff and a decreased ability to handle fu-
> ture stressful situations. He or she has learned that staff intervention leads
> to more personal punishment, alienation, and rejection.
>
> **B. No-Change/No-Growth Outcome**   The crisis intervention takes
> place, but, unfortunately, the student does not learn from the situation.
> Therefore, the next time the triggering event occurs, the student responds
> in the same characteristic manner, once again losing control. Intervention
> is handled in the same way, and staff end up becoming "firefighters and not

fire proofers." There is no change or increase in the student's ability to deal with future stressful situations.

C. Higher-Level Outcome   An intervention occurs in a beneficial manner. This process involves using life-space crisis intervention (LSCI) skills to help the student learn some insights into the dynamics of the crisis and how to prevent it or handle it more constructively in the future. The student gains a greater trust in the staff, a sense of mastery, support, and an improved self-esteem. This is the planned outcome of a successful LSCI.

THE THREE GENERIC CATEGORIES OF A STUDENT CRISIS . . . .

A student crisis can be triggered by any of the following: (a) a developmental crisis, (b) a destructive personal life event crisis, or (c) a situational crisis.

A Developmental Crisis . . . .

Caplan (1961) has documented that all individuals, from birth to death, go through a series of predictable stress periods or transitional stages that can lead to personal crisis. The developmental crises can include: leaving home and going to school, learning how to read, making friends, belonging to groups, becoming independent, accepting physical development and sexual identity, developing values and beliefs, selecting a profession, and so on. At each of these developmental stages, a student can become temporarily flooded by feelings of anger, excitement, shame, guilt, fury, or fear, and will need the assistance of an adult to resolve the conflict or confusion. Wineman (1959) believes all children and youth at times can profit from crisis intervention, and teachers should broaden their view that crisis intervention is a strategy designed only for troubled students.

> The idea that normal and healthy children don't need any therapy is basically correct. The further assumption that being normal and healthy also means freedom from the danger of being overwhelmed by the complexities of life is a naive illusion. Most healthy and normal kids are equipped with a considerable amount of resilience. They can handle many experiences that would send their more disturbed compatriots into psychotic blow-ups or neurotic convulsions. This, however, does not mean they can manage all of them. Take any child, no matter how well matured, healthy, wonderful, and at some time during some phase of his life, he will find himself in . . . predicaments in which he will need an adult to stand by. Indeed, during such a time it will make a lot of difference just how well this adult handles himself during this crisis. (pp. 3–7)

Developmental crises are particularly active and plentiful during the junior high or middle school years.

A Destructive Personal Life Event Crisis . . . .

This type of crisis is triggered by an event over which the student has no control, but which drastically affects his or her ability to function in school. Unplanned traumatic events might include the shooting of a friend, the death of a family member, a paralyzing illness, sexual and psychological abuse, a sudden move to a new city, or physical threats by alcoholic, drug-addicted, psychotic people in the community. Students experiencing these types of crises will need abundant support and clarity in order to help them focus on the "real" problem and get control over their lives.

A Situational Crisis . . . .

Redl and Wineman (1957) concluded that a number of crises occur in every ongoing group situation for children and youth, and these crises can be used in therapeutic ways to help children and youth cope with their reality frustrations, interpersonal conflicts, and personal problems. Redl and Wineman called this type of crisis intervention life space interviewing (LSI).

All three types of student crises happen in school, and an awareness of these different types becomes helpful in improving the effectiveness of adult intervention.

A BRIEF OVERVIEW OF LIFE SPACE INTERVIEWING . . . .

In 1959, Redl proposed an exciting and effective way of talking with troubled children and youth about some behavior that they could not manage appropriately.

This reality-based verbal technique differs significantly from the structured office interview used by clinicians, although it has similar goals. Most important, life space interviewing (LSI) provides the staff, who have worked directly and have had the most contact hours with troubled children and youth, a therapeutic technique that enables them to be more active and professional as contributors to the treatment team.

THE TWO OUTCOME GOALS OF LSI . . . .

Every student crisis begins with an "issue" or a "life event" that triggers the crisis. Each LSI can focus on one of two outcomes: "Emotional First Aid on the Spot" or "Clinical Exploitation of Life Events." The decision about how a crisis is to be managed does not depend on the instigating "issue" but is determined by a set of staff criteria. If the staff decides the goal is to support this student emotionally by draining off his or her feelings and returning the student to the program ASAP, then the staff outcome goal involves Emotional First Aid on the Spot.

If the staff decides to use the student issue to clarify a pattern of self-defeating behavior that is in need of repair or change, then the staff's outcome goal involves Clinical Exploitation of Life Events. Redl (1959) offers an excellent example of the choice involved in deciding what to do about a crisis issue.

> Let's assume that a group of children are just about ready to go out on that excursion they have anticipated with eagerness for quite a while. Let's assume there is, due to our fault, somewhat more delay at the door because of a last-minute search for lost shoes, footballs, etc., so that irritability mounts in the gang that is already assembled and raring to go. Let's further assume that in the ensuing melee of irritated bickering two of our youngsters get into a flare-up, which ends up with Johnny's getting socked more vehemently than he can take, furiously running back to his room, cursing his tormentor and the world at large, all educators in particular, swearing that he will "never go on no trip no more in his whole life." We find him just about to soak himself in a pleasurable bath of self-pity, nursing his grudge against people in general and adding up new evidence for his theory that life is no good, people are mean "so-and-so's" anyway, and that autistic day-dreaming is the only safe way out. (p. 4)

If the decision is made to be with John during his unhappiness and to help him sort out his many emotions in order to get himself back in shape and to go on the trip, then the appropriate choice is Emotional First Aid on the Spot. However, if the decision is made to use this issue as an opportunity to help John become aware of a pattern of behavior he does not recognize, then the goal of returning John to the group is given up in order to use Clinical Exploitation of Life Events to introduce some personal insight and behavioral changes. The goal of this interview is to use this incident—and previous ones the staff and John have experienced—to demonstrate how John's rude, impulsive, and provocative behavior invites peer rejection, although he may not be aware of this pattern.

Although a staff may begin with one goal in mind, new information or reality factors can force the staff to switch to the other category.

In the next article, Carol Merritt-Petrashek describes Redl's five specific strategies of emotional first aid on the spot. Teachers can use these strategies to patch up a student emotionally and keep the student in the program. These five strategies are similar to surface management techniques and to Fagen's techniques (see page 273) for reducing undesirable behavior. Merritt-Petrashek has developed an effective way of teaching these five strategies, and has offered a teacher quiz.

ARTICLE 7.2

Emotional First Aid:
Bandaids for the Bumps

Carol A. Merritt-Petrashek

Emotional First Aid is one of the strategies of life space interviewing (LSI) characterized by the multiple skills of active listening, decoding behaviors, advocating and sanctioning students' feelings, and supportive decision making by the interviewer. Often a student will require immediate help when his coping skills break down while dealing with a particularly stressful situation. At these painful times, one or more of the five subcategories of Emotional First Aid can be used.

SUBCATEGORIES OF EMOTIONAL FIRST AID

1. *Drain-off of Frustration Acidity or "Look Out, I'm Going to Explode."* Life is frustrating. The release of emotional stress due to frustration is termed a "drain off." Broadly, release of stress is accomplished by the use of sympathetic listening and the decoding of feelings and behavior. In plain language, all the angry feelings must be drained off verbally before the student is able to look at his behavior and the situation rationally. The interviewer encourages this process by sharing and supporting the student's feelings with statements such as, "What you are saying is . . . ," and "I can see you are feeling _____ ('angry,' 'confused,' 'sad,' 'lonely,' 'scared,' etc.) about . . ."

Sympathetic listening is also used to reassure a student of the interviewer's understanding of the frustrating situation. Saying nothing—simply listening—an interviewer can communicate acceptance by nodding, touching, and facial expression. Many students need this quiet acceptance in order to control their intense feelings. At these times, the interviewer does not want to risk decoding prematurely or decoding irrelevant information because it could create a power struggle with the student.

Through the use of these two skills—sympathetic listening to convey acceptance and decoding to focus—the student begins to release the whys, hows, and when of the stressful incident. The more information released or "drained off" by the student, the less confusing and disappointing the painful incident becomes.

"I Can't Take It Anymore!" In the middle of English class, Bob throws his pencil down and yells, "The hell with this! How do you expect me to do this stuff? I hate this goddamn class anyway!" As Bob talks, he rips the paper in front of him and throws it across the room. Angry with his disruptive

---

From *Pointer*. (1981). Vol. 25, No. 2. Reprinted with permission of the author.

behavior, his teacher tells Bob to pick up the paper and observes that the work would have been easier if he had only listened to the directions initially. Bob, furious and insulted, seeks revenge by flipping over his desk and chair. He then leaves the room shouting obscenities.

What technique would have been effective yet not disruptive to others in the class? What form of release could be useful? The next paragraph may provide some suggestions.

The first step is to label the cause for the behavior and anger—in this case frustration with the task and perhaps fear of failure. The second step is to realize that a surface technique, as opposed to an in-depth technique, is needed because of situational factors (i.e., the class is in session, time to deal with the problem is limited, or the issue producing frustration can be remediated rapidly). The third step is the approach. At this point, the teacher has indicated a need to interfere with the student's frustration, release the emotional pressure, and return the student to the program as soon as possible. A possible approach could be as follows:

The teacher should move toward the student instantly, sending up a flag stating, "I hear you." To convey acceptance rather than anger share the understanding rapidly: "This English assignment is frustrating."

Sympathize with the student by decoding what you see and hear. Usually, if a teacher is successful in "draining off" the frustration, both physical and verbal release are quite visible. At this point, both teacher and student should develop a way to tackle the original task without creating a new conflict cycle.

2. *Support for Management of Panic, Fury, and Guilt, or "Let Me Know You Care."* Often, when a student becomes overloaded with, or flooded by, guilt, panic, or fury, interpersonal confusion surfaces. In this frenzied state, the student is capable of losing total self-control. At this time, it is essential for the interviewer to provide *protection for the student and others around him*. A message whether stated verbally and/or physically to a student must convey, "I will be your controls until your own controls take over." This message when communicated gently yet confidently helps the student feel secure and protected as he gathers his internal control. Once the student can endure and control his intense feelings, the interviewer's task is to return him to the daily schedule as soon as possible.

"It's Unfair!" One morning, Chris entered the class in a highly aggressive state. (Chris was suspended from the bus because the driver said he was uncooperative.) He burst through the door of the classroom screaming and yelling obscenities. Running around the room, he threw chairs, knocked over desks, and pitched small objects. With tears running down his face, he screamed over and over again, "That's no fair!" His teacher stood with hands on hips yelling, "Chris, stop this instant!" Unfortunately, Chris did not stop but threw a block, hitting another entering student. The entering student promptly launched a physical attack on Chris. The teacher was rendered practically helpless in attempts to end the struggle.

Did the teacher's behavior escalate Chris's stress? If the teacher had moved toward Chris instantly, could the fight have been prevented? A suggested technique follows.

The student is obviously in a severe state of panic and fury. His behavior should be an immediate signal of needed "support for management of panic, fury, and guilt." The emphasis is placed on the word "support."

The first step requires the teacher to reach the student as fast as possible. Isolate the student's space gently with your own body and words, e.g., "Calm down, Chris" or "I will help you through this, Chris." If the student's behavior decreases, physical restraint is not necessary. Support the student in every way possible, remembering to speak softly and accept all feelings at this time.

The second step occurs if, after verbal controls, the student is still unable to manage his frenzied state. Physical restraint is then used to protect the student, his peers, and oneself from his aggressive behavior. Be prepared for physical and verbal aggression to escalate during the restraint, followed by tears and silence.

3. *Maintenance of Communication in Moments of Relationship Decay; or "I Can't Hear You and You Can't Make Me Listen!"* After an intense conflict, some students are so overwhelmed by their feelings that they withdraw into fantasy or go into a prolonged anger, sulk, and refuse to talk. Unless these reactions can be penetrated, the silent world of fantasy or anger can be more destructive than the world of reality.

A withdrawal into fantasy is best dealt with by engaging the student in any kind of conversation or activities. A quick change of subject to the student's interests, followed by questioning in a non-threatening way, can be helpful. The use of something manipulable may be helpful at this point, or the quiet use of an art medium may lure the student back to words.

"I Deserve More Points." Cathy and her teacher had a disagreement about the number of points earned on a daily behavioral program. Infuriated with the outcome of the total, Cathy glares at her teacher and says, "I hate you." When the teacher ignores this remark, Cathy begins to breathe deeply, folds her arms across her chest, and tilts her chair back. Cathy's eyes become fixed on a decided point on the wall, and her sulk begins. She does not speak, nor does she make or hear any attempts to resolve the issue. This retreat from reality usually continues for ten minutes to an hour, depending on the intensity of the previous conflict. Deciding that the behavior is purely attention seeking, Cathy's teacher chooses totally to ignore Cathy for whatever length of time her stubborn withdrawal lasts.

Does the teacher alter Cathy's behavior effectively? Is Cathy's withdrawal from reality simply a conscious sulk? The following technique may help to answer these questions.

The first step in "Communication maintenance in times of relationship decay" is to decide whether the student is truly withdrawing from reality or seeking attention from the adult. An obvious way of identifying attention-seeking behavior is to gauge the intensity, duration, and frequency of this behavior.

If the student is showing evidence of listening to others but not to you or if the student responds to your direction in one modality but not others, she is obviously in touch with reality. If clarification of reality versus fantasy is still warranted, the following simple method may be helpful. Use a convincing act to entice the student to respond, e.g., say, "Oh, look what's outside the window!" If the student does not budge or blink, he or she has retreated into fantasy.

Once the interviewer has identified the fact that the student is truly losing contact with reality, the reinstatement of communication can begin. Discussion of "safe" and comforting people is helpful, along with the use of favored objects. When successful, this nonthreatening approach usually registers in the student's face. Blinking, smiling, and relaxing of the facial muscles are typical reactions prior to speech. Maintain communication at a gentle pace, ending the discussion only when assured the student is once again based in reality.

When the student enters the world of reality, he or she feels more comfortable with his thoughts. Discussion of the initial conflict can occur after a safe amount of time has passed.

4. *Regulation of Social and Behavioral Traffic, or "Policing the Area."* Although most students understand the rules and regulations of a school, they need to be reminded frequently of where, when, and what they should be doing. The task is to keep the activities, lessons, and transitional periods as free as possible from interpersonal traffic jams by monitoring the pupils' behavior.

"Strike Three, and You're Out!" It is 8:30 A.M. when Bus 305 pulls up to the school. Tom steps off the bus, laughing with John, Bill, and Rodney. Tom begins to flex his muscles, taking playful jabs at Bill. Rodney turns to John and punches him in the shoulder. He is imitating Tom, saying, "Look at me, I'm real tough." The four boys laugh. Tom turns and begins to take playful jabs at Rodney. "Who can hit harder" begins. The supervising adult has been more concerned up to this point with unloading the bus than interfering with four playful boys. Rodney takes a powerful and painful slug from Tom, bringing tears to his eyes. Rodney says, "You bastard, Tom," while John and Bill announce to all arriving students, "Rodney's a baby, look at those tears." "What did you just call me, punk?" Tom demands. Rodney launches a rage-filled attack on Tom, and four adults are needed to separate the fight. What seemed like playful amusement became a brawl. How could this have been avoided?

In the "regulation of social and behavioral traffic," a teacher must always be predicting outcomes of interactions. This foresight provides positive support to students by warning them of the possible hazardous outcome.

When the students began the playful boxing, the following sequence might have been helpful. First, an organizing comment could be used, such as, "All right, guys, on into school." This message reminds them of what should be occurring. If this approach is ineffective, try a clear verbal warning, e.g., "Playful hitting can sometimes become painful. Stop, please." As you are speaking, emphasize your point by moving closer to the students. Your presence, with the use of words, may have altered the playful punching, thus refocusing their attention to appropriate school behavior.

5. *Umpire Service, or "Safe or Out, That Is the Question."* This technique is required in two instances: in umpiring a student's initial conflict with self or in umpiring for several students as you would in a team sport. Both types of problems surface when a conflict causes a student to lose self-control. The interviewer's task in these situations is to appeal to the values of fairness. Also remember umpires are not always cherished people.

"A Quick Hand When Trouble Strikes!" Sue was a rather heavy child, constantly struggling for peer acceptance and often rejected because of her appearance. One day, in the lunch line, after several days of dieting, Sue grabbed a piece of pie and a package of cookies. As she tried to sneak by her teacher in the lunch line, several of her classmates announced her actions. "Sue's breaking her diet!" Sue looked up at her teacher, hoping for a decision. Her teacher simply stated, "You've been doing a great job on your diet, and I notice some weight loss." Smiling, Sue promptly removed the desserts from her tray. The other students were equally supportive.

In this incident, Sue's teacher simply appealed to her "better" self to encourage an appropriate decision. The teacher's remark was supportive, not critical, and helped Sue to feel great about the eventual outcome.

"Let's Change the Rules!" A class of twelve boys were outside playing softball. All members of the two teams agreed on two outs. In the third inning, one team was losing by seven runs. Bob said, "Our team should have three outs to catch up!" All members of his team looked at the teacher for the verdict while the other team protested quite loudly. The teacher simply stated, "How many outs were originally agreed upon?" After the answer had been given, several of Bob's team members said, "We can catch up, Bob! Let's leave it as is." The game went on with two outs.

In this incident, the teacher realized any change in the rules would contribute to chaos. Acting as umpire, the teacher refocused on the original decision allowing better selves to shine here and there on the two teams. The outcome has the appearance of the majority wanting to stick with the original rules.

All the methods mentioned under Emotional First Aid are used on the spot. Immediate attention is offered in the student's present surroundings. Supportive measures are given when coping mechanisms become inadequate or overburdened by life's reality demands.

The emergence of new information through the interview process may cause the interviewer to switch goals to pinpoint the student's needs. Furthermore, as this new information is discussed, the need for in-depth interviewing may become applicable. In this case, the Clinical Exploitation of Life Events offers an interviewer a more extensive interviewing capacity.

Because students in stress create similar feelings in teachers, what emotional first aid techniques can a teacher use to get through the day?

TEACHER'S EMOTIONAL FIRST AID NEEDS: A QUIZ

1. You have just spent several hours developing what you consider to be a wonderful lesson. As you present it to the class, a majority of the students begin to say, "That's dumb!" "We're not doing it!" With time passing, it becomes more and more apparent that you will be unable even to try your lesson. Your stomach tightens, and your face turns purple. All you can think of is how much time and effort you spent. Which method of Emotional First Aid would be helpful in providing ego support for you? (Hint: Identify how you are feeling.)

   a. Regulation of behavior and social traffic

   b. Umpiring

   c. Drain-off of frustration acidity

   d. Communication maintenance in times of relationship decay

   e. Support for management of panic, fury, and guilt

2. You are angry at a student who has been off-task and disruptive all day. However, you notice he has earned just enough points to have free time. Your anger makes you really want to take away his free time; yet he has earned it. When you mention the problem to a fellow teacher, his response is, "Hey, he has earned the points. Maybe you need to tighten up your behavioral system in the future." What form of Emotional First Aid can be offered to this angry teacher?

   a. Drain-off of frustration acidity

   b. Support for management of panic, fury, and guilt

   c. Communication maintenance in times of relationship decay

   d. Regulation of behavioral and social traffic

   e. Umpire services

3. John has been quite verbally abusive and disruptive off and on during the day. It seems no matter what you try, this behavior continues. You feel a tightening in your stomach as John begins again. Enraged by his actions, you confront him. John spits in your face. What technique of support do you need immediately?

   a. Umpire service

   b. Drain-off of frustration acidity

   c. Regulation of behavioral and social traffic

   d. Support for management of panic, fury, and guilt

   e. Communication maintenance in time of relationship decay

4. All students are working independently at their desks on an assignment. Suddenly, it seems each student requires your help now. You hear and feel the anger in the words as you try to meet each student's needs. You can feel yourself becoming overwhelmed and wanting to be somewhere else; consequently, you begin to withdraw slowly. What form of support do you need?

   a. Drain-off of frustration acidity

   b. Support for management of panic, fury, and guilt

   c. Communication maintenance in times of relationship decay

   d. Regulation of behavioral and social traffic

   e. Umpire service

5. All staff members are attending an important meeting. Time is running out, and a decision has not been made. Mrs. Jones raises her hand. Contributing nothing, she talks at a tangent. Members of the staff become irritated. The director of the program interrupts Mrs. Jones and redirects the group to the task by saying, "Remember, we must reach a decision about our new policy today." What is the method the director used? (Hint: The director used the word "remember.")

   a. Support for management of panic, fury, and guilt

   b. Umpire services

   c. Drain-off of frustration acidity

   d. Communication maintenance in times of relationship decay

   e. Regulation of behavioral and social traffic

ANSWERS: (1)e (2)c (3)d (4)c (5)e

. . . .

In the previous article, Merritt-Petrashek described the first category of LSI-Emotion First Aid on the Spot; the second category of LSI is the Clinical Explanation of Life Events.

SUBCATEGORIES OF CLINICAL EXPLOITATION OF LIFE EVENTS . . . .

To achieve this second category of LSI, Redl proposes five different types of interviews for student insight and behavioral changes.

   1. *Reality Rub-in Interview.* This interview is used with students who distort reality and have social blindness because of their level of anxiety. They perceive reality not as it is but as they are emotionally. They frequently hear things, see things, and remember events during a crisis that are not accurate, but they believe their distortions.

2. *Symptom Estrangement Interview.* This interview deals with students who are comfortable with their aggressive, hostile behaviors and believe nothing is wrong with them. They are not motivated to change, and they have no awareness that their behavior is deviant or pathological. They may assault a peer and justify their behavior by saying, "He started it" or "I warned him" and assume the role of the victim and not the victimizer.

3. *Massaging Numb Values Crises.* This interview is conducted with students who act out and then become so guilty they put themselves down emotionally and show self-abusive behavior, such as tearing up their work or hurting themselves. This interview focuses the students' self-worth, self-control, and attacks their irrational beliefs that they deserve to be punished. This interview also avoids any guilt inducing statements.

4. *New Tools Salesmanship.* This interview focuses on the student's lack of social skills, which, in turn, creates new social problems for the student. The interview is the precursor of the social skills training curriculum, as developed in the 1980s.

5. *Manipulation of Body Boundaries.* This interview helps a student understand how manipulation by "group forces" or a "false friend" encourages him or her to act out the group's wishes in exchange for personal acceptance.

These five clinical interviews involve knowledge of group dynamics, developmental psychology, and psychodynamic theory, and are based on the following beliefs:

1. When a student crisis occurs, it is to be perceived by staff as a unique opportunity for change and not as a disaster to be avoided. It is a time for benign instruction and not a time for punishment and student alienation.

2. LSI is a verbal firefighting strategy that leads to developing fireproofing skills. It takes place in the student "here and now."

3. LSI is a humanistic approach in which the staff serves as the student's advocate.

4. LSI is initially nonjudgmental, but if the student is not motivated to change the inappropriate behaviors, further staff intervention is grounded on clear ethical values about how people live and treat each other in group situations.

5. LSI assumes a student in a crisis initially will deny, project, and rationalize any responsibility for the aberrant behavior. During this time, the student is his or her own worst enemy and will make the situation worse.

6. If logic, order, responsibility, and resolution are to happen during a crisis, the staff must be well trained to understand and manage a student's inner thoughts, feelings, and behaviors.

7. A successful LSI will have the following benefits for the student, staff, and school board.

The student will learn that:

- A crisis doesn't mean adult rejection or estrangement.
- An adult can accept him or her at his worst and still extend respect.
- The important relationship between his or her thinking, feeling, behaving, and consequences.
- To identify a chronic pattern of self-defeating behavior.
- To accept responsibility for personal behaviors.
- New ways of managing frustrations by learning more appropriate social skills.
- To have more trust in the staff.

The staff will benefit by:

- Feeling empowered as professionals.
- Learning successful ways of deescalating a crisis.
- Learning different strategies of responding to a crisis therapeutically.
- Developing more supportive staff relationships.
- Providing a safer school environment.

The school board will benefit by:

- Providing a more successful resource for "high-risk" and "troubled" students.
- Reducing the level of violence in schools.
- Reducing the number of lawsuits filed against the school system.
- Improving public relations with the community.

THE TRANSLATION OF LSI FOR EDUCATORS . . . .

Morse (1980) was the first educational psychologist to adapt the LSI concept into an understandable process for school staff use. In his published "Worksheet on Life Space Interviewing for Teachers," he described a seven-step process for carrying out a successful LSI. His translation of the LSI made the clinical issues of LSI more understandable and teachable to educators. Table 7.1 on page 438 delineates the differences among LSI, psychodynamic, and traditional approaches to conflict resolution.

THE EVOLUTION OF LIFE SPACE INTERVIEWING TO LIFE SPACE CRISIS INTERVENTION . . . .

From 1970 to 1980, behavior modifications theory and programs dominated special education practices, and, in the majority of the teacher training programs, LSI instruction faded into disuse.

TABLE 7.1   MORSE'S WORKSHEET ON CONCEPTUAL VARIATIONS IN INTERVIEW DESIGNS WITH CHILDREN

	Psychodynamic	Life Space or Reality	Traditional
1. Instigating condition	General personality problem, long-term, not responding to supportive and growth correctional effort	Specific incident (or series) of behavior usually calling for "on the spot" managerial interference	Both implied, but interpreted as moral issue
2. Goal	Long-term expectations of gradual emergence of more healthy personality, possible regression followed by integration and eventual independence	Degree of behavioral compliance accompanied by life space relief fostering adjustment	Induce an immediate character change, exterior change
3. Setting	Office isolation away from immediate life pressures, formal setting, sequence timed	Direct use of milieu reality aspects; choice of time and place to enforce or mitigate as needed	Isolated, integrated, frequent use of group or setting for pressure
4. Relationship	Classical transference, resistance to interpersonal relationship	Emphatic, child identified role by adult	Adult role of authority; paternalistic, autocratic
5. Content	Conscious and unconscious, fantasy, early conflicts, projection, focus on feeling, impulse exploration	What went on, reality exploration, reconstruction with attached feelings and impulses recognized and accepted	Emphasis on the standard morality interpretation of event
6. Processes	Transference, resistance, interpretations, insight, identification, acceptance of impulses (interpretations of unconscious material), high verbal permissiveness, acting out interpreted	Causal behavior "accepted," clinical exploitation of life space events, ego-level interpretation, impulse-control balance critical, support given, explanations fostered, ego support, hurdle help, "skills" depicted, behavior implications faced	Appeal to value system, threats, admonition, exhortations, denial of impulses
7. Resolution	Eventual transfer to life situations	Support and milieu planning to mitigate critical conditions	Surface compliance or rejection

In 1981, Long and Fagen published a new monograph on LSI to promote its use among special educators as they struggled to mainstream students with emotional behavior problems into the regular classroom. LSI had a fresh and important role in special education, but still lacked a teacher-friendly instructional model. In 1991, Wood and Long published *Life Space Intervention* and filled this void. In 1992, Long and Fecser took LSI to the next step and developed a certification program in life space crisis intervention (LSCI), sponsored by the Institute of Psychoeducational Training. These two resources provided the professional structure and the standards for trainer preparation in LSCI, which resulted in an unprecedented resurgence of this concept.

THE FOUR MODIFICATIONS OF LIFE SPACE INTERVIEWING TO LIFE SPACE CRISIS INTERVENTION . . . .

LSCI developed out of the LSI theory proposed by Redl, Wineman, and Morse in the 1950s and 1960s. The basic concepts of LSI have not been changed; they only have been upgraded, expanded, and made more functional. Just as a modern fire department has improved its effectiveness by integrating new technology into its firefighting tactics by using better heat-resistant apparel, more reliable oxygen-breathing apparatus, and more effective water nozzles, LSCI has been enhanced and intensified to meet the new social concerns about the increase of student aggression, hostility, and violence in schools. In an effort to cope, four updating changes were made in LSI.

1. The name life space interviewing was modified to life space crisis intervention. The reasons for modifying the name were carefully considered, and they outweighed the obvious disadvantages of changing the name of an established concept. LSI originally was used in clinical settings with seriously disturbed students. LSI is now used more frequently in educational programs, correctional facilities, and group homes. The word *interview* seemed too restrictive and gave the impression of interrogating or extracting information from a student to obtain admission of some wrongdoing. It also appeared to be a one-time experience in a highly structured, adult-dominated setting. Finally, the pervasive emotional needs of many troubled students required more support and help that could be provided by the psychodynamic model of understanding and by talking with an accepting adult. As an alternative to these concerns, the words *crisis intervention* were substituted to indicate that LSCI also involves the integration of many theoretical concepts and skills, including psychodynamic theory, cognitive theory, social learning theory, and behavioral theory. The word *intervention* is a broader and more realistic term than *interview* in describing how LSCI is currently being taught and used in schools during a crisis.

2. LSI was based on sophisticated clinical insights and skills. All too often, they reflected the personality of the interviewer. As a result, LSI was difficult to teach and often was misinterpreted and misused by new staff.

The appeal of this concept was so magnetic that learners believed they knew about LSI before they understood it. LSI sounds easy to learn and practice, but it is a highly complex and demanding skill. To counter these concerns, Long and Fecser analyzed the LSI process and identified 26 baseline competencies that are necessary to learn before one is qualified to practice LSCI. These 26 foundation concepts and skills took the mystery out of LSI and provided a quality control standard for LSCI training while emphasizing the importance of the "helping staff" to enter the student's world relatively uncontaminated by their own life history.

3. One of the problems with LSI is the ease with which the helper can get lost, sidetracked, and confused by the irrational, defensive, and disorganized world of a troubled student in a crisis. Too many staff begin an LSI appropriately, only to become bewildered and perplexed by the intensity of the student's feelings and issues.

To clarify the LSCI process, a cognitive map was developed to "cue" the staff to specific student/staff stages. Morse's worksheet on LSI was modified, and the new LSCI guidelines propose six sequential stages of the process with identifiable student/staff issues.

THE SIX STAGES OF THE LIFE SPACE CRISIS INTERVENTION PROCESS . . . .

Stage One: Student Crisis Stage and Staff's Deescalation Skills . . . .

The goal of this stage is to drain off the student's angry feelings to the point where his or her behavior is driven by rational processes and not by emotions.

- *Drain off emotional intensity.* Reduce the amount of emotion around the incident; acknowledge that the emotions the student feels are acceptable.

- *Support a student engulfed in intense emotion.* Use time out or physical restraint when a student is so flooded by emotion his behavior is out of control; protect the student and others from his temporary rage; communicate that an adult will temporarily protect him.

- *Use all deescalation and affirmation skills to maintain communications.* Beware of staff counteraggression.

Stage Two: Student Timeline Stage and Staff's Relationship Skills . . . .

Assist the student in a detailed step-by-step recounting of the entire incident, beginning with a point in time when the problem did not exist. Use attending, active listening, observing, and responding skills.

- Frequently validate or *affirm* and acknowledge feelings and behaviors that were "appropriate" under the circumstances.

- *Clarify* "questionable" points. "What you are saying is very important and I want to be sure I have it right." See the sequence of behavior from the student's point of view.

- *Watch for* "*red flags,*" seemingly insignificant comments or asides that may signal a personal issue. If one appears, try repeating the key word or phrase, or try a follow-up question. Don't push it if the student doesn't want to continue, but remember the comment and return to it at another time.

- *Observe* the student's *body language* very carefully. Denial, agitation, interest, or silence is sometimes indicative of being on a meaningful track.

- *Use reflecting* often, to clarify, signal support, and keep the conversation going.

- *Decode* or interpret the student's comments.

- *Stop and summarize* what you have heard so that the student can see the sequence of his or her thoughts, feelings, behaviors, and reactions. Use the Conflict Cycle model whenever possible.

Stage Three: Student Central-Issue Stage and Staff's Differential Diagnosis Skills . . . .

- *Find the central issue.* Decide whether the issue is representative of the student's chronic patterns of perceiving, thinking, feeling, and behaving or is merely a situational conflict.

- *Assess the student's perception, insight, and motivation to change.* Decide whether the student is capable of participating in an LSCI.

- *Select the appropriate therapeutic goal.* This will decide whether the focus of the interview will be Emotional First Aid or one of the seven interventions.

Stage Four: Student Insight Stage and Staff's Clinical Skills . . . .

- *Carry out the appropriate intervention*—should lead to some student insight regarding one's pattern of self-defeating behavior and to learn more effective social skills.

- *Get a commitment.* Help the student to commit to the solution. What will the student see as a satisfactory solution that can be "owned"?

Stage Five: Student New-Skill Stage and Staff's Empowering Skills . . . .

This is the prosocial teaching time.

- *Rehearse new behaviors.* Role-play under as realistic conditions as possible.

- *Anticipate consequences.* Discuss the possibility of discomfort when the student tries out the new behavior for the first time. How will the student deal with the possibility of a less-than-desired outcome?
- *Affirm potential benefits.* Review the commitment and the positive results hard work can bring.

Stage Six: Student Transfer-of-Training Stage and Staff's Follow-up Skills . . . .

- *Set the expectation to participate with the group.* What is the ongoing activity that the student will be expected to join? What rules and expectations are in place?
- *Prepare for reactions of the peer group.* Anticipate how peers will receive the student as he or she enters the room. How will the student handle possible problems?
- *Support and follow-up.* Do what you can to help the student make a successful attempt at using the new behavior modification plan. Speak with colleagues to let them know what to expect and how to encourage the new behavior. Check in with the student and show that the new plan is important to you.

4. In the final change, the five clinical interviews have been expanded to seven identifiable patterns of self-defeating behavior. This decision was based on analysis of over 300 school crises in which two new clinical interventions emerged: (a) *the red flag crisis intervention*, in which a student carries in or expresses an explosive personal issue in school, and (b) the *double struggle crisis intervention*, in which a staff inadvertently misperceives or mishandles the student's crisis and ends up making the conflict worse. The seven crisis interventions are:

1. Red flag
2. Reality rub
3. Symptom estrangement
4. Massaging numb values
5. New tools salesmanship
6. Manipulation of body boundaries
7. Double struggle

To help improve the clarity of these patterns of self-defeating behaviors, each of the seven crisis interventions is described in greater detail according to the student's issue, the student's perception, the staff process, the outcome goals, and the student's new insight (pp. 443–451).

CLINICAL INTERVENTION 1

Red Flag Crisis Intervention
CARRY IN; TAP IN; CARRY OVER

Student Issue

Students who demonstrate any of the following types of self-defeating behaviors—screaming, crying, threatening, attacking, or running away—*overreact* to normal school rules and procedures. They are motivated to escalate their behavior into a blatant "no-win situation" power struggle with staff that will result in more rejection and feelings of alienation as a way of avoiding a personal home/community crisis.

Student's Perceptions

"Life is unfair. My life is troubling me. Nobody understands my situation and personal pain. I feel like a volcano about to explode. I don't think I can keep it together. I really don't care what happens to me! F_____ it!"

Staff Process

1. To perceive that the student's behavior is different or bizarre today.

2. To deescalate the self-defeating behaviors and to determine the source of the intense feelings and inappropriate behaviors.

3. To control the adult's counteraggressive feelings toward the student while working through the multiple layers of student resistance.

Outcome Goals

1. To identify the source of the red flag problem:

    (a) *Carry in:* This usually occurs within the first 40 minutes of the school day. The problem has its source in the home or the community—physical or sexual abuse, parent illness or separation, harassment on transportation, and other causes.

    (b) *Tap in:* This occurs when a discussion, a movie, or a curriculum task triggers a personal issue—abandonment, death, physical or sexual abuse, bodily mutilation, sexual identity, and so on. The overwhelmed student then acts out.

    (c) *Carry over:* This frustration which occurs in one class or school event and is carried over and acted out in the next class.

2. To identify the "dynamics of displacement" in each of these three types and to acknowledge that the problems the student caused in school are not the causes of the student's problems.

3. Focus on the real problem and how the school can help.

4. To practice new ways of managing the home/school problems and the thoughts that arouse intense feelings.

Student's New Insight

"Someone does understand my personal pain and can read beyond my behavior. I need to talk to staff about my real problems and not create new ones at school!"

CLINICAL INTERVENTION 2

Reality Rub Crisis Intervention
ORGANIZING REALITY

Student Issue

Students who demonstrate any of the following five patterns:

1. Personal anxiety due to emotional stress, fatigue, or drugs that alter perception of reality.

2. Selective attention or tunnel vision, seeing only one aspect of the event.

3. Accurate perception of the event, but have faulty thinking and come to a wrong conclusion.

4. Acting out to avoid confronting an event that may cause greater psychological distress.

5. Tests of the limits of the setting.

Student's Perceptions

1. "I don't understand why everybody and everything is going against me!"

2. "I have a right to be upset! No one can see it my way!"

3. "No matter what I do, nothing works out right! Everything is always so unfair!"

4. "I don't want to hear about this again! I just want [them] to forget it!"

5. "I just wanted to see what they'd do if "I" didn't follow the program!"

Staff Process

To organize the student's perceptions into an accurate and logical sequence of events, to bring order to confusion, and to demonstrate a cause-and-effect relationship (i.e., nothing comes from nothing).

Outcome Goals

1. To correct interpersonal distortions and misperceptions.
2. To identify defenses such as rationalization and denial.
3. To connect behavior to feelings.
4. To connect feelings to a stressful incident.
5. To connect a stressful incident to irrational beliefs.
6. To help the student accept a natural consequence as a function of poor decision-making skills.

Student's New Insight

"I only saw and remembered one part of my problem. Now I understand why the crisis happened, what I did to make it worse, and what I need to do to make it better."

CLINICAL INTERVENTION 3

Symptom Estrangement Crisis Intervention
BENIGN CONFRONTATION OF UNACCEPTABLE BEHAVIOR

Student Issue

Students who justify their aggressive behavior and are not motivated to change cast themselves into the role of victims who have been exploited by others and now must protect themselves. They frequently receive secondary pleasure and status from their peer group, are narcissistic, and believe nothing is wrong with them.

Student's Perception

"I will do whatever I have to do to take care of myself. I won't be pushed around. Nobody can tell me nothing. I have a reputation to maintain. There is nothing wrong with me. I'm OK, but you're messing with me."

Staff Process

To obtain a time line; appeal to their narcissism; highlight past vs. current responses; accept *feelings* and not behaviors; clarify the "Law of the Streets" vs. the values of a therapeutic treatment program; benignly confront the defenses and irrational beliefs in an effort to create some *anxiety* about the behavior.

Outcome Goals

1. To drop a pebble of a new idea into students' pool of thought! To have them *think* that maybe they are tricking themselves into believing that it is OK to take the law into their own hands. If they can convince themselves that it is OK, then they can be cruel, hurt others, steal, and so on, without feeling guilty. The goal is to expose their self-deception slowly while still maintaining a caring relationship.

2. To have them realize they are too smart to continue their self-defeating behavior. They are paying too great a price for their momentary pleasure.

Student's New Insight

"Maybe I'm not as smart as I tell myself. Maybe I have been cruel and have been tricking myself into believing it is OK to hurt others. Maybe I am paying too great a price for my deception because I'm in treatment and I am not free."

CLINICAL INTERVENTION 4

Massaging Numb Values
Crisis Intervention
STRENGTHENING SELF-CONTROL SKILLS

Student Issue

Students who act out impulsively and then feel guilty about their behavior, and/or students who are burdened by intense feelings of remorse, shame, and inadequacy, and seek out additional forms of punishment to cleanse their guilt. Frequently, these students have a history of being abused, neglected, abandoned, and deprived, and have low self-esteem.

Student's Perception

"I'm a terrible person. I can never do anything right. I can't control myself so I need to be punished."

Staff Process

To avoid any guilt-inducing statement; to manage all self-destructive behaviors first; to attack the irrational beliefs about *magnification* and *emotional reasoning* (i.e., "I'm a terrible rotten person"). To give abundant affirmation and reflections about existing desirable attitudes, traits, and behaviors such as kindness, fairness, and friendship. To focus on the control side of the issue and not on the impulsive side.

Outcome Goals

1. To *massage* students' awareness that they have more self-control than they realize.
2. To help them accept the belief that accidents happen, that they can make mistakes and poor decisions without feeling they are worthless.
3. To help them listen to and improve their self-control system.

Student's New Insight

"Even under tempting situations and group pressures, I have the choice and the capacity to control myself. Because I made a mistake this time, it doesn't mean I'm a terrible person. There is a part of me that can learn the skills to say 'Control!' I can stop myself!"

CLINICAL INTERVENTION 5

New Tools Salesmanship Crisis Intervention

TEACHING NEW SOCIAL SKILLS TO STUDENTS WHO LACK AGE APPROPRIATE SOCIAL BEHAVIORS

Student Issue

Students who have the *correct attitudes* toward adults, peers, and learning, but who lack the appropriate social skills to be successful.

Student's Perception

"I want to do the right thing but somehow it always comes out wrong."

Staff Process

To obtain an accurate time line; to *review* it with the student and make the *connection* or interpretation between the student's intentions and behavior (i.e., "Oh! You're telling me that you grabbed his hat because, in your mind, you were trying to make a friend!"). Once the student can focus on a right attitude instead of a wrong behavior, the staff affirms the student's right attitude and reinforces that the student and the staff are on the same side. The student wants to make friends (learn, relate, etc.) and the staff wants him or her to make friends, improve academically, and relate to adults. Once this positive relationship is established, then move to the outcome goals.

Outcome Goals

1. To teach the student new "age-appropriate" social skills by using prosocial skills training strategies. While all Life Space Crisis Intervention involves teaching the student new social skills, a New Tools Salesmanship Crisis Intervention is reserved for those students who initially wanted to do the "right thing!"

Student's New Insight

"I have the right attitude and now I am learning the right behaviors to make new friends, improve academically, and get along with adults."

CLINICAL INTERVENTION 6

Manipulation of Body Boundaries Crisis Intervention

EXPOSING EXPLOITATION BY PEERS

Student Issue

Students who are either:

1. neglected, isolated, or loners and develop a self-defeating friendship with an exploitative classmate. In this relationship, the dependent

student frequently maintains the relationship by acting out his "friend's" inappropriate wishes; or

2. are "set up" and "controlled" by a bright passive aggressive student. In this relationship, the aggressive student is unaware of being manipulated by the passive aggressive classmate and reacts inappropriately to the provocation.

Student's Perception

1. "It is important to have friends even if I get into trouble."

2. "I'm not going to let that jerk tease me. I will go over and teach him a lesson!"

Staff Process

1. If the issue is *false friendship,* it is essential for both students to be involved in the interview. The strategy is to get the exploitative friend to act out the "manipulation" in front of the victim and staff, thereby demonstrating how the manipulator uses the victim for personal needs.

2. If the issue is not "false friendship" but *being set up* by others, then the aggressive victim can be seen alone. The focus is to demonstrate how the aggressive student is in trouble when reacting to the other student's manipulation.

Outcome Goals

1. To demonstrate that a friend is someone who will help and make life better, not worse. A friend doesn't exploit willingly.

2. To demonstrate that the aggressive student is giving his or her controls and freedom to the manipulative passive aggressive student when the aggressive student reacts to the provocation.

Student's New Insight

1. "I want a friend who will help me solve problems and feel good, not someone who is false and exploitative."

2. "I will not react to the manipulation because _____ wants me to act out and get into trouble. I will ignore the tricks, not fall into the traps, and then feel good about myself."

CLINICAL INTERVENTION 7

Double Struggle Crisis Intervention

BENIGNLY CONFRONTING STAFF REGARDING ONE'S INAPPROPRIATE BEHAVIOR DURING THE CONFLICT

Staff Issue

Staff who inadvertently fuel conflict for any of the following reasons:

1. They become caught in the student's Conflict Cycle.
2. They hold rigid and unrealistic expectations regarding normal developmental student behavior.
3. They are caught in a bad mood.
4. They are caught in prejudging a problem student in a crisis.

Staff's Perceptions

1. "I'm not going to take his abuse! If he wants to challenge me, I'm ready!"
2. "She'll conform to my demands with a smile or she's out!"
3. "That's the last straw! I won't take any more of his garbage behavior!"
4. "I knew it would be her again!"

Staff Process

To benignly confront the staff by using the Conflict Cycle to help the adult gain insight into his or her role in the incident.

Outcome Goals

1. To acknowledge the adult's good intentions in dealing with the crisis.
2. To share information about the student or the incident that the adult may not have had at the time of the crisis.
3. To correct misperceptions about the student's role in the crisis.
4. To use the Conflict Cycle as a way of understanding student and adult stress during a crisis.
5. To support the adult with affirming statements rather than blame.
6. To help the adult accept a new and accurate perception of the incident.
7. To help the student understand the situation from the adult's point of view.
8. To facilitate reconciliation and problem resolution.

Staff's New Insight

"Now I understand the situation from the student's point of view and I recognize how I contributed to the problem."

. . . .

The skills involved in carrying out these seven different interventions can be learned, but the first task is to understand the differences among them. To offer an opportunity to test the cognitive differences among these interventions, a differential spot quiz follows.

THE DIFFERENTIAL DIAGNOSIS OF THE SEVEN LSCI INTERVENTIONS: A QUIZ . . . .

Read the following seven documented crises, identify the central issue of the crisis, and then select the appropriate intervention:

    A. Red Flag Crisis Intervention
    B. Reality Rub Crisis Intervention
    C. Symptom Estrangement Crisis Intervention
    D. Massaging Numb Values Crisis Intervention
    E. New Tools Salesmanship Crisis Intervention
    F. Manipulation of Body Boundaries Crisis Intervention
    G. Double Struggle Crisis Intervention

1. Barry, an overweight 8-year-old, walks into the classroom late because of an incident on the bus. Several of his peers had teased him by calling him "Blimpy the whale," and Barry reacted by spitting on them. Barry is very attracted to his teacher, Mrs. Wade, and shouts "Hello" to her. Mrs. Wade is working with another student and responds by putting a finger to her lips, indicating that she is busy and Barry should be quiet. Barry misperceives her signal and is convinced she is rejecting him. He goes over to his seat, kicks his chair, and slams his books on the desk. In a few minutes, Mrs. Wade comes over to Barry and says in a kindly way, "Barry you seem to be in a grumpy mood today." Barry blows up, screams, and says, "Don't call me dumpy, why are you teasing me about my weight. I hate you!" (_____)

2. Tyrone, a 14-year-old walks into school with his cap on although he knows it is against the rules. Mr. Garcia sees Tyrone and asks him to please take off his hat. Tyrone swears at Mr. Garcia and walks into his classroom. He refuses to sit down and threatens his classroom teacher by saying, "What are you staring at, bitch. Mind your own business." Additional

staff arrives, the behavior escalates, and Tyrone has to be physically re-strained. (____)

3. Jason is a hyperactive first grader. His class is watching a film strip run by Ms. Yelfin, the classroom aide. Jason walks over to the film projector and starts to examine it. Ms. Yelfin tells him to sit down but Jason ignores her and continues to look at the machine. Ms. Yelfin again commands Jason to go back to his seat. Jason replies, "If you make me go back to my seat I will hit you." Ms. Yelfin, who is frustrated, says, "Go ahead; go ahead and hit me and see what happens to you!" With this encouragement, Jason hits Ms. Yelfin in the arm. Ms. Yelfin is shocked and angry. She grabs Jason and marches him to the principal's office demanding Jason be suspended for staff assault. (____)

4. Clarese is a 10-year-old abused girl who has been placed in four different foster homes. She is beginning to develop a relationship with Mr. Quinn, the school principal. Mr. Quinn is walking around her classroom, commenting on the students' progress, when Clarese reaches out to touch him. Inadvertently, she grabs the pocket of his jacket and, as Mr. Quinn turns, the pocket rips. Clarese is horrified and apologizes. Mr. Quinn acknowledges her concerns and is not upset, but has to leave the classroom immediately because of a telephone call.

The next period, Clarese refuses to do her work and doesn't earn her points for the Friday treat, begins to scribble on her attractive shirt, and tears up all of her artwork. (____)

5. Warren, a 16-year-old street-wise student, walks over to Doug during a silent reading period and slugs him in the chest so hard Doug falls to the ground and starts crying. The teacher is surprised by Warren's behavior and says, "Warren, what happened?" Warren replies, "Doug has been staring at me all morning. At lunch time, I gave him a warning and told him I would punch him out if he didn't stop. I was trying to read, but I looked up and there was Doug giving me the bug eyes, so I hit him. I should have hit him harder, but I gave him a break because we were in class. So talk to Doug. It's his problem, not mine." Warren appears comfortable with his behavior; he has no intention of accepting any responsibility for his hostility. (____)

6. David is a 13-year-old student who has a history of being immature and regressive. David is walking to his next class when he sees Tom opening his locker. David would like to have Tom as his friend, so he says, "Hello." Tom doesn't hear him so David taps Tom in the head harder than he had planned. Tom hits his head against his locker, hears David laugh, turns, and hits David in the stomach. David is surprised and angry, and is brought to the crisis room saying, "It's not fair. Everyone is mean to me." (____)

7. Larry, an aggressive 12-year-old, is group leader of his class. Larry decides to befriend Daryl, who is usually ignored by his peers. Daryl is excited to have Larry as a friend and looks up to him with admiration. Several weeks later, Larry brings a cap gun to class and, just before school ends,

shows it to Daryl. Larry says, "Daryl, the teacher is in the back of the room. Let's have some fun. Let's shoot off this cap gun and surprise Ms. Gallagher. As my closest friend, I'll let you go first!" Daryl takes the cap gun, pulls the trigger, startles the entire class, and leaves a trail of smoke rising from his desk. Ms. Gallagher follows the smoke to Daryl, identifies him as the offender, and takes him to the principal's office. (____)

ANSWERS

1. Reality Rub Intervention
2. Red Flag Carry In Intervention
3. Double Struggle Intervention
4. Massaging Numb Values Intervention
5. Symptom Estrangement Intervention
6. New Tools Salesmanship Intervention
7. Manipulation of Body Boundaries Intervention

HOW EFFECTIVE IS AN LSCI? . . . .

The modifications of Life Space Interviewing that created Life Space Crisis Intervention have maintained the theory of LSI while also making LSCI a significant and critical skill for all professionals who provide direct service to troubled students.

 In the next article, Long and Dorf provide a comprehensive illustration of an actual Life Space Crisis Intervention. This example demonstrates the many skills required in order to enter a crisis and turn it into a rewarding experience for the student and staff.

ARTICLE 7.3

A Red Flag Carry-in Life Space Crisis Intervention: The Tip of the Iceberg

Nicholas J. Long and Ruth Dorf

The iceberg is one of my favorite analogies. It is a floating mountain in which seven-eighths of its mass is underwater. Psychologically, it highlights the difference between overt and covert behavior. What you see is not what you get. It demonstrates how the magnitude of the problem is out of sight; and, as the captain of the "indestructible" Titanic learned, it does not give you any advanced warning before you run into its hidden part.

A similar hidden destructive force threatens our public schools. Students come to school after experiencing overwhelming abusive situations

---

From *The Journal of Emotional and Behavioral Problems*. (1994). Vol. 3, No. 2. Reprinted with permission.

at home or in the community the previous night. Fearing for their physical and psychological safety, they are unable to confront their abusers; but they come to school filled with emotional pain, which they quickly dump onto their peers and teachers.

Like the iceberg, these students do not give the staff any advanced warning. They do not come to the staff and say they are angry or depressed. They do not talk about their traumatic life experiences. Instead, they come to school and, within the first 40 minutes, they fight with staff and peers over insignificant comments or standard school procedures. They overreact to such normal requests as "Take off your hat," "Open your book," or "Take your seat." They create blatant "no win" situations and openly engage their peers and staff in self-defeating power struggles. Their behaviors are irrational. They shout, "I don't give a shit what happens to me!" "I hate this school!" "I hate you!" "I hate everyone!"

For persons who try to manage these students' crises, the problem is complex and upsetting. These crises are examples of the Conflict Cycle in hyperaction. The Conflict Cycle's basic principle is:

"A student in a crisis will create in the staff his feelings; and, if the staff is *not* trained, the staff will mirror the student's behavior."

This means the staff will "pick up" the student's massive feelings of anger; and since the staff feels they are being treated unfairly by the student, the staff also can experience intense feelings of "Righteous Rage" (for example, "I don't deserve to be treated this way," or "This student is too disturbed to be in this setting"). Because these feelings are real, they frequently block any staff from realizing that this troubled student is his or her own worst enemy.

A Red Flag Carry-in Crisis can escalate into a school-wide problem, frequently ending with staff being assaulted, the police being called, and the student being suspended from school. When this occurs, the original source of the student's problem is never identified; the local newspaper article reads, "Student Goes Berserk and Assaults Teacher!"

In the following Red Flag Carry-in Crisis, the student, Claudia, was very fortunate to have Ruth Dorf intervene and manage her crisis. Ruth Dorf had just completed her certification in Life Space Crisis Intervention and demonstrated the following intervention skills:

- she recognized that Claudia's behavior was different;
- she recognized and controlled her own counter-aggressive feelings;
- she de-escalated the crisis by using decoding and affirming skills;
- she helped Claudia recognize the real source of her anger;
- she helped Claudia identify the concept of "displacement";
- she helped Claudia accept the consequences of her behavior; and
- she helped Claudia realize the need to use the staff the next time she is upset, thereby avoiding her self-defeating pattern of behavior.

Most important, it illustrates how a student crisis can be used in a therapeutic way.

BACKGROUND INFORMATION

Claudia is a 15-year old African-American female who lives with her biological parents and 2 younger siblings. At one time, the father left the house because of accusations of physical and verbal abuse. He has since moved back into the home. Claudia has said on various occasions that she hates her father.

Claudia also has a very serious problem with personal hygiene. Unless she is reminded by the school nurse, she does not shower, change her clothes, or brush her teeth on a regular basis. As a result, she is not very popular with her peers. Claudia is a learning-disabled student who is doing poorly in her studies. She is friendly toward the other youngsters, but she constantly accuses others of "picking on her."

INCIDENT

Claudia walked into the school building with a scowl on her face. It was quite obvious that she had not showered or changed her clothing from the previous day. She entered the breakfast room and sat in the far left corner, alone. As she got up to get her breakfast, she shouted at Diane, "Leave me the f_____ alone!" As she walked back to her seat with her breakfast, she suddenly stopped and threw her breakfast tray at Diane, hitting her in the leg with her food. Diane jumped out of her chair, ran over to Claudia, and struck her in the face with her fist. The fight escalated, and it took three staff members to separate them.

DRAINOFF STAGE

I happened to observe the fight and told Claudia she needed to come with me to my office. She came reluctantly but yelled all the way, "Who the f_____ does she think she is?" "I'm gonna get the bitch!" "Why'd she smack me upside my head?" "Wait till I get her outside!" "You'll see which one of us starts crying!"

I told Claudia I could hear how upset she was with Diane, but I was more concerned to determine if she was physically hurt. She looked herself

N.J.L.

up and down and said she was okay. I said I was glad that she wasn't hurt; but if it was all right, could I look at where she was hit? She agreed and took a seat.

I asked her if she'd like breakfast. She replied, "Yeah! But they won't give me another one." I told her to relax and let me handle it. I asked her to remain in the office and remain quiet. She agreed. When I returned with the breakfast, Claudia thanked me and began to eat. I complimented her on how she was able to remain quietly in the office when she was so upset. Much to my surprise Claudia gave me a little smile. I allowed her to finish her breakfast in peace.

After she was done, I asked her if she could calmly tell me about the incident. She said she didn't know. I gave her a few minutes to think about it. All of a sudden, she tried to blurt out all sorts of things that were not making any sense to me. After she got it out, I asked her if we could go over all the issues again, one by one, since I wanted to get it straight. I told her how pleased I was she could share her concerns with me.

TIME LINE

After her initial outburst of words, I asked her how she was feeling when she came into school today. Having some knowledge of Claudia's homelife, I felt that this was a good place to begin. I asked her if she felt happy, sad, worried, upset, etc. She shouted, "Okay!" I continued to probe, and she told me she was tired. "I want to be left alone!"

I responded by saying, "Let me understand what happened so far. You came into school feeling okay. But, you are also tired and want to be left alone. Do I have it right, so far?"

Claudia shook her head in agreement. I said, "Okay, now let's get to the breakfast room. You walked in quietly, and where did you sit?"

Claudia said, "I sat in the corner, away from everyone."

I affirmed that was a good decision, since she was tired and wanted to be alone. I again asked her if she was sure she felt "Okay" when she came into school.

She said, "Yeah! I'm okay, but I was a little mad!"

I responded by saying, "Wait a minute. Let me make sure that I understand what we've been talking about. You came into school feeling okay, tired, wanted to be left alone; and now you're saying that you were a little mad. Did I get it right?"

"Yeah!"

I then said, "I give you a lot of credit for coming to school feeling the way you did. Most students would have skipped school when they are feeling so tired and mad. I don't know if I'd be able to do what you've done. You should be proud of yourself. I'm proud of you!"

After this comment, Claudia completely calmed down and began to get very involved in the LSCI.

A RED FLAG INTERVENTION

RD: Tell me about your event last night.

Claudia: It was all right. (Body language showed some tension.)

RD: Did you sleep well?

Claudia: Yeah.

RD: What time do you get up in the mornings?

Claudia: I don't know, about 7:00.

RD: That's good. I get up early, too.

Claudia: Today, I got up at 6:00.

RD: Tell me why you got up so early this morning? No wonder you're so tired!

Claudia: I had to wake my father up at 6:00.

RD: Doesn't he have an alarm clock?

Claudia: No! He doesn't have shit!

RD: So, he didn't have an alarm clock so you had the responsibility of waking him up. Do you have to do this often?

Claudia: No.

RD: So, did you wake him up on time?

Claudia: (with tears in her eyes) Yeah!

RD: What did he say or do when you woke him up?

Claudia: He yelled at me.

RD: Here you are doing a favor for your father and he yells at you for waking him up. I'd also be mad. Tell me, what did he say? How loud did he yell? How did you feel?

Claudia: I hope he dies! He's a real bitch!

RD: So you were real upset with him. What did he actually say to you?

Claudia: (tears are coming down her face) He called me a bitch and a whore.

RD: That must really have made you feel sad! Is that all he said?

Claudia: No, he asked me why I woke him up?

RD: Did you tell him that he asked you to wake him last night?

Claudia: Yeah. He told me to drop dead and that I'm a filthy bitch.

RD: Anything else? Was he drinking last night?

Claudia: Yes, he was. He said I was an idiot, I can't get anything right, and that I'm no good!

RD: So you carried out your responsibilities and got him up on time, and he says you can't get anything right! Do you believe him?

Claudia: He's a f_____ing bastard!

RD: You are really angry at him! Would you like to go and wash your face and freshen up a little?

Claudia: Would you come with me? (a positive sign)

RD: Certainly!

Claudia: Am I gonna get suspended for throwing the food?

RD: Let's finish with one issue at a time before we solve the next one. What did you do when your father stopped yelling at you?

Claudia: I went to the bathroom and got dressed and left.

RD: So, when you got to school you weren't really feeling okay, and I don't blame you, you were really mad and wanted to be left alone.

Claudia: Yeah, I guess.

RD: Now, let's go back to the breakfast room. Someone started to bother you by calling to you, remember that.

Claudia: Yeah.

RD: Do you remember what you said?

Claudia: Yeah! I said, "Leave me the f_____ alone!"

RD: When you heard your name being called, did you know that it was Diane?

Claudia: No.

RD: If you had known it was Diane, do you think that you would have thrown your food at her?

Claudia: Yeah! I wanted to be left alone!

RD: What I'm hearing is that you would have acted in the same manner no matter who it was.

Claudia: Yeah!

RD: Have any of us or Diane done anything to you this morning to get you mad at us?

Claudia: You all bother me!

RD: What Diane did to bother you was to try to get your attention, right?

Claudia: Right!

RD: Did Diane know that you were very upset with your father this morning?

Claudia: No.

RD: Then she didn't try to upset you on purpose.

Claudia: No.

RD: Since she is one of your friends, maybe she wanted to help, since you looked upset.

Claudia: Yeah.

RD: Can you tell me who you really are mad at?

Claudia: My father—but, he always yells stuff like that at me!

RD: So you were really upset with your Dad, but you took it out on . . .

Claudia: Diane.

RD: Yes you did. But does Diane deserve it?

Claudia: No.

RD: But, she got your anger. You gave it to her when you were upset at your . . .

Claudia: Father.

RD: Claudia, do you think this is a pattern you use when you are upset?

Claudia: I don't know. (Her body language indicates she is feeling anxious about her answer.)

RD: Do you think it was true today?

Claudia: Yes.

RD: Did this fight with Diane solve anything, or did it make your life worse?

Claudia: It made my life worse. Now Diane is mad at me.

RD: That's another problem which you will need to solve. But if you get upset at home again, and come to school angry, what can you do to avoid creating more difficulty for yourself?

Claudia: I can talk to someone at school about it.

RD: I know you have talked to Mr. Gallagher in the past. The two of you seem to get along. What if I arrange a meeting with him so he will understand how difficult your life can get? Now, I know it is not easy to talk to someone, but we need to be good to ourselves and not beat ourselves up when we are feeling sad and angry. You have had enough psychological pain in your life.

Claudia: I will try.

RD: Shall we practice? I'll be you and you be Mr. Gallagher. (I thought this process was very helpful to Claudia.)

OUTCOME GOALS FOR CLAUDIA

- To have Claudia understand the dynamics of displacement and that the real problem was with her father, not Diane.
- To have Claudia understand that there are other people in this school who will listen to her and support her when she comes to school upset.
- To have Claudia solve her conflict with Diane.
- To help Claudia return to class and participate in her classes without further difficulty.

RETURN TO CLASS

Claudia and I discussed what she would do if someone began to "bother" her in class.

Claudia: I won't bother with them.

RD: Yes, but that might be hard to do. What then?

Claudia: Tell the teacher or ignore them.

RD: Very good, but what if they continue to bother you?

Claudia: Leave the room and go to the Dean's office.

RD: What if the teacher will not excuse you from class?

Claudia: I'd tell her I'd rather get into trouble for leaving the classroom without a pass than for fighting.

RD: That's terrific! I'm really proud of you! Ready to go to class?

Claudia: Yeah.

POSTSCRIPT

I made sure to speak with all of the teachers for the day. They were informed to keep an eye on Claudia and give her a pass to my office if she asked for one. Claudia came to my office once during the course of the day to tell me she was ready to speak with Mr. Gallagher.

. . . .

INSTRUCTIONAL COMMENTS . . . .

An explosive crisis situation usually escalates into punishment, alienation, and rejection. Instead, Ruth Dorf turned it into an opportunity for personal insight and support. Claudia left the session with renewed hope that someone understood her personal pain and could see beyond the tip of her internal iceberg. Ideally, she will learn that this act of displacement is a self-defeating pattern of behavior that should be understood and stopped. Her goal is to talk to the school staff about her real problems rather than about the ones she creates in school.

I was impressed with Ruth's Red Flag Carry-in Intervention, but some minor issues are worth discussion. During the timeline stage, most students never tell what is troubling them, but they drop little clues that we need to pick up. For example, when Claudia said she came to school tired, this would be important to explore:

> Tell me how tired you were, on a scale of 1–10. Help me to understand if you are tired because you went to bed late, couldn't go to sleep, woke up in the middle of the night, or got up early?

By exploring these personal events, we frequently can get to the central issue of the intervention earlier.

I also want to emphasize Ruth's skills in managing her counteraggressive feelings when Claudia was swearing as she walked to the office. Equally important were Ruth's nurturing and affirming skills, such as checking to see whether Claudia was hurt, getting her a second breakfast, and affirming Claudia's self-control skills. I noticed that Claudia was much more available to this process once Ruth spoke about and met some of Claudia's emotional needs.

In summary, the Red Flag Carry-in Intervention is the most difficult to do, because these students are the most resistant to help. However, the Red Flag Carry-in Crisis is becoming the number-one source of crises in schools, and staff will need to be trained not to act on their feelings if these students are to be helped. With training, staff can quickly see the tip of the iceberg and avoid the fatal crash!

R.D.

HOW LSCI CAN BE INTEGRATED INTO THE SCHOOLS ...

If the schools are serious about meeting the needs of high-risk students and including students with special needs in the regular classroom, then the schools must have well-trained staff who are responsible for handling student crises.

It is our belief that *at least* two staff members of every school should be certified in LSCI, from among: a special education teacher, a school counselor, a school psychologist, or the school principal.

 In the next article, Morse proposes the ideal arrangement for schools by advocating the need and resources of a crisis teacher.

ARTICLE 7.4

The Crisis Teacher
William C. Morse

One of the most encouraging aspects of recent Michigan public school planning for emotionally disturbed students is the flexibility which is anticipated. Suggestions include special classes, consultant teachers, and individually designed experimental programs. It is recognized that these new programs are supplemental to efforts for overall school mental health and the services of visiting teachers, psychologists, school nurses, and guidance workers.

A few school districts have already been operating small classes for the emotionally disturbed: in several instances evaluative efforts have been incorporated.

The plan presented in this new report is not a substitute for any of the present services or their anticipated legitimate expansion. Nor is it proposed that the school become a psychiatric institution. Rather, the plan is an immediate school rescue operation designed for the point of problem origin through the use of a new educational device, the crisis teacher. If the regular school is to function, it is mandatory to keep the classrooms as free from teacher-exhausting, group-disrupting students as is possible. Conversely, the school has recognized the responsibility to offer additional assistance to these students when they cannot benefit from a well-modulated classroom learning situation. The small but appreciable educational "fall out" presents a difficult situation: authoritative handling seldom resolves the problem, and many cases go year after year until a negative school adjustment becomes fixed.

What are some of the school conditions which are necessary to keep a reasonably constant learning flow in classrooms? First, there must be an immediate resource for the teacher when there is significant disruption of the classroom group learning process. Help must be available without stigma or recrimination or even the implication of overburdening the administrator. The truth is the principal has so many duties his availability is limited. A new hand is required, but of a special type. Not only must the new person help the school at large, but he must provide immediate succor to the students as well. It is easy to forget that the student is in real need at his time of stress. And he needs help with two things—his school work and the feelings which distort his efforts at the moment. Of course, this is true for the acting out student who disrupts the class. But it is also true for the withdrawn, unhappy, quiet underachiever.

The "crisis teacher" is the school resource designed to meet this situation. This teacher must really know curriculum at the school level served, must be steeped in remedial teaching techniques and must be skilled in life-space crisis interviewing, a style of interviewing essential for the teacher who must handle diverse types of behavior problems. The space provided may include a small classroom with a pleasant anteroom. Books and materials of all sorts are at hand.

Since each school is unique, modus operandi are derived from the specific needs of a given school. There are several observations, however, which may serve as guides.

1. The crisis teacher can be effective only to the degree that the whole staff is concerned about understanding and helping the troubled student. Case conference and strategy planning meetings involve all the teachers. Some planning for particular children can be done on a sub-group basis. The general principle is, that all the adults who deal with the student take part in devising the plan and evolving the strategy. Many failures in school relations are due to faulty communication among teachers who do not work together on their common problems. Merely providing another specialist will not make the necessary impact on the school environment. Also, regardless of what is accomplished in the special work, its real purpose is to help the student to get along properly in the regular classroom. The classroom teacher continues to spend more time with the student than any specialist does, and plans for assistance will have to consider her work as well as the time the student spends with the crisis teacher. Since many students are skillful manipulators, little will be gained unless all adults are aware of the case dynamics and have thought through the most appropriate management procedures. Frequently, after an encouraging start, an improvement plateau is reached and new plans must be evolved on the basis of a more complete understanding of the student and how he reacts.

2. Referral procedures are the responsibility of the total staff. When a teacher feels that a student cannot be helped in the classroom alone, this student becomes a potential candidate for the crisis teacher. It is important to note that this does not await a complicated diagnosis or parental permission, because the student is not in the usual sense a special case. His behavior "in situ" makes the referral. If possible, plans for assistance are

worked out in advance; but the regular teacher may take the student directly to the crisis teacher and present the situation in a nonrejecting non-moralistic but frank manner. This special service is not a dumping ground or a discard heap. Rather, the two teachers discuss sympathetically the educational complexity at hand. Cues relative to the student's attitude about the referral are faced directly and the crisis teacher goes over possible goals. Afterward the student returns to the classroom only when he is considered ready to resume his progress in that setting.

Thus, the crisis teacher does not have a regular class or group. Students may come and go, sometimes on a more or less regular basis as seems advisable, but often on an episodic basis when specific pressure accumulates. Of course, at particular times, the special teacher may be working with more than one student. As crisis demands decrease or vacillate there are always underachieving students to be given individual help.

3. The work which goes on in the special setting is determined by the student's problem. Students seldom compartmentalize their relationships or their quandaries. Home, school, and play are all intermixed. General attitudes and school work motivation are a confused combination. Consequently, the teacher has to take a broad humanistic approach in crisis teaching. The interaction may take on characteristics of a "man to man" talk, a parental surrogate, or a counselor, besides involving the general teacher role. Free of large group responsibilities, immediate achievement goals and time restrictions, the able teacher can operate with a new flexibility. Perhaps it will be individualized tutoring, an informal talk, a diversionary activity, or an intensive life space interview session around the feelings and tension evinced in the student. In short, what is done is what any teacher would want to do were it possible to determine action by the needs of the student rather than the large group learning process in a classroom. At times several students may be involved, and group work is called into play. The difficulty may turn out to be a learning frustration, an interpersonal conflict, or an internal feeling. As the crisis teacher sizes up the situation, plans are made for immediate and long-term steps. This teacher may get the outpouring of the student's inner conflict and must be prepared to handle whatever the student brings, as well as to refer special problems to other services. It is particularly important for the student to learn he will be listened to and that his problem will be considered, even to the point of initiating joint sessions with his regular teacher to discuss conditions as he sees them. There are few of the secrets and confidences which some professional school workers make much of at the expense of exchanging information needed to solve the student's school problem. While it is obvious that this work takes utmost skill and sensitivity, it should also be clear that co-equal members of a staff can be open with the student, and no professional worker is "handling" another. All too soon we are faced with the fact that the total staff, with all the insight we can muster, will still not be able to influence the lives of some of these children at any better than a surface level. On the other hand, if we can help a student meet what are for him

reasonable social and academic school expectations, this is itself a worthwhile goal, though other problems remain.

4. While a student does not have to be certified as any type of a special student for this service, some of the clientele will already have been studied intensively in the normal course of events. Other students will present baffling difficulties to the crisis teacher and staff. Here psychological study, visiting teacher investigation, or material from a psychiatric examination may be in order. Perhaps it becomes evident that the student's needs are for individual case work or family contact which can best be done by the visiting teacher or counselor. Since these specialists participate in the planning meetings, trial decisions are the product of mutual discussion. The sharing of cases becomes the sharing of a problem-solving venture. In this way, the school principal, specialists, crisis teacher, and classroom teacher work as a team: possessiveness and contention are a luxury schools cannot afford. With adequate research it may eventually be possible to predict which student will respond to such a program. At present the value is in the improved learning climate provided for the whole school, as well as helping the particular student.

. . . .

SUMMARY . . . .

This chapter was organized to describe the essential concepts and skills of managing a student crisis using the concept of Life Space Crisis Intervention. LSCI is an effective and therapeutic concept involving staff who are a natural part of the students' school experience. LSCI provides staff with the skills to talk with students about specific target behaviors and personal problems that frequently escalate into destructive experiences. Finally, the LSCI dramatizes the value of assisting students to talk about themselves, how they see life, and how they view their troubles in the context of school. The LSCI supports a powerful and insightful approach to problem solving by singling out the student's difficulty for instant, unmuddled, and undisguised supportive handling—at the time and place the difficulty occurs.

What makes LSCI a powerful and effective strategy is the knowledge that students in a crisis, regardless of how angry, depressed, fearful, or anxious they are, want to tell their story.

REFERENCES . . . .

Caplan, C. (1961). Preventing mental disorders in children. New York: Basic Books.

Long, N. (1986). *The nine psychoeducational stages of helping emotionally disturbed students through the reeducation process. The Pointer* (Vol. 30, No. 3). pp. 5–20.

Long, N., & Fagen, S. (1981). *Pointer: Life space interviewing* (Vol. 25, No. 2). Washington, DC: Heldref.

Long, N., & Fecser, F. (1992). *Life space crisis intervention training manual.* Hagerstown, MD: Institute of Psychoeducational Training.

Morse, W. (1965). "Worksheet on Life Space Interviewing." *Conflict in the Classroom.* Belmont, CO: Wadsworth.

Morse, W. (1980). Worksheet on life space interviewing for teachers. *Conflict in the classroom* (4th ed., pp. 267–271). Belmont, CO: Wadsworth.

Positive education program. (1995). *Crisis prevention/crisis intervention training manual: Competency 1: Safety/crisis management* (pp. 3–6). Cleveland, OH.

Redl, F. (1959). The concept of life space interviewing. *American Journal of Orthopsychiatry, 29,* 1–18.

Redl, F. (1966). *When we deal with children.* New York: Free Press.

Redl, F., & Wineman, D. (1951). *Children who hate.* Glencoe, IL: Free Press.

Redl, F., & Wineman, D. (1952). *Controls from within.* Glencoe, IL: Free Press.

Redl, F., & Wineman, D. (1957). *The aggressive child.* Glencoe, IL: Free Press.

Tompkins, J., & Tompkins-McGill, P. (1993). *Surviving in schools in the 1990s.* Lanham, MD: University Press of America.

Wineman, D. (1959). *The life space interview, social work,* Vol. 4, #1, 3–7.

Wood, M., & Long, N. (1991). *Life space intervention* (pp. 34–36). Austin, TX: PRO-ED.

8

The Psychoeducational Classroom: Strategies and Skills of Successful Methods and Social/Emotional Curricula

The major school intervention channel to help troubled students lies in what is taught and the methods used. In practice, curriculum and method cannot be separated: they are two sides of the same coin. An exciting curriculum innovation can become boring if presented with poor teaching methods. Conversely, exciting teaching can be wasted on dull and nonrelevant curriculum. Finding legitimate motivations that will bring troubled students to the learning table is frequently the primary task.

In selecting curricula, one is confronted with a philosophical issue: What are schools for in a democratic society? We all agree at an abstract level that schools are for producing responsible citizens who can function in the world of work and society, but when we get specific, especially concerning handicapped pupils, the right curriculum is anything but simple. Presuming the student will return to the mainstream, should the curriculum and method replicate what goes on in the regular setting? Or, because many troubled students have other handicaps as well, such as learning disability (LD), should we concentrate on specialized methodologies?

The rapid expansion of the possible knowledge base, the new skills needed for negotiating tomorrow's world, and the difficulty of predicting what an individual student will need, all add to the problem of curriculum selection. Answers to "What are schools for?" depend both on predictions of what society will be like in 20 years and on values held by the debaters. Essentialists, being content-centered, would have a set, basic academic curriculum taught to all, with an emphasis on high achievement and mastery learning. For them, the school should not become a quasi-mental health agency. On the other hand, developmentalists, being child-centered, would prioritize on the basis of individual children's needs. In the current educational ferment, diverse models reflect differing philosophies for what the schools should be doing and how they should do it. Each professional needs to clarify his or her personal view of what schools are for and what is the role of specialized educational programs, lest friction come from differing but unarticulated visions. Regarding troubled students, is the purpose of school different than for regular students? Is the goal to make the pupil fit into the mainstream (whatever it is), or to help a child become as successful as possible in life? These issues face all teachers, but especially those teaching students who are not successful in the regular school.

As we turn our attention to strategies for curriculum, it is clear that the term itself is used in several ways: what the schools teach, the course of study, a precise sequence with specific content components, a specific educational activity planned for a given student at a given time, or all the experiences the child has while at school. The so-called covert curriculum consists of those self-feelings (self-esteem) and attitudes about peers, schooling, and authority that are generated by the school experience. Because each pupil responds in a unique manner to what goes on in school, one can say each student attends his or her own school with a particular curriculum—sort of a selective, personal IEP. When a parent asks a student what happened in school today, the response is selective and seldom matches what the teacher would report.

The degree to which a teacher can select the classroom curriculum differs by districts. There is no national curriculum, but some states and local districts do prescribe to varying degrees some of what must be taught (and may even indicate how). Eleven national professional organizations are currently working to establish standards for content in the various subject matter areas of the curriculum, to prepare students for the year 2000 and beyond. As would be anticipated from subject matter experts, each committee is advocating a very high level of coverage and mastery of its subject for graduation. The standards for excellence will present double jeopardy for our troubled youngsters who are usually behind even the expectations we now have. Some districts have responded by creating dual graduation standards for regular and special students, or providing graduation when IEP goals are met. Incidentally, certain schools have found a quick way to demonstrate improvement in school achievement: they cease to include the scores of special students, and the average goes up.

The other side of the curriculum coin is method. How can teachers gear instruction so that pupils are highly motivated to learn the content and skills in the curriculum? Accountability no longer rests in the process of how one teaches, but in the outcomes of teaching. What has actually been learned by the pupil? How close have we come to the expectation in the IEP or alternate goals? Our problem students are generally academically deficient: their knowledge and skills reveal acute lags in formal school accomplishment. Studies show that the vast majority do improve when given special help, but they remain below the norms; only a very few make spectacular gains. No wonder teachers feel as though they are in an impossible bind with the goals set in some state *Education 2000* plans.

such as: "All pupils shall be up to grade level before moving to the next higher level." Underlying most methods is the aim of motivating troubled students by high-interest materials at a level that ensures success while still permitting as much choice as possible. For problem behavior in the classroom, curriculum and method can work as a cause or a cure.

Decisions of how best to teach troubled pupils rest on one's theory of how individual children learn. The constructionists hold that, by active interaction with external stimuli, youngsters create their personal knowledge bank. As Piaget and Dewey demonstrated, learning is an active, explorative, and individual process. This view is in stark contrast with notions of the learner as a passive absorber, a sitting sponge for absorbing didactic presentations. Many of the formal research studies on how children are presumed to learn are of limited value to the teacher because the research has been done under such atypical conditions that we do not learn how children perform in actual multifaceted classrooms. Incidentally, attention to cultural differences in learning style is especially important, given that ethnic minorities are overrepresented in the population of school-designated troubled children.

The wide diversity in selecting curriculum is matched by the diversity in overall methodology. Behavior modification emphasizing external rewards as motivators still dominates practice and will continue to have a role, especially in learning social skills. There is a growing effort to make schools caring places because consistent caring is missing in the lives of so many troubled students. One of the interesting times in some classes is when a group of obstreperous adolescents are read to by the teacher. Flopping around relaxed, members may even doze off: this is the bedtime storytelling they never had. Group processes such as cooperative learning vie with individual competitiveness. The use of pupil folios for evaluating learning is competing with typical normative and teacher-made tests. Teaching to cognitive intelligence only is challenged by the concept of multiple intelligences. Whole-language and integrated subject matter projects contrast with workbook and subject drills. Expecting traditional schools to meet all the needs of high-risk and problem students contrasts with integrated community wraparound services in the full-service school. In some places, attention to continuity of personnel who can really get to know the students through continuous progress is replacing the sequence of grade-level transitions and brief episodic, piecemeal professional contact. Failure can be eliminated by continuous progress. Not all innovations will help all troubled students, but we should be working to eliminate system and bureaucratic hazards. By improvident procedures, schools produce troubled students whom the schools then resent.

Many conflicting voices are speaking out on schooling for problem students and high-risk pupils. Observers report examples of some of the most sterile teaching and some of the most trailblazing, often next door to each other. Generally, the evidence on inclusion of troubled pupils is that little is done to alter the traditional mainstream curriculum or methods, even if there is a special pupil IEP.

On the other hand, a wide variety of adjustments to curriculum method are currently being practiced by some thoughtful teachers in both inclusive programs and pullout designs. Some of these efforts represent creative planning; others seem more like taking an easy out. Close collaboration with social agency colleagues is being encouraged. Some special programs only play academic catch-up because problem youngsters are usually behind. Dull remedial drills may be employed, often repeating the same processes that failed the student previously. Other efforts may employ a maximum use of computers as an aid to learning. Special programs may water down both the curriculum and expectations, with the intent of ensuring success at all costs. When the task is the traditional curriculum, a teacher may concentrate on external rewards because troubled youngsters are not noted for a zest for learning school material.

A promising approach for highly resistant students is an alternative curriculum where basic skills and life survival skills are taught through real-life hands-on experiences in the community. When money-earning work experience is incorporated, school finally makes sense for the first time. For adolescents, the alternative curriculum is usually combined with vocational planning. Carefully planned individual crisis support can sometimes fit the troubled student into even a conservative regular school curriculum.

Some professionals are so fixed on structure as a universal solution that they fear anything but a traditional classroom for troubled students, lest more open methods such as cooperative learning or integrative projects result in increased problem behavior. In general, high-risk and problem students benefit from a curriculum that includes survival skills, basic academics, social learning, and vocational experiences—all presented around pupil interests in innovative ways. Abstract courses of study, such as civics, are approached in a concrete fashion: What actually happens to delinquents is learned through visits to the court rather than through reading a book chapter. The methods for teaching troubled students run the gamut from the most traditional to the cutting edge. There is no better "method" than a zestful, creative, and enthusiastic teacher who ensures excitement in the classroom. Teaching a group of youngsters is a fluid, ever-changing process in which the stability provided through the organization of the day can give way to prime teachable moments that arise at the most unexpected junctures. There is no certain solution, no prearranged always-works methodology: Teaching is a profession, not a trade. The examples that follow provide glimpses of a few ways in which successful teachers practice this profession.

The first article presents the widely emulated Re-ED program designed by the late Nicholas Hobbs with the collaboration of others, including William Rhodes. Re-ED offers a clean break with the past, both in theory and practice. Fecser, our author, is the Quality Improvement Coordinator for the Positive Education Program (PEP) in Cleveland, Ohio. PEP serves 1,200 children and youth in day treatment, early intervention, and case management programs. One of the essentials is an ecological focus that keeps close liaison with the family life. Fecser says that four critical concentric systems are necessary in classrooms, to foster positive behavioral change in troubled children. He starts with a clear enunciation of the classroom's pervasive values. Much is made of group process in classroom meetings. Specific individual needs of each student are addressed. Caring adults are essential. Teachers often ask: "What are the elements of a thorough program for troubled students?" Fecser provides an answer in the model of a Re-ED classroom.

ARTICLE 8.1

A Model Re-ED Classroom for Troubled Students

Frank A. Fecser

What are the key ingredients for designing a successful learning environment for troubled and troubling children?

Those of us who work with troubled and troubling students are fortunate that a wealth of great thinkers share our profession. These clinicians and researchers have shaped new ways of thinking about emotional and behavioral problems and their remediation. Now, as our field matures, we are moving from "one true light" presumptions, acknowledging the need to blend the best of divergent approaches in meeting the complex challenges presented by these children and youth.

The Re-ED model represents a system for integrating practices known to facilitate positive behavioral change in students with emotional disturbances. This article describes a Re-ED classroom model developed at the Positive Education Program (PEP) in Cleveland, Ohio. This model is conceptualized as a series of four concentric systems, beginning with the foundation of values and focusing inward to the personal needs of the student. A successful program must attend to critical variables on each of these four levels.

THE VALUES SYSTEM

A clearly stated values system is the foundation of any community, be it an entire school or a single classroom. Our values system establishes the ethics of good practice and provides a standard against which our decisions can be measured. The values system also provides a common language for communication and consultation among colleagues.

From *The Journal of Emotional and Behavioral Problems*. (1993). Vol. 1, No. 4. Reprinted with permission.

Level I of the PEP model reflects the 12 principles of Project Re-ED (Re-Education of Emotionally Disturbed Children and Youth), developed by the late Dr. Nicholas Hobbs in the early Sixties. These principles are the operating beliefs of our model Re-ED classroom:

1. Life is to be lived now, not in the past, and lived in the future only as a present challenge.
2. Trust between child and adult is essential, the foundation on which all other principles rest, the glue that holds teaching and learning together, the beginning point for re-education.
3. Competence makes a difference; and children and adolescents should be helped to be good at something, especially at schoolwork.
4. Time is an ally, working on the side of growth in a period of development when life has a tremendous forward thrust.
5. Self-control can be taught, and children and adolescents can be helped to manage their behavior without the development of psychodynamic insight. Symptoms can and should be controlled by direct address, not necessarily by an uncovering therapy.
6. The cognitive competence of children and adolescents can be considerably enhanced; they can be taught generic skills in the management of their lives, as well as strategies for coping with the complex array of demands placed on them by family, school, community, or job. In other words, intelligence can be taught.
7. Feelings should be nurtured, shared spontaneously, controlled when necessary, expressed when too long repressed, and explored with trusted others.
8. The group is very important to young people, and it can be a major source of instruction in growing up.
9. Ceremony and ritual give order, stability, and confidence to troubled children and adolescents, whose lives are often in considerable disarray.
10. The body is the armature of the self, the physical self around which the psychological self is constructed.
11. Communities are important for children and youth, but the uses and benefits of community must be experienced to be learned.
12. In growing up, a child should know some joy in each day and look forward to some joyous event for the morrow.

The Re-ED values reflect an integration of disciplines and promote the creative blending of the best practices of different theoretical models.

Not only must teachers and administrators work from a values base, but the classroom itself should have a system of operating values that the students understand and accept. Our classroom values might include the following:

- Everyone has the right to feel safe and will be protected from physical and psychological abuse.
- Everyone has the right to personal space, and this right will be protected.
- The personal property of each class member will be respected and protected.
- Learning and classroom activities are important and will be protected despite interruptions.
- Each member of the class is important and will be treated with respect.

Our belief system sets forth the fundamental values by which the classroom operates. Any correction of behavior or disciplinary action can be traced back to a violation of the classroom values. The adults actively model and mediate these values so students can come to understand how they are interpreted through behavior.

CLASSROOM STRUCTURE

Many troubled students find change confusing and distressing. They do not adapt well to shifts in routine or situations in which expectations are unclear. These students perform best when the environment is predictable and the behavior of adults is consistent. Level II of the PEP model identifies four structural components that interact to create a psychologically safe and predictable learning environment: (1) level system and data collection; (2) rules, rituals, and routines; (3) schedule; and (4) organization of the environment.

Data Collection and Systems

The first step in collecting data is to decide what information will be useful in tracking progress. Most teachers will want data in at least two broad areas: student conduct and academic behavior. Student conduct behaviors might include following directions, keeping hands and feet to self, and appropriate verbal interactions. Academic behaviors might include completing assignments on time, completing assignments to accuracy, and completing homework.

Some of the many ways to collect data include awarding points on a timed cycle (e.g., every hour), subtracting points for violating standards, or periodically assessing behaviors on a rating scale. Students receive feedback on their ratings or counts and thereby come to understand behavioral expectations and how they measure up to them. Of course, these expectations are reasonable, attainable, and held constant and are, therefore, predictable.

Feedback hour by hour and day by day is helpful, but the impact of data collection can be made stronger by tracking behavior over many days and helping students see their own patterns of conduct. Charts and graphs give a good deal of information in an uncomplicated form. An accompanying level system can help motivate behavior gains by linking them to status or privileges in the classroom.

Level systems can be simple or quite complex, depending on the ages of the students and the design of the classroom. Simply, the system acknowledges student progress by according increasing privileges and increasing independence and trust as students move to higher levels. Increasing responsibilities also are incorporated for both conduct and academics. For example, an entry-level student may have homework once a week, but a student on an advanced level has homework three times weekly. Entry-level students must have a teacher escort in the halls at all times, but higher-level students may use a pass and walk through the halls unescorted. This may seem a privilege to students but, in effect, it is practice in building responsibility. The student is learning to act responsibly without adult supervision.

The level system adds continuity to the environment, is a mechanism for feedback, and provides a stable measure of progress.

Rules, Rituals, and Routines

Another systems-based feature of the classroom is the concept of rules, rituals, and routines. In a predictable environment, the rules are concrete and definite. For example, when we enter an art museum, there are signs everywhere stating that we are not to touch the exhibits. In addition, there are uniformed guards posted throughout. Occasionally, a guard can be heard cautioning a too-curious visitor. There is absolutely no question about the rules of conduct at the museum. On the other hand, a person visiting a Japanese restaurant for the first time is faced with unfamiliar menu items, unfamiliar seating styles, and unfamiliar utensils. The rules are somewhat uncertain and, therefore, so is behavior.

Effective classroom rules are unambiguous, posted clearly, and reviewed at least daily. There are only as many rules as students can remember (five, plus or minus two), and they are stated positively. Stating rules positively enables us to praise students for adhering to them. It is effective to say, "Thanks for raising your hand, Joe." but ineffective to say, "I'm glad you are not talking out." The rules are drawn directly from the classroom values.

Routines are, essentially, good habits. Many students live in environments where life is turbulent and good habits are not easily formed. There may be no established household routines, family dinner hour, or bedtime convention. The absence of regular patterns of expected behavior raises anxiety because uncertainty prevails. Regular routines in the classroom bring a sense of order and stability, and they help create a feeling of security. Typical routines include establishing when one can take a water break, how to let the teacher know that work is completed, and how to fill time acceptably when work is finished before the period is up. When consistently followed, routines can eliminate a good deal of confusion and conflict.

Rituals are first cousins to routines and are especially helpful in bringing structure to a troublesome situation. For example, imagine that a group of intermediate students has difficulty settling in after gym. The walk from the gym to the classroom is a noisy race to the water fountain. Once in the classroom, there is milling about and loud talking. It takes ten minutes for transitions before everyone is settled and ready for math. The teacher might introduce a ritual to solve the problem. First, the group lines up in the gym before going out into the hallway. Next, they review the rules for appropriate behavior in the hall, then walk halfway to the room and stop at a pre-determined point. (Naturally, the teacher enthusiastically affirms individuals and the group for their performance.) Everyone enters the classroom without getting a drink. Once all are seated in their areas, the group takes a ten-second quiet time. Students are called individually or in small groups to go to the water fountain and are publicly appreciated for their courtesy.

Rules, rituals, and routines carefully followed in the classroom reduce anxiety by making the environment safe and predictable. There are no surprises concerning what is expected of the student, and the adult's behavior is consistent.

The Schedule

A good daily schedule is the heart of classroom structure. The schedule establishes the events of the day and helps motivate students through difficult tasks. Using the Premack principle, the day is divided into manageable units of time, so that something generally considered "difficult" is followed by something generally considered less difficult. For example, math is followed by group meeting, which is followed by reading, which is followed by recess. In order to get to recess, the group must get through math, group meeting, and reading within the allotted time. Group meeting is not as attractive as recess, but it may be more attractive than math. Therefore, the student is motivated to complete math and move on to group meeting with the objective of recess in mind.

The teacher follows the schedule very closely and uses it to cue students to complete tasks: "You've completed six of your ten math problems. If you keep working, you'll finish in time for group meeting in fifteen minutes." If the student doesn't finish, participation in group meeting is still required; but his math assignment must be done before he goes to recess.

Maintaining the daily schedule eliminates any confusion about the planned events of the day and relieves the teacher of making arbitrary decisions. For example, sometimes one of our groups will have a difficult day. There's been lots of arguing, task avoidance, and oppositional behavior. Finally, during gym, the group is cooperating for the first time all day in a game of kickball. The teacher looks at the clock with dismay, noting that it's time to return to the classroom. What is the better decision: let a good thing continue a little longer, or take on the formidable task of ending the game at a high point of excitement? The teacher might be wise to take a lesson from the producers of television mini-series; end the game now so it will retain attractiveness as a contingency later on. If the teacher violates the schedule this time, the students get the message that the schedule is not really important and is negotiable or subject to the teacher's fansy. Does this mean there is to be no spontaneity in the classroom? Of course not. Spontaneity is exciting and novel by definition. As long as it happens on occasion and is not "standard operating procedure," it is a wonderful motivator for learning.

Organization of the Environment

In keeping with the objective of predictability and order, we can do much to further the cause by organizing the environment. Organization of the environment fits hand in glove with the three R's: rules, rituals, and routines. A well-organized classroom has a place for almost everything. Each student has a desk and a prescribed area for it. There is a place to hang coats, store boots, and place lunch bags. Students know where to put folders, where books are shelved, and how and when to access "free time" materials. The classroom is divided into individual and group work areas, with attention to strategic location. There may be special areas for play and others for projects. Such a setting adds to a student's sense of well-being and "ownership" of the classroom by clarifying expectations and projecting a sense of order and predictability.

It is equally important to create a classroom environment that "belongs" to the group. The teacher should post student-created artwork, therapeutic pictures and sayings and personal artifacts, just as we would decorate our own work space with symbols of our personalities and experience.

CLASSROOM CLIMATE AND GROUP PROCESS

The conditions for growth are established by the values system and by the elements that bring structure and predictability to the environment. The four components included in Level III are:

- Instructional style.
- Management style.

- Group meetings.
- Responses to feelings and emotional well-being.

These components create the emotional climate of the classroom and embody the "art" of effective teaching. We know that students who experience academic difficulties, are struggling, or are anxious or alienated, perform best in classrooms where there is a positive, personal, noncompetitive approach. The components discussed here combine to create such an environment.

Instructional Style

The Re-ED values system highlights the importance of competence in schoolwork and suggests the significance of effective instruction. There has been much written about what makes for "good teaching," yet research on effective teaching of students with behavior disorders is rather limited. Early work by Kounin (1970) has had a strong impact on the field. Using sophisticated videotaping apparatus, he collected extensive samples of teacher and student behavior from more than 80 classrooms. Observations include non-handicapped students as well as a subsample of mainstreamed students. In analyzing the tapes for student work involvement and prevention of misbehavior, Kounin discovered dimensions of teaching style that correlated significantly with students' behavior and work environment.

Effective Behavior Management (Kounin)

With-it-ness and overlapping. Effective teachers have eyes in the backs of their heads. They are attuned to the behavioral "tone" of the group. Kounin called this phenomenon "with-it-ness." Overlapping refers to the teacher's ability to deal simultaneously with multiple competing responsibilities. For example, an effective teacher can be working with a small group and keep them going while she assists an individual student who has approached her for help.

Smoothness and momentum. Effective teachers manage transitions well, keep things moving along in the classroom, and have little "down time."

Group alerting and accountability. Effective teachers maintain group focus during recitations in contrast to becoming immersed in a single child. They hold students accountable by making sure assigned tasks have been completed and following up on conditions set forth in the classroom.

Valence and challenge arousal. Effective teachers enhance the attractiveness of classroom activities. They arouse motivation to meet the challenge.

Seatwork variety and challenge. Effective teachers program independent learning activities with variety and intellectual challenge, especially in seatwork settings. The work is just challenging enough to give the student a sense of accomplishment.

Kounin concluded that these management techniques apply to normal students, to boys as well as girls, to the group as well as to individuals, and across all grade levels. He emphasized that effective application depends on an awareness of ecological variables and teacher sensitivity to students needs.

Management Style

Three concepts highlighted in the Re-ED principles offer guidance in the development of a management style: self-control can be taught, symptoms should be addressed directly and trust between the child and adult is essential. The keys to effective management are: (1) affective sensitivity and (2) knowledge of behavior management principles as applied to the classroom.

Affective sensitive teachers know students well. They know their ecologies, histories, vulnerabilities, strengths, weaknesses, fears, and aspirations. They know when they're losing involvement and how to gain it. Based on their knowledge of the student, they can design behavioral strategies and motivation techniques. They know when to "come on strong" and when to "back off" to maximize impact on the student. They can follow through on contingencies and enforce consequences, yet maintain a relationship with the student. They are sensitive to the needs of the student and make arrangements for those needs to be met at the antecedent level in socially appropriate ways. In short, the teacher applies behavior management principles in a "personalized" fashion. Management style is largely based on trust between child and adult.

Group Meetings

"The group is very important to young people, and it can be a major source of instruction in growing up." (Hobbs, 1982, p. 22) Within the structured environment of the classroom, under conditions of trust, students can be helped to share self-evaluations with classmates. Sharing of vulnerable moments, when this risk-taking is supported and accepted, can have a strong effect on the development of group cohesion. Students can begin to take the risk to trust others. We can establish the conditions under which such connections can begin and grow in the classroom through guided group meetings.

All meetings begin with a review of the group meeting rules, which include being recognized to speak and respecting the contributions of others. At first, meetings are run by the adults to model the process. As students become proficient at participation, leadership is passed to the group. Three types of group meetings can be conducted in the classroom:

Business meetings. These low-threat meetings might be used to facilitate the acceptance of the "meeting" concept. Business meetings are held to discuss such class projects as fund raisers or special events and follow a structured agenda.

Positives meetings. Positives meetings are held daily, usually at the close of the day. In a group format, each person says something positive about himself or herself and something positive about at least one other member of the group. The comments are focused affirmations and relate to an observation made during that day. Because they receive affirmations so infrequently, many students find it as difficult to accept affirming feedback as they do corrective feedback. Positives meetings offer practice at becoming comfortable with praise.

Evaluation or goal meetings. The most challenging of the three meetings to conduct are daily goal meetings. At the beginning of the week, each student selects a goal and makes a commitment to achieve it. The goal is usually a social one and addresses a behavior that may affect the group in some way. For example, "keeping area clean and organized" represents a low-threat goal. A skillful teacher can facilitate meetings so that the group has input into the selection of the goal for each member and the development of a "plan" for attaining the goal. Often, the plan involves support from the group.

It may take several sessions to establish goals for all students. Once that is done, the group meets daily to review goals and plans. The teacher and group members give individual feedback on the prior day's goal attainment. Ideally, each student will give a self-evaluation, identifying specifically what he or she did to meet the goal or identifying the roadblocks that prevented him or her from doing so. Plans are amended to provide a greater opportunity for success. At the end of the week, those students who have attained their goals are rewarded with a pre-determined bonus. New goals are selected as students master current goals. However, if a student is struggling with a goal for two or more weeks, it is appropriate to put it aside and select a goal with which a student can be successful.

Social skills training also is conducted in a group setting in which students give and receive feedback. Although the content is instructional, these sessions, when conducted in a warm and positive environment can build esteem and carry considerable emotional content.

Responses to Feelings and Emotional Well-Being

This is certainly the most intangible of the components of an effective classroom and, perhaps, the most important. "Trust between the child and adult is essential, the foundation on which all other principles rest, the glue that holds teaching and learning together, the beginning point for re-education." (Hobbs, 1982, p. 22)

Morgan (1976) studied empathy in the classroom and concluded: It does not appear to be practical or judicious for educators to merely adopt or adapt the assessment devices used in psychotherapy. Teaching necessitates a more active and directive type of interaction than that which occurs in the classic therapy situation. Indications are that empathy in teaching is different, in that more is required than verbal communication of understanding. (p. 167)

In an attempt to define empathy in the classroom, Morgan (1979) developed a questionnaire and administered it to children in special education settings for emotionally disturbed students and to a control group of non-handicapped students. The results of the interviews indicated a qualitative difference between responses of the handicapped and non-handicapped students. Non-handicapped students related almost entirely to the teacher in terms of the teacher's ability to make academic work understandable, whereas handicapped students attended predominantly to the affective sensitivity of the teacher. The responses of students to the interview questions focused on what the teacher said and did that gave them a sense of security and comfort about personal as well as academic difficulties. The majority of responses by handicapped students referred to action-oriented teacher behaviors that, when codified, fell into four clusters. From these, Morgan derived the following delineation of modalities and behaviors by which teachers of emotionally disturbed students express empathy:

Teaching with Empathy (Morgan)

Management of instruction

- Devises legitimate reasons to change an activity when the child is frustrated.
- Begins with a guaranteed success.
- Personalizes lesson to teach concepts.

Organization of the environment

- Gives the child a time and place to be alone and quiet.
- Does not send the child to someone else for punishment.
- Room itself (space and furnishings) is organized and uncluttered.

Responses to feelings and emotional well-being

- Senses when the child is on the verge of trouble and offers help before it's requested or a blow-up occurs.
- Identifies for students feelings they are unable to verbalize.
- Stays physically close and lavishes assurances.

Interpersonal qualities

- Has a sense of humor.
- Is warm and can openly show affection for the child.
- Appears calm and relaxed, speaks softly, and smiles frequently.

REFERENCES

Hobbs, N. (1982). *The troubled and troubling child.* New York: Jossey-Bass.

Kounin, J. S. (1970). *Discipline and group management in classrooms.* New York: Holt, Rinehart & Winston.

Long, N. J. (1986). The nine psychoeducational stages of helping emotionally disturbed students through the re-education process. *The Pointer, 30,* 5–20.

Morgan, S. R. (1976). Assessing the empathic potential of student teachers of the emotionally disturbed. *American Journal of Othopsychiatry, 46,* 163–167.

Morgan, S. R. (1979). A model of the empathic process for teachers of emotionally disturbed children. *American Journal of Othopsychiatry, 49,* 426–435.

. . . .

Aggressive behavior has permeated both our schools and our communities, and what to do about aggressive, troubled children in school is a major concern. Nothing exhausts a teacher more than confronting a steady stream of aggressive behavior and using tactics that produce no improvement. Alternative programs to teach prosocial behavior are in order, rather than reliance on punishment and exclusion. Arnold Goldstein, of Syracuse University, is a recognized leader in providing tested programs teachers can use. He pulls no punches in telling it how it is. He works directly with troubled students who produce the kind of aggressive behavior teachers face everyday. His curriculum has a sound theoretical base, but the content evolved from his hands-on work with very aggressive adolescent boys and girls (aggression is no longer just a male display). His premise is to teach alternatives rather than expect reduction by suppression. To accomplish this goal, he presents a prosocial curriculum. Teachers may also wish to consult his books and films. The latter present scenes of his program in actual practice.

ARTICLE 8.2

Prepare: A Prosocial Curriculum for Aggressive Youth

Arnold P. Goldstein

It has been convincingly demonstrated during the past decade that aggressive behavior is *learned* behavior. Though the belief in instinct, not learning, as the primary source of human aggression dies hard, evidence to the contrary is overwhelming. Not only is aggression primarily learned,

---

Abridged from *Perceptions.* (Fall 1988). Used with permission of the author.

but the manner in which such acquisition occurs has been shown in an extended series of social learning investigations to be no different from how all other behaviors—both antisocial and prosocial—are also learned. Thus, manipulativeness, cheating, teasing, bullying, as well as altruism, cooperation, sharing and empathy, and aggression, appear to be learned largely by means of either observational, vicarious experiences (e.g., seeing others perform the behavior and receiving reward for doing so) or direct experiences (e.g., enacting the behavior oneself and receiving reward for doing so).

Chronically aggressive youngsters are characteristically individuals with a life history in which, from their early years on, aggression was frequently used, and used successfully, by family, peers, media figures, and others constituting the youth's real-world environment. Such aggression by others, increasingly learned and used by the youth himself, is very often richly, reliably, and immediately rewarded. It pays; it pays off; it is reinforced—thus making it behavior which is quite difficult to change. The fact that such youths are often markedly deficient in prosocial alternative behaviors, that is, in achieving life satisfactions and effectiveness via prosocial, rather than antisocial routes, makes their chronic aggressiveness all the more difficult to change.

And prosocially deficient they are. A substantial body of literature has directly demonstrated that chronically aggressive youngsters display widespread interpersonal planning, aggression management and other prosocial skill deficiencies. Patterson, Reid, Jones, and Conger (1975), studying chronically aggressive youngsters, observe:

> The socialization process appears to be severely impeded for many aggressive youngsters. Their behavioral adjustments are often immature and they do not seem to have learned the key social skills necessary for initiating and maintaining positive social relationships with others. Peer groups often reject, avoid, and/or punish aggressive children, thereby excluding them from positive learning experiences with others. [p. 4]

Teacher and school administration response to aggressive, disruptive, difficult youngsters in America's secondary and elementary schools, as well as parental response to such behaviors in the home, has characteristically involved heavy reliance on one or another method designed to reduce or inhibit such negative behaviors, with relatively little companion effort explicitly directed toward increasing the frequency of alternative constructive behaviors. We have, in fact, become reasonably competent in at least temporarily decreasing or eliminating fighting, arguing, teasing, yelling, bullying, and similar acting-out, off-task behaviors. But in a relative sense we have attended rather little to procedures designed to teach negotiation skills; constructive responses to failure; management of peer group pressure; means for dealing effectively with teasing, rejection, accusations, anger, and so forth.

A central point with regard to the several means in use for reducing aggressive behavior in the classroom, home or community—whether corporal punishment, reprimands, or much more benign punishers as extinction, time out and response cost—is that none teaches alternative constructive responses. They suppress, but offer no substitutes. As we have commented elsewhere:

> A reprimand or a paddling will not teach new behaviors. If an aggressive youngster literally is deficient in the ability to ask rather than take, request rather than command, negotiate rather than strike out, all the . . . scolding, scowling, spanking and the like possible, will not teach the youngster the desirable alternative behaviors. Thus, punishment, if used at all, must be combined with teacher efforts which instruct the youngster in those behaviors he knows not at all. (Goldstein & Keller, in press)

Constructive alternatives to aggression can be effectively taught to chronically aggressive youngsters. The present paper outlines our efforts in developing a comprehensive, prosocial curriculum for doing so.

PROSOCIAL INSTRUCTION—AN HISTORICAL OVERVIEW

Prosocial instruction in general, and the proposed PREPARE Curriculum in particular, have their roots in both Education and Psychology. The notion of literally seeking to teach prosocial behaviors has often, if sporadically, been a significant goal of the American educational establishment. The Character Education Movement of the 1920s and more contemporary Moral Education and Values Clarification programs are three prominent examples.

Thus, though both Education and Psychology have begun to seriously seek to meet the challenge of developing means for enhancing positive behaviors. It is in this latter spirit that we began the development of the PREPARE Curriculum, and in that spirit we seek the opportunity for its further development and refinement.

THE *PREPARE* CURRICULUM

General Considerations

There are a number of qualities of the proposed curriculum which we wish to briefly comment upon, before considering its constituent courses, namely its intended purpose, planned comprehensiveness, relevance, complementarity of courses, prescriptiveness, and open-endedness.

Purpose   It is our hope, and our goal, to develop a means for teaching chronically aggressive adolescents and younger children the prosocial competencies they need to lead effective and satisfying lives with minimal need to resort to antisocial routes to these same desired life goals. We have named the proposed curriculum PREPARE in the literal hope that that is precisely what it will accomplish.

Comprehensiveness   Most interventions provided aggressive, disruptive or even delinquent youth in school, clinic, community or incarceration settings are far, far too piecemeal in their impact. A youngster's daily living experiences for ten or more years may have taught him such lessons as "aggression pays," "might makes right," and "take, don't ask." Surely, we are wearing blinders to hope that a weekly counseling session, or occasional use of time-out, or three days of in-school suspension can make a dent in altering such life-long learning. To have even a chance of success, our interventions must be encompassing, long-term, and powerful. We intend that PREPARE be a step in just such a comprehensive direction.

Relevance   The curriculum's constituent courses, it is our aspiration, will be functionally useful and valuable from the perspective of the youth to whom they will be taught, as well as to the major figures in their real-life environments. To maximize this quality of relevance, the prosocial competency areas we plan to develop into courses were selected based upon not only the relevant professional literature, but also in active and continuing consultation with both teachers and other youth-care professionals and, especially, with adolescent and younger child "consultants" themselves.

Complementarity   The several competencies which the proposed curriculum seeks to teach are optimally used in the real-world functioning of its recipients in sets, subsets, patterns or combinations. We intend to design its constituent courses with this patterning goal in mind, and will later point to specific examples of groupings and sequencing of courses in such a manner that their respective gains have the potential for building upon one another.

Prescriptiveness   We believe strongly that offerings such as the proposed curriculum will yield maximal effectiveness when employed in a tailored, differential, prescriptive manner. Different courses, course combinations, and course sequencing for different youths are components of effective implementation. While such a goal is clearly as much a matter of assessment of deficit as the course offerings per se, preparation for prescriptive usage begins with attention to course development parameters. Thus, the courses to be developed must vary not only in content or focus, but also on such dimensions as difficulty, abstractness/concreteness, immediacy of usage, media employed, and other prescriptiveness-permitting parameters.

Open-Endedness   To plan and develop the proposed curriculum we have and will draw upon the relevant bodies of professional literature; our own decades of curriculum building and evaluation experience, and that of a panel of real-world teachers and youth-care consultants; feedback from adolescent and younger child trainees themselves; as well as systematic evaluation research. While we are *temporarily* pleased with the comprehensiveness of the curriculum, we are well aware of the manner in which new research findings, emerging societal needs, and developments in the pedagogy of curriculum delivery each may make desirable the addition to this curriculum of yet other courses, and the deletion from it of existing courses. Our intention, therefore, is decidedly open-ended, with a willingness and even eagerness to be responsive to such change considerations as our efforts progress.

Course Offerings

The courses described below (see Figure 8.1) are of three types: (a) courses in place—those fully developed and evaluated already (courses 1, 2, 3); (b) courses in development—those partially developed and currently undergoing evaluation (courses 4 and 5); and (c) courses in initial planning—those still very early in their formation (courses 6–10).

Course 1. Interpersonal Skills Training

Via a sequence of didactic procedures we termed Structured Learning, we have since 1970 sought to teach an array of interpersonal, prosocial competencies to aggressive youth and children (Goldstein, 1973, 1981; Goldstein, Carr, Davidson, & Wehr, 1981; Goldstein, Sprafkin, Gershaw, & Klein, 1980). In this approach, small groups of chronically aggressive youngsters with shared prosocial skill deficiencies are (1) shown several examples of expert use of the behaviors constituting the skills in which they are weak or lacking (e.g., *modeling*); (2) given several guided opportunities to practice and rehearse these competent interpersonal behaviors (e.g., *role playing*); (3) provided with praise, re-instruction, and related feedback on how well their role playing of the skill matched the expert

FIGURE 8.1   PREPARE: A Prosocial Curriculum for Aggressive Youth

Course 1	Interpersonal Skills Training
Course 2	Anger Control Training
Course 3	Moral Reasoning Training
Course 4	Problem-Solving Training
Course 5	Empathy Training
Course 6	Social Perception Training
Course 7	Anxiety Management
Course 8	Cooperation Training
Course 9	Building a Prosocial Support Group
Course 10	Understanding and Using Group Processes

model's portrayal of it (e.g., *performance feedback*); and (4) encouraged to engage in a series of activities designed to increase the chances that skills learned in the training setting will endure and be available for use when needed in the school, home, community, institution or other real-world setting (e.g., *transfer training*).

By means of this set of didactic procedures, we have been able to teach such youngsters a 50 skill curriculum, organized into six groupings:

A. *Beginning Social Skills*, e.g., "Starting a Conversation," "Introducing Yourself," "Giving a Compliment."

B. *Advanced Social Skills*, e.g., "Giving Instructions," "Apologizing," "Convincing Others."

C. *Skills for Dealing with Feelings*, e.g., "Dealing with Someone Else's Anger," "Expressing Affection," "Dealing with Fear."

D. *Skill Alternatives to Aggression*, e.g., "Responding to Teasing," "Keeping Out of Fights," "Helping Others."

E. *Skills for Dealing with Stress*, e.g., "Dealing with Being Left Out," "Responding to Failure," "Dealing with an Accusation."

F. *Planning Skills*, e.g., "Setting a Goal," "Arranging Problems by Importance," "Deciding What Caused a Problem."

We have conducted approximately 30 investigations evaluating the effectiveness of this interpersonal skills training approach. Skill acquisition (Do they learn it?) is a reliable outcome, occurring in well over 90% of the aggressive adolescent and younger child trainees involved (Goldstein, 1981; Goldstein, et al., 1980; McGinnis & Goldstein, 1984). Skill transfer (Do they use the skills in real-world settings?) is a less frequent outcome thus far, occurring in about half of the trainees involved. Of great importance here, however, is the manner in which we have been able to show that transfer can be and is increased to the degree that one's training effort incorporates a series of recently developed transfer-enhancing techniques (Goldstein & Kanfer, 1979). Clearly, Interpersonal Skills Training is an established and valuable part of a prosocial instructional curriculum.

Course 2. Anger Control Training

Anger Control Training was developed by Feindler and her research group at Adelphi University (Feindler, Marrion, & Iwata, 1984), and substantially modified by us in separate programs involving disruptive elementary school children (Keller, Goldstein, Wynn, & Glick, in progress) and incarcerated juvenile delinquents (Goldstein, Glick, Reiner, Zimmerman, & Coultry, 1986). In contrast to the direct facilitation of prosocial behavior in Interpersonal Skills Training, Anger Control Training facilitates indirectly, by teaching means for inhibiting anger and loss of self-control. Participating youngsters are taught, over a one-term span, how to respond to provocations to anger by: (1) identifying their external and internal triggers; (2) identifying one's own physiological/kinesthetic cues which signify anger; (3) using reminders, which are self-statements designed to function opposite to triggers; [i.e., to lower one's anger-arousal level]; (4) using reducers, to further lower anger via deep breathing, counting backwards, imagining a peaceful scene, or contemplating the long-term consequences of one's anger-associated behavior; and (5) self-evaluation, in which one judges how adequately anger control worked, and rewards oneself when it worked well. Our implementation of Anger Control Training was systematically evaluated for effectiveness as part of a three course set, to be discussed below.

Course 3. Moral Reasoning Training

Armed with both the ability to respond to the real-world prosocially, and the skills necessary to stifle or at least diminish impulsive anger and aggression, will the chronically acting-out youngster in fact choose to do so. To enhance the likelihood that such will in fact be his frequent choice, one must enter, we believe, into the realm of moral values. In a long and pioneering series of investigations, Kohlberg (1969, 1973) has demonstrated that exposing youngsters to a series of moral dilemmas, in a discussion-group context which includes youngsters reasoning at differing levels of moral thinking, arouses an experience of cognitive conflict whose resolution will frequently advance a youngster's moral reasoning to that of the higher level peers in the group. While such moral reasoning stage advancement is a reliable finding, as with other single interventions, efforts to utilize it by itself as a means of enhancing actual overt moral behavior have yielded only mixed success—perhaps, we would speculate, because such youngsters did not have in their behavior repertoires either the actual skill behaviors for acting prosocially or for successfully inhibiting the antisocial. Consistent with our curriculum development goal of course complementarity, we thus reasoned and have in fact been able to show that Kohlbergian Moral Education has marked potential for providing constructive directionality toward prosocialness and away from anti-socialness in youngsters armed with the fruits of both Interpersonal Skills Training and Anger Control Training (Goldstein, et al., 1986).

Course 4. Problem-Solving Training

Aggressive adolescents and younger children are frequently deficient not only in knowledge of and ability to use such prosocial competencies as the array of interpersonal skills and anger control techniques taught in Courses 1 and 2, but they may also be deficient in other ways crucial to the use of prosocial behavior. They may as Ladd and Mize (1983) point out, be deficient in such problem-solving competencies as "(a) knowledge of appropriate *goals* for social interaction, (b) knowledge of appropriate *strategies* for reaching a social goal, and (c) knowledge of the *contexts* in which specific strategies may be appropriately applied." (p. 130)

An analogous conclusion flows from the research program on interpersonal problem solving conducted by Spivack, Platt, and Shure (1976). At early and middle childhood, as well as in adolescence, chronically aggressive youngsters were less able than more typical youngsters to function effectively in most problem-solving subskills, such as identification of alternatives, consideration of consequences determining causality, means-ends thinking, and perspective taking. The course under development here seeks to provide just such an effort. In our early pilot development of it, it is a longer-term (than existing programs) sequence of such graduated problem solving skills as reflection, problem identification, information gathering, perspective taking, identification of alternatives, consideration of consequences, and decision-making. Our initial evaluation of this sequence with an aggressive adolescent population has yielded significant gains in problem solving skills thus defined substantially encouraging further development of this course. These results give beginning substance to our assertion made earlier that

> Individuals can be provided systematic training in problem solving skills both for purposes of building general competence in meeting life's challenges, and as a specific means of supplying one more reliable, prosocial alternative to aggression. (Goldstein, 1981)

Course 5. Empathy Training

We are especially interested in the inclusion in the PREPARE Curriculum of a course designed to enhance the participating youth's level of empathy for two reasons. Expression of empathic understanding, it seems, can simultaneously serve as an inhibitor of negative interactions and a facilitator of positive ones.

The notion of empathy as a facilitator of positive interpersonal relations stands on an even broader base of research evidence. Our recent review of the literally hundreds of investigations inquiring into the interpersonal consequences of empathic responding reveal such responding to be a consistently potent promoter of interpersonal attraction, dyadic openness, conflict resolution, and individual growth (Goldstein & Michaels, 1985). It is a most potent facilitator indeed.

This same review effort led us to define empathy as a multi-stage process of perception of emotional cues, affective reverberation of the emotions perceived, their cognitive labeling, and communication and, correspondingly, to develop a multi-stage training program by which these four constituent components could be taught. At the time of this writing, we are in the process of developing concrete lesson plans and materials so that this Empathy Training course can be both implemented and evaluated for its empathy-enhancing effectiveness.

Course 6. Social Perception Training

Once armed with the interpersonal skills necessary to respond prosocially to others (Courses 1, 2, 3), the problem-solving strategies underlying skill selection and usage (Course 4), and a fuller, empathic sense of the other person's perspective (Course 5), the chronically aggressive youngster may still fail to behave prosocially because he or she "misreads" the context in which the behavior is to occur. Emotionally disturbed youngsters, as well as those "socially maladjusted" in other ways are characteristically deficient in such social perceptiveness. Furnham and Argyle (1981) observe:

> . . . it has been found that people who are socially inadequate are unable to read everyday situations and respond appropriately. They are unable to perform or interpret nonverbal signals, unaware of the rules of social behavior, mystified by ritualized routines and conventions of self-presentation and self-disclosure, and are hence like foreigners in their own land. (p. 37)

We believe that the ability to accurately "read" social situations can be taught, and we intend to do so with this proposed course. Its planned contents will be responsive to the valuable leads provided in this context by Brown and Fraser (1979) who propose three salient dimensions of accurate social perceptiveness, (1) the *setting* of the interaction and its associated rules and norms. (2) the *purpose* of the interaction and its goals, tasks, and topics, and (3) the *relationship* of the participants, their roles, responsibilities, expectations, and group memberships.

Course 7. Anxiety Management

We have oriented each of the preceding course descriptions toward either directly enhancing prosocial competency (e.g., Interpersonal Skills Training, Moral Reasoning, Social Perceptiveness), or reducing qualities that inhibit previously-learned or newly-acquired prosocial competency (e.g., Anger Control Training).

Individuals may possess an array of prosocial skills in their repertoires, but not employ them in particularly challenging or difficult situations because of anxiety. A youth may have learned well the Interpersonal Skills Training skill "Responding to Failure," but his embarrassment at a failing grade in front of his teacher or his missing a foul shot in front of his friends may engender a level of anxiety which inhibits proper use of this skill. A young woman may possess the problem-solving competency to plan well for a job interview, but perform poorly in the interview itself as anxiety, as it were, "takes over." Such anxiety—inhibition as a source of prosocially incompetent and unsatisfying behavior—may be especially prevalent in the high peer conscious adolescent years.

A series of self-managed procedures exist by means of which anxiety may be substantially reduced. It is these procedures which form the contents of the proposed Anxiety Management course. Participating youngsters will be taught systematic deep muscular relaxation, meditation techniques, environmental restructuring and related means for the management, control and reduction of anxiety.

Course 8. Cooperation Training

Chronically aggressive youth have been shown to display a personality trait pattern quite often high in egocentricity and competitiveness, and low in concern for others and cooperativeness. We propose herein to design and offer a course in Cooperation Training not only because enhanced cooperation among individuals is a valuable social goal, but also because of the several valuable concomitants and consequences of enhanced cooperation. An extended review of research on one major set of approaches to cooperation training, namely "cooperative learning" (see below) reveals outcomes of enhanced self-esteem, group cohesiveness, altruism and cooperation itself as well as reduced egocentricity. As long ago as 1929, Maller commented:

> The frequent staging of contests, the constant emphasis upon the making and breaking of records, and the glorification of the heroic individual achievement . . . in our present educational system lead toward the acquisition of competitiveness. The child is trained to look at the members of group as constant competitors and urged to put forth a maximum effort to excel them. The lack of practice in group activities and community projects in which the child works with his fellows for a common goal precludes the formation of habits of cooperativeness . . . (p. 163)

It was many years before the educational establishment responded concretely to this Deweyian-like challenge, but when it did it created a wide series of innovative, cooperation-enhancing methodologies, each of which deserves long and careful application and scrutiny both in general educational contexts as well as, in our instance, with particularly non-cooperative youth. We refer to the cooperative learning methods: Student Teams—Achievement Divisions, Teams-Games-Tournaments, Jigsaw Classrooms 1 (Aronson, 1978). Group Investigation and Co-op (Kagan, 1985). Using shared materials, interdependent tasks, group rewards, and similar features, these methods (applied to any content area—mathematics, social studies, etc.) have consistently yielded the several interpersonal, cooperation-enhancing, group and individual benefits noted above.

In our proposed course, we wish to sort through the existing methods, adding aspects of our own, and seek to prescriptively tailor a cooperative learning course sequence of special value for chronically aggressive youth. In doing so, we will make use not only of the many valuable features of the cooperative learning approaches noted above but, in addition, responding to the physical action orientation typical of such youth, we will also in our course contents planning rely heavily on cooperative sports and games.

Course 9. Building a Prosocial Support Group

Aggressive youth quite typically are regularly exposed to highly aggressive models in their interpersonal worlds. Parents, siblings, and peers each are quite frequently chronically aggressive individuals themselves. Simultaneously, there tend to be relatively few, countervailing prosocial models available to be observed and imitated. When they are, however, such prosocial models can apparently make a tremendous difference in the daily lives and development of such youth. In support of this assertion we may turn not only to such community-provided examples of prosocial modeling as Big Brothers, Police Athletic League, Boy Scouts, and the like, and not only to the laboratory research consistently showing that rewarded prosocial behaviors (e.g., sharing, altruism, cooperation) are quite often imitated, but also to more direct evidence. For example, Werner and Smith (1982), in their impressive longitudinal study of aggressive and non-aggressive youth, *Vulnerable but Invincible,* clearly demonstrated that many youngsters growing up in a community characterized by high crime, high unemployment, high school drop out and high levels of aggressive models, were indeed able to sail on through as it were, and develop into effective, satisfied, prosocially-oriented individuals if they had had sustained exposure to at least one significant prosocial model—be it parent, relative, or peer.

Since such models are often scarce in the real-world environments of the youth PREPARE is intended to serve, efforts must be put forth to help these youth identify, encourage, attract, elicit, and at times perhaps even create sources and attachments to others who not only—as models—function prosocially themselves, but who can also serve as sustained sources of direct support for the youth's own prosocially-oriented efforts.

Our course contents for teaching such identification, encouraging, attraction, elicitation, and creation skills will rely in part on both the teaching procedures and certain of the interpersonal skills which constitute our Structured Learning skills training curricula for adolescents (Goldstein, et al., 1980) and younger children (McGinnis & Goldstein, 1984). In addition, other relevant procedures and materials, yet to be determined, will also be employed.

Course 10. Understanding and Using Group Processes

Adolescent and pre-adolescent acute responsiveness to peer influences is a truism frequently drawn in both lay and professional literature on child development. It is a conclusion resting on a very solid research foundation. As a curriculum designed to enhance prosocial competencies, it is especially important that PREPARE include a segment giving special emphasis to group—especially peer—processes. Its title includes both "understanding" and "using" because both are clearly its goal. Participating youth will be helped to understand such group forces and phenomena as peer pressure, clique formation and dissolution, leaders and leadership, cohesiveness, imitation, reciprocity, in-group vs. out-group relations, developmental phases, competition, within-group communication and its failure, and similar processes.

For such understanding to have real-world value for participating youth (the "using" component of our course title) this course's instructional format will consist almost exclusively of group activities in which, *experientially,* participants can learn means for effectively resisting group pressure when one elects to do so, for seeking and enacting a group leadership role, for helping build and enjoy the fruits of group cohesiveness, and so forth. Examples of specific activities of apparent value for such group-experiential learning include such group simulations, structured experiences and gaming as "Assessment of Leadership Style," "Committee Meeting: Demonstrating Hidden Agendas," "Process Observation: A Guide," "Top Problems: A Consensus-Seeking Task," "Dealing with Shared Leadership," "Conflict Resolution: A Collection of Tasks," "Group on Group," "Line Up and Power Inversion," "Polarization: A Demonstration," "Not Listening: A Dyadic Role Play," "Towers: An Intergroup Competition," and "Peer Perceptions: A Feedback Experience," (Pfeiffer & Jones, 1969; Thayer & Beeler, 1975).

The foregoing prosocial courses developed, in development, and planned for development constitute the proposed PREPARE Curriculum. As a group, they comprise our curriculum development plans for the next two years. But earlier we stressed the continuing value, even necessity, of openendedness in curriculum planning—for aggressive youth or otherwise. In this spirit, we wish to indicate that, in addition to the full development of the courses described above, our immediate plans also include the initial, feasibility-study examination of a number of other possible courses in such prosocial competency areas as Negotiation Training, Parenting Training, Creativity Training, Dealing with Authority Figures, and others.

Curriculum Delivery

Substantial gains in prosocial competency will occur in youth receiving the proposed curriculum not only if the *contents* of its constituent courses are creatively and prescriptively developed, but also if the *delivery* of the courses is conducted in a creative and prescriptive manner. There are a number of special problems associated with teaching chronically aggressive youth, and the PREPARE Curriculum we believe, must attend to them in order to maximize its probability of success. The *Teachers Guide* we will prepare will address four concerns.

1. *Assessment of deficit.* For prescriptive programming of the PREPARE courses to be possible, each youth's proficiency–deficiency status on course-relevant dimensions must be reliably ascertained. Four complimentary approaches to deficit assessment will be addressed: naturalistic observation, role play or simulation testing, interviews with the youth and significant others, and skill competency inventories.

2. *Classroom Management.* The rate of aggressive, disruptive, off-task behavior among youth for whom PREPARE is intended is likely to be high. In other contexts, we have devoted a great deal of attention to means for effectively managing such behaviors and getting on with teaching activities (Goldstein, Apter, & Harootunian, 1984; Goldstein & Keller, in press). The *Teachers Guide* we will prepare will seek to address this area of concern in depth.

3. *Enhancing prosocial motivation.* It serves both society and the youth participating in PREPARE rather little if they learn its substance well but rarely use it. *Functioning* prosocial competency means knowing what to do (what, where, when, with whom), and being motivated to do so. Prosocial competency training must address this crucial motivational concern, and we plan to do so along both achievement motivation paths (Alschuller, Tabor, & McIntyre, 1980; DeCharms, 1976; McClelland, 1965), via procedures for the enhancement of internal self-regulatory mechanisms (Bar Tal & Raviv, 1982; Kochanska, 1984), and by use of approaches designed to alter one's attributions and increase one's expectancies for successful outcomes.

4. *Transfer and maintenance of learning gains.* An effective curriculum not only imparts new knowledge and skills, but does so in such a manner that material learned is retained and available for use by the learner in other than classroom settings (i.e., transfer) and enduringly over time (i.e., maintenance). The development and evaluation of techniques for enhancing both transfer and maintenance has been the primary focus of our own research program for the past 15 years, and a number of effective enhancers have been developed and identified (Goldstein, 1981; Goldstein & Kanfer, 1979). Most recently, we have sought to fine tune this thrust in development research concerned with transfer and maintenance enhancement when working with aggressive individuals (Goldstein & Keller, in press). This focus will be a major emphasis in the planned *Teachers Guide.*

The four curriculum delivery arenas we have addressed do not exhaust the special concerns which fruitfully will be examined in our planned *Teacher's Guide* for the PREPARE Curriculum. What other concerns additionally ought to be included will, we are certain, emerge from the course development efforts which lie ahead.

Curriculum Evaluation

Our research group has conducted a great many evaluation studies bearing directly upon the PREPARE Curriculum. Most are in the Interpersonal Skills Training domain (see Goldstein, 1981 for a comprehensive report of these 30 investigations). Recently, however, we completed a two-year evaluation of a subset of PREPARE courses (Courses 1, 2, and 3) which we labeled, as a group, Aggression Replacement Training. This subset, it should be noted, yielded an extended series of substantial positive changes in prosocial competency in samples of highly aggressive adolescents, (Goldstein, et al., 1986).

We are eager to continue our evaluation program, focusing progressively on all of the PREPARE courses as their initial development is completed and their sustained classroom utilization occurs.

REFERENCES

Aronson, E. (1978). *The jigsaw classroom.* Beverly Hills, CA: Sage.

Brown, P., & Fraser, C. (1979). Speech as a marker of situations. In K. Scherer & H. Giles (Eds.), *Social markers in speech.* Cambridge, England: Cambridge University Press.

Feindler, E.L., Mamon, S.A., & Iwata, M. (1984). Group anger control training for junior high school delinquents. *Cognitive Therapy and Research, 8,* 299–311.

Furnham, A., & Argyle, M. (1981). *The psychology of social situations.* New York: Pergamon Press.

Glasser, W. (1969). *Schools without failure.* New York: Harper & Row.

Goldstein, A.P. (1981). *Psychological skill training: The structured learning technique.* Elmsford, NY: Pergamon Press.

Goldstein, A.P. (1973). *Structured learning therapy: Toward a psychotherapy for the poor.* New York: Academic Press.

Goldstein, A.P. (Ed.). (1978). *Prescriptions for child mental health and education.* New York: Pergamon Press.

Goldstein, A.P., Apter, S.J., & Harootunian, B. (1984). *School violence.* Englewood Cliffs, NJ: Prentice-Hall.

Goldstein, A.P., Carr, E.G., Davidson, W.S., & Wehr, P. (1981). *In response to aggression.* New York: Pergamon Press.

Goldstein, A.P., Glick, B., Reiner, S., Zimmerman, D., & Coultrs, T. (1986). *Aggression replacement training.* Champaign, IL: Research Press.

Goldstein, A.P., & Kanfer, F. (1979). *Maximizing treatment gains.* New York: Academic Press.

Goldstein, A. P., & Keller, H. (in press). *Aggressive behavior: Assessment and intervention.* New York: Pergamon Press.

Goldstein, A.P., & Michaels, G.Y. (1985). *Empathy: Development, training and consequences.* Hillsdale, NJ: Erlbaum.

Goldstein, A.P., Sprafkin, R.P., Gershaw, N.J., & Klein, P. (1980). *Skill-streaming the adolescent: A structured learning approach to teaching prosocial skills.* Champaign, IL: Research Press.

Kagan, S. (1985). Co-op: A flexible cooperative learning technique. In R. Slavin, S. Sharan, S. Kagan, R. Hertz-Lazarowitz, C. Webb, & R. Schmuck (Eds.), *Learning to cooperate, cooperating to learn.* New York: Plenum Press.

Keller, H., Goldstein, A.P., Wynn, R., & Glick, B. (in progress). *Aggression prevention training.* Unpublished manuscript, Syracuse University, Syracuse, NY.

Kohlberg, L. (1969). Stage and sequence: The cognitive-developmental approach to socialization. In D.A. Goslin (Ed.), *Handbook of socialization theory and research*. Chicago: Rand McNally.

Kohlberg, L. (Ed.). (1973). *Collected papers on moral development and moral education*. Cambridge, MA: Center for Moral Education, Harvard University.

Ladd, G.W., & Mize, J. (1983). A cognitive-social learning model of social skill training. *Psychological Review, 90*, 127–157.

Maller, J.B. (1929). *Cooperation and competition: An experimental study in motivation*. New York: Teachers College, Columbia University.

McGinnis, E., Goldstein, A.P., Sprofkin, R.P., & Gershaw, N.J. (1981). *Skill-streaming the elementary school child: A guide for teaching prosocial skills*. Champaign, IL: Research Press.

Pfeiffer, J.W., & Jones, J.E. (1969). *A handbook of structured experiences for human relations training*. LaJolla, CA: University Associates.

Spivack, G., Platt, J.J., & Shure, M.B. (1976). *The problem-solving approach to adjustment: A guide to research and intervention*. San Francisco: Jossey-Bass.

Thayer, L., & Beeler, K.D. (1975). *Activities and exercises for affective education*. Washington, DC: American Educational Research Association.

Werner, E., & Smith, R. (1982). *Vulnerable but invincible: A study of resilient children*. New York: McGraw-Hill.

In addition to their need for social skills, increasing numbers of troubled students lack the values on which social skills training builds. There is an emerging realization that we must cultivate empathy and respect for the democratic values incorporated in the U.S. Constitution. Our social fabric is in jeopardy because too many youngsters have not been raised with these values. In addition to information, the teacher demonstrates how we should respect each other. Ethical issues are discussed as they arise in the classroom. Age-appropriate ethical decision making based on the democratic ethos has replaced the old affective education that concentrated on feelings. The school and the classroom have to be laboratories for cultivating the democratic values stated in our Constitution, Bill of Rights, and later amendments. Beane (1990) has done essential work on this issue of "moral education" the topic of considerable public debate.

REFERENCE

Beane, J. A. (1990). *Affect in the curriculum toward democracy, dignity, and diversity*. New York: Teachers College Press.

 We turn now to several somewhat more specific curriculum examples. William Rhodes has devised what he terms a "postmodern psycho-educational" curriculum to empower troubled students. In the following article, Professor Kathy Piechura, now at Stetson College, describes how she taught this curriculum to her class of very disturbed youngsters. The Life Impact Curriculum empowers troubled students to gain control of their lives through simple psychological "experiments" that students do to acquire new perceptions. These experiments deal with very fundamental processes such as time, space, categorization, and perceptual uniqueness. The lessons are not intended to constitute the total school experience but rather to teach core skills to help a student grapple with life problems. The specific exercises the author presents could be tried out by any teacher to get the feel of this different approach, working from the concrete to the theoretical base.

Empowering the Minds of Children and Youth

Kathy Piechura

It is the purpose of the Life Impact Curriculum to teach children how to learn, instead of what to learn. Children should see themselves in relation to their world and understand how they participate in the projection and creation of that world. Learning in the emerging paradigm is seen as an act of construction of knowledge not simply the reception of knowledge. The Life-Impact Curriculum is broken down into three main components which are meshed together holistically, so that the childrens' experiences are unified. It is the belief of the authors that the whole is greater than the parts, and that the parts viewed separately do not necessarily make a whole. The Curriculum allows children to experiment with life constructions, and during their experimentation, discover new ways to pattern themselves in their personal realities. A better understanding of their personal realities gives them the ability to align themselves more closely with the agreed-upon reality of society.

Behaviorally disordered students, part of the larger category of "at risk" students, have historically been described as out of touch with reality. They are reminded by their teacher that the way they view the world is not reality. Yet, as educators, we rarely look at what the child's reality is, let alone accept that the child's view may be more appropriate in his life-space than the teacher's. The underlying premise of the Life Impact Curriculum is that there are multiple realities, and that society and its subcultures, during a particular place and time, define what reality is. The Curriculum stresses that the reality of a child, who is labeled emotionally disturbed, is

From *The Journal of Emotional and Behavioral Problems*. (1992). Vol. 1, No. 2. Used with permission.

not right or wrong, but different from that of the consensus of society. Most importantly, the Curriculum teaches every child that they possess the power to change reality.

The teacher's role during the experiments takes a non-traditional direction. The teacher is no longer the giver of vast information, but instead, becomes a facilitator of learning and ultimately learns with the children. Each new group of students and each teacher encounter different experiences as they use the Curriculum, because each individual brings a unique reality to the process.

The overall design of the Life Impact Curriculum teaches children to generate and pattern three interpenetrating areas of reality construction: Multiple Realities Generation and Patterning, Personal (inter- and intra-personal) Generation and Patterning, and Context Generation and Patterning (object, space, time, and causality). In each of these areas, we use a specific "workshop" instrumentality. In Multiple Reality Generation and Patterning, we use the Reality Workshop, in Personal Construct Generation and Patterning we use *Me Books,* and in Context Generation and Patterning we employ *Think Books.*

The following diagram shows the components and instrumentalities of the Curriculum design.

Generation & Patterning Activities, Experiments and Instruments

Curriculum	Instrument
Multiple Reality Generation	Reality Workshop
Personal Construct Generation & Patterning	Me Books
Context Generation & Patterning or Constructive Thinking	Think Books

THE WEB DESIGN

The experiments or activities are designed in a webbed fashion. For example, the concept of sorting and classifying is used in the Context Generating component, and the Personal (Inter- and Intrapersonal) construct, as well as the Reality Workshop component of the Curriculum. Presently, these components are taught in a 50 minute class period labeled Social Personal. Later in this article, I will discuss ways by which I integrated the Curriculum into other traditional subject areas holistically in spite of the fragmented nature of the district-mandated curriculum.

All three areas (Context Generating skills, Multiple Reality, Personal Construct) of the Life Impact Curriculum are taught weekly. The remainder of the article will give specific examples of the various components and will describe how they web together so that the child learns to view the world holistically.

TEACHING THE GENERATION OF REALITY

A component of the Curriculum is the generation of Multiple Realities. During these experiments, the child learns there are multiple realities and that one view of reality is not necessarily the correct view. The child also learns to look at reality more flexibly and in more than one context. Usually in the beginning of the semester, conflicts arise over whose reality is correct and whose is wrong. These conflicts allow the facilitator to demonstrate some of the concepts related to multiple reality projection. As an example, we use inkblots which the students make themselves.

During this activity, the students are shown several ink blots on an overhead projector. They write down their first impressions of each blot. After viewing all the transparencies, the class re-examines each blot. The students then report on what they saw. After all of the students have committed their initial responses to paper, the group then is allowed to discuss what each of them perceived. An interesting phenomena that almost always occurs is the contagion of a thought or idea. For instance, I saw a Chinese dragon in the above inkblot. None of my students saw the dragon until I pointed it out. Suddenly, all of the students were able to see the dragon. The idea of contagion is discussed with the students, allowing them to experience how ideas (realities) diffuse through groups of people.

It is almost certain that several students in the group might have written down the same response. It is during this time that the concept of agreed-upon realities is discussed. Agreed-upon reality is defined as the societal consensus of what reality actually is. The inkblot was described by several of my students as a Teenage Mutant Ninja Turtle. I, at the time, was ignorant of what a Teenage Mutant Ninja Turtle was. However, it was evident by their insistence that the inkblot was a Teenage Mutant Ninja Turtle. The class had come to a group consensus, and I found that I was out of synch with their agreed-upon reality. The students have learned through experiences such as this that reality is what the group agrees that it is. The question was then asked of the group whether I was wrong because I was out of synch with their reality. It was decided that I was not wrong, but rather that I viewed the situation differently.

Each week the students are introduced to either a webbed offshoot of the original multiple reality lesson, or an experiment that webs cognitive experiments into life-conflict-resolving skills. Most of the material used in the reality workshop portion of the Curriculum is of a projective nature. We utilize figure ground reversals, hidden pictures, ink blots, role playing, and other techniques.

CLARIFYING REALITIES

Helping the students understand the implications of their realities is another aspect of the reality workshop. The use of non-threatening statements and guidance of their conversation can assist the students in clarifying their views of reality. For example, sometimes the child's view of reality is hostile, and the child chooses to express his hostility. As a facilitator, the teacher can explore the implications of the way the child views reality in the following manner:

Yes, you can view reality that way. However the rest of that group seems to view it differently, like _____ .

What problems do you see that might come up if you continue to view reality differently than others?

How do you think you could modify your thoughts to align more closely with theirs?

Is this something you would like to do?

Is having a different opinion (reality) worth the conflict that may arise if you continue to view reality this way?

These are questions only the child can answer, but as his teacher, I can stand by the student as a support system. As mentioned above, it is during the role-playing activities that Multiple Reality Generation in the reality workshop directly links with the Personal Construct component of the Curriculum.

CONFLICTS COLLIDING REALITIES

None of the three components of the Life Impact Curriculum are independent of the others. For instance, in the component dealing with generating and patterning personal constructs, we include an exercise which blends with the Multiple Realities Workshop. The students are required in the Personal Construct portion of the Curriculum to document "conflicts" in their daily lives. The students use these recorded conflicts as scripts or plots for role playing. The web between the child's personal conflicts and role playing allows the child to understand multiple realities while at the same time gaining a greater insight into his/her own behavior. After the conflict is played out expressing one person's reality, the actors then switch roles. This allows each student to experience the other's reality in a nonthreatening environment. Through role playing multiple realities, the children learn that the way they project their world is personal, and that each person has control over their own projection. As a facilitator, accepting and allowing children to express multiple views of reality cuts down on arguments and power struggles that many times accompany children with behavior disorders. This leads us into the Personal Construct Generation and Patterning portion of the Curriculum.

PERSONAL CONSTRUCT

The Personal Construct component is referred to by the students as Me Books. It is in their Me Books that the students discover the constructs or characterizations that they use to perceive themselves and their world.

It has been somewhat difficult to get the students to examine their own personal (inter- and intrapersonal) attributions and the way they have patterned these. As is the case for most people, it is difficult for them to look at themselves. We have tried several different approaches and are still perfecting the approach that will prove to be the most effective. In an effort to better web the Curriculum, we relied on already practiced skills that the students mastered in the Context Generating component (which is discussed later in the Curriculum).

It should be noted, again, that the Curriculum is holistic, therefore, each section is intrinsically webbed to the others. The children experience one lesson in each component every week. This reinforces each concept and allows the children to conceptualize the process as a whole.

The beginning exercise in the personal construct component is the sorting, ordering, and classifying of human figures. This is accomplished by using magazine pictures. The students first treat the human figures as objects (utilizing the same skills learned in the Context Generating or Constructive Thinking component discussed later). They classify inanimate human figures on the basis of color, size, and shape. The next step is to get them to treat the figures as subjects, and apply human characteristics (attributes) to the figures. Instead of categories such as tall, short, black, or white, they focus on behavioral, social, and cognitive qualities. These might include happy-sad, good-bad, kind-mean, and so on. The students are then instructed to sort and classify the cut out figures using the human attributes they have identified.

The classification of human attributes allows the students to begin to verbalize the personal attribute repertoire that they use to perceive their world. Class discussions and sharing of the student's personal attribute system using magazine cut-outs allows the students to begin to understand multiple psychological classification systems. The students also begin to understand that the attributes that they use to describe their system are personal and can be changed. Discovering that personal attributes are "thought constructs" is much like the students discovering there are multiple realities and the concept that they have the power to change the way they project their world.

In a follow up activity, the students learn how to sort, classify, and rank their personal attribute systems, constructs, and systems used to identify people whom they like and dislike. By classifying their attribute systems, they begin to use their thinking skills to sort themselves as they compare, contrast, and classify themselves with others. The same mental operations are employed during the Context Generating or Constructive Thinking skills activities to sort and rank attribute beads and blocks. The activity of sorting, ranking, and classifying the magazine figures now becomes personally meaningful. The children gain insight into their connectedness and relationship between themselves and others.

The next step is to allow children to experiment with the way they project themselves onto their world. The insight that children gain from monitoring their personal construct system allows them to recognize patterns associated with their behaviors. Once a child has identified the personal construct system, the teacher as a facilitator, sets up situations in which the child can practice modifications or changes in the qualities or attributes in this construct system. We have already discussed role-playing as one method. Another method conceptualized, but not yet fully tested, is that of personality projection. In a tape-recorder or on paper, the child uses the personal construct repertory to describe self-perception at the present time. Then the child describes an ideal personality. The teacher and class, through discussions, develop various scenarios, suggesting how the child's ideal personality can be actualized. The child then decides which scenario to practice, and, either through role-playing or real life situations, the child experiments with the new attributes (personality traits). It should be noted that some of the projected changes are dramatic, and it may be advisable to use role-playing, to allow the child to experience negative outcomes without fear of real-life failure.

It is during the personal construct portion of the Curriculum that the child incorporates individual projections of reality and utilizes mastered cognitive skill training to gain control over life.

CONTEXT GENERATION

The Context Generation or Constructive Thinking skills component is the final web of the Curriculum. Its purpose is to enhance and develop the tools children use to construct their contextual world. The basis of the Context Generating or Constructive Thinking component arises from Piaget's work dealing with the concepts of object, space, time, and causality, so that the child gains control over the mental processes that construct physical reality. The child learns that objects, space, time, and causality are modes of thought, rather than set conditions in the universe. The following experiments are examples of how practice in object, space, time, and causality can be effectively webbed into the previously described components of the Curriculum. Incidentally, these exercises should be very familiar to teachers. They are used as precursors to math and science skills. We also web them directly into other subject-matter skills.

Piaget has shown that "object" is the first construct that the child learns. Sometime during the child's first discoveries of the attributes associated with objects, the child learns to differentiate himself from other objects in the world. This is the beginning of the self. Therefore, we begin our experiments by studying the attributes of objects. One of the earliest activities, "stringing beads," teaches the students the attributes of color, size, and shape. The students are shown a pattern of beads for approximately twenty seconds. Then, they are asked to repeat the pattern by memory at their own desk. Initially, the only attribute difference is that of color. As the students become more proficient in their ability to recall the pattern, the attributes of size and shape are added. We also use blocks and other materials to teach patterning abilities. After the exercise is over, the students discuss the methods they used to remember the patterns. The students then record in their Think Books the methods they employed to remember the pattern.

THINK BOOKS: OBJECTS

The Think Book is an important aspect of the critical thinking skills section of the Curriculum. The children record the thought processes they used to come up with their solution. The children also practice loud think. Loud think encourages the children to think through the problem orally. This is another method that demonstrates to the children that there are multiple ways to view and solve a problem. For example, in the stringing beads activity, Ken numbered the color pattern for easier memorization. He repeated 1, 2, 3, 3, 2, 1. Several of the other students couldn't figure out why he was repeating numbers. Ken explained that 1 signified yellow, 2, red, and 3, blue, and that the pattern was an easy 1, 2, 3, that repeated itself backwards. Many of the students adopted Ken's number pattern, instead of memorizing the colors. This made the activity easier once the attributes of size and shape were added.

Once the children learned object attributes, they had the mental construct patterns to manipulate objects in their mind. Kelly figured out that she no longer had to move her bedroom furniture around in the middle of the night, because she could move it around in her mind. Incidentally, it is not unusual for children to have such "ah-ah" experiences while participating in this curriculum. We have developed many activities that teach children the attributes, classification, sorting, and enumeration of objects. The student's ability to mentally manipulate objects allows us to move into Piaget's second mental construct—"space."

THINK BOOKS: SPACE

The students' understanding of space was quite limited. Many of these physically, mentally, and economically abused children expressed that the reason they needed to learn about space was to find places to hide. Because of their limited spatial awareness, we begin with very simple activities. We first experimented with the concepts of right, left, forward, and backward. I found that many of the students had problems with right–left literality. However, the students felt that they didn't have any problem differentiating their right and left (differing realities?). Therefore, I brought in my old Twister game. This game incorporates the attributes of color with spatial coordination. The students found that the game was not as easy as they thought, and many times got tripped up on their rights and lefts. After the students gained a better understanding of right and left, we began working with a floor compass.

The floor compass is a round circle labeled north, south, east, and west. Through verbal directions, the students must orient themselves in space and express the direction they should be facing. For example, the children are instructed that they are facing towards the east. They are then asked which way they would be facing if they were to turn three times to their right, once to the back, and once to the left. This exercise is repeated several times, and each child gives instructions, acts as the pointer, and guesses the directions. When just beginning to work with the compass, the students are allowed to watch the person acting as the pointer. As the students become better acquainted with directional space, they are only allowed the use of a model of a compass. It is the purpose of these and the other spatial experiments to teach the children to conceptualize spatial directions in their minds. Therefore, through activities such as the one described above and others which incorporate map skills, the children gain mental constructs regarding spatial relationships.

THINK BOOKS: TIME

After the students have strengthened their ability to conceptualize objects and space, they are ready to move on to Piaget's third construct: time. (Incidentally, Piaget did not see these constructs as independent of one another. They were parts of the whole in the child's construction of reality.) Einstein defined time as objects moving through space. With this definition in mind, one can understand why emotionally disturbed children are often referred to as excessively tardy, slow, too fast, disorganized, unable to schedule their time, or easily upset if order is disrupted. The emotionally disturbed child's inability to conceptualize time may be inhibited by poor conceptualization of objects and space. As with the concept of space, the children found it difficult to understand that time was a concept developed by man to measure the passage of objects moving through space. For example, when asked when they thought that time measurement began, they replied that time was always there. It just was. When questioned how time was measured, they replied, "With watches, of course." When asked if they thought that cave dwellers wore watches, they replied, "No." The next question was, "How did cave dwellers measure time?" After much debate, the movement of the sun and the moon was agreed upon, confirming my original definition of time as an object moving through space. I then pointed out that a clock's hand is just an object moving through space. After this original philosophical question was understood, the class could begin to view time as a construct, thereby allowing the students to mentally manipulate the construct of time.

One favorite class activity was that of solar-system time-travel. We pretended that we could live on any planet that we wanted. In order to do so, we had to develop a calendar and clock for each of the nine planets. This activity forced the children to think about how long the day and the year on each planet would last. A ten-year-old boy found it quite fascinating that he would be 130 years old on Mercury (it takes Mercury 28 Earth days to revolve around the Sun). However, it has taken quite a while for the students to grasp these concepts. Denny, a fourteen year old, when told that in California many people were still sleeping (Denny's time was 10:00 AM EST), exclaimed that he was moving to California, because people there got to sleep in. The concept of time to Denny was not personal. It was something that he felt he had no control over. Once he gained a better understanding of time, he was able to sort time priorities, classify time differences, and schedule his personal time to better fit the constraints that others placed on him in their agreed-upon time frames.

As in the Reality Generating or Reality Workshop portion of the Curriculum, the students learn that as a society we have agreed-upon time zones, calendars, and measurements. In our personal lives, we adjust to these agreed-upon times and the adherence of the importance to meeting agreed-upon timelines. Children learn that being slow is relative to the person who is measuring the task. Time, like reality, has multiple ways of being interpreted. However, all relate to the self.

In a recent discussion with Denny, he questioned what exactly was Daylight Savings Time. I threw the question back to him to see how he conceptualized Daylight Savings Time. He said, "I don't know—maybe the sun moved." When I discussed with him that, in effect, society agreed to move the clock in order to best utilize the amount of sun, he replied, "What would happen if a city decided not to adopt Daylight Savings time?" He was informed that did happen once, in Kentucky. Denny figured out that Kentucky would be one hour different then the rest of the east coast. His only concern with Kentucky's differing time was that their *TV Guides* would really be off, or they would have to print their own *TV Guide*. Denny's view exemplifies how the effects of time differ for each individual person. Denny's life-impact revolved around his love for television.

WEBBING MEANING INTO SCHOOL LIVES

The activities associated with the concepts of objects, time, and space can easily be webbed into the teacher's general subject matter curriculum. Skills developed in mathematics are utilized during many of the activities. For example, during map making the students measure distances, calculate ratios, and deal with geometric figures. Science subject matter, such as the solar system, as well as history is webbed into time exploration. Geography is intricately related to spatial relations, and biology utilizes the concepts of attributes and classification. It is the intent of the Curriculum to web into as many subject oriented activities as possible. By doing this, the child learns there is relevance in the subject matter that can be applied to personal skills. The classification systems in biology no longer are viewed as pieces of trivia, but instead as a method of practicing everyday skills. In a recent interview, Denny stated that he uses classification every week when he sorts his laundry. He is in the process of developing a stacked container for his closet, so that he doesn't have to sort his laundry later. This invention would cut down on the mess in his bathroom. He commented that once he designed it, he was going to make it in shop. This is a wonderful example of how Denny learned to solve the spatial problem he had in his room by developing an object that will save him time in the long run.

Denny's invention is just one example of the transference and transformation that the Curriculum fosters. Throughout the year that I dealt with the Curriculum, students invented and designed activities related to our studies. Kelly and Tina loved playing Twister. When the class progressed to North, South, East, and West, they developed a Twister game utilizing the different objects studied (squares, circles, triangles) and the directions on a compass. They had transformed their dilemma of not being able to play Twister in class into a solution by creating a new game. There were many examples of how students transformed personal likes and dislikes into the Curriculum. One student's love of jewelry was expressed during an activity in which we took apart old appliances. She utilized the copper wire inside a blender to create earrings, necklaces, and bracelets. The necklaces she designed displayed washers, bolts, and springs and became very popular with the student's neighborhood peers. By allowing children to explore and expand on the concepts that are being taught, the children learn that education is personally meaningful—holistic. They also learn through the transformation and acceptance of ideas that they have control over what happens in their lives.

TRANSFORMATION

It was part of our research team's intent to transform the Life-Impact material to better fit the curriculum that was being taught by the other teachers in the school, so that the concepts learned in Social Personal class could be generalized to the students' other classes. During Social-Personal, where the Life-Impact Curriculum was being tested, I was teaching the students that by gaining a better grasp of attributes, classification, and enumeration, they were experimenting with the tools used to construct their world. By sharpening these tools, the student gains a better understanding of thinking about thinking. By teaching the students in the Social Personal class to think about thinking, we transformed the notion that students are slates waiting to be written upon, into thinking of students as experimentors—scientists of life. Their roles as scientists were expanded to creators, as they helped to develop the curriculum.

The students were informed that we (my students and myself) were creating a curriculum, and that their ideas would help shape what they learned. It was explained that we had to cover the basic curricular content outlined by the county, but that if they could think of any other way in which we could make the activities more life impacting or fun, they just had to ask.

WEBBING TO SUBJECT MATTER COURSES

I taught in a secondary program in a center for severely emotionally disturbed children. I was responsible for teaching English, reading, science, and social personal skills. Most of the secondary students in the school were assigned to my classroom one class period, and some for more than one. It should be pointed out here that the other teachers in my school were not invested in emergent teaching or the new holistic paradigm. This made the students' job even more challenging—How could they integrate and find wholeness in the time-space of their day when the other teachers were fragmenting their learning material? As facilitator, I made sure that I was abreast of the subject matter that the others were teaching so that I could point out similarities and web activities into an integrated whole. Having to integrate fragments of other teachers' lessons makes teaching in a resource or secondary program more challenging. It is the intent of the researchers of the Life-Impact Curriculum in the future to experiment with self-contained classrooms, so that the concepts of the Life-Impact Curriculum can be integrated into the holistic teaching approach, as opposed to a 50 minute time-slot.

Working with the Life-Impact Curriculum gave me the basis for webbing the activities that the students learned in Social Personal class with other basic curricular constructs that they learned in other classes. The following are two examples as to how my students and I webbed their learning into their lives.

As stated before, the Life-Impact Curriculum bases many of its curricular constructs on Piagetian concepts of classification, conservation, and attributions. The students, while studying objects, space, time, and causality, are encouraged to discover the conceptual bases that help organize objects and space. Thus, by integrating these concepts into all of their total curriculum (not just in my classes), the children discover that there is embeddedness in their learning.

TRANSFORMATION SCIENCE

Take, for instance, general science. In seventh grade, a basic concept to be learned is that of the classification of the scientific world. Students are introduced to applied biology and the plant, animal, fungi, and monad kingdoms of the world. My class could not understand why a grasshopper had to become an arthropod, and they didn't seem to care that a shark was a vertebrate. The students in Social Personal class had previously learned that classification systems were personal. They had already discovered that objects can be classified in many different ways. My next step was to connect their ability to classify in Social Personal with classification in science. By having the students create their own animal kingdom in Social Personal, I bridged Social Personal with science. Their science assignment was to bring in several of their favorite tapes and records (personally meaningful items). They quickly divided the tapes into rap, heavy metal, rock, country and that stuff that old people listen to (the Beatles). We once again discussed how classification systems allow us to have a common language to discuss something. One of the students pointed out that if we didn't classify music, it would take forever to find a record in the record store. That observation prompted an intense discussion of how stores set up merchandise in groupings or classifications to make shopping easier. Tina suggested that the students select a store at the mall, then determine how that store classifies their merchandise. She had woven her love for the mall in with her learning about classification. It was explained that everyone uses classification systems every day of their life. Scientists, on the other hand, use a larger classification system to sort out plants and animals. Classification allows scientists from any part of the world to talk to one another and understand what they are studying. In biology, we need to learn the classification system of science to enable us to talk about and understand what it is that scientists are talking about. That year's group of students learned the phylum classifications much faster than had the class the previous year. They had webbed together the concept of classification as a tool for learning and the use of that tool in science. They also retained the information longer. About six to seven months after those lessons, Ray came running into my classroom screaming, "I just saw the largest arthropod." Sure enough, on the sidewalk outside of my room was a grasshopper that was about four inches long.

TRANSFORMATION ENGLISH

I then decided to web the ideas of classification into our English lesson. I asked the students what classification has to do with parts of speech. For a few minutes, they were unsure. Suddenly, Ray exclaimed that nouns, verbs, adjectives, and adverbs were the phyla of English. He was able to make the connection between classification systems in science with the classification systems in English. He had learned to generalize the concepts originally learned in Social Personal with other subject areas. The homework assignment about the mall became an English assignment in which we listed all of the adjectives and nouns that were found in each store. To further expand the web, the students designed a store setup of their own, and I introduced prepositional phrases. The students created any kind of store that they wanted, but they had to make sure that the model was drawn proportionally. I learned from their math teacher that several of them were starting metric measurement, so their models had to be done in metrics. By showing my students connectedness, I helped them understand that learning is always occurring and that English, science, and math are tools we use to discover our lives.

STUDENT GENERATED CURRICULUM

Throughout the year, the students came into English, reading, or science excited about something they were studying in another class or had seen on TV. I would ask them how we could web their ideas into the subjects being taught in our class. Their creativity was endless. Their ideas prompted many trips to the library and many projects I had never intended to do. Their ideas also stimulated a lot of learning, not just for them, but for me, too. My role as a teacher of the Life-Impact Curriculum was unclear in the sense that I was unsure of who was teaching whom. I found that focusing on a holistic approach and strengthening my student's tools to think independently gave my students ownership of their education, and together, we discovered many exciting things.

The concept of transformation and acceptance is reinforced in all three components of the Curriculum. It is through transformation that the children learn that personality attributes are changeable and that reality projection is a personal matter. As teachers, we need to encourage children to experiment with transformation by strengthening the tools (object, space, time) that children use to construct physical reality. The holistic design of the Curriculum allows the children to conceptualize the relevance between education and life. It is the hope of the authors of this Curriculum that our Curriculum will empower children to the point that they are confident and happy with the way they project reality, thereby transforming themselves into productive members of society.

The Life-Impact Curriculum teaches children how to construct their lives. It is designed to fit the constructivist message of the emerging holistic paradigm which says that human beings play an active role in the direction their reality takes. Such researchers as Piaget also point out that this constructive ability is relative to the level of development of processes and schemas in the child's mind. Our Curriculum tries to address these processes and schemas.

. . . .

Many teachers observe that a troubled student faltering in formal academics has unusual talent in other areas or high competency in street smarts. All of us have seen children with special facility in other than the verbal-linguistic skills and logical-mathematics ability on which success in the typical school curriculum depends. Howard Gardner, of Harvard University, has ascertained that at least five other intelligences can be added to these two. He has been working with teachers in several schools that are revising their programs to accommodate a broad range of abilities. As a researcher-practitioner, Gardner has put his concepts to the test in public school classrooms. Many troubled students need just such an expansion in the breadth of teaching and learning to experience school success and an accompanying increase in self-esteem. Bruce Campbell organized his third-grade classroom to engage all seven intelligences, thereby enhancing pupils' opportunities for success. No group needs an expanded school learning environment more than our troubled students. This is a way we can reduce the number of school losers. An interesting application is to plot one's own intelligence profile. Which intelligences are most necessary for those electing to teach troubled students?

ARTICLE 8.4

Multiple Intelligences in the Classroom

OF THE SEVEN DIFFERENT WAYS WE LEARN, SCHOOLS FOCUS ON ONLY TWO. ADD THE OTHER FIVE, AND YOU INCREASE THE CHANCES OF SUCCESS

Bruce Campbell

If we are to achieve a richer culture, rich in contrasting values, we must recognize the whole gamut of human potentialities, and so weave a less arbitrary social fabric, one in which each diverse human gift will find a fitting place.—Margaret Mead

In recent years, new definitions of intelligence have gained acceptance and have dramatically enhanced the appraisal of human competencies. Howard Gardner of Harvard University in his book, *Frames of Mind: The Theory of Multiple Intelligences,* suggests that there are at least seven human intelligences, two of which, *verbal/linguistic* intelligence and *logical/mathematical* intelligence, have dominated the traditional pedagogy of western societies.

The five non-traditional intelligences, *spatial, musical, kinesthetic, interpersonal,* and *intrapersonal,* have generally been overlooked in education. However, if we can develop ways to teach and learn by engaging all seven intelligences, we will increase the possibilities for student success and create the opportunity to, in Margaret Mead's words, "weave a social fabric in which each diverse human gift will find a fitting place."

From *In Context.* (1993). No. 27.

HOW CAN THE MULTIPLE INTELLIGENCES BE IMPLEMENTED IN THE CLASSROOM?

To implement Gardner's theory in an educational setting, I organized my third grade classroom in Marysville, Washington, into seven learning centers, each dedicated to one of the seven intelligences. The students spend approximately two-thirds of each school day moving through the centers— 15 to 20 minutes at each center. Curriculum is thematic, and the centers provide seven different ways for the students to learn the subject matter.

Each day begins with a brief lecture and discussion explaining one aspect of the current theme. For example, during a unit on outer space, the mornings lecture might focus on spiral galaxies. In a unit about the arts of Africa, one lecture might describe the Adinkra textile patterns of Ghana. After the morning lecture, a timer is set and students—in groups of three or four—start work at their centers, eventually rotating through all seven.

WHAT KINDS OF LEARNING ACTIVITIES TAKE PLACE AT EACH CENTER?

All students learn each day's lesson in seven ways. They build models, dance, make collaborative decisions, create songs, solve deductive reasoning problems, read, write, and illustrate all in one school day. Some more specific examples of activities at each center follow:

- In the Personal Work Center (Intrapersonal Intelligence), students explore the present area of study through research, reflection, or individual projects.

- In the Working Together Center (Interpersonal Intelligence), they develop cooperative learning skills as they solve problems, answer questions, create learning games, brainstorm ideas and discuss that day's topic collaboratively.

- In the Music Center (Musical Intelligence), students compose and sing songs about the subject matter, make their own instruments, and learn in rhythmical ways.

- In the Art Center (Spatial Intelligence), they explore a subject area using diverse art media, manipulables, puzzles, charts, and pictures.

- In the Building Center (Kinesthetic Intelligence), they build models, dramatize events, and dance, all in ways that relate to the content of that day's subject matter.

- In the Reading Center (Verbal/Linguistic Intelligence), students read, write, and learn in many traditional modes. They analyze and organize information in written form.

- In the Math & Science Center (Logical/Mathematical Intelligence), they work with math games, manipulatives, mathematical concepts, science experiments, deductive reasoning, and problem solving.

Following their work at the centers, a few minutes are set aside for groups and individual students to share their work from the centers. Much of the remainder of the day is spent with students working on independent projects, either individually or in small groups where they apply the diverse skills developed at the centers. The daily work at the seven centers profoundly influences their ability to make informative, entertaining, multimodal presentations of their studies. Additionally, it is common for parents to comment on how much more expressive their children have become at home.

WHAT ARE SOME OF THE RESULTS OF THIS PROGRAM?

During the 1989–1990 school year, an action research project was conducted in my classroom to assess the effects of this multimodal learning format. A daily teacher's journal was kept with specific entries recording the following:

- general daily comments
- a daily evaluation of how focused or "on-task" students were
- an evaluation of the transitions between centers
- an explanation of any discipline problems
- a self-assessment—how the teacher's time was used
- tracking of three individuals, previously identified as students with behavior problems.

In addition, a Classroom Climate Survey was administered 12 times during the year, a Student Assessment Inventory of work at the seven centers was administered nine times during the year, and a Center Group Survey was administered eight times during the year.

The research data revealed the following:

1. *The students develop increased responsibility, self-direction and independence over the course of the year.* Although no attempt was made to compare this group of students with those in other third grade classes, the self-direction and motivation of these students was apparent to numerous classroom visitors. The students became skilled at developing their own projects, gathering the necessary resources and materials, and making well-planned presentations of all kinds.

2. *Discipline problems were significantly reduced.* Students previously identified as having serious behavior problems showed rapid improvement during the first six weeks of school. By mid-year, they were making important contributions to their groups. And by year's end, they had assumed positive leadership roles which had not formerly been evident.

3. *All students developed and applied new skills.* In the fall, most students described only one center as their "favorite" and as the one where they felt confident. (The distribution among the seven centers was relatively even.) By mid-year, most identified three to four favorite centers. By year's end, every student identified at least six centers which were favorites and at which they felt skilled. Moreover, they were all making multimodal presentations of independent projects including songs, skits, visuals, poems, games, surveys, puzzles, and group participation activities.

4. *Cooperative learning skills improved in all students.* Since so much of the center work was collaborative, students became highly skilled at listening, helping each other, sharing leadership in different activities, accommodating group changes, and introducing new classmates to the program. They learned not only to respect each other, but also to appreciate and call upon the unique gifts and abilities of their classmates.

5. *Academic achievement improved.* Standardized test scores were above state and national averages in all areas. Retention was high on a classroom year-end test of all areas studied during the year. Methods for recalling information were predominantly musical, visual and kinesthetic, indicating the influence of working through the different intelligences. Students who had previously been unsuccessful in school became high achievers in new areas.

In summary, it is clear that students' learning improved. Many students said they enjoyed school for the first time. And as the school year progressed, new skills emerged: some students discovered musical, artistic literary, mathematical and other new-found capacities and abilities. Others became skilled leaders. In addition, self-confidence and motivation increased significantly. Finally, students developed responsibility, self-reliance and independence as they took an active role in shaping their own learning experiences.

WHAT IS THE TEACHER'S ROLE IN A MULTIPLE INTELLIGENCE PROGRAM?

The teacher's role also transforms in this type of program. I developed skills different from those I would develop by standing in front of a class lecturing each day. I need to observe my students from seven new perspectives.

In planning the centers, I find I am pushing my students from behind rather than pulling them from in front. Also I am working *with* them, rather than *for* them. I explore what they explore, discover what they discover, and often learn what they learn. I find my satisfaction in their enthusiasm for learning and independence, rather than in their test scores and ability to sit quietly. And most importantly, because I am planning for such a diversity of activities, I have become more creative and multimodal in my own thinking and my own learning. I can now comfortably write and sing songs. I am learning to draw and paint. I see growth and development within myself. I sometimes wonder who is changing the most, my students or myself.

WHY IS A MULTIPLE INTELLIGENCES MODEL SUCCESSFUL?

The reasons for the academic and behavioral success of the program appear to be twofold. First, every student has an opportunity to specialize and excel in *at least* one area. Usually, however, it is three or four. In the two years since this program was initiated, I have not had one student who was unable to find an area of specialty and success. Secondly, each student learns the subject matter in a variety of different ways, thereby multiplying chances of successfully understanding and retaining that information.

Many student needs are met through this program. Their intellectual needs are met by constantly being challenged and frequently exercising their creativity. At the same time, their emotional needs are met by working closely with others. They develop diverse strengths, and they understand themselves better as individuals.

The emphasis in such a program is upon *learning* rather than teaching. The students' interests and developmental needs dictate the direction of the program. Such a model adapts to students, rather than expecting students to adapt to it. From my own classroom experiences, I believe that teaching and learning through the multiple intelligences helps solve many common school problems and optimizes the learning experience for students and teachers alike. Again following Margaret Mead, if we educate to engage the "whole gamut of human potentialities" in the classroom, society will benefit by enabling "each diverse human gift to find its fitting place."

FOUR FACTORS IN EDUCATIONAL REFORM

Many of us interested in efforts at educational reform have focused on the learner or student, be she a young child in preschool or an adult bent on acquiring a new skill. It is clarifying to have such a focus and, indeed, any efforts at reform are doomed to fail unless they concentrate on the properties and potentials of the individual learner. My own work on multiple intelligences has partaken of this general focus; colleagues and I have sought to foster a range of intellectual strengths in our students.

But after several years of active involvement in efforts at educational reform, I am convinced that success depends upon the active involvement of at least four factors:

1. Assessment. Unless one is able to assess the learning that takes place in different domains, and by different cognitive processes, even superior curricular innovations are destined to remain unutilized. In this country, assessment drives instruction. We must devise procedures and instruments which are "intelligence-fair" and which allow us to look directly at the kinds of learning in which we are interested.

2. Curriculum. Far too much of what is taught today is included primarily for historical reasons. Even teachers, not to mention students, often cannot explain why a certain topic needs to be covered in school. We need to reconfigure curricula so that they focus on skills, knowledge, and above all, understandings that are truly desirable in our country today. And we need to adapt those curricula as much as possible to the particular learning styles and strengths of students.

3. Teacher education. While most teacher education institutions make an honest effort to produce teaching candidates of high quality, these institutions have not been at the forefront of efforts at educational improvement. Too often they are weighted down by students of indifferent quality and by excessive—and often counterproductive—requirements which surround training and certification. We need to attract stronger individuals into teaching, improve conditions so that they will remain in teaching, and use our master teachers to help train the next generation of students and teachers.

4. Community participation. In the past, Americans have been content to place most educational burdens on the schools. This is no longer a viable option. The increasing cognitive demands of schooling, the severe problems in our society today, and the need for support of students which extends well beyond the 9–3 period each day, all make it essential that other individuals and institutions contribute to the educational process. In addition to support from family members and other mentoring adults, such institutions as business, the professions, and especially museums need to be involved much more intimately in the educational process.

Too often, Americans have responded to educational needs only in times of crisis. This is an unacceptable approach. Education works effectively only when responsibility is assumed over the long run. We have made significant progress in this regard over the past decade. There is reason to be optimistic for students of the future, as dedicated individuals continue to collaborate in solving the challenging educational problems of our time. — Howard Gardner

. . . .

Even when assigned individual seat work or placed in booths, pupils still spend considerable effort in surveillance, to keep up on what their peers are doing. Although most schools still concentrate on individual, competitive achievement, students remain vigilant toward peers and respond to every movement. All eyes leave the task to watch the first hand raised to indicate the assignment is done. Cooperative learning provides not only a way of co-opting peer interest when teaching content but becomes an ongoing laboratory for social learning. Yet many programs for troubled children eschew the use of cooperative methods as high-risk. Some teachers fear the potential for disruption and off-task behavior when pupils work in small groups. They anticipate that control will disintegrate, which does sometimes happen. Actually, cooperative activity may be a better avenue to teach reasonable social interaction, group problem solving, and cooperation than special abstract units on social skills. When there are difficulties, the teacher, working with the group, can sort out the problems and work out solutions. David Johnson and Robert Johnson (from Educational Psychology, and Curriculum and Instruction, respectively, at the University of Minnesota) are the recognized leaders in the Cooperative Learning movement. They do not rest on the mechanics but show how cooperative learning can foster positive peer relationships, a highly desirable goal for troubled children who are often lonely and alienated. Cooperative Learning also facilitates caring teacher relationships. This method is especially appropriate for inclusion programs. A word of caution: There is no method that will compensate for boring, nonrelevant curriculum.

ARTICLE 8.5

Cooperative Learning: What Special Education Teachers Need to Know

David W. Johnson and Roger T. Johnson

Consider two special education students. Ralph walks into the school knowing that today he will learn more about English and math but that no one would miss him if he were absent, no one would care if he were sick, and no one would care if he could not do the required work. Fred walks into the school knowing that he has friends who are waiting to see him, who truly care about him as a person, who would miss him if he were absent, who would feel bad if he were sick, and who will give him the help he needs to succeed.

From *Pointer*. (1989). Vol. 33, No. 2. Used with permission.

THE IMPORTANCE OF LONG-TERM CARING RELATIONSHIPS

It is difficult to overemphasize the importance of the relationships special education students form with peers and teachers. If these pupils are isolated individuals who have no meaningful and lasting relationships with peers or teachers, school is less than wonderful and their future may be less than promising. If special education students form caring, committed, and permanent relationships with peers and teachers and are part of an ongoing support group, then school is terrific and their future is bright. Lonely, isolated, and alienated students do not do well in school. Popular, liked, accepted, and respected students do. Although learning academic material is important and should not be deemphasized, the relationships built with peers and teachers dominate the school life of special education students.

In order to create caring and committed relationships among students, cooperative learning has to dominate the classroom. Competitive and individualistic learning experiences do not promote caring and committed relationships among students, nor do they provide a context in which social skills may be learned, practiced, and perfected. Relationships and social skills are built out of working together to get the job done.

At least one cooperative group, the base group, should last for a number of years. Most schools assume that relationships are either undesirable or of no consequence. Students and teachers are usually assigned to classes as individuals as if it does not matter who a student's classmates and teachers are, especially in secondary school. Teachers and classmates, for example, usually have a temporary, 1-year relationship with any one student. It is important for special education students to have a base group made up of nonhandicapped as well as special education students that stays together for a number of years.

Social skills training has to be emphasized for both special education and nonhandicapped students. Working in cooperative learning groups takes leadership, decision-making, communication, trust-building, and conflict-resolution skills. Building and maintaining long-term caring and committed relationships require the same skills. These skills have to be systematically taught, used, reinforced, and emphasized.

Finally, although mainstreaming is preferred, when it is not possible, cooperative learning should dominate special education classes. The advantages of cooperative learning exist in the self-contained as well as the mainstream classroom. Cooperative learning, furthermore, needs to be used within special education classrooms in order to prepare students for cooperative learning in regular classrooms. When mainstreaming is possible, nonhandicapped members of a cooperative group should be waiting in the regular classroom to "claim" the special education student as "one of us," to welcome him or her into their group and class, and to provide the student with ongoing social support.

In order to create the constructive relationships and social support system so necessary for special education students' success and well-being, special education teachers need to understand the meaning of cooperative learning, the essential elements required to ensure that cooperative groups are productive, the teacher's role in structuring cooperative learning groups, the impact of cooperation on learning outcomes, the variety of ways cooperative groups may be used, and how to solve some of the common problems in integrating special education students into cooperative learning groups with nonhandicapped peers.

WHAT IS COOPERATIVE LEARNING?

"I want to be able to hear a pin drop in this room." "Don't copy." "I want to see what you can do, not your neighbor." "Save the talking for the hallway." These are familiar teacher statements exhorting students to work by themselves without interacting with their classmates. In many classrooms, in every part of the country, these statements are becoming passé. In classrooms with cooperative learning and in schools with collegial support groups, we are returning to the North American tradition of cooperation.

What is cooperative learning? Cooperation is working together to accomplish shared goals, and cooperative learning is the instructional use of small groups so that students work together to maximize their own and each other's learning. Within cooperative learning groups, students are given two responsibilities: to learn the assigned material and to make sure that all other members of their group do likewise. Thus, a student seeks an outcome that is beneficial to him- or herself and beneficial to all other group members. In cooperative learning situations, students perceive that they can reach their learning goals only if the other students in the learning group also do so. Students discuss the material to be learned with each other, help and assist each other to understand it, and encourage each other to work hard.

Cooperative learning may be contrasted with competitive and individualistic learning. In the competitive classroom, students work against each other to achieve a goal that only one or a few students can attain. Students are graded on a curve, which requires them to work faster and more accurately than their peers. Thus, students seek an outcome that is personally beneficial but detrimental to all other students in the class.

In the individualistic classroom, students work by themselves to accomplish learning goals unrelated to those of the other students. Individual goals are assigned, students' efforts are evaluated on a fixed set of standards, and students are rewarded accordingly. Thus, the student seeks an outcome that is personally beneficial and ignores as irrelevant the goal achievement of other students.

We, the authors, know a great deal about competition. As brothers 1½ years apart in age, we competed intensely with each other for about 18 years. Having experienced firsthand what competition can do, we decided to cooperate when we became colleagues at the University of Minnesota in 1969. We combined expertise in social psychological work on cooperation with that in classroom teaching. Ever since, we have been reviewing and synthesizing the existing knowledge about cooperative, competitive, and individualistic efforts; building theoretical models about how each may be used appropriately; conducting a systematic program of research to validate the theory; creating operational procedures for teachers and administrators to use; and building a national and international network of school districts implementing cooperative learning in the classroom and collegial support groups in schools and districts on a long-term basis.

BASIC ELEMENTS OF COOPERATIVE LEARNING

Simply placing students in groups and telling them to work together does not in and of itself promote higher achievement and more positive relationships among students. There are many ways in which group efforts may go wrong. Less able members may "leave it to George" to complete the group's tasks (i.e., the free-rider effect), more able group members may expend less effort to avoid the sucker effect, or the group may engage in all the explanations and elaborations (i.e., the rich-get-richer effect) (Johnson & Johnson, in press). Group efforts can be characterized by self-induced helplessness, diffusion of responsibility and social loafing, ganging up against a task, reactance, dysfunctional divisions of labor, inappropriate dependence on authority, destructive conflict, and other patterns of behavior that debilitate group performance (Johnson & Johnson, in press). It is only under certain conditions that group efforts may be expected to be more productive than individual efforts.

Suppose that in a Minnesota fifth-grade classroom, a teacher gives her students a set of math story problems to solve. She assigns students to groups of three, ensuring that there is a high-, medium-, and low-performing math student and both male and female students in each group. The instructional tasks are to solve each story problem correctly and to understand how to do so.

In order to make this lesson cooperative, five basic elements have to be included. The first is positive interdependence, wherein students perceive the lesson as a "sink or swim together" situation. Students need to feel that their work benefits their groupmates and their groupmates' work benefits them. Teachers structure positive interdependence by requiring each group to agree on what the answer to each problem is and how it is derived and assigning students the complementary roles of reader (reads each problem aloud to the group), encourager (encourages all members of the group in a friendly way to participate in the discussion, sharing their ideas and feelings), and checker (makes sure that all members can explain how to solve each problem correctly).

The benefits of cooperation are not maximized unless there is considerable face-to-face, promotive interaction—the second element—among students. Group members need to encourage, support, help, and assist each other's efforts to learn. There are cognitive processes and interpersonal dynamics that occur only when students become involved in explaining their reasoning to each other.

The third element is individual accountability, which exists when the performance of each student is assessed regularly. Group members need to know who needs more assistance in completing the assignment. Members should perceive that they must fulfill their responsibilities in order for each individual and the group to be successful. Because students are required to certify that each group member has the correct answer written on his or her answer sheet and can correctly explain the answers, individual accountability is structured by picking one answer sheet from the group or randomly asking one member to explain the group's answers.

Fourth, the social skills emphasized in the lesson are checking and encouraging. Learning groups are not productive unless members are skilled in cooperating with each other. Cooperative skills include leadership, decision making, trust building, communication, and conflict resolution. These skills have to be taught just as purposefully and precisely as academic skills. Procedures and strategies for teaching students social skills may be found in Johnson (1986, 1987); Johnson and F. Johnson (1987); and Johnson, Johnson, and Holubec (1986).

Finally, at the end of the period, the groups process their functioning by answering two questions: (1) What is something each member did that was helpful for the group? and (2) What is something each member could do to make the group even better tomorrow? Group processing is the discussion of how well group members are learning and maintaining effective working relationships among members.

These five elements represent a conceptual approach to cooperative learning that allows teachers to become educational engineers who structure their existing lessons, materials, and curricula. Teachers can tailor lessons to their instructional needs, circumstances, subject areas, and students. Thus, teachers who have learned a conceptual model of how to make lessons cooperative can use cooperative learning within all subject areas, and they can adapt and modify cooperative lessons to take into account the specific social, emotional, and learning problems of special education students.

Besides understanding the five basic elements, teachers also need a set of procedures that define their role in structuring cooperative lessons.

THE TEACHER'S ROLE IN IMPLEMENTING COOPERATIVE LEARNING

Imagine you are a principal walking down the halls of your school during a normal school day. In one classroom, students sit in rows, quietly working on individual worksheets and taking notes while a teacher lectures. In another classroom, students busily work in triads, encouraging each other and explaining and elaborating to each other the material they are working on, while the teacher moves quietly from group to group to see which ones may need assistance in understanding the material or in working together effectively. Which classroom is more productive?

For years, the quiet classroom has been perceived to be the productive classroom. Noise level was an informal index of classroom control and on-task behavior. No longer. We now know that working together to achieve joint goals has numerous advantages over competitive and individualistic efforts. But how do you do it? How does a teacher structure learning situations so that students cooperate with each other? Theory can only guide practice if theory is translated into a set of concrete and practical procedures that teachers can use to implement cooperative learning.

When using cooperative learning, you, the teacher, function as both an academic expert and a classroom manager to promote effective group functioning (Johnson & R. Johnson, 1987; Johnson, Johnson, & Holubec, 1986, 1987). First, you specify the objectives for the lesson. Second, you make a number of preinstructional decisions, such as how large the groups will be, how students will be assigned to groups, what roles should be assigned to students, and what materials each group needs. Third, after the lesson is planned, you explain to the students the learning task, the positive interdependence, and related instructions for working with each other. It is at this point that you teach the academic concepts, principles, and strategies that the students are to master and apply. Fourth, while the students work in groups, you monitor students' effectiveness in completing the assignment and in working together cooperatively. You provide task assistance (such as answering questions and teaching math skills and strategies) and assist students in increasing their interpersonal and small-group skills. You instruct students to look to their peers for assistance, feedback, reinforcement, and support. You expect students to interact with each other, share ideas and materials, support and encourage each other's academic achievement, orally explain and elaborate the concepts and strategies being learned, and hold each other accountable for learning. Finally, you evaluate students' achievement and help them process how well they cooperated with each other. A criteria-referenced evaluation system is used. Detailed descriptions of each of these steps may be found in Johnson, Johnson, and Holubec (1986) or Johnson and R. Johnson (1987).

Implementing cooperative learning is not easy. It takes considerable effort and time to gain expertise in it. With special education students, furthermore, the specifics of how cooperative learning is structured may need to be adapted. There must be careful consideration of which students in a mainstreamed classroom work with the special education student, what roles he or she is given, which criteria the special education student's performance is based on, and which social skills are emphasized within a lesson. Once teachers gain some expertise in structuring lessons cooperatively, such modifications become easy and natural.

WHAT DO WE KNOW ABOUT COOPERATIVE LEARNING?

Working together to maximize one's own learning and the learning of other group members can have profound effects on students. In trying to understand how cooperation works, and in continually refining our understanding of how to implement cooperation most effectively, we have conducted a 20-year program of research that has resulted in over 80 published studies. These studies have included lab-experimental, field-experimental, field-evaluation, and large-scale survey research. From these studies we can conclude as follows:

1. More caring and committed relationships between special education and nonhandicapped students tend to result from working together to get the job done than from competing to see who is best or working independently from classmates.

2. The positive relationships and social support found within cooperative learning situations tend to increase students' self-esteem and healthy psychological adjustment.

3. Cooperative learning experiences, compared with competitive and individualistic ones, tend to increase students' social skills and competencies.

4. Cooperative experiences promote higher achievement, more frequent discovery and use of higher-level reasoning strategies, and greater critical thinking than do competitive and individualistic ones.

Whether special education students are taught in self-contained classrooms or mainstreamed into regular classrooms, the primary goal is to involve them in constructive relationships with nonhandicapped peers. When cooperative learning is emphasized, that goal is accomplished along with a number of other important instructional outcomes such as higher self-esteem, general improvement in psychological adjustment and health, greater social skills, increased achievement, and higher level reasoning skills. With the amount of research evidence available, it is surprising that classroom practice is so oriented toward individualistic and competitive learning.

TYPES OF COOPERATIVE GROUPS

There are three types of cooperative learning groups that special education teachers may use. Ad hoc cooperative learning groups consist of brief and temporary tasks such as "turn to your partner and answer the following question." Formal cooperative learning groups are carefully structured to complete assignments that last for several hours, days, or weeks. Base cooperative groups are long-term groups whose role is primarily one of peer support and long-term accountability. It is especially important for special education students that they are members of an ongoing base group that is permanent and, preferably, lasts for several years. To be truly caring and committed, relationships have to be more than temporary "shipboard romances" based on a single assignment or unit. Students need to know that their relationships are permanent and that they have to work together and get along for years. This diminishes anonymity and increases accountability to peers who have a long-term investment in a student's well-being and success.

Working in any cooperative group takes social skills. Whereas competitive and individualistic learning situations require students to work quietly without interacting with classmates (thus preventing the learning, use, and refinement of social skills), cooperative learning is based on the appropriate use of leadership, communication, decision-making, and conflict-resolution skills. Teaching students these skills and then encouraging their use become important responsibilities of the special education teacher.

Finally, in order to sustain the long-term implementation and in-classroom help needed to gain expertise in cooperative learning, special education teachers need support groups made up of colleagues who are also committed to mastering cooperative learning. Good collegial relationships require as much careful structuring and monitoring as do cooperative learning groups.

INTEGRATING SPECIAL EDUCATION STUDENTS INTO COOPERATIVE LEARNING GROUPS

When special education students are mainstreamed into cooperative learning groups, there may be a number of problems that both special education and regular classroom teachers need to attend to. By carefully structuring positive interdependence, individual accountability, face-to-face promotive interaction, the use of social skills, and group processing, teachers can prevent or reduce problems that special education and nonhandicapped students have in working together. Three of the most common problems are the special education students' fear and anxiety, the nonhandicapped students' concern about having their grades affected, and special education students' passive uninvolvement. Some suggestions for dealing with such problems follow.

WHEN SPECIAL EDUCATION STUDENTS ARE ANXIOUS

Many special education students may be fearful and anxious about participating in a cooperative learning group with nonspecial education peers. The following steps may alleviate their anxiety:

1. Explain the procedures that the learning group will follow.

2. Give the special education students a structured role so that they understand their responsibilities. Even if students cannot read, they can listen carefully and summarize what everyone in the group is saying, provide leadership, and help to keep the group's work organized. There is always some way to facilitate group work, no matter what handicaps the students may have.

3. Coach the special education students in the behaviors and social skills needed within the cooperative group. Pretraining in social skills and periodic sessions to monitor how well the skills are being implemented will increase the special education students' confidence.

4. Pretrain the special education students in the academic skills needed to complete the group's work. Try to give the special education students a source of expertise that the group will need.

WHEN NONSPECIAL EDUCATION STUDENTS ARE ANXIOUS

Many nonspecial education students may be concerned that the special education student will lower the overall performance of their group. Three major ways of alleviating their concern are as follows:

1. Train nonspecial education students in helping, tutoring, teaching, and sharing skills. The special education teacher may wish to explain to the group how best to teach the special education group member. Many teaching skills, such as the use of praise and prompting, are easily taught to students.

2. Make the academic requirements for the special education students reasonable. Ways in which lessons can be adapted so the students at different achievement levels can participate in the same cooperative group are to

    a. use different criteria for success for each group member;

    b. vary the amount each group member is expected to master;

    c. give group members different assignments, lists, words, or problems, and then use the average percentage worked correctly as the group's score; and

    d. use improvement scores for the special education students. If it is unclear how to implement these procedures, consult with the special education teacher to decide what is appropriate for the specific special education student.

3. Give bonus points to the groups that have special education members. This will create a situation in which nonspecial education students want to work with their special education classmates in order to receive the bonus points.

PASSIVE UNINVOLVEMENT BY
SPECIAL EDUCATION STUDENTS

When special education students are turning away from the group, not participating, not paying attention to the group's work, saying little or nothing, showing no enthusiasm, or not bringing their work or materials, the teacher may wish to jigsaw materials so that each group member has information the others need. If the passive, uninvolved student does not voluntarily contribute his or her information, the other group members can actively involve the student. Another strategy is to divide up roles and assign to the passive, uninvolved student a function that is essential to the group's success. Or the teacher may reward the group on the basis of their average performance, which will encourage other group members to derive strategies for increasing the problem member's involvement.

SUMMARY

Caring and committed relationships are derived from cooperative efforts, not from competing to see who is best or from working alone. The heart of school for special education students is the relationships they form with their classmates and teachers. Lonely and alienated students do not learn well. Students who are liked and accepted by their classmates are much more likely to acquire the skills and competencies needed to learn and to maintain their relationships.

Just placing students in groups and telling them to work together does not usually result in a cooperative effort. To be a cooperative learning group, five basic elements must be present. Students must (1) believe they sink or swim together (positive interdependence), (2) interact face-to-face to help each other learn, (3) be individually accountable to learn, (4) have and use required interpersonal and small-group skills, and (5) process how to improve the effectiveness of their group.

Special education teachers need to be especially expert in constructing cooperative learning situations that are engineered to promote constructive relationships and maximize the achievement of students regardless of their social, emotional, and learning problems. The anxiety special education students feel about working with nonhandicapped peers, the anxiety nonhandicapped students feel about working with special education peers, and the withdrawal of special education students from the group effort are three of the problems that may be prevented and solved through modifying the way cooperative learning groups are structured.

Finally, it is important that at least some of the cooperative relationships are permanent, special education students are specially taught the social skills they need to be productive group members, and special education teachers are part of an ongoing teacher collegial group that provides the support and assistance needed to persist in gaining expertise in using co-operative learning.

REFERENCES

Johnson, D. W. (1986). *Reaching out* (3rd ed.). Englewood Cliffs, NJ: Prentice-Hall.

Johnson, D. W. (1987). *Human relations and your career* (2nd ed.). Englewood Cliffs, NJ: Prentice-Hall.

Johnson, D. W., & Johnson, F. (1987). *Joining together: Group theory and group skills.* Englewood Cliffs, NJ: Prentice-Hall.

Johnson, D. W., & Johnson, R. (1987). *Learning together and alone: Cooperative competitive and individualistic learning.* Englewood Cliffs, NJ: Prentice-Hall.

Johnson, D. W., & Johnson, R. (in press). *Cooperation and competition: Theory and research.* Hillsdale, NJ: Erlbaum.

Johnson, D. W., Johnson, R., & Holubec, E. (1986). *Circles of learning.* Edina, MN: Interaction Book Co.

Johnson, D. W., Johnson, R., & Holubec, E. (1987). *Structuring cooperative learning: Lesson plans for teachers.* Edina, MN: Interaction Book Co.

· ·

There are many ways to reach troubled children in school and some of the most effective are least utilized, as we were reminded by Gardner. Bibliotherapy, caring for pets, horticulture, music, art, play, dance, free writing, and drama are examples of such curricula, sometimes called action-oriented therapies (Nickerson & O'Laughlin, 1982). Such healing activities can constitute a significant part of the student's school experience. Typically, troubled students are not selected for the cast of a class play lest they mess up the performance. Their artwork may be too revealing or bizarre for adult comfort, and their writing might contain forbidden words. The reluctance to use action-oriented therapies reflects the fact that those who need a thing most are left out because of the difficulty they might cause. On the other hand, skillful teachers have recognized that many troubled pupils may begin to find themselves through such activities. Participating in a chorus can encourage a sense of belonging. Or, consider how the dramatization of a historical event contrasts with just silent reading and answering a series of questions on a worksheet.

REFERENCE ·

Nickerson, E. T., & O'Laughlin (Eds.). (1982). Helping through action. *Action Oriented Therapies.* Amherst, MA: Human Resource Development Press.

Lanell Hileman teaches at the Southard School at the Menniger Foundation. As Hileman says, teachers have to adapt these ideas to their own setting. Both group presentations and videotaping are exciting possible products. Some pupils are, in a play, able to assume roles that are foreign to their usual behavior; they enjoy an opportunity for practicing new roles. Drama is also an excellent opportunity to combine groups and coteach. A deeper level of psychological process often accompanies dramatic participation. Drama offers a nondidactic mode to teach about emotions, explore character, and analyze options in stressful situations.

ARTICLE 8.6

Exploring Drama with Emotionally Disturbed Adolescents

Lanell R. Hileman

Drama can be a great source of fun and exploration, as well as a therapeutic process for emotionally disturbed youth. It encourages utilization of all the senses and fosters mental, physical, social, emotional, and spiritual growth needs. In planning a drama program, the drama teacher must exercise much caution to ensure that selected activities will enhance the well-being of the students. Furthermore, these activities should not cause a great deal of stress, since emotionally disturbed youth are already facing many stresses daily. The teacher should emphasize reality-based situations rather than highly imaginative or fantasy ones, because of the difficulty some students have in distinguishing fantasy from reality. When this problem occurs with younger children, they may have a hard time separating from their acting role when drama class is over.

The teacher must make the rules of the class clear. Discipline is essential to dramatic expression. Students should experience feelings of freedom and pleasure, but must also feel the security that discipline provides. There are many ways to establish group rules, and each teacher can decide upon a method suitable to his/her leadership style. Mood planning or motivation is another factor to be considered when establishing a drama class. The arousal of thinking, feeling, and expression in students takes much teacher planning because an experience must get inside a child before s/he can create from it. Students need to visualize a character or idea in their minds before they can create from it. Therefore, the drama teacher will need to have a plan for developing character feeling.

Finally, the drama teacher must have a final goal for each student's and the group's participation. A fairly structured course outline is vital to

From *Pointer*. (1985). Vol. 30, No. 1. Used with permission.

the success of a drama program. It is important that the teacher find out as much as possible about the students enrolled in the class. With this information, the teacher can determine individual and group goals and objectives.

I have established a summer drama workshop at Southard School in elementary and secondary programs. The course for elementary children meets for 30 minutes daily. This time frame seems to work best because the children have short attention spans. The secondary class meets for two consecutive hours daily. These periods provide time necessary for students to initiate projects, participate in projects, and complete cleanup. The courses incorporate a multimedia approach designed for use with children and adolescents in my institutional setting; however, the courses could be implemented with modifications in other settings, if necessary.

A week-by-week description of the secondary course is provided in this article. Materials used to supplement the activities are listed at the end of each week's description. Samples of materials used in the course are included at the end of the article.

SECONDARY DRAMA PROGRAM

Week One

Students are presented with copies of the course outline, general information sheets, activities sheets, and other necessary information. Each of these items is carefully explained so that students know expectations. A sheet describing classroom rules is circulated for each student's reading and signature. I keep this sheet on file in case arguments about rules arise. Students also receive a teacher-made drama word search assignment called "nest egg" points. The "nest egg" points accumulated on the word search, which total no more than 100, may be used to replenish points lost throughout the course due to inappropriate behavior and/or unexcused absences.

While students work on this activity, I meet with each one individually to discuss I.E.P. goals and to establish personal objectives for the course. I have found this valuable for discovering how students feel about themselves, what their idiosyncrasies are, and, most importantly, their attitudes toward drama.

There are two long-term assignments to be completed by students on their own time: a drama notebook and play critiques. Students are required to complete activities indicated on the information sheet and keep them in a spiral notebook to be turned in the last week of class. They are also required to read three plays of their choice and write a synopsis and critique of each, also due the last week of class.

Since most of the enrolled students have had little or no background in theater, a brief history of drama is presented. Students take notes as I write on the blackboard. At the end of each class period the notes are reviewed. A short, open-note exam is given over all the material presented that week. My purpose for beginning the course in such a way is twofold. It provides background information important to understanding drama basics and it allows students to acclimate themselves to peers, my teaching style, and classroom surroundings before "jumping into" acting.

Week One Resources

Whiting, F. M. (1969). *An introduction to the theater.* New York: Harper & Row.

Ommanney, K. (1960). *The stage and the school.* St. Louis: McGraw-Hill Book Co.

Week Two

During the second week, students are introduced to various areas of drama and theater arts such as storytelling, scene design, makeup, costuming, puppetry, filmstrip production, and mime. One of the favorite mime activities involves the students' free choice of a song to which a mime routine is developed and performed. Recent successful routines included Michael Jackson's "Beat It," Culture Club's "Do You Really Want to Hurt Me?" and "Singing in the Rain." Each student selects two of the above drama areas to be included in a project presented to the drama class. Extra credit is given to students who choose to present their projects to the elementary class; most decide to do so.

Weeks Three and Four

For the next two weeks, students spend class time creating and making preparations for the presentation of their projects. A great deal of socializing takes place during this time. Support systems evolve which make presenting projects much easier. For example, a small group may be cutting felt cloth figures for backdrop scenery in a low-keyed atmosphere. Students are not threatened, and they feel free to ask questions that require evaluative responses, e.g., "Does this horse look muscular?" The students are learning to respond candidly, but with sensitivity, e.g., "The horse is beginning to look strong. Have you thought of making a wide curve near the shoulder?"

I may arrange seating for pair activities so that a student with initiative and a positive attitude is adjacent to a withdrawn student. As we all work together, we have discovered the potential for group support, sometimes unobtrusively prearranged as described. My time is spent helping students work on techniques and project media. Some students require encouragement in imaginative thinking, whereas others will need to have their imaginations directed into productive paths.

Students schedule their presentations for one of two predetermined dates. They are required to respond to a self-critique sheet, stating the grade they feel they deserve after the project has been completed and presented. The course content emphasizes each student's ability to evaluate him/herself objectively. Each self-critique contains items such as (a) Did you feel comfortable in front of the audience? (b) Would you feel comfortable in front of a strange audience? (c) What was easiest for you to do in the project? (d) What was the most difficult to do? and (e) What did you learn about yourself? I critique each individual's performance, making sure that my feedback is tactfully delivered and understood by the student. My critique includes items relevant to (a) body posture and gestures, (b) eye contact and facial expression, (c) organization of material, (d) choice of words, (e) vocal expression, and (f) poise and self-control.

Weeks Two, Three, and Four Resources

Corson, R. (1975). *Stage makeup.* Englewood Cliffs, NJ: Prentice-Hall, Inc.

Foley, K., Lud, M., & Power, C. (1981). *The good apple guide to creative drama.* Carthage, IL: Good Apple, Inc.

Gousseff, J. (1974). *Pantomimes 101.* Chicago: Dramatic Publishing.

Hudson Photographic Industries, Inc. (1968). *"U" film.* Irvington-on-Hudson, NY.

McCaslin, N. (1974). *Creative dramatics in the classroom.* New York: David McKay Co.

Nobleman, R. (1979). *Mime and masks.* Rowayton, CT: New Play Books.

Sawyer, R. (1970). *The way of the storyteller.* New York: Viking Press.

Siks, G. B. (1958). *Creative dramatics: An art for children.* New York: Harper & Row.

Stolzenberg, M. (1979). *Exploring mime.* New York: Sterling Publishing Co.

Weeks Five, Six, Seven, and Eight

At this point in the course, I look closely at the group and determine whether these remaining weeks should be spent on acting techniques and activities, or on preparing a short, simple one-act play to be presented to the school. Most of this decision rests on my evaluation of students' abilities in drama, their willingness to perform in front of a large group, and the availability of a play suitable to this group. If the decision is to perform a play, the remaining weeks are spent analyzing the play, reading parts aloud, memorizing lines, designing the set, preparing program handouts, and working on scenes, timing, and line delivery. The latter involves an assortment of activities such as the delivery of a specific line to portray a situation or to convey an emotion. For example: "Oh, I see." (You have just figured out the answer to something.) "Oh, I see." (Convey the emotion of disappointment.) "Yes, but what can you do?" (You are being counseled by someone.) "Yes, but what can you do?" (Convey the emotion of frustration/despair.)

Videotape equipment is used frequently during this phase to acclimate the students to being filmed and give them "reflective" feedback. Students watch videotapes of plays performed by former drama classes to give them an idea of a successful "finished product."

Weeks Five, Six, Seven, and Eight Resources

Catalog of Hard-to-Find Theatre Drama & Communication Arts Resources. (1984–85). Colorado Springs, CO: Contemporary Drama Service.

Dias, E. (1971). *One-act plays for teen-agers.* Boston: Plays, Inc.

Murray, J. (1979). *Fifteen plays for today's teenagers.* Boston: Plays, Inc.

Zapel, T. (1982). *What makes an actor: An introduction to the fundamentals of acting* (Filmstrip). Colorado Springs, CO: Contemporary Drama Service.

If the decision is to work on acting techniques and activities, the remaining weeks are filled with a combination of teacher-made and commercial activities. The class views a filmstrip on making the self-mask. Each student constructs one and uses it during various activities. These self-mask activities are good initial drama experiences for students who are apprehensive. A student can begin acting behind a mask, which enables him or her to hide some nervousness. The students also view a film on acting, and work on timing and line delivery. We play charades, use makeup, act out improvisational situations, and role-play. Writing and performing several duet acts is the final activity.

Weeks Five, Six, Seven, and Eight Additional Resources

Can of Squirms. (1971). Colorado Springs, CO: Contemporary Drama Service.

Gilbert, E. R. (1982). *The self-mask: A filmstrip demonstration of how to construct and use the self-mask.* Colorado Springs, CO: Contemporary Drama Service.

Zapel, T. (1982). *What makes an actor: An introduction to the fundamentals of acting* (Filmstrip). Colorado Springs, CO: Contemporary Drama Service.

SAMPLE OF DRAMA COURSE ACTIVITIES

Selected Drama Notebook Activities

- Discuss the statement "Discipline is essential to creative expression."
- Read one children's story of your choice. Write the title, author's name, and a synopsis of the story to include the theme, plot, and characters.
- Observe an animal, bird, or insect for 10–15 minutes and write your observations. Consider movement, expression, and use of space.
- Provide three observations for each of these feelings: anger, frustration, sadness, elation, and disappointment. For example, if a person is feeling rejected, the head may drop down, the shoulders slump, and the feet shuffle along slowly.
- If you could be an actor/actress anywhere in the world, where would you act? Why?

Accelerated students are challenged with questions such as:

- Why was the Renaissance an exciting era for artists?
- Choose a character from any Shakespeare play. Design the makeup for that actor by filling out a makeup form.
- Discuss the history of the art of storytelling in the old and new world. How were the stories spread throughout the world?

Exercise 1 is entitled "You" and contains 20 items (Siks, 1958), including:

- What would be a good adventure for you today?
- What thoughts cause you to soar high in spirit?
- What smell do you like to smell the most?
- Where is treasure?
- What is a friendly sound at night?

Selected Items from Midterm and Final Quiz

Each test included true-false, fill in the blank, multiple response choice, matching, and short answer items. Among these are:

- True or False: In every being there exists the impulse to play.
- Name three of the five reasons for developing an imagination.
- Circle the five main parts of a story: introduction, plot, theme, conclusion, characterization, climax, setting, style, motivation.
- Identify the stage areas.
- For straight face makeup, show where to apply each.

SUMMARY

Students who have participated in the drama workshop have grown in many ways. They have discovered some of their strengths and weaknesses. Their interactions have improved significantly because they have learned how to offer and receive criticism and support, as well as how to share responsibilities and rewards. Now when they meet major obstacles they know how to reduce them. Many have begun to learn how to enjoy life.

I continually evaluate the program to expand or enrich the drama learning experiences. This article contained material and lesson descriptions from which others can select for their classroom dramas. Teachers need to select materials judiciously to meet each group's "personality," and to select materials with which they are comfortable. Each year I revise and update my drama program. What I have going now in our treatment facility is quite successful for my students and for me.

Staff and friends have asked "What makes your work worthwhile?" My reply is "feedback." We feel ecstatic when standing ovations, words of appreciation, and acknowledgment of success are given. We enjoy receiving comments from younger students, adolescent peers, faculty, and other staff. The feedback is our evaluation of the performance's success.

REFERENCE

Siks, G. (1958). *Creative dramatics and art for children* (pp. 83–84). New York: Harper & Row.

. . . .

Teachers remark that they learn more about pupils in one weekend of camping than in a year in school. Teacher and pupil roles change in an outdoor setting. As Outward Bound has illustrated, adolescent–adult contention is deflected to cooperative efforts in dealing with natural problems in a less familiar environment. Jack Howell is Vice President for Professional Services of the Eckerd Family Youth Alternatives, which operates a system of wilderness camping programs in Florida and the Eastern states. The author explains the intricacies of how camping can serve adolescents. As his summary suggests, camping offers much in addition to learning about bugs and other natural phenomena.

ARTICLE 8.7

Adventure Boosts Empowerment

Jack N. Howell

Adolescent rebellion is not an inevitable phase in human development. She asserts that the power struggle between generations, which seems impossible to avoid, is a result of a patriarchal pecking order in our society which keeps teenagers at the bottom of the chain of command at the very time in their lives when the individuation process and the need for autonomy are at full bore.

When we take a careful look at the issue, it seems clear that parents and adults in general tend to set themselves and the adolescents in their life up for unnecessary battles which, though usually beginning over a relatively insignificant issue, can often escalate into full scale war ultimately resulting in a domestic apocalypse. When such conflict continues to escalate

From *The Journal of Emotional and Behavioral Problems*. (1992). Vol. 1, No. 3. Used with permission.

without intervention, alienated, angry, frustrated youth may run away from home, become delinquent, turn to substance abuse, and/or require psychiatric hospitalization.

While the failure of adults to properly respond to their adolescents' individuation process and autonomy needs is only one of many factors which lead to delinquency, substance abuse, and psychiatric disorders among adolescents, it may be the most common and is certainly the most preventable. The prevention strategy is simple: as adolescents begin to carve out their own space in the world, the adults who have controlled, sustained, and protected them begin to let go. In fact they do more than gradual passive concession; they pro-actively challenge their youth to challenge themselves.

The reflexive reaction of adults who are used to being in charge is to squeeze harder when their charges begin to push the boundaries. This happens in part because adults who have appropriately kept tight reins on their children are unable to adjust quickly enough to the rapid and often instantaneous changes as their children pass into puberty and become adults in process. Teenagers sense instinctively that they are ready for a gradual increase in freedom, autonomy and responsibility. Adults have to be hit over the head with the same realization. Adults often tend to increase their teenager's responsibilities (such as adding more and more household chores) without increasing their autonomy. When teens defy the added expectations, parents assume they cannot handle added autonomy when it is likely that the expectations would have been fulfilled had added autonomy come with the package.

Once adolescents are in crisis and require clinical and/or judicial intervention, the traditional approach is to squeeze even harder, to break their will, to take out the fight, to wear them down into compliance, using rigidly structured behavior modification programs. These programs often appear to be effective with many youth in the short term in the sense that they become "manageable," but at what cost to their self-actualization? This is not to suggest that behaviorally oriented clinical programs don't have their role, but, rather, to say that the attempt to control inappropriate behavior without a component which concurrently addresses the adolescent's need and right to develop autonomy and individuality is doomed to fail.

There is growing momentum in the movement to empower youth as a means of prevention and intervention. The student volunteer movement is spreading rapidly across the country, making community service of some sort a prerequisite for high school graduation. Progressive leaders in youth ministry in many churches are changing the format of their programs from education and entertainment to intergenerational integration and leadership training. While initial results are non-conclusive, it would appear that where adolescents are offered progressively more control over their lives, more input into decisions and policies directly affecting them, more room to risk, and more respect for their evolving beliefs and ideas, they are willing and able to accept more responsibility, achieve more academically, and contribute more to their families and their society. Assuming other factors are conducive to healthy development, it would appear that adolescent rebellion can be avoided or minimized by offering appropriate opportunities for autonomy, individual expression, and responsibility.

This strategy seems equally promising as an intervention with youth already in crisis, once other psychiatric issues, if possible, have been addressed. Empowerment programs such as utilized by the Eckerd Therapeutic Wilderness Camping System, for example, serve to interrupt the cycle of adolescent acting out by offering them the very things they have struggled so violently to achieve. Instead of bearing down harder on residents as they struggle harder and instead of simply letting them go to wreak havoc upon themselves and others, such an adventure offers a third alternative: the opportunity to take control of their lives within an appropriate structure. The structure serves as a wooden frame or mold might serve when cement is being poured. As the soft, malleable character forms and solidifies, the structure is there to offer support. Once the concrete is firm the external supports are extraneous and are removed. Once the program succeeds the structure is removed and the youth is able to utilize autonomy appropriately and become a functional, productive citizen. The structure in this case is composed of the confines and methods of the Eckerd camping program. By removing the youth from their homes and community environments and placing them in therapeutic residential wilderness settings, their potential for inappropriate behavior is limited and the factors of family dynamics and home-peer influences are removed. Then, rather than making the emphasis of the program on rules and restrictions, the focus shifts to challenges and opportunities.

For example, on extended wilderness trips, residents are responsible for meeting many of their own needs. By placing them in a vulnerable position in a sate but uncontrolled environment alien to them and giving them the responsibility for providing for their own comfort and safety, three things occur. First, there is a shift in their own sense of priorities. Other things which previously seemed important to them, issues over which they were willing to fight to any extreme, suddenly seem quite insignificant when their own "perceived" survival is on their shoulders. Then, by being given the challenge of caring for their basic needs, residents experience true autonomy for the first time and realize they have been given what they had been fighting for, yet it wasn't by "fighting" that they gained it and only by cooperation and appropriate behavior will they keep it. Finally, because the role of staff in the camping program is to work side by side with the residents as team-members rather than to direct them as authority figures, the residents begin to learn to trust adults and also are further reinforced in their sense of autonomy and individuality.

This reinforcement by caring adults of the adolescent's newly acquired sense of autonomy must not be minimized or confused with his or her capacity of "knowing" autonomy and translating it into action. In fact, after an empowering river trip (or any other wilderness adventure experience), residents still need help in interpreting the meanings and implications associated with being more fully in charge of their own lives. The understandings that they gain solely from experiencing a "power of life" adventure are simply far from complete and mature. Two secondary extensions help to maximize the academic and therapeutic benefits inherent in the primary adventure: 1) drawing out from the residents the personal learnings associated with the adventure, and 2) exposing residents to the ideas and feelings of others who have also participated in the adventure or who have had a related-type of experience in the past. Both of these secondary experiences extend the first-hand base experience and further strengthen the resident's understanding of his or her own growing independence.

Calling forth and welcoming the residents' personal response is easily achieved by giving them individual time to talk about the experience and to express their ideas and feelings in a variety of ways. This sharing time allows opportunity for the resident to reorder the experience, give it shape, and integrate it into his or her thinking. (It is necessary in this instance to recall that when residents are unable to express their understandings verbally, other avenues of expression must be available to them. e.g., art, music, drama, and writing.) This added "sharing component" complements the "experience component" and further empowers residents who, in the process, also extend and strengthen their personal skills of communication (listening, speaking, writing, reading).

Bathing residents in a wardrobe of language, ideas, and values from others takes them beyond themselves to places that are concerned with persons and their capabilities, capabilities that include being more aware of oneself, of being concerned about things in the world, and of ultimately living more authentically. This sense of additional empowerment is promoted as residents have multiple opportunities to hear the ideas and thinking of their counselor-teachers and peer group members. Through their reactions and responses to one another's ideas, a new dynamic for teaching emerges. Learning is transformed and individual "knowing" is expanded as each group member pays attention to what the other has to say. By comparing and contrasting the variation of personal ideas associated with the primary adventure, residents retrieve alliterative thoughts about success, recognition, and importance, and are exposed to healthy interpretations of power and control. In the process of sharing with one another, residents are influenced as they continue to re-create, clarify, and expand their own personal perspectives. This additional opportunity for reflection represents a vital link to meaning. It is achieved by a two-way process of address and response to what the individual residents and supporting adults have to say about responsibility vs. irresponsibility, about dominance vs. submission, about dependence vs. independence, and, ultimately, about the power of love and compassion. These additional perspectives serve as springboards for ever-widening knowledge and give residents options as they try them out in the course of real life challenges and human interactions.

The Eckerd camping system pays attention to adolescents' desire and need for greater independence and responsibility. It recognizes that they demand to be treated as adults and that they want and need control over significant portions of their lives. This gaining of independence is, therefore, central in planning for the residents' needs. We believe that there is no easy substitute for primary wilderness experiences (ones that do not require reading and writing to be successful) for providing the raw material or launching pad for empowering young people. The experiences refresh and heighten their consciousness so they see the things they look at and hear the things they listen to in interaction with environments rather than in detachment from them. We also believe that caring adults and peers must be readily available to residents so that sharing of experience is facilitated. We recognize that exercises and workbooks are poor substitutes for the "acts" of listening, speaking, singing, dancing, and writing out of experience and within real communication settings. When these efforts are further supported by bringing residents in contact with the wide range of literature that is available, residents discover new dimensions of selfhood and confirm and extend existence in relationship to others.

Pro-actively empowering adolescents in these ways requires adult leaders within the camping system who are sensitive to developmental needs and individual differences among residents, and it entails providing structure when needed and decreasing it when it stifles growth. Empowering young people in the "Eckerd Way" involves both caring adults and peers encouraging one another to open environments that open the world. It involves working and talking together so that experiences and the words are exchanged, for it is experience and shared words that are integral and indispensable parts of the process of teaching fuller understanding. It is in sharing that the door is open and the resident discovers new dimensions of his or her own emerging independent selfhood and is simultaneously awakened to a sense of interdependence with others.

How significant it seems then to recognize that the individual adolescent has something to contribute! What an opportunity exists for the resident in the dialogue with peers! How encouraging and powerful when counselor-teachers are deeply acquainted with residents and committed to creating conditions and experiences for them that foster human interaction, personal accountability, and boosts of empowerment.

REFERENCES

Loughmiller, C. (1965). *Wilderness road.* Austin, TX: Hogg Foundation for Mental Health.

Schaef, A.W. (1987). *When society become an addict.* Cambridge: Harper and Row.

Schorr, L.B. (1988). *Within our reach: Breaking the cycle of disadvantage.* New York: Doubleday.

. . . .

For most of us, trying new curriculum ideas and methods involves risk. There are many barriers to overcome, especially in rule-bound settings. Each of us has to ask, "How much risk capital do I possess?" Schools are reluctant to depart from the most traditional, even though the traditional has failed our troubled students. At the same time outcome studies indicate that, in spite of higher costs, we are still not doing well with troubled pupils. Critics continue to point to low graduation rates, failures in employment, and a low quality of adult life as the destiny of too many troubled students. The accepted remedy has been to demand higher standards, seek more traditional therapy (which is not available), and ignore the therapeutic potential of a reinvigorated curriculum.

It is not always easy to be a lone innovator. Teachers need to collaborate, discuss their efforts, and evaluate new ventures. It is a good idea to start in an area of natural talent and comfort. Try setting aside one time during the week for experimenting with new curriculum methods. Team up with a colleague for exchanging ideas. Above all, consult with and share your intent with the youngsters themselves. They can be the staunchest of allies once they are assured that there are many ways to learn skills and acquire knowledge. Students need assurance that they will not fall further behind when less traditional approaches are employed. Pupils need to participate in discussions of what curriculum is crucial for them. A simplified explanation of metacognition serves to clarify that all pupils do not learn in the same way and that the mastery of different tasks anticipates variant processes. Curriculum method is the core of school-based efforts to help troubled students, although the teacher is the advocate for a full-service program, the elements of which have been described in this book.

So much depends on the professional character of the teacher. We come with a set of beliefs about good teaching and how students should respond, and then we face troubled students. The reflective teacher discovers that we learn about teaching as we teach and make sense of what transpires. Teaching is a profession for entrepreneurs.

9

Beyond the School: Enhancing Family Support

The school has an anonymous role in relating to students' families. Increasing diversity characterizes family patterns found in students' homes. Schools seldom relate to families as such. Even in two-parent families, the "mother" usually is the only contact. With increasing frequency, this contact is done by a surrogate for the biological mother—a grandmother, stepmother, or foster mother. Thus, a teacher must learn to relate to a wide variety of family patterns that go far beyond personally familiar or traditional patterns. Ethnic and cultural variations must also be considered.

We know that family and school collaboration is as necessary as it is difficult. Many of the program descriptions using traditional efforts turn out to be on-paper-only when closely examined. They enlist euphemistic hopes rather than reality. When one listens to parents' actual experiences, one hears tales of unbelievable bureaucratic obstinacy. Evidence of teacher–pupil–parent unity finally brings hope to some overwhelmed parents. We know that family participation is crucial in supporting troubled students. It is therefore mandatory that we search out new approaches to involve families. We must continue to explore effective ways to relate to families, recognizing the wide variety of family structures and circumstances of our youngsters before the start and after the end of each school day. The day when families could be scapegoats for school failures has long since passed, and has been replaced by the goal of helping to restore whatever family function we can.

Regarding special education, families have legal rights but not legal responsibilities. Schools have responsibilities. Schools are sometimes guilty of trying to dominate parents, but parents have the right of veto over any school proposal. Parents are the final arbiters, even to the point of taking court action.

The role of the family in work with troubled children has now made a complete cycle: the emphasis has rotated from the family as the cause of the student's problems to the family as the best source of the solution to the student's problems. Current family literature is permeated with family preservation doctrines. Wraparound family and student services are considered essential.

There are several reasons for this change. First, it is evident that substitutes for the family child-raising function are very difficult and very expensive to accomplish, especially for troubled youngsters. Witness the risks of foster placements and the special care required for adoptions, when such alternatives are deemed necessary and are available. The reason is the fundamental psychological attachment a child develops to his or her generic roots as the source of identity. The youngster seeks or invents explanations when the generic family does not provide its expected support functions. Sometimes, resentment becomes a core theme. In some "Million-dollar cases" on record, a lavish sequence of services has been provided for a youngster to no avail because the family did not change to provide the anchor of concern.

Second, replacing the family with professional or even quasi-professional personnel costs society a great deal of money because the natural family is a volunteer agency. Thus, it is economically as well as psychologically astute to invest maximum resources in family support and preservation. The change in ideology from family as cause to family as cure does not mean the task of family restoration has become any easier. It just means that we must try harder and in more diverse ways. The commonly used term *dysfunctional family* has to be reexamined. In what specific way is it dysfunctional? What family supports are needed if a given family is expected to become functional? Support can range from a critical piece of psychological advice on child-raising to an intensive crisis wraparound team being available 24 hours a day.

Each student is unique in the kind of support he or she needs from the family. Some children survive and become resilient in a chaotic family. Others feel abuse and rejection where there is none. The study of individual child vulnerability/resilience and family systems has not yet advanced to a point of prediction, and the family is only one of the support systems that a child needs. For example, the school can provide the student with compensatory developmental support and become part of the solution rather than add to the problem. As the African proverb goes, "It takes a whole village to raise a child."

Overall, the family support systems for troubled students have been weak except in brochure descriptions. A bonding of family and program in a unified effort for the student does happen but is not typical. Even educational programs with significant mental health components have difficulty in maintaining positive and reciprocal relationships with parents, and, if the families have serious multiple problems, there are few settings with adequate resources for them. In preparation for the readings on this topic, we identify five reasons why schools have difficulties when they try to reach out to be helpful to families.

1. Many efforts still rest in a nostalgic fantasy about the nature of the American family, which never was and certainly is not now. We need a realistic base for considering assistance, as Bronfenbrenner has so well documented. Otherwise, fantasy about families produces fantasy assistance. The child-raising process has been drastically altered to fit current cultural conditions. Primary changes have arisen in the number of mothers working outside the home, the high divorce rate, single parent families, and poverty.

2. Family preservation is not easy to provide. Families have power and are inviolate in our system. They may refuse cooperation even if help is offered with empathy and caring. Unless declared legally neglectful or abusive, a family retains the right to go an independent way. Establishing provable neglect or abuse is an invasive, complex, and time-consuming task. Sometimes, the goal of preservation (establishing a reasonably stable family) may be too high. We must try at least to mitigate the stresses because minor improvement can often result in making an impossible situation tolerable.

3. Frequently, the professionals who conceive and conduct the family liaison programs lack the necessary sensitivity and empathy for the real family circumstance because of their own vastly different life experience. Studies show that families see many help givers as arrogant peddlers of unrealistic advice. Parent conferences that are missed because of a lack of transportation may be labeled "resistance to discuss the issue." Parents see little interest in accommodating the meetings to their schedule, providing child care during conference time, or arranging for more convenient locations. To the school personnel, meetings are part of the job, and it is easy to forget that attendance often requires a parent to take time away from a job, get a sitter, and/or arrange transportation. The list of parents' complaints reminds us that schools can do many things to improve family communication, ranging from attitudinal factors to convenient hours. Teachers find that moving conference locations to the home is in some cases much appreciated and, in others, a resented intrusion. Only by listening to parents' stories of their difficulties and frustrations in trying to help a troubled student will teachers tap into the empathy required to be useful.

4. Often, a child's difficulty, although central to the school, is peripheral to a family struggling just to survive. The son got into a fight, yes, but the rent is overdue. Is the teacher supposed to solve the family financial problem? Is the parent supposed to become highly involved in the son's aggression?

Seldom does a family face a single difficulty: there is usually an accumulation of difficulties. For increasing numbers of families, the issue is the overpowering problem of poverty or marginal income in a society of advertised glut materialism. For these families, the problem is bread, not bicycles. It is getting the plumbing fixed, not a room for each kid. It is plain, sturdy shoes for a youngster who lives in the world of Reeboks. Health and dental care have to wait.

5. There is finally a growing recognition that the school, when functioning by itself, usually cannot generate family preservation. Granted, work with the family is primary—it is a community responsibility that requires the resources of all community agencies in collaboration, from those providing welfare and health to those engaged in job training. This total collaborative push has fostered the growth of full-service schools (FSS)—local schools where community service agencies have representation on the school campus, and the total needs of pupils and their families are considered. Several states have strong developments of this nature. Needed services are defined with the family and subsequently monitored and evaluated by a case advocate. Teachers, especially those of troubled students and special students, had best become advocates for FSS's more rational and thorough approach for meeting the needs of families. Because schools are where the students are, they are the natural places to focus local child and family services.

Helping families of troubled students, though essential, is far from easy. Usually, the school is a natural channel and the teacher is the logical first contact when problems arise. Teachers are assisting parents by providing nonpejorative communication, consultation, crisis help, and parent meetings. As we see, especially in the workings of preschool special education programs where the family IEP replaces a child IEP, joint home and school participation can be one of the most binding forces in human relationships. Liaison is more difficult to achieve as the child grows older. Most families wish the best for their offspring and are willing to sacrifice to that end. They want to learn how to be more effective. The role of the teacher is not to imply or state parental blame.

 School–Home Communication by Magnusson and McCarney is a frank discussion of the reality of collaboration between teacher and parent, grounded as it is in legal statutes. Both authors are professors at the University of Missouri, Columbia. McCarney is coordinator of programs for the behavior-disordered; Magnusson is coordinator of programs for the orthopedically handicapped/multihandicapped. The authors explain the negative effects of "problem-only" communication from school to parent. As one mother said, "It is so nice to be called about a success for once." Magnusson and McCarney go beyond theory to present specific forms to use in establishing positive parent relationships.

ARTICLE 9.1

School–Home Communication
A POSITIVE-CONTACT APPROACH

Clifford J. Magnusson and Stephen B. McCarney

Successful school-to-home communication can be accomplished by reaching out to parents in ways that demonstrate respect, consideration, and sincere desire for cooperation. Examples of mutually beneficial activities include: open houses, newsletters from school, parent-teacher conferences, and informal contacts made when parents visit classes or when teachers see parents in the community.

Unfortunately, parent-teacher communication often originates with a problem situation. Therefore, both parents and educators are likely to feel threatened and ill at ease. A much more promising approach to school-home relations is to establish *positive contacts* on a planned, continuous basis. This article describes a systematic, positive contact approach, incorporating six communication devices: (1) letter of introduction; (2) information memo; (3) student progress report; (4) appointment form; (5) parent communication record; and (6) report card communication. The purpose and rationale for the use of each of these positive contact strategies will be presented.

LETTER OF INTRODUCTION

Purpose

- To establish an important early contact between the teacher and the parents of students entering her classroom

Rationale

- Gives the school the opportunity to take the initiative in developing a positive contact
- Demonstrates an interest in the student and the family
- Marks the beginning of a personal relationship
- Provides a stimulus for a reciprocal contact by the parents
- Guarantees one positive contact

From *The Pointer*. (1980). Vol. 25, No. 1. Reprinted with permission.

February 5, 1980

Mr. and Mrs. Parent
360 Learner Road
Scholar, MO 65201

Dear Mr. and Mrs. Parent:

I'm looking forward to having Charles in my class this year. Our curriculum for class gives us the opportunity to use Unit instruction in the student's interest areas along with providing the three R's. This year we're planning two field trips and there'll be some additional emphasis on career education. People from the community will be invited in to tell us about their career choices.

I'll be sending additional information as the year progresses.

I hope you'll feel free to call me if you have questions or suggestions regarding our program for this year.

Sincerely,

Ima Teacher

P. S. If there is anything about Charles that would help me know him better or better work with him, please share it with me.

- -
(cut and return)
Dear Ima Teacher: _____

_____

INFORMATION MEMO

Purpose

- To communicate necessary information parents often request from the school and/or teacher; can accompany the initial letter of introduction

Rationale

- Offers a reference for pertinent information
- Provides information regarding the most commonly asked questions at the beginning of the school year
- Satisfies a need most parents have to be informed about basic school and classroom information

---

Dear Mr. and Mrs. Parent:

I thought you might be interested in the following information:

Teacher:	Ima Teacher
Principal:	R. A. Principal
School:	New Educator Elementary
	Educator Avenue
	442-3871
Building hours:	8:00 a.m. - 4:30 p.m.
Student's schedule:	8:45 a.m. - 3:15 p.m.
Room:	105
Number of students:	31 (16 boys, 15 girls)
Lunch period:	12:00 - 12:30 p.m.
School lunch:	65¢
Drinks:	20¢ (included with lunch)

Our class uses the *Weekly Reader* ($1.25 per student per year)

Typical materials students need include: tissue, ruler, looseleaf notebook, pencils, apron (paint shirt)

Needed: Room Mothers and Fathers for special class activities; volunteers to accompany class on field trips

Please let me know if you want to help. Call me at school (442-3871) or at home (474-3939).

STUDENT PROGRESS REPORT

Purpose

- To provide the parents with one or more informal positive communications—following the initial contact and before the first conference on report cards—concerning their child's behavior, academic performance or other current information

Rationale

- Provides an opportunity for more frequent communication regarding progress
- Affords an additional opportunity to reinforce progress
- Builds on a positive communication process and encourages interaction
- Offers an opportunity for early identification of special needs

Dear Mr. and Mrs. Parent: Date_____

You can be proud of

Dear Mr. and Mrs. Parent: Date_____

You can be proud of _____

(s)he is having real success _____

_____

_____
Teacher's Signature

If you have any questions or comments please write them here and return this form (or call me at 442-3741).

_____

_____

_____

_____

_____

_____

_____

_____

_____

APPOINTMENT FORM

Purpose

- To facilitate arrangement of conferences or meetings and to provide specific background information to help parents understand the purpose of the meeting

Rationale

- Helps teachers to be specific about the reasons for a meeting
- Provides parents with a reason or reasons for a meeting
- Avoids creating unnecessary parental anxiety

Dear Mr. and Mrs. Parent:

I'd like to meet with you regarding:

    report cards   projects

    improvements I've seen   a problem for which
                                  I need your help

    other: _____

Specific Information: _____

_____

_____

_____

_____

_____

_____

_____

Would you please indicate a time and place we could meet to talk about this?

times   days   places

_____   _____   _____

_____   _____   _____

_____   _____   _____

- Permits parents to prepare for the meeting
- Promotes the exchange of information

PARENT COMMUNICATION RECORD

Purpose

- To facilitate record keeping and to document parent-teacher contacts regarding the child's educational experience

Rationale

- Provides a record of all meetings
- Offers continuity in the communication process
- Serves as a ready record for both short-term and long-term progress
- Promotes teacher accountability
- Documents responsible professional behavior

Teacher: _____   Date: _____   Grade or Level: _____

Parent(s): _____   Student: ____   Type of Class: _____

Other School Personnel: _____   _____

I. Type of Communication: Letter ____ Note ___ Telephone _____

    Parent Visit to School _____ Teacher Visits to Home _____

    Out of School Location _____   Other _____

II. Initiation of Communication: School Scheduled Meeting _____

    Teacher Initiation ____ Parent Initiation ___ Other _____

III. Nature of Communication: Information Sharing _____

Progress Update _____   Problem Identification _____

Other _____

IV. Communication Summary (Copies of Written Communication Should
    be Attached):

    _____

    _____

V.   Expectations for Further Communications: _____

    _____

    _____

    _____

    _____

    _____

REPORT CARD COMMUNICATION

Purpose

- To respond to the criticism that "the report card is just not enough" to describe school progress

Rationale

- Helps the teacher prepare to discuss each student's progress
- Provides parents with documentation of all past communications
- Indicates a present level of performance
- Expands on and personalizes the report card date
- Provides an opportunity for sharing anticipated intervention strategies

In addition to the positive contact strategies suggested for classroom teacher use, school districts can creatively develop a variety of activities to enhance school-home communication. The following examples of activities were generated by the Columbia Public Schools, Columbia, Missouri, during the past year.

Student: _____   Teacher: _____ Date: _____

Parents: _____ _____

Areas of most progress:

Areas of success:

Areas of concern:

Proposed Intervention:

Parent Comments:

Columbia School District Newsletter: Published four times yearly; contains general information about the School District; mailed to parents.

Activities Line: A telephone number to be called to learn details of activities sponsored by the Columbia Public Schools.

Shopping Center Visits: School District officials set up an information booth on five or six Saturdays per year in one of two enclosed malls; a different topic is emphasized each time, e.g., reading, mathematics, vocational education; parents and other citizens can ask questions concerning the topic of emphasis or any other topic.

Radio Show: Following each Board of Education meeting, a member of the Board appears on Dial 1400, a news information program, to discuss the actions of the Board at the previous night's meeting.

Board of Education Meetings: The Board of Education encourages individuals and groups to attend Board meetings; individuals in the audience are permitted to speak on the issues being discussed by the Board.

Letters and Handbooks to Parents: Each secondary school sends a letter and a new handbook to parents in August preceding the opening of school each year; the handbook contains information, including rules and regulations.

Class Newsletters: Several classes in the elementary schools send home monthly newsletters containing information about C1355 activities.

Grandparent Days: Each elementary school sponsors a Grandparents' Day; children invite their grandparents or other older citizens to accompany them to school for a special day of activities.

Surveys: Each year a random sample of parents and other citizens are surveyed by the School District to determine feelings and attitudes on important school-related issues.

Parent and Senior Citizen Volunteers: Between three hundred and four hundred parent and senior citizen volunteers serve the schools in some capacity: their active involvement acquaints the volunteers more thoroughly with the school program, and they serve as information givers in the community.

Coffee with the Principal: Many elementary and secondary principals schedule monthly coffees at the school and invite the parents to come for a visit and to bring their questions.

The means are available to communicate with parents and provide them with opportunities to respond. Educators can be optimistic about facilitating the communication process. By planning for positive contacts, communication with parents can become a valuable and informative experience.

. . . .

For two-thirds of our students, a single-parent family is the expectation for some part of their growing up—and the ratio is increasing. For high-risk and troubled students, the figure is even higher. Myra Olson, of the University of South Dakota, speaks from both personal and professional experience in her discussion of strategies to help single-parent families. Because she has been in receiving and producing roles in teacher and parent exchanges, she is in a position to dispel common myths concerning the impact that having only one functioning parent has on children. At least two consequences derive from reading this article: (a) there will be a cleansing of the stereotypes about one-parent families that most of us have hidden somewhere in our belief systems; and (b) the author provides not only sensitivity to the situation but suggests specific teacher strategies to support both parents and children in these families.

ARTICLE 9.2

Five Ways Teachers Can Help Children from Single-Parent Families

Myrna R. Olson

My interest in single-parent families grew out of my own experience as a single parent. I also have conducted research that included interviews with more than 30 other single parents. The strategies offered in this article

From *The Journal of Emotional and Behavioral Problems*. (1993). Vol. 2, No. 4. Reprinted with permission.

came out of my personal experience, the interview data, and my own conviction that schools need to make some adjustments to meet the needs of children from single-parent homes.

MAKE NO ASSUMPTIONS

While many studies have sought to compare the behavior and well-being of children from intact homes with those from single-parent homes, none are conclusive. Recent family research emphasizes that family behavior determines a child's self-concept, not family structure. Furthermore, there is clear evidence that income, not family structure, is responsible for many of the differences seen between these two groups of children. Finally, we know that children tend to see themselves, and consequently act, in ways consistent with the expectations of people important to them.

While single parent families may seem to have more problems than "traditional" families, it is important to remain open-minded when one searches for an explanation to problems children are having. One mother in my study related the following to me:

> My son was four years old and had been enrolled in a local preschool program. After two weeks of tears, I went in to discuss his unhappiness with the director. My son's explanation for his unhappiness was that he was there with the "babies." I mentioned this to the director, and she told me that the time slot I had chosen for my son happened to be for 18-month to three-year-old children. However, she felt certain his needs were being accommodated within the program. She then told me that if my son was unhappy, she was confident it related to my recent divorce from his father. I was furious with her lack of sensitivity and disappointed that an expert in early childhood education could overlook the importance of socialization with same-age peers.

Teachers are very important to children. It is imperative that teachers not stigmatize children for residing in single-parent homes. A good beginning is for teachers not to use the term "broken home" when referring to the homes of these children. "Broken" implies that something is defective, not to be valued, and even discarded.

Every child from a single-parent home is unique and comes from a unique set of circumstances. *Just* a few dimensions on which single parents differ are the following: 1) reason for single parenting (that is, death of spouse, prolonged separation, divorce, abandonment, never married, single adoption); 2) time elapsed since becoming a single parent; 3) number of children and their respective ages and personalities; 4) age and personality of parent; 5) relationship with other parent, if alive; 6) financial situation; 7) occupational demands; 8) experiences from family of origin and family of construction; 9) self-esteem and attitude; and 10) support received from family, friends, and institutions.

Obviously, there is no single template for understanding or making assumptions about children from single-parent families. It is imperative that teachers remain open-minded about all children—affirming and supporting them for who they are.

TEACHING ABOUT DIFFERENCE

At the beginning of each school year, it is important to teach a unit on difference. Such a unit will set a background for discussing that there are many ways of being in the world—including the kind of family structure within which one lives.

Teachers must model acceptance of difference and give examples of it. With respect to single-parent families, it is important to acknowledge that not everyone has a mom and a dad living in the home. Children must be given opportunities to talk about and write about their families. Teacher-selected books that feature different kinds of family structures might be shared with children at this time.

Preschool/Elementary

- Williams, V. B. (1982). *A chair for my mother*. New York: HarperCollins.

  Child lives with mother and grandmother.

- Steele, D. (1989). *Martha's new daddy*. New York: Bantam.

  Child of divorced parents experiences remarriage of her mother.

- Christiansen, C. B. (1989). *My mother's house. My father's house.* New York: Penguin Books.

  Parents are divorced and child lives with both.

- MacLachlan, P. (1985). *Sarah, plain and tall*. New York: HarperCollins.

  Two children anticipate the remarriage of their father after their mother dies.

Junior/Senior High

- Wilson, B. (1988). *Breakdown*. New York: Scholastic Books.

  Two children experience a change in their father after their mother dies.

- Klein, N. (1972). *Mom, the wolfman and me*. New York: Avon Books.

  A girl whose mother never married deals with the change in her life as her mother becomes serious about a man.

- Klein, N. (1988). *Now that I know*. New York: Bantam Books.

  A young girl living with both parents after a divorce deals with each parent having a new partner.

- Paterson, K. (1988). *Park's quest*. New York: Puffin Books.

A young man searches for information on his own when his mother refuses to talk about his father, who died in the Vietnam War.

Finally, at gift-making time, teachers have the opportunity to introduce the concept of "who is special" to each child. By encouraging children to share who the special people in their lives are, the focus on moms and dads is somewhat broadened. Children should subsequently be allowed to make the number of gifts they deem appropriate.

FACILITATING PARENTAL CONNECTION TO THE SCHOOL

We all know that it is in the best interest of children to have their teachers communicate effectively with their parents. Many single parents have limited financial resources and are unable to provide food or money for school activities. Furthermore, their jobs may preclude them from volunteering in the classroom or from attending conferences at assigned times. Unless a teacher is aware of such difficulties, he or she may interpret the single parent's lack of involvement as disinterest in the child's education.

A phone call made to every parent at the beginning of each school year will provide a valuable link to all parents. It is possible that a single parent can come in and share a hobby, chaperone a field trip, or assist with a party. On the other hand, it is important to find out that a parent's schedule will not accommodate traditional ways of being involved with schools. It is possible that even the parent-teacher conference will have to be accomplished over the telephone to allow for a single parent's particular set of circumstances. The purpose of phone conversations is to help the parent feel a connection to the teacher, to the school, and to the child's education within the school. The parent must feel valued regardless of his or her ability to be physically present in the school.

A child who has lost a parent by death may need increased support on the anniversary date of that parent's death. The parents I interviewed appreciated teachers who asked for this information and were prepared before the school year got under way.

SHARING GOOD NEWS WITH PARENTS

When our son, Nathan, started kindergarten, there were custodial proceedings still taking place. As his father and I sat down with his kindergarten teacher at the end of the first reporting period, the air "dripped" with tension. The teacher's first remark was, "I realize that the two of you are probably not very comfortable being here, considering all that you have been going through. I appreciate that you both came and must begin by complimenting you. Nathan is a very happy, well-adjusted little boy. Despite your differences, you have both obviously done something right!" The tension in that room was immediately reduced. She had affirmed us as parents and told us that something was going well in our otherwise difficult lives. It is rare that teachers cannot find a single good thing to say to parents. I think it is fair to say that most of us do not set out to be ineffective parents, though we may make mistakes along the way.

ALTERING WRITTEN COMMUNICATION AND RECORD KEEPING

Without teachers realizing it, children from single parent families often suffer discomfort related to written notices and school records. There are two situations responsible for the discomfort.

Often, only the custodial parent receives report cards, school bulletins, and letters written to parents. This practice not only causes stress for the parents but also puts the child in the middle of his or her parents. When the custodial parent and the noncustodial parent do not get along, the child often is made responsible for keeping both parents informed about school events and progress reports. Teachers can alleviate any problems in this area by simply sending all written communication to everyone who parents a child.

The school directory is another potential source of trouble for children from single-parent homes. These children may have names different from those of their parents, and they often have parents living at different addresses and responding at different phone numbers. A simple remedy for teachers is to request that the office send out forms with ample space for listing custodial and noncustodial parents or two parents who share custody equally but reside apart. The school directory (which often is compiled from these forms) can then designate biological parents with a star and custodial parents with an underline—giving all pertinent addresses and phone numbers for each. Again, allowing parents to feel valued, regardless of their custodial status, can serve to enhance the lives of their children.

If we want to advocate for children from single-parent families and nurture their emotional well-being, we must first *make no assumptions about these children.* Further, it is important to *teach children about difference,* to subsequently help children understand different types of families, and to model acceptance of those families. Teachers are in a position *to facilitate parental connection to the school* by arranging for conferences and school visits that are scheduled around work and child-care obligations. Too often parents hear from teachers only when children are doing poorly. It is crucial that teachers *share good news about children* as well. Finally, parents will feel more valued by the school if teachers try to *alter written communication and recordkeeping.* This means sending all school correspondence to everyone who parents a child and making school directories that properly acknowledge these individuals as well.

. . . .

Aggressive students comprise a large segment of a school's troubled population. Their parents are especially complex for teachers to assist: consequently, the parents are often recipients of nothing but blame. John Mordock is the assistant executive director of Astor House and child guidance centers in Duchess County, New York. He has extensive direct clinical knowledge of both aggressive children and their parents. Mordock has examined the parental dynamics that are common in families with aggressive children. The parents often come from families that failed them, leaving a residue of strong need to be nurtured themselves. Angry marital disputes are not resolved, and the child may become a third party in the role of scapegoat. Although these parents often hold reasonable values, their intentions are not joined to appropriate parental behavior. Low parental self-esteem results in anger against children and then in ineffective punishment. Parents may see their aggressive children as monsters. Mordock further indicates a failure of bonding; the parents do not feel close to the children. Family life becomes chaotic, driven by unrealistic expectations and denial (Mordock, 1988).

In the following article, Mordock describes family dynamics to provide strategies for working with these often strongly resistant parents. The significance of the processes advocated by Mordock is that they are based on the family dynamics he has presented but do not require the teacher to become therapeutically entwined in the parents' lives, which would be a low-yield option. Knowing about the dynamics of parents of aggressive students is essential for a teacher; assuming the role of family therapist (unless adequately trained) is not a teacher's option. The author is particularly relevant in discussing crisis meetings, because a teacher is easily seduced into trying to work through conflicts that would require next-to-impossible personality changes. Even as he describes the dynamic aspects, this author is not neglectful of possible biological components in aggressive behavior.

ARTICLE 9.3

Working with Parents of Aggressive Children

PRINCIPLES AND TECHNIQUES FOR INTERVENTION

John B. Mordock

In Part 1 of this presentation (Mordock, 1988c), we described parents of aggressive children as having the following characteristics: unfulfilled dependency needs, low self-esteem, bonding failure, disturbed identity formation, cognitive immaturity, denied affects, chaotic lifestyles, and social isolation. Each characteristic needs to be addressed in any plan to engage these parents in treatment designed to free their child from being enmeshed in the

From *The Pointer*. (1988). Vol. 33, No. 1. Reprinted with permission.

parents' problems. The child can then respond positively to educational efforts.

Although eliciting the cooperation of families or engaging them in counseling is a major problem in special educational programs for aggressive children, almost no literature exists in the special education field to guide the psychoeducational staff in how to do this. Parents' problems can seem overwhelming to clinicians. Without guidelines to assist them in setting realistic goals for clients and for themselves, they are subject to burnout, resulting in lowered self-concept, dehumanizing attitudes toward clients, and increasing inflexibility. Such clients rarely, if ever, give positive feedback to the counselor about their progress, a factor contributing heavily to burnout.

This article will attempt to fill the void previously mentioned and provide special educators and counseling support staff with a philosophy and specific procedures designed to optimize the engagement effort. The format is modeled after Stanton and Todd (1981), who set forth principles for engaging families of drug abusers. The material is divided into various content areas. Within each of these areas, one or more principles are set forth. Although every rule has its exception, these tenets have been arrived at after multiple failures in one of the Office of Mental Health's first licensed day treatment programs for emotionally disturbed children in New York State. Interagency discussions between day treatment staff and the staff of the Duchess County Board of Cooperative Educational Services, which also runs classes for aggressive children, indicate that these principles can also be applied in less intensive psychoeducational treatment settings.

STYLE OF INTERVENTION

Educational staff members need to be sensitive to parents' needs for self-determination. These parents have had "advice" and direction from others all their lives. Their experiences of being in control are limited. A nonjudgmental, nonintimidating attitude is essential in initial efforts to engage such parents. This brings us to our first principle.

Initially emphasize collaboration. The parents are asked for their help in understanding the child and in helping school staff to attend to their child's needs. Feedback from parents indicates positive reception to counseling efforts that are viewed as collaborative.

Ask for their help before and immediately upon enrollment. The closer the counselor's first contact with the parent is to the time of enrollment, the greater are the chances for involving the family, even when meaningful involvement may actually occur much later. Many children placed in classes for the disturbed are in crisis prior to placement. Once the placement has occurred, the family often feels the problem is resolved. Magical thinking prevails. If your contact is delayed, the parent may think that you are handling the problem—"Why ask for my help now after you've had my child for three months?"

The counselor must be accessible and dependable. The counselor must pursue the parents regularly through home visits, phone calls, letters, and invitations to the school (Stanton & Todd, 1981). The contact must be *personalized.* Such parents are unforgettably impressed by particular incidents that appear to them as beyond the call of duty. Birthday cards, get well cards, and visits to parents when they are sick can help them feel that someone cares. A rather dramatic example of personal involvement occurred when a child in treatment died and the counselor attended the child's funeral. A breakthrough in the family's resistance happened, and the counselor was able to help the parents deal with other problem children in the family. But don't expect them to feel grateful for such efforts. Expressing grateful feelings interferes with the parents' need to express anger, and this need will remain strong for some time; otherwise, they choke on their own rage.

INITIAL PHASES OF COUNSELING

Accept the parents where they are. If the parents blame you or the school, listen to these accusations. Don't defend yourself or other school staff— such a response merely escalates parental anger or precipitates their flight. Listening to the parents is the first step. No one has listened long enough for them to feel understood and for their anger to subside. Take responsibility for their anger—"You're right; we should have been more careful with Jimmy. Maybe he was upset because we kept him from gym; perhaps that was a mistake on our part." Many of these parents have never heard anyone in their life acknowledge a mistake or apologize to them. Even if you didn't err, say you did so. The same techniques that work well with aggressive children work well with aggressive parents—"I must have given you the wrong problems today, Bill; I'm sorry. Here. Let's try these." (Teacher substitutes easier problems for ones a child has angrily thrown to the floor.) "I'm sorry, Mrs. Jones, for the transportation problem; I must have relayed the wrong information to the transportation department."

If the parents say the child is to blame, listen to that, too. Revenge begins early. The three-year-old whose father forgets to bring him a desired object from work retaliates by refusing to let his father carry him up to bed, stating, "I want Mommy to do it." (Friedrich & Boriskin, 1976). One mother laments that every night she makes a special dinner for her teenage son, turns back his bed, and lays out clean, ironed clothes for his next day. Yet her son repeatedly stays out late, often never comes home, and never acknowledges her for these efforts. Mike Tyson, current heavyweight champion of the world, talks of the degree of hatred and indifference between a child and his parents:

> If a kid knew his mom was going out with money and didn't want to steal it
> himself, he'd tell me where she was going, what time. I'd wait for her and
> rob her, then we'd split it. (Smith, 1988, p. 74)

Accept the parents' explanations for their problems and acknowledge
their difficulties. Angyal (1965, p. 18) says that we only come to life by
being understood and acknowledged by someone else. The worst punishment is to be unnoticed by everyone.

Reduce demands upon parents to achieve control of the child. Achieving control of their child's aggression is a long-term goal of parents. Early
efforts at control can result in stronger hostility toward the child. Behavior
modification techniques suggested too soon can be used inappropriately on
the child and then later rejected because "I've tried that already." In addition, the inappropriate use is experienced negatively by the child, and he
escalates his anger at the parent and at program staff, who he knows gave
his parents the misused approach.

*Avoid initiating interactions between family members that can create
additional conflict.* Do not encourage expression of emotionally charged
issues or conflict resolution between family members. Listen to their views
about these conflicts, identify them as problems, but don't bring family
members together in an effort to resolve these difficulties. Encouraging family members to interact around highly charged issues may release destructive behavior of intolerable proportions (Weitzman, 1985). These families
are not necessarily committed to working through conflict with one another
for the sake of more adaptive family functioning. They are more likely to be
seeking to establish a prior level of functioning or distance from the problem. Escalating the conflict further causes even more erosion of the equilibrium (Weitzman, 1985).

*Remember that the parent's psychological equilibrium is intimately tied
to the child's sick role.* Allow the parent to project blame onto the child.
Use a symptom-oriented approach and help organize the parents or other
family members around the child's symptoms. Pittman (1982, p. 366) remarks, "Therapists know better than to side with the battered child, since
the battering parent already respects the love and sympathy given the
child."

Both the parents and the child are unduly sensitive to criticism. Because the child has internalized destructive aspects of his parent's personality, he experiences both rage and loyalty at the family. If the child feels
that the staff blames his parents, the child is likely to try and defend them.
Weitzman (1985) presents the case of a nine-year-old boy who set a therapist's car on fire because he thought his treatment team was too critical
of his depressed father. The children do not merely react to a distressed
family system, but they also act on the system as well, sometimes destruc-
tively, even after parents start improving.

Use life cycle explanations to reduce their self-blame. Every family
experiences stress at various stages in family life. Explain that their troubles

result from these normal stresses—"It's no wonder you have these problems, considering your son's approaching adolescence." "Your unemployment makes things difficult." "You never learned how to parent from your parents." "You expect too much from yourself at this time in your life." "Considering your background, you've done quite well."

Confront the unrealistic self-ideal. Discuss the cultural myths that unrealistically guide much of the parents' thinking. Work on their unrealistic "shoulds."

Acknowledge their good parenting efforts. "It was a good parental decision allowing your child to come to school here." "You presented your views of your child well to members of the Committee on Special Education." Help build feelings of self-confidence. Acknowledge that the parents have overcome great odds. Their self-contempt and periodic self-denigration keep them locked in guilt feelings (feelings you don't see because their expression is defended against by anger at you). Praising parents' good efforts, no matter how small, helps to uncover buried assets to increase self-esteem. The parents can discover that they are seen, with all their shortcomings, as likable, worthwhile human beings. Such efforts will take a long time to bear fruit. Many individuals with low self-esteem turn any evidence of self-worth into the opposite because their self-contempt is so fundamental.

Self-love must be encouraged and new forms of gratification found. Because adequate self-esteem cannot be obtained in daily life, self-love must be developed and encouraged in practical ways.

MIDDLE-PHASE PROBLEMS

In middle phases of counseling, the worker can become a potential source of the parenting the mother or father never experienced. A client's fears of intimacy are proportionate to the intimacy the parent has with his or her own inner feelings and the feelings of intimacy experienced in prior relationships. Because some parents have felt abandoned in past intimate relationships, increased feelings of intimacy in the counseling relationship become a threat to that kinship.

Intimacy fears combined with conflicts over primitive needs for nurturing intensify the parents' struggles with their wish for gratification, their expectation of rejection, and their guilt over their relationships with their own parents. They will test the worker in ways designed to provoke rejection to resolve these conflicts. They will break appointments, make unreasonable demands, and withdraw from treatment, leading to the next principle.

Set firm limits on their behavior. "I will talk to you when you calm down and stop shouting; call me back when you're calm." Such limits should be set only after a relationship has been established and the parent trusts that you're setting these limits for his or her own good—"I can't really understand you when you shout so loudly."

Make a concentrated effort to change the position of the husband-father in the family. Numerous writers have stressed the importance of involving fathers in family treatment. Engaging fathers in treatment is particularly difficult for inexperienced counselors.

L'Abate (1975) has suggested a number of ways to involve resistant fathers. In general, ignore statements by the mother that he won't let you see him, and call him directly (Stanton & Todd, 1981). Once he is involved, the chief task is to help him build bridges between the competent areas of his life, usually his work but also his hobbies and interests, and his family functioning. Many of his work-related competencies include interpersonal, organizational, and problem-solving skills, which are in contrast to his inability to operate effectively as a husband and father within his family. The bridges that need to be built are those that translate work skills into his home life and help the family to accept these skills into their life.

Examine biological factors. While family and individual difficulties abound, many aggressive children also have subtle neurological problems and a history of mental illness in their families. In addition, the presence of neurological problems makes impulse control more difficult and takes some of the blame away from the parent for the child's difficulties. The parent may fear a neurological examination of his or her child because of fear that the child may be considered "crazy." Consequently the parent will need education and training about subtle neurological problems and how they affect their child's behavior.

THE LATER PHASE

In this phase, parents have become more open about their backgrounds and more dependent upon the counselor for assistance. At this time, the counselor should focus discussions around the parents' relationships with their own parents.

Help parents sort out intergenerational patterns and conflicts. Help parents to see their own parents' weaknesses and how their relationship with them resulted in their current problems. Help them to recognize their own parents' limitations and suggest how they might improve this relationship. Once the parent has begun to sort out the intergenerational patterns of conflict and distortion, education in basic parenting can begin. It is also during such discussions that feelings previously experienced as not belonging to the self begin to be owned by the parent. Current emotions begin to be experienced in terms of attachments to past emotions, often referred to as "earlier similars" (Van Ornum & Mordock, 1983).

Gradually turn over executive powers to the parents. Help parents become firm with their children without being mean. Review in detail their concrete disciplinary efforts so you can see where they could improve. Teaching them approved physical holding techniques can also be helpful.

Be patient and wait for a trigger event. As we will see in clinical vignettes (Mordock, 1988b), parents can resist involvement for long periods. Frequently a crisis will facilitate their involvement. For example, a father who had resisted treatment efforts for several years sought help from school staff when his wife absconded with his children, and he was awarded custody upon their return. He had never had to parent and admitted the need for help.

Be prepared to use power tactics to reduce ambivalence. As the clinical examples will illustrate, parents may reach a point where their ambivalence is so strong that the counselor and program staff may have to take a firm stand in order to overcome parental ambivalence that blocks further progress—"Our only alternative is residential treatment." "We can't continue to work with him without your help—we are recommending discharge."

Set realistic goals based on a thorough ongoing family assessment. Many families will not respond as favorably to our developmentally oriented, ego-supported efforts as we would like. We must assess families in terms of three levels of attainability (Terkelsen, 1980). The highest level is *full restoration.* At this level the family recaptures its capacity to promote the need attainment of all its members. The second level is *supplementation.* Here we do not expect the family to attain sufficiency in and of itself. The treatment plan deliberately includes creation of some more or less permanent attachment between the family and an external helping agent (Lamb, 1980). The family becomes semiautonomous. Involvement in self-help support groups or continual support by school staff will always be required to preserve family stability. The lowest level is *replacement.* Too much is missing in the family, resulting in the family needing extensive supplementation to function adequately. One or more of its members will require periodic placement in foster homes, group homes, or other institutions (Mordock, 1988a). These supplemental services should be used in the context of the relationship established with the parent and with awareness of the parent's needs for control. Whereas some staff may view the use of such facilities as treatment failure, their use may create some family stability. The parent should participate in the finding, planning, and utilization of these services. Such planning helps to promote the parent's growth, the ability to cope more effectively, and self-esteem. When concrete services are provided outside of this context, strong regressive tendencies are encouraged and only temporary and sporadic relief occurs (Newman & Martino, 1973).

REFERENCES

Angyal, A. (1965). *Neurosis and treatment: A holistic theory.* New York: John Wiley & Sons.

Friedrich, W. N., & Boriskin, J. A. (1976). The role of the child in abuse: A review of the literature. *American Journal of Orthopsychiatry, 46,* 580–590.

L'Abate, L. (1975). Pathogenic role rigidity in fathers: Some observations. *Journal of Marriage and Family Counseling, 1,* 69–79.

Lamb, H. R. (1980). Therapist-case managers: More than brokers of services. *Hospital and Community Psychiatry, 31,* 762–764.

Mordock, J. B. (1971). Behavioral problems of the child with minimal cerebral dysfunction. *Physical Therapy, 51,* 398–404.

Mordock, J. B. (1988a). Evaluating treatment effectiveness. In C. E. Schaefer & A. J. Swanson (Eds.), *Children in residential care* (pp. 219–250). New York: Van Nostrand Reinhold.

Mordock, J. B. (1988b). Working with parents of aggressive children: Clinical vignettes. *The Pointer, 33*(1), 22–25.

Mordock, J. B. (1988c). Working with parents of aggressive children: A description of their problems. *The Pointer, 33*(1), 13–17.

Newman, M. B., & Martino, M. S. (1973). The child and the seriously disturbed parent. *The Journal of the American Academy of Child Psychiatry, 12,* 162–181.

Pittman, F. S., III. (1982). Book review of family violence literature. *Family Process, 21,* 363–367.

Smith, G. (1988, March). Tyson the timid, Tyson the terrible. *Sports Illustrated,* 72–80, 82–83.

Stanton, M. D., & Todd, T. C. (1981). Engaging resistant families in treatment. *Family Process, 20,* 261–293.

Terkelsen, K. G. (1980). Toward a theory of the family life cycle. In E. A. Carter & M. McGoldrick (Eds.), *The family life cycle: A framework for family therapy.* New York: Gardner Press.

Van Ornum, W., & Mordock, J. B. (1983). *Crisis counseling with children and adolescents.* New York: Continuum.

Weitzman, T. (1985). Engaging the severely dysfunctional family in treatment: Basic considerations. *Family Process, 24,* 473–485.

. . . .

Educators need all the assistance they can get in how to be effective helping families. Naomi Karp, of the Federation of Families for Children's Mental Health, in *Collaboration with Families: From Myth to Reality,* provides help on two levels: (a) she gives us a new family-friendly conceptualization of the teacher–parent relationship, and (b) she provides a checklist to test the level of our collaboration versus our authoritarianism as we move from working *on* families to working *with* families. The dual checklist covering both teacher and family could be used at the first parent meeting to explain how the teacher hopes to work collaboratively with the family. Karp challenges the diagnosis of "dysfunctional family" and suggests specific ways to increase parental involvement. It becomes clear that old-style collaboration will not be sufficient: we are facing a transformation in the way schools do their business, if our efforts together are to be authentic. Families want to be supported, not supplanted.

ARTICLE 9.4

Collaboration with Families: From Myth to Reality

Naomi Karp

Over the past decade, the field of children's mental health has undergone a series of changes that is upgrading the quality of services delivered to children who have emotional, behavioral, and mental disorders, and their families. Gradually, mental health service providers are shedding traditional roles and are examining the ways in which they approach and communicate with families. Instead of "we" and "they," professionals and families gradually are becoming partners in the therapeutic process.

The Federation of Families for Children's Mental Health grew out of a 1988 "Next Steps" conference, convened by Portland State University and the U.S. Department of Education. The goal of that conference was to set an agenda for children's mental health. Subsequently, 17 family members decided to meet again to form a national organization. That was the beginning of the Federation of Families for Children's Mental Health, the first advocacy organization dedicated solely to children's mental health and family-support issues. Four years later, the Federation has a strong impact on improving services, policies, and laws affecting children with mental health disorders and their families.

Unfortunately for families and children, educators often do not live up to legislative requirements to collaborate with families, and persons who deliver mental health services have no mandate to form partnerships with families. Therefore, families would like to have the professional disciplines understand what is meant when families talk about "partnerships" and "collaboration."

COLLABORATION CHECKLIST FOR PROFESSIONALS

____ Do I really believe that parents are my equal, and, in fact, are experts on their child?

____ Do I show the same respect for the value of families' time as I do for my own time by educating myself about an individual child's case before appointments or group sessions?

From *The Journal of Emotional and Behavioral Problems*. (1993). Vol. 1, No. 4. Reprinted with permission.

_____ Do I speak plainly and avoid professional jargon?

_____ Do I actively involve parents in developing a plan of action and then review, evaluate, and revise the plan with the family?

_____ Do I make appointments and provide services at times and places convenient for the family?

_____ Do I share information with other professionals to ensure that services are not duplicated and that families do not expend unnecessary energy searching for services and providers?

COLLABORATION CHECKLIST FOR FAMILIES

_____ Do I believe I am an equal partner with professionals and do my share of problem solving and planning to help my child?

_____ Do I clearly express my own needs and the needs of my family to professionals in an assertive manner?

_____ Do I treat each professional as an individual and avoid letting past negative experiences get in the way of a good working relationship?

_____ Do I communicate quickly with professionals when significant changes and events occur?

_____ When I make a commitment to a professional for a plan of action, do I follow through and complete the commitment?

_____ Do I maintain realistic expectations for professionals, myself, and my child?

The preceding checklist challenges both professionals and families to approach each other in ways that embody values of respect, consideration, and empathy for others. A Vermont parent perhaps best summarizes why family-professional collaboration, based on family-centered principles, is important: "Parents should be thought of as scholars of experience. We are in it for the distance. . . . We have our doctorate in perseverance. We and the system must be in concert or the vision shrinks" (D. Sylvester. Cited in Thousand and Villa, 1989).

The composition of the American family is no longer the stereotypical "mom, dad, and two kids, and a dog." Rather, a family may be a single parent who relies on a maternal grandmother for child care; a teen-age couple who speak little English; or any configuration of people living under the same roof. Therefore, it is essential that mental health providers think about "parent" collaboration in new ways. One of the first steps toward a new way of thinking is to use new language. The term "parents" should be replaced with "family," since so many children do not live with both parents or, in many cases, with either parent. A comprehensive, inclusive definition of "family" should be used when mental health professionals are trying to collaborate with adults who are responsible for a child's well-being. The following definition was adopted by family leaders from across the country at a recent Office of Special Education and Rehabilitative Services (OSERS) conference:

A family is a group of people who are important to each other and offer each other love and support, especially in times of crises. In order to be sensitive to the wide range of life styles, living arrangements, and cultural variations that exist today, the family in OSERS programs can no longer be limited to just parent/child relationships. . . . Family involvement . . . must reach out to include: . . . mothers, fathers, sisters, brothers, grandparents, neighbors, and other persons who have important roles in the lives of people with disabilities (Family and Integration Resources, 1991).

Support is a key ingredient for family success and coping. Families of children with emotional and behavioral problems would like to see the term "dysfunctional family" erased from the vocabularies of professionals. Service systems are inflexible and not responsive to families' individual needs. They create unnecessary stress and overwhelming responsibilities for families. Professionals often misperceive families as being "dysfunctional" when these families are, in fact, experiencing normal reactions to the serious lack of appropriate affordable accessible community-based services and supports. It is service systems that are dysfunctional when they do not respond to families' needs. The term "dysfunctional family" is the system's way of blaming someone else and must not be used.

Additionally, families would like professionals to not "assess the family's deficits" and dwell on them. Rather, they would like professionals to talk with them and to find out what types of services and supports would build on the family's strengths and really make a difference in the lives of the whole family. Further, families want professionals to share their visions and expectations for children. Daring to dream about what might be, in terms of services and outcomes, is an essential part of a sound, collaborative partnership.

True family-professional collaboration can be built only on a shared set of values about children and families. Here are some examples of values that teams may want to affirm jointly:

All children and youth are to be valued as people.

All children and youth have strengths and can learn to make positive contributions to their families, friends, and society.

All families have a variety of strengths and coping styles that should be identified and enhanced.

Diversity and individual differences are to be valued and respected.

The values, choices, and preferences of families should be respected.

Families are sources of wisdom and knowledge about their children and should be recognized as experts.

After professionals have jointly developed a set of values about children and families, displaying them in a place where families can see them will help lay the foundation for collaborative partnerships. The next task is to put our values into practice. It is of paramount importance to develop strategies that will include families from all cultures and all walks of life as equal partners in their children's treatment programs.

As a final note, families increasingly are asked to serve on local, state, and national policy-making boards and councils. Most family members are delighted and honored to be asked to serve. However, families across the country are voicing a number of common complaints. These problems and our timelines for solutions are listed below:

- Only one family member is invited to serve on a board. This can be intimidating to the solitary "nonprofessional" in the group. Tokenism of any kind cannot be tolerated. Therefore, balanced representation on boards and councils is desired by the year 2000.
- Conferences frequently have a "family theme," but no family members are invited to plan the conference, present their views, or participate in a major or minor way. To have a meeting about families and to not include families is like studying anatomy without a body. By the year 2000, families would like to be equal partners in conferences and meetings.
- Families participate on boards and councils but are not compensated for their time. Child care, transportation, time away from one's job, and a host of other factors are not considered when families are asked to devote countless hours to improving systems and policies. Families' consulting skills have to be recognized and paid for just as any professional is compensated for her or his time.
- Families participate on boards and councils, but their ideas and opinions frequently are discounted. For example, large numbers of families said that they took part in developing their states' P.L. 99-660 Plans. However, many families' ideas never appeared in the finished proposals. This is another form of tokenism that families would like to see obliterated long before the year 2000.

REFERENCES

Family and integration resources. (1991). Second Family Leadership Conference. Washington, DC: U.S. Dept. of Education.

Thousand, J.S., & Villa, R.A. (1989). Enhancing success in heterogeneous schools. In S. Stainback, W. Stainback, & M. Forest (Eds.), *Educating all students in the mainstream of regular education.* Baltimore: Brooks.

. . . .

There is a difference between parental cooperation with a school program and parental involvement in actively dealing with a child's difficulties. Parents are finally being accepted as sources of new ideas and encouraged to become coteachers in parent-to-parent meetings. To get increased participation, parents' communication with their peers is far more effective than official notices.

Teachers should know parents' expectations from the program and their hopes and fears for the future. In particular, special education has the reputation of outpromising the potential and then blaming parents for the shortfall. Parents' collaboration is a matter of sharing not only ideas and agendas but also power. Taking risks with teacher power is required to encourage involvement in education programs. Some teachers hold periodic focus groups with parents to get their ideas about the program. Many parents say this is the first time they were ever asked for their opinions on any school matter. A principal in a community where "parents would never come to school" describes his way of getting high attendance. He has their kids perform, and slips in a carefully selected brief parent educational film. He reports, "You can't keep them from coming to see their own on stage." All of the meetings feature children. As the articles in this chapter illustrate, if school programs are going to be serious about preserving families, new strategies must be employed. We end by reemphasizing three basic concepts:

1. The complicated state of most of our families requires more than school-related assistance. Community agencies must be engaged through full-service schools.
2. Our own family experience is so deeply imprinted that we must understand what it has meant to us, lest what happened to us, whether positive or negative, be transferred to our expectations and responses for our students' families. Otherwise, hidden agendas can confound our efforts.
3. While the literature discusses various family "patterns," in truth each family is a unique entity, just as each person is unique. The use of stereotypes is both erroneous and prejudiced. Only by extensive listening can a teacher learn how an individual family functions with a given array of assets and limitations.

Index